A Hodder Christi

JOYCE H...

**Listening to God
Listening to Others
Finding Freedom**

Roshnada

Blessings & peace,

Joyce Huggett

Also by Joyce Huggett

Open to God (and cassette)
The Smile of Love
Teach Us to Pray (cassette)
Encountering God

Joyce Huggett Omnibus

Joyce Huggett

**LISTENING TO GOD
LISTENING TO OTHERS
FINDING FREEDOM**

Hodder & Stoughton
LONDON SYDNEY AUCKLAND

Unless otherwise indicated, Scripture quotations are taken from
the HOLY BIBLE, NEW INTERNATIONAL VERSION.
Copyright © 1973, 1978, 1984 by International Bible Society.
Used by permission. All rights reserved.

Bible references which are not taken from the NIV are quoted with the
following abbreviations: AV (Authorised Version),
GNB (Good News Bible), JB (Jerusalem Bible), JBP (J. B. Phillips),
KJV (King James Version), LV (Living Bible)

The quotation from *Prayers of Life* by Michael Quoist is reproduced
courtesy of the publishers, Gill and Macmillan

Listening to God copyright © 1986, 1996 by Joyce Huggett
Listening to Others copyright © 1988, 1996 by Joyce Huggett
Finding Freedom copyright © 1994 by Joyce Huggett

This omnibus edition first published in Great Britain 1998

The right of Joyce Huggett to be identified as the Authors of the Work has
been asserted by her in accordance with the Copyright, Designs and
Patents Act 1988.

1 3 5 7 9 10 8 6 4 2

British Library Cataloguing in Publication Data
A record for this book is available from the British Library

ISBN 0 340 67896 8

Printed and bound in Great Britain by
Mackays of Chatham PLC, Chatham, Kent

Hodder and Stoughton
A division of Hodder Headline PLC
338 Euston Road
London NW1 3BH

Listening to God

For Andrew, whose friendship I value, whose experience of God whets my appetite all over again and whose adventure into prayer is both an inspiration and joy to watch.

And in memory of Tom, who first taught me to listen to God.

Contents

Acknowledgments

Countless people have contributed to this book in one way or another. Most of them remain blissfully ignorant of that fact. Nevertheless I would like to express my thanks to a few of them.

I shall always be indebted to the monks of Mount St Bernard Abbey whose life and witness and worship made such a major contribution to my early explorations into contemplative prayer. I shall always be grateful, too, to the sisters of St Hilda's Priory in Whitby who welcomed me into their fold with such warmth and generosity even though I was a complete stranger. And my very special thanks to the Sisters of the Love of God, particularly certain sisters at Boxmoor, who have offered me, not simply endless support in the pilgrimage of prayer, but lasting friendship also.

The Rt. Revd. Stephen Verney, the Bishop of Repton, has been a constant source of inspiration and encouragement. The members of the original prayer group at St Nicholas' Church, Nottingham, similarly shaped my prayer life. While thanking them, I must include, too, my husband and children who sacrificed family togetherness time to set me free to adventure into listening prayer and who also helped me to evaluate my findings.

Twelve people prayed for me while I was giving birth to this book. Without their love and intercessory prayer this book would never have been completed and I am glad of this opportunity to thank them publicly. Carolyn Armitage, my editor, is someone whose wisdom, insights and concern I have grown to value through the writing of this book and to her I give another verbal bouquet. As for my typist and friend, Joan Edlin, I cannot thank her enough for typing and re-typing the manuscript without complaint and for the endless encouragement she gives me.

Preface

Ten years have elapsed since I tentatively sent the manuscript of *Listening to God* to my then-editor, Carolyn Armitage. The book lay finished in the drawer of my desk for three months before I plucked up the courage to post it. Even though Carolyn had given me endless encouragement, I found myself riddled with fear at the prospect of this particular book being published. How would the Christian public react to it, I wondered. Would evangelicals understand why I had drawn on the insights of Catholic authors? Would they reject me? Would charismatics understand and identify with my expressed belief that my call to stillness and solitude was the beckoning of God's Spirit? Would my contemplative friends be offended by the gentle challenge which I give in the final chapter of the book? In short, would I find myself misunderstood, friendless, isolated by those who had become dear to me?

I need not have worried! In fact, sometimes I still smile as I remember my own neurosis. Even before the book was published, the editorial team who then worked at Hodder and Stoughton sought me out at the Christian Booksellers' Convention, thanked me for the book and prophesied that countless readers would be grateful for it. When the book *was* eventually published, I marvelled that their prophesy proved to be correct. For well over two years, I received letters every day from readers all over the world. Many of these readers confessed that their prayer pilgrimages found so many parallels in my own that, in very many ways, they could have written the book themselves. They also expressed gratitude that *Listening to God* had given them permission to respond openly to the Spirit's nudging. Such letters still reach me. Every time I read and reread one of them, I breathe a prayer of gratitude to God, not only for inspiring me to write the book in the first place, but for his faithfulness and for giving me the grace to summon up the courage needed to send the completed manuscript to the publisher.

So much has changed since that day when I *did* take the manuscript to the post. Internationally things have changed in that, today, many more Christians from an evangelical and charismatic background seem to be responding to God's plea: 'Be still, and know that I am God' (Ps. 46:10) and to Jesus's invitation: 'Come with me by yourselves to a quiet place and get some rest' (Mark 6:31).

My own circumstances have also changed. I no longer live in England in a seven-bedroomed house where I had the luxury of a quiet room for a prayer place. I now live in a one-bedroomed apartment in Cyprus and my prayer place, like that of Jesus, is the great outdoors or the tiny church near my home.

My husband has also changed. He is no longer the Rector of a thriving church in the English Midlands. Like me, he is a Mission Partner with Interserve. Like me, he has learned the value of stillness and retreats. Together we now lead retreats for other Mission Partners – some from our own society and some from other missions. Together we teach ways of meeting God in stillness and solitude. Together we seek to help Mission Partners to listen to God through meditating on his Word, on creation and in the ways I have sketched in this book.

These retreats never take place in the kind of palatial, well-appointed retreat houses we took for granted in England. As I write this new Preface, we have just returned from a five-week trip in the two-thirds world where our retreats were held in places with no heating, often no electricity, sometimes no running water, yet we never heard our Partners complain and we saw God work in the deep places of people's lives. So we rejoice.

On my desk, as I write, lies a prayer card on which is written:

> *CHANGE*
> *GOD*
> *tossing us –*
> *gently –*
> *from one hand*
> *to another*
> *GOD can*
> *CATCH!*
> *PRAISE BE*[1]

As I look at that card from time to time, it reminds me of the appropriateness of change. Prayer is a journey. A pilgrimage. I was reminded of this in one of the retreat centres on that trip I mentioned above. It sits on a high promontory overlooking a meandering river. While the retreatants were meditating or praying, I would sometimes sit and gaze at that river which lay, like a giant, sleeping snake in the gorge below. Its curves and bends reminded me of the twists and turns in my own life.

In *Listening to God*, I have shared one stretch of my own journey through life – a phase of the pilgrimage that lasted for some fifteen years. That phase, as I have explained, was preceded by another, longer period of nearly forty years. Now I have moved into a new phase which I shall refer to again in the postscript to this book.

As I explained in the Preface of the original manuscript, there were two reasons why I described in detail that middle phase of my spiritual pilgrimage. One was because so many of the people I was meeting were asking the kind of questions I had asked in the 1970s: Does God speak today as he did in Bible times? If so, *how* does he speak? How do I know whether it is his voice I have heard? What must I do if I want to learn to tune in to God's still, small voice? This book was written with such people in mind. It went to publication with the sincere prayer these people would find the answers to some of their questions as my own story unfolded. It was produced because, deep down in my heart, a conviction had taken root that God still speaks today and he is actively seeking Christian people who will take his command to listen seriously.

In the course of my work and my travels, I still meet Christians, young and old, who are asking the same questions so I am grateful to the publisher for giving this particular book a new lease of life. I continue to pray that people will find parallels here with their own faith journey.

There was another reason why I decided to write about listening to God. It can best be summed up with the word obedience. I sensed that God was asking me to draw together three threads of spirituality which, at certain stages of the Church's history, had remained so separate that they seemed incompatible: the richness of the evangelical tradition with its faithfulness to the Bible, the freshness of the charismatic movement with its openness to the energising and empowering of God's Holy Spirit, and the deep-down stillness of the world of contemplation with its emphasis on encountering God and being encountered by him.

In the book, I describe how these three strands have been intertwined in my own life. I relate some of the joys, some of the sorrow and some of the surprises that met me as this work of God began in my life twenty years ago. I attempted to show how, in one life, *my* life, God had been breaking down the barriers of suspicion and prejudice that used to divide Christian from Christian; how he had impressed on me the fact that Christians in many camps not only have much to teach one another but they actually need one another if they are to become whole and embrace the whole Gospel. There is a sense, then, in which this book is about reconciliation as well as listening prayer.

In the preface of the original book, I wrote this:

I offer the book to readers in whom the Holy Spirit of God is working similarly with the encouragement not to fear the strange changes you may find happening to you, but to rejoice in them. For God invites us, not to stagnate in our spiritual life, but to change and to go on being changed.

Ten years farther along the path I believe that claim even more fervently than when I first typed it into my computer. I believe it because I myself have changed considerably since writing the book. My experience of God has not been frozen between the pages of *Listening to God*. It continues to evolve. To develop. To deepen. That is why I have added a postscript. It is why I have called the postscript '*Moving On*'. God is always moving us on. One of the places through which he leads us is the desert. As he expresses it through the prophet Hosea:

I am now going to allure her;
I will lead her into the desert
and speak tenderly to her.[2]

That has been my experience. As I explain, I have discovered that the desert, that place where we encounter spiritual dryness and spiritual darkness, has a friendly, fruitful face. It is not a place to be feared but rather a place to be welcomed. It is the place where we are refined, the place where we are being watered, the place where we are being prepared for eternity – where we shall meet the Beloved face to face.

As this book is reprinted, I echo the prayer I first prayed way back in 1985 – that it may become a bridge on which the Christian earnestly desiring to hear God's voice and the God who yearns to communicate with his children may meet, embrace each other and journey through life together listening in love to one another.

Joyce Huggett
Cyprus 1995

Chapter 1

Learning to Listen

Prayer became the warp and woof of my life very early on in my childhood. My father wove the first prayer-threads into the fabric of my experience. It was not that he taught me prayers, nor that he prayed with me, so far as I can remember. Instead, he taught me the value of prayer by allowing me to watch *him* at prayer.

I can see him now. Every evening, after work, he would settle himself into the armchair next to the coal fire which always blazed in the hearth of our tiny living room in winter. He would read the local newspaper from cover to cover, listen to the news on the wireless, then reach for his big, black, gilt-edged, leather-bound Bible. I would watch him out of the corner of my eye. I loved the smell of that leather and the rustle of the India paper and the shimmer of the gold pages. And I loved the look on my father's face as he read this treasured book. Reading it seemed to bring him contentment and joy even when times were hard, like when he was made redundant. When he had finished reading the Bible and the notes, I knew what he would do next. He would hand the Bible to my mother who sat in the armchair at the other side of the fire. While she flicked through the pages, he would close his eyes, bow his head and bury his apple-red face in one hand. And often I would contemplate his wavy, auburn hair and sit very still while I watched his thin lips move. Even when I was very young, I understood that at such moments I was not to interrupt. But when he lifted his head again, I would sometimes climb on his knee, snuggle into his arms and play with his floppy ear-lobes before giving him a smacking kiss on the cheek nearest the fire: the cheek which would be warm.

Our terraced house boasted only two bedrooms. My brothers shared one and I slept on a child-size bed in the corner of the other, sharing it with my parents. Often, I would still be awake when my parents came to bed and I would watch as my mother folded back the flamingo-pink satin bedspread before kneeling with my father on the cold, pink lino beside their bed. My father would frequently linger in this attitude of prayer and again, I would study his prayerful form and watch the silent movement of his lips.

Children are great imitators of people they love. Perhaps it is not surprising, then, that I cannot remember a time when prayer did not feature in my life.

Among my earliest memories is a picture of myself kneeling by *my* bed in prayer and the recollection of a regular routine. I would lie in bed with the light on and sing at the top of my voice until someone came to tell me to stop. My favourite song was one my father taught me and which we used to sing in Sunday school:

It is a thing most wonderful
Almost too wonderful to be
That God's own Son should come from heaven
And die to save a child like me.

I sometimes think about the cross
And shut my eyes and try to see
The cruel nails and crown of thorns
And Jesus crucified for me.

And I would close my eyes, visualise Jesus hanging on the cross, and my heart would be strangely warmed. God's love for me caused a stirring in my heart. Even at a tender age I wanted to respond by giving him the love that welled up inside me as I thought of him hanging on the tree for me.

By the time I reached my teens, a personal pattern of prayer was well established. Every evening, like my father, I would read the Bible, study the passage with the aid of Scripture Union notes and kneel beside my bed to pray. The deepest desire of my heart was to live life God's way. But what was God's way?

I remember puzzling over this when I fell in love for the first time. I was fourteen and my hero was an athletic fifteen-year-old. He would meet me from school and we would cycle home together and kiss and cuddle in the park near my home. No one ever talked to me about the ecstasy of falling in love. No one ever explained to me how a Christian should behave with members of the opposite sex, so even though I enjoyed the kissing and the cuddling, at the same time I was anxious. The only person I talked to about the situation was God. He had my complete confidence. At night I would kneel by my bed and tell him everything. And I would ask him a whole string of questions: Is it right to feel this way about a boy? Is it wrong to do these things in the park? Is this partner the one you want me to marry? My heart was full of trust and sincerity as I unburdened myself. The problem was that no answer came. I would rise from my knees as perplexed as before.

The same ceiling of silence met me when another boyfriend asked me to marry him. I was eighteen at the time and working hard at my 'A' levels. I remember being flattered and confused, stunned and excited all at the same time. Unable to talk to my parents about such things, I knelt in my usual spot that night – on the rug beside my bed – and begged God to show me what I should say to this infatuated young man. No audible answer came. Only silence.

Throughout my student days, the love of God drew me irresistibly. Prayer intrigued me, attracted me, and occupied several hours of my time each week. As a theology student I was obliged to study Church history. I envied the

early monks and hermits I read about who had devoted
their entire life to prayer. But I never discovered the secret
of how to hear God. Neither did I meet anyone else who
had learned this art. Prayer, for me, was like a telephone
conversation where one person did all the talking. I was
that person. I seem to remember being taught that prayer
was the way man communicated with God. Bible reading
was the way God chose to speak to man.

Whether I was actually taught that or not, this was what
I believed and each day I would make time both to talk to
God and to try to listen to him by reading the Bible. One
of my tutors in the Theology Department discovered this
personal pattern of prayer. It earned me and others like
me the label 'God-botherers'. But we didn't mind. Prayer
mattered.

From our honeymoon on, my husband and I prayed
together as well as apart. In prayer, we would chatter away
to God. When we needed an answer to an urgent question
we would hope that a verse from the Bible would leap out
from the page and point us in the right direction, or that
circumstances and the advice of friends would coincide
and that in this way God would make his will clear.

When our son was born, we taught him to pray. When
our daughter arrived, we prayed over her and with her and
for her. While I breast-fed her in the early hours of the
morning, I would enjoy the stillness and pray. Prayer was
one of the pivotal experiences of our family life. Yet prayer
somehow created a hunger. It was as though a whole piece
of the jig-saw was missing.

Listening to God

When our son was eleven years old, my husband accepted
a job in Nottingham. He was to pastor a church in the
centre of the city. Our new home would border the city's
busy inner by-pass at the front and Woolworth's at the
back. 'It's ideally situated for lunch-time meetings for
businessmen,' we decided before we even settled in.

Every Wednesday lunch-time, a handful of businessmen
would meet in our lounge, drink soup, eat sandwiches,

listen to a talk and pray. One of the most regular attenders was a retired member of our own congregation: Tom. From time to time, members of the group would lead the meeting for themselves rather than invite an outside speaker to address them. Whenever Tom's turn came round he would speak about a dimension of prayer he called 'listening to God'. He would insist that when a person listens to God, God speaks, and when a man obeys, God works.

Tom once described how this process of listening to God had turned his marriage inside out. While listening to God on one occasion, he sensed that God was urging him to ask his wife's forgiveness for the way he had failed in the past. That night, he made his confession and suggested that he and his wife should be quiet together. The result of this act of obedience was that his wife rededicated her life to Christ.

From that time on, Tom and his wife set the alarm for 6 a.m. every morning so that they could enjoy a time of quiet together. They would read the Bible, pray and listen for God's still, small voice. Whenever they sensed God was speaking to them, they would write down the instructions or challenges or directions they received. They determined to obey to the best of their ability. Because of this rekindling of spiritual awareness, life opened up for them in a new way. The life and standards of Jesus became the pattern on which they cut their lives. Their love for one another deepened, their marriage was enriched, and the new quality of their lives touched their many friends and acquaintances.

Tom also described how during his times of attentive listening to God, creativity flowed and plans were hatched. On one occasion, he came to God burdened about the strike action which was paralysing the printing firm of which he was a director. God seemed to implant in his mind, not only a method to end the strike, but ideas which, when implemented, created a new spirit in the firm. On another occasion God seemed to place a burden on his heart for a Marxist friend of his. During his early morning period of quiet, ideas flowed which, when put into practice, resulted in this man's conversion to Christ.

Tom's testimony both fascinated and frightened me. I admired Tom. Kindness overflowed from him and his wife to my family and me. His genuineness, honesty and transparency could not be denied. But although I detected a fluttering of desire in the pit of my stomach whenever he described his experience of detecting God's still, small voice, a certain memory filled me with dread and blocked the path of progress for me. Indeed, I shuddered as I recalled the tragedy of Jim, a friend of ours, who mistook wishful thinking for God's whisper.

Jim had been an undergraduate with my husband and me. We knew him well. Just after our wedding, he wrote to us to tell us that God had told him to marry a mutual friend of ours, another fellow undergraduate, Jenny. 'But that's stupid,' I protested when I read the letter. 'Jenny's engaged to Geoff. They're getting married in three months' time.' We resisted responding to Jim's letter. Jenny married Geoff. Several months later, another letter arrived from Jim insisting that God had told him to marry Jenny. This time, David, my husband, wrote to Jim to break the news. Jenny was married.

Undaunted, Jim jumped on the next train and came to our home protesting that Jenny had made a mistake. Indeed, at first he refused to believe that Jenny was married. Only after inspecting the marriage register in the church where the wedding had taken place was he convinced that Jenny was now committed to Geoff 'for better, for worse'.

Jim's reaction strained our own relationship with him and brought considerable distress to the newly-weds, Jenny and Geoff. The recollection of this distressing incident caused me to question whether Tom's apparent hot-line to God was authentic. I could tell that it was important to him, but I was not convinced that the Bible encouraged us to listen to God in this way and so, somewhat reluctantly, I dismissed his prayer recipe, and was even slightly suspicious of it.

God has his own way of breaking through our personal prejudices. Francis Thompson's poem, *The Hound of Heaven*, a favourite poem of mine, reminds us of this glad fact:

I fled Him, down the nights and down the days;
I fled Him, down the arches of the years;
I fled Him, down the labyrinthine ways
of my own mind, and in the mist of tears
I hid from Him . . .
From those strong Feet that followed, followed after.[1]

I was not aware when I discounted Tom's experience of listening to God that I, too, was a would-be escapee. But it seems that that is how God saw me. And, as always, the hound of heaven pursued gently, sensitively, persistently. Once again, he conquered. But this time, *I* became his willing victim.

Chapter 2

Tuning in to God

By this time the city centre church where we were working and worshipping was humming with new life. One reason for this was the influx of students who worshipped with us on Sundays. They came from Nottingham University and the polytechnic. In the autumn of 1976, two years after our arrival in Nottingham, the chaplain of the poly invited us to attend a weekend conference which he was organising for some of his students and to speak to them on the subject of prayer. 'We'll be holding the conference at Mount St Bernard Abbey,' he explained. 'It's a Roman Catholic monastery about forty minutes' drive from Nottingham.'

David and I each prepared our talks and duly arrived at the monastery. I had never darkened the doors of a monastery before, but as we entered the tree-lined drive, I remember smiling at our arrogance. 'Why on earth have *we* come to do the speaking?' I asked David. 'These monks have given their lives over to the work of prayer. Surely they know more about it than we do?'

I was to speak first. A white-robed, bald-headed monk sat at the back of the meeting and from time to time I wondered what his evaluation of my lecture would be. When the students broke up into small discussion groups, therefore, I engineered the grouping to ensure that I sat in the same group as this expert on prayer. I was eager to hear what he would say.

The aim of the discussion was to encourage each person

to explain to the others the methods of prayer which had proved beneficial to them. The monk listened, nodding and smiling from time to time, but not speaking. Towards the end of the discussion we invited him to divulge the secret of his prayer life. His reply was to haunt me for weeks. 'Oh,' he replied, his eyes twinkling merrily as he spoke, 'I find that a rather difficult assignment. You see, most of my praying these days is done in silence.' I failed utterly to understand how someone could spend most of their life in prayer and yet by-pass words. The mystery of this statement bothered me every time I thought about it in the weeks that lay ahead.

The monk befriended my husband and me that day and planted a suggestion in our minds.

'Why don't you come here and make a retreat on your own one day?' The very phraseology, 'make a retreat', sounded suspiciously Catholic to our Protestant ears, but something about this prayer sanctuary had hooked us. Early in December, we arrived to make our first retreat.

I shall never forget that first sip of real stillness. The retreat demanded nothing of us except simply to be in the presence of God. Coming, as we had, straight from the activism of parish life in a busy city-centre church, this absence of the driving need to achieve was therapy in itself. The monastery, with its prayer-saturated walls and fabric, its quiet rhythm and its God-centredness, seemed to us a welcome oasis. We were being nourished, renewed and refreshed. We each rejoiced to watch the other relax in the warmth of the felt love of Christ, a phenomenon which seemed rare at home.

From time to time during our forty-eight hour retreat, the monk met us and explained some of the mysteries of his experience of prayer. He also lent us a book which was to change my life. As I read John Powell's, *He Touched Me*, I was deeply moved. Here was a man who understood my quest, who voiced my struggles, and who was unafraid to expose his personal vulnerability by expressing how he had stumbled across answers to the kind of questions I had been asking.

How does God communicate himself to me? How does
he disclose who he is after I have revealed myself to
him? Do I have to wait hours, days, weeks or even
years to see what God will do with and about my
open-ness to him? Or is there a more immediate and
direct response? . . . Can God put a new idea directly
and immediately into my *mind*! Can he give me a new
perspective in which to view my life with its successes
and failures, agonies and ecstasies? Can God put new
desires into my *heart*, new strength into my *will*! Can he
touch and calm my turbulent *emotions*! Can he actually
whisper words to the listening ears of my soul through
the inner faculty of my *imagination*? Can God stimulate
certain *memories* stored within the human brain at the
time these memories are needed?[1]

I had never had the courage to voice questions like these
even though they had burned in my heart every time Tom
talked to me about listening to God. With eagerness, I
read on. John Powell's conclusion filled me with child-like
excitements:

Of course I feel sure that God can and does teach us in
these ways. I think of the whole Bible as simply a written
record of such religious experience, of God invading
human history and human lives, of God speaking to
men. I also believe that this God is available and
anxious to speak to you and me. Yes, just as anxious
as he was to speak to Abraham, Isaac and Jacob, Isaiah
and Jeremiah.[2]

'But would he come to me?' This question penned by John
Powell also found an echo in my own heart. His testimony
left me with an insatiable thirst:

The Lord . . . puts his ideas into my mind, and especially his perspectives. He widens my vision, helps me to
see what is really important in life, and to distinguish the

really important from the unimportant . . . He comes to
me, in the listening, receptive moments of prayer, and
he transfuses his power into me.[3]

This man had an experience of prayer which was like
a foreign language to me. I determined to learn that
language. I wanted what he had found and I was prepared
to make sacrifices for this pearl of great price.

The finger of God
Just as the father detected the early stirrings in the heart
of the prodigal son, it seems that God's all-seeing eye took
note of my fresh longings for him. He made an entry into
my life in a dramatic, gentle and sensitive way.

For eight years I had fought against the charismatic
movement. Its extremes and eccentricities disturbed and
alarmed me and I determined to steer clear of what seemed
to me mere emotionalism. But two weeks after this retreat
at Mount St Bernard Abbey, a trusted friend telephoned
late one night to tell me that he had been filled with the
Spirit and he thought he had been speaking in tongues.
I was angry. I remember the shudder which shook my
body as I noted the excitement in his voice. I recall my
response: 'Oh dear! Perhaps we should talk about this
after the meeting tomorrow night.' I did not give voice
to my determination to knock this nonsense out of his
head, neither did I react verbally to his parting comment:
'Joyce, I think there's something in this for you.' But I
dreaded our encounter and hoped it would not mark the
end of a happy friendship.

After the meeting that Monday night, this member of
our congregation and I talked long and late. I knew him
well and I could not deny that God had touched him. It
would be useless, I knew, to talk him out of a religious
experience which had so clearly revitalised his love for
God, renewed his thirst for Bible reading and empowered
his prayer life. It was that night, as we prayed, that the
hound of heaven caught up with me. I could no longer fight
off the new surge of life with which he filled me. I have no

words to describe what happened. I simply remember that I tingled with joy. The next day I was buoyant with this joy. As I put it to my husband, 'I suppose this is what it means to be filled with the Spirit of God.' I no longer felt hungry in prayer. I could not stop myself praying. I prayed as I walked to the shops. I prayed as I met the children from school. I prayed when I went to bed and when I got up in the morning. But the nature of the prayer had changed. It ceased to be a string of requests, a tirade of questionings, beseechings and plaguings. Instead, the sense of the presence of God's life within stunned me into silence. This awed silence gave birth to wordless praise, wordless adoration and wordless consecration of my life to him. Silence. Wordlessness. This was what the monk had been describing. A fresh touch from God. This was what John Powell had experienced.

The still, small voice

A dark-haired, brown-eyed school teacher we shall call Joan used to come to our home with a crowd of other young people most Sunday evenings at this stage of our church's history. She was shy and though I made several attempts to befriend her, I never felt I met the real person behind the dark eyes. When the phone rang one morning and Joan's voice cried out for help, I was surprised but pleased that she could trust me. Joan came round and explained that her mother had collapsed quite suddenly, that a diagnosis had been made and that she was suffering from a brain tumour which was thought to be incurable.

I felt helpless. After Joan left me, I asked God to heal this woman. Instead of promising to do that, I sensed that God was asking me to visit her in the nearby hospital. I am not claiming to have heard a voice. I did not. I am saying that an inner awareness which I shall refer to as a 'voice' spoke to me so clearly that I could not escape its implications. Indeed, it was so real that I argued with it. 'But, Lord, I don't even know her. What am I supposed to say?'

The voice simply replied, 'You go and I'll tell you

what to say when you arrive.' The realisation that God wanted me to visit this sick woman would not go away. So I went.

As I walked through the hospital gates, my eyes lighted on a statue in the niche of a wall. The sculptor had chiselled out a sensitive representation of a shepherd holding a helpless lamb. The voice spoke again. 'Describe that statue to her.' In my faithlessness, again I protested. 'But, Lord, she's not a Christian. She won't understand what it means.' The reply came back. 'Never mind. Tell her.'

When eventually I found the patient, I talked to her about her illness, about her daughter, about the nurses. Just before I left, I described the statue I had seen. She listened, and seemed pleased that I had come, so I promised to return.

For several weeks, I visited this patient and a trusting friendship sprang up between us. Somehow I sensed that God was at work in her life. Even so, when she told me one afternoon that she was ready to die now that she knew the Good Shepherd for herself, I was stunned. She told me that she had thought a great deal about that statue and God had shown her himself through it. A few days later, she died.

This experience persuaded me that God can speak, that he does speak, and if we obey the inner prompting remarkable things can happen.

Another incident reinforced this realisation. A few weeks after Joan's mother's death, I received a phone call from a distressed clergy wife. She was dying of cancer and the treatment left her depressed and weak. I used to visit her from time to time until she was hospitalised. Then I wanted to avoid intruding on family visiting time, so I simply prayed for her at home.

One afternoon, I could not get this woman out of my mind. The voice I was learning to recognise as God's pushed me into visiting her. As I sat by her bedside, holding her bony, parchment-yellow hand, the same voice whispered, 'Remind her of the hymn, "Just as I am".' My reply shows how slow I was to learn to obey. 'But, Lord, she's from a high-church tradition. She won't appreciate *that* hymn.' The reply came. 'Never mind. Quote it.'

As I started the first line, I hoped I would be able to remember the first verse. The whole hymn tumbled out of my lips:

> Just as I am without one plea
> But that Thy blood was shed for me
> And that Thou bid'st me come to Thee
> O Lamb of God, I come . . .
>
> Just as I am, Thou wilt receive
> Wilt welcome, pardon, cleanse, relieve,
> Because Thy promise I believe
> O Lamb of God, I come.

When I had finished, her weak hand squeezed a thank you and, quietly, I left.

A few days later, she died. When I attended the funeral, I was startled to find that one of the hymns her husband had chosen was this same hymn, 'Just as I am'. Later, he explained. 'The words of that hymn brought her such consolation and peace even in the middle of all the suffering of the final pain-wracked hours on earth. She would often ask me to read it to her.'

Again, I was deeply touched. I could no longer deny that God speaks today.

In these action-packed weeks, I seemed to be discovering for myself that Tom's claims were correct. The indwelling Spirit of God does speak today and he wants us to listen. What is more he wants us to act as well as hear. This discovery swung open a door into a whole new spiritual realm for me. Like Lucy in C. S. Lewis' book, *The Lion, the Witch and the Wardrobe*, I found myself in a world which was connected with our own but which was mysteriously other. Like Lucy, I was filled with wonder, awe, and spine-tingling excitement. I identified with the mixture of emotions C. S. Lewis describes when God surprised him by joy:

I was overwhelmed . . . the long inhibition was over, the dry desert lay behind, I was off once more into the land of longing . . . There was nothing whatever to do about it: no question of returning to the desert. I had simply been ordered – or, rather, compelled – to 'take that look off my face.' And never to resume it either.[4]

Chapter 3

A Taste of Silence

Whenever I could I would go to Mount St Bernard Abbey
to pray. Sometimes all I could spare would be a few hours.
Sometimes I managed to stay for a whole day. Very
occasionally I would make a retreat of thirty-six hours.

What was it that drew me? A recent visit helped me to
pin-point the power of the place. I had driven through haz-
ardous conditions to reach the abbey, along snowpacked
lanes, through a blinding blizzard; on the way my car had
skidded and in doing so had collided with another, bigger
car. Even so, when eventually I had parked outside the
abbey guest house, picked my way through ankle-deep
snow-drifts and lifted the latch of the oak chapel door, I
became aware of a peace invading my spirit.

The hush of the prayer-saturated chapel seeped into
me. Within seconds, I had fallen to my knees, aware of
my surroundings, the smell of fresh furniture polish, the
sound of the monks shuffling into the choir stalls, the wind
howling round the building, yet intensely aware of a love
which drew me to itself, the love of God.

The sense of God's presence and love was so strong that
it banished all memories of the traumatic journey. This
love called from me a response. While the monks worshipped, like a sponge which had lain hard and shrivelled I
opened every cell and fibre of my being to the warmth, the
radiance and beckoning of the love of the living Lord.

'And this was how it always was,' I reflected. 'In this

place the Lord calls me from my preoccupation with self and my overbusyness to focus on him and him only. In this place he touches me, the real me which often I hide from the world. He touches me through the winsomeness of the music, he touches me through the visual stimulus of the cross, he touches me through the powerful, prayerful atmosphere, he touches me through the flickering candle which somehow stills my harassed heart.'

When the monks left the church, I would linger there, as I did on this occasion. And I would be aware that every part of my being – body, mind and spirit – were open, attentive to the divine presence. I had done nothing to prepare myself for this eventuality. God had done it. The initiative was his. The miracle was his. By beaming his love on to me in a way I could feel, parts of me which normally remain closed, unfolded. I suppose I was rather like the water lily which opens itself when it can bask in warm sunshine but which closes its petals when cloud or rain obliterate the sun.

What I heard in those times of listening was more than a voice. It was a presence. Yes. I heard the Lord call my name. But I also 'heard' his tenderness. I soaked up his love. And this listening was on a level which runs deeper than mere words. Sometimes it seemed as though Jesus himself stood in front of me or beside me or above me. This encounter with him overwhelmed me. Was it his radiance? Was it the tenderness of his gaze? Or was it the fact of his gaze? The only way I can describe it is to liken it to the overwhelming a person feels when they love someone very deeply. That person's heart burns with pure pleasure at the joy of being in the presence of the loved one, that person's eyes sparkle or shine or mist over with warmth and deep-felt emotion, but that person does not speak. No words are necessary. They might even be intrusive for they could trivialise the love. And nothing must spoil the ecstasy of their encounter which may be all too brief in any case. They are content simply 'to be' in one another's presence. But that silence is packed with warm communication.

I had never delighted in God in this way before. And it had never occurred to me that God wanted me to linger in his presence so that he could show me that he delighted in me. Until now, my prayer had been vocal, busy, sometimes manipulative, always achievement-orientated. To kneel at the foot of a cross, allow music to wash over me so that I could 'just be' with God in a stillness which convinced me that 'he is', that 'he is God', was a new experience. But to 'waste time' for God in this way was changing my life, changing my view of God, changing my perception of prayer, changing my understanding of listening to God.

The problem was that, while I could achieve this kind of stillness in a place where people prayed day-in, day-out, I was married, the mother of two teenage children, heavily involved in helping my husband in a busy parish. I could never be a monk. I might fantasise about becoming a hermit, but my vocation, I realised, was not simply to prayer but to marriage, to motherhood, to service in the community. How was I to take what I experienced of God at Mount St Bernard Abbey and translate this into my everyday spiritual pilgrimage?

While I was still puzzling over this problem, glandular fever knocked me sideways. Perhaps it was God's way of giving me the time and space I needed to sift my priorities? Perhaps it was his opportunity to speak in tones I could not have detected had I been living life at the normal pace? C. S. Lewis rightly reminds us that pain is God's megaphone through which he speaks to a deaf world.

I do not know why this illness removed me from the front line of activity for months. What I do know is that a book which a friend gave me while I was ill presented me with the answer to my question, 'How can I draw near to God in the busyness of my everyday routine?' It also answered another question which was bothering me at the time but which I had not yet had the courage to face. Was this facet of prayer, which no one had told me about before, and which I scarcely dared to mention in the circles in which I moved, simply an emotional, me-centred

trip? Or was it a well-tried path of prayer of which I was
so far ignorant?

The name of the book was *Poustinia* which, in Russian,
means 'desert' or 'hermitage'. The author, Catherine de
Hueck Doherty, was born in Russia but defected to the
West after the October revolution in 1917. Eventually she
settled in Canada where she began to teach spiritually
hungry people an approach to God which had been her
heritage in her homeland. Her thesis is that modern man
needs silence just as much as his fore-fathers needed it:

> If we are to witness to Christ in today's market places,
> where there are constant demands on our whole person,
> we need silence. If we are to be always available, not
> only physically, but by empathy, sympathy, friendship,
> understanding and boundless *caritas*, we need silence.
> To be able to give joyous, unflagging hospitality, not
> only of house and food, but of mind, heart, body and
> soul, we need silence.[1]

This paragraph struck an immediate chord in my heart.
And it was quickly followed by another observation which
seemed to have been written just for me: 'This silence is
not the exclusive prerogative of monasteries or convents.
This simple, prayerful silence is everybody's silence – or
if it isn't, it should be.'[2] The author develops her thesis
by explaining that a poustinia means a quiet, lonely place
where people retreat because they desire to encounter God
and because they seek to listen to him. She makes the claim
that God reveals himself in a rare fullness to the person
who withdraws from the maelstrom of life in this way. It is
a place where we can be still and know that God is God,
where God can fulfil his promise: 'I will lead her into the
desert and speak tenderly to her' (Hos. 2:14).

I was lying in bed when I read this book. By the time
I reached her practical suggestions about such a retreat
place, I was sitting bolt upright from sheer enthusiasm.
She emphasises that a poustinia need not be completely
away from the haunts of men. Some people had reserved

in their homes a small room to which they went to pray and meditate, which some might call a poustinia.

Within four months of reading this book, we had moved to a rambling four-storey house with seven bedrooms. Even before we moved, the attic-type bedroom at the top of the house was earmarked for silence. I would make it into a prayer room where I could adventure further into silence without having to withdraw from the family so frequently.

Going deeper

At this time, my friendship with the lady chaplain at Nottingham University took on a new significance. This friend was a nun, a sister on loan to the university from a convent in Whitby. She used to visit me as I recovered from glandular fever and we would talk about prayer, particularly silent prayer. With pride I showed her my prayer room tucked away at the top of the new house.

As the summer holidays approached, Sister Stella Mary prepared to spend the vacation back in the community. Just before she left Nottingham, she sprang an invitation on me: 'Why don't you come to Whitby for a few days while I'm there and taste *our* silence? The quiet of the convent and the sea air would do you good – hasten your healing.'

The idea attracted me for several reasons. First, I liked the idea of seeing this friend's 'home' for myself. Second, since it was an Anglican community, I knew I would be able to take communion there, something which I could not do at Mount St Bernard Abbey since I am not a Roman Catholic. Third, the thought of four days of solitude in congenial surroundings beckoned me after months of weariness and sickness.

My family warmed to the idea, too, so in August they drove me to the imposing grey stone castle now converted into a convent and a school.

I was spoiled: by God and by the sisters. For the four days I was there, the sun bathed the building and garden with warmth and light. I found a sun-drenched niche in the garden and there I sat, among the hollyhocks, with my back against the red brick wall and my face upturned to the sun, and for hour after hour I relaxed, read, drank in the peace, prayed and meditated on God's Word. From time to time I would relax, too, by striding along the seashore, watching the seagulls and envying their strength, but suddenly feeling as free as they looked. And I lapped up the kindness showered on me: like the day when I was observing total silence and a sister brought my coffee to the garden complete with home-made biscuits *and* a chocolate wrapped in gold foil.

But what made the most profound impact on me was the depth of the silence. I ate in the refectory with the sisters – in silence. I prayed in the chapel with the sisters each morning – in silence. Like them, I spent most of my day in silence.

I had never eaten in silence before. And I had never prayed with a group of people before without using any words. The power this silence generated stunned me.

Yes. I had sipped silence at Mount St Bernard Abbey, as I have said, and this had become precious. But Mount St Bernard Abbey flings wide its doors to people like me: people just beginning to explore the depths of prayer, people needing instruction, people needing help of varying kinds. Such people cannot sustain silence for long periods and so the peace of the place is punctuated by conversation in the guest house. From time to time noise pollutes the guest wing and it is probably appropriate that it should do so.

But here, at Whitby, guests do not disrupt the rhythm of the monastic way of life. They are fewer and they are absorbed by the community, its customs and its stillness.

This sustained stillness softened my spirit, making it receptive to the new seed-thoughts which were about to be sown.

Sister Stella Mary was shrewd. As we talked about God and about my longings for him, she detected that I was being called to contemplation. On the first evening of my visit, she lent me a book which I had never seen before, *Prayer and Contemplation* by Robert Llewellyn. It was another of those books which seemed to have been written especially for me.

From it, I learned that there is a close correlation between the charismatic experience which had crept up on me by surprise, and the yearning for solitude which I was currently experiencing. Robert Llewellyn explains that only the Holy Spirit can teach us how to pray. Indeed, prayer is his work within us. He is not only our teacher but our assistant. It is he who comes to help us in our weakness. When we are at a loss to know how to pray, 'the Spirit himself intercedes for us with groans that words cannot express' (Rom. 8:26). 'Groans that words cannot express', or as the RSV puts it, 'sighs too deep for words', or as one commentary paraphrases it, 'inexpressible longings which God alone understands'. This is one definition of contemplative prayer. Such contemplation is a gift of God's Spirit. Sometimes he teaches us to plumb the depths of silence. At other times he teaches us to vocalise spontaneous prayer. At other times again he encourages us to pray in tongues.

As I pondered on revelations like these, two thoughts struck me with the force of a flash of lightning. The first was that the kind of prayer which was drawing me again and again to Mount St Bernard Abbey had a name: contemplation. The second was that this thing called contemplation was a gift God gave to his people through his Holy Spirit, a gift which enabled them to unfold to the presence of God.

With that intuitive knowing which is, of itself, a gift of God's Spirit, I knew that God was inviting me not simply to receive this gift but to unpack it; that he had brought me to Whitby with this primary purpose in mind.

This hunch was confirmed as I read more of Robert Llewellyn's book and particularly his description of the call to contemplation.

He suggests that it sometimes happens that a Christian is initiated into the life of prayer by learning to take a passage from the Bible, read it, examine it, ponder it, and consider how it affects his life-style and relationships with others. At the end of this period of Bible study, the person concerned will pray some kind of free, vocal prayer. I saw myself reflected in this description. It was the pattern I had practised for years.

He goes on to suggest that there may come a time when these occupations, though valuable in themselves, do no more than touch the fringe of our longing in prayer. They leave us with a sense of emptiness rather than fullness. Indeed, it becomes almost impossible to continue using these well-tried methods. What I read next persuaded me that God was trying to set my feet on a well-trodden path of prayer for which, as yet, I had no map, no compass, and no guide. Robert Llewellyn claims that when such changes are accompanied by a deep longing for God, when we find ourselves wanting him and him alone, then we may take this as a clear indication that the Holy Spirit is leading us into contemplative prayer. There is then only one option left: to yield to the impress of God's Spirit.

God used statements like these to show me his beckoning finger. Not knowing quite what I was surrendering to, since I had never consciously heard of contemplative prayer before, I said my 'Yes' to God. I wanted to be completely open to anything his Spirit had to give me.

Parched places inside me craved for more of the life-giving water of the Spirit which Robert Llewellyn implied was available. In the light of this I knew I could no longer be content with thoughts about God – either my own or other people's. I had to encounter him for myself; to meet him and be met by him. I could be content with nothing less. If necessary, I would go on making sacrifices for the privilege of pursuing this path of prayer. I was therefore ready to respond to God's further challenge:

Any who find within their hearts an answering cry to St Augustine's great words, 'Thou hast made us for thyself and the heart of man is restless till it finds its

rest in thee,' and who are ready in the grace of God
to face the testing experiences of the way, should go
forward, nothing doubting, in the path which the Spirit
is now calling.[3]

Chapter 4

Called to Contemplate

Refreshed, and in the full flush of joyful enthusiasm, I returned home. Contemplative prayer became a passion. My response to this call to contemplation was wholehearted.

'Is there a technique for this kind of prayer, a kind of do-it-yourself guide to contemplation?' I wondered. If there was I was determined to unearth it.

Robert Llewellyn's book, which I had had to leave at the convent, had offered several hints to beginners. I had recorded many of these in the big, brown, battered exercise book I had taken to Whitby and which I now guarded with my life. Sister Stella Mary, too, sensing the spiritual metamorphosis which was taking place in me, was a walking warehouse of practical suggestions which she shared with me most generously. But she was in Whitby and I was in Nottingham. I needed a more permanent mentor and guide.

God has a marvellous way of bringing people, events and books into our lives just when we need them. As I stood at this cross-roads in my pilgrimage of prayer, my search for guidelines at its peak, another friend said to me one day, 'I thought you might be interested to take a peep at this.' 'This' was a booklet which she had borrowed from a friend. Its title *A Method of Contemplative Prayer* drew me in the same way as I imagine honeysuckle attracts bees on a summer's evening.

The author, James Borst, is a teacher of prayer who lives in India. I warmed to him immediately when I learned from the foreword to the booklet that, like me, he was a teacher and counsellor whose diary was so full that he had to create time to pray. And I felt further drawn to him when I read his own preface to the booklet. There he emphasises the two spiritual steps which had laid the foundations for his own prayer life: first, the step of accepting Jesus as his Lord and Saviour; second, the step of opening himself to an infilling of the Holy Spirit of God. He explains that this second step, for many people, is the open sesame to contemplative prayer; the beginning of a new life in the Spirit in which the love of God becomes an experienced reality rather than an acknowledged fact only.

I was eager for this new life in the Spirit, as I have said, so I thumbed through the pages of the sixty-page booklet. To my joy and astonishment, James Borst was applying himself to the self-same questions which were whirling round my brain: 'What is contemplation?'; 'How does one go about it?'; 'What does this kind of prayer achieve?'; 'How does it help us to listen to God?' A quick glance at the no-nonsense answers which the author offers in response to these questions persuaded me that this book was exactly what I needed at this stage of the prayer adventure.

Imagine my dismay when my friend explained that she had promised to return the book that evening and that I would not be able to buy a copy of my own because it was out of print. There and then I sat in her flat and copied out whole pages of the book in longhand. I knew I could not afford to allow such spiritual gems to slip through my fingers.

The time was not wasted. As I wrote, my understanding of the nature of contemplative prayer deepened. I saw that contemplative prayer is essentially listening prayer. But it would not necessarily be words that I would be hearing. Rather, it would be an awareness of the presence of the indwelling Christ. I might start the prayer by using words like, 'Our Father in heaven'. But these words would not be the complete prayer. They would be like the sounding of a gong whetting my appetite and alerting me to the fact that the Father could be met and heard and loved. This broad definition of contemplative prayer was as tantalising to my spiritual palate as the smell of fresh ground coffee is to the natural taste buds. It reawakened the desire which had been quickened in me first at Mount St Bernard Abbey and then at Whitby.

With eagerness I noted the practical suggestions the author makes for those who respond to God.

A place and a time

The first requirement, he claims, is a place, preferably the privacy of one's own room. He reminds his readers of Jesus's example in this. Jesus himself 'often withdrew to lonely places and prayed' (Luke 5:16). And he recalls Jesus' exhortation: 'But when you pray, go into your room, close the door and pray to your Father, who is unseen' (Matt: 6:6).

I was privileged. My place was prepared. I read on. I wanted to know how I could make the best use of it.

He underlined the need we have to examine our commitments – family, profession, church, recreation – and within that framework to plot a daily appointment with God which we endeavour to keep as faithfully as possible. Progress would not be made in this pattern of prayer unless a definite time was fixed and kept, he claimed. Where possible, an hour a day should be set aside for this purpose.

A whole hour a day! As I looked at my diary, I wondered just where I could create an hour-long slot for prayer. But God challenged me through James Borst's observation, 'One full hour a day represents just about four per cent of all the time we live.'[1] Was I really saying that I could not consecrate four per cent of my life to attentiveness to God and him alone? Had I not noted in my exercise book:

If we are called to contemplative prayer and are to respond to the Spirit's call, we must face the fact that this will call for sacrifice of time, for courage to

perserve . . . That is one side of the work, the side
which is costly to the giver, and we may well ask, who
is sufficient for these things?[2]

The least I could do was to try. At that time, my
children were old enough to travel to school alone and
my husband's office was not in our home as it normally
is. By 8.30a.m. therefore a hush fell over our home after
the early morning scurry to school and work. The best
time to pray, I knew, would be from 8.30a.m. to 9.30a.m.
If I earmarked that time for stillness before God I could
be reasonably certain of being undisturbed. To guarantee
this still further, I began to make it known in the parish
that, except in emergencies, I would be grateful if phone
calls could be delayed until after 9.30a.m.

To my surprise, people were not offended. They
responded. This taught me two important lessons. If I
am really serious about listening to God, I must fix my
prayer time first and fit other things round it. If I am bold
enough to make my plan public, others will support and
encourage me in keeping my commitment.

Bodily posture

Just as a time and a place are basic to the life of prayer,
so is attention to bodily posture. As I read this further
claim in James Borst's booklet, I smiled. I had learned
to pray from my father, as I have said. Copying him, and
others whom I respected, usually when I prayed I would
bend my body in two as though I had stomach cramp, and
hold my head in my hands, a pious gesture which might
have looked to the uninitiated onlooker as though I had
a headache, or was trying to shield my eyes from the sting
of shampoo, and to God may well have looked as though I
was trying to hide from him rather than open myself to his
love and his Word. But it had never occurred to me that
the body can make a positive contribution to prayer, that
different bodily postures correspond to different moods
and emotions.

My mind went back to Whitby. There I had observed

a woman stretched out on the floor, face down, lying prostrate, her arms held out, her body thus forming the shape of a cross. At first I had felt embarrassed. 'Was she all right? Would she mind someone seeing her in this position?' The more I thought about that woman at prayer: the harmony which was being expressed between her body and her spirit, the more profound the impact it made on me.

With James Borst's challenge came the desire to experiment. I would sometimes lie prostrate on my prayer room floor. I found that this bodily posture expressed penitence, unworthiness, or my inner yearning for God far more eloquently than any words of mine. So I adopted it as a language all of its own. And when I came to prayer exhausted, I would sometimes lie in this position and voice a simple prayer: 'Lord, there are no words to express what I long to say to you. Please interpret the language of my body lying prostrate before you.' At such times I would sense a strange warmth which I took to be the support, the strengthening or the cleansing of God.

I am glad, looking back, that no one made a video recording of my experimentations with bodily posture. To the observer, certain postures must look very comical. But I found that when my body, mind and spirit were co-ordinated, an air of expectancy pervaded my prayer and an alertness to God characterised my listening.

Sometimes I would stand as I came into God's presence in the same way as many of the Old Testament prophets did.[3] At the same time, I would cup my hands, a gesture I use to show God that I am ready to receive whatever he wants to say or give to me. Sometimes I would tremble with anticipation as my body and my spirit waited attentively for a fresh visitation from God.

Usually, I would move from the standing position to kneeling. Sister Stella Mary had introduced me to the value of a prayer stool, an oblong stool nineteen centimetres high and eighteen centimetres wide which, when placed across the calves, supports the body, prevents the body's weight from cutting off the blood supply to the legs, and therefore enables a person to kneel for long periods in comparative comfort. A member of our congregation made a portable prayer stool for me, a gift I still value.

And my hands played an increasingly important part in my prayer. Sometimes I would hold them in my lap, palms upturned, a gesture of receptivity indicating that I was ready to receive anything God wanted to give me. At other times, as I knelt, I would bring my arms parallel to my body, spreading them out and tilting my palms very slightly as I turned them towards the front. Using this posture, my body says to God: 'I am your listening servant. I am yours. What is your will for me?'

When a sense of unworthiness swept over me, I would frequently fold my arms across my chest. And like Job and the Psalmist, I began to experiment with expressing praise and adoration to God, not simply with words, but by raising my hands and arms.[4] Occasionally, I would dance to some of the worship choruses I was growing to appreciate.

Gradually, I discovered that, in my body, I possessed an ally; a part of me which responded to the word of God's Spirit with greater ease than my mind; an ally who seemed able to assist the Holy Spirit in his work of revealing God's truth to my innermost being. There were times, which increased as the years fled by, when I would be still before God; I would stand or kneel, and stretch out my hands to receive from him whatever he wanted to give me; and, with my body receptive, an awareness of the presence of the living God would overwhelm me. In the stillness, I *knew* with my body, my mind and spirit that he *is* God. This convinced me early on that I must not ignore my body or neglect it, but rather must view it as an essential part of listening prayer, a part of me God created for his glory.[5]

Distractions

Even though my place of prayer was prepared and I had carved out a chunk of the day for listening to God, and even though I was training my body to co-operate rather than distract in this art form of prayer, it would frequently happen that as soon as I closed the prayer room door and settled down on my prayer stool my mind would buzz with noise. What would happen day after day is that I would remember that there was no bread in the bread-bin or that there were no eggs in the fridge, or stillness would be the time when I would remember certain letters which really should be written, or phone calls which should have been made.

Distractions of other kinds crowded in on me too. There was the blue-tit which sat on the window-sill of my prayer room while I prayed, and knocked on the window with his beak. And there were the pigeons which perched on the sloping roof and cooed gently but persistently while I tried to focus on God. At first both these internal and external distractions irritated me. I felt guilty, too, fearing that my progress in listening to God must be painfully slow if I could be side-tracked by such trivia.

But James Borst seemed to take such intrusions for granted. Robert Llewellyn, too, assumed that the Christian called to contemplate would encounter such difficulties. Both gave practical suggestions which helped me leap this hurdle.

Robert Llewellyn suggested that when we pray we imagine that we are rather like motor launches. Coming downstream float flotsam and jetsam of every kind. We are to keep our eyes on the goal, Jesus, and simply allow all this paraphernalia to pass us by. Meanwhile, we push our way through it, steadfastly heading for our destination: God and attentiveness to him.

I enjoyed taking authority over disrupting noises in this way. I would keep a piece of paper and a pen beside me. If I remembered some shopping which needed to be done urgently I would jot down the necessary items and return to the work of listening. When other thoughts vied for attention, I would steer my way through them, as Robert Llewellyn suggested. As for the blue-tit, the pigeons and the occasional troublesome motor-bike roaring past the house, I learned to *use* these sounds; I learned to translate

them into prayer rather than to fight them as though they
were enemies of God. I would hear the blue-tit's beak tap
against the window and simply say: 'Thank you, Lord, for
being nearer to me than that blue-tit; for your love which
is more persistent than the sound of his hammering.' I
would return to prayer and the noise would disappear,
not because it had stopped, but because it had been dealt
with, leaving me free to listen.

As I phased in and out of prayer like this, the name
Jesus was often on my lips. I was not using the Lord's
name as a mantra. Rather I used it as a reminder of
my goal in prayer: to encounter the living God, to be
met by him, held by him, commune with him and hear
him. Somehow it seemed natural, therefore, to call him
by name. As I come to prayer today, I still repeat that
name often. And if my concentration is broken for any
reason, I return to the stillness by repeating that name
slowly and silently. While I do this, I find that my
breathing deepens automatically. James Borst suggests
that these two methods – using a word of love, like
the name Jesus, and consciously breathing more deeply
– bring us back from the siding into which distractions
shunt us, and on to the main track of prayer. I find this
a helpful concept, one which I still use.

Phasing-in to stillness
John Donne used a memorable phrase to describe the
prelude to prayer: 'To tune the instrument at the gate'.
Both James Borst and Robert Llewellyn emphasised the
need for a phasing-in period: a few moments when we
can re-focus from the concerns of the day, relax and open
ourselves to attentiveness to the Spirit of God which is
contemplation.

I found in the early days of exploration into stillness that
I needed this re-orientation phase. I still need it.

Sometimes I would delay shutting the prayer room door
quite deliberately. Instead, I would tidy the house while
I composed myself and prayed a mental prayer: 'Lord,
quieten my mind and my heart as I prepare for this time

with you.' Sometimes I would go to my prayer room immediately my time for prayer came round. There I kept a tall, fat, red candle and I used to light this whenever I came to pray. It held no theological significance for me, only a practical one. If my mind was spinning like a top, as often it does, I would watch the flame flicker, listen to the wick splutter and spit, take careful note of the poker-still body and ask God to bring *me* into that kind of alive stillness.

The focal point of my prayer room was a cross. During this prelude to prayer, I would sometimes simply kneel at the foot of that cross and gaze at it. The cross of Jesus, that compelling symbol of sacrificial love, challenges me to centre my thoughts, not on *my* needs, *my* worries, *my* fears, *my* wants, but on Jesus. And as I gazed, I would find that in the wordlessness of silent wonder Jesus would emerge from the background of my mind and become the principal character in this drama of listening prayer.

Occasionally, as I phased into stillness, I would resort to a method of prayer made famous by one of the mystics. In my prayer room, in addition to the candle and the cross, I had a chair, an old wicker-work one painted white. Particularly if I came to prayer exhausted or hurting for some reason, I would imagine Jesus sitting in this chair. I would lay my head on the cushion, as though it were his lap, and weep or sigh or 'just be' in his felt presence. This kind of preliminary to prayer was therapy; on many occasions it infused my whole being with a sense of God's healing and peace; it was a form of listening which defies definition.

Preparing to listen

More and more, meditative music helped me to drop into the inner stillness which, for me, became the pre-requisite for alert, attentive and accurate listening to God. Almost always I would refer to the notes I had taken from James Borst's booklet and make my own response to them:

Just sit down and relax. Slowly and deliberately let all tension flow away, and gently seek an awareness of

the immediate and personal presence of God . . . You
can relax and let go of everything, precisely *because*
God is present. In his presence nothing really matters;
all things are in his hands. Tension, anxiety, worry,
frustration all melt away before him, as snow before
the sun.

Seek peace and inner silence. Let your mind, heart,
will and feelings become tranquil and serene. Let inner
storms subside: obsessional thoughts, passionate desires
of will and emotions. 'Seek peace and follow after it'
(Ps. 34:14).[6]

If I was still conscious of tension, I would tighten every
muscle in my body quite deliberately. Then, starting with
the facial muscles, I would relax them. At the same time,
I would ask God to spread his life and his energy through
me. And almost always I became aware that I was being
impregnated by God's peace.

In this way, I began to serve my apprenticeship in the
art of listening to God. Increasingly, I came to value the
simple techniques I have mentioned: a quiet, private place,
a fixed time, the language of my body, dealing with distractions and the relaxation which enables the personality to
unfold in the warm rays of the felt love of God. I still value
them and find them essential, though, with the years, the
emphasis I place on them has changed.

For me, learning to listen to God in this way has
been rather like learning to drive a car. When I was
a learner driver, between lessons I used to rehearse
mentally the process of changing gear and think carefully
about the technique of the three-point turn. In time, with
experience, these procedures became almost automatic
and required little thought.

Similarly, the prayer techniques I have described became
a regular part of my routine. This did not result in
complacency, however. I was always greedy for more.
I say this with no sense of pride. With the realisation that
prayer is a gift of God came the awareness that even the
desire to pray had been engrafted by God himself. No one

could work himself up to want to meet God in the way I thirsted for his presence at that time. It was a pure and precious gift.

Why was God enriching my life in this way? Why was prayer becoming such a profound experience? I was no super-saint, just an ordinary Christian leading an ordinary life, trying to be a good wife, a good mother and an effective witness for God in my neighbourhood.

For months no answer to that question was given, so I pressed on, growing all the time in my appreciation of silence, solitude and stillness before God. With the art of stillness came a greater ability to hear God. Phillip Keller has described the situation well:

> It is within this inner stillness, within this utter quietness, within this sweet solitude, that the Spirit of the living God speaks most clearly to our spirits. It is there, alone with him, that he makes himself real to us. It is there we 'see' him most acutely with the inner eyes of our awakened conscience. It is there he communes with us calmly through the inner awareness of his presence, speaking to us with ever-deepening conviction by his own wondrous word.[7]

This was becoming my experience. It filled me with awe. At the time there were few people I could confide in about this pilgrimage in the Spirit. That seemed unimportant. What was more important was that I pursue this purposeful prayer. Perhaps the time to talk would come later.

Chapter 5

Preparing to Contemplate

Contemplative prayer was to be a rich source of listening
to God. Day by day I would sit or stand or kneel in my
prayer room, relax, allow tensions to slide away, focus
on God, and a miracle would happen. As I closed my
eyes to shut out visual stimuli, and as I closed my ears,
as it were, by dealing authoritatively with the distractions
which threatened my ability to tune in to God, it was as
though, on the one hand, I closed a series of shutters on
the surface level of my life, thus holding at bay hindrances
to hearing the still, small voice of God, and on the other
hand, I released a trigger which gave deeper, inner, hidden
parts of myself permission to spark to life. As I attempted
to focus, deliberately and unashamedly, on the presence
of Christ, I would sometimes detect an inner stirring as
though secret antennae were being aroused and alerted
to pick up any and every signal the indwelling royal guest
might choose to give.

This attentiveness, alertness and sense of anticipation
was not unlike the in-tuneness I experienced when my
children were babies. I would be cooking or gardening,
reading or even sleeping, yet at the same time I would
be alert to their feelings: their pleasure, their glee, their
discomfort, their pain. Just as I had wanted, as a young
mother, to be responsive to my offspring, so now I longed
to respond to God in this intuitive way.

But there was so much more to learn. I loved the

learning process. My highway code, which stayed with me almost always in the early days, was James Borst's booklet, *A Method of Contemplative Prayer*. At first I scarcely ever veered from this step-by-step guide to attentive stillness. Eventually, as I grew in confidence and experience, inevitably I developed methods of my own in my pursuit to refine the art form of listening to God. Each person who seeks to stand before the living God will discover his own way of doing so. This must happen. The secret of true prayer is to place oneself utterly and completely at the disposal of God's Spirit. Sometimes the Spirit might cause us to dance or to jump for joy; at other times the same Spirit might draw us into the depths of silence where all is too mysterious for words. Even so, while remaining flexible and responsive to the wind of the Spirit, there is value in being aware of formulae used by others which one can then adapt in one's own time and way. James Borst's formula was the launching pad which thrust me into orbit.

James Borst suggests that there are certain phases which the person eager to reach the presence of God either passes through or dwells in during the course of any one period of prayer. He suggests that, in contemplative prayer, there are nine such phases. Some of these are preparatory phases, one is the contemplative phase itself, then there is the afterglow. The person at prayer might move from one phase to the next during their hour of prayer. Alternatively, depending on circumstances or personal needs, the one praying might stay in one phase only on a particular occasion if that seems most helpful. The contemplative phase will not necessarily be reached during every prayer time.

Phase of relaxation and silence

The first phase, I found, was indispensable. This is the one I have already described where, deliberately, I relax and let go of everything: tension, worry, anxiety, frustration. It is the period of prayer when I attempt to obey God's commands given through the psalmist: 'Be still, and know that I am God' (Ps. 46:10).

James Borst suggests that, if necessary, the whole of one's prayer time should be devoted to this activity. I soon saw the reason for this suggestion. Until our bodies, minds and spirits let go of the clutter we bring to our places of prayer, we automatically tune out the still, small voice of God. Unless we come into stillness before God we do not detect either the fullness of his presence or the winsomeness of his voice.

This phase of prayer has a value all its own. As we stop struggling before God we make it possible for him to impregnate us with his Spirit. During this prelude to prayer I would sometimes imagine myself as a meadow being saturated and refreshed by a gentle fall of dew. At other times I would think of myself as a tree; I would feel the sap surge through my roots and the sun shine on my leaves and I would know myself nourished by God. Sometimes, during this initial phase of prayer, I would picture myself as a rock on the seashore and I would enjoy the warmth of the sun of God's love and the washing of the water of his Spirit lapping over me. At such times I felt cherished by God.

Phase of awareness of his presence

I found that unless I took the trouble to unwind in God's presence in this way, I failed to appreciate the next phase of prayer: the few minutes when I opened myself to an awareness of God's presence, attentiveness and care. And it was this part of prayer which was revolutionising my life, so it was worthwhile spending time to prepare for it.

I am not conscious that anyone had ever suggested to me that, having relaxed in the presence of God, I should take time to recollect that he dwells at the core of my being; that as my Father he is as attentive to my cry as a mother to the slightest whimper of her new-born baby; that his gaze is focused on me as eagerly and devotedly as a father fixes his love on his new-born child. But as I began to spend time in recognising that God delights in me in this way, that he desires intimacy with me more than I long for oneness with him, I was filled with a profound sense of security.

I think, for example, of an occasion when I was suffering from an acute sense of loneliness. As I entered my prayer room, removed my shoes, relaxed, and concentrated, not on the growing emptiness within, but on the presence of God, I seemed to see myself as fragile, helpless and vulnerable as a new-born baby. But I was not lying alone, unloved. No. The arms of God were cradling me, his finger was stroking my cheek, his eyes were twinkling down at me. I felt loved.

I could have read those consoling words, 'Underneath are the everlasting arms', (Deut. 33:27), and I could have meditated on God's promise, 'I have loved you with an everlasting love', (Jer. 31:3), but to see those arms and to experience that love caused the assurance in my head to trickle into my heart and to lodge there. It is one of the rich dividends of contemplative prayer, I find, that in the stillness familiar truths make an impact on my experience in a way which is healing, consoling or challenging.

Phase of surrender

The more practised I became in finding the still point before God where I could taste his love and feel his warmth, the more I longed to surrender every part of my being to him. I wanted to be able to make the claim Paul once made: 'I no longer live, but Christ lives in me' (Gal. 2:20). I wanted to move from my prayer room into my corner of the world 'pregnant with Christ', to borrow Catherine de Hueck Doherty's phrase. And so, most days, I would make a conscious attempt to hand back to God all that I am, all that I possess, all that I do and all that I feel: my counselling, my teaching, my writing; my personality, my sexuality, my love, my friendships; my home, my pain if I am hurting, my successes or failures. I would echo the prayer James Borst uses: 'Take me and all I have, and do with me whatever you will. Send me where you will. Use me as you will. I surrender myself and all I possess absolutely and entirely, unconditionally and forever, to your control.'[1]

Whenever I paused to think seriously about this far-reaching prayer and could pray it with integrity, I would notice the level of joy and love for God rise measurably inside me. My heart would burn with love for God. My ability and desire to make sacrifices for him increased. This is hardly surprising. As Thomas Merton once put it, 'The deepest prayer at its nub is a perpetual surrender to God'.[2]

As I pray with others from time to time, I notice that there seems to be a law which links the awareness of God's presence with surrender to him. I think of an occasion when I was praying with a close friend of mine. He had asked me to pray for him that the parched places of his life might be revitalised by the life-giving waters of the Spirit of God. That night God met him in a most moving way. On a subsequent occasion, sensing that the Holy Spirit was leading him along the route I had travelled, the path of contemplative prayer, we again opened ourselves to receive whatever God wanted to give us. Then we kept total silence for several minutes.

It was my friend who broke the silence temporarily: 'I feel light-headed,' he admitted, 'and my heart is pounding.' The sense of the presence of God filled my study where we were praying. 'I believe these sensations are the Spirit's work,' I suggested. 'Let's just remain silent and open to him.' After several more minutes of complete silence, my friend, a young man who is not given to sentimentality or emotionalism, slumped back in his chair and sighed: 'I love him. I really love him. I could sing the chorus, "I love you Lord," right now, and really mean it.'

He said no more. There was no need. I could see on his face the look of longing love he felt for Jesus at that moment as he contemplated him. It did not surprise me that, from time to time after this overwhelming of the Spirit of God, this young man talked to me about offering himself to God for full-time service. The awareness of God's presence and the surrender of all our faculties belong together. If they do not, prayer can simply degenerate into self-indulgence.

Phase of acceptance

The fourth phase of prayer recommended by James Borst almost always causes me discomfort, to the same extent as the first few phases bring the overwhelming of the Spirit's presence. This is the time when we invite God to put his finger on specific situations, sins or attitudes which would block our ability to listen to God.

Jesus reminded us that part of the Holy Spirit's mission in life is to convict us of sin, to cross-examine us until we admit our failure. The further I progressed on this path of listening prayer, the more ruthless God seemed to become in highlighting inconsistencies in my life, showing me where he required me to change. At times I rebelled. At other times I squealed. God's demands are absolute, uncompromising. When he exposed sin I knew there would be no peace in prayer until I had played my part and obeyed his command to renounce it.

I think, for example, of an occasion when my husband and I had quarrelled. I made no attempt to hide my anger and bitterness from God. And he made no attempt to hide his requirement from me.

'Forgive David,' he said. 'Go and apologise.'
'But, Lord, it was *his* fault, not mine,' I protested.
'Never mind. You make the peace,' came the uncompromising reply.

On another occasion, as I gave God the opportunity to highlight areas of my life which he wanted to change, the dislike of a member of our congregation rose to the surface of my mind. The degree of irritability I encountered shocked me. This realisation drew from me a prayer: 'Lord, give me *your* love for her.' As though in answer to that prayer, I became aware of this girl's suffering. God seemed to pour into my receptive heart a great compassion for her, the compassion which is identification with another's pain and the desire, where possible, to alleviate that person's loneliness.

I still find this phase of prayer by far the most disconcerting. It is the part of prayer I most frequently omit. And my life is impoverished because of it. I recognise why I avoid this listening. One reason is that I am afraid: afraid of the sacrifices which may be demanded of me. Another reason is that, so often in my listening prayer, I am more concerned to receive the consolations of God than the God of consolations, the one who sets out to show me the truth about himself and the truth about myself, the one whose mission is to change me into his likeness.

Phase of repentance and forgiveness

Thomas Merton claims that 'to pray means to change'. He adds: 'Prayer if it is real is an acknowledgement of . . . our open-ness to be changed.'[3] Whenever I gave God the opportunity to show me myself and the areas of life which he wanted to prune or purge, I passed, with thankfulness, into the fifth phase of prayer. This is the place where James Borst urges the would-be contemplative to be ruthlessly honest: 'We face God as we are: sinful, spiritually handicapped and disabled in many ways, chronic patients. And we accept these handicaps and disabilities because he accepts us as we are and because he loves us as we are.'[4] James Borst is not suggesting that we become complacent about the sin which soils our lives. On the contrary, his challenge to cast it at the foot of the cross is compelling. But for me, the startling part of this phase of prayer is his insistence that we not only confess but *receive* forgiveness.

The introvert, particularly if that person comes from an evangelical background, is good at confessing and notoriously bad at receiving forgiveness. I am an introvert and an evangelical. These words never cease to amaze me even though I have been reading them for nine years.

> We are not permitted to nurse a sense of guilt: we must fully and completely accept and embrace his forgiveness and love. Guilt feeling and inferiority feeling before

God are expressions of selfishness, of self-centredness: we give greater importance to our little sinful self than to his immense and never-ending love. We must surrender our guilt and our inferiority to him; *his goodness is greater than our badness. We must accept his joy in loving and forgiving us.* It is a healing grace to surrender our sinfulness to his mercy.[5]

'His goodness is greater than our badness.'

'We must accept his joy in forgiving us.'

I recorded in my prayer journal an occasion when God wormed these words into my realisation. My emotions were in turmoil at the time. The problem was that I was working with a male colleague whose warmth and gentleness, tenderness and spirituality I was growing to appreciate. He was eliciting from me a response which was equally warm and this resulted in a special closeness which seemed like a gift from God.

Whenever God entrusts us with something of value and beauty, Satan sets himself the task of destroying or distorting it. In this instance he tried to soil this friendship by bombarding my mind with day-dreams and suggestions, thoughts and fantasies which, if translated into practice would turn *philia*, warm, compassionate, tender love into *eros*, a romantic love which would threaten my marriage and my integrity as a person.

At first, knowing that there is a close correlation between spiritual closeness and sexual awakening, I resisted each temptation firmly. A civil war raged inside but I fought to win. But gradually, my efforts weakened and I surrendered my imagination to the impure pictures which flashed frequently on the screen of my mind. While masquerading as a God-pleasing person, this poison was polluting me. Consequently, the reservoir of prayer dwindled to a mere puddle. The yearning to listen to God waned. And peace evaporated.

God disciplines those he loves. And he disciplined me. It was while I was sitting in church one Sunday morning that his voice reached me through the tangle of my emotions.

'You've lost your cutting edge', was all he said. And I knew that he was correct.

A deep, dark sadness crept over me as I reflected on this home-truth. 'What do I do, Lord?' I whispered. My answer came through the sermon. 'If you have lost your effectiveness for God because you have been sinning, admit it, acknowledge your failure and apply the blood of Jesus to the stain so that you may be forgiven.'

Later that day, I sat in the garden with my prayer journal and did just that. In a letter to God I poured out my repentance. When I had finished writing, I paused to listen. Into my mind came a picture of a pair of hands holding a piece of white fabric which was soiled and stained. I sensed the hands were God's hands and the piece of fabric represented my sin-spoiled life. As I watched, the hands held the fabric into a vat containing liquid. After several minutes, they gathered up the length of cloth and lifted it from the detergent. The stain had disappeared. The material was whiter than it had ever been. And God's voice seemed to whisper: 'My blood, shed for you, is the best detergent in the world.' I was so deeply moved that I wept tears of gratitude. I was so amazed at this sheer, undeserved goodness that I felt numb for several hours. I was so overwhelmed that I recorded the awe in my prayer journal. I was responding to the verse which claims that when God forgives, there is 'nothing left against you.' And I wrote:

'Lord, I can scarcely drink in this good news. Can it be true that you have wiped the slate clean of *all* the sin of the past few months? Yes! With my mind I know it. May that word NOTHING echo through the labyrinths of my entire being. NO THING. Not one single thought. No fantasy. No lust. NOTHING! Zero! The score against me from the divine perspective is nought. What relief! What joy! I am free: free from the guilt, free from the stain, free from the power of the Evil One, free to say no to all his fiendish suggestions. For this miracle, my Lord and Master, my Saviour, I praise you. May I be a faithful steward of the mystery of this grace of forgiveness. May I be a faithful steward, too, of *your* gift of love.'

God's forgiveness and love cannot be earned. It is always undeserved. Nevertheless it is to be received with humbleness and brokenness of spirit. It is to be relished. It is to be accepted with thanksgiving. It reflects the victory Jesus won at Calvary. It turns our disgrace into trophies of his grace.

Listening prayer, I was discovering, operates when we are in the pits, needing to be rescued by God, and it is operative, too, when we soar to unexpected spiritual peaks. And, of course, God goes on speaking in the ordinary, in-between days when life seems mundane, even monotonous. He not only speaks, he woos us, calling us to receive him into our lives, persuading us to fix our gaze on him.

Chapter 6

Continuing to Contemplate

I preached at a friend's wedding just before I began to write this chapter. After the ceremony, the bride and groom invited those who had taken part in the service to congregate on the steps of the church to be photographed. The group formed: the bride, the groom, the vicar of the church, a friend who had officiated at the service, the two people who had read Bible passages, a young man who had sung a solo, and me. We smiled – and shivered, because it was a cold, grey day. One photograph was taken and we began to move away. But the photographer cried out: 'Hold it! I want to take another one just like that.'

'Hold it!' Perhaps that is the simplest and most accurate definition of contemplative prayer: the deepest, most mysterious method of listening to God which I know of.

In the last chapter, I described the way I went about preparing to contemplate. The phases of prayer are rather like pieces of a jig-saw puzzle. When you fit them together, you realise that God has been preparing you for the moment when you 'hold it'; when your heart and mind and will are relaxed, focused on him, surrendered to him, cleansed and renewed so that you are ready to gaze on him in adoring love and to know yourself the object of his undivided affection and attention.

Archbishop Anthony Bloom captures the nuances of this dimension of listening prayer with a simple story of a peasant who had formed the habit of slipping into a certain church at a certain time of day with clockwork regularity. There, day by day, he would sit and, apparently, do nothing. The parish priest observed this regular, silent visitor. One day, unable to contain his curiosity any longer, he asked the old man why he came to the church, alone, day in, day out. Why waste his time in this way?

The old man looked at the priest and with a loving twinkle in his eye gave this explanation: 'I look at him. He looks at me. And we tell each other that we love each other.'

This is contemplation in a nutshell. This is the essence of listening prayer. Though I was a mere beginner, and still consider myself to be no more than a novice, this was the gift God was giving me. This was the reason why I carved out a whole hour a day to abandon myself to the stillness in which the love of Christ could be felt. This was why I was at pains to use the phases I have described to opt out of the crazy whirlpool of ceaseless activity into which I am so quickly sucked and to reach the calmer waters of the prayer of silence. Phillip Keller captures the benefits of this stillness well:

> For the man or woman who has come to know and love the Lord God in the depths of such intimacy, the times of solitude are the most precious in all of life. They are a rendezvous with the Beloved. They are anticipated with eagerness. They are awaited with expectancy . . . For the person who has found in God a truly loving heavenly Father, gentle interludes with him alone are highlights of life. For the one who has found Christ the dearest friend among all the children of earth, quiet times in his company are the oases of life. For the individual conscious of the comradeship of God's gracious Spirit in the stillness of solitude, these intervals are the elixir of life.[1]

Such was my experience. Indeed, such *is* my experience. No words of mine can hope to do justice to the encounter with God which takes place in such silence. It is as hard to recapture with a pen as it is to describe the scene outside the cottage window which I have been gazing at for the past five minutes. I can tell you that raindrops glisten as they hang like pearls from the rose bush which almost touches my window pane; that the fronds of the weeping willow are waving to the cars which wind their way along the valley; that a blackbird is surveying the moors as he sits on the telephone wire and sings; that the sun is trying to shine on the rain-drenched hills. I can describe the colours: the purple aubrietia cascading over my neighbour's grey stone walls, the yellow pansies in her garden, the coral pink of her rhododendron bushes, the scarlet of her tulips, and the variegated virgin greens which cover the countryside in spring. But this is only a fragment of the scene which delights me. You cannot hear the thrush trilling nor hear the chaffinches chattering nor see the buds bursting with life, nor feel the creative energy of the countryside in May. If you would appreciate the full extent of the beauty before me you must witness the glory of this place for yourself.

Similarly, the wonders of contemplation can be appreciated only by those who contemplate, for as Stephen Verney, the Bishop of Repton, rightly says, 'contemplation is an opening of the eyes . . .'[2] It is losing oneself in what one sees and hears in the same way as one loses oneself in a spectacular sunrise or a magnificent view from an aeroplane.

Stephen Verney suggests that there are three stages of contemplation: first, 'it is me and him'. I come to prayer conscious of myself, my need, my desires. I pour these out to God. Second, prayer becomes 'him and me'. Gradually, I become more conscious of the presence of God than of myself. 'Then it is only him.'[3] God's presence arrests me, captivates me, warms me, works on me. It is mystery, reality, certainty – awesome. As an unknown author of the thirteenth century put it: 'While you are quiet and exist in a calm and simple awareness of his presence, your heart seeks him out and opens to receive his love. It is a prayer which is wordless, fed by a quiet ardor.'[4] Or, as another contemplative has struggled to express the inexpressible:

You turn yourself entirely to his presence. You steadily look at him. His presence becomes more real to you. He holds your inward sight. Your glance simply and lovingly rests on him. Your prayer is nothing but a loving awareness of him: I look because I love; I look in order to love, and my love is fed and influenced by looking . . .'[5]

What does the contemplative see when he gazes in this way? I cannot speak for anyone else. I can speak for myself. For me, the seeing varies from day to day.

In the early days I would often dwell on the vision of Christ contained in the Book of Revelation. As I contemplated, I would catch my breath as a hint of the glory of the wounded, wondrous, much-worshipped Lamb of God would impress itself on me:

Then I looked and heard the voice of many angels, numbering thousands upon thousands, and ten thousand times ten thousand. They encircled the throne and the living creatures and the elders. In a loud voice they sang:

Worthy is the Lamb, who was slain,
to receive power and wealth and wisdom and strength
and honour and glory and praise!

Then I heard every creature in heaven and on earth and under the earth and on the sea, and all that is in them, singing:

To him who sits on the throne and to the Lamb be praise and honour and glory and power, for ever and ever!

The four living creatures said, 'Amen', and the elders fell down and worshipped (Rev. 5:11–14).

In the early days, too, while the cross was the visual focus in my prayer room, the sufferings of Christ, physical, emotional and psychological, would often fill my horizon as I fixed my attention on love crucified.

Since my visit to Israel, where the aliveness of Jesus struck me with fresh force, and where a bronze statue of the Lord leaping with resurrection joy made a deep impression on me, often, as I kneel or stand or sit in an attitude of listening prayer, God's strength, vitality, power, authority and even sense of fun overwhelm me and intermingle with the pain and glory I have already mentioned.

This morning, for example, God delighted me with the reminder of the *joie de vivre* which is an expression of the abundant life Jesus enjoyed as well as promised to others. As I focused my attention on God, C. S. Lewis' vigorous account of the resurrection flooded back into my mind. In his children's fantasy, *The Lion, the Witch and the Wardrobe*, Aslan, the lion, who represents Jesus, was sacrificed and then mysteriously brought back to life:

> 'Oh children,' said the Lion, 'I feel my strength coming back to me. Oh children, catch me if you can!' He stood for a second, his eyes very bright, his limbs quivering, lashing himself with his tail. Then he made a leap, high over their heads, and landed on the other side of the table. Laughing, though she didn't know why, Lucy scrambled over it to reach him. Aslan leaped again. A mad chase began. Round and round the hill-top he led them, now hopelessly out of their reach, now tossing them in the air with his huge and beautifully velveted paws and catching them again, and now stopping unexpectedly so that all three of them rolled over together in a happy laughing heap of fur and arms and legs.[6]

I could never predict beforehand what the result of the listening would be. Nor could I anticipate how long the sense of the awareness of God's presence would last. Usually, I find the moments of acute in-touchness with God are fleeting, but real. I soon discovered that I must be content with what God gave, enjoy it and benefit from it without trying to cling or crave for more. He might choose to reveal himself momentarily, he might linger. That is his responsibility. Mine is simply to be ready.

Phase of receiving
And I wanted to be ready always. As bulbs in spring stretch their green fingers upwards in response to the warm rays of the sun, so I was responding to the felt, experienced presence of God. And I discovered that the phase of contemplation is not the final phase of prayer. There is an afterglow to be enjoyed. The first phase after the moment of contemplation is the phase of receiving. As James Borst puts it, '"Seek and you will always find" becomes "Seek and you will always be found."'[7]

Having spent years in prayer asking God for things, this phase of the afterglow was sheer delight. At first I scarcely dared to believe James Borst's claim:

'He responds: He turns to me. He seeks me. He is anxious to invade my spirit. He wants that his Spirit possess me. I bask in the warmth of his love. I feel his gaze upon me. Jesus, my Lord, is eager to possess my heart with which to love his Father, and with which to radiate his love . . . His presence brings a deep spiritual peace, a share in his 'sabbath' rest, a greater serenity, ability to accept and to suffer, a lifting of despair, a welling up of joy and love, a floodlight, a strong desire to praise and thank him.'[8]

But these claims became true to my experience.

Eighteen months after my initiation into this life of listening prayer, I began to keep a prayer journal where I recorded some of the things I wanted to express to God as well as some of his responses. In the autumn of 1978 I wrote:

I find prayer exciting because I never know in advance how God is going to meet with me. The Divine Lover

sometimes comes as the Father, the one who is saving the best robe for the worst child, the Father
who gave his own Son, such is the generosity of
his loving. Sometimes my Lord comes as the loving,
searching Shepherd, sometimes as life. Sometimes as
energy.

I recorded the sense of awe which overwhelmed me with
every realisation that it is *God* who takes the initiative in
this kind of prayer:

My knowledge of God is becoming deeper. It is far less
an intellectual knowing and progressing towards the
intimate knowing experienced by a husband and wife:
union. Sometimes he comes to me as the Bridegroom
to his Bride and in that knowing there is such awesome
love. As I write that now, it seems too wonderful that
Almighty God – the generous one – should meet *me* in
that way and yet that is part of his generosity that it is
he who takes the initiative.

All my life, the teaching I had received on prayer had
placed the responsibility for my relationship with God
firmly on my shoulders. I had been taught to seek God:
in his Word, in church, in the fellowship. Even when I
had had a conversion experience at the age of seventeen,
the emphasis seemed to focus on *my* commitment: it was
me giving *my* life to God. But now the emphasis had
changed. God seemed to underline the true situation: that
the initiative in the prayer of listening was not mine but
his. The initiative of love, similarly, was not mine, but
his. As Thomas Merton puts it: 'True contemplation is
not a psychological trick but a theological grace. It can
come to us *only* as a gift.'[9] And as the author of *The
Cloud of Unknowing* reminds us, '*He* kindled your desire
for himself, and bound you to him by the chain of such
longing.'[10]

These facts penned so poignantly by Stephen Verney
stunned me into silent worship and wonder:

This is the nature of the encounter, not that I am stumbling towards the Abba Father, but that the Abba Father is running towards me. It is not that I love God but that God believes in me. The discovery at the heart of contemplation is not that I am contemplating the divine love, but that the divine love is contemplating me. He sees me and understands and accepts me, he has compassion on me, he creates me afresh from moment to moment, and he protects me and is with me through death and into life beyond.[11]

To know oneself loved, believed in, understood, accepted, trusted and constantly renewed by God is a humbling experience. At least, I found it so. And it took time for the realisation of these truths to trickle from my head into my heart. As, gradually, they lodged there, the phase of receiving began, not only to make sense to me but to become a priority.

Jesus now featured in the dialogue of prayer in a new way: not just by whispering into my ear but by acting on my behalf.

I think of the time when I wondered whether the glandular fever germ would ever leave my body, when my body was weary and I was lonely. One day, as I prayed, I poured out my frustration to God. During the phase of receiving in prayer, I found myself re-enacting the parable of the Good Samaritan. But in the video which played through my imagination, I seemed to be the wounded person lying helpless on the deserted road. As I opened myself to receive from Jesus, he came to me displaying all the tenderness and skill attributed to the Good Samaritan. The encounter was so powerful that I could sense him anointing my emotional wounds, entering into my loneliness, picking me up and pouring into me the courage I needed to carry on.

A recurring picture which never ceased to amaze and comfort me also found its roots in one of Jesus's parables. I would picture myself as a forlorn lamb which had lost its way and lost its companions. While I was busy bleating or panicking or running round in small circles, I would see Jesus striding towards me. I would sometimes see his smile. I would sense his immense strength. Sometimes I would feel him put me on his shoulders and carry me back to the proper path. At other times he would simply stand and cuddle or chastise me.

Receiving God's love in this vivid way reinforced for me the reality of the God who is always there, the God who cares. It encouraged me to open myself to the surge of God's love and not to dictate to him how he might or might not express this love.

Phase of Praise and Thanksgiving

It also carried me across the threshold into another phase of prayer: the phase of praise and thanksgiving. From time to time God would challenge me to learn to receive life as a gift from himself instead of living life at such breakneck speed that there was no time to think thankfully.

As I responded to this challenge, I learned to savour the good gifts God sends: a perfect rose, the scent of honey-suckle, the embrace of a friend, the taste of bacon. As this savouring became a part of life, I would thank God for the gift of electricity when I used my cooker instead of taking modern technology for granted. And as I fell asleep at night, I would watch an action replay of the previous twenty-four hours in my mind and select particular people and events for which I wanted to praise God. At such times life became a symphony of praise.

As time went on, this heart-felt gratitude to God began to be expressed in a whole variety of ways. One morning, a few months after this journey into contemplative prayer had begun in earnest, having gazed at the features of the Lord I was learning to trust in a deeper, richer way than ever before, I took up my guitar and started to sing a song of praise to its accompaniment. After a few minutes I was playing a chord sequence I had not learned and singing a tune I had never heard before. The language I used was not English, but tongues, a method of praising God I had once considered weird and superfluous, but which I now value immensely.

But the times when I wondered whether my heart would burst with praise almost always happened at the convent which eventually became my spiritual home. At 9.0 a.m. each morning, the sisters celebrate Holy Communion and I would join them for this highlight of the day's worship. Usually it was a simple, short service lasting not more than half an hour. There would be no music, just the liturgy, Bible readings, prayer and the sacrament – the bread and wine. At the close of the service, everyone would kneel in silent adoration of Jesus, the one who had fed us with these symbols of his body and blood. It was then, having been brought into silence, having been brought face to face with the mystery of God and having been fed by him, that praise would surge from somewhere deep inside of me and beg to be expressed: either in silent wonder, or in sighs and groans, or in a burst of song. The urge to sing was so strong sometimes that after Communion I would go to the bottom of the garden where no one could hear me and sing under the pine trees, or I would take my guitar to the garden shed and strum it and sing to God there. To be gripped by such praise was intoxicating, and I realised that very often I approach prayer, praise and thanksgiving from the wrong angle. I rush into God's presence, blurt out some superficial sentences of gratitude, but never pause to encounter him. When the encounter comes first, I realised, the level of praise is deepened, the experience more real.

Phase of Intercession

And I learned that having dropped into the stillness of God, contemplated him, received from him and given thanks for who he is and what he has done, I was ready to intercede for others. But the nature of intercession changed. The focus of the prayer was not the person for whom I was praying, as it had been in the past. No. The focus of my intercessory prayer was Jesus himself. This refocusing revolutionised my practice of interceding for others. The acute awareness of the presence of Jesus persuaded me that I need not fumble for fine words in order to present to Jesus the needs of others. All that was needed was that I should pass the person or situation into his all-knowing, all-wise, all-capable and all-caring hands.

The consciousness of Christ's presence changed my prayer for another reason also. Instead of dictating to God what he should do to alleviate a certain person's suffering or to sort out a complex crisis, I learned, as I held the situation to him, to listen for an answer to the question: 'Lord, is there anything you would like me to do for this person to show them that you are in control or that you care?' I found that God is faithful in responding to that sort of question and very often requires me to form a part of the answer to my own prayers.

There never seems to be enough time to complete such intercession in my specific prayer time. Most of my interceding spills over into my day, so I lift people and circumstances to God while I am hoovering or walking or driving the car or resting after lunch. God hears. He acts. In this prayer we simply sidle alongside the great intercessor, Jesus himself, and enjoy the privilege of becoming his prayer partner.

I could never be certain from day to day which of these phases of prayer would occupy most of my prayer time. What I could be certain of was that my experience of God would leave me panting for more. St Bernard said of contemplative prayer: it is a 'searching never satisfied but without any restlessness'. And Gregory of Nyssa observed: 'The one who looks up to God never ceases in that desire.' In a small way I was beginning to testify to these twin feelings and I wanted to press on because more experienced prayers persuaded me that one of the rewards of this particular search is to go on searching.

Chapter 7

Back to the Bible

I was troubled. People in my church fellowship were becoming suspicious of my prayer pilgrimage. One girl put the anxiety of many others into words: 'I think you're going overboard. You're allowing those mystics to influence you too much. You're in danger of betraying your evangelical heritage.' Others refrained from expressing their ambivalence at the time but confessed to me later, 'We thought we'd lost you to silence for ever.'

I understood this fear. Nevertheless it hurt. It hurt because it seemed as though I was not trusted. And it hurt to hear mature Christians express so much criticism and suspicion of those whose experience of God was somewhat different from their own. Whenever unfair comments were made about Catholic spirituality, for example, tears would prick my eyes and I would catch myself crying inside.

I am not saying that it was inappropriate for my friends to question what I was doing. Neither am I saying that I could not see why they were doing it. Until this phase of my life, I, too, had been bitterly prejudiced against 'high church practices' and particularly against Catholicism. My father, a staunch Baptist, had refused so much as to buy a Christmas card with a candle on it because to him it smacked of being Catholic. Ingrained in me from childhood was the belief that no good thing could come from Rome. But now I was beginning to catch a glimpse of how misguided that prejudice was. I am not saying that I accepted everything Catholic spirituality stands for. Neither am I saying that it ever occurred to me to become a Roman Catholic or even a high Anglican. What I am saying is that the monks I met at Mount St Bernard Abbey challenged the hard crust of contempt which covered me, not by anything they said, but by the life they lived: particularly by the quality of their prayer. I could see for myself that these men had plumbed depths of prayer which no one from my spiritual tradition had ever shown me. And I wanted what they experienced. Moreover, I believed that God wanted it for me, that he had provided these nursery slopes of prayer for me. And I recognised early on in my quest that I did not have to buy the whole Catholic package in order to benefit from their experience of prayer. Neither is God bound by the confines of our denominations.

Even so, I was torn in two. My husband, I could tell, was worried about me. Occasionally we attempted to discuss my growing interest in silence, meditation and contemplative prayer. But our minds failed to meet. He was afraid that I was travelling up a cul-de-sac which would result only in disillusionment. I was afraid that he was trying to squeeze me into a spiritual mould from which I had been set free. 'What am I to do?' On the one hand I seem to be standing on the threshold of a dynamic dimension of prayer which is revolutionising my life and on the other hand I seem to be alarming a number of people, including my husband. I put this kind of question to myself on several occasions and the absence of an answer left me even more confused. I recorded this confusion in my prayer journal on one occasion. Writing to God, I said:

> I want to confess to you the confusion I feel over the whole area of prayer. I so long to follow your leading in this – into silence. But I see this creating a bigger and bigger gulf between David and me . . . Father, I feel resentment. Why have you led me this way? Why can't he understand? I feel deep anger and sorrow that over the years I have listened to and assented to

untruths about many of your children [meaning Roman Catholics]. Yes, I want to be caught up in your work of reconciliation. But it hurts and I sometimes feel so alone . . .

But I was troubled for another reason, too. Although I sensed that God was giving me a priceless pearl in this gift of prayer, I had been taught that I was to be a 'guardian of the gospel' and to ensure that my philosophy of life and my behaviour were always in alignment with the clear teaching of scripture. So far, although I had been fascinated and helped by the rhythm of prayer I dropped into at Mount St Bernard Abbey, at Whitby, and now at home, and although I was thrilled by the teaching on prayer I was receiving from the books I have mentioned, references to the Bible's teaching on listening to God were only oblique. I could not say for certain that the belief that God still speaks today is firmly rooted in scripture.

How can John Powell be sure that God is as available to speak to us today as he was to speak to Abraham, Isaac, Jacob and Jeremiah? How can James Borst be certain that it is *God* who will manifest himself in stillness? How can I decide whether the overwhelming spiritual experiences originate in God?

These questions and others like them bothered me, not only because I loved the Bible and was firmly committed to live biblically, but also because I knew that many Bible-believing scholars pour scorn on voices and experiences. In the circles in which I lived and worked the counter-claim prevailed: that God has spoken through his Son and through his revealed Word, the Bible. Since this revelation contains everything we need 'for teaching, rebuking, correcting and training in righteousness' (2 Tim. 3:16), God has no more need to speak.

Jim Packer describes this viewpoint powerfully and more generously than many:

While it is not for us to forbid God to reveal things apart from scripture, or to do anything else (he is

God, after all!), we may properly insist that the New Testament discourages Christians from expecting to receive God's words to them by any other channel than that of attentive application to themselves of what is given to us twentieth-century Christians in holy scripture.[1]

Trapped between this teaching, the anxiety of my friends and an irresistible thirst to know more about listening to God, there seemed only one way forward. I would have to search the Bible for myself to see whether it describes the kind of listening to God which had struck a chord within my heart.

'I'll do my own research. I'll comb the scriptures and apply to them three questions: Does the Bible address itself to the subject of listening to God? If so, what exactly does it say? How did God speak to men and women in the days when the Bible was written?'

Having made this resolve, I determined to be as thorough as possible. I raided my husband's study and collected every version of the Bible I could find, gathered together a stack of Bible commentaries, unearthed the fat, red New Bible Commentary I had used in student days, treated myself to a brand new Concordance and reorganised my own study to accommodate the booklets and articles and books on prayer which had helped me in some way. Thus surrounded by studies of prayer written by teachers of prayer and people of prayer from a variety of Christian traditions, I began my own quest into the Bible's teaching on listening to God.

God's promises

One of the first passages of the Bible I turned to intrigued me. It was the familiar passage from the fourth gospel: 'I am the good shepherd; I know my sheep and my sheep know me . . . I have other sheep that are not of this sheep pen. I must bring them also. *They too will listen to my voice*, and there shall be one flock and one shepherd' (John 10:14–16, italics mine). Two sentences from this passage gripped me. First, Jesus's claim to be 'the Good Shepherd'. Second, his promise. 'They too will listen to my voice.'

I began to tease out what might have been in Jesus's mind when he described himself as the Good Shepherd, a pen-picture which does not necessarily communicate itself accurately to the Western reader.

As I meditated on these words: 'Good Shepherd', my mind flew first to Greece where we had travelled on one occasion. I remembered commenting to my husband as we drove through mile upon mile of arid countryside: 'Have you noticed that you never see sheep here without an accompanying shepherd? At home it's the exact opposite. You scarcely ever see a shepherd, just fields full of unaccompanied sheep.'

My mind wandered from Greece to Israel. Tired of the heat and narrow streets thronging with tourists, my husband and I wandered out of Nazareth to picnic on a grassy slope we could see in the distance. There we met a youth carrying a new-born lamb, a shepherd boy.

He showed us his lamb with obvious pride. 'It's mine. It's not quite twenty-four hours old.' He also pointed to the other sheep grazing peacefully in the long grass. This boy was in charge of seventeen sheep including the baby lamb. Each sheep had a name. Each responded to that name. When the shepherd called, they followed. His relationship with these sheep, which belonged to his father, was intimate. He treated them not as possessions, but as persons. So he whispered in the lamb's woolly ear in the same way as a mother would coo over her baby. He told his little flock his news as they walked from pasture to pasture. He chided them when they wandered away from him or when they strayed near a dangerous precipice. And as they walked home in the evening, he explained to them what was happening and told them of his plans for the next day. This encounter with eastern shepherds provided me with a new perspective on the familiar image used by Jesus.

In order to deepen my understanding of Jesus's claim,

I turned to the Old Testament and to the descriptions it contains of faithful shepherds.

> [The Sovereign Lord] tends his flock like a shepherd; he gathers the lambs in his arms and carries them close to his heart; he gently leads those that have young (Isa. 40:11).

> The Sovereign Lord says: I myself will search for my sheep and look after them. As a shepherd looks after his scattered flock . . . I will search for the lost and bring back the strays. I will bind up the injured and strengthen the weak . . . (Ezekiel 34:11; 16).

> The Lord is my shepherd, I shall not be in want.
> He makes me lie down in green pastures,
>   he leads me beside quiet waters,
>   he restores my soul.
> He guides me in paths of righteousness
>   for his name's sake.
> Even though I walk
>   through the valley of the shadow of death,
> I fear no evil,
>   for you are with me;
> your rod and your staff,
>   they comfort me (Ps. 23:1–4).

I meditated on these passages for several days. The picture of the Good Shepherd which rose up before me was of a man who expresses his faithfulness through his availability: 'he leads me, restores me, is with me.' The good shepherd is one who involves himself in the life of his flock: he gathers the lambs together, carries them, leads the ewes with gentleness. The Good Shepherd is a dedicated person: he searches for the lost, heals the sick, bandages the wounded. Communication between sheep and shepherd seemed a two-way affair: the helpless sheep looked to the shepherd for guidance, wisdom and direction. These resources were given constantly. The relationship which grew between a sheep and his shepherd was one of intimacy.

Not only does Jesus *imply* that, as the Good Shepherd, he will communicate with his flock. Here he *promises* that the Holy Spirit will be a talking, teaching, acting agent of God whose mission will be to show us the truth by transmitting God's messages and to further lead us into the truth by revealing to us 'what is yet to come'.

Peter takes up this theme on the day of Pentecost. When he quotes from the prophet Joel he hints that the Holy Spirit has at his disposal a whole variety of ways to ensure that God's will and Word are made known to man:

> In the last days, God says,
> I will pour out my Spirit on all people.
> Your sons and daughters will prophesy,
>   your young men will see visions,
>   your old men will dream dreams, (Acts 2:17 quoting Joel 2:28).

Paul repeats the refrain in his letter to the Corinthians. The gifts of the Spirit are, in the main, gifts of communication: prophecy, tongues, discernment and knowledge (1 Cor. 12). It is as though Paul is reminding us that the God who yearns to communicate will find a variety of ways to convey God's message and apply God's revealed word to his people. Can this really happen *only* through the text of scripture?

The writer to the Hebrews, quoting from Psalm 95, assumes that God will continue to speak to his people. Three times he quotes the Holy Spirit as saying: 'Today, *if you hear his voice*, do not harden your hearts . . .' (Heb. 3:7–8, 15 italics mine).

And John the Divine, contemplating the glorified Lord, builds on the foundations already laid in both the Old Testament and the New. Through him Jesus invites believers and unbelievers alike to hear his voice: 'Here I am! I stand at the door and knock. *If anyone hears my voice* and opens the door, I will come in . . .' (Rev. 3:20, italics mine).

I turned to the Old Testament. There I noticed God talking to Adam, to Abraham and to Moses 'as a man speaks with his friend' (Exod. 33:11). Similarly, David and Solomon, Elijah and Nathan, to name but a few dignitaries, heard the voice of God.

And my survey of the books of the Bible highlighted another truth. Over and over again, when God communicated with those he loved, it was he who took the initiative, by preceding the person and providing him with an awareness of his presence or speaking in clear unmistakable ways. So the psalmist cried out in wonder, 'Thou, God, seest me.' Jacob acknowledged, 'Surely, the Lord is in this place and I was not aware of it' (Gen. 28:16). Mary Magdalene heard that one, welcome, economical word at the tomb, 'Mary!' And the disciples on the road to Emmaus enjoyed the companionship of the stranger whose company and conversation caused their hearts to burn within them.

Several of Jesus's parables encourage us to expect God to take the initiative in this relationship of love. The father waits and watches for the return of the prodigal and gathers up his skirts so that he is free to run to greet the returning wanderer. The woman searches until she finds the coin she has lost. The good shepherd searches ceaselessly for the sheep who has wandered away.

The more I delved into the pages of the Bible, the more convinced I became that the thread which runs right through the Old Testament and the New is of a God who spoke to his people incisively and intimately in times past, a God who is the same yesterday, today and forever, a God whose constancy and consistency do not permit him to 'change like shifting shadows' (Jas. 1:17), a God who is therefore committed to communicate in creative ways throughout history: through the written word, through his Son (Heb. 1:2), through dreams, through visions, through angels, through the prompting of the indwelling Spirit, through nature, indeed, through any method he chooses. As David Watson puts it: 'God did not finish speaking to us when the scriptures were completed . . . God is the living God, the God of today; and every day he wants us to enjoy a living relationship with him, involving a two-way conversation.'[2]

Convinced and thrilled by these early investigations into the Bible's view of listening to God, I read on. The outcome was a whole chapter of surprises.

Chapter 8

Commanded to Listen

The God who spoke in times past still speaks and will continue to speak throughout history. God's word is powerful, full of majesty (Ps. 29:4), accurate and active (Heb. 4:12). These solemn truths overshadowed me as I continued to survey the Bible's teaching on listening to God. Michael Mitton expresses it in this way:

> The life of man is impoverished if he does not communicate with his Creator . . . Man is created as a responding creature – he must respond to his Maker. By doing this, to use Martin Buber's language, he becomes 'I' as he communicates with 'Thou'. If God does not communicate to us, he is only an 'It'; if he speaks to us, and we speak with him, he becomes 'Thou'.[1]

That God is a 'Thou', a person as opposed to an object, I had no doubt. That God yearns to communicate, similarly, I had no doubt. But what I learned next about the God of the Bible took me by surprise.

I had turned from meditating on the shepherding of Jesus to contemplate the Transfiguration. Embedded in Matthew's account of this unique revelation of Jesus's glory, lay a command which I had never bumped into before: 'There he was transfigured before them. His face shone like the sun, and his clothes became as white as the light . . . and a voice from the cloud said, "This is my Son,

whom I love; with him I am well pleased. *Listen to him!*'"
(Matt. 17:2, 5, italics mine).

I looked at this verse long and hard and found it difficult
to believe that it does not say, 'This is my dear Son, talk
to him.' Nor does it read, 'This is my dear Son, ask him
for things.' Neither does it encourage, 'This is my dear
Son, tell him your diagnosis when someone is sick.' No.
It reads, 'This is my Son . . . *Listen to him.*'

Why had I never noticed this verse before? Why had
I never heard anyone preach a sermon on it? Why was
the emphasis always on asking God for things when we
pray rather than on listening to him? Did this verse mean
simply that God's people are to obey his words which have
been recorded in the Bible or does it imply something more
than that?

With this clear command to listen to God staring me
in the face, these questions puzzled and bothered me.
When I unearthed a whole string of commands to listen
to God, I became even more perplexed and asked myself
why some people claim that it is presumptuous to expect
God to speak when God's call to listen runs through the
Old Testament and the New in the same way as a theme
tune runs through a film.

I found God's call to listen highlighted most movingly
in the history of the youth Samuel:

> The Lord called Samuel a third time, and Samuel got
> up and went to Eli and said, 'Here I am; you called
> me.' Then Eli realised that the Lord was calling the
> boy. So Eli told Samuel, 'Go and lie down, and if
> he calls you, say, "Speak, Lord, for your servant
> is listening."' So Samuel went and lay down in his
> place. The Lord came and stood there, calling as
> at the other times, 'Samuel! Samuel!' Then Samuel
> said, 'Speak, for your servant is listening' (1 Sam.
> 3:8–10).

The same command to listen punctuates the book of
Isaiah: 'Consult me' (30:2); 'Listen' (44:1); 'Hear this

. . .' (51:21); 'Listen to me' (55:2); 'Give ear and come
to me; hear me . . .' (55:3).

Jeremiah takes up the theme: 'Hear the word of the
Lord, all . . . who come through these gates to worship
the Lord' (7:2).

And Ezekiel commands nature itself to listen to God:
'Prophesy to these bones and say to them, "Dry bones,
hear the word of the Lord!"' (37:4).

The same command to listen throbs through the early
chapters of the book of Revelation like a persistent
drum-beat:

> If you have ears, then, *listen* to what the Spirit says
> (2:7)
> If you have ears, then, *listen* to what the Spirit says
> (2:11)
> If you have ears, then, *listen* to what the Spirit says
> (2:17)
> If you have ears, then, *listen* to what the Spirit says
> (2:29)
> If you have ears, then, *listen* to what the Spirit says
> (3:6)

I found that, according to Micah, political leaders do not
escape the divine interdict: 'Listen . . . you rulers of the
house of Israel! Should you not know justice, you who
hate good and love evil' (Mic. 3:1).

Amos reminds rebels to listen: 'Hear this word, you
cows of Bashan on Mount Samaria, you women who
oppress the poor and crush the needy and say to your
husbands, "Bring us some drinks!"' (Amos 4:1).

Old men are exhorted to listen to God. 'Hear this, you
elders' (Joel 1:2). Idle women must listen: 'you women
who are so complacent, rise up and listen . . .' (Isa. 32:9).
Whole families are required to listen: 'Hear the word of
the Lord . . . all you clans of the house of Israel. This is
what the Lord says . . .' (Jer. 2:4). These people were not
listening to the written Word only. They were expected to
hear and obey God on a day-to-day basis.

The more I burrowed into the Bible, the clearer it became that men and women of God heeded this command; they expected God to speak to them because he had promised to do so and because he had commanded them to listen.

The impression I gained from my study is that men and women in the Bible were not unlike my milkman in one respect. My milkman does his entire round tuned in to a voice other than his own or the cheery comments of his customers. In the pocket of his white, nylon overalls he carries a personal portable radio. Into his ears he tucks its tiny headphones and his face, indeed, sometimes his whole body, responds to a sound which is not audible to anyone but him. Men and women in the Bible seemed similarly plugged into and responsive to God. When they listened and responded obediently to the will of God, their life ran smoothly. When they refused to listen, God's heart broke. God's reaction to man's failure to listen sent a stab of pain right through me and further convinced me of his longing to communicate.

God's disappointment

Jeremiah puts the situation powerfully: 'I spoke to you again and again, but you did not listen; I called you, but you did not answer. Therefore . . . I will thrust you from my presence, just as I did all your brothers, the people of Ephraim' (Jer. 7:13, 15).

Zechariah, too, exposes the anger which burns in the heart of God when his people refuse to listen.

'My people stubbornly refused to listen. They closed their minds and made their hearts as hard as rock. Because they would not listen to my teaching . . . I became very angry. Because they did not listen when I spoke, I did not answer when they prayed.' (Zech. 7:10).

And I found God spelling out his displeasure through the lips of Isaiah also:

The people do as they please. It's all the same to them whether they kill a bull as a sacrifice or sacrifice a human being . . . They take pleasure in disgusting ways of worship. So I will bring in disaster upon them – the very things they are afraid of – because no one answered when I called or listened when I spoke – They chose to disobey me and do evil. (Isaiah 66:3–4).

Against this back-cloth, I placed the success stories: occasions when the voice of God was obeyed. Two such incidents in Acts thrilled me:

The Spirit told Philip, 'Go to that chariot and stay near it.' Then Philip ran . . . (Acts 8:29–30).

The Lord told him [Ananias], 'Go to the house of Judas on Straight Street and ask for a man from Tarsus named Saul, for he is praying. In a vision he has seen a man named Ananias come and place his hands on him to restore his sight.'
. . . Then Ananias went to the house and entered it. Placing his hands on Saul, he said, 'Brother Saul, the Lord . . . has sent me so that you may see again and be filled with the Holy Spirit.' Immediately, something like scales fell from Saul's eyes, and he could see again (Acts 9:11–12, 17–18).

The result of Philip's obedient listening is well known: the Ethiopian turned to Christ. Similarly, the punch-line of the Saul and Ananias story is familiar: Saul's sight was restored and the direction of his life changed.
I found similar miracles recorded in the gospels. A well-known story fired my imagination:

When evening came, [Jesus] said to his disciples, 'Let us go over to the other side.' Leaving the crowd behind, they took him along, just as he was, in the boat . . . A furious squall came up, and the waves broke over the boat, so that it was nearly swamped. Jesus was in the stern, sleeping on a cushion. The disciples woke him and said to him, 'Teacher, don't you care if we drown?'

He got up, rebuked the wind and said to the waves, 'Quiet! Be still!' Then the wind died down and it was completely calm (Mark 4:35–39).

And the terrified disciples asked each other, 'Who is this? Even the wind and the waves obey him!'

Again my mind wandered back to Israel, to an occasion when my husband and I were caught in an unexpected storm on the Sea of Galilee.

We had been lazing on a tiny beach on the shores of the lake. After we had sunbathed, collected miniature shells, imagined Jesus standing in a fishing boat teaching the crowds in the open-air auditorium, and wandered through some wheat fields, we decided to head back for Tiberias.

As we travelled, the weather changed. A grey cloud crept over the sun and spread right across the sky. A wind began to howl from the surrounding hills. And the white pleasure-boat rocked and rolled as the storm whipped the waves into a fury. Unlike the other passengers, David and I braved the wind and the rain and the spray which soaked us as great waves crashed against the sides of the boat. Perhaps we had hoped to live through a sudden squall like this? It helped us identify with the disciples' panic. It also stirred in our hearts a sense of wonder as we realised that Jesus had only to speak to giant waves like this. They heard. They subsided.

No voice silenced the storm that day, yet I recalled that Jesus is still the sustainer of the universe. He still holds the whole world in his hand. The cosmos is still dependent for its existence 'on every word that comes from the mouth of God' (Matt. 4:4).

The facts before me seemed inescapable. The Bible does address itself to the subject of listening to God. Indeed, the God of the Bible is portrayed as a God who aches to communicate: he promises to speak, he commands the entire world to listen. When we refuse, we hurt and anger him, but when we obey, he showers us and others with undeserved and unexpected gifts. But what of this counter-claim that the only method God now uses to speak is through his revealed Word, the Bible?

I thought long and hard about this while I tramped the hills of Derbyshire one day. 'Is it possible to hold in tension two apparently opposite and opposing view points?' I wondered. As I walked and wondered, certain facts clarified in my mind:

- God has spoken.
- Christianity is a revealed religion.
- In his written Word, the Bible, and the incarnate Word, Jesus, God has given full expression of the fundamentals and foundations of our faith.
- As Christians, therefore, we shall not expect to receive any further revelation of *doctrine*.
- The Bible contains the complete Word of God and everything must be tested by this yard-stick.

But does this full and complete revelation condemn a Creator-God to silence? I looked at the hills which I love. I gazed at the sky which was changing in colour from pearl to purple, then to pink. And the force of the 'Surely not!' which burst into my brain took me by surprise.

To suggest that this full and complete revelation which we have in scripture condemns a Creator-God to silence would be like denying the same God the creativity of the seasons, or saying that he must paint the sky the same colour every night at sunset.

I looked again at the familiar hills and the nearby woods, and I recollected that every time I go to Derbyshire, a place to which I frequently retreat to write, 'my' hills and woods are always the same, yet fascinatingly different. These hills which were created 'in the beginning' by God are still subjects of his artistic flair. In winter, they are sometimes snow-hushed, in autumn they are resplendent in their russets and reds, in spring the virgin greens which clothe the countryside cause us to catch our breath in wonder every year.

God created; and God still creates. Similarly, God has spoken; and God still speaks. This was the conclusion I reached. When we listen to God, we do not expect God to say anything new *doctrinally*. Of course not, the doctrine of our faith has been spelt out by God once and for all. What we do expect is that, when we listen to God, the indwelling Holy Spirit will speak to the situation in which we find ourselves, but whatever comes from him will be in alignment with the Bible's teaching.

I checked this conclusion with my husband on one occasion. I have always respected his integrity and unwavering faithfulness to the Word of God. I knew that he, too, was learning to value some of the insights on prayer which I had gleaned and which he could tell were of increasing value to my spiritual life. As we talked, he seemed to put his finger on the nub of the matter with a memorable observation: 'Listening to God is not about *newness* but about *nowness*. It is receiving the applied Word in whatever form God chooses to make it known.'

For me, that summed up the situation well. The hurt and anxiety with which I had begun my study on listening to God vanished. I was convinced that claims like the one Richard Foster makes are correct: 'Jesus Christ is alive and here to teach his people himself. His voice is not hard to hear, his vocabulary is not hard to understand. But we must learn how to hear his voice and obey it.'[2]

In the light of this conviction, I set myself the joyful task of learning God's vocabulary. The prayer Eli taught Samuel found an echo in my own heart: 'Speak, Lord, for your servant is listening' (1 Sam. 3:9).

Chapter 9

How God speaks: Visions and Dreams

'Man needs every word that God speaks.' Commenting on this claim, David Watson observes: 'The word "speaks" (ekporeuomeno) means "is continually coming out of" the mouth of God. Since God is the living God, he is constantly trying to speak to us and we in turn need to listen to him . . . If we are to keep spiritually alive and alert, we need every word that God is continually speaking.'[1]

Anxious as I was to 'keep spiritually alive and alert', indeed, to grow in Christian maturity, statements like this tickled my taste-buds. And now that I had established for myself that the Bible gives positive encouragement to the Christian not only to listen to God's written Word, the Bible, but also to attune to the living Word, the Spirit of Jesus, I was eager to forge ahead in the discipline of listening.

The kind of pondering on God which the gift of contemplation had opened up for me featured for several key people in the Bible. After Jesus's circumcision, Mary and Joseph 'marvelled' (Luke 2:33). After Jesus's first visit to Jerusalem as a boy, we read that 'his mother treasured all these things in her heart' (Luke 2:51). To marvel and to treasure the mysteries of the faith is contemplation. The apostle John, similarly, contemplated the mysteries of the faith in the gloom of the empty tomb on the morning of the Resurrection: 'He saw and believed' (John 20:8) implies that he contemplated the strips of linen used to

embalm Jesus's body and slowly the realisation dawned
that what Jesus had predicted had, in fact, happened.
Similarly, we find Simeon contemplating the Christ child:
'Simeon took him in his arms and praised God, saying:
. . . "My eyes have seen your salvation"' (Luke 2:28;
30). This is no cursory glance Simeon is referring to. It
is the long, lingering, adoring gaze of the contemplative at
prayer. The Old Testament, too, teems with images which
highlight the art of contemplation: 'Lord, you have been
our dwelling place' (Ps. 90:1); 'He who dwells in the shelter
of the Most High will rest in the shadow of the Almighty'
(Ps. 91:1); 'He will cover you with his feathers, and under
his wings you will find refuge' (Ps. 91:4). Daniel, Isaiah,
Ezekiel and Moses knew what it meant to lose themselves
in the awesomeness of adoring, listening prayer.

But God has a variety of methods of communication at
his fingertips. A quick glance at the Old Testament and
the New convinced me that God frequently conveyed his
purpose and plan to man pictorially as well as verbally. The
vision seemed to be a favourite means of communication.

By profession, I am a teacher of the deaf. I reflected
that when I used to teach deaf children, it would never
occur to me to try to teach them anything without some
form of visual aid. Communication experts assure us
that we remember what we see far more permanently
than we store the words we hear. In the light of this,
I was fascinated to find God transmitting very ordinary
messages to his people by means of a method which we
pride ourselves is 'modern'.

It was through a vision that God promised the veteran
couple, Abraham and Sara, that they would give birth to
a much longed-for baby:

> After this, the word of the Lord came to Abram in a
> vision: 'Do not be afraid, Abram. I am your shield,
> your very great reward' . . .
>
> And Abram said, 'You have given me no children;
> so a servant in my household will be my heir.'
> Then the word of the Lord came to him: 'This man

will not be your heir, but a son coming from your own body will be your heir.'

He took him outside and said, 'Look up at the heavens and count the stars – if indeed you can count them.' Then he said to him, 'So shall your offspring be' (Genesis 15:1, 3–5).

Isaiah, similarly, received his life-changing vocation through a memorable vision:

In the year that King Uzziah died, I saw the Lord seated on a throne, high and exalted, and the train of his robe filled the temple. Above him were the seraphs, each with six wings: with two wings they covered their faces, with two they covered their feet, and with two they were flying. And they were calling to one another: 'Holy, holy, holy is the Lord Almighty; the whole earth is full of his glory.'

At the sound of the voices the doorposts and thresholds shook and the temple was filled with smoke.

'Woe to me!' I cried. 'I am ruined! For I am a man of unclean lips . . .'

Then one of the seraphs flew to me with a live coal in his hand, . . . With it he touched my mouth and said, 'See, this has touched your lips; your guilt is taken away and your sin atoned for.'

Then I heard the voice of the Lord saying, 'Whom shall I send? And who will go for us?'

And I said, 'Here am I. Send me!' (Isa. 6:1–8).

In the New Testament, God continues to use this colourful and profound method of communication. He used it to impress on Peter the fact that God is not simply a God for the Jews but rather a God whose salvation embraces gentiles also. The picture God gave Peter to prepare him for this revelation is curious:

Peter went up on the roof to pray. He became hungry and wanted something to eat, and while the meal was being prepared, he fell into a trance. He saw heaven opened and something like a large sheet being let down to earth by its four corners. It contained all kinds of four-footed animals, as well as reptiles of the earth and birds of the air. Then a voice told him, 'Get up, Peter. Kill and eat.'

'Surely not, Lord!' Peter replied. 'I have never eaten anything impure or unclean.'

The voice spoke to him a second time, 'Do not call anything impure that God has made clean' (Acts 10:9–14).

Luke records that while Peter was still thinking through the implications of this startling mental picture, three men arrived on his door step asking Peter's help for the gentile, Cornelius. The Holy Spirit gave Peter clear instructions: 'Do not hesitate to go with them, for I have sent them' (Acts 10:20). Little by little, the message concealed in God's picture emerges. When Cornelius makes his request for instruction in the Christian faith, Peter understands why the vision occurred when it did and in the way it did. He makes this comment to Cornelius: 'You are well aware that it is against our law for a Jew to associate with a gentile or visit him. But God has shown me that I should not call any man impure or unclean' (Acts 10:28).

Through this pictorial message, God had liberated Peter from the prejudices and perspectives of his upbringing. The economy and dynamic of these pictures with the immediacy and urgency of their message made a deep impression on me. It seemed a powerful and unforgettable way for God to make his will and way known to his people.

Other visions seemed to fall into a different category. These were glimpses of God's glory and future kingdom given to ordinary men by God while they were 'in the Spirit', gazing at God alone. Daniel records the revelation God gave him: 'I looked up and there before me was a man dressed in linen, with a belt of the finest gold round his waist. His body was like chrysolite, his face like lightning, his eyes like flaming torches, his arms and legs like the gleam of burnished bronze, and his voice like the sound of a multitude' (Dan. 10:5–6).

And he tells us what he heard from the man's lips: '"Now I have come to explain to you what will happen to your people in the future, for the vision concerns a time yet to come"' (Dan. 10:14).

Ezekiel, similarly, met a man in a vision 'whose appearance was like bronze; he was standing in the gateway with a linen cord and a measuring rod in his hand . . .' (Ezek. 40:3). Ezekiel's vision with its detailed description of the temple he saw, takes up pages of his book.

In contrast, some visions seemed ordinary, almost mundane: 'The word of the Lord came to me: "What do you see, Jeremiah?"

"I see the branch of an almond tree," I replied' (Jer. 1:11).

That kind of vision encouraged me because it seemed more attainable than the extravagance of Isaiah's vision or the revelation of God's glory which John describes in his last book of the Bible, or the double-edged prophecy which Daniel goes on to give in Daniel 10.

While this academic appraisal of visions was in progress, I began to talk to people about visions to discover whether God still speaks in this way today. I was soon to discover that God did not stop using this technicolour language when the last full stop was added to the book of Revelation. He is still comforting and cajoling and challenging people through this medium today.

A friend of mine explained to me how God had met her in the depths of despair through a vision.

She was married to a pastor but had indulged in an affair with a married man. Eventually, the realisation dawned that she had reached a cross-roads. Either she must leave her husband and children and cause untold hurt to numerous people, or she must give up her lover. She chose the latter.

Having repented of the illicit love-affair, she wandered

into the woods to think and to pray. As she continued to pour out the bitterness of her soul to God, she described her life to him as nothing more than fragments of her former self. While she stood, silent and still before God, into her mind came a picture of the fragments she had described: they littered the ground like so many pieces of red clay. As she gazed at the broken vessel representing her life, into the picture came Jesus. She saw the tenderness of his face and observed the sensitivity of his fingers as he stooped down and started to turn over those forlorn fragments. 'Suddenly, he started to piece them together,' she told me. 'He assured me that, though the vessel was a mess, every tiny piece of the pot was precious. I watched the skill with which he put the pieces together again. He re-created that vessel. He showed me that it would be even more beautiful than it had been before and much more useful. Then, he glazed it and held it up for me to see. I couldn't see a single sign of the joins where the cracked parts had been pressed back together.'

For that woman, this vision came to her as a promise from God which guaranteed her future with him. It also communicated the much-needed message of healing and forgiveness which motivated her to walk away from the sin of the past and to work at her marriage again.

God had already spoken to this woman through his written Word. When she first confessed her sin to him and repented of it, she turned to 1 John 1:19: 'If we confess our sins, he is faithful and just and will forgive us our sins and purify us from all unrighteousness.' She believed this revealed Word. In her head she knew that God had forgiven her. But sexual sin affects not our heads only, but our entire being: body, mind, personality, emotions, imagination, spirit. God knows this. The series of images he planted into this woman's sin-saddened mind touched her in a way words never could. The vividness of the vision engraved God's revealed truth on to her heart and set her free to become the gifted person for him he had always intended that she should be.

It was not long before God began to give me mental

pictures like the one which had transformed my friend's life. Sometimes these would come while I was still before God and in prayer. Often these would build up my faith or deepen my awareness of God's presence. On one occasion, while I was praying, a picture of a beautiful oasis rose before my eyes. The water in the pond was still and pure; the trees which surrounded it were stately and offered shade from the scorching sun. Beside the pond stood an animal: a deer which seemed to be looking for something. When a fawn appeared, the deer showed his delight. They nudged each other affectionately. The fawn snuggled into the deer's warm body. They drank together from the pool before resting in the warm grass. When I asked God what this delightful picture meant, he seemed to assure me that this was a representation of my listening prayer. The time I set aside to develop my relationship with him becomes an oasis. In this still place he waits, more eager for an encounter with me than I am to encounter him. He seemed to show me that on the occasions when I come to this place of refreshment, I must be unashamed to delight in him; that he, similarly, will show me that he delights in me; that I am the focus of his love, the object of his affection and care. During these times he would nourish me. Like the bride in the Song of Songs I would sit under his shade and taste the fruit of his love.

On other occasions, a picture would unfold in my mind while I was counselling. On those occasions, the counselling interview would often be far more incisive and effective than when I was relying on counselling skills only. I began to realise that these visions were promptings from the Holy Spirit which frequently brought me to the heart of the person's need.

I remember praying for a girl on one occasion who was sobbing uncontrollably yet unable to voice the anguish the tears were trying to express. While I prayed silently for her and she continued to weep, I saw in my mind's eye the picture of a little girl in a playground at school. Her playmates were teasing her mercilessly.

When the girl stopped crying, I described the school

scene to her and asked her if it made any sense. 'Why, yes!' she exclaimed. 'That's me. I'd forgotten all about it but I used to be teased at school such a lot.'

This picture proved to be the key which unlocked the door into the emotional hurt which was paralysing this young Christian. I marvelled. God had shown me in seconds what counselling might have taken weeks to disclose.

Dreams

The borderline between visions and dreams is thumb-nail thin. When a person sees a vision, he sees a series of images while he is wide awake and attentive to the Holy Spirit. When a person dreams, on the other hand, he, too, sees a series of images but does so while he is fast asleep.

As I delved into the Bible to discover how frequently God resorted to this means of conveying a message, I was taken by surprise. I found that the book of Numbers implies that visions and dreams are perfectly valid means of prophetic revelation: 'When a prophet of the Lord is among you, I reveal myself to him in visions, I speak to him in dreams' (Num. 12:6). I found that Jeremiah endorses the fact that a prophet might receive a prophetic dream: 'Let the prophet who has a dream tell his dream' (Jer. 23:28). Indeed, Jeremiah himself describes such a dream in which God describes the peace and harmony and obedience which he will bestow on his chosen people (Jer. 31:26). And Joel foresees the day when God's Spirit will be poured out on all mankind and when the links between prophecy, dreams and visions will be crystal clear:

I will pour out my Spirit on all people.
Your sons and daughters will prophesy,
    your old men will dream dreams,
    your young men will see visions. (Joel 2:28 quoted
    in Acts 2:17).

Dreams feature frequently in the New Testament. Matthew, for example, records several dreams in connection with the birth of Jesus. God spoke to Joseph through a dream on two occasions: in the first, to instruct him to go through with his intended marriage to Mary and, in the second, to advise him that Herod's death had paved the way for the family to return to Nazareth. Similarly, it is through a dream that the magi received God's warning not to return home by the proposed route, by way of Herod's palace, but to travel a different way from the way they had come. And later in the gospel Matthew refers to the dream which threw Pilate's wife into turmoil: "'Don't have anything to do with that innocent man [Jesus], for I have suffered a great deal today in a dream because of him'" (Matt. 27:19).

With this data in front of me, I began to reflect on a vivid dream I had had on the last day of a sun-splashed holiday in Greece one spring.

With David and Kevin and Christina, our children, I had shoe-horned myself into the cabin of the passenger boat which ploughs between the island of Rhodes and Athens. We had torn ourselves away from the delights of Lindos with its tiny harbour, its cobbled streets, its colourful bazaars and its famous donkey transport. After the night voyage, we would collect our dormobile and start the long haul home by road.

That night my sleep was disturbed by a dream in which I saw our dormobile being towed away by a lorry. The vehicle was a total wreck. In the dream, I watched the rescue lorry disappear from sight taking most of our possessions with it.

I woke from that dream, lay in the darkness and, with uncharacteristic calm, prayed: 'Lord, if that should happen to us, please give me the courage to cope.' The prayer offered, with a peace which does not match my personality, I fell asleep.

On the following day, in high spirits, I drove from Athens to Skopje in Yugoslavia where I handed the driving over to my husband. The dream forgotten, I settled on to the back seat of the dormobile to read the map and relax. I don't know what made me glance up at my husband.

What I do remember is the grim, grey look on his face as I watched him juggle with a steering wheel which clearly was out of control. With incredulity, I watched him drive through mid-air and head for a silver-birch tree. I heard my nine-year-old daughter scream, 'No! No!' And I felt the dormobile bounce off the trunk of the tree before somersaulting down the steep embankment.

Some minutes later, I lay on the grassy bank, conscious of a dull pain between my shoulder blades, aware of blood pouring from a head wound and staring at the twisted machinery before me which six months earlier had been our brand new, blue Volkswagen dormobile. But I was not surprised. Nor shaken. It was as though I had lived this moment the night before in my dream. This was simply an action replay of a familiar event. Through the trauma of the chaotic days which followed, my heart stayed at peace.

Two days later, while I lay in a primitive hospital north of Skopje wearing a crown of bandages on my injured head, a lorry towed the dormobile containing most of our possessions to the scrap heap – just as my dream had foretold.

While I was regaining strength in this hospital, news filtered through that my father had died tragically and suddenly of a heart attack. By the time we reached home, the funeral was over. I was never able to say my final farewell to him.

My husband referred to the accident and the bereavement and the dream in a sermon on one occasion soon after we arrived back in England. A surgeon happened to be in the congregation that morning. After the service, he told my husband something which we had not appreciated at the time: that if someone was to suffer the kind of head injuries I sustained and be so quickly subjected to the added pain of bereavement, this dream was the kindest possible preparation they could have. The trust the dream engendered ensured that, at the time of the tragedies, I was relaxed, conscious that I was held by a love which would not let me go.

Thinking back to that time, I remembered that when my husband had passed on this piece of medical information my heart had missed a beat. I had wanted, there and then, to believe that this dream had originated with God, that through it he had been assuring me of his protective love and constant care. But I had never allowed this to take root. I had been taught that God speaks to us only through the Bible, not through dreams. But now that that shibboleth was becoming a notion of my past, and in the light of the facts before me – that God's use of dreams was a well-tried and often-occurring method of communication – I was forced to re-evaluate the situation. Like Mary, I marvelled at God's faithfulness and treasured this memory with its hidden message of love, constancy and compassion.

John Sherrill, in his introduction to Herman Riffel's book on dreams, makes the claim that dreams are a secret code and advises that we learn to unravel this code.[2] Herman Riffel believes that dreams can 'be a valuable computer in a man's unconscious realm'.[3] I do not have sufficient insight into dreams and their interpretations to assess whether these claims are accurate or not. What I do know is that, in the past, God used dreams to transmit messages to his people. What I also now know is that, on one occasion at least, he has spoken to me in this way.

Chapter 10

How God Speaks: Voices and Angels

When a man catches a glimpse of God's glory through a vision it is but a fragment of that full revelation of God which we shall enjoy when we meet him face to face. And when a man encounters God in a dream this is but a pale reflection of the splendour we shall one day savour. Nevertheless, such revelations are to be recognised for what they often are: manifestations of God's presence, his tap at the window of our souls.

But God does not always resort to picture parables when he wants to make his purposes known. My Bible survey suggested to me that a favourite means of message transmission was nothing less than the clear, unmistakable, uncompromising voice of God communicating clearly with his people.

Indeed God reminds Aaron and Miriam that it is his intention to speak to certain people in this way:

> When a prophet of the Lord is among you,
> I reveal myself to him in visions,
> I speak to him in dreams.
> But this is not true of my servant Moses . . .
> With him I speak face to face,
>   clearly and not in riddles;
>   he sees the form of the Lord (Num. 12:6–8).

Moreover, the Bible is full of references to situations in which other individuals heard God speak, not through pictures, which always require an interpretation, but through an uncontrived conversation with God. Noah heard God's voice: 'God said to Noah, "I am going to put an end to all people . . . So make yourself an ark of cypress"' (Gen. 6:13,14). Similarly Abraham heard God's voice: 'God tested Abraham . . . God said, "Take your son, your only son, Isaac . . . Sacrifice him."' (Gen. 22:1, 2). And Adam heard God's call: 'The Lord God called to the man, "Where are you"' (Gen. 3:9). God spoke to the prophets in this crystal clear manner: 'The word of the Lord that came to Hosea . . . "Go, take to yourself an adulterous wife and children of unfaithfulness"' (Hos. 1:1, 2). 'The word of the Lord came to me, saying, "Before I formed you in the womb I knew you, before you were born I set you apart"' (Jer. 1:4). 'The word of the Lord came to him [Elijah]: "Go at once to Zarephath of Sidon and stay there"' (1 Kgs. 17:8–9).

The same awareness of God's voice is recorded in the New Testament. As might be expected, Jesus himself heard it, as Peter testifies: 'For he received honour and glory from God the Father when the voice came to him from the Majestic Glory, saying, "This is my Son, whom I love; with him I am well pleased." We ourselves heard this voice that came from heaven when we were with him on the sacred mountain' (2 Pet. 1:17–18).

Saul heard it as he travelled along the road to Damascus:

As he neared Damascus on his journey, suddenly a light from heaven flashed around him. He fell to the ground and heard a voice say to him, 'Saul, Saul, why do you persecute me?'

'Who are you, Lord?' Saul asked.

'I am Jesus, whom you are persecuting,' he replied (Acts 9:3–5).

John heard it after he had been exiled to the Island of Patmos: 'On the Lord's Day I was in the Spirit, and I heard behind me a loud voice like a trumpet, which said:

"Write on a scroll what you see and send it to the seven churches . . .'" (Rev. 1:10–11).

Isaiah seems to hold out a promise that future generations will also hear that voice. 'Whether you turn to the right or to the left, your ears will hear a voice behind you, saying, "This is the way; walk in it"' (Isa. 30:21). And Jesus reinforced that message by implying that his gentle inspirations and awakenings would continue: '[My sheep] will listen to my voice' (John 10:16); by guaranteeing, too, that the voice of his Spirit would never be silenced. 'But when he, the Spirit of truth, comes, he will guide you into all truth. He will not speak on his own; he will speak only what he hears, and he will tell you what is yet to come' (John 16:13).

Since this voice peals so persistently through the pages of the Bible and since Jesus at least hints that it would never be lost, it seemed relevant to investigate whether that same voice is still being heard today. I soon discovered several people who claimed that they had heard God speaking to them. Indeed, just as I was about to write this chapter, a woman came to tell me of an experience of that voice which had changed the direction of her life.

The woman, an unbeliever, lay in her hospital bed knowing that she was suffering from cancer. In intense pain, she longed for the injection which would prepare her for the operation she was to undergo that afternoon. Since there was no sign of the nurse, she lay back on her pillow, closed her eyes and tried to relax. All of a sudden, standing by her bedside, she 'saw' a priest and another person whom she took to be Jesus. Jesus stretched out his hand and held hers. A calmness spread through her body. Jesus invited her to trust him for the future. She promised him that if she recovered from the anaesthetic, she would live life his way. She did survive. And she kept her promise. She had come to excite me with the delicacies of her new-found faith in God. Over the months I have watched her change even more. She has certainly turned her back on the past and turned to face the living God.

Or I think of a woman I met in Singapore. She told me

of a holiday she and her husband planned on the tropical
island of Penang. Their flight was booked. Their cases
were packed. But on the day of the trip, a voice seemed
to urge this woman not to travel by the planned flight.
She telephoned her husband and persuaded him to cancel
the trip. He did. That day, the air-bus travelling from
Singapore to Penang crashed killing all the passengers.

I sense I sometimes hear that voice myself. One Sunday
night, I had prayed for a young man whose spirits had
sunk very low. Early on Monday morning, I woke with
this young man's need weighing heavy on my heart. As
I prayed for him, I decided to telephone before he left
for work to assure him of my continued prayer. 'I'll ring
at eight,' I decided, and started to work on a book I was
writing. At 7.45 a.m. a voice broke in on my concentration:
'Ring now!' I looked at my watch and decided there was
no hurry. But the voice repeated: 'Ring now.' I rang.
The young man thanked me for ringing when I told him
the purpose of the call. 'Perfect timing too!' he teased.
'Why? When do you leave for work?' I asked. 'Oh! In
two minutes' time,' he said. When I heard this, I offered
silent praise to the God who, I believe, prompted me to
act in time.

Or I recall one harvest time when again God's voice
burst in on my awareness and changed my carefully made
plans for the day. On the day after the harvest services in
our church, members of staff distribute gifts of flowers and
fruit to the elderly. When I was parcelling up these gifts,
the voice told me first to visit a lady who had recently been
widowed and then to call on one of the pensioners attached
to the church.

When the widow opened her door, she clung to me.
She was sorting through her husband's possessions and
had longed for company and someone to pray with her.
A similar scene greeted me on the second visit. That
morning the pensioner had received a letter telling her
that her sister, to whom she was very close, had suffered
a nervous breakdown. When I arrived she was still reading
and re-reading this letter, still trying to drink in the tragic

news. She, too, had longed for a listening ear and some prayer support. I returned home that day marvelling at God's faithfulness, deeply thankful that he had shunted me into the right place at the right time to be the funnel through which his consolation could be poured.

While I was concentrating on the God who takes the initiative in communicating to his people, through dreams and visions and voices and a whole variety of other ways, God seemed to bring across my path illustration after illustration which suggested to me that he has never, in fact, been silent. There was the mystic, Julian of Norwich, whose revelations of divine love are an unashamed attempt to pass on to others what she believed God had said and shown to her. There was St Francis of Assisi whose personal encounter with the living Lord turned his life inside out. There was St Augustine, whom his mother Monica despaired of, but whose experience of God proved so overwhelming that he cried out in response: 'Too late have I loved thee . . .' And there was St Symeon, a theologian of the eleventh century, who tells how Christ revealed himself in a vision of light:

You shone upon me with brilliant radiance and, so it seemed, you appeared to me in your wholeness as with my whole self I gazed openly upon you. And when I said, 'Master, who are you?' then you were pleased to speak for the first time with me, the prodigal. With what gentleness did you talk to me, as I stood astonished and trembling, as I reflected a little within myself and said: 'What does this glory and this dazzling brightness mean? How is it that I am chosen to receive such great blessings?' 'I am God,' you replied, 'who became man for your sake; and because you have sought me with your whole heart, see from this time onwards you shall be my brother, my fellow-heir and my friend.'[1]

All down the ages, it seems God has spoken.

Angels
So far, the truths I was unearthing from the pages of the
Bible, from history and from personal testimonies, my own
and other people's, thrilled me to the core of my being and
caused the level of expectation within me to soar to new
heights. But when I bumped into angelology, a systematic
statement of biblical truth about angels, my reaction was
different. I did not want to believe in angels.

Did my resistance stem from the fact that I had frequently been an angel in nativity plays at school and
had therefore relegated these heavenly beings with their
shining countenances and translucent wings to the world
of make-believe or fantasy? Was it that I had never, to
my knowledge, met a single Christian who believed in the
existence of angels? Or was it because I feared that an
angel was a kind of 'spiritual will-o'-the-wisp', to borrow
Billy Graham's phrase, a figment of man's imagination?

I don't know why my resistance to angels was so strong.
What I do know is that my survey of the scriptures persuaded me that if I was to be a Bible-believing Christian,
it was imperative that I take the belief in angels seriously.
The Bible does. Moreoever, the Bible leaves us in no
doubt about the nature and purpose of the existence of
these heavenly beings.

Angels, according to the author of the letter to the
Hebrews, are 'ministering spirits sent to serve those
who will inherit salvation' (Heb. 1:14). Myriads of these
exotic, glorious, non-material beings shuttle through the
pages of the Bible fulfilling their ambassadorial vocation; they offer guidance and give specific instructions
to men:

See, I am sending an angel ahead of you to guard you
along the way and to bring you to the place I have
prepared. Pay attention to him and listen to what he
says. Do not rebel against him . . . since my name is
in him (Exod. 23:20–21).

An angel of the Lord appeared to Joseph in a dream. 'Get up,' he said, 'take the child and his mother and escape to Egypt' (Matt. 2:13).

They give advance warning of certain events:

The angel of the Lord appeared to her and said, 'You are sterile and childless, but you are going to conceive and have a son' (Judg. 13:3).

The angel said to her, 'Do not be afraid, Mary, you have found favour with God. You will be with child and give birth to a son, and you are to give him the name Jesus' (Luke 1:30).

They protect and deliver God's people:

The angel of the Lord encamps around those who fear him, and he delivers them (Ps. 34:7).

They are messengers of God's mercy and promise, God's secret agents:

While I was still in prayer, Gabriel . . . came to me in swift flight . . . He instructed me and said to me, 'Daniel, I have now come to give you insight and understanding' (Dan. 9:21–22).

These divine beings, appointed by God to be extensions of his right hand, usually appear in human form, like the three strangers who descended, without warning, on Abraham and Sara (Gen. 18). It seems that sometimes their voice is heard even though they, themselves, remain invisible (Gen. 21:17).

These spokesmen sent from God stunned me by their glory and silenced my unbelief. I was forced to admit that, in the days when the Bible was penned, angels existed, angels spoke and angels acted.

But does God still send angels? This question puzzled me as I pressed on with my investigation into the methods God chooses to speak today.

I had never seen an angel. Neither did I know anyone who had seen one. But I started to read Billy Graham's thrilling book, *Angels: God's Secret Agents*, and realised that he, at least, is in no doubt that God still communicates through these heavenly beings, who still appear in human form today. To prove it, he records one of God's modern miracles:

> The Reverend John G. Paton, a missionary in the New Hebrides Islands, tells a thrilling story involving the protective care of angels. Hostile natives surrounded his mission headquarters one night, intent on burning the Patons out and killing them. John Paton and his wife prayed all during that terror-filled night that God would deliver them. When daylight came they were amazed to see the attackers unaccountably leave. They thanked God for delivering them.
>
> A year later, the chief of the tribe was converted to Jesus Christ, and Mr Paton, remembering what had happened, asked the chief what had kept him and his men from burning down the house and killing them. The chief replied in surprise. 'Who were all those men you had with you there?' The missionary answered, 'There were no men there; just my wife and I.' The chief argued that they had seen many men standing guard – hundreds of big men in shining garments with drawn swords in their hands. They seemed to circle the mission station so that the natives were afraid to attack. Only then did Mr Paton realise that God had sent his angels to protect them. The chief agreed that there was no other explanation. Could it be that God had sent a legion of angels to protect his servants, whose lives were being endangered?[2]

A shiver of excitement ran down my spine as I read story after story like this in Billy Graham's book. It would seem that God still sends his agents to protect and direct us:

When I was visiting the American troops during the Korean war, I was told of a small group of American marines in the First Division who had been trapped up north. With the thermometer at 20° below zero, they were close to freezing to death. And they had had nothing to eat for six days. Surrender to the Chinese seemed their only hope of survival. But one of the men, a Christian, pointed out certain verses of scripture and taught his comrades to sing a song of praise to God. Following this they heard a crashing noise, and turned to see a wild boar rushing towards them. As they tried to jump out of his way, he suddenly stopped in his tracks. One of the soldiers raised his rifle to shoot, but before he could fire, the boar inexplicably toppled over. They rushed up to kill him only to find that he was already dead. That night they feasted on meat, and began to regain strength.

The next morning, just as the sun was rising, they heard another noise. Their fear that a Chinese patrol had discovered them suddenly vanished as they found themselves face to face with a South Korean who could speak English. He said, 'I will show you out.' He led them through the forest and mountains to safety behind their own lines. When they looked up to thank him, they found he had disappeared.[3]

Testimonies like these, placed against the backdrop of biblical teaching which had already convinced me of the existence of angels, transformed my prayer life. At first this amounted to no more than an inclusion of the mention of them in vocal prayer: 'Lord, send your angels to protect us as we travel.' It wasn't until the first draft of this chapter had been written that I 'saw' an angel in prayer.

I was suffering from a severe and unexpected bout of depression which left me curiously insecure. The situation eventually distressed me so much that I asked two friends to pray with me. The night before we had agreed to meet, I asked God to show me if there was anything from my past which was blurring my perspective of the present.

At 4.00a.m. I woke up re-living a vivid memory from my teen years. I was in a beauty spot in Devonshire where I had lived at the time. I could see the sun shining through the beech leaves, hear the brook gurgling its way down the gorge, feel the firmness of the stepping stones on which I had stood to contemplate this beauty. But a chill cloud passed over the entire scene as I became conscious of a man approaching me whose look was sinister, whose intentions clearly were far from pure, who put his arm around my shoulders and tried to kiss me. At this stage of the action replay, I froze and switched the memory off. It had become too painful to watch alone.

That evening, I told my friends about this memory. We recognised that seeds of distrust had been sown on that occasion when this man, a so-called friend, had planned to molest me. They asked God to touch my memory and to remove from it anything which would distort my view of people in the present and leave me with feelings of insecurity.

The sense of evil stayed with me for several days. At times, I seemed to be overwhelmed and over-shadowed by it: the same sense of evil which had spoiled the beauty of that lovely day in Devon. One morning, in the stillness of my prayer corner, again I re-lived the memory. It seemed important that I should do so. This time, I saw not only myself standing on the stepping stone and my assailant coming towards me: this time, I also saw an angel standing on the same stepping stone as me. His outstretched wings formed a shelter into which I could creep. I knew that under his wings I could find safety. The voice of God seemed to come to me clearly. I recorded them in my prayer journal:

> Joyce! Think not so much of the powers of evil
> The powers of destruction
> But of my power to protect.
> I watched over you
> I shielded you from harm
> I held you in *my* arms

The arms of pure love.
In this relax and rejoice
For I am your God
And you are the apple of my eye.
I am your God
Your best interests are tucked into the
    creases of my Father-heart
I am your Father.

And the words of Psalm 91 rang in my ears like a peal of
joyful bells:

He will cover you with his feathers,
    and under his wings you will find refuge;
    his faithfulness will be your shield and rampart.
You will not fear the terror of night,
    nor the arrow that flies by day . . .
then no harm will befall you . . .
For he will command his angels concerning you
    to guard you in all your ways;
they will lift you up in their hands,
    so that you will not strike your foot against a
stone . . .
'Because he loves me,' says the Lord, 'I will
    rescue him' . . .
I will be with him in trouble.

The sense of wonder which filled me was as profound
as the pain had been. Though the memory had bruised
me emotionally, standing in the wake of the brightness
of God's messenger, the angel, and sheltering under the
protection of his wings, brought healing and peace. Some
weeks later, I happened to drive past that particular beauty
spot in Devonshire. As I did so, I noted that the fear and
dread had vanished. I could see the grandeur of God's
creation and praise him for it and remember the past
with peace.

God still uses angels, it seems, to speak even to someone
as cynical about their existence as I had been. And

when God speaks, no matter what method he uses, the encounter proves powerful. Anthony Bloom puts it well: 'It is possible to lend an ear to the Living God who speaks to us and then all other thoughts die out, all other emotions come to an end because he who is life, he who is the Word, speaks.'[4]

Chapter 11

How God Speaks: Through Nature and the Imagination

'God speaks to those who keep silence.'[1] God speaks through visions and dreams, through angels, and with a voice as penetrating as the sound of a trumpet. And God also speaks through nature.

When I came to terms with the fact that the created world exists, not simply for our enjoyment, but as a language, my heart did a little, gleeful, hop, skip and a jump. I love nature: the first aconites heralding spring, ripening lilac, scarlet poppies, a mackerel sky. If these could speak to me of God in a deeper way than I had experienced so far, in a way which actually brought me to the Creator, there was a whole unexplored dialect right on my doorstep which I was eager to learn.

Down the ages, I recollected, men and women have heard God speak through the eloquence of nature. God spoke to David in this way so powerfully that the psalmist was inspired to pen Psalm 8:

When I consider your heavens,
   the work of your fingers,
the moon and the stars,
   which you have set in place,
what is man that you are mindful of him? (Ps. 8: 3–4).

Through Isaiah, God challenged his people to contemplate creation:

> Who has measured the waters in the hollow of his hand,
> or with the breadth of his hand marked off the heavens?
> Who has held the dust of the earth in a basket,
> or weighed the mountains on the scales
>   and the hills in a balance? . . .
>
> Surely the nations are like a drop in a bucket;
> they are regarded as dust on the scales;
> he weighs the islands as though they were fine dust . . .
> Before him all the nations are as nothing (Isa. 40:12, 15,17).

God, similarly, invited Job to look away from the darkness within his own soul to the objective orderliness and beauty of the created world:

> Who shut up the sea behind doors
>   when it burst forth from the womb,
> when I made the clouds its garment
>   and wrapped it in thick darkness,
> when I fixed limits for it
>   and set its doors and bars in place,
> when I said, 'This far you may come and
>   no farther;
> here is where your proud waves halt' . . .
>
> Can you bind the beautiful Pleiades?
>   Can you loose the cords of Orion?
> Can you bring forth the constellations in their seasons
>   or lead out the Bear with its cubs?
> Do you know the laws of the heavens?
>   Can you set up God's dominion over the earth?
>   (Job 38:8–11; 31–33).

When Jesus came striding across the pages of history,

he reiterated the challenge: look carefully at the birds, contemplate the lilies, (Matt. 6:26, 28); an extraordinary invitation for a bunch of uncouth fishermen. But Paul explains why God persists in this way. God's invisible qualities are made visible through the things which he creates. His power and majesty and mystery are encapsulated in some measure in the work of his hands (Rom. 1:20).

The mystics learned to read this visible language. Take St Anthony for example. To his hermitage in the desert came one of the wise men of the time who said, 'How can you endure to live here, deprived as you are of all consolation from books?' Anthony replied, 'My book, philosopher, is the nature of created things, and, whenever I wish, I can read in it the works of God.'[2]

Brother Lawrence glories in the changing seasons which speak to him of the constancy of God.[3] And Prince Vladimir Monomakh of Kiev writes in similar vein: 'See how the sky, the sun and moon and stars, the darkness and the light, and the earth that is laid upon the waters, are ordered, O Lord, by thy providence! See how the different animals, and the birds and fishes, are adorned through thy loving care, O Lord!'[4]

When, one day, I read Carlo Carretto's invitation: 'Contemplate what lies before you. It is God's way of making himself present.' I was conscious of a restlessness within. This was exactly what I ached to do but I was not sure how to go about it. Yes. I could look at a purple anemone, wonder at its velvet petals, feel its texture, touch its tough stem and that small flower in my hands would bring me to the threshold of the mystery of the God who could manufacture such intricacies, but I sensed there was something more to contemplating the creativity of God.

By this time, a small group in my church had joined me in my quest to listen to God more effectively. They were as anxious as I was to plumb the depths of the parables of nature, to use the language of Carlo Carretto, so we decided to devote one Saturday to learning this art. Stephen Verney, the Bishop of Repton, agreed to introduce us to a form of meditation which many people of prayer use in an attempt to hear God speaking through very ordinary objects: a flower, a tree, a telegraph post.

I recall the Saturday well. The sun shone on the Derbyshire hills which encircle the bishop's house. The hedgerows and meadows were studded with wild flowers: harebells, buttercups, meadow-sweet, cowslips. We stood on the terrace of the bishop's home, drank coffee, and drank in, too, the magnificence of the countryside in summer. Then we went inside.

As we sat in a circle in the lounge, the bishop invited us to focus our attention on a bowl of wild flowers on a small table in the centre of the circle. 'Just waste time looking at them,' he invited. After a few minutes he turned to Matthew 6 and read Jesus's command: 'Consider the lilies . . .'. 'This word "consider" really means "contemplate",' the bishop suggested. 'When we contemplate something, we look at it from many angles, we touch it, feel it, smell it and learn from it. That is what I propose we do this morning.'

He passed the bowl of flowers round the room and invited each person to choose one. 'Now let's first spend time contemplating the flower we have chosen,' he said.

I had chosen a marguerite, the kind of big, wild daisy I love to watch waving in the breeze on a summer's day. But I had never looked at one so closely before. I gazed at its golden eye and felt its flimsy, fur-like petals. I squeezed its firm stem and turned it over to examine the pinkish underside.

The bishop's voice broke in on my contemplation: 'What is God saying through this flower?' he asked. The words which came to me immediately were simple and straightforward: 'I made that,' God seemed to say. I thought about that statement for several minutes. When my children or friends make something with their own hands, I treasure it. This common marguerite, the kind I trampled on in the fields every time I went for a walk in summer, was a portion of God's creativity. A treasure. An expression of his personality.

The bishop's voice filtered into my consciousness again: 'What is God saying to *you* through this flower?' he was asking.

I fingered the flower lovingly, respecting it now because of the one who manufactured it. And a verse from the Psalms imprinted itself on my mind:

> I praise you because I am fearfully and
>   wonderfully made;
> your works are wonderful,
> I know that full well (Ps. 139:14).

The flower, I could see, was fearfully and wonderfully designed by the master-craftsman of the world. I marvelled at his handiwork.

'Now I'd like to invite you to imagine how it would feel to *become* that flower.' The Bishop's voice interrupted my train of thought once more.

At first I thought it sounded a silly idea to try to *become* a flower. But I respected Stephen Verney and knew him to be a man who had ventured much further along the path of prayer than I had, and in doing so had gained the experience I coveted, so I decided to lay aside my pride and try to 'become' a marguerite.

To my surprise it was easy. I identified all too readily with the feelings a marguerite might feel if it were sentient: the vulnerability of being plucked from its moorings, sorrow at the violence of man whose greed demands that he possess the beauty he sees, emptiness at being removed so suddenly from the sustenance nature normally supplied.

'What is God saying to you now?'

The verse from Psalm 139 which had already been engraved on my heart, returned with fresh force. Through it, God seemed to show me that, though at times, I am as vulnerable and frail and helpless and misused as the marguerite, I am still a part of his creation, uniquely designed, the object of his care, cherished.

This reassurance brought a rich measure of healing that day. Assured that I was cherished by God, I reached out to him and opened myself to the energy which he longs should pulsate through our bodies, minds and spirits.

'I'd like you now to imagine yourself surrounded by your relatives and colleagues and friends,' the bishop said. 'Imagine that they are standing around you in a semi-circle. Picture them. Name them. Ask God to show you how you can convey to them the riches which he has given to you this morning.'

I thought of my husband, my two children, certain members of the church and my neighbours. I asked God to show me practical ways in which I could offer them his love. I was amused to discover how down-to-earth some of the suggestions seemed to be: 'You'll have been away for the whole day; express your thanks by cooking them a favourite meal!' I thought of one person I was counselling at the time. She needed to hear what I had heard from God: that she was valued by God and would be sustained by him. I prayed that I might communicate this message to her in a way she could imbibe.

Before we parted, the bishop invited us to turn to the person next to us and to attempt to explain what we had learned from God through the flower. When I voiced what I had experienced, it underlined the truths which God had been imparting. As I spelt out these truths my gratitude grew.

At first I kept this kind of meditation for my structured times of quiet with God. But some months after this group Quiet Day, a poem inspired me to look for God in this way anywhere and everywhere:

I hear you
   in the cry of the gull
   in the wind chasing the last leaves of fall
   in the whisper of a child

I see you
   in the animal shapes of cumulus clouds
   in the trees ten times my age
   in the wrinkled face of a woman over ninety . . .

I touch you
   in the smooth bark of a white birch
   in the rock beneath the summit tearing my hands
   in the texture of wet and dry sand.[5]

This poem pushed me into walking around with my eyes and ears open. I would be walking in the Derbyshire hills watching the sunset. God would speak to me of his majesty as he splashed the sky with golds and reds. Again, God would speak as I watched the clematis buds tilt their faces to the spring sun. I became acutely aware that everything God made pulsates with his uncreated energy; all things are sustained by him and, in one sense, are a theophany. Whether I was walking or sitting on the beach or in the garden or travelling in the bus, I would meditate on God's world, asking myself:

- What is God saying through this scene or object?
- What is he saying to *me*?
- What happens when I become that object?
- How can I take what I have learned into my world?

Just before starting to write this chapter, I wandered through the woodland walks in the rhododendron gardens near my home. At the moment they blaze with colour: pinks, vermilions, sherbet-lemon yellows, purples, creams, whites. As I gazed at such extravagance it was as though I was being embraced by God. When I walked into the gardens it seemed as though God greeted me, as though he had been searching for me and was glad that I had come. When I stretched out my hand to touch this beauty, I became aware that I touched a beauty which is part of him. The music of this visual harmony had been composed by him. The boundless ever-newness of this extravaganza leaves me spell-bound. But as I contemplate his creativity I catch, too, a glimpse of his glory.

As I learned to welcome him more and more, to hear him speak through the language of his world, I was introduced to the mystery of God in a new way. The mystery is that God is not so much the object of our knowledge as the cause of our wonder. The mystery is that I shall never know God exhaustively yet I may know sufficient to feel compelled to fall at his feet in wonder, love and praise. The mystery is that he is both hidden and revealed. The mystery is that he reveals his greatness through everyday objects: in the teaching of Jesus, through the coin which the woman had lost, through the yeast which caused her bread to rise, through the children who played in the market square and in the annals of Jeremiah, through the potter who shaped and re-shaped his clay.

On more than one occasion, God trickled healing, holding love into my grazed emotions through contemplating such ordinary objects.

It was September and, as is my custom, I had prepared a bowl of potting compost, buried a hyacinth bulb in it and thrust it into a deep, dark cupboard. While I was attempting to pray later that day, God seemed to give me a glimpse of the activity which would soon cause that bulb to change: the white roots which would push their way out of the shrivelled up bulb and into the nourishing soil; the green poker-like shoot which would nudge its way above the surface of the earth; the tiny flowers which would unfold and, in bursting open, would fill my study with fragrance.

I was suffering from a prolonged and painful bout of depression at the time. When the voice which I was learning to recognise as God's whispered, 'This is what the darkness of depression will do for you; it will result, eventually, in prolific growth and wholeness,' I felt strangely comforted. When the depression did its worst, it was to this visual promise that I clung.

It has never worried me that this kind of meditation leans heavily on the use of the imagination. I came across a phrase which C. S. Lewis uses, 'the baptised imagination', and this encouraged me to believe that when our imagination is soaked in the living waters of the Holy Spirit, God can use it. Similarly, John Powell makes the claim: 'God has access to us through the power of imagination.' He quotes a short excerpt from George Bernard Shaw's play, *St Joan*:

Robert: How do you mean? voices?
Joan: I can hear voices telling me what to do. They come from God.
Robert: They come from your imagination.
Joan: Of course. That is how the messages of God come to us.[6]

I, too, firmly believe that when the imagination is handed over to God, it is a powerful tool in the hand of a God who seeks to communicate his message of healing love through a whole variety of ways.

And the fear of pantheism, which keeps many Christians from hearing God speak through nature, does not trouble me either. I am clear in my mind that when I claim to hear God speak through the lips of a tulip, he speaks, not because he *is* the tulip, but because, as the creator of the tulip, he is giving expression to facets of himself through its design, its texture, its shape, its size and the streaks of red which he paints on the yellow petals with one stroke of his brush.

As my experience of listening to God through nature increased, I echoed the assurance of St Symeon:

I know the Immovable comes down:
I know the Invisible appears to me;
I know that he who is far outside the whole creation,
Takes me within himself and hides me in his arms . . .[7]

Chapter 12

How God Speaks: Tongues, Prophecy, Words of Wisdom and Knowledge

I was greedy, always thirsting for the 'something more' which God delights to give to his children. I took to heart the advice of St Isaac the Syrian which I had read: 'Thirst after Jesus and he will satisfy you with his love.'[1]

As I read the teaching Paul gave to the Corinthian Christians on listening to God, I recognised that there were yet more lessons to be learned:

> Now to each one the manifestation of the Spirit is given for the common good. To one there is given through the Spirit the message of wisdom, to another the message of knowledge by means of the same Spirit, to another . . . prophecy . . . to another speaking in different kinds of tongues, and to still another the interpretation of tongues (1 Cor. 12:7–10).

I smiled as I read those verses and recalled the days when I feared the gift of tongues. Even when God had taken me by surprise and overwhelmed me with his Holy Spirit's life and joy, I insisted that I would never speak in tongues. Now that I viewed prayer as a developing friendship with God, this gift of the Spirit was no longer something I despised. It was something I valued. I saw it as a love-language with which I could express the adoration which sometimes burned in my heart when I worshipped God. I saw it as a means of expressing the spontaneous praise which sometimes leapt from the inner recesses of my being rather like the jet of a giant fountain. I saw it as a method of communicating to God the wonder, love and awe I felt, which even the Psalms could not adequately put into words.

As I became less embarrassed about this supernatural language, I would use it sometimes when praying with people who had come to me for counselling. From time to time this would give birth to an interpretation which would speak incisively to the situation we had been discussing or which would bring immediate and profound comfort and peace to a person in distress.

If tongues could contribute to my personal prayer life and benefit others, I felt sure that the other pieces of God's grammar and syntax which Paul mentions here must have equal value. But so far, I knew little about the supernatural gifts of wisdom, knowledge and prophecy, so I set myself the task of discovering what these terms meant and whether I could expect God to speak to me in this way.

The Word of Wisdom

David Watson's book, *One in the Spirit*, had already dispelled many of the irrational and childish fears which had prejudiced me against the work of the Holy Spirit and, in particular, the gift of tongues. So I decided to refer to this book again. In it David Watson suggests that the word of wisdom is the God-given ability to speak an appropriate word on every occasion, to make the right decisions, to discern between good and evil. He reminds us of the remarkable demonstration of this gift recorded in 1 Kings 3:16–28. Two women approached Solomon and brought with them two babies. One was alive. The other dead. Each mother insisted that the living baby was *her* baby. Solomon, exercising the gift of wisdom, proposed slicing the live baby in two so that both mothers could keep one half. This elicited a protest from the real mother. She refused him permission to murder her child, thus revealing her true identity. The bogus mother would have been content to watch the baby being butchered.

Solomon had prayed for this gift of wisdom: 'O Lord my God, you have made your servant king in place of my father David. But I am only a little child and do not know how to carry out my duties . . . So give your servant a discerning heart to govern your people and to distinguish between right and wrong' (1 Kgs. 3:7–9).

Solomon's prayer brought joy to God. As I meditated on it and the dynamic way in which God answered it, it stirred up in me a heart-hunger. I, too, longed to rely, not simply on skills which I had learned and acquired through experience, but on *God's* wisdom. This, I sensed, could transform my counselling ministry. In his epistle James encourages us to ask God to invest his wisdom in us. So I made my request.

Meanwhile, I stumbled on an amusing contemporary illustration of this gift in Keith Miller's challenging book, *The Taste of New Wine.*

One of the battlegrounds which troubled Keith Miller's marriage in the early days, it seems, was the conflict which erupted over role delineation. When they married, Mary Allen, his wife, assumed that he would empty the pedal bin in the kitchen each day. He, meanwhile, felt insulted by the suggestion. This was woman's work in his view. He refused to capitulate to his wife's demands.

After his conversion to Christ, Keith Miller tried to convince his wife that he had found something wonderful in God, that God was changing her husband's personality. In an attempt to convince her of the strength of this claim he looked for ways of demonstrating this truth by his behaviour.

He goes on to explain how the word of wisdom flashed into his awareness: 'While I was looking around for some . . . way to convince my wife that I had really changed, my glance fell on the waste basket standing full by the back door. "No, Lord," I groaned quietly to myself. "*Not* the waste basket. Take my income, anything."'[2]

After a struggle, he obeyed. He emptied the waste basket. 'Without saying a word I took it out, and didn't even mention it to her.'

Mary Allen, of course, took note of this change in attitude. She continued to refuse her husband's invitations to Christian meetings but she did begin to ask a friend penetrating questions about the Christian faith. These discussions resulted, in time, in her own conversion to Christianity. When she retraced the way God had wooed her to himself she recognised that her husband's gesture that day he emptied the waste basket had been one of the prongs God had used to prod her in his direction.

Situations like these taught me that the word of wisdom, God's incisive word given for a specific occasion, comes winged with power and authenticity. Often it comes laced with humour also.

The word of knowledge

I was to learn that, just as God grants a person the gift of wisdom, so he speaks powerfully, precisely and economically through words of knowledge. A word of knowledge is an insight implanted by God about a particular person or situation for a specific purpose. Alex Buchanan, in a talk given to our fellowship on one occasion, summarised the gift helpfully:

The word of knowledge may be the revelation of the whereabouts or the doings of a man, the nature of his thought, or the condition of his heart. It is a gift of revelation. It becomes vocal when shared with others. It is a fragment of divine knowledge which cannot be attained by study or consecration. It is a divinely granted flash of revelation concerning things which were hopelessly hidden from the senses, the mind, or the faculties of men.

I was to discover that Jesus exercised this gift. His use of it astounded the Samaritan woman who talked with him at the well. Although Jesus had never encountered this woman before, so far as we know, he seemed well informed about her sex life. 'You have had five husbands, and the man you now have is not your husband' (John 4:18). This word of knowledge not only astonished this woman, it resulted in a complete change of life-style.

I found Jesus exercising this gift again after the Resurrection. The disciples were fishing on the Sea of Galilee. Although the lake normally teemed with fish, on this trip, they caught nothing. Jesus called to them from the shore: 'Throw your net on the right side of the boat and you will find some.' John records the result of the disciples' obedience to this word of knowledge: 'When they did, they were unable to haul the net in because of the large number of fish' (John 21:6).

God still speaks, convicts and consoles through these flashes of inspiration. The first time God spoke to me in this way I was both startled and amused.

My husband and I were house-parents at a houseparty for students and, during the course of the conference, I had spoken on boy/girl relationships and on prayer.

One evening, a young man asked if he could talk to me. He told me that his prayer life was dry and arid, that when he prayed his words seemed to hit the ceiling and bounce back at him like a boomerang. I listened and we talked about his prayer life for nearly half an hour but somehow I realised we were not really communicating. Without warning, and for no other reason than the prompting of the Holy Spirit, the word 'masturbation' lodged in my brain. At first I tried to push it away. But the voice within refused to be silenced. 'His prayer problem is a guilt problem. He's feeling guilty about a masturbatory problem,' the voice insisted.

Feeling rather nervous and foolish, I steered the conversation away from prayer *per se* and on to the subject of guilt. The young man blushed and then started talking about 'his besetting sin'. When eventually I mentioned the word masturbation he sighed with relief and real communication began.

Left to rely on my own insights, I would have failed utterly to make a direct connection between prayer and masturbation. On that occasion, and on many subsequent occasions, I have thanked God for the time-saving inner prompting of the gift of knowledge. It does not replace counselling skills or sensitivity or the need for solidarity with a person's pain. But it is a valuable tool with which God equips us as we seek to bring people to wholeness.

This gift is not for super-saints. It is for everyone. If we are open to God, he uses it, not only in the way I have described above, but to nudge us into prayer and action when and where prayer is specially needed.

I had written one third of this chapter of this book when I decided to take a coffee break. As I filled the kettle with water, the name of a friend popped into my mind and I sensed this person needed my prayers. There in the kitchen, I lifted him into the all-loving hands of God. Two minutes later, the phone rang. I should not have been surprised to hear this friend's voice at the end of the phone: 'Will you pray for me please?' he said. 'I'm off work today and I've just come back from the doctor. It's suspected appendicitis.'

That kind of connecting happens so regularly now that I am no longer tempted to believe it is mere coincidence. I take such promptings as God's promptings and try to act on them appropriately.

Prophecy

Another discovery I made is that words of wisdom, knowledge and prophecy intertwine and overlap with one another. David Watson described prophecy in this way: 'Prophecy is a message from God, which is not necessarily anything to do with the future: a forth-telling not primarily a foretelling . . . It is a word from the Lord through a member of the body of Christ, inspired by the Spirit, to build up the rest of the body' (1 Cor. 14:3–5).[3]

Alex Buchanan helped me enormously as I sought to understand this gift. He suggests that this gift as we have it in the church today finds three expressions. There is 'low level prophecy', where God might encourage a person or a congregation with a simple statement: 'The Lord says: "Don't be afraid. I am with you."' There is a 'higher level' of prophecy where God reveals something about the situation in a particular church at a particular time. And there is the 'highest level' of prophecy which causes people to bow down and worship God in awe and wonder because they know, 'The Lord has spoken.'

I noticed that Paul exhorts us to 'eagerly desire spiritual gifts, especially the gift of prophecy . . . everyone who prophesies speaks to men for their strengthening, encouragement and comfort' (1 Cor. 14:1,3). And so I became covetous for this gift too.

On one occasion, at a student conference where I was speaking, one of the other speakers gave a word of prophecy which would fall into Alex Buchanan's third category: the highest level of prophecy. The speaker spelt out the vision of God which he could see in his mind's eye. It was reminiscent of parts of the book of Revelation or of Isaiah's vision of God. We, the listeners, were scarcely conscious of the words. Jesus filled our entire horizon. When the words stopped, a powerful hush silenced the group, a silence pregnant with worship, adoration and wordless praise. God had spoken, to strengthen, encourage and uplift us. I was left in no doubt that God still speaks in this way today.

God also demonstrated to me that his use of prophecy to warn his church is as accurate, painful and uncomfortable as it was in Old Testament times.

I was invited to speak to a group of church leaders on one occasion but had been out of the country on sabbatical leave for four months, so knew little of what had been going on in that church in recent weeks. While I was preparing for the conference, a sense of heaviness overwhelmed me. I quote from the notes I made as I listened to God for that occasion: 'There are some leaders here who are battle-scarred, weary, resourceless from over-much pouring out. There are others who are blatantly disobedient. Unless their life-style changes, they will be weeded out of leadership by our Lord himself. He will not use dirty vessels.'

I felt extremely vulnerable as I gave this talk. What if I was wrong? What if *God* had not revealed these things . . .?

Within a year, five leaders had resigned, unable to cope with the pressures of family, responsible jobs and leadership in the church; several key people had resigned because they were committing gross sexual sin.

At this time, a member of that congregation was given a word of prophecy for the church which she offered with hesitancy and an open-ness to be corrected. The prophecy reads: 'I am raising up the debris of society to take the leadership you will not take. Those you count as nothing . . . who know their need and acknowledge their dependence on me, will overtake you and leave you as nothing.'

Today, former leaders in that church have fallen away. A whole new leadership is emerging. It consists of many unlikely people. The prophecy, it seems, is being fulfilled.

As I looked more closely at the gift of prophecy, I saw that if a prophetic word is from God, it will edify or exhort or comfort (see 1 Cor. 14:31). It will not necessarily be painless. Indeed, it will cut into a situation and cause pain, even fear. This is not unlike the incision the surgeon makes with his scalpel. It is the pain which precedes purging and healing, which is, in fact, an act of love.

The prophetic word is not only a word of love; it is also a timely word in the sense that it is necessary for that person or that group of people at that particular time. It is also an accurate word. Its accuracy survives the test of time. If it originates in God, the minutest details will be fulfilled.

On the day of Pentecost, as we have already seen, Peter quoted Joel's prophecy:

In the last days, God says,
I will pour out my Spirit on all people.
Your sons and daughters will prophesy,
    your young men will see visions,

Your old men will dream dreams.
Even on my servants, both men and women,
I will pour out my Spirit in those days,
    and they will prophesy (Acts 2:17,
    quoting Joel 2:28–32).

I began to realise that we live in those exciting 'last days'. And I began to realise that Christians who open themselves to the Holy Spirit of God will, as occasion demands, be entrusted with the supernatural gifts of wisdom and knowledge, prophecy and visions. I would now go further. Like David Watson, I recognise that these gifts are 'tremendously important for every age'. They are 'not made redundant by the completion of the God-given revelation in the scriptures.'[4] Rather, they are made available for us by God through the anointing of his Holy Spirit.

God speaks through very ordinary, everyday events and objects. And God speaks through the supernatural. That God speaks at all today still sent a shiver of anticipation down my spine whenever I turned to prayer. I expected God to speak. And he did.

Chapter 13

Many Mistakes

Listening to God is not always as straightforward as it seems. At least, this is my experience. At times it can even seem quite frightening.

I am a person who likes to keep at least one toe on the ground while swimming in the sea. Similarly, I like to keep well within my depth in a spiritual sense. But there were times when the tide seemed to sweep me along with it and I was forced to respond to the challenge to become a stronger swimmer.

The problem was that although I knew that God speaks today and that his messages are transmitted in a multitude of ways and although I had experienced the fact that he wants to gain *my* attention, to communicate to me, I was also becoming increasingly aware that the pictures I saw, the dreams I dreamed, and the inner voice I heard did not always originate in God. If my suspicion was correct, then where did these phenomena spring from? And how was I supposed to discern the real from the spurious?

One night, for example, a vivid dream startled me. My husband and I were on holiday in Austria at the time. David is a keen photographer and, like a mountain goat, he will sometimes leap to seemingly precarious places in order to 'get a better shot'. In my dream, David and I were walking in the mountains in the way we love to do. Suddenly a breath-taking scene of snow-capped mountain cones framed by an expanse of cornflower blue sky opened up before us. David edged himself on to a wobbly ledge to capture the scene on film when, all of a sudden, he fell. At first, fear paralysed me. But then it propelled me into action. I ran and ran as fast as I could until I reached the spot where he lay. But I was too late. His body was slumped in a heap. He was dead.

Next morning, fear seemed to hold me in a vice-like grip. For some reason I cannot fathom even now, I was unable to voice this fear to David. Perhaps I was afraid that if I described the accident it might even happen? That evening we had a minor accident in the car. All that happened was that we demolished a bollard at the edge of the road but my nerves, still shattered by the vividness of the dream, gave way. Hysterical, I clung to David, sobbed, and poured out the details of the dream which was making me so miserable. The panic only subsided after we had prayed together.

On a previous holiday, God *had* spoken to me through the dream I described in an earlier chapter. Of that fact I was now convinced. But this dream clearly had not come from the same loving source. Where *had* it come from?

Some months later, David and I attended an interview for a new job. While I was praying on the day of the interview, I sensed God was telling me that we would be appointed to this new post. I was glad. I would enjoy a series of new challenges.

Three days after the interview, the expected phone call came but the voice at the other end did not give the anticipated message. On the contrary, it said: 'We'd like to thank David and yourself for giving up your time to attend the interview. I am sorry to tell you we are unable to offer you the job. Someone else is now considering the post. We will confirm this in a letter in a day or two.'

I placed the phone in its cradle and was relieved that the house was empty. The shock left me numbed. Had God not kept his promise? Impossible. Had the interviewers made a mistake? Unlikely. So many people had prayed about this appointment. Then I must have been mistaken in my listening. Listening to God was not as straightforward as I imagined.

Other people were having problems with separating the real from the spurious, too. I knew of this because some of them were honest enough to tell me.

There was the woman who said, 'The Lord has told me to write a book. I'm to write the story of my life.' She spent years writing her book but was unable to find a publisher. Had her listening been accurate? Had *God* told her to write the book?

There was the Christian student who confessed to me that he had been sleeping with his non-Christian girlfriend for several months. He told me that, since it would be impossible for them to marry for several years, but since they were committed to one another, God had told him it was permissible for them to have sexual intercourse. What did I think?

And there was the person who asked to see me because she was utterly confused. 'Joyce! I don't know what to do any more. You see, I keep hearing all these voices in my head telling me what to do. I think it's the Holy Spirit talking to me. I used to read my Bible regularly and do what it told me to do. But now I don't know which to believe. So I've stopped reading my Bible and just do what the Holy Spirit says.'

Without ever realising what they were doing, these people helped me to face up to the fact that those of us who embark on the adventure of listening to God are going to make mistakes. For listening to God can be the most sublime and joy-filled privilege in the world or it can become the most absurd exercise we ever embark on.

For sheer absurdity, I have never encountered an example which surpasses the one quoted by Jim Packer:

There was once a woman who sincerely wanted to listen to God about the details of her life. Each morning, having consecrated the day to the Lord as she woke, she would then ask whether she was to get up or not. She would not stir until the still, small voice told her to dress. As she put on each article she asked the Lord whether she was to put it on. Very often the Lord would tell her to put her right shoe on but to leave the other off. Sometimes she was to put on both stockings but no shoes and sometimes both shoes and no stockings. And thus listening to God she would deal with every article of dress in turn.[1]

Mistakes! Mistakes! Mistakes! When I read stories like this, counselled people like the ones I have mentioned above and smarted over the situations I mishandled myself, there were times when I was tempted to abandon my quest. But a claim Thomas Merton makes in one of his books lodged in my mind and prevented me from abandoning all that I had learned to treasure. Thomas Merton says of mistakes that the only one which is really a mistake is that from which we learn nothing. I had also heard David Watson's maxim: 'The antidote to *abuse* is not *disuse* but *right* use.' In the light of these challenges I determined to allow a whole string of mistakes to become, not my censors, but my teachers.

Recognise the source
A talk given by Jean Darnall at a Swanwick conference I attended cleared away the mists of confusion which swirled round my brain and my emotions. 'Test the spirits,' she challenged. 'Make certain that what you are hearing comes from God.' She pointed us to the scriptures: 'Dear friends, do not believe every spirit, but test the spirits to see whether they are from God, because many false prophets have gone out into the world . . .' (1 John 4:1).

Later, when I followed this theme up for myself, I noticed that this solemn warning has been woven into the fabric of the New Testament's teaching. Jesus warned us to beware of the wolves who come to us in sheep's clothing. Paul begs us not to quench the Spirit by putting out his fire, nor to treat prophecy with contempt, but he also urges us to 'Test everything. Hold on to the good.' (1 Thess. 5:19). In James, I found advice which further clarified my own position: 'The wisdom that comes from heaven is first of all pure; then peace-loving, considerate, submissive, full of mercy and good fruit, impartial and sincere' (Jas. 3:17).

When I applied this verse to my two dreams, I saw the difference immediately. The one I dreamed in Greece which had prepared me to face up to imminent tragedy was 'peace-loving' in the sense that, horrifying though it was, it left my heart and mind full of God's peace rather than full of terror. The dream which interrupted my sleep in Austria, on the other hand, was not only terrifying in its attention to detail, but it left me panic-stricken. The lack of peaceableness, had I known about this verse in James at the time of the dream, could have been my clue. This dream had not emanated from God.

Three possible sources

If my dream was not sent from God, where did it spring from? Again, it was Jean Darnall who showed me that dreams and visions and voices and thoughts come from three possible sources:

- the Holy Spirit
- my own spirit
- the Evil One.

That made immediate sense. I reflected on my second dream again and saw that it had not been prophetic but simply an expression of my neurotic fear that David would one day slip over the side of a precipice while taking photographs. I laughed. The laughter brought a new perspective: of course the dream described my neurosis in technicolour detail. God would only feature in it if I were to hand the fear over to him.

I thought, too, of 'the word' which assured me that we would be appointed to the new post. Again, I smiled in a wry kind of way. How easy it was to listen to the voice of pride and wishful thinking and hang the Lord's name around their neck. I realised that I was still wearing L plates where listening to God is concerned. Probably I always will. As Thomas Merton observes: 'We do not want to be beginners. But let us be convinced of the fact that we will never be anything else but beginners all our life!'[2] For this reason I was grateful to Jean Darnall for the practical advice she gave me at that time. 'If you believe God has told you to do something,' she advised, 'ask him to confirm it to you three times: through his word, through circumstances, and through other people who may know nothing of the situation.'

For the next twelve months I became far more cautious about listening to God. I tested the ground in the way Jean suggested. And I was grateful for the apprenticeship, which enabled me to grow in confidence.

I now realise that we can never be one hundred per cent certain that the picture we see or the voice we hear or the prophecy we speak out is winged to us from God. That is why listening to God is hard, why speaking out in the name of God is costly and leaves us feeling vulnerable.

If the voice is truly from God, it will have an ice-cutting quality about it. Someone will hear it and say, 'Oh yes! I see!' If the voice comes from our own hurt spirit or over-anxious or over-loving spirit, no lasting harm will be done so we need not worry. But we shall be able to tell the difference between this and God's voice because there will be a lack of authority and dynamism about what is shared. The word or picture will probably fall flat on its face like a badly told joke.

But what if a word or a picture or a dream or an intuition is planted in one's heart by the Evil One? This seemed to me far more serious and, I admit, the possibility worried me. Satan, I know, loves to fake spiritual gifts. He is skilled in the art of the counterfeit.

Know the Father-heart of God

While I was still worrying over this question, Alex Buchanan, whom I had first met when he was on the staff of St Michael-le-Belfrey Church, in York, and whose friendship my husband and I had grown to value, made one of those pronouncements whose divine origin one recognises immediately. On a visit to our home he said, 'If you want to be certain that you are truly listening to God, you must know the Father-heart of God.' I was glad that there were others in the room when he turned that statement into a question. 'Do you *know* the Father-heart of God?'

I knew what he meant by this question. He was asking whether we knew the mind of God, whether we understood the personality of God, whether we were acquainted with the will of God and the way he normally acts and reacts in certain situations. He was asking whether we were familiar with the pronouncements God has made on certain subjects. He made it clear that the way to distinguish between God's voice and Satan's voice was to become acquainted with what lay in God's Father-heart.

That made sense to me. That very week I had taken a phone call for David which had demonstrated to me the value of knowing someone's mind in this intuitive way. A friend had telephoned one evening and asked to speak to my husband. David was out. 'Oh well, Joyce, you'll do,' the voice said. 'I was going to ask whether he would be interested in a new job. I'd like to put his name forward if I may.'

'Well,' I replied, 'I'm ninety-nine per cent certain that David would say that at the moment he feels God is asking us to stay in Nottingham.'

When David came home, I asked him, 'If someone was to ask if they could put your name forward for a new job, what would you say?'

David used almost the same words I had used earlier: 'I'd say that I feel that we're being asked to stay in Nottingham at the moment.'

I live with David. We have spent years working at the art of communication. I know his mind. I know his personality. I know his plans. I talk to him and I listen to him. Was it possible to know God in this intuitive way also?

I was preparing to preach a sermon on Daniel at the

time. Daniel seemed conversant with the Father-heart of God. Daniel offered me the master key. It came in the form of a pithy observation: 'I, Daniel, understood from the scriptures . . .' (Dan. 9:2). To understand means here: to consider in detail, to go through carefully, to examine, to scrutinise. Daniel knew the Father-heart of God because Daniel applied his *mind* to the hard work of understanding God's Word so that he could understand God himself.

The psalmist was another man whose writings reflect an intimate knowledge of God. When I searched for his secret, I discovered his, too, was an open secret. David familiarised himself with the Father-heart of God by familiarising himself with scripture. David delighted in God's Word, treasured it, steeped himself in it, respected it, memorised it, pored over it, examined it and determined never to veer from it.[3] He meditated on God's revealed word day and night and exhorted others to follow his example (Ps. 1:2).

That these men built a close relationship with God because they applied their energies and time and minds to the study of God's Word came as a sharp and salutary reminder. God seemed to be warning me again that listening to him is not just a matter of openness or willingness to hear his still, small voice. It is not just a matter of meditating, internalising the message or contemplating him, it is also a matter of hard work and application. When listening to God, inspiration and perspiration walk hand in hand.

God gave this same warning through John Wesley: 'Do not ascribe to God what is not of God. Do not easily suppose dreams, voices, impressions, visions, revelations to be from God without sufficient evidence. They may be purely natural, they may be diabolical. Try all things by the written Word and let all bow down before it.'

If my student friend had done this, I reflected, there would have been no need to ask my advice about his relationship with his girl-friend. The Bible makes it quite clear that to be unequally yoked with an unbeliever is to accept second best in marriage, not God's best. The Bible also makes it clear that sexual intercourse has one context and one context only: marriage. Any voice which tells an unmarried person that they are absolved from this clear biblical teaching must therefore be rejected. It is not God's voice. God will not contradict himself. God's truth is not negotiable.

Similarly, I thought of my friend who had abandoned Bible reading in favour of listening to the voices in her head. I understood now why anger had burned inside me when she told me of her decision. I had not been angry against her but against that serpent, Satan, who still bewitches us and uses all and every means to side-track us from the narrow path which leads to life.

There could be no finger pointing on my part. I was too busy making my own mistakes and learning from them to have time to wage war against others. But I knew that in future I must test my listening by asking four questions:

- Is the result of this piece of listening in alignment with scripture?
- Do the circumstances substantiate what I heard? Has it come true?
- Is my attitude Christ-like, characterised by humility, or is it reminiscent of Satan, the rebellious one?
- Is this still, small voice prompting me or others to live in a way which honours God and obeys him, or will the suggestion bring his name and honour into question or disrepute?

As I pondered on these criteria for accurate listening, I recognised that here was a charge from God. If I am to listen to God for married people in trouble, as I do, I must first know what God's Word says about marriage. If I am to help unmarried people with sexual problems, as I do, I owe it to them to be certain what lies in the Father-heart of God concerning their problems and their person.

God had challenged me. However fascinated I became

with his presence, his power and his ability to communicate, I must not allow my knowledge of the scriptures to grow rusty. At the same time, I took comfort from Francis Schaeffer's reassuring observation. Speaking of people who steep themselves in the gospel, maintain a high view of scripture *and* give a proper emphasis to God's Spirit he maintains that God will use them even if they make mistakes, as undoubtedly they will: 'If we preach the gospel clearly, have a strong view of scripture with a strong emphasis on content and give adequate place to the Holy Spirit, God will use us even if we make mistakes – and, I repeat, none of us are free from mistakes.'[4]

Use your intelligence

Even so, I wanted to avoid making mistakes wherever possible. To speak in the name of Christ must not be done lightly. Mistakes must be taken seriously. Since it was becoming clear that my fallibility could cloud God's clarity, I determined to take on board two other suggestions which God seemed to underline. First is the need to submit what I hear to others so that they can weigh the word or picture language, sift it and determine its origin. Second is the responsibility I have not to neglect my intellect but to sharpen my powers of thinking. I took seriously a warning given by no less a listener than St John of the Cross who says on several occasions that we should not demand supernatural intervention when we are capable of understanding a situation for ourselves. God gave us our intellect to be used and used to the full. When the light of my own human intelligence is sufficient for the task in hand, he will not superimpose on it spiritual enlightenment. I thought of Jim Packer's story of the woman who waited for God to tell her what to wear, and asked to be delivered from the laziness which masquerades for a super-spirituality. And I resolved to become, to use the language of John Wesley, *unius homo libri*, a person of one book, the Bible.

Chapter 14

The Bible: the Touchstone of Listening

In all our listening, the most penetrating word we shall ever hear is God's written Word, the Bible, that sword which slips into the inner recesses of our being, challenging us, changing us, and renewing our minds. As we saw in the previous chapter, those who urge us to steep ourselves in the scriptures bring a vital, indispensable emphasis to the art form of listening prayer. The Bible is the touchstone of all our other listening. What is more, it has a power all its own.

J. B. Phillips testified to the power of this Word which springs from the Spirit of God. While he was translating the New Testament he discovered that God's Word was moulding his thinking: 'Although I did my utmost to preserve an emotional detachment, I found again and again that the material under my hands was strangely alive; it spoke to my condition in the most uncanny way.'[1]

Campbell McAlpine claims that this book, the Bible, 'is the *living word of the living God*'.[2] And Jesus lived by this Word. Moreover, he anticipated that the lives of believers would be shaped by it. He expected that all theological thinking would be tested in the light of his Father's 'letters from home', to borrow St Augustine's phrase. Thus when the Pharisees quizzed him about the marriage relationship, Jesus referred them to first biblical principles: 'Haven't you read . . . that at the beginning the Creator 'made them male and female', and said, 'For this reason a man will leave his father and mother and be united to his wife, and the two will become one flesh?' (Matt. 19:4;5, quoting Gen. 2:24).

Jesus assumed his followers would possess a thorough working knowledge of the scriptures. When lack of biblical insight blinded their eyes, Jesus rebuked them. So, on the road to Emmaus, Jesus found fault with his ignorant companions: 'How foolish you are, and how slow of heart to believe all that the prophets have spoken! Did not the Christ have to suffer these things and then enter his glory? And beginning with Moses and all the prophets, he explained to them what was said in all the scriptures concerning himself' (Luke 24:25–27).

In the view of Jesus, it seems, the written Word contained in scripture is the Word of God. Jesus expresses this dramatically when, in the desert, he confronts Satan face to face. With authority and poise, he withstands the Enemy with one economical phrase: 'It is written . . .' (Luke 4:4, 8).

For Jesus, as Jim Packer reminds us, 'It is written' was the end of the argument. 'There could be no appeal against the verdict of scripture for that would be to appeal against the judgement of God himself.'[3] For Jesus, the Old Testament taught and expressed God's mind and will. For this reason scripture was to be heeded, heard and obeyed, David Watson underlines these facts powerfully: 'The Bible is our final court of appeal for what God has said. Here is the God-given objective test for our belief and behaviour.'[4]

If I was to learn to listen to God accurately, to avoid the trap of tuning into my own emotions and mistaking these or wishful thinking for the voice of God, I knew it was incumbent on me to take these solemn words seriously. I must make time for Bible study.

Bible Study

In one sense this was not difficult. As a theology student who also read history and loved English literature, I learned to enjoy studying the Bible: Paul's epistles, the prophets, the historical books, the poetry and, of course, the gospels. I owe this enjoyment of the discipline of Bible study chiefly to my scripture teacher at school. A committed Christian who clearly relished God's Word herself, she passed on to me the desire to understand the written Word of God as well as the longing to interpret it accurately and to allow it to direct and renew my perception of life.

As an undergraduate, I sat at the feet of scholars whose love and respect for God's Word was equally profound. As I listened to them expound portions of scripture, like the psalmist, I delighted in God's revealed Word and felt nourished by it. In those days I never tired of the daily diet of Bible study.

When the demands of motherhood crept up on me, I grew lazy, even sloppy, in my attitude to the Bible. Although I struggled to have a Quiet Time most days and although this would include the reading of a portion of scripture and a cursory glance at some Bible reading notes, I could scarcely claim that Bible *study* featured in my life. But now, with this insatiable thirst to unearth methods of listening to God, I made Bible study a priority once more. God's word would give me the objective, scientific, revealed framework into which the prophecies and visions would fit if they were born of him.

For a while, I studied the Bible every day. I applied myself to it with diligence. I analysed it, concentrated on it, sought to understand what the original author intended to communicate when he wrote what he did, then sought to understand why God had left us with this particular message for all time. I tried, equally, to apply what I read to my own circumstances. And I dug deep. When I came across commands which now seem obsolete because the structure of society has changed here in the West ('Slaves, obey your masters'), I used my thinking powers to try to ascertain what the lasting underlying principles of such commands might be. I wanted to be an *informed* Christian.

I rejoiced to be grafted back into God's Word. I remember shutting myself in my study one Saturday, littering my desk and floor with Bibles and commentaries, and concentrating on Psalm 119 for the entire day. By evening I was euphoric. Not only had God given me a special love for that psalm, with its one hundred and seventy-six verses, but I could re-echo much of it.

> Oh, that my ways were steadfast in obeying your decrees! (9).
> My soul is consumed with longing for your laws at all times (20).
> Turn my heart towards your statutes and not towards selfish gain (36).

As I write this chapter Bible study is still, for me, a joyful privilege. I have just returned from two weeks away from home. While I was away on a retreat-holiday, I immersed myself in the first book of Kings. It is years since I read about the decline and fall of Israel and the spiritual downfall of Solomon and his successors to the throne. But through this application of my mind to his revealed Word, God reminded me of some salutary truths: enthusiasm for him is not enough, wisdom is not enough, fame is not enough; obedience to him is crucial for the person intent on progressing in the Christian life.

It is not only solo study which thrills me. Whenever I have the opportunity to attend Bible readings given by those gifted by God to present God's revealed Word in a systematic, scholarly way, I find my love for God rekindled. I crave for the richness of this diet. And it reminds me of the salient truth that God speaks to us first and foremost through our minds. No matter how skilled we become in tuning in to his multi-level methods of communication – 'hearing' prophecies and dreams and visions and 'vibes' – the starting point and check-point must always be God's Word revealed in the pages of the Bible. Unless we know what this Word contains we can never discern whether what we hear runs counter to the Bible and must therefore be discounted since God will not contradict himself.

Because Bible study has come to be of such importance in my listening prayer, it no longer features in my daily devotional time. I consider it too crucial for that. When a project becomes vital to my way of life, I carve out priority time for it. So, no matter how busy my schedule, I reserve quality time to spend with certain people, like my husband. Similarly, having recognised that Bible study is an indispensable part of listening to God, I create regular, leisurely opportunities when I can give myself to the commentaries and Bible dictionaries and the serious intellectual enquiry into the words which God has spoken and which are recorded for us for all time. I cannot concentrate on God's Word in this way on a *daily* basis, but I can commit myself to such study regularly.

Bible meditation

I am not saying I do not *read* the Bible every day. Most days I do. I am saying I do not study the Bible in an academic way each day. Instead I remind myself of God's truths by meditating on a portion of scripture.

My first introduction to this simple but profound method of Bible reading came through a book which boasts the simple title: *You*. I think I was attracted to the book by its sub-title: *Prayer for beginners and those who have forgotten how*. In it the author describes a reading technique which he calls 'super-slow reading'. Super-slow reading is reflective reading. You take a verse of scripture or a familiar passage and instead of studying it analytically, you read it as slowly as possible, presenting yourself to the situation described so forcibly that you begin to experience, with your imagination, the sights, sounds and feelings that are painted for you by the author.

The first time I experimented with this art of super-slow reading, Mark's account of the Crucifixion stunned me by its solemnity, then bruised my emotions with almost physical force:

At the sixth hour
darkness came over the whole land

until the ninth hour.
And at the ninth hour Jesus cried out in a loud voice,
'Eloi, Eloi, lama sabachthani?'
which means,
'My God, my God, why have you forsaken me?'
(Mark 15:33–34).

I knew those words so well I could probably have recited
them without reference to the text. But as I practised
superslow reading, I pictured in my imagination the hill
of Calvary where Jesus was strung up on his cross:
Golgotha, the place of the skull. I could feel the intense
heat of the mid-day sun burning his body. That phrase,
'darkness came over the whole land', terrified me as I saw
the blackness descend like a blanket over the whole of
Jerusalem and the surrounding countryside. The awfulness
of that darkness sent a shudder right down my spine. It
was my spine that reacted again as I heard the anguish of
Jesus's shout pierce the gloom: 'My God, my God, why
have you forsaken me?'

That day, I read these two verses from the gospel
narrative and that was all. It was enough. This scene
had changed my life. When you see Jesus writhing on
the cross before your very eyes in the way I did that day,
you have to make a personal response of humble, grateful
surrender to such depths of loving.

For a while, I concentrated solely on this method of
Bible reading. It transformed my attitude to the gospels.
This was of particular value for me because I had attended
Sunday School from the age of three. Consequently, I
knew all the Jesus stories inside out (or I thought I did).
Because I knew the punch-lines, the gospels had lost much
of their drawing power. Paul's epistles held far more
appeal than the accounts of Jesus's earthly pilgrimage.
But super-slow reading changed all that.

So did another method of Bible reading which is attributed to St Ignatius of Loyola and is described by him in
Spiritual Exercises. This method of reading the scriptures
involves replaying in one's mind and heart a particular

episode from the Bible. The idea behind the technique is that the reader relives the event which the gospel writer describes. Instead of standing on the fringe of the story as an observer, however, he becomes an active participant, immersing himself in what is happening and experiencing for himself with each of his five senses every detail of the story.

In other words, instead of simply reading about the woman who stretched out her hand to touch the hem of Jesus's garment, you *become* that woman and take the personal risk of reaching out to touch him. Instead of merely reading about the paralysed man who sat helplessly beside the pool of Bethesda, you *become* that man. You encounter Jesus for yourself. You talk to him. You hear his voice. You respond to his challenge: 'Do you want to get well?'

John Powell, in his book, *He Touched Me*, had encouraged me in the belief that God could speak through our five senses: sight, hearing, smell, taste and touch. This so-called Ignatian method of Bible reading convinced me of the authenticity of this claim.

Perhaps it is because God has endowed me with a vivid and virile imagination that these meditations quickly became one of the ways God spoke to me. As I 'became' Mary, the mother of Jesus, sitting astride the back of a donkey on my way to visit Elizabeth, and as I pondered on the stupendous news Gabriel had just brought, 'You are to be the mother of the Messiah,' my heart leapt with joy at the sheer wonder of it all. Despite the intrusive noise I could hear – the clip-clop of the donkey's feet – praise rose from somewhere deep within me: 'My soul glorifies the Lord . . .'

In this meditation, I was not nursing grandiose opinions of myself, mistaking my mission, believing myself in reality to be the mother of Jesus. Rather, I was identifying with Mary as fully as my senses would allow in order that the Holy Spirit of God could break through with fresh insights. He did. The wonder of the Annunciation and the Incarnation: the Creator of the world lying in a cradle; God coming to be found and seen and touched by mankind, bowled me over with an impact a mere reading of the words had never done.

I began to write my own meditations and to use them personally. One Ascension time, in my imagination I climbed the Mount of Ascension with the disciples and watched Jesus's departure from earth using this guideline:

Imagine that you have been allowed the privilege of walking with the eleven, out of Jerusalem to the Mount of Ascension.

Stay behind them as you leave the noise and clutter and the stifling heat of Jerusalem behind.

Feel the heat warming your body as you start the steep climb.

Feel the warm dust creeping into your sandals.

What can you see . . .?

What can you hear . . .?

What can you smell . . .?

Take time to picture the whole scene as vividly as possible.

Become an integral part of it.

How do you feel?

Look at your companions, the eleven disciples.

What sort of people are they?

How are they dressed?

What are they talking about?

Is there anything you'd like to ask them – or say to them?

Now you are nearing the place where Jesus promised to meet you.

How does it feel to be about to meet him?

And now – there he is – standing in front of you!

How does it feel to see the risen Lord?

What do you want to do as you meet him?

Take a good look at Jesus –
  at those hands still bearing the wounds of love
  at those hands hovering over you to bless you.

What do you want to say to Jesus?

Watch carefully. He is leaving you now, being lifted out of sight. Soon he will be hidden by the cloud of God's presence.

Is there anything you want to do?

Anything you want to say?

Look at the two men dressed in white.

How does it feel to be in their presence?

Drink in their message:
  this same Jesus will come back.

'Jesus is coming back.'

Say that over and over to yourself.

How do you want to respond?

Stay silently on the mountain top for a few minutes.

Allow God to speak to you.

Be caught up in the wonder of the moment.

The others are going back to Jerusalem now.

Go with them.

Is anyone saying anything?

How do they seem to feel?

How do you feel?

See the city come into sight again.

Notice the dome of the Temple.

Hear the sounds
  see the sights   } of the city.
    smell the smells

Go into the Temple with the others.

Try to drink in what you have seen and heard.

Thank God for it.

Whenever I embarked upon this type of meditation, it made a profound effect on my life. My meditation resulted in a genuine encounter with the living Christ. The result was a deep, inner communion with the Lord I love. Instead of just reading the Bible or expending effort on studying it, both valuable in themselves, its message was becoming internalised and personalised and therefore grew ever more precious. And my view of Jesus and my relationship with him was changing. On the one hand we were becoming more intimate, on the other more distant. I use the word 'distant' deliberately, not to suggest that Jesus was moving further away but to show that intimacy was laced with reverence and stripped of all hint of over-familiarity. I found I could not encounter Jesus in this genuine way and be 'matey'. That cheapened this 'tremendous lover'.

With the heart in the head
Campbell McAlpine says of meditation: 'Meditation is the devotional practice of pondering the words of a verse or verses of scripture, with a receptive heart, allowing the Holy Spirit to take the written Word and apply it as the living Word to the inner being . . . Someone has described meditation as "the digestive faculty of the soul . . ." Meditation is inwardly receiving the Word of God, illustrated by eating or feeding. God spoke to Ezekiel and emphasised this truth: "But you, son of man, *listen to* what

I say . . . open your mouth and *eat* what I give you" (Ezek. 2:8, italics mine).[5]

For me, meditation was proving a most nourishing method of feeding on the Word of God.

It was much later that I discovered the value of *lectio divina*, or 'divine reading' as it is sometimes called. I had seen these two latin words on the timetable of the monastic day and had dismissed them thinking they had nothing to do with me, a layman. How wrong I was! *Lectio divina* is sometimes described as 'reading with the mind in the heart'. Basil Pennington strives to capture its value.

> [it is] reading with God, with the Holy Spirit – walking with Jesus on the way and letting his Spirit within us set our hearts ablaze as the scriptures are opened to us. This little method . . . is more than reading: it is prayer, a real communication with God that opens out to us the depths and the heights – the depths of intimacy, the heights of transcendent contemplation . . . It is not a question of reading a paragraph, a page, or a chapter. It is, rather, sitting down with a friend, the Lord, and letting him speak to us. We listen. And if what he says in the first word or the first sentence strikes us, we stop and let it sink in. We relish it. We respond from our heart. We enjoy it to the full before we move on. There is no hurry. We are sitting with our friend . . . We let him speak. We really listen.[6]

I used this method of Bible reading more and more, interspersing it with the Ignatian approach and super-slow reading. Because, for me, ideas flow most fluently when I hold a pen in my hand, I would respond to the Lord and the passage before me in writing, recording my thoughts in my prayer journal. On one occasion, as I was reading the Song of Solomon meditatively, conscious because of certain sins that were cluttering my life, that I was unworthy of God's love, the familiar verse, 'He brought me to his banqueting table' begged me to stop. Among other things, this is how I responded to each word in turn:

HE: Lord, it is you, the Lord of Lords and King of Kings, who have prepared that banqueting table. Such knowledge is too wonderful for me to take in. HE brought me. The high and lofty one, the Creator of the universe. I can call you my Beloved. You are mine. This is sheer, undeserved love. Last night I bewailed my own wretchedness and unworthiness to approach you, yet here this morning I hear your persistent, gentle, loving invitation. No. It is more than an invitation. You know that if you merely invited me at the moment, probably I would refuse to come. At least, I would be shy and hesitate. And so because you really want me to be there you

BROUGHT: me. What persistence! What desire! You love me enough to carry me, albeit struggling, to your banquet: the feast you have specially prepared. And if you are doing the carrying, all I have to do is to rest and relax and allow you to do what you will. With that, I am content and humbly thank you . . .

ME: I begin to see the banquet – carefully and lovingly laid out. I smell the fruit, see their colours, handle them, savour them in anticipation. And I see that it has been lovingly prepared. Amidst all this grandeur, as *your* specially invited guest, I see myself, and my heart cries out, 'Why me? I shouldn't be here!'

I go on to record the joy of receiving the forgiveness and cleansing and renewal with which God feasted me at his banqueting table on that occasion.

Richard Foster says of *lectio divina*: 'It is a kind of meditative spiritual reading in which the mind and the heart are drawn into the love and goodness of God . . . We are doing more than reading words . . . we are pondering all things in our heart as Mary did. We are entering into the reality of which the words speak.'[7]

As this happened in my experience more and more, the Bible assumed even greater importance in my listening to God. It was not just the framework into which all the other listening was required to fit. It was, of itself, the chief piece of listening equipment at my disposal. As such, it was always at my fingertips; whether studying it or memorising it or singing it or meditating on it, I would seek to open myself to God through its pages. Even so the problems did not disappear. On the contrary, they seemed to multiply, so much so that at times, for reasons I shall explain in the next chapter, I was tempted to give up.

Chapter 15

Tempted to Give Up

Ladislas Orsy makes the claim that, just as a skilled surgeon will operate on a patient better and faster than a medical student who has to keep referring to his text books, so an habitually prayerful person will discern God's still, small voice more quickly and more accurately than one whose prayer is spasmodic and dissipated.

This challenged me. I thought back to the early years of learning to listen, the honeymoon months when listening seemed pure delight. Then, the dire warnings I read and heard, 'listening to God is the most difficult yet most decisive part of prayer,'[1] and 'listening to God requires effort, practice and discipline,'[2] had puzzled me. Now the pressure was on me. The temptation to give up was one which plagued me often.

The pressing problem was busyness. Until 1981 I believed God was calling me to a life of listening prayer. This was to be the life-giving stream which never ceased to flow under the surface even while I managed my home and worked alongside my husband in the parish. I had carved out a place for God: in my home, in my heart and in my timetable. I determined, each day, to give him my undivided attention, quality time. And in the rhythm of the life which was mine at that time, I tried to lay the foundations of listening to God faithfully, through study and through prayer.

But in 1981, my first book was published. It was not

that I believed myself to be an author by vocation. I wrote this one book because I was invited to do so. As far as I was concerned, it was a one off. But this book on Christian marriage spawned another book on engagement. Its publication coincided with a prophecy I was given which hinted that, since I would have no more children (I had just had a hysterectomy) I was to give birth to books!

To my surprise, what I wrote seemed to strike a chord in people's hearts. I was invited to speak at various meetings. The number of couples queueing for counselling increased. Suddenly, it seemed, I was catapulted from the obscurity I relished into the whirlwind of activity I had so often despised in others. Dispossessed of time, my carefully planned routine lay in ruins. Concentrated listening seemed a thing of the past.

A whole hour for prayer became a luxury, a fond memory. Indeed, when ideas for a book or magazine article flowed, prayer would often be squeezed out altogether. Even if I lit my candle and contemplated the cross of Christ in my prayer room, stillness evaded me. Quietness and privacy simply swung open the door to a flood of creativity: ideas for the next chapter of the book or for the next talk I was to give would spring up like the magic genies in children's stories.

Inwardly, I despaired. How was I to listen to God if I had lost the art of stillness? At times I felt cheated. It was as though my pearl of great price had been stolen almost overnight. At other times guilt crushed me. What kind of a Christian was I? God had given me such a valuable training in prayer and here was I allowing it to be eclipsed by activity.

In August 1982, I poured out some of the pain, frustration and anguish in a letter to my friend and editor, Derek Wood. I began the letter by complaining of a 'holy restlessness, a yearning, an urgency to return to stillness – not in an escapist way but to redress a balance.'! 'I'm in conflict, inner turmoil. I know God has called me to a work of prayer. I know that power and authority and inspiration come in the stillness . . . And yet I now take less time to be still. Whenever I'm involved in a project, I find stillness crowded out by thoughts and ideas which jostle and vie for attention.' Yet I wanted to be creative also: 'I have to be creative – God has shown me that. But that creativity has to arise from the silence . . . What *is* the answer? How do I combine these seemingly incompatible responsibilities: to listen to God in the stillness *and* become a careful steward of the gifts he has entrusted me with?'

A few weeks before I wrote that letter I wrote in similar vein to another friend of mine, a hermit who is also a writer. As a fellow-traveller on the path of prayer, and as one who is far more experienced than I am, I awaited her advice with eagerness. Faithful friend that she is, she did not tell me what I wanted to hear: hang on to the luxury of your prolonged times of quiet; cling to this as your right. No. Instead, she explained that she believed that God was moving me on, that the luxury of the prolonged periods of prayer I had enjoyed in the past had served their purpose. By them God had brought me through my apprenticeship and at the same time had poured a great deal of healing into my life. Now, listening prayer was to serve a different purpose, among other things it was to fuel the fire of creativity rather than become an end in itself. In practical terms this meant that when I attempted to be still before God and ideas seemed to crowd God out, I must write the ideas down, see them as a part of the prayer, not enemies of it, recognise their source – God himself – and give him thanks.

The letter went on to warn that the intense activity in which I was now engaged must be punctuated by periods of uncluttered silence during which I could creep back into God for sustenance. This was essential for the survival of my life of listening. We have to be big for God. As prayerful people, God wants us to grow even bigger for him. But we need to be very little too, so little that we know the joy of being carried and held by him.

These insights coincided with my editor's reaction to my letter:

Your hermit friend wrote wisely I think. We do move
from one of God's emphases for us to another. I am
in need of learning more how to be silent. You have
done that and need to learn how to use it, not as an
end in itself, but as a means to a deeper friendship
with God and a means of releasing your creativity.
On the 'friendship with God' approach I can't help
recalling what our church warden said about prayer.
'It's what God and I come up with together.' This
describes creativity well, I think.

These letters had a certain ring of truth about them.
Nevertheless, for several months I feared that I would
never be capable of holding in tension the two vocations
which were so dear to my heart: to be rooted in God and
to be creative for him.

As I look back, with the wisdom of hindsight, I recognise
that God was teaching me a vital lesson. I am a pilgrim.
Pilgrims must be always on the move. A pilgrimage is a
journey, often a steep ascent. I must face the challenge of
the climb with a willingness to respond to the beckoning
of God's finger no matter what it costs me. When he
calls me to leave behind past securities and to face new
challenges, I must obey, gladly and with child-like trust.
Inherent in the Christian's calling is the belief that new
life comes through death; the grain of wheat has to die so
that it can produce new life. For the Christian, constant
change is an inevitability.

But I had not learned these vital lessons at this stage of
the journey and so I mourned for the loss of the pattern of
prayer I had learned to value. And when God asked me
to dismantle my prayer room and to pray, instead, in one
corner of my study, this seemed yet another bitter blow,
the loss of something else I had held dear.

Again, looking back, I understand what I did not
appreciate at the time: God was asking me to piece
together my work and my prayer. To move my cross
and my candle and my prayer stool into my study simply
symbolised this essential integration. But, at the time, I

was full of pain. Clearly I had not yet learned another vital lesson the person of prayer must learn: to hold lightly to things and people and the past!

The underlying pain in me was not really touched until I read a book by Henri Nouwen in which he describes how his pursuit of prayer similarly had been disrupted by lecturing, writing, teaching. His honesty disarmed me:

> While teaching, lecturing, and writing about the importance of solitude, inner freedom, and peace of mind, I kept stumbling over my own compulsions and illusions . . . What was turning my vocation to be a witness to God's love into a tiring job? . . . Maybe I spoke more about God than with him. Maybe my writing about prayer kept me from a prayerful life. Maybe I was more concerned about the praise of men and women than the love of God.[3]

Henri Nouwen plucked up the courage to clear his desk and his diary and become a Trappist monk for seven months. There, in the monastery, he reassessed his priorities with the help of the abbot. As his seven months of solitude drew to a close, he asked the abbot, John Eudes, how he was to combine prayer and creativity when he returned to the maelstrom of the college where he taught. John Eudes' advice to Nouwen reinforced the routine God had been suggesting to me through my friends:

- Establish a new rhythm of prayer, make it known, and make it a priority.
- Make a daily discipline of listening prayer a must by plotting periods of the day when you determine that you will 'waste time' with God.
- Recurring days of retreat will be really fruitful only when this daily discipline is firmly established.
- Integrate prayer and work: 'Lecturing, preaching, writing, studying and counselling . . . would be nurtured and deepened by a regular prayer life.'[4]

As I pieced the jig-saw together, the picture which began to emerge pleased me. It presented me with the possibility of increased harmony in my life as I learned to blend personal preparation, time with people and prayer. I record in my prayer journal the joy that coursed through me as I re-apprenticed myself to the practice of listening prayer.

That is not to say I overcame the obstacles easily. I did not. Indeed, I still struggle to orchestrate prayer and work. But there were valuable lessons to be learned on the way.

The chief lesson God repeats to me over and over again is that if I am to receive his message into myself so that it strikes root, germinates and bears fruit, I need silence. This silence – 'Be still, and know that I am God' (Ps. 46:10) – is difficult to achieve. But it is the prerequisite of listening, and it involves telling myself, firmly and authoritatively, to stop chattering, to shut up!

Discipline is the answer. I find, for example, that when I resist the temptation to go straight from breakfast to my desk and start writing but, instead, move to my desk via my prayer corner, the quality of my work improves because, deliberately, I take time to drop anchor into God. I know this to be true. I have proved it over and over again.

Lack of obedience

But busyness was not the only hindrance to listening to God. Difficulties had pressed in on me before I started to write, problems of a more subtle nature. The chief problem was sin.

As I re-read my prayer journals today, the cacophony of anger, jealousy, resentment, poisoned memories and blatant disobedience which I describe in detail fills me with horror. There was the occasion when I poured out page after page of anger against a certain member of our congregation. Suddenly, it seemed, I stopped and wrote: 'Lord, I've just heard the birds singing. My anger has been shouting so loudly, I haven't heard them until now.' I had been sitting in the garden for a whole hour!

But it was the disobedience which seriously threatened my relationship with God. With shame, I now read my own accounts of my struggle to give God the mastery in certain relationships which were corroding my friendship with Jesus. I wanted the best of both worlds: my way and God's.

When God faced me with the inevitable choice – my way *or* his – I squealed. For months I was so full of self-will that I heard little from the still, small voice of God. Bible meditation ceased, Bible study stopped. I would dip into the Bible from time to time but it communicated nothing. This was hardly surprising. I had not yet learned that God's Word is not simply to be studied, read or personalised. It has to be obeyed. But as William Barclay warns: 'There are people into whose minds [and emotions] the word has no more chance of gaining an entry than the seed has of settling into the ground that has been beaten hard by many feet.'[5]

There are many things which can close a person's mind. Disobedience is the most effective. As someone aptly said: 'The one who truly listens is also the one who truly obeys.'

It hurts to recall the failures. It is the kind of hurt I felt once when I watched a family on the beach in Cyprus. The parents were trying hard to give their children a happy holiday. The sun was shining, the sandy beach stretched for miles, white waves tickled the shore. And the children were squabbling over a small, red, plastic spade.

I am like those children. God's generosity to me had known no limits. Yet I was throwing his love back in his face because the attractions the world offered seemed to possess a greater magnetic power than the wonder of his presence. At times I rejected him altogether. At times I feared my life of listening was a closed chapter.

But the Holy Spirit continued to bombard my ears with messages from God: uncomfortable messages, disconcerting messages, messages which troubled me and caused me to struggle to survive. I would hear these messages and take careful note of them. And I would respond to them in my prayer journal, not recognising that the Spirit's work is not always to notify us of God's love but rather to bring us up with a jolt: to show us his displeasure.

Little by little, my response grew stronger. Eventually, God showed me what had to be done. A load of rubble had to be tipped out on the dumping ground of the cross where he would take responsibility for it. Slowly and thoughtfully I made a reappraisal of my life: where I was going, what I was wanting, what God was asking of me. Anything which obstructed the path would have to go. Equally slowly, but quite deliberately, I cleared out the clutter which had kept me from Christ.

I see now what was happening. God emptied me of so much of self that he created within me a greater capacity for him. He had read the signs which showed that, at the deepest level of my being, this was what I wanted. When my Bible lay unused, a hunger would grow inside me. When my prayer time became nothing more than good and evil waging war within, a holy dissatisfaction filled me. It gave birth to the realisation that I cannot live without him, that a life devoid of listening to him, loving him and being met by him spells emptiness and not fullness. The good would therefore have to win.

I would like to be able to present a neat formula which I used to steer me through these sticky patches. Alas! I know of no such aerobics guaranteed to keep me spiritually trim and fit to listen. The struggles I have described still dog my path of prayer from time to time just as they have done in the past.

Obedience, I know, is the key, the 'open sesame' to listening. For years God engraved that word on my heart. For this reason I have studied the salutary warnings the Bible gives to the disobedient. I have combed the pages of the Bible in an attempt to discover what God requires of me in certain situations: as a wife, a mother, a friend, a business woman; as a sexual being, a female and, one entrusted with Christian leadership. I know that disobedience can lock and bolt the door against God's still, small voice. Even so, I find it easier to write about obedience, read about obedience and preach about obedience than to obey. I know how to leap this hurdle: simply discover God's will and do it. But I find it hard.

The same stubbornness characterises my current attitude to stillness. I love it. I benefit from it. Yet I neglect it because I persuade myself that the pressures on me do not allow it space. I know the way out of the problem: respond to the wooing of God. Yet I ignore his courtship.

But God's patience seems infinite. When I do succumb to my self-imposed discipline, I recognise that the long apprenticeship was not wasted. I drop into stillness easily and quickly. The awareness of God's life springs into being equally rapidly. That is hardly surprising since God is never reluctant to come to our aid but responds gladly to every advance of ours. The joy of surrendering to him is usually sweet. A privilege. And being found, held, and loved by God all over again and receiving his activity deep into the inner recesses of my being fills me with fresh awe and wonder and praise. The encounter is usually so powerful that it leaves me asking the question: '*Why* don't I make more time for this more often?'

Because such encounters with God seemed fleeting and few and far between I discovered that my hermit friend was correct when she recommended uncluttered times with God away from the normal, hectic routine. I am now busier than I was when I first faced the crisis I described at the beginning of this chapter. For this reason I try to spend a day away each month when God and I can 'just be' together in the quietness of a prayer saturated place. I aim to arrive at 9.30 a.m. and not to leave before 7.0 p.m. During these quiet days of reflective, listening prayer, time seems to stand still. Nine hours seem like twenty-four. On some of these days apart, I asked God to show me how to be more effective in integrating my work and my prayer. It was on one such occasion that the phrase 'praying my life' captured my imagination and encouraged me further to perfect the art of finding God in everything.

Chapter 16

Some Helps along the Way

Martha, the one distracted by a thousand tasks, and Mary, the one who lost herself in the wonder of Christ's company, can co-exist in the same person. And this need not result in spiritual schizophrenia. Certain practical methods of prayer make this unlikely marriage possible.

When this realisation burst in to my awareness, I began to ask God to help me to tune into him, not only in times of stillness, but at odd times during the day. In order to thus pray my life more effectively, I used one retreat to explore how others did this. From there I went on to experiment for myself.

The first suggestion which fascinated me was what Guy Brinkworth calls 'the method of the godly pause'.[1] In his book, *Thirsting for God*, he explains how this occasional pause during the day to say the name of Jesus or simply reflect on the fact that he is concerned for us can be a valuable 'booster' to the prayer of listening.

This seemed so sensible, almost obvious, that I adopted this practice immediately. When taking paper out of my typewriter or making myself a cup of coffee or waiting at traffic lights, I would turn my mind God-wards quite deliberately. Often God would communicate his presence to me in some felt way.

And a phrase of Catherine de Hueck Doherty captured my imagination also. She speaks of the 'little pools of silence' which punctuate one's day and goes on to demonstrate how prayer might feature in these so that the desert experiences of our life might be irrigated constantly. Whilst washing up, ironing, hoovering, dusting, gardening, walking to the post, driving to the shops, or travelling by public transport, therefore, I would try to listen to God as intently as in my place of prayer. It worked.

Soon after my resolve to tune into God all day and every day, I was caught in a sudden, heavy snowstorm which caused traffic chaos almost immediately. It took me four hours to drive along a route which normally takes half an hour: an excellent way to put into practice my intention. That day I learned the truth of Catherine of Siena's claim: 'Every time and every place is a time and place for prayer.' I also understood why it was said of St Teresa of Avila that she could find God 'so easily among the pots and pans' and why Brother Lawrence testified that even when, as cook of the monastery, he was elbow-deep in potato peelings, he could converse with God, entreat him, rejoice with a thousand thanksgivings; how his very soul, without any forethought, could be lifted above all earthly things and be held by God.

Even bedtime became a time of resting in God as I tried to follow the psalmist's example:

On my bed I remember you;
I think of you through the watches of the night (Ps. 63:6).

The more I pursued this path of prayer, the more I would wake in the night, not from insomnia but with a burden to pray: for a particular person, for nurses on duty, for people who become suicidal in the loneliness of the long night hours. One night I woke with the name of a member of our congregation ringing in my mind: a pregnant wife. I prayed. I was moved the next day when her husband telephoned to say that his wife had given birth to a daughter in the middle of that night.

And in my waking hours, I delighted to discover the

reality of another of Guy Brinkworth's prayer boosters: the recollection of the constant companionship of Christ: 'As I work, a Loved Presence over my shoulder, as I drive a Loved Passenger beside me. In my reading, cooking, studying, whilst teaching, nursing, accounting: in the maelstrom of the supermarket or waiting for the bus or train – ever the loving sense of a Presence – always that nostalgia for my Creator.'[2]

Gradually I learned to phase in and out of a loving awareness of Christ and his presence on and off during the day. I found that the warmth of the encounter with Christ in the early morning stillness need not vanish as I apply myself to work. Rather, the experience was not unlike the love which holds two friends together. They may not meet, but they will think about one another during the day, wonder how the other is faring, picture the other, even make a mental note of snippets of news to be shared when they next telephone or see one another. Thus the friendship is kept alive in the absences; the communication between them never really ceases.

Short ejaculatory prayers can help to keep this love alive. A prayer of Amy Carmichael's was one I used often: 'Holy Spirit, think through me till your ideas become my ideas.' And John Wesley's words expressed my desire to stay in tune all day: 'Jesus, strengthen my desire to work and speak and think for you.' Especially while writing or counselling. Samuel's short prayer frequently found an echo on my lips: 'Speak, Lord, your servant is listening.'

Using simple, practical techniques like this, I discovered that listening prayer need not be divorced from my everyday routine, but could become an integral part of it. As Guy Brinkworth puts it: 'a background yearning for God can be sustained in the middle of any activity as a kind of "celestial music while you work".'[3] 'The internal burning sign of love need not, with practice and adaptation, interfere with the efficiency of the "secular" side of the contemplative's activity.'[4] In-tuneness with God's will and mind need not cease when we take up a pen or a newspaper or a gardening fork.

I am not saying I became a Martha, so harassed by frenetic activity that I could see God only out of the corner of one eye; I am saying that I began to experiment with allowing the Mary who is a part of me to sit at the feet of Jesus in leisurely, listening and adoring prayer at the beginning of the day, but to give the Martha, who is also a part of the real me, permission to live life to the full without losing the sense of Jesus's attentive presence. Sometimes this seemed easy. At other times, almost impossible.

Spiritual reading

Spiritual reading featured largely in the life of the people of prayer whose pilgrimage was influencing my own, as indeed, I discovered, it had done in the lives of the great teachers of prayer of the past. St Teresa of Avila, the Carmelite mystic, often went to prayer with a book in her hand. She once wrote: 'Often the mere fact that I had it by me was enough. Sometimes I read a little, sometimes a great deal.'[5]

Spiritual reading usually takes one of four forms:

- instruction: when we read about prayer in particular or the spiritual life in general
- inspiration: when what we read encourages us to grow in the life of listening to God and our entire relationship with him
- preparation: reading matter which prepares us to tune in to God
- meditation: when our reading acts as a prayer guide.

I learned so much from the sayings of the Early Fathers and from the classics on prayer: Thomas Merton, Pierre de Caussade, Thomas à Kempis, Carlo Carretto, to name but a few, that the temptation was to substitute reading about prayer for the discipline itself of listening to God. But I was particularly grateful for the instruction and inspiration spiritual reading gave me. I remember reading St Bernard's reflections on the difficulty which dogged

me – of combining action and contemplation – and the
relief with which I reacted to *his* suggestion that, since
Martha and Mary are sisters, they should live together
harmoniously under the same roof. They should seek to
complement one another.

And I recall the hope that surged through me as a
powerful picture from *Poustinia* whetted my appetite for
more effective listening to God:

> The world is cold. Someone must be on fire so that
> people can love and put their cold hands and feet
> against that fire. If anyone allows this to happen . . .
> then he will become a fireplace at which men can
> warm themselves. His rays will go out to the ends of
> the earth.
>
> The English word 'zeal' usually means intensity of
> action. But real zeal is standing still and letting God
> be a bonfire in you. It's not very easy to have God's fire
> within you. Only if you are possessed of true zeal will
> you be able to contain God's bonfire. We must allow
> God to 'contribute' through us . . .[6]

Or again: 'The Lord is calling us to *stand still before
him while walking with men*. Yes, the next step . . . is the
ability to walk with men and be contemplatives while we
are walking.'[7]

A Prayer Journal

Michel Quoist's *Prayers of Life* were a constant source of
inspiration. In them, the author, a Roman Catholic priest,
points out his true feelings to God, then records God's
response:

> I'm at the end of my tether, Lord.
> I am shattered,
> I am broken.
> Since this morning I have been struggling to escape
>   temptation, which, now subtle, now persuasive, now

tender, now sensuous, dances before me like a glam-
our girl at a fair.
I don't know what to do.
I don't know where to go.
It spies on me, follows me, engulfs me.
When I leave a room I find it seated and waiting for me
in the next . . .
Lord, Lord, help me!

Son, I am here.
I haven't left you.
How weak is your faith!

You are too proud.
You still rely on yourself.
If you want to surmount all temptations, without falling
or weakening, calm and serene,
You must surrender yourself to me . . .
You must let yourself be guided like a child,
My little child.[8]

This method of communication with God attracted me.
When, in the course of my spiritual reading, I bumped
into the suggestion that the beginner in listening prayer
should attempt at least some writing, I needed no further
invitation. As I have explained, I found that, for me, writing was a powerful method of concentrating. With a pen
in my hand and a note-book on my knee, I would write my
daily letter to God, telling him how life was treating me.
In this way, my own thoughts and emotions would clarify.
I would then pause, listen, maybe meditate on a Bible
passage or an object, and go on to write down anything
I believed God was saying or showing me in response. As
I look back now on nine years of such journal keeping, I
marvel at the way God used this method of communication
both to deepen my relationship with him and to point out
some uncomfortable home truths about myself.

Once, when I complained that there was so little time
to pray on Sundays, God seemed to say: 'What about

church services?' I laughed. As a vicar's wife, going to church came into the 'work' category. I think of Sunday as a working day. My husband and I have our 'Sabbath' in the week. At church there are people to see, people's needs to minister to, responsibilities to shoulder. But God turned this attitude inside out so that I began to go to services expectant: waiting for God to say at least one thing which was pertinent to my walk with him at that moment, listening, too, to the wonder of who he is as expressed by the composers of some of our magnificent hymns, and of course, listening to his Word, the Bible.

And more and more God 'spoke' through music. In church, if I was battered emotionally for any reason, music would be the ointment the Holy Spirit applied to the inner wounds. If I came to my place of prayer fraught by the pressures of the day, music would woo me into the stillness where God's presence is most powerfully felt. Through meditative music, God would seem to speak: of his longing to invade my spirit with the Spirit, of his consoling love, of his agony on the cross, of his gift of forgiveness. Some music would cause a stirring in my heart and set a fountain of praise playing inside me. It was as though the many layers of my personality responded to God in different ways. Music filtered through to touch and communicate with the secret, hidden parts which rarely respond to words.[9]

But the word which percolated from God through each of these methods of listening was 'obedience'. It was as though he was underlining constantly the fact that listening to him must result in obeying him. God's lament over the disobedient filled me with pain:

> If only you had paid attention to my commands,
> your peace would have been like a river,
> your righteousness like the waves of the sea. (Isa. 48:18).

And Jesus's stern observation reinforced the realisation that obedience is a prerequisite for rootedness in God:

> Therefore everyone who hears these words of mine and puts them into practice is like a wise man who built his house on the rock. The rain came down, the streams rose, and the winds blew and beat against that house; yet it did not fall, because it had its foundation on the rock (Matt. 7:24–25).

Such obedience to the Father, I knew, characterised the life of Jesus. Such obedience was the source of the psalmist's joy (Ps. 119:111). Such obedience brought happiness to the author of Proverbs (Prov. 8:34). The implication was clear: if I wanted to enjoy unruffled peace and if I wanted to keep the lines of communication open between God and me, I, too, must progress in the life of obedience. As Kenneth Leach rightly reminds us, 'There can be no spiritual life if ethical demands are bypassed or sins ignored.'[10]

I was grateful that, from time to time, God brought across my path people of prayer who could help me in this superhuman task. I would have floundered abysmally without their spiritual direction.

Contemplative prayer and listening to God are disciplines which lay the Christian wide open to eccentricities, extremes and errors. To protect them from sallying forth on some mystical ego-trip most people find that a mentor and guide to set them on course from time to time is essential. Thus St Basil (330–379) urges his readers to find a man 'who may serve you as a very sure guide in the work of leading a holy life', one who knows 'the straight road to God'. He warns that 'to believe that one does not need counsel is great pride.'[11] St Jerome (340–420) pleads with his friend Rusticus not to set out on an uncharted way without a guide. And St Augustine (354–430) is emphatic: 'No one can walk without a guide.'[12]

Not everyone would agree that spiritual direction should be given by a friend. Nevertheless, I was grateful for the friendship I enjoyed with those to whom I turned for help along the way. To me, they were 'soul friends', to borrow Kenneth Leach's memorable phrase.

A soul friend is the intimate stranger who, as a person experienced in the life of prayer, will commit himself to you in an adult/adult relationship in an attempt to set you on the path of prayer, assist you in discerning the breathings of the Spirit, bring you to a place of greater self-knowledge and self-acceptance and help you find the will of God. The soul friend will avoid encouraging excessive dependence on himself, but will accept you as you are as well as confront and challenge when occasion demands. A soul friend might draw alongside the person of prayer as he confesses his failures to God. Or he might be God's instrument of healing using prayer counselling, the laying-on of hands or anointing with oil. To those of us who have been privileged to receive the help of a soul friend, a certain Celtic saying elicits a loud 'Amen': 'Anyone without a soul friend is a body without a head.'[13]

It was my soul friend, a spiritual guide, who listened to my confusion on more than one occasion. With him the jumble of conflicting thoughts and emotions would tumble out. With him I could express my uncertainties and fears. He would listen, attune his ear to the Holy Spirit of God, disentangle the threads, present them with order and clarity and explore with me what God was asking of me. He would make suggestions but never demand that I obey him implicitly.

I remember clearly one of those horrifying patches when God seemed to have absented himself never to return, when I recorded in my prayer journal that a complete revulsion for prayer swamped me. Engulfed by this darkness, and in panic, I telephoned this friend and asked if I could see him. Sensing the depths of my despair he fixed an appointment for the following day. As I described the darkness, the fear, the nothingness, the pain, I also voiced my self-doubts: Had I sinned? Was that why God had disappeared? Was I deluding myself about this pilgrimage of prayer? Was I expecting too much, expecting to encounter God in the way I had enjoyed? Or were the doors to contemplation and listening to God closing?

When my tale of woe had been told, this wise man of

God closed his eyes, held his head in his hands, and went quite silent. I knew him well enough to know that he would be praying. A hush stole over the room and I waited.

After several minutes he looked up and I noticed that his eyes twinkled and an excited smile spread across his face. 'Joyce!' he said, 'I feel so excited by this darkness of yours. You see, when you stand in the howling desert like this, you never know how God will next come to you. What you do know is that he will come. I believe God is encouraging you to look for him round every corner because he *is* coming – and he's coming soon.'

This calm, sensitive, positive challenge, this absence of blame or finger-pointing criticism, this freedom to talk in this way to someone who understood the inner turmoil because he was an experienced navigator on the voyage of prayer was precisely what I needed. That day we knelt together in silence in his prayer room. The presence of a fellow-voyager symbolised, for me, the objective fact that God had not left me. When my friend left, I lingered. As I gazed at the crucifix hanging on his hessian-covered wall, with its reminder that Jesus, himself, had known the darkness of separation from the Father, courage flowed right into my grazed and troubled spirit. Later, having absorbed the stillness and basked in it, the heaviness lifted; my steps were lighter as I walked away.

It was this friend who taught me how to reap the harvest of meditation and share the fruit with others. It was he who instilled in me the courage to face myself as I really am: not the successful, coping person I like to project to the world, but the mixture of success and failure, honesty and deception, saint and sinner which I really am. It was he who confronted me with the need to change. His own pilgrimage of prayer proved to me that listening to God is a journey whose joys are found as much in the travelling as in the arriving. His child-likeness in prayer drew from me a child-like eagerness to reach my destination even when the destination, I knew, lay at least in part on the other side of eternity.

These aids to listening spurred me on. I was always hungry for more. Someone has described this urgency well:

Saint Catherine of Siena, Lord,
said you are like the sea.
The more we know of you,
    the more we find;
And the more we find of you,
the more we want.
Yet we never really understand you.

I don't like that idea at all.
I want to know about you, Lord.
Just as I want to know about the sea
or space or electricity.
But if it's true that I can't know it all
Then keep me wanting to know.[14]

Chapter 17

More Helps along the Way

To listen to God I need silence: internal silence and external silence. But our world is polluted by noise which, like a persistent drum-roll, drowns God's voice, or at least distorts it.

Screwtape, the senior devil in C. S. Lewis' book, *The Screwtape Letters*, divulges one of the reasons for this perpetual cacophony:

> Music and silence – how I detest them both! . . . no square inch of infernal space and no moment of infernal time has been surrendered to either of those abominable forces, but all has been occupied by Noise – Noise, the grand dynamism, the audible expression of all that is exultant, ruthless and virile . . . We will make the whole universe a noise in the end. We have already made great strides in this direction as regards the Earth. The melodies and silences of Heaven will be shouted down in the end.[1]

There were times when the external noises in my own home banished the still, small voice of God. Ordinary, domestic noises – the sound of the radio, the shriek of the telephone, the songs my husband sings in the mornings – could prevent me from putting up the shutters of the senses to drop deep into the silence of God. For this reason, the regular Quiet Day and an occasional retreat quickly became priorities as I have said. I learned to plot these in my diary first and to fit other engagements round them because these times when God and I could 'just be' together became vital times of renewal, refreshment and reappraisal.

The Anglican convent near my home is a hiding place where I delight to spend a day in quietness. A large converted manor house, it stands in spacious grounds and overlooks acres of farmland. When I go there for a day, I accept this solitude as a gift of God's grace. To me the time and place are sacred.

The first points around which I plan the day are the Communion service and lunch. Within that framework I create space for a leisurely time of listening prayer which will not be short-circuited by a gong or a bell or the need to depart. Apart from these three focal points, I expect to benefit from a period of spiritual reading, meditation and writing in my prayer journal. Work is refused permission to come with me unless part of my listening is to ask God whether I should accept a particular invitation to speak, or to seek guidance about a piece of writing I am working on.

I try to begin the day by dropping consciously into the creativity of God's silence. The garden helps. I might stand under the ancient cedar tree and gaze at its strength, the circumference of its branches and the size of the cones. Or if the weather is warm I might sit beside the pond, contemplate its plump gold fish and mull over those words of one of the mystics: 'We are in God as a fish is in water.' Or I might wander among the daffodils or the bluebells or sit under the japonica. I refuse to hurry. Most of my week I rush from one meeting to the next or scamper from one appointment to the next. As my body adapts to walking instead of hurrying, my mind and emotions wind down also. At the same time the level of expectancy rises as I realise that I am in this place for one purpose only: to hear God speak. I try to be open to him at every stage of the day and in every corner of the convent. Sometimes he creeps up on me when I least expect it: as I absorb the beauty of his creation in the garden, while I muse on the sufferings of Christ depicted in the stations of the cross in the chapel, while a sister reads as we eat in the refectory in silence. On these holy days God always seems to drop something into my quietened heart which I need to hear. That is why it seems sensible, not selfish, to organise my activities around this stillness. Through it, I catch my spiritual breath, rest in him afresh, and gain his perspective.

This is the purpose of a Quiet Day. One of the desert fathers expressed it simply but powerfully. Into a jar he poured water and some sand. As he shook the jar, the water became murky, but as he allowed the jar to rest the sand settled to the bottom and the water became clear again. Using this visual aid, he taught his disciples that the pace people live their lives normally clouds their spiritual perspective. Those who dare to settle themselves into God's stillness find that the water of perception becomes clear again.

I value these sacred spaces more and more and know that my life and ministry are impoverished when I permit them to be elbowed out of my diary. The busier I am, the more I attempt to find God in everything, the more I need to stand in that still point with God where my looking becomes a beholding, my listening an attentive hearing, my touching a deep awareness, and my tasting a silent savouring. God's gift of a Quiet Day provides me with a sip of some of these spiritual liqueurs.

By admitting that this need to withdraw from the world's whirlpool is an urgent one, I am not saying that it is impossible to 'find God everywhere and in everything'. What I am saying is that in times of quiet it is easier to listen to God attentively. Listening to God, as we have seen already in this book, involves so much more than the narrow sphere of hearing a voice. It involves a tuning-in to a multi-level method of communication: hearing a voice, yes, but a presence also – and signs and non-verbal communication and everything which goes into creating a relationship.

It is rather like my relationship with my husband. He and I work hard at communicating with each other. We give one another quality time most days because in this way we believe we keep our marital love alive. Even so our holidays are a highlight: an indispensable part of the oneness we enjoy. On holiday we draw closer to one another than ever before because we have the leisure to listen to each other with every fibre of our beings.

Similarly I need to take time out to be with God. For me, a day seems too short to descend into the depths of the grand silence of God. A three or four day retreat gives far more scope for the letting go of anxieties and distractions and obsessions which is a precursor of in-depth listening to the awareness of God.

Again I am fortunate. Seven years ago a friend suggested that I should make a retreat at one of the houses of another Anglican community, the Sisters of the Love of God. This was more easily accessible to my home than Whitby and its size and intimacy appealed immediately: only five or six sisters live and pray together there. In Holy Week 1978 I spent three days there and it has been my spiritual home ever since. There I hide occasionally for three or four days and my prayer journal reminds me how rich and healing, how challenging and life-transforming these days have been.

The cross which hangs from the ceiling of this chapel is unique. On one side the artist has painted a picture of the crucified Christ. On the other he has painted a portrayal of the resurrected Lord. I love to kneel at the foot of that cross and savour the mysteries of our salvation. Usually, my concentration focuses on Christ's suffering and sacrifice. But one morning, after Communion, as I stayed in the chapel to pray, the Holy Spirit drew my attention to the living Lord. What I 'heard' in the silence was not new factually. It *was* new experientially. I revelled in the revelation, took my prayer journal to the bottom of the garden, sat on a log under the pine trees and tried to capture the wonder:

Lord, thank you. I feel as though I've taken one delicious bite, the first of many, from an exotic fruit. I *know* that you are alive. It's as though I've never heard that message before. It is exhilarating; wonderful . . . You are alive. You are life. You are my life . . .

Lord, I began to realise that for forty years, and particularly for the past four or so, I've contemplated Gethsemane and Calvary and Easter Saturday but I've never, in fact, identified with Easter Day. But that gap between Calvary and Pentecost leaves an inexplicable void. Thank you that you've filled in the gap – placed in my hands the missing piece of the jig-saw. It's exciting . . . Oh! How much joy has yet to be entered into.

Revelations like these broadened my view of God. Sometimes God spoke to me about the nitty-gritty of life, like my marriage. One day, I marvelled at the way God was bringing healing to our marriage:

Thank you, dearest Lord, for this retreat: for the weather, the hot days, the golden dawns and dusks. Thank you for time to reflect on our marriage. Thank you that for twenty years David has coped with all my immature comings and goings and with all my struggling and striving. Thank you that his has been the love that will not let me go and which is enabling the butterfly to emerge from the chrysalis. What a wonderful husband you provided me with. Thank you, dear Lord, for this provision for my deepest need. And thank you for this love of ours which goes so much deeper than superficialities and anchors us in one another and in you.

Sometimes God's word winged its way into my awareness with supernatural force. At a time when I was crawling out of the tunnel of depression but still dogged with a recurring death wish, I bumped into this quotation in one of Alexander Schmemann's books: 'I shall not die but LIVE and declare the works of the Lord.' I wept. I knew God wanted me to echo those words. In many ways, this was a turning point as I received from him the courage to make those words my own.

I do not always go to a convent to make my retreat. Sometimes I use a cottage in the country where I read and meditate and reflect and study God's word and pray. The advantage of a cottage retreat, for me, is that, surrounded by the wonders of God's creation, I open hidden parts of myself to God which remain closed elsewhere. I listen as I walk. God speaks through the silent eloquence of the countryside.

But to retreat in the context of a worshipping, praying community adds an indefinable ingredient to this time of attentiveness to God. And so I vary my venue.

If I stay in a convent, I drop into the rhythm of life observed by the sisters: I eat when they eat, worship when they worship, read when they read, and sometimes work in the garden alongside them. I sleep more than they do. I am not embarrassed to make this confession. I am usually in need of rest when I retreat. Sleep is a gift of God and the ability to listen increases when the body is rested.

These retreats are not necessarily sublime mountain-top experiences. Sometimes they prove painful, often challenging. On one retreat, I recorded my resolve:

- to rid myself of the rubble of resentment: 'prayer and resentment cannot co-exist'
- to re-instate Jesus on the throne of my life: I cannot listen accurately to him if he has a rival
- to try harder to respond to the challenge of intertwining listening prayer and writing.

At times I record the specific instructions God seemed to be giving: at a time when the music group in our church was without a leader, God seemed to nudge me in that direction in a way that took me completely by surprise. I spent much of the retreat resisting God's challenge but

eventually capitulated: 'Lord, if the music group is where
you want me, I *am* willing. Make me more ready to accept
the cost which I have counted.'

When I make a three or four day retreat, I bring to it
four main aims:

- to realise more clearly the presence of God in the
  inner sanctuary of my being
- to assess the response I have been making to God's
  loving overtures since my last retreat
- to discern what God's will is for me in the here
  and now
- to readjust my life in the light that God gives.

In my prayer journal, I usually spell out my hopes and
fears to God almost as soon as I arrive. Day by day I write
to him and record his response. I often scribble quotations
from my spiritual reading in this fat note-book. The fruit
of my meditations is also captured there. At the end of
the retreat, I keep a page called 'Retreat Resolves'. On
this page, I write down God's re-commissioning for the
coming months.

Several questions require examination and an honest
answer during these times apart:

- Does anything in my life stand between God and
  me?
- Is anything preventing me from giving myself freely
  to fulfil God's plan for my life?
- What have I been doing for God?
- What am I doing for him at present?
- What ought I to be doing?

This ruthless self-examination usually results in a pro-
longed period of confession. Keeping short accounts with
God in this way is essential. When sin curdles within,
I am not in a position to hear God speaking. Isaiah
reminds us of the solemn fact that sin separates us from
God: 'Your iniquities have separated you from your God;

your sins have hidden his face from you, so that he will not hear' (Isa. 59–2). Simon Tugwell, commenting on his gulf, warns the would-be listener that to fail to see this is sloppy. And Henri Nouwen observes that if the person of prayer persists in clutching sin in his clammy hands as though it were a priceless treasure, he is unable to receive from God in the here and now.

Slowly and gradually God convinced me of the uselessness of rummaging around in my own sin and of the value of confession. Confession precipitates the desire to change. It gives birth to repentance: the determination to live differently. It syringes the ear which would tune in to God.

Almost always I would confess my failings to God privately. But there came a time in my life when God persuaded me to take the Bible's advice seriously; to avail myself of the opportunity of confessing my sin in the presence of a shrewd and trusted friend (Jas. 5:16).

The depression with which God entrusted me pushed me into laying aside my pride and seeking help of this nature. While the cloud of depression hung over me, from time to time I would struggle with suicidal tendencies as the desire to live evaporated. At times I sunk so low that I considered it my right to think this way.

When a friend pointed out to me one day that this desire to cease to be was not so much a sickness as a sin, I was shocked. If this was true I had sinned seriously and persistently. When I tried to confess this deep-seated rebellion to God I became guilt-ridden, inwardly tortured, introspective. The realisation dawned, therefore, that I had nothing to lose and everything to gain by taking this sin to God in the presence of a prayerful friend. The same friend I mentioned in the last chapter agreed to pray with me as I repeated my confession to God.

Of course, I was not confessing *to* the spiritual guide. I was clear in my mind that it was God I was addressing. I used the form of confessional which is recognised in the Anglican Church: a short formal prayer which does not give scope for excusing oneself or blaming others but which encourages the penitent to take full responsibility for what he has done: 'I confess . . . I have sinned.'

When I heard myself name the sin 'suicide', it stripped me of all the pretence with which I had clothed myself for months. This was valuable in itself. But when I heard this spiritual guide pronounce the absolution from John's epistle: 'If we confess our sins, he is faithful and just and will forgive us our sins and purify us from all unrighteousness' (1 John 1:9), and I heard him proclaim in the name and on the authority of Jesus: 'You are totally forgiven . . . Christ has set you free,' it was as though the shackles of guilt and condemnation fell from me. I knew I was free to walk away from these chains which had bound me.

The confession made, we talked about the implications of what I had just done. First, this counsellor, friend and guide suggested that I should read a book entitled *The Cloud of Unknowing*. I had read this classic on prayer before. As I re-read it, I understood why he had recommended it as a follow-up to the ministry I had received. The book contains invaluable insights on sin and failure and persistence in approaching God.

The reading of this book was to be my 'penance'. The word startled me. True Protestant that I am, I had always reacted negatively to the word 'penance'. I thought it meant punishment. Indeed, the Pocket Oxford Dictionary defines the word in this way: 'punishment inflicted on oneself especially under priestly direction'. Now I saw that penance need not mean to rub the penitent's nose in his own filth, nor to force him to pay the penalty of his misconduct. Rather it can have positive connotations. Penance can make a constructive contribution to the spiritual growth of the Christian.

My own first taste of confession and penance is a good example. I could have come away from this experience feeling condemned by God and my confidante. Instead, my friend and I talked about the reason for my visit: the death wish. This spiritual guide made no attempt to excuse my sin. What he did do was to disentangle the sin from the need which had given birth to the sin: emotional wounds which would not stop bleeding. He explained that the sinful element had been dealt with through the confession and Christ's forgiveness; the emotional need would be met in a different way. By inviting me to read the book, *The Cloud of Unknowing*, he believed that some of my confusion would be clarified and I would glean insights which were essential to this stage of the pilgrimage of prayer. When I read the book, the mists of confusion did lift. I was delivered from the stranglehold of introspection and I rejoiced in this particular piece of penance.

Such positive penance given by an experienced and wise soul friend can be a constructive way of setting us on our feet again after we have fallen. It is one of the contributions a soul friend makes to our spiritual growth. As an objective observer he can discern more clearly than oneself where God wants to purge and prune and where he wants to bind up and heal. Kenneth Leach suggests other reasons why a soul friend is of value: he helps us to laugh at ourselves, relax, not to take ourselves too seriously, not to assume a false piety. I needed this spiritual guide to do this for me.

Fasting

Fasting, I found, was another sin-and-pain detector. I would embark on a thirty-six hour fast and expect to feel super-holy. Instead, by the time the fast had finished, I might have snapped at my children, been irritable with my husband or chewed over some resentment which I had been scarcely aware of earlier. Richard Foster explains why fasting highlights huge inconsistencies or seedling sins germinating in our life:

> Fasting reveals the things that control us . . . We cover up what is inside us with food and other good things, but in fasting these things surface. If pride controls us, it will be revealed almost immediately . . . Anger, bitterness, jealousy, strife, fear – if they are within us, they will surface during fasting. At first we will rationalise that

our anger is due to our hunger, then we know that we are angry because the spirit of anger is within us.[2]

But fasting, I found, not only exposes the large lumps of wax in my spiritual ears, it makes a positive contribution to listening prayer. Perhaps its major contribution is the uncluttered, purposeful space it provides for the act of listening to God. When I fast, with no meals to prepare and no clearing up to do, I can linger in my prayer corner and listen to God without having to keep an eye on the clock.

In one sense, fasting of itself does not aid my ability to concentrate on God in that I am often acutely aware of my rumbling tummy or the headache which often plagues me at such times or the occasional dizziness which reminds me that I have not eaten for several hours. Yet, in another sense, the discipline of the fast, with its non-verbal commitment to hear God's presence or voice, makes a major contribution to listening prayer. The physical symptoms remind me of the purpose of this fast: prayer and attentive listening to God.

Catherine of Siena and Teresa of Avila, whose teachings on prayer have inspired Christians down the ages, believed that unless a Christian spends time tuning in to an awareness of God, then much of the energy spent in other things is a waste of time. As this belief lodged itself in me, more and more I experimented with these aids to prayer, adopting Archbishop William Laud's prayer: 'Lord, I am coming as fast as I can.'

Chapter 18

Another Piece of the Scaffolding: the Listening Group

'No man is an island,' claimed John Donne. No Christian attempting to pray is an island either. My individual listening, if it is to bear lasting fruit, must be healthily integrated into the Body of Christ. For this reason, I need others.

For years the independent part of me which enjoys going it alone rejected this need for others. But when God added to me a group of like-minded people, as intent on learning to hear the Spirit's breathings as I was, a whole new dimension of listening to God opened up for me. I found that to approach God *with others* added depth and texture and colour to my personal prayer in a way no amount of solo prayer could have done. That is not to say that I abandoned private prayer. Rather, I learned that private prayer and shared prayer overlap, affect and feed one another.

The first of these prayer groups came into being when a number of people in our church fellowship began to express an interest in listening prayer. We had all worked through considerable pain and animosity to reach this stage; their suspicion of my prayer pilgrimage subsided; my bitterness against those who questioned what I was doing had been dealt with, ruthlessly, by God. The meeting of our paths was sweet.

Our mid-week church fellowship had grown: from a prayer meeting attended by seven people who met in the rectory lounge to seventy people who congregated in the church hall each week. They wanted teaching as well as the opportunity to pray. For an experimental period, therefore, we set in motion a variety of workshops: on evangelism, on Bible study, on the Holy Spirit, to name but a few. One option open to anyone who wanted to come was a workshop on prayer.

For an hour a week, a group of us explored together the basics of listening to God. Together we experimented with various ways of entering into stillness. We tried a number of bodily postures, had fun in discovering together that deep, rhythmical breathing acts as a kind of metronome in prayer, spent time writing in our prayer journals, and learned to meditate in the way I have described in this book: on creation and on God's Word.

To some of the group God gave the gift of contemplation. When the trial period was over, they were hungry for more. We would therefore meet for an occasional Quiet Day when the exploration into collective silence would continue. One Saturday, we travelled to Derbyshire to spend the day in the quietness of the Derbyshire hills. The day began with worship when we re-focused from the busyness of the week on to God. It continued with a meditation on the story of Bartimaeus, followed by an opportunity to walk or sit, to enjoy 'just being' amidst the splendour of God's creation: a rare treat for city dwellers. The day concluded with an opportunity for anyone who wished to express to the others what God had been saying in the re-creative silence.

On another Saturday we visited a farm not far from our home. We ate in silence and learned the value of listening as someone read to us while we ate instead of indulging in ceaseless, superficial chatter. Together we meditated on the claim of Jesus: 'I am the vine'. In our prayer journals we recorded some of the insights we had gleaned. And we celebrated Christ's death together in a quiet service of Holy Communion.

It has been said that Communion is the peak of contemplation. Prepared as we were, that day, by hours of delicious, fruitful stillness, we certainly soared to new heights of silent, corporate praise and adoration after we had received the sacrament. The awareness of the mystery, the majesty, the humility and the generosity of the God who was ever drawing us to himself filled us with a deep and intense joy.

But just as I, personally, was finding that a Quiet Day was frustratingly short, so we as a group would separate after a Quiet Day conscious that we had been brought to the threshold of a banqueting room whose door must again bar us from the feast inside. For this reason, weekend retreats became a feature of our group prayer twice a year.

We would start the retreat on Friday night, continue in silence until Sunday afternoon, then return to our church in time for the evening service. These retreats always incorporated a number of ingredients: worship, stillness, teaching, mutual ministry, liturgical prayer and intercession. Sometimes we would use the guesthouse at Mount St Bernard Abbey, sometimes the guesthouse at the Convent of St Laurence in Belper. Both were equidistant from our home: a drive of some forty minutes, which we considered to be long enough for a weekend retreat.

The main aim of the retreat never varied: we wanted to meet God face to face, as a living reality, and to support one another in this pursuit for an encounter with the risen Lord. A secondary aim was to learn together how to pray 'with our mind in our heart', to borrow a phrase popular among contemplatives. In other words, we wanted to explore for ourselves the well-tried methods of listening we were reading about: methods which enabled others not simply to know the theory about God but to know him in depth.

The pattern rarely varied. On Friday evening we would arrive in time for supper during which we would exchange news. Between supper and the short service of compline, we would unpack and prepare ourselves for the stillness to come. After compline we would meet but not talk. The grand silence had begun and we wanted to become a part of it.

I cannot speak for the others, but during this time, when almost always we sat in a circle in a room which was lit only by a large candle, I would begin to express to God what I hoped for from this time apart with him. Then I would place the spotlight, not on me and my hopes and my anxieties, but on to him. This half hour together became, for me, a time of de-location, the godly pause which Guy Brinkworth has described so well which is 'reminiscent of the hush of concentration of the high jumper or competition diver just before the supreme effort.'[1]

After breakfast on Saturday, we would meet to study some of the basic principles of prayer. On our first retreat, one of the monks at Mount St Bernard Abbey urged us, if we were serious about learning to listen to God, to take prayer seriously. Among the notes I scribbled in my prayer journal are the following facts which I return to time and time again:

- Guarantee God a certain time each day: five minutes in the morning, perhaps, and five minutes in the evening. Don't set your sights too high. You can always give God *more* time than you promised initially but if you earmark half an hour and manage only five minutes your listening will be drowned by guilt feelings.
- The most unselfish prayer is the prayer you pray when you least feel like it. Then you pray out of love for God, not because it appears to benefit you.
- The crucial time is when we are not formally praying at all. True prayer must be integrated into our life. There is something phoney about the person who 'lives' in church but has a very bitter tongue.

We would take time to respond to simple ground rules like these and tease out what God was saying to each of us personally in connection with our life of listening prayer. We would spend part of the day reading: either the Bible or a book about prayer, or both.

Bible meditation of one form or another always featured on our programme and as the group became a cohesive unit we learned to value these more and more.

I remember one Sunday morning in Belper when we read together the account of the healing of the woman who suffered from haemorrhaging for twelve years. We tried, at first, to visualise the scene: the pressing crowd, the poverty-stricken woman, and Jesus. We then tried to put ourselves into the scene in the way I described in an earlier chapter: to *become* the sick woman whose need to touch the hem of Jesus's garment was so urgent. As much as our imaginations allowed, each of us felt the hot, sweaty bodies of the crowd jostle him and identified with the desperation that woman must have felt; in our own time and manner, each of us stretched out his hand and touched the bottom of Jesus's robe. And each of us saw Jesus turn, heard him ask that curious question, 'Who touched me?', basked in his acceptance and approval, savoured his living, loving presence and allowed ourselves to be drawn to him by that magnetism of his which never ceases to attract people to himself.

I have said that 'each of us' entered into the meditation in this way. That is not quite accurate. One member of the group, a housewife and mother, described to the group rather tearfully that she had spent the entire meditation carrying a sick friend to Jesus. When she heard other members of the group relate how Jesus had touched and spoken to them, she felt envious. She had been so busy interceding for another that she had not stopped to have her own needs touched by the Son of God. 'That's typical of my life at the moment,' she admitted. 'I'm so busy caring for others that I don't give Jesus a chance to care for me.'

As leader of the group, I asked her if she would like to be touched by Jesus. After all, there was still time. She confessed that she would like a fresh touch from God.

Most of the group held her into the love of God quite silently but supportively. Two or three of us laid hands on her head and prayed, again quite silently, that she would take courage in both hands as the woman suffering from the haemorrhage had done, and reach out to touch the home-spun garment of Jesus for herself. She did. There was no emotionalism. There *was* deep-felt joy as we watched her strained face break into a peaceful smile and as we saw the tension in her body disappear; as we saw her relax. When this young woman opened her eyes she became aware of the group's love and told us what had happened in the silence: Jesus had turned to her and touched her. She had looked into his eyes and seen sensitivity, gentleness and compassion – not only for her friend, but for her. This prayer ministry had taken less than ten minutes but it had proved life-changing for this young mother.

We were not day-dreaming or playing the child's game 'let's pretend' in these times of meditation. No. To God a thousand years are but yesterday; he is the same yesterday, today and forever. It seems a valid use of the gospel narrative, therefore, to meet the incarnate Christ, not only in its pages, but with our imagination and our senses also. To see and hear and touch him who came that man might see and hear and touch him seems a most natural approach to the Bible, a valid way to cross the time-vault together.

I learned to value this group more and more. It was to them that I submitted some of my own listening so that they could test whether what I was hearing was from God or wishful thinking. It was with them, therefore, that I grew in confidence. And it was with them that I realised that, though I could listen to God on my own, listening to God in the context of a community brought a wholeness and wholesomeness which no amount of praying in isolation could bring. In the group I put down roots. We belonged. It was as though the group was rather like a womb in which our listening prayer gestated and matured and in which we grew as individuals also.

New discoveries

At one stage the group met monthly in my prayer room. On Saturday evenings we would go there to be still together for an hour to prepare ourselves for Sunday and to give one another support. In this way we became soul friends to one another. We discovered that Jesus's promise to be especially present to the twos and threes who met in his name was relevant for us. The sense of his presence and power seemed almost tangible at times.

As time went on, a whole new dimension of listening prayer unfolded for us. It would sometimes happen that one member of the group would ask for prayer for a particular decision which had to be made, or for a seemingly insoluble problem. We rarely discussed the situation. Instead, in our customary silence, we would hold the person and the expressed need to God. As we did so, we would find that very often first one member of the group, then another, would receive an insight in the form of a picture, a passage of scripture, a thought, or a prophecy. This began to happen so frequently that, as leader of the group, I encouraged individuals to share such insights so that the entire group could test the source of the listening to ensure that it came from God, and so that we could piece together the fragments to make up the whole picture. What emerged was fascinating. I remember an occasion when I asked the group to pray for me because I was unsure whether to undertake a particular piece of counselling. After a prolonged period of silence one person quoted a verse of scripture which had impressed itself on her mind while she was praying. Another gave a word of prophecy in which God seemed to be promising to bring the person to be counselled through great darkness into light. At this, one girl gasped. 'That makes sense of a picture I've been seeing in my mind but couldn't make sense of,' she said. 'The picture is of a large swimming pool. I've watched you, Joyce, dive into the deep end of the pool with another person. For some considerable time you were both lost to sight – presumably you were swimming under water. Then you emerged in a different part of the pool. You were both bathed in light.'

The result of this piece of listening was that I embarked on the counselling situation. The picture of the swimming pool in particular, encouraged me when the person I was trying to help seemed to make little progress. But this dimension of listening fascinated me for another reason. It demonstrated to me, again, the value of the group. Alone, I hear the whisperings of the Spirit of God in mono only. With others, we have the capacity to hear in stereo. On my own, I am capable of detecting only minute fragments of the whole purpose of God. But many pairs of ears pick up other fractions of God's vision. When we respect and learn from each other, we can put together our gleanings and gain a far more accurate impression of what God is trying to communicate.

Moving on

I said in an earlier chapter that God is always moving us on, that change for the Christian is an inevitability. One winter we became increasingly conscious that the group had fulfilled its function: we had served our apprenticeship in collective listening; it was time now to move back into the mainstream of the church. God would give us others with whom we would work in listening prayer.

I found it hard to disband the group. Once again I was forced to learn the lesson of detachment: to accept God's good gifts when he gives them but to be willing, when the time is ripe, to surrender them, trusting that what he removes with one hand, he replenishes with the other.

Looking back, I see one reason why the group had to break up. We could have become a ghetto. But God wanted us to leaven the lump of the fellowship. Today, members of that original listening group are teaching others to listen to God and are heavily involved in a listening ministry; four of them are Elders in our church – essentially a group which sets itself the task of listening to God; others lead 'link groups' (our term for house fellowships), others are members of the music group

which leads the worship of the church but leans heavily
on listening to God. Though we never meet today as we
used to in the old days, the oneness between us has never
been broken: we value one another, respect one another
in a whole variety of ways, not least in the ministry of
listening and intercessory prayer.

All kinds of listening
Since those early days of group listening, I have enjoyed
a rich and varied diet of listening to God with others, and
the learning has been enlightening.

On one occasion I visited a Greek Orthodox monastery
where, for three days, I joined in the rhythm of prayer
practised by the monks and nuns who live there. The
special feature of this monastery, for me, was the use
these people made of what is known as 'The Jesus prayer',
a prayer which consists of the words, 'Lord Jesus Christ,
Son of God, have mercy on us.'

For two hours every morning and two hours every
evening, the community meet in the chapel to pray. They
use these words and these only: 'Lord Jesus Christ, Son
of God, have mercy on us.' As I prepared to visit this
monastery, I feared that to recite this prayer would be
nothing more than vain repetition. What I found as I
joined in the prayer with these men and women was
that, for four hours each day, I was listening to God
on a profound level. I cannot speak for the others who
participated in this prayer cycle, but, for me, I became
acutely aware of two realities: the holiness of God and
my own innate sinfulness. In one sense, this was not new.
In another sense, it *was* new because of the manner in
which I 'saw' the mystery and the 'otherness' and the glory
of God and because of the manner in which I became
equally conscious of my own nothingness before him. The
fact that I am nothing, he is everything, and yet he loves
me, hit home to me in a new and powerful way.

The music in this particular monastery conveyed to me
more powerfully than any other music I have ever heard
the fact of God's unending love. At various points in the

day – before and after meals and during the communion service in particular – the entire community would break into unaccompanied, six-part harmony. It was not frothy, pseudo-praise but a plaintive, compelling form of communication which helped to quench my insatiable thirst to be filled with the love of God.

When it comes to the artistry of 'wasting time' with God – contemplating him for who he is and what he has done – I still find this comes more easily and readily in the context of a group. I have just returned from a convent where, on my retreat, I rested in God after a particularly hectic conference. There, in the convent, morning by morning after the communion service, I knelt with the sisters and dropped into the kind of silence where each of us was captivated by the love of Christ: where we were privileged, once again, to be lost in wonder, love and praise. Exhausted as I was, I doubt whether I could have managed this alone. But in this silence, supported by others, Christ came. I heard him. And rejoiced.

Chapter 19

Some Results of Listening to God

Whenever I close my eyes in an attempt to listen attentively to the sounds around, I am amazed at the mixture of noises which I had failed to hear until that moment: the humming of the fly, the hoot of the owl, the final faint song of the chaffinch, the creak of a chair. Similarly, whenever I tune into God's still, small voice the medley of experiences he gives astounds me. I can never anticipate beforehand what he will say or how he will act. What I can foretell is that whatever he gives will be worthwhile.

Early on in my prayer pilgrimage, I discovered that listening to God did not necessarily result in mystical experiences. Often, it was not other-worldly at all. Rather, it was a deeply practical affair.

I remember an occasion when the concept of listening to God seemed strange and new. While I was praying the words, 'Ring Valerie' kept pounding through my brain. Valerie was a close friend who lived eighty miles from my home. Feeling rather foolish, I telephoned. Valerie gasped when she heard my voice. We had not made contact for several months. 'What made you ring tonight?' she asked. 'Pam's here with me. Her husband died suddenly last night and I don't know what to say to her. She's just been saying, "I'd love to talk to Joyce." Will you speak to her?'

Pam was a mutual friend. She had expressed care for me after my father died. Now God gave me the privilege of drawing alongside her in her bereavement.

On another occasion, a young married couple came to me for counselling. For several years they had tried to start a family. When the wife failed to conceive they both subjected themselves to the necessary tests. These tests revealed that the husband was infertile. Should they adopt a child? Should they follow the advice they had been given and conceive a child with A.I.D.?

While they talked about their disappointment and moral dilemma, the Holy Spirit of God seemed to whisper the words, 'Pray for a miracle' in my spiritual ears. I had never prayed for a miracle baby before and was not sure that my faith would stretch that far. But the voice persisted so eventually I asked, 'Has it ever occurred to you that God might want to perform a miracle and give you a baby by natural means?'

The wife's face lit up. She, too, had sensed that this might be God's answer to their problem. The husband was uncertain. 'Supposing we pray and nothing happens?'

By this time the conviction in me was so strong that I suggested the husband borrowed the combination of his wife's faith and the little I could muster and we prayed that God would give them the gift of a child.

Six months later, the phone rang. I know the husband well and recognised his voice: 'Joyce! I've got something to tell you. My wife's pregnant.'

Thomas Merton once wrote:

Meditation has no point and no reality unless it is firmly rooted in *life*. Without such roots, it can produce nothing but the ashen fruits of disgust, *acedia*, and even morbid and degenerate introversion, masochism, dolorism, negation.[1]

And Richard Foster adds:

Often meditation will yield insights that are deeply practical, almost mundane. There will come instruction on how to relate to your wife or husband, on how to deal with this sensitive problem or that business situation. More than once I have received guidance on what attitude to have when lecturing in a college classroom. It is wonderful when a particular meditation leads to ecstasy, but it is far more common to be given guidance in dealing with ordinary human problems.[2]

The practical nature of listening to God prompted me to keep these questions in my mind when I prayed:

- What is God saying?
- What is God giving to *me personally*?
- What is God asking me to take from this time with him into my world: to my husband, my children, my colleagues, my friends, my neighbours?

Just as Jesus's times alone with the Father overflowed to enrich the lives of the disciples, indeed of the entire world, so I wanted to avoid a me-centredness in my listening: to ensure that listening became the launching pad for more effective service and incisive ministry instead of degenerating into a bless-me club with a membership of one.

Praise, wonder

But listening to God need not be earthbound. It can transport one into worship, praise and adoration.

I recall an evening when I was meditating on the resurrection of Jesus. John's gospel lay open on the floor at my feet. I read chapter 20 as slowly as I could applying my senses to the unfolding scene. So I watched Mary steal to the sepulchre in the grey darkness of pre-dawn. I sensed her dismay as she saw, not the sealed tomb, but a yawning hole where the stone should have been. I heard her run to alert Peter and John, observed their race to the grave and, in my imagination, I went with Peter into the belly of the rock. I, too, saw the strips of linen lying there, 'the burial cloth that had been around Jesus's head. The cloth was folded up by itself, separate from the linen' (John 20:7).

And I gazed from the neat piles of linen to John who had crept quietly into the sepulchre. As wonder spread across his face and as he worshipped, my heart leapt with joy. I fell on my face and worshipped the resurrected Lord, not from any sense of duty, but with well-springs of praise which rose from somewhere deep inside me.

Pain

But just as listening to God can elicit paeans of praise so it can plunge the person at prayer into a deep and terrible pain. When this first happened to me and prayer triggered off uncontrollable weeping, I wondered what was happening. Now, I think I understand.

When we stand before God and tune into him, we pick up some of the heart-break he feels for a needy world. In this way God gives us the privilege of 'knowing him' and entering into the 'fellowship of his sufferings', to use the language of St Paul.

As I write this chapter a series of news bulletins on the radio has triggered off this inner weeping within me. Four young Buckinghamshire schoolboys were swept off the rocks at Land's End by a huge wave two days ago. Their bodies have not yet been found but they are presumed dead. News percolates through that the town in which they lived is in a deep state of shock. When I pray, my heart goes out to the mourning parents, the dazed pupils and the staff of the school.

This, I believe, is more than one mother empathising with another. It is an identification with the sorrow in God's heart as he contemplates human suffering. I do not understand why one tragedy can affect me in this way while another can leave me cold. What I do know is that in prayer I must hold this pain into the healing hands of Christ so that his compassion and man's heartache can meet and be matched. This is the solemn responsibility of the person of prayer.

This weeping sometimes creeps up on us in curious ways. Just before I mapped out the outline for this chapter, a friend called to see me. He is a schoolteacher, a person

God is drawing into listening prayer. He spelt out the horror he felt as he watched certain pupils in his school fight one another physically, just like little tigers. 'It hurts even to think about it,' he admitted. 'I don't understand why they want to be so cruel to each other.' I suggested that his inner turmoil and pain might have found a mooring in his heart for a purpose: because God wants him to weep and groan in prayer, not just for the situation at school, but because peace in the world has been pillaged, because in the world at large strife sets man against man on a bigger scale than this school scene.

Resting

Just as listening to God can produce pain and heartbreak, so it can result in a delicious resting in God. Thomas Merton puts this well when he describes the condition of 'resting in him whom we have *found*, who loves us, who is near to us, who comes to us to draw us to himself'.[3]

I recall the relief that has filled me on a number of occasions when I have come to prayer, weary but wanting to listen, and God's invitation has come so clearly: 'Don't talk. Just rest.' And I nestle in his arms and enjoy being held.

Re-creation

Listening to God, when the hearing prompts obedience, is always a re-creating experience. This may not be the re-creation of the comfortableness and contentment I have just described. To listen to God might mean to change. In God we are always on the move. He calls us from deep to deep. He requires us to be in his hands as clay submits to the hands of the potter. Those hands re-mould and reshape us and the experience may be far from comfortable. As we listen he shows us how he wants these changes to take place.

Many pages of my prayer journal remind me of the way God put his finger on areas of my life and showed how they cripple me or distort his image.

I once expressed hatred of someone who had hurt me.

God challenged me. The real reason for the hatred was that my pride had been wounded because friendship with me was a lower priority on this person's list than it used to be. God forced me, too, to face my jealousy. 'Pride and jealousy are sins to be confessed,' the Holy Spirit whispered, 'not rights to cling on to.' He gave me no peace until this sinful rubble was tipped out at the foot of the cross.

Sometimes the changes God wanted to bring about in my life took years rather than minutes. For months, pages of my prayer journal were devoted to the anger and frustration which poisoned my life and which stemmed from the growing tensions in our marriage.

In prayer I would whine to God about my husband: 'It really feels as though he doesn't care about me at all . . . How little is his understanding and how very limited his compassion.' In prayer I would throw down the gauntlet and challenge God to change my husband so that the quality of our marriage could improve. In prayer I would pour out the self-pity that filled me to the brim: 'There's a big part of me, Lord, which is tired of trying, weary of forgiving, exhausted with the agony of gingerly putting my nose out of my hedgehog prickles only to have it stepped on again.'

And in prayer, God would come to me, hear me out, absorb my bitterness, touch my bruised and battered heart, and gently but persistently show me, not where David needed to change, but where *I* must change. Comments like this recur in my journal: 'And yes I hear your voice again. Forgive! Not just seven times but seventy times seven.'

In addition, God would give clear, specific directions. On a day when my prayer journal reads like the ranting of a petulant child, the instructions God gave me read like a letter from a marriage counsellor:

- Take your own advice to others seriously: *listen* to David and his needs.
- Make time to be with him. You haven't done that for a whole week.

- Don't try to read his mind. Clarify what he really does feel about you and current circumstances. Make time for this clarification to take place.
- Look at the tensions in your marriage carefully. Learn from them. See where you must grow. Let them show you where you need healing. Let them highlight where sin stains the relationship. Respond to the challenge: change.

By God's grace we both changed so that the sharing of our lives today is more mutually fulfilling and fun-filled than it has ever been. Painful though it was at the time, I look back with gratitude at the patient surgical skills with which the Holy Spirit operated on me to break me, re-create me and to rid me of spiritual diseases in the hospital of prayer. Through this I learned that God gives the gift of listening prayer not primarily to provide us with warm feelings towards him, though he does enrich our lives in this way, but to impress on us the need to grow. Listening prayer may not give us cosiness. It will bring us into wholeness, the *shalom* which is the integration of body, mind and spirit.

The dark night of the soul
One of the methods God uses to bring about this inner harmony in some people is an experience which is sometimes called 'the dark night of the soul'. This phrase describes the phases of the spiritual journey when the senses no longer pick up the felt presence of Christ but seem to be conscious, instead, only of nothingness. During this winter of the senses God seems to be, not present and attentive and loving, but completely absent. Thomas Merton refers to this experience often and describes it variously: 'spiritual inertia, inner confusion, coldness, lack of confidence'.[4] 'What at first seemed rosy and rewarding suddenly comes to be utterly impossible. The mind will not work. One cannot concentrate on anything. The imagination and the emotions wander away.'[5]

In my prayer diary, I record the pain and bewilderment

which the apparent absence of God brings: 'I ache for fellowship with you, Lord, but you seem so silent. You, whom this time last week I held and loved and cherished seem to have gone away again. Come, Lord Jesus, with healing hands . . .'

What I am referring to here is not simply an absence of warm feelings in prayer but something more profound than that: a definite sense that God had vanished, even abandoned me.

The first time I encountered the horror of this seeming separation from God, I was on retreat. Faced with four whole days of solitude, instead of the sense of anticipation which normally filled me at such times, I was seized with a sudden, severe sense of panic, even fear. I dreaded the moment when I must cross the threshold into silence.

In the convent where I had retreated to pray lived a nun who knew me well. In her I confided: 'Please pray for me. I don't know what's happening but I'm terrified of going into silence. God seems to have disappeared. He just isn't there any more and I'm left with this awful emptiness.'

She smiled and seemed quite unperturbed by the nature of the problem. Friend and confidante as she was, she prayed with me and for me and opened my eyes to the fact that in the school of prayer this particular seminar is a training ground for those who would graduate in the art of listening to God. In the first place, it increases our longing for God.

This became my experience. The darkness which crept over me in the convent on that occasion caused me to shudder and draw back, but it drew from me a call for Christ which came from the very depths of my being and which I experienced as a near-physical pain. It set me on a search for him which was both urgent and full of anguish. Was it, perhaps, the kind of search which sent Mary to the tomb very early on that Easter Day, full of longing to find the love which had been snatched away so suddenly? Was it reminiscent of the anxious hurt of the bride for her bridegroom in the Song of Songs? (3:1–2). Certainly, it seemed an identification with the pain David expresses so poignantly:

> As the deer pants for streams of water,
>   so my soul pants for you, O God.
> My soul thirsts for God, for the living God.
>   When can I go and meet with God? (Ps. 42:1–2).

And it echoed his cry of bewilderment: 'Why have you forgotten me?' (Ps. 42:9).

But it did more than expose my genuine desire for God. It sharpened my spiritual ears. God seemed to be hiding. But he had promised never to leave me or forsake me. He must, therefore, be there – somewhere. My spiritual antennae quivered with eagerness and alertness to detect even the faintest sign of his presence.

Meanwhile the nothingness which engulfed me forced me into some necessary sifting. As I thought about my normal programme of priorities – the people I spent time with, the activities I enjoyed, the work I found so fulfilling – I recognised the truth of the situation that in comparison with Christ and his presence the best the world can offer is but a mean and paltry offering. Thus the world lost more of its lure and lustre and what the mystics describe as the *capax Dei*, the capacity for God, increased. And deep down this was what I wanted. If this yawning emptiness was the enlargement of my inner capacity for God, then I would welcome these desert experiences. The intermingling of cautious trust and longing expressed in a prayer I once heard became *my* prayer:

> You, oh lord, are the thing that I long for
> And yet
>   I'm not sure that I can bear the emptiness that this
>   longing will involve
> If I really long for you then there will be no room for
>   the clutter
>   of a lot of other longings . . .

I must be hollowed out
To become a capacity for you.
I shrink from the pain that that will involve
But I must needs feel the poverty of my emptiness
And my poverty meets with your giving in the silence
    of lovers.

And, of course, when he saw that the time was ripe,
God overwhelmed me once more with his felt presence.
Meanwhile, having dispensed with the debris within, I
had been enlarging the reservoir into which he could pour
the life-giving waters of his Spirit's loving, invigorating
presence. And when the 'tremendous lover' did return,
the wave of joy which broke on the shore of my soul
gave birth to a song of heart-felt thanksgiving and relief.
And I realised I had learned another valuable lesson: that
I must not depend on feelings nor dictate to God *how* he
will appear to me. If he has spoken in a certain way on
one occasion, I must not expect that necessarily he will
visit me in that way a second time. I must allow God to
be God. And I must recall that he is not here to meet my
neurotic needs nor to kow-tow to my whims and fancies.
He is here to transform me into his likeness. The work of
God's Spirit is to grow me up into the likeness of Christ.
Just as one third of our earthly existence is spent in physical
darkness, night, so God in his wisdom ordains that from
time to time my prayer life must work a few night-shifts
also. The mystery is, as the psalmist reminds us, that the
darkness is not dark to him: 'The night will shine like the
day' (Ps. 9:12).

I learned, too, that this darkness is a relative phenomenon. As someone once explained it to me, 'When you've
been looking into the sun, you turn round and everything
seems dark. Similarly, when you've been gazing at Jesus,
everything else lies in his shadow.'

Thomas Merton makes the claim that these night times
of the senses increase in frequency as time goes on, that
there is a sense in which they can be taken as signs
of progress provided the pray-er does not give up but

determines to respond to the challenge, refuses to view this hollowness as spiritual doom or punishment for sin, but sees it, rather, for what it really is: the opportunity for growth.

Speaking personally, I still shudder when prayer dries up on me, when I listen and hear nothing, when I yearn for God and find emptiness, but I am learning, slowly, that the darkness is but the shadow of his hand, silence but the herald of his call, and nothingness the space prepared for the return of never-ending love.

As we listen to God, the pendulum swings from practicalities to ecstasies, from joy to pain and back again. But always our aim in prayer is to listen to the persistent tick-tock of his voice. When we do this, others take notice, benefit from the overflow, and give glory to God. As the pagan Queen of Sheba put it, reflecting on Solomon's intouchness with God: 'Praise be to the Lord your God, who has delighted in you' (2 Chr. 9:8).

Chapter 20

Pray as you Can

Early on in my prayer pursuit, I heard a wise maxim: 'Pray as you can, not as you can't.' In other words, pray and listen to God in a manner which holds meaning for you personally. Beware of falling into the trap of aping another person's prayer style. For the would-be listener to God this advice is priceless.

All kinds of components make up the complete listening package, as we have seen. Not everyone will gain access through each component. To some, God will communicate his purposes in one way, to others he will reveal his plans in a completely different manner. At different times and in different places he may communicate to the same person in a whole variety of ways. As we noted in chapter nineteen, we must allow God to be God, to take the initiative as he will. Our responsibility is to be ever-ready to receive his transmissions as and when he sends them.

I have tried to demonstrate, through the pages of this book, some of the ways in which I have grown in my understanding and experience of listening to God. Even so, I am conscious that I have not yet 'arrived', but still have much to learn.

Although I consider myself to be no more than an undergraduate where the study of listening prayer is concerned, I propose to devote this final chapter to a question I am asked frequently by fellow seekers: 'How can *I* learn to listen to God more effectively?'

Know your background

My first response to this question is to suggest that you take stock of your spiritual background.

Speaking personally, I dislike the man-made labels we use frequently to compartmentalise ourselves and others and I try, whenever possible, to resist the words 'evangelical', 'contemplative', or 'charismatic'. However, there are occasions when such words form a convenient shorthand and to this shorthand I shall resort in this chapter.

If you are an evangelical, and you are coming to the end of this book thirsting to hear God's voice more adequately, the first thing to do is to be grateful for the tools which your background has, in all probability, placed at your disposal already: a thorough working knowledge of and love of the Bible.

I have shown elsewhere in this book that informed biblical thinking is an essential component of listening prayer. Indeed it is the touchstone of all our listening.

Having said that, it would be foolish to imply that the Christian from an evangelical background has at his fingertips *all* the tools which the skilled listener needs. Very often he has not. Some evangelicals are rather like the bee I watched the other day. It perched on the outer petals of a peach-coloured rose, crawled right round the perimeter, presumably appreciated its fragrance, but flew away without bothering to penetrate the heart of the rose where the pollen collects.

What I watched reminded me of the evangelical I had talked to a few hours earlier. He and I were attending the same Christian conference. He clamoured for more biblical teaching, insisting that his mind must be fed. Yet in a quiet moment, he admitted to me that he was living promiscuously and was certain that this was all right.

If we would learn to listen to God more effectively, we evangelicals must learn that listening to God involves much more than cerebral activity. It demands a living response: obedience. And it demands attentiveness to God at many levels: intellectual, emotional, spiritual, volitional. In other words, the challenge to the evangelical

may well be to tune into God with his emotions, his will
and his spirit as well as with his mind. As Jesus put it,
love for God involves a whole-hearted dedication of heart,
mind, soul and strength. Until we give this, we miss the
very heart of the gospel and tune out much of what God
is attempting to say.

The evangelical Christian who is anxious to listen to God
more attentively may have other disciplines to master. We
in evangelical circles are not very experienced in keeping
quiet. We have to *learn* to 'be still', to know that God
is God. We have to learn 'to be' and not necessarily to
achieve. We may even need to be persuaded that God
is prepared to speak to us in unexpected ways, through
nature, other people, our imagination, as well as through
his revealed Word, the Bible.

There was a second bee on the peach-coloured rose
I mentioned earlier. This one also crawled round the
perimeter of the flower, then it pushed its way among the
petals and hummed as it carried its collection of pollen
away in its pocket. For the evangelical Christian, listening
to God can be as productive as that. He has already landed
on the right flower. If he will learn to value and adopt the
insights of others, if he will learn to meditate as well as
study, feel as well as think, he can discover far more to
listening than he formerly believed was possible.

The contemplative

The contemplative Christian who asks this same question,
'How can *I* listen to God more effectively?' also has cause
to thank God for the richness of his spiritual heritage. In all
probability he has been schooled in the art of stillness.
And such stillness is a prerequisite for listening to the
still, small voice of God as Ladislas Orsy reminds us:
'Discernment requires contemplative persons, well-versed
in finding God's presence by instinct. A gentle sensitivity
to the gentle movements of grace is necessary to the point
of being an indispensable condition. Without it there is no
wholeness in discernment.'[1] The contemplative may well
have achieved a heightened awareness of the presence

of Christ, particularly in the communion and in the community. He may also have become quite skilled in reading some of God's signs, seeing him in nature, or in the face of a child, or feeling him in the force of the wind.

But just as the evangelical has to learn that listening to God goes beyond the narrow sphere of reading words, so the contemplative, in refining the art form of listening to God, may need to turn back from mere signs and the teaching of the church to the scriptures – to study them, to become conversant with them. The desert fathers and teachers of prayer have passed on much wise counsel and it is sheer folly to ignore the wisdom they have imparted down the ages. Nevertheless, if we would know the mind of God we must heed the Word of God. *It* must become our chief delight. *It* must lodge in our hearts and minds. *It* must govern our thinking. If we do not know what the Word of God contains we may be sinning against God without ever intending to do so.

We contemplatives may face other challenges also. God is always on the move, as we have seen. If we cling to fossilised forms of worship, if we are frightened of departing from the rubric, if we are suspicious of every movement of the Spirit which we cannot explain, we will bolt the door on God and shut out his voice. We contemplatives may need to be persuaded to believe that Jesus says of himself 'I AM', not 'I WAS'. He is living and active and communicating today in supernatural ways and unless we accept this, his multi-layered communication will fall on deaf hearts and minds. Moreover, we may fail to discover the 'new thing' which God is always creating.

Just as the evangelical may find himself with unexpected avenues to explore, so the contemplative faces a life of fruitful exploration if he is prepared for the challenge which listening brings in its wake: to study, to re-evaluate, to discern every movement of the wind of the Spirit.

The charismatic

The charismatic asking the question, 'How can *I* listen to God?', similarly, has a certain head start and severe limitations.

We charismatics need no persuading that God is at work today, changing people's lives in a supernatural way. We have seen it for ourselves. We rejoice. We want to be open to everything God wants to do and to say.

But this very enthusiasm can be our greatest handicap. Our spontaneity can be the greatest obstacle we bring to the work of listening to God. For God says, in effect, 'Shut up!' 'Listen!' And shutting up is a discipline in which we do not excel!

The charismatic Christian whose hunger to hear God is real can learn from the contemplative to stop talking, stop clapping, stop praising for a while. And listen. In the stillness all that is phoney is stripped away. In this stillness authentic adoration is born which can later be expressed in exuberant praise if need be. In this stillness the desire for the spectacular is replaced by a deeper desire to know God for himself alone, not for anything he can do.

And we charismatics, like the contemplative, must follow the example of Jesus and steep ourselves in the scriptures. We must sharpen our thinking powers and use them. Unless we do so, we may find ourselves making pronouncements in the name of Christ which run counter to the Word of God. To do so is serious. God cannot contradict himself. If we are to speak out in the name of God, we must make it our responsibility to know what the Word of God contains.

Like the evangelical and the contemplative, the charismatic brings certain strengths to listening prayer but if the gift is to be perfected, for most of us, a great deal of hard work lies ahead.

To any Christian who, with genuineness, asks the question, 'How can *I* listen to God more effectively?' the way ahead is plain, in my view. We must recognise the skills already entrusted to us by God, give thanks for them, and use them efficiently. Then, instead of falling into the trap of *criticising* Christians from other traditions, we shall begin to ask, not, 'How can I prove that they're wrong?' but rather, 'What can I learn from them?' We shall not expect to agree with everything a person from another tradition believes in or stands for. Nevertheless, if we are to obey the command of Jesus, to love them as he loves them, we shall learn to accept and value all that God is doing in them and, in the area of listening to God, to take on board disciplines which clearly assist them in the task in hand: to listen to God with accuracy. In this way, too, we shall be captivated continually by the expanding vision of God which creeps over our horizon. We shall realise, in the language of J. B. Phillips, that for all our life so far, our God has been too small.

Know yourself

Just as the would-be listener can learn to discern his strength and limitations by acknowledging the insights his background has provided and areas in which his particular fellowship is deficient, so the would-be listener can improve his ability to listen to God by becoming aware of his personality.

The analyst, Carl Jung, divided people into personality types: the extrovert and the introvert. One is not better, more mature, than the other; they are different. He went further and subdivided each of these personality types in four ways according to the manner in which they approached life: through sensation, intuition, thinking and feeling.

There is great value in admitting to yourself where your chief bias lies because, in all probability, you will hear God speaking to you in certain ways which fit your personality.

For example, the extrovert who is a thinking person is more likely to hear the voice of God through the study of the Bible, the reading of commentaries, the evaluation of doctrines and the clarifying of theological positions than through nature and the imagination. The introvert who is a thinking person, on the other hand, will seek to hear God through Bible *meditation*, the slow reading of scripture, devotional reading. One is not better than the other. They are different.

Similarly, the extrovert who is motivated to a high degree by sensations may seek a fresh touch from God by attending celebration services. By watching or participating in spiritual dance, drama or the singing of scripture choruses, he will tune in to God. The introvert, who is governed by sensations, on the other hand, will seek God's presence in the calm of a convent, in the quiet of contemplation, or a country walk, or in the peace of a place preserved for prayer. One is not better than the other. They are different. The extrovert will seek to hear God outside of himself because, by definition, the extrovert turns outwards. The introvert, on the other hand, will seek attentiveness to God by paying attention to the world within because, by definition, the introvert feeds the inner world. One is not better than the other. They are different.

The challenge to those of us who would listen to God is to 'pray as we can'; to recognise the particular bias which we bring to the discipline of listening because of our personality, to start from there and then to move outside of these self-limiting boundaries to explore methods of listening which are valued by people with personality types which are different from our own.

Let me explain what I mean. I am an introvert. If I moved within the restricted sphere of my personality type, I would restrict myself to silence, Bible meditation, slow reading of scripture, contemplating God in nature, hearing God with the vividness of my imagination. But I married an extrovert and early on in our marriage we set ourselves the task of learning to find value in what the other enjoyed. My husband loves services of celebration, intellectual discussions and drama. Over the years, while I have been seeking to discover why he values such things, I have discovered that God speaks to me, not only in ways I would expect as an introvert, but in ways I would expect him to speak to my extrovert husband also. This not only enhances my listening, it brings a sense of completeness and wholeness. In the same service I can now drop into the stillness of the presence of God *and* praise him with my tambourine!

Know your Lord

It is not enough to know our background and know ourselves. We must know our Lord as well. Jesus has a wonderful way of making his presence known to all kinds of personality types and to people from a variety of backgrounds.

Think of the Resurrection appearances of Jesus, for example. Early in the morning, on the first Easter Day, Jesus appeared to Mary around whose neck we might hang the label 'contemplative', or 'introvert'. While Mary wept out her grief at the mouth of the empty tomb, Jesus appeared to her. He gave her the luxury her heart pined for: a long, leisurely opportunity to gaze at the Master she adored; the opportunity to drink in the Lord's one loving word to her, 'Mary', her own name.

Or think of the disciples who tramped the road which stretches from Jerusalem to Emmaus. Perhaps these two were extroverts: thinking types. As Jesus drew alongside them in their grief, his approach was quite different from his meeting with Mary. He appealed, not to their emotions, but to their minds. He expounded the scriptures, opened the eyes of their understanding, and rebuked them for neglecting to use their thinking powers. And by the end of the journey they heard him. In meeting them in their need he had used a language they could understand.

Think, too, of Peter, the extrovert who reacted to situations rather than responding to them after careful thought. For Peter, Jesus performed a miracle. After Peter's abortive all-night fishing trip, Jesus pointed out where a massive shoal of fish could be found. And as though that was insufficient, Jesus took his disconsolate disciple on one side and reinstated him, assuring him in a language Peter could interpret, that his denial of his Master was forgiven.

These different people with different personality types
and different needs had one thing in common. They
encountered the living Lord Jesus in a way which was
unique to them.

While I have been writing this book, the conviction in
me has deepened that this living Lord Jesus still yearns
to communicate: through his Word, through his people,
through circumstances, through nature, and through a
whole variety of ways which only a creative God could
devise. While I have been writing this book, I have
also become increasingly aware that large numbers of
Christians in the world today are crying out for a deeper
encounter with this Creator God. It is my prayer that
what I have written may contribute in some small way
to a matching of the two: that this book may, perhaps, become a bridge on which a communicating God
and some listening Christians encounter one another
in love.

For me, as I have said, fasting, prayer journals, Quiet
Days and retreats, Bible study, Bible meditation, slow
reading and the contemplation of nature have all contributed to my growth in listening to God. But that does not
necessarily mean that each of these will feature in *your*
life in a significant way. I repeat: 'Pray as you can, not as
you can't'.

The young mother may long for a Quiet Day but be
unable to shed her responsibilities for such a luxury. Five
minutes of silence will be bliss indeed. A family living in
cramped conditions could not hope for a prayer room. A
person living in the inner city may see little sign of God
in creation.

Not everyone will take on board all the aids to listening
I have mentioned all of the time. Some will help and
encourage others at different phases of their life. My
advice is: experiment. See what works for you. If a
particular method of listening seems to be an asset in
refining your ability to listen to God, use it. If it does
not help, leave it on one side without any sense of guilt
or shame.

Five minutes for God

But be disciplined. Christians who are serious in their desire to listen to God embark on a journey. It is full of surprises which make of it an adventure. But as I have already hinted, it is an ascent, a climb, hard work. Most of us can reserve a chair in a corner as a prayer place if we are disciplined. Most of us can carve out five minutes each day for God if we are disciplined. Most of us can learn to weave prayer into our chores if we are disciplined. Many of us *can* fast and even manage a Quiet Day if we are disciplined. And without discipline we shall never learn to listen. That is partly why we need each other.

God is always more anxious to speak than we are to listen. Speaking personally, the awareness of this fact spurs me on.

As I write, propped up in my prayer corner is Ulrich Schaffer's book, *Into Your Light*. On one page, the contemplative camera has captured the underside of a leaf, photographing the web of veins which give it life. On the facing page, the poet records his response to God's invitation to course through his life in like manner:

I sense your drive
To flow through me
Into the smallest blood vessels
Because you want to be my heartblood
In all the passages of my life
And you want to become visible in the leaves
And the fruit that I bear.

Spread out in me
Press forward, penetrate, pierce and flow
Even if, at times,
I want to repeal this invitation
Being afraid of your ways in me.

Circulate in me
Change and renew
Because I know

That only your Spirit
Can bring real life and fruit.[2]

As one who is spiritually full but never satisfied, who has
been found but still searches, who has heard but still waits
in listening love, I, too, echo that prayer. Spread out in
me, Lord Jesus, until I see you face to face.

Moving On

'God is always moving us on.' He invites us, 'not to stagnate in our spiritual life, but to change and to go on being changed'. That's the claim I make in the revised preface to the new edition of this book.

Often, when I reflect on the mystery of this inner movement, I liken it to the journey a river makes from its uncertain beginnings – perhaps as a trickle of mountain water percolating through heath and curving through mountain peaks – to that moment when it flows confidently into the sea. If the river could tell its own story, it might describe how it forced its frosty passage through glacial lakes, how it tumbled and splashed down pebbled paths, how it squeezed itself through a series of spectacular chasms, meandered past gentle meadows and snaked its way through the wilderness before rushing relentlessly towards the beckoning ocean.

'Snaked its way through the wilderness'. When my publisher invited me to add a postscript to this book, I reflected on my own spiritual journey, picturing myself as a river. As I did so, I recognised that, since the publication of the first edition of this book, my prayer pilgrimage has taken me through long stretches of wilderness. I have referred, albeit briefly, to such periods of spiritual dryness in Chapter 19. There I have shown how this phase of prayer is sometimes known as 'the dark night of the soul' because methods of prayer which once reaped rich reward suddenly cease to yield the expected harvest: the felt presence of God. I no longer fear this phase of the journey. On the contrary, I am excited by it. The writings of Thomas Green have helped me to understand it so that I now realise more clearly than ever before that those who are serious in their desire to go deeper into God will almost certainly be drawn into a 'vast, purifying dryness'.[1] The spiritual desert.

Stages of Spiritual Growth

Thomas Green suggests, and I agree with him, that most people experience three stages in their Christian growth. These stages vary in duration and intensity from person to person but, when we look back over our lives and trace our own histories, we may well discern their presence.

The first stage is rather like the uncertain beginnings of the river I have described. To change the image from meandering rivers to relationships, it is rather like the beginning of a friendship where we are drawn to someone by the kind of chemistry we call 'attraction' or 'falling in love'. It is the stage where we long to get to know the person and spend hours doing so. In our relationship with God, we are so drawn to him, even infatuated with him, that we earmark time and use up considerable energy in prayer and Bible study, or Bible meditation and contemplation as well as the kind of listening prayer I highlight in the earlier chapters of this book. Much of our knowledge during this phase, however, is head knowledge. We store into the computer of our brain a great deal of information *about* God.

But close friends or lovers are never content simply to get to know each other. They have an insatiable longing to be together. They yearn to move from this initial stage of the friendship on to the next – where knowing about becomes the deeper knowing we call intimacy; where head knowledge becomes heart awareness. Fondness. Affection. Love. In our relationship with God, during this second phase of the journey, the truths which we have stored in our brain gradually trickle, if slowly and gradually, from our heads into our hearts. Prayer becomes less achievement-orientated and more still. We recognise that God longs that we should, at times, simply be with him. He woos us with his love in the way I have described in Chapter 3. He spends a great deal of time convincing us, as Henri Nouwen puts it, that *we* are the beloved, God's beloved.[2] During this stage of our growth, we may experience periodic spiritual dryness – the kind I describe in Chapter 19. As I have emphasised in that chapter, these short-lived periods, when God seems more absent than present, will put us in touch with an incurable ache for him. They will also be punctuated by forays into spiritual oases where, with our senses and our emotions, we will recognise and enjoy to the full the presence and the love of God.

Just as the relationship between close friends or married couples changes over the years so that their love becomes based more on the will than on the emotions, so our relationship with God changes with time. Thomas Green suggests that it is in this third phase of prayer that we move from loving to *truly* loving God. We learn what it means to love with that part of our being the Bible calls 'the heart'. The heart means our innermost being. It includes the emotions, certainly. It also includes the will.

One way God teaches us to engage our will is to take us into the spiritual desert where our well-learned, much-practised, cherished ways in to God cease to be of help. The intellect dries up, so Bible study may seem fruitless, even boring. The imagination dries up, so Bible meditation may become equally arid and meaningless. The feelings dry up, so that when previously we may have sensed the presence of God, now we experience only his seeming absence. We may well find ourselves wondering whether we have, at best, lost our first love or, worse, lost our faith.

Some examples

I sense I see the apostle Peter passing through these three phases of spiritual growth. Having been introduced to Jesus by his brother Andrew (John 1:41) Peter is given

the privilege of spending an entire day with Jesus. As
that day dawned, he listened to Jesus's teaching. As the
day wore on, he witnessed Jesus perform the miracle of
the shoal of fish (Luke 5:3ff). We are not told what else
happened between these two men as they spent the day
together on the Sea of Galilee. We are told that a certain
magnetism we would call attraction drew Peter to Jesus
so irresistibly that, when Jesus invited him to 'Follow
me', Peter pulled his boat up on the shore, abandoned
everything and followed his new Master.

Almost three years later, when Jesus was praying in
private yet in the company of Peter and the other members
of his little community, he asked his companions that
pertinent question: 'Who do the crowds say I am?' This
was quickly followed by that even more pertinent question:
'But what about you? Who do *you* say I am?' As so often
happened, it was Peter who blurted out the answer to the
question: 'The Messiah of God' (Luke 9:20).[3]

This clear statement of faith shows that Peter had not
only listened to and learned from Jesus's teaching about
the Kingdom, he had discerned Jesus's identity. He had
gleaned a great deal of head knowledge.

Being with Jesus for three years gave birth in Peter,
not only to an awareness of who Jesus was but also
to a deep-down love for the Master. It was protective,
though misguided love that prompted Peter to protest
when Jesus declared his intention of moving from Galilee
to Jerusalem. It was love that caused Peter to recoil,
albeit inappropriately, from having his feet washed by
the Beloved (the kind of love that often leaves the loved
one feeling totally unworthy of the love of the other).
It was love, however feeble, that drew from Peter the
futile promise, 'Even if all fall away on account of you,
I never will . . . Even if I have to die with you, I will
never disown you' (Matt. 26: 33, 35). In the event, these
promises proved empty and futile but, when they were
made, they were sincere and well-intentioned.

The refining of Peter's love came later – after the
Resurrection. The watershed came at the Crucifixion.

For three years Peter had lived with Jesus, learned from Jesus, loved Jesus. On that first Good Friday something died. Jesus died. And with him died the second phase of Peter's spiritual growth. Never again would Peter make such extravagant, emotional claims as those I have quoted above. Never again would Peter enjoy the privilege of a day-by-day, almost moment-by-moment encounter with the Beloved. Even after the Resurrection when Jesus surprised Peter with that unexpected love-gift of a personal encounter somewhere in the streets of Jerusalem (Luke 24:34). Even after Jesus had met with Peter and the others on at least two occasions in the Upper Room in Jerusalem, the relationship between the two men went through an inevitable change. Peter now had to grow up – to learn that he could enjoy Jesus's felt presence only fleetingly. Just as Mary Magdalene had had to hear from Jesus those probably painful words, 'Don't cling' (John 20:17), Peter needed to hear them too.

It would appear from the Gospels that Peter found this transitional dryness difficult to handle. This is understandable. For him, transitional dryness meant that, one minute he was with Jesus enjoying his presence as he had known it for those three precious years, while the next minute Jesus had disappeared again. On one of those occasions when Peter felt keenly the absence of the physical presence of the Master, he announced to anyone who was listening: 'I'm going fishing' (John 21:3). Was this return to his old profession a sign of restlessness or of disillusionment? Perhaps. Later that same morning, Jesus warned Peter that there was worse to come. The day would come when Peter's expressed love for the Lord would be further refined. 'I tell you the truth, when you were younger you dressed yourself and went where you wanted; but when you are old you will stretch out your hands, and someone else will dress you and lead you where you do not want to go' (John 21:18). John explains that Jesus was here referring to the way Peter's life would end – in the death of crucifixion. If we take Peter's writing seriously and read it sensitively, it quickly becomes obvious that it meant more than that. It referred to the refining and purifying of Peter's person and love.

Until the Crucifixion of Jesus, Peter's love had been an emotional love. As Thomas Green explains, 'The emotions . . . are essentially self-centred. They grasp at whatever pleases and gratifies them . . . Thus, love which is strongly emotional is essentially self-seeking, concerned with its own pleasure and delight.' He adds that, 'the well of emotion will surely run dry'.[4]

While Jesus was alive and Peter was a respected, loved, key member of the Jesus community, he enjoyed a great deal of kudos, excitement and fulfilment. It is true that he had made considerable sacrifices to follow Jesus. It is also true that he worked hard for the Master. In the early post-Resurrection, post-Pentecost days, he would continue to pour himself out for Christ and his Church. But here, on the shore of the Sea of Galilee, Jesus seems to be warning Peter that the day was fast approaching when he would need to hand over the reins to God. To let God be God. Like clay in the hands of the potter, Peter was to be softened and reshaped. His role would change. Instead of being the one who took the initiative in work or in prayer, he would need to be as submissive and compliant as clay. Now *God*, the heavenly potter, would take the initiative while Peter would learn the sometimes-difficult lessons of acceptance and receptivity. If we compare the up-front leadership style of the Peter of the Acts of the Apostles with the sensitivity of Peter the author of 1 Peter, we see that he had travelled a long way down the path of sanctification before his crucifixion. That path of sanctification led him through the howling wilderness where, at times, he could neither see nor feel nor hear the Jesus he loved but where, mysteriously, he knew that his Master's promise would be kept. Jesus would *never* leave him or forsake him. Even though he seemed, at times, to be absent, he was there – unseen yet gloriously present, unheard yet still speaking, unfelt yet still wonderfully in control.

The spiritual desert

Just as Peter needed to pass through phase three, so do we. Thomas Green goes so far as to suggest that, 'It is only when we come to *love* the desert, and to *prefer* it to the oases, that we are well on the way to God. It is an 'upside-down world indeed.'[5]

Since the publication of *Listening to God*, I have found the river of my life being forced to push its way through the wilderness. This does not mean that I have abandoned the methods of listening to God which I have outlined in the book. I still use them. I still find them valuable. I now realise, however, that the initiative is not mine but God's. It also means that I recognise that I cannot manipulate God. Just because I set myself the task of listening on any given occasion, that does not mean that God will necessarily choose that moment either to reveal himself to me or to speak to me. I am learning to let God be God – to let him control the flow of words, of felt love, of healing, of the sense of his presence. There are times when he seems gloriously present, there are other long stretches of time when it *feels* as though he has disappeared but faith assures me that he is as close as he has always been and, when he discerns that the time is ripe, he will make his presence and his love felt again.

As I explained in the Preface, much in my life has changed since I served my apprenticeship in listening prayer and as I explored stillness and solitude. Now that I live and work overseas, I have been stripped of many of the props that I took for granted when I lived in England. When I prepare to lead retreats in the kind of condition I describe in the Preface, I sometimes identify with Peter. It feels as though I am frequently being taken to places which I would prefer not to visit. And yet, as a friend pointed out to me recently, do you realise how often you write in your letters, 'I am deeply, deeply happy. Content'? Until she reflected this back to me, I had not seen it.

As I reflect on that comment and on my personal experience of the desert, I realise that the claims that are made about this phase of our spiritual growth are

accurate. The desert is the place where, gradually and
slowly, we are stripped of our love of self and even our
love for God is refined. The desert is the place where we
are taught not to cling to anything or to anyone – not
even to God. The desert is the place where our prayer
matures and is purified. In the desert we realise that,
even in prayer, God does more and more, we do less and
less. We pray, not because we receive the consolations of
God as a result but because God prays through us and,
increasingly, the longing of our heart is that our life should
revolve, not around self, but around him. He has become
our heart's desire.

Curiously, the desert is the place where seeds of faith
germinate. As I look out of my study window as I write,
nature presents me with a parable. It is the famed Cyprus
springtime. The grass is virgin green. Rows of spring wheat
grow alongside carpets of yellow mustard. Pink blossom
peeps from the almond trees and white blossom spreads
its fragrance throughout the orange groves. And mother
earth, which for nine months of the year lies parched and
dry as though it is crying out for water, has given birth to a
myriad of wild flowers: miniature cyclamen, purple vetch,
paper-white marguerites, wide-eyed marigolds, deep-blue
speedwell, tiny, pale-blue irises, creamy-lemon narcissi
and dancing daffodils, to mention a few. It reminds me
that all that these plants have to do is to be in the place
where they were planted – to be receptive to the nurture of
the sun and the seasonal rain. The result of this receptivity
is that they will germinate and grow, they will bear fruit
and be a delight.

The spiritual desert is like that. It is the place where
we recognise our littleness, our utter dependence on God
even for the life of prayer. It is the place of receptivity,
of germinating faith. Paradoxically, it is the place where we
discover that the seeming dryness contains all the water
we need. It is the place where the seeming darkness turns
out to be blinding light. It is the place where seeming
barrenness bears prolific fruit – the kind of fruit which
the world, sometimes even the Christian Church, passes

by or tramples on, but the kind of fruit which the heavenly
Gardener and those who have tramped this desert path
recognise and value. For, as Isaiah reminds us, where
the Spirit is, there the desert becomes a fertile field (Isa.
32:15).

Whenever I speak to groups about this desert experience, this third stage of spiritual growth, I find that
dedicated, devoted people of prayer prick up their ears
and appear to drink in every word. Many thank me for
throwing light on what is seen, in some Christian circles,
as a negative experience.

Possible causes of darkness

Not all spiritual dryness has a positive face, of course.
When we find ourselves wandering in the spiritual desert,
therefore, we do well to ask ourselves some pertinent
questions:

- Am I here because I have never learned that prayer
  is not a duty to be performed but a relationship with
  God to be enjoyed? Have I allowed prayer lists and/or
  someone else's method of prayer to become a burden
  rather than envisaging prayer as time spent with the
  Divine Love?
- Am I dry because I have allowed busyness to elbow
  out time with God?
- Do I need, like Mary, to make time to sit at Jesus's
  feet?
- Do I rush in and out of God's presence without
  'tuning the instrument at the gate' – preparing myself
  reverently to meet a holy God?

Has someone or something become more precious to me
than God? Do I need to learn to hold that person or
that thing on an open palm so that my open hands are
ready for God to take or restore them and so that I
am ready to receive whatever or whoever he sends into
my life?

Is my life revolving around self rather than around God? If so, this is the essence of sin and needs to be confessed?

Or could it be that this dryness is not self-imposed but rather comes as a love-gift from God?

One way of discerning whether spiritual dryness is a sign that priorities need to be examined and maybe changed or whether it is a gift to be received is to ask ourselves some questions:

- Does it seem as though this dryness finds parallels with the kind of transitional dryness Peter experienced? Sometimes Jesus's presence is recognisable and real while, at other times, he seems more absent than present?
- What kind of fruit am I bearing? (According to Jesus, a good tree cannot bear bad fruit.)
- Whose Kingdom am I serving – the Kingdom of God or the kingdom of self?
- Does this prolonged dryness seem like an invitation to grow – to dance to God's tune – to cease to demand that God dances to mine? To change the metaphor, could it be that God is asking me to become as malleable clay in his hands or like a patient entrusting himself into the hands of a skilful surgeon? Could it be that this God who has my best interests at heart is using my work, my relationships, my frustrations and the other circumstances of my life as instruments which, though they might hurt, are bringing about healing, wholeness, shalom?

Listening to God in the Desert

One way of discerning the reason why you are in the desert is to ask yourself some questions:

- What kind of fruit am I bearing? (According to Jesus, remember, a good tree cannot bear bad fruit.)
- Whose kingdom am I serving?

If we take time most days to pause and ask God to show us where he has been at work in our lives giving birth to the fruit of the Spirit: love, joy, peace, patience, kindness, goodness, faithfulness, gentleness and self-control (Gal. 5:22), he will honour that prayer and help us to discern where his Spirit is working in the hidden recesses of our being. And if we ask him to show us, from time to time, if possible most days, whose kingdom we have been serving with our time and our energy, our activities and our attitudes, he will honour that prayer also.

I suspect that many of those readers who wrote to me ten years ago to tell me that their journeys found many parallels in my own story may, by now, have found themselves drawn by God into the desert. My prayer is that all of us, when we are entrusted with this privileged time of testing, may draw strength from God's promises:

This is what the Lord says –
   he who made a way through the sea,
a path through the mighty waters . . .
Forget the former things;
   do not dwell on the past.
See, I am doing a new thing!
   Now it springs up; do you not perceive it?
I am making a way in the desert
   and streams in the wasteland . . .
to give drink to my people, my chosen,
   the people I formed for myself
that they may proclaim my praise

(Isa. 43: 16, 18–21).

'I am now going to allure her;
I will lead her into the desert
and speak tenderly to her.
There I will give her back her vineyards . . .
There she will sing as in the days of her youth

(Hos. 2:14).

Although God was originally speaking through Isaiah to the Children of Israel and to Hosea about his unfaithful wife Gomer, I believe that there are spiritual truths we who must spend some of our time wandering through the wilderness can draw from these promises. As we do, we may well find ourselves agreeing with Bob Brown, Director of the Tasmanian Wilderness Society: 'We need wilderness. The concrete canyons, asphalt plains and plastic flowers of the modern city are no substitute for nature's wide open spaces.'[6] We might find ourselves adding our own qualifying clause: 'We need wilderness because . . .'

As I reflect on my own experience of the desert, my mind goes back to a retreat I once made in Canada. There, I meditated on Teresa of Avila's claim: 'The water is for the flowers.' In other words, when God comes into our lives, for with his felt presence or with the kind of spiritual gifts I have highlighted in *Listening to God* it is for one purpose – that he may be glorified through the spiritual harvest that is reaped as a result. This prompts me to claim that we need wilderness so that our life ceases to revolve around self and, instead, revolves around the God in whom we live and move and have our being.[7]

Notes

Preface
1. Community of All Hallows
2. Hosea 2:14

Chapter 1
1. Francis Thompson: *The Hound of Heaven*. Mowbrays, pp 4–6

Chapter 2
1. John Powell: *He Touched Me*. Argus, 1974, p 70
2. Ibid, p 71
3. Ibid, p 74; p 77
4. C. S. Lewis: *Surprised by Joy*. Fontana, 1962, pp 173–4

Chapter 3
1. Catherine de Hueck Doherty: *Poustinia*. Fountain, 1975, p 20
2. Ibid, p 21
3. Robert Llewellyn: *Prayer and Contemplation*. Fairacres, 1975, p 29

Chapter 4
1. James Borst: *Contemplative Prayer*. Ligoun Publications, 1979, p 43. (A revised version of *A Method of Contemplative Prayer*.)

2. Robert Llewellyn: *Prayer and Contemplation*. Fairacres, 1975, p 33
3. See, for example, Ezekiel 2:1–2
4. See, for example, Psalms 88:9 and Job 11:13
5. For further information read *The Body at Prayer* by H. Caffarel. SPCK, 1978
6. James Borst: *A Method of Contemplative Prayer*. MHM, Asian Trading Corporation, 1973, p 11
7. W. Phillip Keller: *Solitude for Serenity and Strength*. Decision Magazine, August-September 1981, p 8

Chapter 5
1. James Borst: *A Method of Contemplative Prayer*. Asian Trading Corporation, 1974, p 12
2. Thomas Merton: *Contemplative Prayer*. DLT, 1973, p 13
3. Ibid, p 7
4. Ibid, p 8
5. Ibid, p 15 (italics mine)

Chapter 6
1. W. Phillip Keller: *Solitude for Serenity and Strength*. Decision Magazine, August-September 1981, p 8
2. Stephen Verney: *Into the New Age*. Fontana, 1976, p 90
3. Ibid, p 92
4. James Borst: *The Cloud of Unknowing. Quoted Contemplative Prayer*. Ligouri Publications, 1979, p 59
5. Dom Vitalis Lehodey. Quoted ibid, p 58
6. C. S. Lewis: *The Lion, the Witch and the Wardrobe*. Puffin 1966 p 148
7. James Borst MHM: *A Method of Contemplative Prayer*. Asian Trading Corporation, 1974, p 18
8. Ibid, pp 18–19
9. Thomas Merton: *Contemplative Prayer*. DLT, 1973, p 115
10. Anon.: *The Cloud of Unknowing*. Penguin, 1977, p 51
11. Stephen Verney: *Into the New Age*. Fontana, 1976, pp 91–2

Chapter 7

1. J. I. Packer: *God's Words*. IVP, 1981, p 39
2. David Watson: *Discipleship*. Hodder and Stoughton, 1981, p 149

Chapter 8

1. Michael Mitton: *The Wisdom to Listen*. Grove Pastoral Studies no 5, 1981, p 10
2. Richard Foster: *Meditative Prayer*. MARC Europe, 1983, p 3

Chapter 9

1. David Watson: *Discipleship*. Hodder and Stoughton, 1981, p 143
2. Herman Riffel: *Your Dreams: God's Neglected Gift*. Kingsway, 1984, p 9
3. Ibid, p 48

Chapter 10

1. Kallistos Ware: *The Orthodox Way*. Mowbrays, 1979, p 21
2. Billy Graham: *Angels: God's Secret Agents*. Hodder and Stoughton, 1975, pp 12–13
3. Ibid, pp 154–5
4. Anthony Bloom: *Taped Talk on a Quiet Day*, made privately, so unavailable to public.

Chapter 11

1. Charles de Foucauld
2. Quoted Kallistos Ware: *The Orthodox Way*. Mowbrays, 1979, p 54
3. See *Practising the Presence of God* by Brother Lawrence
4. Quoted Kallistos Ware: *The Orthodox Way*. Mowbrays, 1979, p 4
5. Ulrich Schaffer: *Into your Light*. IVP, 1979, pp 43–4
6. John Powell: *He Touched Me*. Argus, 1974, p 79
7. Kallistos Ware: *The Orthodox Way*. Mowbrays, 1979 p 58

Chapter 12
1. Kallistos Ware: *The Orthodox Way*. Mowbrays, 1979, p 88
2. Keith Miller: *The Taste of New Wine*. A Word Paperback, 1970, p 93
3. David Watson: *One in the Spirit*. Hodder Christian Paperbacks, 1973, pp 90–1
4. David Watson: *Discipleship*. Hodder and Stoughton, 1981

Chapter 13
1. J. I. Packer: *Knowing God*. Hodder and Stoughton 1973 p 264
2. Thomas Merton: *Contemplative Prayer*. DLT, 1973, p 43
3. Ps. 119:16, 162; 11; 15, 27, 48; 2, 115, 129; 13; 52; 97, 99, 148, 94, 110, 157
4. Francis Schaeffer: *The New Super-Spirituality*. Hodder and Stoughton, 1972, p 24

Chapter 14
1. Quoted in *The Practice of Bible Meditation* by Campbell McAlpine, Marshalls, 1981, p 20
2. Ibid, p 20
3. J. I. Packer: *God's Words*. IVP, 1981, p 35
4. David Watson: *Discipleship*. Hodder and Stoughton, 1981, p 147
5. Campbell McAlpine: *The Practice of Bible Meditation*. Marshalls, 1981, p 75
6. M. Basil Pennington DCSO: *Centering Prayer*. Image Books, 1982, p 193
7. Richard Foster: *Meditative Prayer*. MARC Europe, 1983, pp 23–4

Chapter 15
1. Mother Mary Clare SLG – Talk on tape.
2. Andre Louf: *Teach us to pray*. DLT, 1974
3. Henri J. Nouwen: *The Genesee Diary*. Image Books, 1981, p 14

4. Ibid, p 135
5. William Barclay: *The Gospel of Matthew* Vol. 2. Saint Andrew Press, 1975, p 60

Chapter 16

1. Guy Brinkworth, SJ: *Thirsting for God*. Mullan Press
2. Ibid, p 16
3. Ibid, p 12
4. Ibid, p 13
5. Quoted in *You* by Mark Link. Argus, 1976, p 53
6. Catherine de Hueck Doherty: *Poustinia*. Fountain, 1975, p 70
7. Ibid, p 93
8. Michel Quoist: *Prayers of Life*. Gill & Macmillan, 1966, pp 101–2
9. For suggestions of music to bring one into stillness, see Appendix
10. Kenneth Leech: *Soul Friend*. Sheldon Press, 1977, p 170
11. Quoted in *Soul Friend* by Kenneth Leech. Sheldon Press, 1977, p 41
12. Quoted Ibid, p 44
13. Quoted Ibid, Frontispiece
14. *Pray with* . . . Bro. Kenneth CGA and Sister Geraldine Dss. CSA C10, 1977, p 15

Chapter 17

1. C. S. Lewis: *The Screwtape Letters*. Fontana, 1956, p 114
2. Richard Foster: *Celebration of Discipline*. Hodder and Stoughton, 1980, p 48

Chapter 18

1. Guy Brinkworth SJ: *Personal Renewal and Formal Prayer*. Convent of Mercy, 1970, p 32

Chapter 19

1. Thomas Merton: *Contemplative Prayer*. DLT, 1973, p 45

2. Richard Foster: *Celebration of Discipline*. Hodder and Stoughton, 1978, p 17
3. Ibid, p 32
4. Ibid, p 44
5. Ibid, p 44

Chapter 20
1. Ladislas M. Orsy: *Probing the Spirit*. Dimension Books, 1976, p 14
2. Ulrich Schaffer: *Into your Light*. IVP, 1979, p 29

Moving On
1. Thomas Green SJ: *When the Well Runs Dry*, 1992, p 12
2. For readers entering or dwelling in this phase of prayer, I recommend Henri Nouwen. *The Life of the Beloved*. Hodder and Stoughton, 1992.
3. Eugene Peterson's translation from *The Message*
4. Thomas Green: op cit, p 24
5. Thomas Green: op cit, p 12
6. Bob Brown: *Wild Rivers*. Peter Dombrovskis Pty Ltd, Tasmania, Australia, 1983, p 29. Bob Brown's graphic description of some of the rivers of Tasmania has inspired my own perception of life as a meandering river.
7. I would recommend that those who want to explore the nature of the spiritual desert further should read three books by Thomas Green. *When the Well Runs Dry, Drinking From a Dry Well, Darkness in the Marketplace* – all published by Ave Maria Press.

Bibliography

During the past ten years, the market has been flooded with books on spirituality. In this bibliography, I mention some of those which have been most helpful to me and which I believe could help and inspire readers of *Listening to God*.

To help us come into stillness

Jim Borst	*Coming to God*	Eagle
Gerald O'Mahoney	*Finding the Still Point*	Eagle
Joyce Huggett	*The Smile of Love*	Hodder and Stoughton

(Joyce Huggett has also produced two audio cassettes to help people come into stillness: *Teach us to Pray* and *Teach Me to Pray*)

Spiritual Dryness

Thomas Green	*When the Well Runs Dry*	Ave Maria Press
Thomas Green	*Darkness in the Market Place*	Ave Maria Press
Thomas Green	*Drinking From a Dry Well*	Ave Maria Press
Heather Ward	*Streams in Dry Land*	Eagle

Listening to God

Michael Mitton	*The Sounds of God*	Eagle
St Margaret Magdalene CSMV	*Jesus: Man of Prayer*	Hodder and Stoughton
David Runcorn	*Space for God*	DLT
Ian Petit OSB	*The God Who Speaks*	DLT Daybreak
Klaus Bockuehl	*Listening to the God Who Speaks*	Helmers and Howard
Mark Vikler	*Dialogue With God*	Word

General books on Prayer

Richard Foster	*Prayer*	Hodder and Stoughton
James Houston	*The Transforming Friendship*	Lion
Joyce Huggett	*Explaining Prayer*	Sovereign World

(This is a simple booklet on prayer written, primarily, for people whose first language is not English)

Gerard Hughes	*God of Surprises*	DLT
Henri J. Nouwen	*Reaching Out*	Fount
Henri J. Nouwen	*The Genessee Diary*	Image
Henri J. Nouwen	*The Life of the Beloved*	Hodder and Stoughton
Henri J. Nouwen	*The Return of the Prodigal*	DLT

Prayer and Personality

Lawrence and Diana Osborne	*God's Diverse People*	DLT

When Prayer is Difficult

Joyce Rupp	*Praying Our Goodbyes*	Eagle
Paul Wallis	*Rough Ways in Prayer*	SPCK Triangle

About Meditation

Peter Toon	*Meditating Upon God's Word*	DLT
Peter Toon	*Meditating As a Christian*	Collins
Joyce Huggett	*Open to God*	Hodder and Stoughton
Peter Dodson	*Contemplating the Word*	SPCK

Prayer in Ordinariness

Joyce Huggett	*Finding God in the Fast Lane*	Eagle
Margaret Hebblethwaite	*Finding God in All Things*	Fount
Macrina Wiederkehr	*A Tree Full of Angels*	Harper and Row

On Spiritual Direction

Kenneth Leach	*Soul Friend*	Sheldon Press
Margaret Guenther	*Holy Listening*	DLT
William A. Barry William J. Connolly	*The Practice of Spiritual Direction*	Harper and Row
Tilden Edwards	*Spiritual Friend*	Paulist Press
Wendy Miller	*Spiritual Friendship*	Eagle

Keeping a Prayer Journal

Brian Hawker	*Your Life in Your Hands*	Fount
Joyce Huggett	*Prayer Journal*	HarperCollins

In addition, of course, certain classics on prayer continue to have an ongoing and significant ministry:

Author unknown	*The Cloud of Unknowing*	Penguin Classics
Thomas à Kempis	*The Imitation of Christ*	Penguin Classics

Pierre de Caussade	*Self-abandonment to Divine Providence*	Fontana
Thomas Merton	*Contemplative Prayer*	DLT
Thomas Merton	*Seeds of Contemplation*	DLT

Some of the music I use to bring me into silence
Music from Taize – particularly from three cassettes: Laudate, Alleluia, and Songs and Prayers from Taize

Worship tapes
Open to God: cassette (Hodder and Stoughton)
Give Thanks: Classical Praise Piano. Keith Routledge (Monarch)
Worship with Violin and Piano: Living Water Lynette Webster and Barbara Yates
   Come to Me Lynette Webster and Barbara Yates
(Sold in aid of The Lyttleton Well Project. Available from Malvern Priory, Malvern, Worcestershire)
God's Springtime: cassette (Eagle) – particularly:
Broken for Me
When I survey the wondrous cross
The Name of Jesus
Come as you are
Coming Softly to the Father (The Master's Collection) – particularly:
Be Still
Worshipping the Lord our God
Coming Softly to the Father
Children, I am Waiting
Do you know who I am?
He Touched Me
Come Back to Me
Holy One of Israel: (all Marilla Ness MLM)

Instrumental Music
Simeon and John's Music – particularly:
Reaching Out
In the Beginning: (both Eagle)

Listening to Others

The author and publisher have endeavoured to trace all copyright holders for the material quoted in this book but apologise for any inadvertent omissions, which will be rectified in any reprint.

For permission to use copyright material they are grateful to the following sources:

David Augsburger, extract from *Caring Enough to Hear and be Heard,* Herald Press; Michael Jacobs, extract from *Swift to Hear,* © 1985 by Michael Jacobs, SPCK; Francis MacNutt, extract from *Healing,* Ave Maria Press; Henri Nouwen, extract from *Compassion,* © 1982 by Darton, Longman & Todd; John Powell, extracts from *Will the Real Me Please Stand Up,* ©1985 by John Powell, SJ. Printed by Tabor Publishing in the United States of America. Used with permission; John Stott, extract from *Issues Facing Christian Today,* © 1984 by John Stott, Marshall Pickering.

Contents

For

Anne

to whom I owe so much

Preface

'When someone listens to you – attentively, lovingly, reverently – how do you feel?' That's a question I sometimes ask when I am leading seminars on prayer or marriage or relationships in general. These are some of the responses I have received: 'I feel valued', 'I feel comforted', 'I feel as though I can carry on living even though things are tough', 'I feel loved'.

'I feel loved.' What an amazing claim! When someone listens to us, hears us and shows that they care, we feel deeply loved. As the Swiss psychiatrist, Paul Tournier, put it, 'He who feels understood feels loved and he who feels loved feels sure of being understood.'

This means that, when we listen to someone, we are offering them a priceless gift. But giving this gift is not as simple as it sounds because listening does not come easily to most people. It is therefore an art form that needs to be *learned* and relearned and improved upon. This book is for those who want to learn that art, those who want to improve their skills, those who believe that listening, of itself, can be a ministry.

Since writing this book in 1988, my own perception of listening has changed. As I explained in the Preface to the original manuscript, I used to view listening to others as a part of my prayer. I still do. I believe passionately in Peter Dodson's claim that contemplation is paying rapt attention to God and his world.[1] I believe, too, that

St Benedict was right when he claimed that the activity of true prayer is both vertical and horizontal. Vertical in that the person praying is united with God and horizontal in that the pray-er unites himself with the world of which he is a part. But I also now recognise that, in a curious way, when we are listening to others – whether we are listening to their joy or their pain, we are, in fact, ministering to the Lord himself. I make this claim as a result of meditating on Matthew 25 where Jesus's parable of the sheep and the goats is recorded. Here Jesus describes, in picture language, the happenings that will amaze us when he returns:

> When he finally arrives, blazing in beauty and all his angels with him, the Son of Man will take his place on his glorious throne. Then all the nations will be arranged before him and he will sort the people out, much as a shepherd sorts out sheep and goats, putting sheep to his right and goats to his left.[2]

The king will then applaud those on his right saying:

> I was hungry and you fed me,
> I was thirsty and you gave me a drink,
> I was homeless and you gave me a room,
> I was shivering and you gave me clothes,
> I was sick and you stopped to visit me,
> I was in prison and you came to me.[3]

Amazed, 'the sheep' will ask when they ministered to the king in this way.

> Then the King will say, 'I'm telling the solemn truth: Whenever you did one of these things to someone overlooked or ignored, that was me – you did it to me.'[4]

Giving a meal to a person who is starving, responding to the unuttered cry for help of a sick person, providing clothes for those who are clad in rags is a profound form of listening. And so is listening to a person's pain or turmoil or joy. When we listen to such people – in the hiddenness of our homes or in the hubbub of the work place or while we're enjoying a day off, we are ministering, in some strange way, to Jesus himself.

So I rejoice that my circumstances have changed since I first wrote *Listening to Others*. Then, I lived in England and was involved in much public speaking, a certain amount of writing and some counselling. Now, I am a Mission Partner with an organisation called Interserve. I live in Cyprus where my main ministry is not to mount the public platform, nor to write, but to listen – to listen to Mission Partners who live in or can travel to Cyprus or to listen to Mission Partners in far-flung parts of the world which my husband and I are privileged to visit. As a result, my belief in the transforming power of listening with love and in partnership with God has deepened. Our work is not so much counselling as retreat giving. When Mission Partners attend our tailor-made retreats, we invite them to tell us what they are hoping for from their 'holiday with God'. We also ask them how they are. When we have listened to the portion of their story which they choose to share with us, we invite them to meditate on a passage of Scripture and to meet with one of us the following day so that we can continue the process of listening and discerning. Our aim is not to draw these people to ourselves but rather to take them deeper into God's love. We feel greatly privileged to be entrusted with this task and have been awed to see the way in which God uses it – to individuals and to groups.

Although I am now involved full-time in the ministry of listening, I still find that I need to return to the basics from time to time – the kind of insights I enumerate in this book. And because Christians working overseas often have no one near with whom they can share at depth, many of them keep in touch with us through letter or cassette or telephone. Similarly, now that I, too, live overseas where

I am stripped of many of the props which I used to take for granted in England, I am forced to do much of my communicating through the media of letters and faxes, cassettes and phone calls and unvoiced cries for help. I am indebted to those who have learned how to listen sensitively to this kind of communication – those who have a gift for listening to and responding to letters, those who pick up vibes and respond to them in love, those who listen to the 'holy hunch' to telephone or fax or speak into a cassette and send it. That is why I have added a Postscript to the original book. It will, I hope, broaden the horizons of some of my readers and inspire them to believe that we do not necessarily have to be 'on the spot' to listen well. All of us *can* learn how to listen – to relatives and friends and acquaintances near and far. Some readers may wonder why I chose to write the book autobiographically rather than in text-book fashion. There were two chief reasons. One was to show that learning to listen is an art form which comes to most of us gradually – often when we go through personal crises. The second was to highlight the vulnerability of those who need a listening ear. Such vulnerability need not be seen as weakness. On the contrary, it *can* be one of the qualifications which equip us for this privileged, costly, healing ministry.

Joyce Huggett
Cyprus 1995

Acknowledgments

'Who we are, what we become, depends largely on those who love us.' This claim of John Powell's took on new meaning for me as I wrote this book and realised more fully than ever before just how much I owe to certain people. I am glad to be able to express in public my thanks to a few of those who have shaped my life by caring for me at cost to themselves.

The first accolade must go to my husband, David, for honouring his wedding vows and loving me through the worst as well as the joyful times. And the second to Anne Long who, on so many occasions, allowed herself to be God's instrument of healing to me. Without the dedicated love and ongoing care of these two people, I might never have been rescued from my brokenness; might never have reached the degree of maturity I enjoy today.

I would like to thank my brother, Ray, too, for all the love he showered on me, his 'baby sister' both in Roberts Road days and more recently in Perth, Australia. His memory of our childhood is so much better than mine. Without his help I would not have recalled the names of some of our neighbours.

I am also indebted to those who prayed for me while I was giving birth to this book. This particular 'labour' was prolonged and, at times, painful. But these faithful friends refused to give up praying. One family even provided me with a place where I could 'duck under', be fed and press on with the praying and the writing in peace. I know no adequate words to sum up just how much I appreciate their co-operation, concern and care.

Among those who gave practical help and advice were my editor, Tim Anderson, and my personal assistant, Charlotte Swan. Tim is a great encourager. Talking with him so sharpens my thinking that I have grown to value this editor-author partnership more and more. Charlotte, too, believed in the book even when it was gestating. She read and re-read the manuscript, made shrewd suggestions, and relieved me of mundane, time-consuming tasks like proof reading, compiling the bibliography and checking references – behind-the-scenes work which she does so faithfully and efficiently.

I would have loved to be able to thank personally each member of the Roberts Road community for the rich start in life which they gave me. Alas, this has not been possible. What I have been able to do is to make contact with Arthur and Doreen Drowley again and I thank them for inspiring David and me to offer for the full-time ministry.

My final thanks go to Elaine, the secretary who once worked with us and who unwittingly triggered off so much of the pain I describe in this book. When the manuscript was finished, I wrote to ask her permission to make public our once-strained relationship and her reply was heart-warming: 'You have more than my permission or goodwill. If there can be one word spoken, one song sung, one word written to bring wholeness to our broken world then may God richly be served and praised.'

This forgiving, reconciling letter, full of undeserved love, humbled me – and amazed me. Elaine records that her lasting memories of her year with us are: 'Your wonderful, smiling, intelligent son and daughter and your laughter in the house.'

She sent me a photograph of herself and her husband and her lovely children. They now smile at me from my study wall.

Reaching Out

I feel your pain
and long to touch the hurt
and make it melt away.
Yes, I know
that I can't really see
the breadth
and depth
of this dark valley you're in.
I can't truly know
just how sharp the knife is
in your soul –
for it is you in its path,
not me.
But I have known other valleys,
and in my heart
still bear knife-wound scars.
Even so,
I would walk your road
and take your pain
if I could.
I cannot.
And yet, perhaps
in some way
I can be a hand to hold
in the darkness;
in some way, try to blunt
the sharpness of pain.
But if not –
it may help a little
just to know I care.

(Christine Rigden)

Chapter 1

Catching Compassion

The shiny black Daimler seemed to slip slowly and silently between number 24 Roberts Road, where I lived, and the red-brick church hall immediately opposite. I followed its progress as it inched its way past Webber's quaint and poky grocery shop which graced the corner of Roberts Road and Franklin Street, past Bolt's the butchers which stood at the junction of Roberts Road and Temple Road and past the undistinguished dairy where Mrs Hart did most of her shopping. Mrs Hart, with her husband and small son Barry, lived almost opposite the dairy. And it was outside their tiny terraced house – number 5 – that the Daimler stopped on the dot of 2 p.m.

When the car purred past number 24 no one in the street below would have known that the bedroom of our house was being used as a lookout. Heavy lace curtains concealed my mother and me. Even so, since my mother lifted the curtains away from the window ever so slightly, we had a grandstand view of the limousine, the man-in-black driving it, and his companion who was also dressed in black.

Full of four-year-old curiosity I crept under the curtain, pressed my nose against the window-pane and waited.

No one in Roberts Road owned a car, so when one was parked in the road it attracted a flurry of interest. This one was no exception. Within seconds, it seemed, a small knot of women had congregated outside the church hall and were now standing near the scarlet telephone box staring at the Harts' house like newspaper reporters scenting a scoop.

My mother showed no sign of leaving her post, so I lingered beside her, equally eager to discover what would happen next. Several minutes ticked by before she pulled me away from the window, dropped the curtain, and contented herself with peeping through one of the larger holes formed by the lace pattern. I copied her. And again we saw the shiny black Daimler drive past our house. But this time it was being driven up the steep hill towards Radford Road and this time, behind the men-in-black sat a polished box which was overlaid with sprays of flowers of every size, shape, texture and colour – blues, yellows, whites, crimsons, pinks, purples, reds. I had never seen so many flowers before. And I had never seen a beautiful box like that before, so naturally I demanded to know what it was.

While the gaggle of housewives took a long last look at the cortège, my mother explained that Barry Hart had gone to be with Jesus.

I do not remember how my four-year-old mind wove together the multi-coloured strands of that day: the solemn black strands of the funeral proceedings, the mute shades of the child-size coffin, the brightly-coloured hues of the wreaths and floral tributes, the colourless strands of the sudden silence which seemed to have enshrouded our normally busy and happy street. Nor do I remember how I coped with the fact that so much strange sorrow should surround such a potentially joyful occasion as a visit to Jesus, the friend we had come to love in Sunday School. What I do remember is the effect this tragic and sudden death had on my mother and the Roberts Road community.

For the rest of the day my mother withdrew into herself and seemed sad. It was the way she used to behave some Sunday afternoons when I would be sitting at the kitchen table thumbing through the old photographs which were kept in a St Bruno tobacco tin in the sideboard cupboard. The routine was always the same. I would examine each picture in turn, ask 'Who's that?' and listen while one of my parents patiently retold the tale behind the picture which I had heard so often before.

One photograph in particular fascinated me. It was of a tiny grass mound which my parents called a grave.

'What's that?' I would ask.

'That's where Maurice is now,' my father would reply.

'Who's Maurice?' I would persist.

'Maurice would have been your brother but he died before you were born.'

'Why did he die?'

'Because he was born a "blue baby".'

This explanation always silenced my insensitive interrogation and I would turn to the next photograph, which was equally brown with age and curled up at the corners through much handling. Young though I was, I understood the term 'blue baby' because that was the term the grown-ups in Roberts Road used to describe Barry Hart. It was an accurate description. Sometimes I would meet him in the dairy with his mother, and would notice that his lips and face and fingertips were tinged with an inky blue – a sharp contrast to the rosy cheeks with which my own healthy face usually glowed.

With the wisdom of adulthood I can now understand why sadness descended on my mother like a snow cloud that day . . . Barry and Maurice must have been a similar age when they died: just three years old. No wonder I overheard my mother admit to the greengrocer when he called later that afternoon: 'My heart really went out to them.' For her, many painful memories had been buried alive. The sight of another child's funeral brought them surging to the surface once more.

But my mother was not the only person in Roberts Road to be affected by Barry's death. It made an impact on the entire Roberts Road community.

Like Coronation Street, two rows of monotonous red-brick terraced houses provided homes for the residents of Roberts Road. The proximity of one house to the next ensured that no one could keep secrets from the neighbourhood even if they tried. The disadvantage of this was that even private pain soon became public property. The advantage was that problems were shared. People cared. It was care and concern which was being expressed by the group of women outside the street's only telephone kiosk. Everyone understood that this was their way of communicating: 'If there's anything we can do let us know.'

Another advantage was that if one person was in pain the whole of Roberts Road seemed to respect that fact and behave accordingly. On this occasion a hush descended on the neighbourhood which was not unlike the gloom that accompanies fog in February. For several days after the funeral no children played in the street outside our house as they usually did. No ball bounced in the back yards which were the Roberts Road substitute for gardens. No youths whistled on their way home from work as they did on happier days. No one dared even to laugh or to turn up the volume on their radio. To do so would have seemed the height of insensitivity and disrespect. Mourners were mourners. When death visited one home in Roberts Road, it visited them all. When tragedy struck we were in it together. We belonged to one another.

No one had taught these people that the word compassion comes from two Latin words *pati* and *cum* which put together mean 'to suffer with'. No one had taught them that 'compassion asks us to go where it hurts, to enter into places of pain, to share in brokenness, fear, confusion, and anguish'. No one had taught them that 'compassion challenges us to cry out with those in misery, to mourn with those who are lonely, to weep with those in tears . . . to be weak with the weak, vulnerable with the vulnerable, and powerless with the powerless'. No one had taught them that 'compassion means full immersion in the condition of being human'.[1] Yet compassionate was what these people were. For them, compassion was instinctive: doing what comes naturally.

It was into this sensitive compassionate community that I was born. It was deeper into this caring community that I was drawn when war ravaged our historic city. And it was from this caring community that I discovered that concern for others is an essential part of being human. No one ever *taught* me that fact. In Roberts Road caring for others was not taught but caught. And I cottoned on to the concept at a very early age.

Mother's example

Though I failed to recognise it at the time, people's reactions to Barry's death made a big impact on my sensitive personality. When the Second World War disturbed the happy equilibrium of Roberts Road even more, my apprenticeship in compassion and caring took a new turn. As many people who lived through those turbulent years have observed, ties with family and friends were strengthened under the impetus of impending crises.

Our next-door neighbour in Roberts Road was an elderly lady called Mrs Langmead. She was overweight, riddled with rheumatism and hard of hearing. Her body aroused my child's curiosity because, as she hobbled from room to room in her home, her entire form seemed to creak. It was years later that I discovered that it was not her body but her corsets that made this curious sound. My brothers and their friends accused her of being bossy because she would spend hours standing on her doorstep watching them play in the street and if a ball bounced too near her windows or if the level of noise rose above her threshold of tolerance, she would wave her stick angrily and shout at them to go and play elsewhere.

But she was not always cantankerous. Occasionally she would be in gentler mood. On such occasions she would invite my mother and me into her home and I would perch on her black leather pouffe, feel the furry texture of the black velveteen cloth which covered her big round table and gaze at the black-lead hearth which formed the focus of her otherwise cheerless living room. That hearth was the home of an equally black kettle which always seemed to sing and sometimes spewed blobs of water on to the flames, turning them blue. Above the stove, on the mantelpiece, a pair of black and white china dogs with black china chains round their necks stared down at us. Between them stood an antique clock which marked every hour with a pretty chime and which delighted me so much that, when I heard its preparatory whirr, I would put my finger to my lips and say 'Shh!' to the adults who insisted on talking through the chime. When Laing (as I nicknamed her) invited us in on winter afternoons my cup of happiness would be full because then I would watch her reach for a long wax taper and light the gas lights which were the only form of lighting she would allow in this home cluttered with Victoriana.

When war broke out my mother worried about Laing. One clap of thunder was enough to worry the old lady out of her wits and send her into hiding in the coal cupboard under the stairs. How was she to cope with the constant wail of sirens and the heart-chilling scream of dive-bombers?

To quieten my mother's fears and to guarantee Laing's safety, we worked out a way of communicating through the cardboard-thin walls which separated her house from ours. As soon as the whine of the sirens built up to its stomach-churning crescendo, our entire family would wedge themselves into the cupboard under our stairs: the only place which was considered safe to protect us from the danger of falling debris. Likewise Laing would manoeuvre her stiff over-size body into *her* cupboard. When we were all in position we would knock on the wall and Laing would make three raps in response. Then we would rest assured that she was safe, and in number 24 we would remain huddled together in our hidey-hole until the 'all clear' was given. As soon as that welcome sound was heard one of us would go into number 26 to check that Laing was unharmed.

I loved to take upon myself the responsibility of caring for Laing in this way. Before the moan of the siren had died away I would rush into the cupboard under our stairs, push past the gas masks which hung on improvised hooks, press myself against the far wall where the gas meter ticked loudly and banging on the wall as loudly as I could, I would shout at the top of my voice: 'Laing! Laing! Can you hear me?'

One memorable day, when the customary warning pierced the peace of the neighbourhood, I leapt into the cupboard as usual, knocked on the wall with my right fist and though I knocked and knocked until my knuckles were red and sore, Laing did not reply. Clearly she had not heard, I would have to go and *tell* her the siren had gone.

By this time our family had acquired a Morrison shelter which had been erected in the front room – the best room which was only used at Christmas and on Sundays in peacetime but which had to double as a refuge during these troubled days. While my father and brothers crept into this shelter I darted towards the front door. Reading my mind, my mother chased after me but I was more nimble than she was and I reached the street first. As I ran out of the bottle-green door I was greeted by the terrifying scream of approaching aircraft. I sped to number 26 but, even as I ran, I could see aeroplanes almost brushing with their bellies the slates of the Roberts Road houses opposite our home. All the more reason for ignoring my mother's shouts and running in to make sure that Laing was safe.

I found Laing shuffling her bulky body towards her cupboard. She had been asleep in her rocking chair and had not heard me knocking but had been startled by the sudden scream of the engines.

'Go back home quickly,' she urged me, waving her stick in the direction of my home. 'Tell them Laing's all right.'

Something about the tone of her voice frightened me so much that I scuttled back to number 24 as quickly as I could.

My mother was outside our house leaning against the neatly-pointed red-brick wall, her face deathly white. And she was angry.

'Go inside at once,' she scolded in a voice I dared not defy. 'You nearly had your mummy killed.' And she dragged me into our house slamming the door behind her.

While she had been pursuing me a curtain of bullets had

been fired from one of the aeroplanes. A piece of shrapnel had missed her by a fraction of an inch, smashed the front-room window and fallen on the steel roof of the Morrison shelter where my father and brothers were huddled.

Whenever my mother told this story to relatives and neighbours, showing them the jagged piece of shrapnel to add spice to her story, I would blush with shame. It filled me with horror to discover that my recklessness had almost caused my mother's death. But it did nothing to dampen my desire to help others. By this time the seam of compassion seemed to have been deeply ingrained in my heart.

Father's example

That is hardly surprising since my father was just as compassionate as my mother. After he had read the newspaper and the Bible in the evening, we would often hear him say: 'I think I'll go and visit old Mrs Davey.' Or, 'I'm going over to see Mrs Jones. Shan't be long.' And he would go and while away his free time with one of these housebound old ladies. And we would accept that life for these women would become more bearable because my father had visited them.

If news reached us that someone had lost his job or had tried to commit suicide or had just come out of hospital or had lost a loved one, it was my father who would visit them. He was one of the world's wonderful carers. Though he had never read a book about compassion, he was so full of that Christ-like characteristic that instinctively he knew that what really counts in moments of pain and suffering is that someone is prepared to stay alongside us, not necessarily providing us with solutions but offering us the consolation and comfort which comes through a supporting presence.

This caring embraced children as well as adults. Indeed it was his concern for working-class children that pushed him into accepting the invitation to become first the lieutenant and then the captain of the 7th Exeter Boys' Brigade Company which met in the church hall opposite our home.

The houses in Roberts Road had no gardens. The pocket-handkerchief-size yards which backed on to the neighbouring streets were too small for the games of boisterous children. Sometimes we would play in the nearby park. But usually we played in the street. For such children organisations like the Boys' Brigade for boys and Brownies and Guides for girls fulfilled a very real need. They provided an outlet for our energy and creativity. And they were character-trainers.

My father threw himself into training the boys in his charge. He took them to camp in the summer and encouraged them to learn to play bugles and drums and cymbals in winter. The band flourished. He always tried to point away from himself as captain to the captain he served: Jesus. Because of the fine work he was doing he earned the respect and affection of many in the neighbourhood including the headmaster of the residential school for the severely deaf near our home.

In the 1940s this headmaster, Mr Kettlewell, approached my father to ask his co-operation in an experiment he was wanting to make. All the children in his school had been born deaf. Since they had little useful residual hearing they had been unable to pick up speech from their parents as hearing children do. One of the chief tasks the teachers in the school faced was to teach these children to speak in a way which would enable them to communicate with hearing people. He believed that one way to hasten the learning process was to encourage them to mix with hearing children. He asked my father if he would be prepared for a group of deaf boys to join the Boys' Brigade Company with this aim in mind. Father agreed.

When the deaf boys began to be integrated into the group, their love for my father became obvious. On Saturdays, when they came to Roberts Road to spend their pocket money in the post office or the newsagent's at the bottom of the road, they would pop in to see us because they knew that they would always find a welcome in our home.

'How d'you understand what they're saying?' I would ask my father.

The boys could pronounce vowels easily enough but most of their words lacked consonants. So when they called my father by his name they would call him '*i-er oo-oo*' instead of Mr Duguid (pronounced Do-good). And that confused me. Most of the time their voices had a nasal quality which I found as distracting and unpleasant as the flat intonation of their speech.

'You get used to it if you're patient and listen carefully,' my father would reply.

'And how d'you talk to them?' I persisted.

Then my father would teach me some of the rules: 'Make sure that the light falls on your face so that they can lip-read. Speak slowly but naturally and carefully and don't mind if they stare at you because they are listening with their eyes instead of their ears.' I would watch him put this theory into practice.

Sometimes even he failed to understand what was being communicated. In this event the boys would 'talk' to each other through sign language before deciding what to 'say' to my father on paper.

My early initiation

Children love to imitate their parents and I was no exception. So when girls from the deaf school joined the Brownie Pack I attended, I did my best to communicate with them by imitating my father. To my delight – and theirs – I found that if I spoke clearly I could make myself understood and if I listened carefully to the sounds they made and to the context of the sentences, I could usually decipher what they were saying. These girls became my trusted friends and it was one of the highlights of my young life when Mr Kettlewell invited me to go to the school on the hill to play with them.

Some Brownies also came from Dr Barnardo's Home. My mother explained to me that this meant that they had no parents or homes of their own so they all had to live together in one big house without a mother and a father. I

could think of nothing more terrible than being without a
mother or father or brothers. So when 'Brown Owl' asked
whether any of us could invite some of these children to
our homes for tea from time to time, I volunteered.

We were always cramped for space in our house. It
boasted only four rooms: two bedrooms upstairs and
two rooms downstairs. Each of these rooms was only
nine foot square. There were few creature comforts: no
bathroom, no hot running water and the toilet was outside
in the back yard. We had little money. Though my father
was a master-baker he earned very little and my mother
supplemented his income by taking a job as a waitress in a
café in the centre of town. Even then their joint salary left
nothing for buying luxuries. But once a month, on Sunday
afternoons, girls from the Dr Barnardo's Home would be
invited for tea and the front room would be filled with
people, fun and laughter. The little we had to offer was all
we could share. The war was still on and food was rationed,
but somehow there was always enough. We all loved it.
And the experience showed me that compassionate people
live a compassionate lifestyle. They refuse to grasp the
little they have but share it gladly with those who need it
most. Compassionate people continue to care even when
such caring costs. In counting the cost and paying it, true
joy is experienced. Though I did not appreciate it at the
time, I was learning a profound lesson about compassion.
Henri Nouwen puts it well:

> Compassion is not a bending toward the under-privileged
> from a privileged position; it is not a reaching out from
> on high to those who are less fortunate below; it is not
> a gesture of sympathy or pity for those who fail to make
> it in the upward pull. On the contrary, compassion
> means going directly to those people and places where
> suffering is most acute and building a home there.[2]

'Going directly to those people and places where suffering
is most acute and building a home there.' My parents had
done that. It was not that they had searched for suffering

and found it. Rather, they found tragedy on their doorstep – the tragedy of bereavement, deafness, homelessness and the helplessness of old age – and they did what they could to touch it with the love of God. Because they were poor, my parents could minister effectively to the poor. Because they had suffered deprivation themselves, they could touch the deprived also. Because their compassion was genuine, it communicated and drew fellow sufferers to itself. And because I was a part of them, I found myself caring from an early age without ever giving it the glamorous name-tag 'ministry'.

The community's example
But I am conscious that my background gave me, not only a vision of how to live compassionately, but the ability to feel compassion. Such an ability seems rare even in some Christian circles today. But in Roberts Road, if people felt an emotion they expressed it. When I was little I saw grown-ups cry quite frequently, particularly during the war years.

I had never seen Mrs Tolman cry until the spring of 1941. Mrs Tolman was a dumpy, cheerful lady who wore high heels and smelt of perfume during the week and who squeezed herself into Salvation Army uniform on Sundays. She had no children of her own but seemed fond of other people's and I loved her because in winter she wore a fox fur round her neck which I was encouraged to stroke. She was a skilled furrier and worked in a shop in Holloway Street. Most days on her way home from work she would wave to me and call 'coo-ee' or my pet name 'Joycee' in a high-pitched, cheery voice.

One morning in May 1941 I was sitting on our doorstep sharing a small patch of warm sun with Snowy, our white fluffy cat, when suddenly I heard the tell-tale sound of Mrs Tolman's high-heeled shoes tapping the pavement. She was hurrying towards her home, her head bowed low. And she was crying. I called out to her expecting the normal greeting. But there was no cheerful wave on this occasion. Instead the sight of me seemed to upset her even more. She let out a loud sob and hurried on without speaking.

Later that day I learned from my father the reason for her distress. In the blitz of the night before a landmine had dropped on Holloway Street, the road adjacent to Roberts Road, and Mrs Tolman had arrived at work that morning to find, not the customary parade of high-class fashionable shops of which their owners were so proud, but a pile of rubble and smouldering ruins. She had lost everything she possessed.

My father did not hide his distress. When the war started, he had volunteered as an air raid warden whose responsibility it was to patrol the warren of streets that backed on to Roberts Road, Franklin Street and Temple Road. Because there had been enemy activity the night before he had been up all night making sure that no chink of light escaped through the blackout which covered people's windows, and searching for leaking gas and hidden bombs. And because he was a baker he had had an early start that morning. Now he held his lined and weary face in his hands while the tears flowed. Like Jesus, he was unashamed to weep openly with those who wept.

I did not know then that, in expressing this anguish, he was giving me a glimpse of the compassion Jesus used to feel when he was faced with similar pain. But now I see certain parallels. Henri Nouwen describes Jesus' reaction to human suffering powerfully:

> There is a beautiful expression in the Gospels that appears only twelve times and is used exclusively of Jesus or his Father. That expression is 'to be moved with compassion'. The Greek verb *splangchnizomai* reveals to us the deep and powerful meaning of this expression. The *splangchna* are the entrails of the body or as we might say today, the guts. They are the place where our most intimate and intense emotions are located . . . When Jesus was moved to compassion, the source of all life trembled, the ground of all love burst open, and the abyss of God's immense,

inexhaustible, and unfathomable tenderness revealed itself . . .

When Jesus saw the crowd harassed and dejected like sheep without a shepherd, he felt with them in the center of his being (Mt 9:36). When he saw the blind, the paralysed, and the deaf being brought to him from all directions, he trembled from within and experienced their pains in his own heart (Mt 14:14). When he noticed that the thousands who had followed him for days were tired and hungry, he said, I am moved with compassion (Mk 8:2). And so it was with the two blind men who called after him (Mt 9:27), the leper who fell to his knees in front of him (Mk 1:41), and the widow of Nain who was burying her only son (Lk 7:13). They moved him, they made him feel with all his intimate sensibilities the depth of their sorrow. He became lost with the lost, hungry with the hungry, and sick with the sick. In him, all suffering was sensed with a perfect sensitivity.[3]

Jesus was full of compassion for people. When people suffered, he suffered with them. Jesus reacted to pain in this way because God reacts to human suffering in this way. Jesus' solidarity with our suffering reveals his Father's identification with the depth of our need. This, as Henri Nouwen reminds us, is wonderful news: 'The truly good news is that God is not a distant God, a God to be feared and avoided, a God of revenge, but a God who is moved by our pains and participates in the fullness of the human struggle.'[4]

In their own way, and in so far as they were able, my parents were like that too. They incarnated the love of Christ to the chimney sweep and the window cleaner, the pilot and the insurance agent, the grocer and the butcher, the greengrocer, the newsagent and the coalman, the policeman, the nurse and the housewives who lived, cheek by jowl, alongside them in Roberts Road. They were not icon saints. They were ordinary working-class people struggling to make a living and, at the same time, trying to live a Christ-like life in the only home they could afford: a rented two up, two down, back-to-back terraced house in a run-down area of Exeter.

Even so they were effective for God in touching the lives of ordinary people. 'Wonderful people,' recalls one of the boys in the Boys' Brigade who is now in his sixties. If anyone had told them that they were reflecting the love of God to the people in our street or that they had a ministry of helping, they would have made light of such labels. Yet this was what they were doing. And in doing it they were making their own response to the great commission of Christ.

In this last and great commission Jesus commands his followers to love as he loved, to care as he cared, to hurt when others hurt. Such love, he said, is the hallmark of the Christian. And such love is one of the basic requirements of anyone who would seek to stretch out a helping hand to others in the middle of life's crises.

It was such compassion that prompted Jesus to heal hurting people. He healed people for one reason only – not to impress them, nor to prove his divinity, but because their pain created such an ache within his own heart that he suffered with them. Because hurting humanity called from him this depth of concern for the sufferer, he stretched out the helping hand which rescued, restored and, in many cases, eventually healed. He was the personification of compassion.

Jesus received this ability to tune in to human anguish and identify with people's pain from his Father, and in turn passed it on to his disciples. He passed it on to Paul who, we read, was filled with tender compassion for the converts in Philippi (Phil. 1:8).

It is a quality all would-be carers and listeners need. For where such Christ-like compassion is absent, stretching out to others sometimes has a hollow ring about it. At best such help can come across as dutiful, brash or insensitive. At worst it can even seem unkind or cruel.

But compassion not duty, kindness not brashness pushed

my parents and the Roberts Road community into supporting others. Because these, my relatives and neighbours,
were well schooled in the art of expressing such care,
this fruit of God's Spirit seeded itself in the fertile soil
of my life. I neither asked for it nor expected it. It came.
And it came early. On that bright May morning when I
encountered Mrs Tolman silenced by the shock of the
atrocities she had witnessed at work, the instinct of my
young heart was to run to her to comfort her, just as my
instinct was to do all in my power to protect the old lady,
Laing, from impending danger.

But the desire to comfort and protect are but small and
immature beginnings – signs that the seeds of compassion
have been sown but not indications that the mature fruit
has yet ripened. I was to discover that if these seeds were
to germinate and grow, they would require rain as well
as sunshine. I was also to discover that the necessary rain
clouds were gathering fast.

Chapter 2

Coping with Crises

The first hint of trouble came with the end of the war. That is not to say that our family did not share in the jubilation and celebration of V Day. We did. The Roberts Road street parties were held outside our front door. Each house in the road sported its own Union Jack. Bunting was draped zig-zag fashion across the road, someone's piano was heaved on to the pavement outside our house and the trestle tables borrowed from the church hall were laden with sandwiches, iced cakes, jellies, trifles and blancmanges. The memory of the reds and oranges, the yellows and greens of the jellies and the pinks and the sweet sickly smell of the blancmanges rises before my eyes still whenever I hear the words 'street parties'.

More treats were in store. The first came in the form of a rumour which was passed round among the children: 'Mr Staddon's making ice-cream again.' Mr Staddon owned the dairy in Holloway Street and we were told that if we took a teacup to his shop he would fill it with freshly made ice-cream. 'Can I go? Can I go?' we all clamoured and since there was no road to cross between Roberts Road and Holloway Street, we were allowed to troop in convoy to Staddon's Dairy. And our mouths would water as we watched Mr Staddon dip his steel scoop into a jug of hot water, scrape a big blob of cream-coloured ice-cream out of a round tub, and plop it into the cups which we held so eagerly up to his counter.

Fresh bananas also appeared for the first time. My mother bought some one day from Mr Major, the greengrocer who used to call at our home. He came by motor bike and we would know when he had arrived because he was the proud possessor of a rubber horn which he used to honk when he arrived at a customer's front door. When he came to our house my mother would reach for the brown leather purse she kept in the sideboard drawer and I would rush out to examine the side-car which was always laden with potatoes and cabbages, carrots and onions, apples and oranges, pears and plums, according to the season.

The first time I saw bunches of yellow crescent-shaped fruit perched on top of the side-car, I voiced my curiosity: 'What's that?' 'Try one,' invited Mr Major and placed a big ripe banana in my hands. 'How d'you eat it?' I asked. Mr Major and my mother laughed as they showed me how to unzip the skin before biting into the creamy flesh inside.

I was seven years old when I was bombarded with all these childhood delights. I was also seven when I realised that, though the war was over, its shadow had not left us completely. The problem was that, though the international crisis seemed to have passed, young men were still being conscripted into the armed forces. And that meant that my eldest brother Ray would soon have to leave home.

Ray was fourteen years old when he left school. He joined the Post Office and became a Telegraph boy. When call-up time drew near Ray made up his mind that, rather than allow others to determine the future for him, he would decide for himself whether he should join the army, the navy or the air-force. At the age of seventeen, therefore, he joined the Royal Navy as a volunteer.

Ray was ten years older than me – more like a favourite uncle than a brother. It was Ray who helped me polish my Brownie badge on Tuesday evenings. It was Ray who spoilt me by giving me extra pocket money. And it was Ray who protected me from the merciless teasing of my other brother, John.

When Ray started to prepare for his departure by

showing me the kitbag marked with his initials R.E.D. (for Raymond Ernest Duguid), the sense of adventure filling him spilt over on to me. And when he dressed up in his naval uniform he became my hero.

But while the anticipated adventure energised Ray and while pride of my big brother inflated me, gloom descended on my mother.

We were a close-knit family living in a close-knit community. When someone left that community, they left a hole which nothing and no one could fill. And when that 'someone' was your eldest son, a mother's grief left her desolate and empty.

Bereavement and depression

My mother would have been unfamiliar with clichés like 'the empty nest syndrome' or 'grief work'. But as the train spluttered out of St David's station carrying away her kitbag-carrying son and leaving her, a forlorn figure, waving a tearful farewell to the fast-disappearing form of this uniformed young lad, a deep and terrible sadness swept over her which left her suffering an emptiness and inner turmoil that hung over her for months.

Such overwhelming time-consuming sadness is normal. Many mothers (and fathers) experience similar crippling emotions when their offspring first leave home to try life their own way. Indeed part of the high cost of loving is to suffer the searing pain which seems to pierce our heart when one we love is torn away for any reason. But coupled with the terrifying sense of loss she experienced was a paralysing sense of anxiety. The terrors of war with the atrocities suffered by the British troops were fresh in everyone's memory. They flooded into my mother's mind uninvited and lodged there. Anxiety, that inner, nagging sense of apprehension, uneasiness and dread which we all experience from time to time, seemed to hold my mother in such a vice-like grip that she lost much of her sparkle and spontaneity. At times she would be weepy and listless. Life lost much of its interest for her.

One way of coping with the sense of severance such

separation brings is to keep in contact with the loved one. At first maintaining physical contact with my brother was not easy. Ray was stationed in Plymouth, some fifty miles from Exeter and most weekends his exeat permitted him to travel only twenty miles. My mother refused to be daunted by such obstacles and weekends would find us boarding the steam train at St David's station, chugging to Newton Abbot, the half-way point between Exeter and Plymouth, and making the long, tiring journey back home again.

Picnicking in a park with Ray in this way, seeing for herself that someone else could feed her son and being reassured by him that he could survive life outside the cloisters of Roberts Road seemed to revive her spirits. At least while the visit lasted. But during the journey home the tears would flow again and the black cloud of depression would descend.

Was this separation from Ray pressing on the unhealed pain of two previous severances: from Maurice, the three-year-old blue baby who died and from the loss she suffered when an earlier baby had been stillborn? I was too young to ask such questions so I shall never know the answers. What I do now know is that it often happens that there is a distinct correlation between the way a person copes with the loss of a significant person in the present with the way that person has coped with similar such separations in the past. Clearly my mother had suffered deeply when her two tiny children had died. In a similar way she was suffering now and she needed help.

Help came in a whole variety of ways. It came casually from people like Mrs Broom at number 33, Mrs Burgess at number 46 and Mrs Bellamy at number 28 Roberts Road. When they walked past our house on the way to Webber's corner shop they would see my mother vigorously polishing the brass doorstep or the matching door knobs and they would stop and enquire: 'How's that big boy of yours?' And my mother would pass on the latest snippets of news knowing that someone was genuinely interested.

None of these neighbours would have dreamed that this

question was a ministry to my mother. The question was prompted by neighbourliness; the concern the Roberts Road community still had for one of its own. Yet this question, lovingly, frequently and sensitively asked, was more therapeutic for my mother than a whole series of counselling sessions would have been. It kept the memory of her son alive during that strange stage of separation when, to one's horror, one can no longer recall what the loved one looks like. It gave her permission to admit that she was hurting because she was missing Ray; that sometimes just to see some of his possessions lying around in his bedroom caused a pang of pain to shoot right through her. And, of course, it brought her into contact with people who cared so that gradually she emerged from the darkness, came to terms with her son's absence and re-negotiated her life on a new set of terms: a life which no longer revolved around Ray.

Other people came alongside my mother in a costly, caring way as she stood at this crossroads of her life. One outstanding carer was my father's sister, Aunt Rene. Aunt Rene seemed to have that God-given knack of arriving just when my mother was reaching her lowest ebb. And Aunt Rene would listen to news of Ray with real interest, look at photographs of him, and somehow communicate to my mother that she understood how hard it must be to have one's child move out of one's immediate orbit. That is not to say Aunt Rene encouraged my mother to wallow in self-pity. On the contrary, she helped her to avoid that pitfall simply by accepting my mother as she was, trying to see life through my mother's eyes and giving her the support she needed as she learned to cope with this hole in our home. Time after time Aunt Rene succeeded in reducing the level of my mother's anxiety and helping her to regain hope and a new perspective on life simply through the genuineness of her love.

This aunt of mine had never trained in counselling. But God had gifted her with one of those 'inherently helpful'[1] personalities which express with loving ease both warmth and sensitivity, understanding and concern, confidence and appropriate optimism. Because she loved my mother as Jesus loves – aching inwardly when she saw how my mother ached – a visit from Aunt Rene was always welcome.

When I took my place in this family circle and listened to this aunt and my mother talk in the intimate way two women often do, I had no idea that I was being taught some of the ground rules of good listening. But now I realise that 24 Roberts Road was one school in which I served my apprenticeship as a listener and carer; that my father's sister was my teacher. For several research studies have shown that effective listening involves not simply theory or techniques, but a personality which is characterised by empathy, warmth and genuineness.

Dr Gary Collins, a professor of psychology and author of several books on counselling, defines 'empathy' by tracing the word back to its German root *einfühlung*, which means 'feeling into', or 'feeling with'. Empathy asks: 'Why is this person so upset?' 'How does she view what is happening?' 'If I were in her shoes, how might I feel?' In other words, empathy seeks to view life through the troubled person's eyes, to experience another person's world as though it were our own while keeping the words *as though* in the forefront of our mind. It involves walking in the other person's moccasins until you feel where they rub. Empathy attempts to show the person in pain that their feelings are both understood and accepted.

Warmth, according to Gary Collins, is synonymous with caring. It is a non-smothering, non-possessive concern for someone which is communicated by a friendly facial expression, a gentle tone of voice, gestures and appropriate touch, posture and eye contact which communicate the clear message: 'I care about you and your well-being.'

And 'genuineness', as described by Dr Collins, is the art of being real. The genuine person is an authentic person. He has no need to pretend or to project a false superiority. Genuineness is authenticity which refuses to contemplate the playing of a superior role. It is openness without phoniness. It is sincerity, consistency and it is full of respect for others.[2]

Aunt Rene embodied each of these qualities in her own sweet and simple way and, though I did not recognise it at the time, as I watched and heard her stay alongside my troubled mother the seeds of compassion which had already been sown in me were being watered by the current crisis.

Physical pain

It has been said that helping people in pain is a skill which, like any other skills, improves with practice. Though this particular problem worked its way out of our family, another storm was brewing which was to hit our household with even greater force and give me the practice I still needed. This crisis erupted four years later – soon after I had thrilled everyone in Roberts Road by passing the Eleven Plus examination.

When Roberts Road children sat the Eleven Plus, everyone in the street became emotionally involved. It was as though the future of the entire community was at stake. It was rare for a Roberts Road child to go to grammar school but when my turn came round to sit the dreaded exam, I was tipped to make the grade. So when it was announced that I had gained a place at Bishop Blackall Grammar School the whole street seemed to celebrate what they considered to be an outstanding achievement. My godfather entered into the joy too by buying me a brand new green Raleigh bicycle, partly as a reward and partly as a means of travelling to this new school which was on the other side of the town.

But this early euphoria faded when my mother became ill. The illness manifested itself in three ways: with frequent severe attacks of asthma which left her gasping for breath, with a cough which racked her body with pain and left her weak and with a mysterious symptom we learned to call 'a turn'. At first it was feared that these turns were epileptic fits. But they were not. Neither were they strokes, though sometimes she gave the appearance of a person suffering a stroke.

When she was sickening for 'a turn', my mother would be overcome with dizziness, her speech would become slurred and eventually she would lose consciousness – sometimes for several minutes, often for several hours and occasionally for more than a day. Her condition distressed everyone who knew her yet it drew from her all the pluck which made her the determined person so many people admired.

But it meant that often my father and I would have to do everything for her. If she had had a turn during the evening we would have to carry her to bed, undress her, slip her nightdress over her and wash her. Carrying her to bed was no easy task because our staircase was narrow – the width of only one person – and there was a sharp bend towards the top which meant that my father would have to walk ahead of me, clutching the top half of my mother's body and I would follow, holding on to her legs. While we heaved her in this way we were always frightened lest we should hurt her, and well aware that in her unconscious state she would not have been able to tell us that we were inflicting hurt. My mother was stubborn too, and even when she felt a turn coming on she refused to give in to it. Consequently, sometimes she would fall and cut, burn or bruise herself and we would administer first aid.

Shortly after I entered the grammar school my mother was bedridden for several weeks. Money, as always, was in short supply so a home-help was out of the question. Before I left for school in the morning I would polish the lino in the living room and the two bedrooms, dust the skirting boards, brush the stair carpet and try to bring a shine to the dressing tables, the sideboard and the dining room table. Though she was ill, my mother was still house-proud and would give me careful instructions and surveillance from her bed.

My father too took up certain household chores. He would polish the brass doorstep every day until we could see our reflection in it as clearly as in the mirror. He would clean the oven after cooking the lunch on Sundays. And he would tackle the washing on Mondays. We had no washing machine. Sheets and pillow-cases were sent to the laundry. Smaller items including towels and tea-towels were boiled up in a galvanised bath on the gas cooker. After the clothes had been boiled and pounded with a wooden stick the bath was lifted from the cooker and carried to the sink. There the clothes were drained and rinsed by hand in cold water before being run individually through the mangle in the back yard.

These chores, which my mother usually did with skill and speed before going off to work, my father and I now master-minded with difficulty. But our efforts were rewarded when, seeing that we could cope with the practicalities, she relaxed and her health began to improve. And this taught me a salutary lesson. Sometimes compassion must be expressed practically rather than verbally. There are times when there are no words. And there are times when actions speak louder than words.

What surprised me was that, though it hurt to see my mother crippled by so much physical pain, and though it was tiring to nurse her *and* clean the house, spend the day at school, come home to homework *and* more nursing of my mother, yet the overwhelming emotion was of joy which used to rise inside me like a mysterious well-spring as I polished or pedalled up the hill to school.

Henri Nouwen offers an explanation for this inner fountain of well-being:

> Wherever we see real service we also see joy, because in the midst of service a divine presence becomes visible and a gift is offered. Therefore those who serve as followers of Jesus discover that they are receiving more than they are giving. Just as a mother does not need to be rewarded for the attention she pays to her child, because her child is her joy, so those who serve their neighbour will find their reward in the people whom they serve.[3]

At the early age of eleven I was given the privilege of proving the truth of this observation. I have gone on proving it. There have been times when my body should have been weary with over-exertion and my emotions wrung out with the strain of performing practical tasks for people in pain, but instead it is as though this energising sense of well-being which seems to radiate from God himself, has flooded every part of me: body, mind and spirit. Looking back I think I was relieved to be able to take the pressure off my parents by giving practical help. I was too young to give them the emotional support they both needed. In due course, others did that. Meanwhile I was learning that sometimes before a person can be brought into emotional, spiritual or physical healing, someone needs to see life through the sick person's eyes and to take immediate and practical action.

Jesus did this so often. That may be one reason why he fed the five thousand. That may be the reason why having healed Jairus's daughter, he reminds her parents that having abstained from food for so long she will be hungry. And it might explain why, on the night before he died, in the absence of the customary slave Jesus himself assumed this role, reached for a bowl and a towel and washed his disciples' dirty sweaty feet. This humble practical gesture demonstrated in an unforgettable way that 'our God is a servant God'.[4] His compassion reveals itself in servanthood – self-emptying. When he calls us to incarnate his compassion and care, he invites us to imitate his servanthood. To be carers.

Every follower of Christ is called to care in this costly way. The call came early to me. I responded by caring practically and trying to be kind and gentle, but I had not yet learned the art of enabling my mother to unburden her frustrations, fear and helplessness.

Our family doctor did what he could. He would spend hours with my mother giving her professional help and endless support. And the vicar of our church helped too. He would cycle from his vicarage to our home, sit with my mother, talk to her and pray with her. But I noticed that my mother never really relaxed with either of these men. A secret smoker, she would stub out her cigarette if she suspected a knock on the door heralded a visit from either of them. And frequently I sensed that she was telling them what she felt they wanted to hear rather than the way she really felt. So although these visits were appreciated by all of us, their usefulness was limited in value.

But, as often happens, a variety of helpers each contributed their unique expression of concern: Aunt Rene again, Mrs Furseman who was a waitress in the same café as my mother, Mrs Tolman who had suffered so intolerably in the war years, Mrs Ford, a retired neighbour who had plenty of that precious commodity, time and plenty of that fruit of the Spirit, patience, who visited regularly, listened and sat with my mother for whole long afternoons while my father and I were out.

These ordinary unqualified women gave my mother what she needed: understanding and the assurance that they would not abandon her but rather would stand by her in her need. This solidarity with her suffering was self-giving which could never be rewarded but which was of inestimable value.

Some recent research suggests that times have not changed. It has shown the value of relatives, neighbours and friends as well as professional counsellors. The role of the professional is obvious. It is vital. But friends and relatives play a key part also. They live close by, are readily available, and often seem easier to talk to than someone who wears the label, 'doctor', 'clergyman', 'counsellor', or 'psychotherapist'.

Encouragingly, research has also revealed that in certain circumstances such friends and neighbours can be as competent as professional counsellors. Several reasons have been offered by way of explanation. One is that a relative or friend knows the person better and can therefore understand the problem better. Another is that the non-professional can often offer more time. And of course friends and neighbours know the person's family, their home environment and their work situation, which is a great advantage in gleaning an accurate assessment of the problem. They use the same dialect, accent or colloquialisms as the person in need so they can chat informally, be natural and lace their help with friendly humour. Perhaps the chief advantage is that helping *this* person emerge from his crisis is the friend's top priority. He is not faced with the daunting realisation that a queue of people are clamouring for his care, so the person in pain never feels like a mere name among a list of clients or patients but knows he is the subject of a sensitive person's love, care and commitment. Thousands of people are saved from emotional drowning by non-professionals. My mother was one of them.

Even so her physical problems persisted and she needed specialised help: from the doctor, the neurologist and, after she had been hospitalised, the occupational therapist. These skilled people turned every possible stone to try to unearth the reason for her 'turns'. No satisfactory diagnosis was found. At times there would be considerable and encouraging signs of improvement. But always, eventually, she would lapse back into another phase of ill health which frequently triggered off discouragement and sometimes depression.

When I left home to go to university my father felt the full brunt of the responsibility. It was a strain he bore gladly and sacrificially – one expression of his love for his wife. Nevertheless it left him tired, worried and drained. So during my vacations I tried to give whatever help I could to relieve him.

Burnout
During my first summer vacation from Southampton University I nursed my mother, tried to keep the house-cleaning up to her high standard, took on a full-time job at British Home Stores to supplement my dwindling grant *and*, most evenings, would try to tackle the academic work I had brought home with me. The result was that by the end of the vacation I was suffering from burnout.

In defining burnout, John Sanford says it is 'a word we

use when a person has become exhausted with his or her profession or major life activity'. It is 'a chronic tiredness of the sort that is not repaired by sleep or ordinary rest and only temporarily alleviated by vacations.'[5]

It had never occurred to me that burnout could be caused by pouring oneself out for another while trying to keep up with a hectic schedule. But this was what had happened to me. The collapse came before the new university term. It happened in the home of a doctor.

The reason why I was in this doctor's home was that I had become Secretary of the Christian Union at Southampton University and it was a tradition that the committee spent a weekend together at the end of the summer vacation before going on to the annual Christian Union pre-term conference. Dr and Mrs Murray Webb-Peploe, who were advisers to the Christian Union, hosted this residential committee meeting in their spacious home, Woodley, London Road, Lymington, Hampshire.

This was my first visit to their home. Before term started I received the following travelling instructions from someone who had been there before: 'You'll be travelling into Lymington on the Southampton Road. Before you reach the town, get off the bus, walk down the road for fifty yards and on your right you'll find a pair of green gates with the name-plate Woodley on them. Walk through these. And you'll find yourself in Paradise: a little bit of heaven on earth.'

I don't know if we shall be overwhelmed by heaven when we arrive there, but my first impressions of this 'little piece of heaven on earth' certainly overwhelmed me. There were no front gardens in Roberts Road. Passers-by would have been able to look straight into the front-room window if there had been no lace curtains to provide a modicum of privacy. But having found the gates of Woodley my feet scrunched up a gravel path, which led first to the cluttered garage and then snaked around the front of the huge Edwardian house separating it from its tree-secluded lawn. While the door bell clanged and I waited for someone to open the big green door, I stared incredulously at the size of the lawn, drank in the beauty of the copper beech trees which gave the garden its shade and gazed at the fruit-laden trees in the orchard. If the garden was like this, I wondered, what was I going to find inside the house.

Once inside everything seemed equally unfamiliar: the giant grandfather clock in the spacious hall which ticked its own story for visitors, the huge oak-framed family portraits in the dining room, the bulging bookcases on the landings, the enormous pine dresser complete with blue and brown Denby pottery in the kitchen and the black lacquered Chinese cabinets which seemed to fill and dominate the drawing room. While Mrs Webb-Peploe poured tea from a silver teapot I studied the Chinese scenes painted in gold on these fascinating pieces of furniture. And I retreated into my shy shell for safety.

But though the house and garden were overwhelming, our host and hostess were quite the opposite. Dr Webb-Peploe was jovial, welcoming and relaxed. He seemed to relish the thought of hosting a houseful of students for a whole weekend. He entertained us with tales and jokes throughout tea and dinner. Mrs Webb-Peploe was quieter but nonetheless welcoming. This petite lady, with her gentle aristocratic features, was dressed in a grey pleated skirt and simple white blouse. Her soft silver hair was persuaded into a pleat at the back of her head, but wavy wisps would sometimes escape from the coil and fall attractively on to her face. She beamed her shy welcome on everyone as they arrived. In her smile there was tenderness and love, and in the twinkle of her eyes I could see that she too looked forward to this weekend with child-like excitement and great anticipation, not knowing *what* God was going to do, yet sensing that something significant was about to happen. I was enchanted by her lilting continental accent. I was enchanted by her serenity. And in particular I was enchanted by the way she talked about God. It was as though her friendship with him was intimate.

On Friday evening the Webb-Peploes left us to our first committee meeting, and after the three-month vacation

we enjoyed the reunion. We were full of zeal, enthusiasm
and vision for the work God wanted to do through us
in the university that year. At least the others were.
But their energy and verve was highlighting just how
exhausted I felt.

By mid-Saturday morning I began to run a temperature.
Instead of tramping in the New Forest with the others on
Saturday afternoon I retreated to bed. Dr Webb-Peploe
summed up the situation and prescribed prolonged rest.
So I missed the remainder of the committee meetings and
the pre-term conference and spent the time instead with
the Webb-Peploes.

In my safe home environment of Roberts Road I
was a confident, outgoing person. But outside of this
working-class environment I frequently felt completely
out of my depth and insecure. I had learned few social
graces and masked my insecurity and uncertainty with
a layer of shyness which it was difficult for anyone to
penetrate. The Webb-Peploes never tried to untie this
mask. Instead they accepted the shy, insecure, silent me
just as I was. Without demanding to know why a young
and otherwise healthy student should collapse at the end
of a three-month so-called vacation, they simply showed
me that they cared and cared deeply.

This was Christian caring with a curious twist; a whole
new pattern of servanthood for me. I was a complete
stranger and yet they were taking me in. There would
never be any way in which I could repay them. Yet they
showered me with kindness, tenderness and understanding
love. Sensitive and skilled in helping others as they were,
they must have realised that there would have been little
mileage in encouraging me to talk about the pressures that
had caused me to collapse. Inarticulate as I was, I would
not have been able to find words to express my feelings to
anyone, least of all to strangers in such an overwhelmingly
new environment. Nevertheless it was in their home that
the coil of tension in me slowly unwound and I relaxed
sufficiently to receive the spiritual healing God gave me
through them.

Not that healing was talked about. To my knowledge the word was not even mentioned. They did not even offer to pray with me and I would have been terrified if they had. What they gave me was richer and deeper, more sacrificial to them and meaningful to me than mere words. They simply provided a healing environment where I could 'just be', soaked me in prayer without threatening my equilibrium by telling me that this was what they were doing, and because of the person she was rather than anything she ever said, Mrs Webb-Peploe in particular took me by the hand, as it were, and led me to the source of healing and refreshment, Jesus himself. The result was that I received for myself the riches of God from God.

I am not saying that she talked to me about God nor that through her I turned to Christ for the first time. I had known about God as a tiny child and committed my life to him when I was in the sixth form at school. No. What I am saying is that, though I knew many people who talked about God, in Mrs Webb-Peploe I was meeting a different quality of Christian. She was someone who showed me that she knew him. She even radiated his love wherever she was and no matter what she was doing.

That transparent love was there when, still wearing her dressing gown, she would bring me my breakfast tray, complete with starched linen tray cloth and a tiny vase of flowers alongside the cereal, the prunes, the toast, the butter and the honey. That love shone through as she stood by my bed, her long silver hair still flowing round her waist and her eyes twinkling even at that time of day. That love shone through the warmth and genuineness of her smile. And that love beamed at me too as she persuaded me to stay in bed for just as long as I liked.

When eventually I sauntered downstairs, I would frequently find her in the dining room, sitting at the table either deep in prayer or reading her Bible or a devotional commentary. And I would detect a fragrance filling the room. It was not unlike the scent of the lilies of the valley which fill my study today as I write. Yet it was not the fragrance of flowers but rather the heady perfume of the sense of the presence of the living God. It sometimes seemed as though, if I had stretched out my hand, I could have touched God for myself. From the serenity which shone from her face and the stillness pervading her whole body it was clear that Mrs Webb-Peploe had enjoyed a fresh encounter with her Saviour. Indeed whenever she spoke of 'de Lord' (she had difficulty pronouncing 'th') it was as though he was closer to her than the husband she adored and whose pet name for her was 'Treasure'.

One morning when I found her deep in prayer she showed me the book she was reading. It was a devotional commentary on the twenty-third psalm by F. B. Meyer. She invited me to dip into it. That day I sat in the sun in the stillness of the garden and read:

WE ALL NEED REST. There must be pauses and parentheses in all our lives. The hand cannot ever be plying its toils. The brain cannot always be elaborating trains of thought. The faculties and senses cannot always be on the strain. To work without rest is like over-winding a watch; the main spring snaps, and the machinery stands still. There must be a pause frequently interposed in life's busy rush wherein we may recuperate exhausted nerves and lowered vitality . . . Be at rest! . . . In all moments of peril and dread, softly murmur His name, Jesus! Jesus! and He will at once comfort thee by His presence and by His voice, which all the sheep know; and this shall be His assurance: 'My sheep shall never perish, neither shall any man pluck them out of My hand.'[6]

I read on eagerly. The author, with his words, was doing what the Webb-Peploes were doing with their lives – pointing me to the Wonderful Counsellor who could cope with my weariness, my fears for my mother, my anxieties for my father, my guilt at leaving behind such a sorry state of affairs for the fun-life of university, and my yearning for friendship. And the Wonderful Counsellor, the Shepherd, was leading me to the well-springs of life which alone can satisfy and refresh at the deepest level, those resources miraculously and mysteriously supplied by his life-giving Spirit. I did not know how to ask for these riches. I simply opened myself in the poverty of my need to the Psalmist's shepherd, sustainer and guide and in ways I shall never fully understand, he met me.

The only way I can describe the sustenance I enjoyed is to liken it to the way a bee crawls into the heart of a rose where it stays and sucks up nectar until it is satisfied. Because peace pervaded the house and garden, the orchard and the mini-farm which was Dr Webb-Peploe's pride and joy, I was able to let go of the pressures, breathe in that peace and discover for myself that still inner centre where this deep spiritual nurturing takes place.

This was God's gift to me through the Webb-Peploes. Their ministry was powerful because it was gentle, unthreatening, appropriate and because it was born out of the womb of listening prayer. They had no need to prise me apart to discover what was troubling me. As they tuned into God, they tuned into my anguish and committed themselves to be the channels through which he could love me and heal me. And he did. Some afternoons Mrs Webb-Peploe and I would sit in the garden shelling peas or just enjoying the spaciousness of God's creation in this oasis of a home. As we sat, she would tell me stories of the way she had seen God breaking into the lives of needy people so that the tormented found unexpected peace and joy again.

I did not know then what I have since discovered: that Mrs Webb-Peploe was a Dutch baroness; that she had suffered greatly while she and her husband were serving God in India; that during the war years, while she was in India, she had been troubled as she thought of her parents living through the horrors of war-stricken Holland. What I did know was that all the anecdotes she told me fanned the flicker of my faith into a flame and that, in listening to her, it was as though the hurts inside me were being touched and soothed and healed by God.

Was it because she was one of God's wounded healers

that she was so sensitive and wise? Or was it because she spent time tuning into the Father-heart of God each morning that she became his instrument of healing to me? I suspect it was a combination of both. Whatever it was, in this home where the silence of eternity was so eloquently interpreted by love, energy flowed back into me.

Were these two servants of God aware, as they stood at the bus stop and waved me off on the first day of the university term, that that short stay in their home had not only healed me of burnout but had made a profound and lasting impression on me? I doubt it. I was too shy to do more than send a polite thank you note. But when we married, my husband and I were to take this couple as our model. Like them, we wanted to be stretched by God, always available to people, yet without being bowed down by the tyranny of pressure. We wanted to provide a home for people where the healing touch of Jesus could be felt. We wanted to reach out to a suffering world with the Father's unpolluted love from the security of a personal relationship with Jesus. We coveted their ability to say the right thing to the right person at the right time; to be able to place the right book in the right person's hand at the right time. And though when I left them that day I would have been incapable of summarising just what it was that I had learned, I knew I wanted to be like them – always.

Chapter 3

A Rabbit-hole Christian

I would like to be able to record that, having been so beautifully helped by Dr and Mrs Webb-Peploe, and having learned from the Roberts Road community the value of listening to people in pain and the need to give practical help to those in need, my final year at Southampton University stands out in my mind as the year when my growth in compassion could be measured visibly. Alas! That is not my memory of it. On the contrary, as I recall it, I was struggling inwardly, asking myself a question which seemed to have no computer-manual type answer. *What is my priority in life: to evangelise or to care for people's practical and emotional needs?*

One reason for this struggle was that from the very early days of my time at Southampton I had become a rabbit-hole Christian, to borrow John Stott's colourful phrase.

The evangelist J. John describes the rabbit-hole student as one whose closest friends share his convictions, who looks around the lecture theatre to find another Christian with whom to sit and who, even in the refectory, will again look out for a cluster of Christians with whom to enjoy lunch; one who sighs contentedly from time to time: 'Isn't it wonderful that God has brought so many of us to the same university?'[1]

The Christians in the hall of residence where I lived when I first arrived at university were like that.

On my first evening in Highfield Hall, where I was to live for the next three years, before I had finished unpacking my belongings, and while feelings of apprehension and excitement familiar to most new students vied for attention inside me, these sincere people drew me into their circle. I was away from home for the first time. I was immature and insecure. I was sharing a room with a girl who could understand neither my need for God nor my desire to make a relationship with him. I needed friendship. When these Christians offered it I received it gratefully.

Before I left home the Captain of the Girl Guide Company I attended in Roberts Road warned me against becoming 'narrow'. The warning surprised me. I had no intention of letting go of any of my four first loves: singing, cycling, studying and sport. I joined the university choir, explored Hampshire by bike, worked hard, particularly at my theological studies which fascinated me, and played for the university netball team twice a week, eventually winning my college blue. Life was rich and full and good. At the same time I joined in the weekly round of meetings organised by the Christian Union: the fellowship meeting on Saturday night when a visiting speaker would give us biblical guidelines about Christian living; the Thursday lunch-time Bible studies when one of the nearby vicars or pastors would expound a Bible passage for us; the Tuesday night meeting for Christians in Highfield Hall when we would pray and study the Bible together; the early morning prayer meetings when we would give ourselves to intercession and the after-church coffee parties which a student arranged in his room.

John Powell once made the claim that who we are and what we become is largely affected by those who love us. Perhaps it was inevitable therefore that, little by little, I should become more and more like these Christians with whom I spent most of my time. Whether it was inevitable or not, a rabbit-hole Christian was what I became.

Conviction

The main reason for this was not weakness on my part so much as conviction. These Christians most nearly resembled the ones who had supported me during the crucial months when God was reshaping my spiritual life. The key person at that time was my boy friend Gerald. He and the others had been left behind in Exeter.

Gerald and I had been friends for years. We had grown up together in the same church. He enjoyed cycling too. And we belonged to the same missionary prayer group. Unlike most students, Gerald stayed at home when he became an undergraduate and read for his degree at Exeter University. It was then that we graduated from being 'just good friends' and enjoyed instead the magic of in-loveness.

When Gerald became president of the Christian Union at Exeter University, he was invited to take a team of Christians from the university to a little town called Plympton, eight miles from Plymouth. The students were to provide back-up for the preaching and ministry of Frank Farley, an evangelist working under the auspices of Youth for Christ.

'Why don't you come too?' Gerald suggested one day.

When he explained that during the day the team would receive training from Frank, go door-to-door visiting and speak at various meetings, such as young wives' groups, I could think of no good reason why I should go. Just the thought of speaking to a group of young married women gave me sleepless nights. Nevertheless I went. On the first night a black and white film about the life of Jesus was shown. I do not remember its title. What I do remember is that the film broke down twice and the sound-track was scarcely audible in places. Even so its message winkled its way into my heart: that during the last tempestuous week of his life on earth, the very people who hailed Jesus with happy hosannas on Palm Sunday were the self-same people who clamoured for his crucifixion with their blood-curdling cries of 'Crucify! Crucify!' on Good

Friday. When it came to the crunch these people chose, not Jesus, but Barabbas.

When the film broke down for the second time, Frank Farley sensitively underlined this thought: 'Tonight you have a similar choice,' he said. 'You can't sit on the fence for ever. Unless you choose Jesus as the Lord of your life, by implication you are rejecting him.' He went on to explain that Jesus longs that we should surrender our entire lives to him and urged anyone who had never done so to make a decision for Christ.

The sights and sounds of the film and now the wooing words of the preacher were finding a niche in my heart. The facts I was hearing and seeing were not new. I had been hearing them for years. What was new was the challenge to make a personal response to God's love. I had never heard anyone give that challenge before. But it made sense. If Jesus loved me enough to die for me, the least I could do was to express my thanks in an act of glad surrender. What was also new was the surge of emotion that welled up inside me, expressing more eloquently than any words the deepest desire of my heart and mind – for both were fully engaged in that moment – to place my life once and for all in the hands of the living God. When Frank Farley later invited those to come forward to the front of the church who would like to make such a commitment to Christ, I pushed my way past Gerald who was sitting at the end of the pew and stumbled up the aisle.

At first Gerald tried to stop me. He thought I had not understood. 'He's talking to the *non*-Christians,' he said in a loud whisper. But I had not misheard. I knew what I wanted to do and was determined to go through with this public abandonment of all I had and all I was to the Christ who had revealed himself to me afresh that night.

Was it the tears that streamed down my face which persuaded Gerald that I needed to go forward? I do not know. What I do know is that that moment was a turning-point in my life: a conversion experience. I meant every word of the hymn we sang:

Just as I am, without one plea
But that Thy Blood was shed for me,
And that Thou bidd'st me come to Thee
O Lamb of God, I come.

Just as I am, though tossed about
With many a conflict, many a doubt,
Fightings and fears within, without,
O Lamb of God, I come.

Just as I am, poor, wretched, blind;
Sight, riches, healing of the mind,
Yea, all I need, in Thee to find,
O Lamb of God, I come.

Just as I am, Thou wilt receive,
Wilt welcome, pardon, cleanse, relieve;
Because Thy promise I believe,
O Lamb of God, I come.

Just as I am (Thy love unknown
Has broken every barrier down),
Now to be Thine, yea, Thine alone,
O Lamb of God, I come.

Just as I am, of that free love
The breadth, length, depth and height to prove,
Here for a season, then above,-
O Lamb of God, I come.

(Charlotte Elliott)

After the service I struggled to express to Gerald a fraction
of the relief and strange joy with which I seemed to be
inebriated. At the team meeting next morning, again I
attempted to put into words the wonder of the afterglow
of the night before. I had no name for the experience. I
could not claim that I had heard about Jesus for the first
time and that, eureka! I had fallen in love with him. On
the contrary, when I accepted the invitation to become
part of the team I did so because I already considered
myself a believer. It was more like an underlining in ink

of what had already been written on my heart in pencil: the love for Christ which had been instilled in me as a child. But it was liberating – and life-changing none the less.

The team were ecstatic. As far as they were concerned I was a very baby Christian and they treated me like one, teaching me all they knew, and in particular drilling me in the art of witnessing. They continued to nurture me in this way when we returned to Exeter. And as far as I was concerned I had nailed my colours to the mast and determined to discover all I could about the Bible.

The aim of the mission where I had had this unexpected encounter with God was to reach the people of Plympton for Christ – particularly those who never darkened the doors of a church. The team recognised that 'in-drag' – expecting such people to pour into a church for an evening meeting – was not the most profitable means of evangelism. They therefore organised open-air meetings, house-to-house visits and small meetings in people's homes so that those who would not come to a meeting in church might still be touched by God. We were also encouraged to 'gossip the gospel' – to talk about Jesus to anyone we met no matter where we met them.

Full of new-found joy in the acceptance I was receiving from Frank, the members of the team and from God, and full of evangelistic zeal I developed the art of this method of 'witnessing'. It outlasted the mission to Plympton. Wherever I went I wanted to witness. Whether the people in my orbit were interested or not, I would tell them my testimony.

My travelling companion in the compartment of the train that carried me from Plymouth to Exeter when the mission was finished heard it. My parents heard it. My scripture teacher at school heard it. My parents and my scripture teacher were thrilled. But I suspect that the stranger who was unfortunate enough to be my travelling companion that day was relieved when the train screeched to a halt at Exeter St David's, disgorged me and left her to continue her journey in peace. My enthusiasm and evangelistic fervour were not, I fear, laced with sensitivity and I had not yet learned the art of earning one's right to speak for Christ by first making a relationship with someone.

The reason why I was so zealous was that, in Plympton, I had seen for myself that God could change people's lives. He was changing mine. He had changed Gill, another teenager who had capitulated to the love of Christ during the mission and who corresponded with me regularly. My longing was to be caught up with the commission of Christ to go into the whole world to win people for him. I wanted to go on seeing God change people's lives.

When I left Exeter to start my university career I left behind the Christians who had nurtured my newly-awakened faith. And after the first term my romantic relationship with Gerald came to an end, so I lacked the support of his twice-weekly letters and occasional visits. But members of the Christian Union in Highfield Hall filled the gap. Together we attempted to tease from the scriptures what it means to live biblically on campus and we shared the same vision. We wanted to witness for Christ in the hall and beyond. This conviction united us. 'Christ is the answer' was our slogan for people in need. Sadly we had not yet learned that until one stops to listen to a person's questions and anguish, that person is unlikely to discover *how* Christ could meet their inner-most needs and thus become the answer to them.

Occasionally people with problems would come to talk to me. There was Pat, for example, who was suffering from claustrophobia and wanted to move out of the small single room the warden had allocated to her. There was the Indian girl who was homesick and worried about the safety of her politician father. And there was the girl who wanted to talk about the problems she was having with her boyfriend. My prayer for each of these students was the same: that they would find Christ. I made the naïve assumption that if they, too, came into a conversion experience their problems would be ironed out overnight. Pat's terrible fear of being crushed or hemmed in would leave her, the Indian girl would settle down, and boyfriend troubles would melt away. So these and countless other opportunities to incarnate the love of God to hurting people were wasted. Instead of bearing my colleagues' burdens (Gal. 6:2) with the care and commitment the Good Shepherd showered on the man who fell among thieves, and in obedience to God, I looked for an opportunity to give my stock answer, 'Turn to Christ', and implied that Christians have no problems. I lent them books and prayed for them but I seemed to have forgotten the lessons I had learned at my mother's side in Roberts Road and the resolve I had made in the bus on the way back to Southampton from the Webb-Peploes' – to love others in the costly compassionate way they had loved me – to express compassion to others simply because compassion is what my heavenly Father is.

I failed to recognise it at the time and would have been appalled if I had even begun to detect that the God-implanted sapling of compassion was being choked. I was becoming more zealous than caring, more enthusiastic than wise. Whether I went to lectures, to choir or to netball matches, I looked for an opportunity to speak to someone about Christ. Indeed when I failed to manipulate the conversation to create an opportunity for such overt witnessing, pangs of guilt would wound me. It had been drummed into me that this was my duty – the only valid form of witnessing. I swallowed the piece of indoctrination without question. It had not occurred to me that though all of Christ's followers are commanded to witness for him the gift of evangelism which I was aping has been entrusted to only a few. Neither had I learned that serving others by meeting their needs in love and with sensitivity is as much a gift from God as the gift of evangelism (Rom. 12:6–8); that indeed some people are attracted to Christ, not by the paucity of people's words, but by the loveliness of a life lived for him like that of Mrs Webb-Peploe whose concern had touched my own hurts so powerfully. Because other members of the Christian Union wore similar blinkers to mine, and because we all shared this dutiful and limited view of evangelism, we were bound together in loyalty and a precarious kind of love.

Persuasion

But there was another reason why I became a rabbit-hole Christian. My theological persuasions pushed me deeper and deeper into the rabbit warren.

I was reading for a theology degree. All my lecturers were liberal theologians. None accepted my evangelical standpoint. The beliefs I cherished were constantly being questioned and challenged and I needed the support of like-minded Christians.

At the same time, as Secretary of the Christian Union, I had occasion from time to time to correspond with the Secretary of the Student Christian Movement – SCM for short.

The gulf between the Christian Union and the SCM had widened over the years. When I was a student in the 1950s it seemed unbridgeable. The SCM by and large attracted students who embraced the theological liberalism which was enjoying considerable popularity at the time. These liberals believed that the essential purpose of Christianity was not to woo individuals into the kingdom of God by challenging them to change but rather to concentrate on transforming society so that the harmony of heaven could be enjoyed on earth. They sought to Christianise society by meeting the material needs of the poor, feeding the hungry and visiting the sick. Philanthropy, not proselytism, was their goal. This was the way to further God's kingdom on earth, they claimed, and they criticised the Christian Union for its evangelistic activity, which came across to them as scalp-hunting, being interested in a person for the sake of saving their soul, but which lacked compassion for the whole person.

The Christian Union (or CU, as it was affectionately known by its members) on the other hand was equally suspicious of the SCM and poured scorn on its 'social gospel' stance, which appeared to reject the clear teaching of Christ: 'I tell you the truth: no one can see the kingdom of God unless he is born again . . . no one can enter the kingdom of God unless he is born of water and the Spirit . . . For God so loved the world that he gave his one and only Son, that whoever believes in him shall not perish but have eternal life' (John 3:3, 5,16).

Every now and again the SCM would invite the CU to join them in philanthropic enterprises and missions. But because their main aim seemed to be to transform society, while the CU's main aim remained unshakeable: to encourage people to allow Christ to transfigure them and to live biblically; these two groups which both wore the label 'Christian' were unable to co-operate with one another. Both groups became more deeply entrenched in their opposite and opposing viewpoints. The CU defended its view of the Bible's teaching with all the ferocity of those fighting with their back to the wall. The SCM defended its 'social gospel' interpretation of Christ's teaching with equal aggression. The CU accused the SCM of liberalism. The SCM retaliated by accusing the CU of narrow-mindedness. The gulf which separated them widened. And those of us in the CU retreated into our rabbit warren, confused, battered and bewildered, completely unable to distinguish between the 'social gospel' of the liberals and the clear challenge of Christ to involve ourselves with those in need.

Against this background perhaps it is scarcely surprising that, as a group, we were in danger of losing sight of the message embedded in Isaiah, that religion without compassion is not only useless but incurs God's wrath and disgust, that his command is clear: 'encourage the oppressed. Defend the cause of the fatherless, plead the case of the widow' (Isa. 1:17). We were in danger too of losing sight of the clear teaching of Jesus: that when we fail to come alongside the hungry, the sick and those in captivity, it is he himself we are neglecting.

We almost lost sight of Galatians 5:22: 'The fruit of the Spirit is love, joy, peace, patience, kindness, goodness, faithfulness, gentleness and self-control.' The love here, which is love-in-action, love with its sleeves rolled up to help the needy, loving until it hurts, had not yet been discovered by our group. Neither had gentleness, the ability to walk a mile in another person's moccasins, to quote the old Indian proverb, so to identify with a person's feelings that no needless pain is inflicted; the ability to pour love in where there has been little or no love. And we were not experienced enough nor wise enough to know that, in some situations, people's pain – depression, bereavement, phobias, loneliness – could not be eliminated with a well-meaning response like: 'Turn to Christ and everything will be all right'; or a loving 'Pray about it.' Such reactions to people's heartaches are too simplistic. But then no one had underlined for us the truth that it is 'those who do not run away from our pains but touch them with compassion [who] bring healing and new strength. The paradox indeed is that the beginning of healing is in the solidarity with the pain.' No one had pointed out to us that 'in our solution-oriented society it is more important than ever to realise that wanting to alleviate pain without sharing it is like wanting to save a child from a burning house without the risk of being hurt'.[2] If we had known these things, I believe we would have behaved differently.

As it was, in our determination to guard the gospel and base our lives on biblical truth, we lost sight of compassion, that Christ-like quality without which much of our evangelism is at best ineffective and at worst crude.

I recall with sorrow that I allowed the good seed of compassion that had been implanted in me as a child to be choked by theological conflict and emotional confusion. In the circumstances I believe this was understandable – but very regrettable.

Immaturity

The third reason why I became a rabbit-hole Christian was that when I went to university I was still in my spiritual infancy. Infants are immature. If they are to grow in confidence and maturity they need, first a womb, then the security of a warm and loving home where guidelines are given and parameters set and explained clearly. The CU was the womb where this infant grew.

The CU's basis of belief and insistence on living biblically gave me the guidelines I needed. And the CU was the home into which I retreated from the challenges of adulthood which I was not ready to face in Christ's name. In CU circles I found the safe place where I was secure enough to discover what a life surrendered to the lordship of Christ meant. Without the fellowship and friendship, the support and the teaching of these like-minded Christians, I might well have wavered in the commitment to Christ I had made while I was still in the sixth form at school. As it was I never turned my back on that life-commitment. And together with the CU friends whose support I cherished, my understanding of certain parts of God's word deepened and grew.

But growth brings change. Babies grow into teenagers. Similarly baby Christians grow into teenage-type Christians. And teenagers rarely accept without question their upbringing and the demands that are made of them.

By the time my final examinations filled my horizon I was becoming a questioning teenager in terms of my spiritual pilgrimage. The weekend before my finals, those examinations which would determine for ever whether or not I emerged from university with a BA degree, the Webb-Peploes again took me into the refuge of their home. I was tense and restless. The year on committee had taken its toll. So had the theological wranglings, long hours working in the library and the constant concern about my mother's health. But again, just being in the Webb-Peploes' home and presence and garden proved to be the therapy I needed. Through the quietness and sensitivity of their concern, the overwound clock of my life learned to tick in time again. Sitting on their lawn soaking up the sun and the stillness, I relaxed into the felt presence of the compassionate Christ. Walking round the garden and the orchard with Mrs Webb-Peploe or the farm with Dr Webb-Peploe, I learned to love so many of God's created things: ripening strawberries and raspberries, clucking hens, grunting pigs and waddling geese, and the shapes and sizes of the trees which towered over the lawn. Once again Mrs Webb-Peploe's serene and prayer-soaked love set the atmosphere where I could experience God's love for myself: the love I knew about in my head but needed so desperately to feel deep inside me. At the end of the weekend I returned refreshed to Southampton to face my final exams.

But this second brief spell at the Webb-Peploes had not only strengthened and encouraged me, it had also caught me off my guard and unnerved me. Their outlook on life seemed so different from ours in the CU. They spent their entire lives seeking to spread the good news that Christ changes lives. They had done this in India and now they were doing it in the New Forest area of Hampshire and beyond. I would listen enthralled as each of them reminisced about the wonderful changes they had seen take place in the lives of some of the people they had met.

A friend recently reminded me of one of the stories Dr Webb-Peploe loved to tell.

Part of his responsibility as a GP was to visit patients in a nearby mental hospital. One of the patients in that hospital was a fellow doctor and Dr Webb-Peploe's heart went out to him in compassion. While praying for this man on one occasion, Dr Webb-Peploe sensed that God was wanting him to share certain verses from the Bible with this man. At first he argued with God, protesting that since this doctor was not a Christian it would be inappropriate to read scripture to him. But the sense of rightness of this course of action deepened, so on his next visit Dr Webb-Peploe chatted to his doctor friend as usual and then asked if he might read the verses to him. The doctor agreed and this is what he heard:

But now, this is what the Lord says . . . he who formed you . . . Fear not, for I have redeemed you; I have summoned you by name; you are mine. When you pass through the waters, I will be with you; and when you

pass through the rivers, they will not sweep over you.
When you walk through the fire, you will not be burned;
the flames will not set you ablaze. For I am the Lord,
your God, the Holy One of Israel, your Saviour . . .
Since you are precious and honoured in my sight, and
because I love you. (Isa. 43:1–4)

These words made a profound impact on the sick man
and when Dr Webb-Peploe had left, he asked for a Bible.
After much searching the nurse found a rather battered
Bible which bore an inscription inside the cover, 'ASHLEY
Baptist Church', and the word Ashley was written in large
Gothic lettering. The man was astonished. The verses he
had heard claimed that 'I have summoned you by name,
you are mine'. It so happened that his name was Ashley.

'How can I enjoy a relationship with Christ?' was the
question Murray Webb-Peploe was asked on his next visit.
And on subsequent visits he was able to see for himself
how God was so touching this man at his point of need and
transforming him that his recovery was being accelerated.
There was real rejoicing on the day he left hospital fit
and well.

In her biography of Dr Webb-Peploe, Katharine Makower
tells another story that the Webb-Peploes loved to recall.
Dr Webb-Peploe had spent three happy days at Cromer in
Norfolk where he helped lead the annual Beach Mission.
On the day he left Cromer he drove along a deserted road
and, as usual, used his travelling time to pray for various
people. To his surprise, out of the blue he was arrested
by an inner voice saying, 'Stop and go back.' He pulled
the car in to the side of the road, switched off the engine
and asked God, 'What does this mean?' The answering
thought seemed very strange: 'Go back to Cromer and
ask Mrs Bulpitt if you can give her and her two children
a lift to Birmingham.'

Mrs Bulpitt's two children had taken part in the activities
organised by the Beach Mission but they had given no
indication that they were in any kind of need. They had
simply said that their father lived in Birmingham and

that they would be joining him when the Beach Mission finished.

Dr Webb-Peploe began to argue with God: 'I can't go and call on a woman I have never met and ask if I can drive her and her two children half across England. It simply isn't done. And anyway I'm late already.' But the impression was so strong that he turned the car round and drove to the hotel where he knew the Bulpitts were staying.

When Mrs Bulpitt came to the foyer, Dr Webb-Peploe explained that he had met her two children at the Beach Mission and then said: 'I am going to North Wales and have to pass through or near Birmingham; may I have the privilege of giving you all a lift home?'

Dr Webb-Peploe recalls:

> I don't know who was the more embarrassed, she or I, but she did what any woman would: began to give every possible excuse why she would not accept the offer: 'My husband is not here. We've made arrangements to go by train', and so on. And then she added, 'And anyway, my daughter is not very well this morning.'
>
> I said, 'I am sorry to hear that. Have you had a doctor?'
>
> She replied, 'No, I don't know any doctor here; I'll wait and see how she is.'
>
> I said, 'I happen to be a doctor and my job is mainly the care of children; would you like me to see her?'
>
> She said, 'I would be most relieved if you could.'

Dr Webb-Peploe diagnosed acute appendicitis in its early stages but explained that, since he was just passing through the town, he was obliged to call the local doctor. The local doctor came, examined the patient and disagreed with Dr Webb-Peploe's diagnosis. They were still discussing the prognosis when the mother returned saying that she had been thinking over Dr Webb-Peploe's offer and would be most grateful if he could take the family back to Birmingham as soon as possible. Within twenty minutes everything was packed up and they were *en route* for Birmingham. Every hour Dr Webb-Peploe stopped the car to take his patient's pulse. And every hour he noticed that her pulse rate was quickening. When they were still an hour away from Birmingham the young girl began to turn grey and Dr Webb-Peploe feared that the appendix might rupture before she could be operated on. He stopped the car again, telephoned the hospital from a callbox and arranged for a bed to be ready and for the surgeon and family doctor to be there so that the operation could take place as soon as they arrived.

Dr Webb-Peploe recalls:

> They were quite splendid, and she was on the operating table within a short time. The surgeon asked if I would like to assist, and I said, 'Yes, very much.' When he had opened up the abdomen and fished out an appendix on the point of bursting, he looked across at me and said, 'You've driven this child half across England; what's the story?' So I told him what had happened, and he said, 'Well I agree; this is the hand of God.'
>
> By this time the father had turned up at the nursing home. He was a wealthy industrialist, I discovered later. He invited me to their home for the night and, after supper, standing up against the mantelpiece in his drawing room he asked me what had happened. So I told him, and he said, 'Yes, I agree; God is in this.' Then he went on, 'You know, I haven't done much about God – I've been too busy making money, I think – but it's about time I did.'
>
> I said, 'I quite agree.'[3]

That night the industrialist found peace with God. Three weeks later Dr Webb-Peploe returned to Birmingham to stay with the family. The child, Millicent, had made an excellent recovery and was eager to hear the full story from Dr Webb-Peploe's own lips. Great story-teller that he was, he enjoyed giving her a blow-by-blow account of the events of that memorable day, suggesting that it was

Jesus who had saved her life. Millicent was so moved that she surrendered her life to God that night, and went on to be used by him to lead a regular Sunday service which was attended by over a hundred children.

Whenever the Webb-Peploes told stories like these, the emphasis was always placed on the sheer goodness of God and the mystery of his wonderful ways. And I would catch a glimpse of the fact that somehow their form of evangelism was in a different league from the kind we were attempting at college. What was their secret?

The penny had not yet dropped that their caring of people was born from the womb of listening prayer and that this was the reason for its effectiveness. Neither had I yet seen that the question is not an either/or: evangelism or caring, but a both/and. And I had not learned to dovetail zeal for souls with a love for people in the winning way H. R. Niebuhr describes: 'When all is said and done the increase of . . . love of God and neighbour remains the purpose and the hope of our preaching of the gospel, of all our church organisation and activity, of all our ministry.'[4]

Instead I was in inner turmoil. Consequently I was glad to be leaving university, the CU and a lifestyle which now seemed out-moded, unsatisfying and unsatisfactory. But such feelings had, of necessity, to be hung on a peg. Exam results appeared on the college notice-board. I had passed. Like most of my friends I found myself caught up in the whirlpool of preparing for the grand finale of these 'salad days': the pomp and circumstance of Graduation day.

Chapter 4

People Matter More than Meetings

The summer of 1959 was one of the hottest on record. Before my final examinations I had spent day after day sitting in the garden revising. During finals the sun beat on the glass roof of the examination room causing several students to faint from the heat. After finals the heatwave continued and my parents came to Southampton for a holiday before taking their seats in the Guildhall where the graduation ceremony was to take place.

Half way through my second year at Southampton I had fallen in love with a post-graduate student, David Huggett. We celebrated the end of my finals and the submission of his thesis by announcing our engagement. Our first task as an engaged couple was to give my parents a good holiday.

My mother was well the entire week. My father relaxed. And at the end of the week their verdict was that this had been the best holiday of their lives. Graduation day, with the presentation of degrees, the speeches and the buffet lunch in the stately grounds of South Stoneham Hall, was a happy highlight and fitting climax. On that day my parents met David's parents for the first time. The pressures of the past year evaporated in the pure pleasures of the present and though I did not realise it at the time, I had turned a significant spiritual corner.

Others

Though we never put the desire into words, I knew David shared my vision that we should take the Webb-Peploe's lifestyle as the model on which we would pattern our lives. This lifestyle was summed up for both of us by the wooden plaque which hung over the mantelpiece in their huge kitchen and on which was engraved a solitary word: OTHERS. During that first week of our engagement it was as though our deepening love for one another overflowed to my parents and we discovered for ourselves the invisible, intangible rewards which come to couples who sacrifice self in the interests of others: the rewards of that inner sense of well-being we call joy.

Back in Roberts Road, with no examinations to cast a shadow over me and no committee duties to occupy my time, I was free to think, to evaluate and to choose how to apportion my days, weeks and summer months. It was early July and I would not be leaving home again until October when I would start my post-graduate studies at Manchester University.

Almost as soon as we arrived back in Roberts Road, my mother's health deteriorated once more. For the whole of that summer vacation she continued to suffer in the way she had done since I was eleven. My father continued to support her by doing the cooking, the cleaning, the shopping and the necessary nursing of her. Aunt Rene continued to come, to listen, encourage and comfort my mother. And many of the same neighbours continued to call. Although I had been away from home for three years, and although my own values and lifestyle had changed, life in Roberts Road was marked by few significant changes. The faithfulness and solid goodness of the people who gave my mother so generously of their time, energy and love made a very deep impression on me.

These people had suffered with my mother in the early years of her illness and they suffered with her still. They were unafraid to show solidarity with her pain and my father's weariness. They ached for my parents because they put themselves in their shoes and felt where these shoes rubbed. As they recognised that the ongoing day-in, day-out nature of their problems brought its own frustrations and difficulties, they continued to give much-needed practical help, like shopping. Their support was both warm and genuine. At first their faithfulness stunned me. During my three years at Southampton, we in the CU had talked about love in action and studied what the Bible said about it but none of us had even begun to translate this theory into practice at cost to ourselves. But here, before my very eyes, were men and women who would never have been capable of dissecting love intellectually but who knew what it meant to love at cost to themselves. It was humbling.

And in a way it was frightening. Most of my neighbours were God-fearing but few darkened the doors of any of the churches which lay in close proximity to Roberts Road. Most would have felt out of place in Christian circles. Few would have understood the religious jargon I had learned to use at university. None had an ulterior motive for caring for my mother – like trying to find an opening to speak about God. No. They simply saw her helplessness and did all in their power to rescue our family. And in doing so they were loving us in precisely the same way Jesus might have loved us if he had lived in Roberts Road. So which of my communities was the most Christian? The students who had signed on the dotted line for Christ and spent hours in prayer, Bible study and meetings where the Bible's teaching was expounded, or these working-class men and women without whom my parents' life would have been a misery? Which lifestyle was more authentic: the life I had known in Southampton where we Christians had been so busy attending meetings that there was little time or inclination to befriend anyone who did not suffer from this 'meetingitis'; or the self-sacrificing, caring way of life I was again witnessing in Roberts Road? I am almost ashamed to admit that I found this question impossible to answer; I was confused. And I was riddled with guilt because I could not bring myself to *talk* to my neighbours about Christ.

The Bible's teaching

In one sense, as I look back, I find it hard to believe that I could show such ignorance. I had just graduated in theology. For my finals I had made a detailed study of the fourth gospel and relished it. It seemed such a privilege to pore over the life and teaching of Jesus. The teaching he had given the disciples only hours before his death had moved me very deeply: 'My command is this: Love each other as I have loved you. Greater love has no one than this, that he lay down his life for his friends' (John 15:12–13).

I knew how Jesus had expressed love when he was here on earth. He had done it by showing immense sensitivity to the feelings of others: the family in Cana of Galilee whose wedding wine had run out, the paralytic he visited personally at the pool of Bethesda, the blind man he met near the pool of Siloam, his grief-stricken friends Martha and Mary with whom he stood at the grave of their brother Lazarus, to mention but a few. I knew that he had taken as much care in communicating with despised blatant sinners – like the woman from Samaria whom he met at the well – as with VIPs – leading Jews and Pharisees, like Nicodemus. I always imagined that one of the reasons why he drew people to himself as a magnet draws iron filings was because he went about touching people at their point of need. And I had observed that his love was a transforming love. Because of who he was, what he did and what he said, people's spiritual eyes were opened. They believed.

This happened to the disciples at the wedding in Cana. It happened to Nathanael. It happened to Nicodemus. And it happened to Martha and Mary and hundreds of others. It was as though his life was a signpost which pointed people to his Father.

Yet somehow his final command before he died: 'Love each other like that', had failed to move me. I knew it in my head but it had not percolated into my will nor did it steer my ways.

I knew that, when Jesus gave us this command, he was

repeating a recurring thought from the Old Testament prophets, for instance Amos. The Book of Amos had featured in my theological studies so I was conversant with the colourful language this great teacher uses to spell out that our religiosity is repugnant to God unless our public worship and private devotions are matched with a concern to improve the lot of the poor. Some of the striking similes and warnings used by this prophet are unforgettable – like the insulting way he refers to the women of Israel as 'cows of Bashan', and like this withering warning: 'I hate, I despise your religious feasts; I cannot stand your assemblies . . . Away with the noise of your songs! I will not listen to the music of your harps. But let justice roll on like a river, and righteousness like a never-failing stream' (Amos 5:21, 23–24).

Yet I had fallen into the trap of intellectualising the words of scripture; noting them, finding them interesting, even amusing, but not allowing them to affect my life – indeed even dismissing them as irrelevant to my life. For example, singing lusty hymns and choruses was one of the things we had enjoyed about our Christian Union meetings, and in the church I had attended in Southampton. I could not yet accept that our expressions of devotion might, in fact, have been offensive to God since it was so rarely accompanied by the compassion the prophet mentions here.

Similarly I was aware that, like a recurring refrain, the theme of love in action features frequently in the letters of Paul; and that James makes a soul-searing attack on those who *say* they have faith but do nothing about it:

What good is it, my brothers, if a man claims to have faith but has no deeds? Can such faith save him? Suppose a brother or sister is without clothes and daily food. If one of you says to him, 'Go, I wish you well; keep warm and well fed,' but does nothing about his physical needs, what good is it? In the same way, faith by itself, if it is not accompanied by action, is dead . . . You see that a person is justified by what he does and not by faith alone . . . As the body without the spirit is dead, so faith without deeds is dead. (Jas 2:14–17, 24,26)

Share with God's people who are in need. Practise hospitality . . . Rejoice with those who rejoice; mourn with those who mourn. (Rom. 12:13,15)

Carry each other's burdens, and in this way you will fulfil the law of Christ . . . Therefore, as we have opportunity, let us do good to all people. (Gal. 6:2,10)

Somehow it had not occurred to me that this teaching included me. There are several explanations for this self-delusion. One is that it is possible to read God's word, to understand it with our intellect but to fail to pick up with our spiritual antennae the message it is trying to convey. I was reminded of this even as I was writing this chapter. A woman came to see me whose husband now shows no interest in the things of God. 'For years he used to come to church regularly,' she confided. 'How *could* he sit under all that superb teaching and not be changed?' Sadly, it is possible. And it is equally possible for Christians to know a great deal about God without really knowing him just as it is easier to be familiar with Christ's commands than to obey them.

Another reason why this clear scriptural teaching by-passed my behaviour was that it was unfashionable in the 1950s to use words with which we are now familiar, like John Stott's 'friendship evangelism' and 'incarnational mission'. Instead evangelists hammered home their own narrow view of evangelism; that witnessing for Christ means talking about him: to the barber, the grocer, the neighbour or the person standing with us at the bus stop. They underlined over and over again that such overt evangelism should be the priority in every Christian's life.

And a third reason why I suffered this terrible spiritual blindness and deafness was that I, and my fellow Christian undergraduates, were children of our age. As John Stott explains so helpfully in his fine book, *Issues Facing Christians Today*, although in the nineteenth century, concern for people and evangelical Christianity were like twin sisters living happily together, during the first thirty years of the twentieth century a major shift took place, which the American historian Timothy L. Smith has termed 'The Great Reversal'. For a variety of reasons, evangelical Christians neglected concern for their neighbour, mislaid their conscience and concentrated instead on the primacy of preaching the gospel.[1]

But in the 1960s a wave of the Spirit of God seemed to sweep over England convincing men and women that 'evangelism and compassionate service belong together in the mission of God'.[2] I was unaware at the time that there was a groundswell of social concern among leading evangelicals. What I did know was that I was uneasy in my spirit about the teaching I had received and the lifestyle that appeared to have been modelled for me by my peers and some of the pastors in Southampton.

Biographies

I have often found that when God is trying to etch something on my heart he softens its clay with a Christian book or biography or film. And that is what happened during this vacation.

My parents owned only a handful of books. But every now and again my father would take one of his musty but precious hardbacks from the shelf in the kitchen and thumb through it. One of these treasured books traced the life and ministry of George Müller whose concern for destitute children in the Bristol area of England prompted him to found a series of orphanages there in the first half of the nineteenth century. The reason why my father treasured this book was that he had spent several years in one of these orphanages as a child and while there his imagination had been fired by the faith of the founder of the homes. He loved to relate one of his favourite passages from this book; to tell of one of the many occasions when George Müller discovered that funds had run out.

The homes were run on a shoe-string budget but George Müller had resolved never to purchase anything unless cash was available to complete the transaction. One day to his horror he realised that no money meant no bread for his three hundred orphans. That night, instead of going to bed, he stayed awake to pray. He reminded God that these were *his* orphans; that he had declared himself the Father of the fatherless; that this work was *his* work and that the honour of his name was at stake. He begged God to prove afresh his faithfulness.

Next morning he came down to the refectory to find that the tables were laid as usual but the bread-plates were empty. Nevertheless, watched by three hundred hungry-eyed children, he said grace thanking God for the food they were about to receive. The children were about to sit down to face a row of empty plates when the sound of cart-wheels on the gravel drive drew every eye to the window. This noise heralded the arrival of the local baker who had felt compelled that night to bake an extra batch of loaves and to bring them as a gift to 'Mr Müller's children' before he began his morning rounds. With a flurry of excitement the cart was unloaded, the hungry children were fed, and trust in George Müller's never-failing God soared.

Because the book meant so much to my father, and because I was intrigued by such stories of the miraculous, I dipped into this life of George Müller for myself. And there I discovered that this great man of prayer was speaking to the very problem that was troubling me. He longed to evangelise – 'to win souls for God', as he put it – but recognised that he would never qualify to be an evangelist until his heart burned with compassion for God's lost and hurting people. By rescuing from the streets of Bristol children whose parents had died of consumption, he learned how to care for the whole person – to feed the hungry, clothe the penniless, provide a refuge for the homeless – to incarnate God's love as well as to talk about it.

Another book which influenced me at this time was *The*

Small Woman by Alan Burgess. The author tells the story of Gladys Aylward the parlourmaid, who was turned down by missionary societies in England but saved her meagre earnings so that she could pay her own passage to China where she believed God wanted her to work and witness to his love.

The reason why I found this book so engrossing was that from a young age I had had a fascination for the Chinese and their culture. When I was seven years old, my Sunday School teacher had recently returned from China where she had been a missionary, and most Sundays she would tell us stories about the Christians in China she had loved and worked with. This interest in the Chinese had been rekindled in my early teens when I had played a part in a dramatisation of Gladys Aylward's life. It was then that I learned to use chopsticks: it was then that I first handled real silk garments: caps and coats embroidered with wide scrolls in many colours: scarlets, blues, greens and golds; it was then that my admiration for this courageous working-class woman was born. And it was then that I realised how hard her life must have been.

For years after her arrival in China she seemed to have few opportunities to win people for Christ. At times she must have despaired and wondered why God had called her to travel half-way across the world to China; why she had sacrificed so much to do so. Nevertheless she made use of the opportunities she did have – to express to ordinary village people how much she cared for them as fellow human beings. She, too, took in homeless orphans. She visited prisoners in the gaol at Yangcheng, thus earning the respect of the prison governor. And when people were sick it was to Gladys that they would turn.

And though she did not realise it her love and concern for people was speaking more eloquently than any words she ever uttered. Over the years this dynamism of love broke down the barriers between the foreign missionary and none other than the Mandarin of Yangcheng. This leading dignitary had despised the tiny ex-parlourmaid when she first arrived in China. To start with she was a female, which in the eyes of a Chinese meant she was socially and intellectually less than dust. And he considered her presumptuous in coming to his country. A cultured Confucian scholar, he would rebuke her for treating his nation as heathens:

'We have produced great art and great philosophy. The Mandarin speech of China is more beautiful and descriptive than any other in the world. Our poets were singing when Britain was but a rocky outpost on the edge of the known world and America was inhabited solely by red-skinned aborigines. Yet you come to teach us a new faith? I find it very strange.'[3]

Over months and years, news of the missionary's exploits reached the Mandarin and he learned to respect her and even consider her his friend. So much so that one memorable day he said to Gladys, whose Chinese name was Ai-weh-deh:

'I am giving a feast which I would like you to attend . . . I have something to say that I wish you to hear.'

When the Mandarin's feast was held, Gladys, to her surprise, found that although as usual she was the only woman present – that had been her privilege for many years – on this occasion she was sitting next to the Mandarin in the seat of honour at his right hand. This had never happened before. All the important personages of Yangcheng were present: the Governor of the prison; two wealthy merchants, several officials; about a dozen in all. The meal was simple, unlike the sumptuous feasts she had enjoyed in early years, and which had lasted for hours.

Towards its close the Mandarin stood up and made his speech. He recalled how Ai-weh-deh had first come to Yangcheng; how she had worked for them; what she had done for the poor and the sick and the imprisoned; of the new faith called Christianity which she had brought with her, and which he had discussed with her many times. Gladys was puzzled by his references. But after speaking for some minutes he turned towards her, and said seriously and gravely: 'I would like to embrace your faith, Ai-weh-deh, I would like to become a Christian!'

Around the table rose a murmur of astonishment. Gladys was so astounded that she could hardly speak. The guests nodded and smiled, and she knew that she was expected to reply. She got up and stuttered her surprise, her appreciation and her thanks.[4]

Afterwards Gladys realised that she had made her most influential convert to Christianity since her arrival in China many years before.

An apprenticeship

These examples of vital, practical Christian love in action moved and inspired me just at the time when I was making preparations for the children's camp where I was to be cook and quartermaster for ten days. This camp was organised by the Church Pastoral Aid Society and the aim was to give children from deprived inner-city areas a good holiday away from the polluted air of the town and an opportunity to hear about Jesus. I had been on one such camp before and was looking forward to returning to Fairlight, a village not far from Hastings in Sussex.

In 1959 Fairlight was a tiny hamlet which boasted a church, a small church hall and a string of cottages straddling the road leading from the church to the nearby fire hills – undulating green hills and cliffs which blazed with colour when the yellow gorse was in flower and which ran down into the grey-green sea.

My task was to plan the menus for the camp, order the groceries, mastermind the cooking and give one of the talks to the children in the evening. We cooked in the church hall. The children slept in bunk beds in the same building and the 'officers' slept in tents in a field opposite the church. On Sundays we swelled the congregation at the morning service in the tiny greystone church.

This year the children were girls from the London area. I can see them now, bundles of excitement tumbling out of the coach which brought them to Sussex. They were wide-eyed and chattering noisily as they explored the tents and the adjacent field of cows and I shall never forget their faces as they took the first memorable walk along the cliff path to the beach. Most of them had never seen the sea before. Most of them had never seen a cow before. And none had slept in tents. So the air would ring with the sound of Cockney voices crying out: 'Coo, Miss! Look at that! A real cow!' 'Miss! I didn't know you could smell the sea!'

I loved hearing comments like these. Coming from a concrete jungle myself, I could still remember my first Girl Guide camp: the spaciousness of the countryside, the soothing sound of wood pigeons, the sight of fields studded with golden buttercups, white marigolds, purple and pink vetch and deep blue harebells, the smell of good fertilised soil and sausages sizzling over a wood fire. Now it was my joy to help provide an environment where other children could enjoy similar pleasures. They would pick armfuls of wild flowers and I would find clean jam jars in which they could place these treasures of the hedgerows. The flowers brightened the trestle tables at meal times. I would teach the children the names of the flowers and watch as they caught their first scent of honeysuckle or squeezed milk from the stem of a dandelion for the very first time.

'You can almost watch these children change colour,' I marvelled as I saw roses appear on cheeks that had been pasty when they arrived. The children spent most of the day swimming or playing games or walking on the fire hills or in the country lanes. Consequently their eyes sparkled, their appetites grew, they learned to appreciate wholesome food. And one of the rewards of the camp was to send them home glowing with health and vitality.

But perhaps the greatest reward came in the evenings

when we all crowded into the church hall to focus on worshipping and learning about Jesus. The children had had a good day. They were happy and relaxed. They knew they were loved. And they settled down to sing, to listen and to think. Just as many of them contemplated nature with a naturalness that seems to be God's gift to children, so many of these girls contemplated the life and love of Christ with the guilelessness of little people whose capacity to trust has not yet been destroyed. We would try to paint an accurate picture of the God who loves them. We would also explain who Jesus was, why he stripped himself of his glory to come and live among us, why he had to die. And we would explain that God's love has to be received and his kingdom entered. The door opens as we surrender our lives to God.

Whenever one of the leaders spoke in this way a hush would descend on the room as the girls pondered the truths that were being explained. It was the hush I have seen steal over even the most extrovert of tourists when they enter a prayer-soaked church. Laced with awe and reverence as it is, it banishes boisterousness for a while and gives the Holy Spirit of God a unique opportunity to work in the hidden recesses of a person's heart. This was what we saw happening to the girls. The eyes and ears of their souls were opened and their hearts warmed by the love of God.

Because I worked in the kitchen, mine was the privilege of seeing for myself some of the ways in which God was working. The girls knew that after the evening meeting, I would be in the kitchen making cocoa. Some – particularly the shy ones – would come to help me and as we worked together side by side, they would make their quiet requests. They called me 'Squirrel' because I hoarded the camp's food. 'Squirrel! Can I talk to you about Jesus?' 'Squirrel! Will you pray with me?'

When children pray they come straight to the point in a way that sometimes disarms adults, and often as I listened to these young girls thank God for sending Jesus or thank Jesus for dying on Calvary's cross, I would be challenged by their clear and uncomplicated faith. And whenever I heard one of these children hand over to God the reins of her life, I thought I caught a glimpse of the reason why Jesus once said: 'There will be . . . rejoicing in heaven over one sinner who repents' (Luke 15:7). This heavenly joy echoed through my own life and through the entire camp also.

Knowing that these girls were going home with more than rosy cheeks and healthy appetites made the hard work of the camp more than worthwhile. And these camps were hard work. We rose early and went to bed late. Before camp began there were tents to put up, talks to prepare, shopping to be done. During camp we sweated over the kitchen stove for much of the day and spent most of our so-called free time talking to the children about their homes and families and troubles and joys. And when, at the end, the girls piled into the coach again, some of them sobbing at the thought of leaving, others waving and calling out their thank yous, there were floors to be scrubbed, toilets to be cleaned, the site to be cleared and food to be packed up so that Fairlight was tidy for the next contingent of campers who would arrive almost as soon as we had left.

I would not have been able to express the conviction coherently at this stage of my pilgrimage, but these camps were giving me something I desperately needed – an opportunity to see how caring for people and witnessing for Christ overlap and intertwine and feed and affect each other. It would have been possible, I realised, to have given these children a really good holiday without mentioning God but that would have deprived them of the most lasting gift we gave them: peace with God and a purpose in life – to serve him always. Equally it would have been possible to spend so much time talking about God that we deprived them of the exercise and fresh air, the good food and stimulating games and the appreciation of God's wonderful world which they so badly needed and enjoyed so fully. Then they would have been less receptive to receive and respond to God's love when it was explained. In other words I saw the importance of the both/and approach to caring for people. I saw more clearly than ever before that overt evangelism and concern for people are both shoots which sprout from the same root – the good news that Jesus came so that we should enjoy wholeness. I had seen for myself that love in action worked, not only for George Müller and Gladys Aylward, but for ordinary children in ordinary summer camps too. What is more, I felt fulfilled as a person. Whole. It was as though my two loves – love for Jesus and love for people – were coming together so that I felt integrated as a person instead of torn apart.

As I packed my cases once more and travelled to Manchester where I was to train to teach deaf children, I was fired with a new vision. I decided that my last year as a student was going to be different from the previous three. I would remain firmly anchored in Christ by having fellowship with like-minded Christians but I would not allow my week to be so cluttered with meetings that I had no time for people in need. It sounded simple and sensible. But the events of the very first weekend were to warn me that this was going to be more difficult than I had anticipated.

Expectations

The problem was that my reputation had gone before me. I suppose I should have expected this. I had, after all, been the Secretary of the Christian Union at Southampton University. I knew that the old-girl network in such Christian circles works well; that the CU in Manchester would have been told that I was to live in Ellis Lloyd Jones Hall for a year. But I had not expected the welcome I received. The Christians in hall invited me to coffee the day I arrived and it was then that I realised that they were looking to me, the graduate, as a guru figure who would help them organise meetings for the mission to the university which was to take place that academic year. Frightened that I might be sucked back into the whirl of CU meetings from which

I had emerged so recently, I panicked inwardly but said nothing.

Meanwhile I was introduced to Margaret. She and I struck up a friendship in the first week of the new term because, like me, she came from Devon. But unlike me, Margaret had not been to university before. She had been teaching primary children for a number of years and had decided to come to Manchester as a mature student to train to teach the deaf. Now, having exchanged her beloved Devonshire countryside for the grim and sooty surroundings of the Old Trafford area of Manchester, she confessed to me that she felt lost, lonely and bewildered.

Margaret was a practising Christian – not the sort to be drawn to Christian Union meetings, but a devout believer none the less. On Sundays she would ask if I would go to church with her. And at first we would troop across town with members of the Christian Union to attend the lively services in the successful 'student church'. But I could tell that these Sunday jaunts and jolly services added to Margaret's feelings of isolation. They were not her scene. So the two of us started to attend a nearby Anglican church. The congregation was small. The vicar was struggling to inject new life into his dispirited flock. No other students were there so he and his wife welcomed Margaret and me warmly. We became a part of the fellowship and recognised that we had something to give as well as enjoying Sunday teas at the vicarage. Margaret blossomed spiritually and emotionally.

But of course this was drawing me away from the 'holy huddle' of the CU. Some of them found it hard to understand how I could worship at a church they considered dead when the church most of them attended hummed with life. Add to this the fact that, frequently on a Saturday evening, I would go to a concert or play or film with Margaret instead of attending the CU meeting and it will be easy to see why certain CU members worried about my spiritual well-being and made it clear that they felt I was losing my cutting edge.

'Perhaps they're right?' The thought worried me. Yet I

was becoming increasingly convinced that people matter more than meetings and I could no longer bear the thought of spending hours at prayer meetings and Bible studies when all around me lived people as needy as Margaret. Because she was not the only one. There was Sin Bee, the lovely, lonely, shy Malaysian girl who lived on my corridor. The cold and the grime of Manchester's concrete jungle left her utterly bewildered. She needed friendship. She needed to learn about English customs. She wanted someone to take an interest in the home-life she had left behind. And she and I clicked like long-lost sisters. So I spent time befriending her.

And there was Pat. I was concerned for Pat. It quickly became clear that she hated Manchester and regretted coming on this post-graduate course. Life in the little garret-like bedroom in hall seemed almost unbearable for her. I would go and sit with her sometimes and try to understand her misery, and though I never seemed able to help her I wanted to go on trying. I knew somehow that I could not keep my integrity as a Christian and abandon this girl to her loneliness by rushing to one meeting after another. Even so it came as a complete shock when, at the end of one weekend, the housekeeper in hall told us Pat would not be returning to college. She had slashed her wrists in the bath at her parents' home and left a farewell suicide note. I was stunned for days, unable to come to terms with the fact that we had failed to hear the depths of her pain. And I became ever more convinced that I could no longer go on dissecting love in an intellectual way, I had to go where people are hurting and practise it. This was the law of Christ.

Misunderstandings

Some members of the CU misread my actions. Because I attended comparatively few meetings and because I could contribute little to the mission meetings, they believed I was backsliding and said so. That both hurt and confused me. How could I tell who was right? If they were right, I was being a big disappointment to God and that seemed unpardonable.

I now believe that my well-meaning fellow Christians were misguided. Yet how could they be expected to understand? No leading evangelical was yet expressing what John Stott has since said so clearly:

> Personal evangelism must be friendship evangelism if it is to be true to its name. Without any doubt friendship is the most Christian context within which to share the good news of Jesus. True friendship involves getting close to people. Friends enter into one another's world.
>
> I believe from scripture that in every unbeliever, even in the jolliest extrovert, there are hidden depths of anxiety and pain. Therefore we can only reach them in truth when we are prepared to enter their suffering and to feel their pain.[5]

No one had explained to us that to hide in our safe Christian ghettos is sheer escapism whereas what God wants is engagement:

> 'Escape' means turning our backs on the world in rejection, washing our hands of it (though finding with Pontius Pilate that the responsibility does not come off in the wash) and steeling our hearts against its agonized cries for help. In contrast, 'engagement' means turning our faces towards the world in compassion, getting our hands dirty, sore and worn in its service, and feeling deep within us the stirring of the love of God which cannot be contained.[6]

No one had pointed out that too many Christians are irresponsible escapists who find fellowship with each other more congenial than serving a hurting and hostile world. No one had shown us that to make our occasional evangelistic raids into pagan territory while shying away from incarnating Christ's love in the community cuts little ice.

If I had known what I now know, and if scholars like John Stott had highlighted the fact that, as Christians, we have a twofold ministry, my years in Manchester would surely have been easier, because instinctively I found myself living truths which are now being presented as *biblical* truth:

If the Christian mission is to be modelled on Christ's mission, it will surely involve for us, as it did for him, an entering into other people's worlds. In evangelism it will mean entering their thought world, and the world of their tragedy and lostness, in order to share Christ with them where they are. In social activity it will mean a willingness to renounce the comfort and security of our own cultural background in order to give ourselves in service to people of another culture, whose needs we may never before have known or experienced. Incarnational mission, whether evangelistic or social or both, necessitates a costly identification with people in their actual situations. Jesus of Nazareth was moved with compassion by the sight of needy human beings, whether sick or bereaved, hungry, harassed or helpless; should not his people's compassion be aroused by the same sights?[7]

But this was 1960. The movement of God's convicting Spirit was still largely hidden. It was seven years later that some leading Anglican evangelicals were to repent in public of their tendency to escape from rather than engage in the pain of the world of which we are a part.[8]

Meanwhile I left Manchester University with a qualification to teach deaf children. But before I took up my first teaching post there was a wedding to look forward to. I married David Huggett on July 16th 1960 and, at our request, Dr Murray Webb-Peploe preached at the wedding service and took the word OTHERS as his theme. With some wedding-present money we bought a dinner service – brown and blue Denby ware. Just like the Webb-Peploes'. For us it was an outward sign of an inner resolve that, like them, we would express our faith with a love which rolled up its sleeves and served others. The die was cast. For us, people must matter more than things or meetings.

Chapter 5

Learning to Listen

A few months before our wedding, my father and mother-in-law moved to Bournemouth and asked whether David and I would like to buy the house that was built for them when they married and in which they had lived ever since.

The Dormers, Pine Walk, Carshalton Beeches, Surrey, as the name suggests, was a spacious detached four-bedroomed suburban house with pretty dormer windows. Its sylvan setting, Pine Walk, with its avenue of pine and larch trees separating one side of the road from the other was both peaceful and pleasing. This rural tranquil atmosphere was further enhanced by the hills and woods which lay within a few minutes' walking distance of our front door, yet we were in London's commuter belt. I used to write to my mother each week and try to capture on paper my new surroundings. One day I tried to describe the garden for her, so set myself the task of counting the trees. Seventy-two larch and pine trees towered over the house in the back garden. Thirty-two more graced the front garden. It was a wonderful home.

David and I spent the summer settling in and putting our own stamp on the house and garden. Homemaking quickly became a hobby. We enjoyed the creativity of unpacking our wedding presents and finding homes for them, decorating the loggia until it was too dark to see, planting vegetables and floribunda roses and doctoring the rockery my mother-in-law had made and which had been her particular pride and joy.

All too soon September dawned, and with it the start of the school term and the beginning of my teaching career. Nutfield Priory School for the Deaf had once been a manor house but was now tastefully converted into a residential school for severely deaf children. To my delight I discovered that my classroom in the wing looked out over the rolling hills of Surrey and beyond to Sussex, Kent and Middlesex. The view changed with the seasons and never ceased to take my breath away. And my work with these profoundly deaf secondary school children proved far more fulfilling even than my wildest dreams.

I had first dreamed of becoming a teacher of the deaf when, as a Brownie, I had befriended girls from the Deaf School in Exeter. 'You'll grow out of it,' my mother warned. But I never did. On the contrary, the desire increased when, as a Girl Guide, I again spent a great deal of time with girls from the Deaf School. And in my final year at Southampton I was overjoyed when my application to train under Professor Ewing at Manchester University was accepted.

To teach deaf children is to tune into pain and frustration. This was a lesson I was to learn in my very first term of teaching. Michael underlined it for me.

Michael was one of the eleven pupils in my class. He was not quite twelve years old but was big for his age and could have passed for fourteen quite easily. Michael was as rude as he was rough and he used his strength to bully and threaten the girls in my class, frequently disrupting entire lessons. At the end of the term when I wrote Michael's report, I expressed concern about his aggressive behaviour. Consequently the headmaster called me to his office to explain the problem. He was embarrassed by what I had written because Michael's father was the school's gardener and his mother worked in the kitchens. Anxious not to lose two valuable workers, Mr Blount suggested that I should talk to them about Michael. I did. And in doing so I learned that Michael's parents too were worried about him.

Nutfield Priory had an excellent reputation and Michael's parents had been determined that their son should complete his education there. To make this possible, his father had resigned from his post in Kew Gardens and assumed the more menial role of school gardener. This had meant a move for all of them and they had watched Michael's insecurity increase when faced with a new home, a new school and new teachers who were struggling to understand his speech. Their sacrifice seemed to have misfired. Had they done the right thing in moving? This was the question they asked themselves continually.

My heart bled for them and after this conversation I tried to put myself in Michael's shoes: growing fast, missing his former home and former friends, feeling utterly bewildered by his new environment, yet because his speech was so undeveloped having no one with whom he could share his frustration; indeed having no one with whom he could communicate freely about anything. Even when he tried to communicate with us, very often even the most experienced members of staff would fail to understand what he was trying so hard to say.

'How would you feel if you were hemmed in by these limitations?' I asked myself. And in answer to that question I sensed that, in Michael's shoes, I would have been angry and frustrated too. 'No wonder he sometimes behaves like a caged animal,' I said to myself.

Thinking the situation through in this way caused my attitude to change. It softened. And as I softened towards him, slowly Michael changed. By the end of the second term we would occasionally see him smile. And by the third term he would co-operate with me and even come to ask my advice about his work. We were beginning to understand and respect each other and when he came to me on his own for speech lessons he would work really hard.

Even so I hurt when I thought of Michael and his parents. Theirs would be an uphill task if he was one day to hold his own in a competitive world of hearing people who make little time to stop to try to understand the world of the deaf.

I hurt too for the sixth-formers I taught. The relationship between a teacher of the deaf and sixth-form pupils is more friend-to-friend than teacher-to-pupil and I valued the closeness that developed between some of the girls and myself. These girls would be leaving school soon and part of our task was to equip them to face the world outside the sanctuary of Nutfield Priory. They learned certain skills like shorthand and typing so that they were qualified to take up employment, but if they were to be employable we knew it was vital that they should learn to communicate with the hearing people they would be meeting – in the office or canteen or other place of work.

For this reason Mr Blount had arranged for his sixth-formers to attend evening classes in the nearby town of Reigate. On Monday evenings therefore I would take a handful of girls there. We learned basket-work, quilting and dressmaking, and the girls discovered how to converse with the women of Reigate who had joined the class to develop their skills. When the girls failed to make themselves understood or were unable to lip read the women, I would act as interpreter. And again I would try to put myself inside the skin of these teenagers; to try to discern the feelings that might well up inside them. And I realised just how rejecting some of them would find the world outside the haven of Nutfield Priory when the time to leave eventually came.

From time to time David and I would invite these sixth-formers to our home for Sunday tea. They loved coming. And we enjoyed providing them with an environment so different from boarding school, where they could relax and enjoy the peace and the beauty of our lovely home.

The bereaved, the lonely, the perplexed

By the time I was five months pregnant it became clear that I could no longer cope with the long daily journey across country to Nutfield Priory nor continue to teach

games and PE as I had been doing. The time had come
to leave. I had been there for less than two years but
my sadness at leaving the school almost overwhelmed
me. I had enjoyed being a working wife. And the few
housewives I knew in the Pine Walk area seemed to
spend most of their time at coffee mornings and talking
about nappies. To exchange the fulfilling life and work of
Nutfield Priory for that seemed to me quite unbearable.

By then David and I were worshipping at St Patrick's
Church in Wallington and had struck up a firm friendship
with Arthur Drowley, the Curate-in-charge, and his wife
Doreen. Most Sundays after the evening service we would
go round to their home for a sandwich supper. It was
to Doreen that I expressed my ambivalence about being
a full-time housewife. I still found it difficult to voice
my innermost feelings but somehow, while we worked
together in the kitchen cutting up tomatoes or grating
cheese, it seemed easier to ventilate the fears and frustrations that were bottled up inside me.

Doreen understood. It was she who helped me to
discover that when God closes a door he opens a window.
The door to teaching deaf children full-time was closed
for the time being but that did not mean that I was to be
condemned to a life of idleness or uselessness. 'Would you
come to our young wives' group and talk about your work
with deaf children?' Doreen asked.

Another of my dreads was women's groups. I feared
that there, too, frustrated women would have nothing
to discuss except nappies and the latest recipes. But I
warmed to the idea of talking about my work. 'I could
show some slides of Nutfield Priory,' I enthused. And I
spent several days sorting out slides and preparing a talk
which would give these women an insight into the world
of the deaf, the joy of being able to teach these children
to speak and the way I had seen God at work in the lives
of some of the children I had taught.

That meeting was a turning point for me. The women
were warm and welcoming. They seemed to appreciate the
way I had opened up a whole new world to them. And I

saw that my prejudices had been misplaced. These were intelligent women whose love for God matched, and in some cases outstripped, my own. I began to attend the group regularly, found it stimulating and was soon to be asked by Doreen to help her to run it. And in saying yes to that, a whole new dimension of ministry opened up for me.

People in need began to come to our home to seek counsel and refuge, and because I was no longer at school all day I was able to give that most precious commodity: time. There was Pat who, like me, was pregnant and finding it difficult to adjust to being 'just a housewife'. There was John, a member of the youth group at church, who was lonely and mixed up about his relationship with the girl he was going out with; and after my baby arrived there was Connie, the mother of five children whose husband had died tragically in a drowning accident.

I wished I knew how to help Connie. Doreen seemed to have just the right touch to gain her confidence and encourage her to talk. I seemed able to do no more than offer her a restful environment away from her own home – and my baby to play with, which seemed therapeutic for her now that her own children were well past the baby stage. I failed to realise at the time how important this was for her. But Henri Nouwen has expressed it well:

When do we receive real comfort and consolation? Is it when someone teaches us how to think or act? Is it when we receive advice about where to go or what to do? Is it when we hear words of reassurance and hope? Sometimes, perhaps. But what really counts is that in moments of pain and suffering someone stays with us. More important than any particular action or word or advice is the simple presence of someone who cares. When someone says to us in the midst of a crisis, 'I do not know what to say or what to do, but I want you to realize that I am with you, that I will not leave you alone,' we have a friend through whom we can find consolation and comfort . . . Simply being with someone is difficult because it asks of us that we share in the other's vulnerability, enter with him or her into the experience of weakness and powerlessness, become part of uncertainty, and give up control and self-determination. And still, whenever this happens, new strength and new hope is being born.[1]

It was twelve years later, after many moves and much change, that I was to discover truths like these.

Our second child was on the way when, although David and I were both content in Carshalton Beeches and fulfilled in our many roles at 'St Pat's', a strange restlessness disturbed us. I have since met other Christians who, when God is trying to effect a radical change in their lives, experience a similar sensation. It seems to be one of the many ways the Holy Spirit uses to speak to us.

David had reached a crossroads in his career. He was now faced with the choice of climbing the professional ladder, which would mean spending more and more time on his subject – aeronautics and space technology – and less and less time with people. Or he must resign his lectureship at London University and concentrate instead on full-time Christian work.

Before we had committed ourselves to discovering what God's will for our future was, David was invited to attend a conference in Sweden. I stayed at home to look after our son. While we were apart God seemed to speak to both of us very clearly, challenging us to offer ourselves for full-time Christian service. One Sunday evening, shortly after David's return, we shared this hunch with Arthur and Doreen. Arthur's response confirmed that God had indeed spoken. He looked overjoyed and simply said: 'I've been praying for this!' and he encouraged David to push the doors to see whether they would open so that he could train for the Anglican ministry.

A year later the Dormers, Pine Walk had been sold, our little family had been uprooted, we had torn ourselves away from the fellowship of St Pat's and we were being transplanted in Bristol where David was to train.

His training included an opportunity to join with the medical students in Bristol in their study of psychiatry, and the added opportunity of working with patients in the nearby homeopathic hospital. Sadly no such training was then available to the wives of ordinands. But in Bristol and then in Parkstone and Cambridge, where David served his curacies, I found that, as a clergy wife, I seemed to attract people with problems. Wherever we lived people in pain would come to our home in the hope of finding some kind of help and support.

In Bristol there was the young mother who was distressed for her son because she needed a hernia operation which would require both hospitalisation and a lengthy period of convalescence. Her little boy Jonathan was the same age as my son Kevin, so Jonathan would come each day and he and Kevin would play happily together, relieving Jonathan's parents of anxiety.

In Parkstone David and I ran the youth group together, and because we lived in a terraced house in the heart of the parish, youngsters would pop in on their way home from school to discuss their problems with us: spiritual problems as well as boy-girl relationship problems.

In Cambridge, because we worked alongside a vicar who was a bachelor, again we were the ones who handled the boy-girl relationship heartaches and the marriage problems.

By the time we moved to Nottingham so many people were presenting me with perplexing problems for which I could find no take-away answers, that I enrolled for the counselling course at St John's Theological College, just three miles from my home.[2] It seemed natural to enrol for this course for two reasons. One, because David and I had already established close links with St John's College. Two, because Anne Long, the lecturer in pastoral counselling, was someone I had learned to admire and respect.

Anne had arrived in Nottingham a few weeks after David and me. We first met at the college at the beginning of the autumn term of 1973. David and I had been invited to speak at the pre-term conference with which the academic year began in those days. I was to speak on the Saturday afternoon and Anne was to introduce me.

'What would you like me to say by way of introduction?' she asked me. I don't remember precisely how I responded to that question. What I do remember is that I confided in Anne that I was feeling strangely nervous and that I supposed it was because this was the first time I had spoken in public since I had been shaken up by a car crash I had been involved in earlier in the year.

What I also remember is the way Anne handled that introduction. She used the opportunity to thank the students and staff of the College for the warmth of the welcome they had given her. The genuineness of her thanks was clearly endearing her to everyone. She then made an enormous impression on me because of the sensitivity with which she introduced me, explained that this was my first public appearance since April and suggested that they should all pray for me.

I still remember that prayer. Not the words. But the hush which descended on the uninspiring lecture room as Anne prayed.

Was it the authoritative but gentle way in which she prayed that drew me to her? Or was it simply that it was obvious when she prayed that she knew herself to be in the presence of the living God? Was it the attractive way she dressed that impressed me? Or was it the quiet wisdom and warmth which gave birth to the desire to spend time with Anne?

I don't know. What I do know is that after that initial encounter, we would meet from time to time and I would ask her about the counselling course which she was organising for the students of the College. The more I learned about the course, the more I longed for the kind of training Anne was giving.

I was surprised and delighted when permission was granted for me to become a student again. The Tuesday afternoon sessions at St John's quickly became the highlight of my week.

The value of listening
One of the first lessons Anne underlined was that the need
for caring people in today's churches is urgent. All of us
cry out for help at some time or another. At such times
there are a variety of ways in which we can be helped.
One vitally important method is the ministry of listening.
If someone will draw alongside us, recognise that simply
to listen is not a waste of time, nor is it less helpful than
offering advice or Bible verses, they can provide us with
untold support by encouraging us to share our innermost
feelings of anxiety or fear or frustration or anger. I have
since heard Myra Chave-Jones, former Director of Care
and Counsel, put this succinctly and helpfully:

> What the person [in pain] wants is that, in our listening,
> we show the ability to stay with her in her pain. There
> is no need to flounder and panic and think we have to
> say something. Sometimes it is enough to stay alongside
> someone silently; to weep with those who weep.[3]

I would sit in the lecture room thinking of the trail of
people who were currently coming to me for help as well
as those who had consulted me in the past. Anne's insights
seemed invaluable. Inexperienced though I was, I had
detected for myself that the cry to be heard is universal.
Whether one lives in the terraced streets of the inner city,
like Roberts Road, or among the wealthy upper-crust
residents of Pine Walk, whether one talks to people in
the seaside town of Parkstone or to the successful dons of
Cambridge, the cry can be heard: '*Please* will somebody
stop what they're doing and listen to me?'

Of course hurting people rarely come straight out with
their request in this way. Usually their cry for help is
more subtle or camouflaged than that. Perhaps that was
why Anne emphasised that listening to others is an art
form which has to be learned. If we are truly to help
others its theory and ground rules must be grasped and
practised until they become a part of life. She likened this
learning to discovering how to drive a car. At first the

work of changing gear requires one's full powers of concentration. But eventually it becomes second nature. For the experienced driver changing gear comes naturally.

I knew I wanted to master this art form. The seam of compassion that had been ingrained in me in Roberts Road had not worn thin. I wanted to find appropriate ways of expressing this learned warmth of personality because I was aware that hurting people drew me towards themselves even when I felt powerless to help them.

What listening communicates

Paul Tournier, the much loved Swiss doctor and prolific writer, once made the claim that when we so listen to a person that he has felt understood, we help him to live and to face even the most difficult of situations without being false to himself. We give him confidence.

Anne fed us with similar insights:

> If you listen to me, I feel valued, you give me your time, acceptance – something I may never have had – and a relationship with another human being – something I may have problems with. You share the burden of my grief, my loneliness, my frustration, my indecision, my guilt. I've been alone with it so far. You let me think my thoughts aloud and sometimes, that way, I find answers – or at least discover where to look for them.[4]

While I was drinking in this kind of teaching I would think back to the people who had listened to me over the years: to the Webb-Peploes and Arthur and Doreen Drowley in particular. Anne was right. When they had listened to my fears and dreads without criticising me, it was as though I glowed inside because I felt that I really mattered even to such 'important' people. Because they expressed their love in this unselfish but costly way they enabled me to discharge my emotions constructively. This was so cathartic that, in purging me of many prejudices and irrational fears, it helped me to re-negotiate life on a new set of terms. And in instilling confidence in me they were modelling to me the never-failing love of the God who listens. I like the way Norman Wakefield highlights this:

> Listening says, 'I want to understand you. I want to know you.' It is one of the most basic ways to convey a sense of respect, to treat another person with dignity. Through this act we affirm to another person that God is willing to listen, that He eagerly waits for His troubled child to come to Him and discover the compassion and deep concern of His loving Father.
>
> Unquestionably, the listening I have been speaking about is a powerful form of ministry. Such listening embodies something of the nature of God Himself. It makes available to the Holy Spirit a channel through which to communicate love and a helpful, appropriate response.[5]

The listeners

And, as Anne had reminded us right at the beginning, this powerful ministry is not the prerogative of the professional, for anyone can learn to listen. Many others would agree with her.

Michael Jacobs, Director of Pastoral Care and Counselling for the Dioceses of Derby, Lincoln and Southwell, for example, suggests that: 'We have as a society effectively deskilled the ordinary man or woman in those tasks which are part of common life.' He goes on to point out that there are many occasions when the ordinary skills at the fingertips of most men and women are quite sufficient to help a person in need. 'What is frequently missing is the confidence to apply them.'[6]

Myra Chave-Jones, an experienced psychotherapist, implies something similar in her valuable primer, *The Gift of Helping*. John Stott sums up her viewpoint in his foreword to the book: 'There are many situations of need in which ordinary Christians can learn how to love and serve people with sensitivity.'[7]

Gary Collins, Professor of Psychology at Trinity Evangelical Divinity School, Illinois, shows that most people in need still turn, not to a professional, but to a friend for help. He claims that 'if these peer counselors . . . can recognise their limitations, they can with very little training make a significant impact on the mental health of people around them. This is real people helping.'[8]

And Roger Hurding, another experienced counsellor, general practitioner and psychotherapist, seems to agree, showing that 'the Psalms, Proverbs, Ecclesiastes, the Gospels and Epistles are full of instructions for believers on the life-long business of helping one another towards maturity.'[9] He also suggests something which Anne and Myra Chave-Jones both emphasise: that though, through God, we can all be enabled to help one another, he does seem to equip certain people with a special ministry of helping and counselling. But he adds an important rider: most of us feel quite unequal to this task.

Paul Tillich suggests that we must lay these feelings of inadequacy on one side for, 'The first duty of love is to listen.'

All this and so much more was précised for me in some words written by George Eliot, which I first found stuck over the sink in Anne's kitchen:

> Oh the comfort, the inexpressible comfort of feeling safe with a person; having neither to weigh thoughts nor measure words but to pour them all out, just as it is, chaff and grain together, knowing that a faithful hand will take and sift them, keep what is worth keeping, and then, with the breath of kindness blow the rest away.

Ground rules of listening

I was so persuaded of the 'inexpressible comfort' of 'just listening' that I lapped up the guidelines to good listening that we were given.

These helped us understand that a person communicates on a whole variety of wavelengths simultaneously. We must therefore listen, not only to the words and sentences a person selects, but also to the non-verbal signals which are being transmitted: the tone of that person's voice, its inflection and the speed with which he speaks – the rush of words at one point in the conversation, the slow and hesitant speech at another, the long pauses in other places and the broken, incomplete sentences. We must listen too to the way in which a person expresses himself – whether his phraseology is coherent or muddled. His facial expression, bodily movements, hand gestures and dress also give vital clues to the way a person is feeling. A depressed person, for example, will often lack the energy to take trouble over the way they dress or do their hair. Their voice will sometimes sound flat, even monotonous. They might yawn frequently as though even to string a few words together takes an effort. They might twiddle their thumbs lazily and endlessly as though their hands were giving expression to their aimlessness.

Good listeners therefore watch as well as listen. They seek to hear the message which is being conveyed through the words. They also make a mental note of the hidden messages which authenticate and embellish the spoken word: 'Di's voice was quiet and she spoke calmly, but her eyes looked full of pain, her face was pale and her shoulders drooped as though her problems weighed heavily on her.'

Michael Jacobs highlights the value of listening to these non-verbal messages:

Non-verbal communication is the very first communication we receive from a person . . . asking for help. Before that person opens his or her mouth, he or she will be showing through non-verbal signs how they feel, perhaps about the interview which is about to take place, or about their general situation. The listener, who now also needs to become the person who watches, can see this basic mood at the point of meeting a person in a waiting room, opening the front door for them if they come to the house, or even when greeted at the person's own front door. Non-verbal clues continue to be observable as people walk into the room, the way in which the person (who is to become the speaker) crosses the room, sits down in the chair, and the position in which he or she remains seated. This is, of course, only the first use of non-verbal communication, but may be very important to the start of an interview, especially if a person looks anxious.[10]

I began to put this ABC of listening into practice. At that time a man crippled with arthritis was coming to me for help. I would watch him limp from the doorstep into the lounge, lower himself gingerly into our soft settee and then wince with pain as he edged himself to the front of the seat where he perched for greater comfort. This man would talk to me about his worries, and as he did so he would mutilate my spider plant which sat on the table next to the settee or take a paper tissue from his pocket and tug at it nervously, tearing it to shreds. As I watched him I realised just how accurately his body was picking up and expressing his emotional stress. The message of those hands, the movements of his pain-racked body and the sorrow which seemed to fill his eyes gave me far more insight into his situation than the few words he managed to stammer out. It was this 'body language' which helped me to empathise with him. And empathy is another ingredient of good listening.

Empathy is not the same as sympathy. Sympathy listens to a person's pain and makes this kind of response: 'Oh! Poor you!' Or if a woman describes the seemingly unreasonable behaviour of her mother-in-law, sympathy says: 'I know just how you feel. My mother-in-law's a bitch too.' Such sympathetic responses often sound superior or patronising and are unhelpful. They can even be intrusive.

Empathy, on the other hand, seeks, not to feel the same as the person in pain, but rather to see the world through that person's eyes without becoming swamped by the other person's troubles or pain. It is the discipline I began to learn when I was teaching at Nutfield Priory and tried to put myself into my pupils' skin so that I could imagine life as they were actually experiencing it. Most of us do this

automatically when we watch a film or read a well written
novel. We identify with the hero or heroine. We enter into
their dread or fear or hope or excitement or joy. In one
sense we 'become' that person for a while.

But true empathy, I discovered, comes in two stages. To
return to the example of the woman complaining about her
mother-in-law's unreasonable behaviour, empathy asks
itself: 'How might I feel if my mother-in-law behaved like
that?' It then moves on to ask itself another question: 'How
is this woman feeling in the wake of her mother-in-law's
behaviour?' In other words, empathy tries to identify with
the emotions troubling another person and feeling into
the situation with them. Rather than assuming that the
message has been accurately received, empathy goes on to
clarify that the message has been understood correctly.

Clarify

David Augsburger, a family therapist in California, has
shown how vital this art of clarification is. The word a
person uses to express a certain emotion may or may
not convey to the listener the precise emotion the person
is feeling. The reason for this, to borrow his colourful
language, is that:

> the word is not the meaning just as the wrapper is not
> the chocolate; the word is not the object it names just
> as the photo is not the person; the word is not the
> experience expressed just as my story is only a small
> part of that moment in history:[11]

600,000
words
are
available
in the English
language.
Of these,
an educated adult uses
2,000.

And the most used
500
have according to
standard dictionaries
14,000
different definitions.
Each common word
must be used to cover
a wide range of 'meanings'.
This pitifully small number of symbols
must describe the infinite richness
of your and my experiences.
(Some words have 100 or more different meanings.)[12]

Empathy therefore must make sure it understands such simple words as 'bad'. When my arthritic friend used to use this word: 'I've been bad this week', sometimes he meant that he was in physical pain. At other times he meant that he felt guilty because he had been drinking heavily. And sometimes he was simply trying to tell me that he was disillusioned with his materialistic lifestyle. I had to learn to check that I really understood what he was trying so hard to tell me by asking simple questions: 'Do you mean . . .?' or 'Are you saying?' or by paraphrasing: 'So you're feeling really fed up with the pain in your knees to-day?'

This was the way I learned to pick up the bass line, as Michael Jacobs calls it, or 'to pick up the vibes', to quote Myra Chave-Jones.

Other helpful hints
My list of ground rules was growing. But there were other principles to grasp: 'Don't be afraid of silences. Worried people often think slowly and need long pauses. Learn to understand silence as much as speech,' Anne told us. 'If a person hesitates or stops talking, ask yourself: Is this a sullen silence or a reflective one; a shocked silence or a thoughtful one? Is the person embarrassed or simply searching for words to describe what is on their heart?'

And listen to the language of tears, Anne further advised. Like silence, tears can convey all kinds of messages: joy, pain, sorrow, frustration and even anger. The wise listener does not assume that they know what the tears are saying. Our eyes and ears can help us to differentiate between hysterical, attention-seeking crying and sobs which come from deep within a person. Even so, sometimes I still find it necessary to ask, gently and sensitively, 'What are those tears trying to say?'

When people came to me for help I would try to put into practice these lessons I was learning. I became particularly interested in people's eyes. Someone has said that eyes are the mirror of the soul. They reflect the emotional secrets we try to hide. I detected such pain and emptiness, anger and sorrow in people's eyes that it sometimes became painful to 'listen' to them. Often I could tell whether the verbal thanks someone was voicing was genuine by the change that had taken place in their eyes. Often it was as though heavy veils had been lifted allowing light and sparkle to shine once more through those bodily windows.

Frequently, in these early days, by the time the person had left me I would find that I was exhausted. I had failed to understand what I now know: that listening to words and emotions and vibes and subtle emphases, trying to remember what has been shared and identifying with the person concerned, takes all one's powers of concentration and a great deal of emotional energy. It was proving a costly form of loving for which I still seemed ill-equipped.

But it was producing rich rewards. People in pain were beginning to say things like: 'Thanks so much for listening.' 'It's so good to have someone to talk to.' 'You've really put your finger on the way it feels.' 'I feel much better now that we've talked.' 'You've been a great help.' On many occasions I had not 'done' anything. I had 'just listened'. I quickly came to the conclusion that 'just listening' was indeed an effective way of helping others no matter whether the person was suffering from a virus or cancer, depression or bereavement, guilt or anger or that common disease of the spirit, loneliness.

I was no nearer understanding *how* it helped. But then, I understand little of what goes on under the bonnet of my car, but I still enjoy using it. I was content to live with the mystery: hearing seems to be one of the ways God brings a person into a measure of healing. Eager student that I was, I determined to learn everything I could about the theory of listening and, I was soon to discover, there were many more lessons to learn.

Chapter 6

The Listening Heart

The foundations were laid. We had learned that good listening requires our full attention; that if we are to listen well, this listening must be three-dimensional: we must tune in to the words a person selects, the language of the eyes, the face, the body and the tears, and we must also learn the art of translating 'vibes' accurately.

The course at St John's College now built on these foundations. Having learned how to listen with accuracy and empathy, we next learned how to respond – and how not to respond – to the person we were trying to help.

The first golden rule seemed to be obvious: *Don't interrupt*. I find it extremely irritating if someone interrupts me when I am trying my best to voice something important. Some people, I realised, were compulsive talkers who seem unable to listen without interrupting every few minutes. But I did not consider myself to be one of these. Nevertheless when I began to compare what I actually did with the rules for good listening I was learning, I was shocked to discover how frequently I caught myself butting in when someone was struggling to express painful emotions.

I think of an occasion when a seemingly-successful businessman told me he had lost his job. He was trying hard to express the emotions that vied for attention in his mind: the hurt and anger, the frustration and fear, the humiliation and hopelessness which tormented him.

I wanted to understand. I wanted to show that I cared. But even though my motivation was high I found myself punctuating some of the pregnant pauses with questions to help him along. And when I reflected on that particular encounter I was forced to admit that most of those questions were unnecessary. Instead of helping him to pour out his innermost feelings they intruded on the thoughtful silences which were an integral part of his story-telling.

I felt ashamed. I knew in my head that good listeners have a good reason for any question they ask; that they do not ask questions out of idle curiosity but only out of the desire to promote the growth of the one they are listening to, but on that occasion I had not translated this helpful theory into practice. I knew too that the questions the listener asks should be open, that is, the kind that draw out more information about a given subject: 'Can you tell me more about that?' or 'How did that feel?' but this time many of the questions I had asked had invited a monosyllabic reply. 'Did that make you feel angry?'

I learned to confess this lack of love for that is how I view such neglect of the rules of good listening. I learned to repent and to receive the forgiveness God delights to give. Even so, despite years of practice, I still find myself interrupting inappropriately from time to time and still catch myself encouraging a conversation to explore an unnecessary cul-de-sac by the questions I ask. But I take comfort from John Powell when he writes:

> Most of us, when we are in the listener's role, feel compelled to be speakers. We feel a compulsive inner urgency to interrupt others as soon as they start to reveal themselves. We feel a strange obligation to advise them, and to support our advice with a few chapters from our autobiographies. We jump in at the first pause, and go on nonstop unless we are exhausted and the other person is near despair. Regrettably, I have done this to others. I have also had this done to me. I have experienced the sadness of not being heard because someone had not cared enough

to listen to my sharing and to learn who I really
am.[1]

That 'strange obligation to advise' which John Powell
mentions was highlighted as one of the snares we should
avoid. 'Don't offer advice,' writes Myra Chave-Jones:

> Most people do not want it and will not use it. It is
> unhelpful to say, 'If I were you I would . . .' or 'I
> think you ought to . . .' because you are not me, and
> your view of what I ought to do is yours . . . The only
> real value of good advice is that it makes the person
> giving it feel better. (Of course, advice which relates
> to factual knowledge – for example, which course of
> study to follow for a particular career – is a different
> matter.)[2]

Again I was somewhat shocked to discover just how
difficult I found it to avoid the trap of becoming a problem
solver for others. Sometimes it seemed so obvious what
course of action a perplexed person should take that I
wanted to tell them so – even take them by the hand
and lead them along the pathway which seemed to me
to be so right. At such times the theory I was learning
at St John's seemed hard to translate into practice. But
of course to act like that would be to manipulate people,
and so Anne Long's reminder was a vital one: 'Avoid
premature solutions offered before the heart of the matter
has been reached. Sometimes your own anxieties will press
for a speedy answer'.

I learned that basic principle twelve years ago and have
been trying to honour it ever since. But even as I write,
I am trying to help a couple in crisis and once again I
have caught myself playing my old tricks: waking up with
'the perfect solution' so clearly in my mind that I have
wanted to telephone them to tell them I have found *the*
way forward. Again I take comfort from John Powell's
disarmingly honest – and very American – confession:

I sometimes have to work at stifling my old urge to turn into a computer printer spitting out all kinds of interpretations and advice. I have personally been working on the technique of the well-placed question. It goes something like this: 'Gee, I don't know what you should do. What do you think? In your judgement, what are the possibilities?' Sometimes a suggestion can be successfully floated into the conversation by way of a question. 'Say, did you ever think of going back to school and getting a degree?'[3]

And I came to recognise the importance of John Powell's observation that 'in the role of the listener we should offer only suggestions and never directions'.[4] He goes on to explain that the reason for this is that if adults are to behave as adults and not overgrown children they must assume personal responsibility for their behaviour and their lives. They must therefore be allowed to have their own thoughts and to make their own choices. The listener who insists on telling another what they should or should not do runs the risk of hindering a person's growth: 'The one sure way not to grow up is to hitchhike on the mind and will of someone else.'[5]

More 'don'ts'

I had no desire to invite hitchhikers to take a ride on my advice or my prayer. Nevertheless I found that certain people did become overdependent on me. This proved disastrous for them and for me. It was disastrous for them because, instead of thinking things through for themselves and taking responsibility for the decisions they made, these people would consult me as though I were an oracle and even reach the point where they believed that my prayers were more effective than theirs. Consequently they failed to grow. And it was disastrous for me because, though at first their confidence in me seemed like a compliment and boosted my ego, my false pride quickly turned to fear as I realised that such people were piling Messianic expectations on me which I could not hope to meet. I am not omniscient. I do not have the answers to everyone's problems. Whenever I tried to behave as though I was omnicompetent, my energy was sapped and my family suffered.

Eventually I saw that I was breaking yet another golden rule of listening: *Don't encourage dependency*. I am still learning the difficult art of coming alongside a person and offering my love and my listening as a crutch but never as an armchair into which they settle comfortably but unhelpfully. Sometimes I seem to get it right, at other times I still get it wrong. It helps, I find, to set boundaries: making it clear to a person when they may telephone and when such a call would be intrusive; when to come to talk about their problems and when I need space. Such boundaries protect me and are reassuring to the person in need. They know that if I say I am happy for them to telephone or to call, I mean what I say.

Gary Collins's book *How to Be a People Helper*[6] helped me to set clear goals when I was trying to help a person through a sticky patch. He uses Jesus' encounter with the disciples on the road to Emmaus to illustrate how best to go about such goal-setting.

First he explains how, in Luke 24:14, 15, we watch Jesus draw alongside the travellers who, from the way they turn the events of the past three nightmarish days over and over in their minds, still seem to be suffering from shock. Jesus takes the initiative and the trouble to establish a rapport with them so that they trust him.

Having built up a relationship, Jesus goes on to explore with them the nature of their problem. Why were they so discouraged? Why were they so stunned? He seems to have listened attentively as they poured out their perplexing tale, giving them ample opportunity to ventilate their frustrations, doubts and disappointments, and having penetrated to the heart of the problem and understood it Jesus decides on a course of action.

With a skilful use of questions and suggestions, Jesus sorts out the confusion by challenging their thinking and encouraging them to think differently about the string of curious events which has precipitated their crisis of faith.

But far from keeping himself detached or aloof, he comes close to his fellow-travellers and joins them for a meal. This fraternising was not an invitation to become dependent on him, however. On the contrary, we read that, quite literally, Jesus vanishes from their sight. This disappearing act seems to have spurred them into action and, on their own initiative, the travellers head back for Jerusalem where they become encouragers of others.

Gary Collins concludes from this that effective listening should include five steps:

1. Building a relationship.
2. Exploring the problem(s).
3. Deciding on a course of action.
4. Stimulating action.
5. Encouraging the person to apply what he has learned by launching out on his own.

At first Jesus' rather ruthless method of confronting his fellow travellers took me by surprise. Don't judge, the teachers of listening warned. But here was Jesus saying, 'How foolish you are, and how slow of heart to believe all that the prophets have spoken!' (Luke 24:25). Wasn't that being judgemental?

'No,' I decided. He had built his relationship with these men. He had tuned in accurately to their confusion. And he had decided that one course of action was to help them to think straight. In order to do this, it was essential for him to point out the discrepancies which lay between their feelings, biblical truth and the situation as it really was. I like to imagine that when Jesus said 'How foolish you are, and how slow to believe', there was a loving twinkle in his eye. Certainly it is unlikely that his challenge was harsh. Rather, he came over so convincingly that he won their hearts, renewed their minds and brought light into their darkness so that within a short while the direction of their life had completely changed. Instead of being caught up in a web of confusion they had been cut gloriously free to spread the good news: 'Christ is risen!'

Similarly I learned that careful and caring listening to a person's pain or confusion gave me permission to challenge discrepancies and distortions of the truth which I detected. The way I usually do this is to ask a question like: 'I wonder if this makes sense to you . . .' and I go on to try to show that though I understand and empathise with the real and powerful feelings which are bothering the person, these feelings may not add up to a correct analysis of the situation.

For example, I think of a girl I once tried to help who said she was suffering from depression. She wept as she told me that the reason, she thought, was that her engagement had broken up. As I explored the situation further, she confessed that she had slept with this young man even though she had known this to be wrong. She was now left with an overwhelming sense of guilt which she had confessed to God many times but nothing had happened. 'I suppose I'm too bad to be touched by God's forgiveness,' she confided.

After I had shown her that I understood the sense of hopelessness which was weighing her down and, while attempting to show her, through touch and the look on my face and in my eyes, and the tone of my voice, that I really cared what happened to her, I simply said: 'I wonder if it makes sense to you that though you *feel* as though you are a kind of spiritual leper, God's word makes it quite clear that the kind of sin you are confessing can be forgiven?'

She looked into my eyes for an instant and quickly looked away again. But that brief glance had been enough. In her eyes I had detected a glimmer of hope. She remained silent for several minutes while this hope struggled to the surface. Eventually she looked at me again and said, 'Yes. I know you're right. What do I do to receive it?' Now that her perspective was clear, my task was comparatively easy. I stood by and watched her guilt being melted by the God who loves to forgive.

In the early days of learning to listen, I would sometimes

feel soiled after a person had been describing their sexual sins. 'I sometimes feel as though a dust-bin has been tipped all over me,' I commented to Anne Long on one occasion. But at the same time I found that, when I really listened in the way I was being taught, it was rarely difficult to care for the people who were telling me about their misdemeanours. One reason was that, as I tried to put myself in their skin and view life from their perspective, I could understand what had prompted them to act in the way they had. That was not to say that I was condoning the sin. It is to say that I was recognising how vital it is at one and the same time to offer acceptance to the sinner without ever condoning the sin which they were confessing.

Some aims

'To offer acceptance.' This was what Jesus had offered me on that day, as a teenager, when I surrendered as much as I knew of myself to as much as I knew of him. This was what the Webb-Peploes had offered me when, as an undergraduate, I had collapsed in their home. And this was what Doreen Drowley had offered me when, as a pregnant mum, I was struggling to come to terms with my seeming lack of status now that my career as a teacher was being interrupted. On these occasions I had been on the receiving end of listening love. I had experienced its transforming power. I had seen for myself that Abraham Schmitt's observation is so accurate: 'To listen totally means that one takes another's whole life into one's being and cares for it.'[7] Now I wanted to pass on this kind of love to others. Twelve years later I am still learning how to do it.

One way, as Myra Chave-Jones stresses so helpfully, is to recognise that to listen to someone is to receive a gift. 'If you give a gift to someone, and they rip the paper off, take a cursory glance and then go off and do something else, it doesn't look as though they have really valued the gift.'[8] But if, on the other hand, you take the wrapped gift, remove the paper with care, turn the gift over and over in your hand, admire it and thank them for it, the giver glows inside and feels valued.

I find it helpful to think of listening like that: receiving a gift; recognising that by listening to someone's story or pain or problem or crisis I am bringing to them a measure of healing because I am communicating that vital message which we all need to hear over and over again: 'You really matter.'

There is a method of listening which at first seemed to me both curious and artificial but which I discovered quickly communicates acceptance and understanding love to the person in need. This method is sometimes called reflective listening.

When a person listens reflectively, they take careful note of the words a person selects and concentrate hard on the content of the verbal gift which is being offered. Then at appropriate moments in the conversation, they repeat back to the person with the problem a summarised version of what has been said.

Let me explain what I mean. Someone suffering from bereavement might arrive at church looking ashen, their eyes might swim with tears and, after the service, they might pour out their anguish that this pain and these tears just refuse to go away; that the sting of being separated from the father who died a few months earlier seems to grow worse rather than better; that time certainly isn't the healer it is claimed to be; that they are angry with God because he seems to have disappeared just when their need for him was desperate. They are even becoming hard and cynical when they hear Christian things talked about.

The listener takes in the 'body language', the words and the vibes, and summarises the situation by saying to the grief-stricken person in the pew: 'You seem to be surprised that it's taking so long to recover and that you still need to cry a lot? And you're angry and cynical because the God who is said to be such a wonderful healer seems to be doing nothing about the pain in you that hurts just as much now as when your father died?'

Although the listener has done nothing more than

receive the bereaved person's verbal gift and begun to unwrap it gently and sensitively, a look of relief will probably pass over the face of the bereaved person. They have been understood. They therefore feel valued. And although this conversation can do nothing to bring back the longed-for father, yet this simple act of listening has given them the courage to go on living and trusting.

Real rapport is established between the person helping and the one being helped when this kind of listening is applied. It then becomes easy and natural to thank the person for giving us the privilege of being the one to hear and handle their innermost thoughts and feelings. John Powell reminds us that it is risky and frightening to put our most sensitive confidences in the hands of another, to examine our failures or to reveal our vulnerability. 'Consequently, we should practise the habit of thanking others for their self-disclosure and for their trust in us.'[9]

This suggestion seemed strange to me at first. But I remember the overwhelming sense of privilege and gratitude which swept over me when, in the early days of taking courage in both hands and putting this theory into practice, I said to someone: 'You know there are many people who would have counted it a privilege to listen to you in the way you have allowed me to do today. So thank you for your trust – for entrusting yourself to *me*.' This genuine expression of thanks took the person completely by surprise. But I could see that at the same time he felt valued because of what I had said.

Of course it would be useless to say something like that if we felt that the person we are helping was being a burden or a nuisance. People are quick to pick up pretence. If truly we are to communicate care, the warm regard which assures a person that they are of unquestionable value, and non-possessive love we must communicate not only with our lips but with our eyes, our hugs, our smiles and our gestures as well. It is this total response that the person in pain will register.

'Non-possessive love.' As I served my apprenticeship in listening I was surprised to discover how emotionally close two people can become when one is sharing confidences and the other is attempting to listen in the attentive, caring way I have described. Such intimacy need not be inappropriate or wrong. It can be healing. But I was to discover the painful truth that it is not my love which heals but God's. Indeed if all I offer to a person is the paucity of my human warmth and acceptance, the person might feel supported, affirmed and valued, but the transformation we are both looking for will not take place. What is needed is not simply that I should feel for and with a person in pain nor that I should be able to express this concern. What I must always remember to do is so to open myself to the love of God that I simply become the embodiment of his love to that person. Agnes Sanford underlined this for me in her book *Sealed Orders*:

> 'Love heals', people say. I do not find that necessarily so. God's love heals, yes. But our own love, if too emotional, may even stand in the way of that great flow of God's love which is an energy rather than an emotion . . . I learned to put Christ between me and the person for whom I was praying, to send my love to Christ and let him do with it what he would. Thus people felt from me or through me, power rather than affection.[10]

Shortly after I had read this resolve of Agnes Sanford's God seemed to highlight its importance for me. I was listening to a friend who was trying to help me to understand how black life felt for her. Suddenly words dried up, she buried her head in her hands and began to sob – just quietly, but from deep inside herself. She was someone for whom I cared deeply and in order to assure her of that love, I went to her and gently placed my arm around her. Instantly, I felt her body freeze. She stopped crying, put on a plastic smile and changed the subject. But her eyes were still filled with pain and the terrible truth dawned on me that I had done the wrong thing. She had needed to cry. This was the only language capable of giving expression to the darkness inside her. And in offering her touch at that moment, she had felt smothered. I had hindered the healing process and not helped it. Whereas if I had placed Jesus between her and me I would have discerned that she needed space to cry and that Jesus would have done the necessary holding.

After this unfortunate encounter I asked God to give me a greater sensitivity to the needs of others so that I would know when such touch was appropriate and necessary and when it should be withheld.

My warm personality intruded in another way too. I was discovering that when I love, I love deeply, and most of us are tempted to cling to the things and people we love. Yet to hang on to a person when the time has come for them to leave is to strangle love.

True love demands that the person be set free when the time is ripe. But I was slow to learn the art of holding such people on an open palm. I was slow to learn that, in pouring out love to others, I must expect nothing from them in return. I was slow too to learn that vital lesson, that when I listen to a person in need I listen for the sake of their well-being, not because I have a need for closeness with others; my real and legitimate needs for friendship and intimacy must be met through the mutuality of supportive friendships – in my relationship with my husband, in the fellowship of Christ's people and through the support of a soul-friend who will listen to me in this caring attentive way.

Dangers

Just as I learned the hard way not to neglect friendships, so I learned the hard way the very real danger of neglecting physical health, sleep and exercise. 'Honour your body, mind, spirit and emotions,' Anne used to warn us. This kind of involvement with people in need sounds glamorous. But it is hard work. It will cost not less than everything. Therefore discover what, for you, is input. To emphasise this piece of teaching, one afternoon

Anne scrawled this equation across the entire width of the blackboard:

OUTPUT = INPUT = OUTPUT = INPUT = OUTPUT

We understood what she meant. If we are giving ourselves to people in this demanding way, we must also receive into ourselves the necessary resources so that we do not burn out in the way I did as a student when I was trying to support my mother, attend to my studies and hold down a full-time job. In other words we must know how to relax, where to go for spiritual and emotional refreshment and how to set definite boundaries which limit our availability to people in need. We must know how to live balanced lives.

Although I understood the wisdom of this teaching, when I first started to erect such boundaries twinges of guilt would trouble me. What right had I to relax when so many people were longing for the kind of help I have described but who knew of nowhere to find it?

I was still struggling to find the courage to put this principle into practice when I heard a tape-recorded talk in which Francis MacNutt, whose book on healing had recently been published, confesses to facing a similar problem. He told us how embarrassed he felt on one occasion when he was speaking on healing at a residential conference. He was expected not only to give a series of talks but to minister late into the night to sick and needy people. And he realised that he was being drained of vital energy.

One of his hobbies was tennis. He had only to play a quick game and he would relax because he would focus away from people's needs and on to the healthy competitive nature of the game. So he decided to spend part of each afternoon on the tennis courts. But how could he possibly bring himself to walk right past a row of people in wheelchairs, who would all like prayer, when he was dressed in shorts, carrying a tennis racquet and obviously looking forward to some exercise. He found he could not do it. Instead he discovered the back door of the conference centre and sneaked out without anyone seeing him.

I identified with his dilemma, admired his limited courage and tried to learn from it, especially when I noticed that Jesus set a similar example.

In Mark 1 we read of a certain Sabbath when Jesus had taught in the synagogue in Capernaum, delivered a man of an evil spirit, healed Peter's mother-in-law, and at sundown had ministered to crowds of needy people. Before sunrise he retreated to a solitary place to be with his Father, but on returning to Capernaum the disciples alerted him to a new set of demands: 'Everyone is looking for you!' Whereupon Jesus replied: 'Let us go somewhere else' (Mark 1:37, 38). And although we are told that the 'somewhere else' was nearby villages where he would preach again, we also know that the walk to those villages would have given Jesus the space and exercise he needed to replenish his own resources.

I took great comfort from Jesus' example, from his command to the seventy-two after their exhausting mission, 'Come apart and rest', and from Francis MacNutt's humble testimony. And I determined to discover how I could best relax, rest and have my spiritual batteries recharged.

I quickly discovered the therapy of the countryside. I love to tramp the hills of Derbyshire and I would try to go there each week to be recreated. Sometimes I would walk on my own, drink in the grandeur of the moors or the stillness of the bluebell woods or the extravaganza of rhododendron gardens or the comfortableness of hollyhocks growing close to dry-stone cottage walls. At other times I would walk with my husband – the only person with whom I feel really free to be me – to shuffle through piles of fallen leaves just like I did when I was a child, to run with the wind in winter or squeal with delight at the surprises of spring, the first snowdrops, premature catkins, newborn lambs. Concerts, the ballet, a good play also help me to unwind.

And creativity, I discovered, is a form of therapy. I

gain immense satisfaction from making my own clothes, weeding a rockery or flower bed, planting hyacinths, preparing a special meal for friends, or spring-cleaning a room. When I am trying to help people whose pain is clearly not going to evaporate overnight, I recognise that I also need to spend time creating lovely things which bring quick returns. Without these, my life lacks balance and I become a dreary, depressed and depressing person.

I discovered too the inestimable value of retreating to a quiet place to be alone with God.

Listening to God

A little phrase Anne used in the course of her teaching had made a deep impression on me because I sensed its importance as soon as she said it: 'We need to listen with one ear to the person who is talking and we need to have the other big ear tuned in to God.'

After I heard this, whenever I knew someone was coming to see me or before I visited a sick or bereaved person, I would try to spend time in my prayer room confessing to God that I knew my own wisdom and insight were insufficient to meet this person's needs and therefore asking him if there was anything he wanted to tell me or to show me which would help me to bring relief or comfort or healing to the person concerned. Then I would spend time being still, waiting and listening.

Sometimes, as I have explained in *Listening to God*,[11] I seemed to have a clear sense of the appropriate course of action. It was as though God had spoken with the same still, small but authoritative voice with which he spoke to Elijah and Samuel. I think, for example, of the occasions when I asked God what I could do to help the arthritic man mentioned earlier in this chapter. Over a period of months I sensed that God was saying: 'I want to heal him of his arthritis.'

At first I was startled by these words; frightened that I was making them up. Our church had not yet started to hold healing services and though we believed that God could heal (he is God, after all) I am not sure that many of us really believed he would.

Yet the voice seemed to insist that he wanted to heal Alistair. I talked to my husband about it. When David Watson came to our home I mentioned it to him, and I also asked for Jean Darnall's advice. Everyone seemed to be of the opinion that this was indeed the voice of God. So I discussed it with Alistair. To my surprise he agreed to receive the laying on of hands and prayer for healing.

I was grateful that Jean Darnall happened to be in Nottingham at the time and gave me the privilege of praying with her. She was experienced in these things. I was a novice. And Alistair had surrendered his life to Christ only twelve hours earlier. Even so, as we prayed it became clear that something dramatic was happening to Alistair's body. When we finished praying he stood up, and as he walked around our lounge an impish grin spread from ear to ear. Next he came over to the settee where Jean and I sat watching him and knelt on the floor in front of us. Alistair kneeling? His knees had been stiff as sticks for years. Now he could bend them without pain.

That whisper I had heard: 'I want to heal him,' had been God's voice. And I was glad I had been given the grace not simply to hear but to take the risk and obey.

On another occasion, while I was waiting on God in preparation for a counselling session with a couple whose marriage was going through a sticky patch, I simply heard one word: 'mother'. I had no idea what it meant. But as I chatted to this couple, it quickly became evident that the man resented his mother because she had smothered him not only when he was a child but as a teenager too. He had always allowed his mother to dominate him, even though he hated himself for it. But now, if his wife began to behave in a way which reminded him of his mother, he reacted angrily and lashed out at his wife in the way he would have liked to have thumped his mother. Again the divine diagnosis had given me a clue. It was clear how I could help this particular couple in crisis.

Sometimes I would sense what *God* was wanting to do.

There was the time when I was listening to a person pour out white-hot anger about her husband, the church, her colleagues and God, for example. I was finding it difficult to be on the receiving end of all this venom and when we prayed together I could find no words. Instead, into the silence came a picture of a hedgehog being held in the curve of a big hand. I sensed that the prickly creature was this woman, that the hand was God's and he was trying to tell me that, despite her anger, he loved her and understood her anguish. There was no need for me to describe this picture to the person concerned. It was sufficient that God had shown me how to pray for her.

But these times of solitude served another purpose too. To share someone else's burden can be like carrying a heavy rucksack: a strain. I would sometimes come to God over-burdened, exhausted and over-identifying with a complaint once made by Michel Quoist:

> Lord, why did you tell me to love all men, my
>   brothers? . . .
> They are bending under heavy loads; loads of injustice,
>   of resentment and hate, of suffering and sin . . .
> They drag the world behind them, with everything
>   rusted, twisted, or badly adjusted.
> Lord, they hurt me! . . .
> They are consuming me! . . .
> What about my job?
>   my family?
>   my peace?
>   my liberty?
>   and me?[12]

At such times I would catch myself worrying about what was going to happen to the person I was trying to help. Like an overwound spring, my mind would cease to function efficiently and I would feel spiritually drained and dry.

In *Listening to God* I have explained that I was learning the value of spending an hour in my prayer room each morning, taking time out to go away for a Quiet Day regularly and making a retreat two or three times a year. I was also exploring the gift of contemplation which I sensed God was giving me; learning that the first phase is relaxation. 'Relax. Let the pressures roll off you. Put your burdens down,' the voice of God seemed to say. And I would picture Jesus standing in front of me with his big strong arms outspread, ready to receive to himself the burdens which were proving too heavy for me to carry. And I would let go of them and the other pressures and anxieties which were paralysing me and, while relaxing, I would become aware of the presence of the living God and open myself up to him completely.

Contemplation is about putting ourselves in the hands of the God who loves us, experiencing that love, basking in its radiance and warmth; being overwhelmed by its power, responding to it; being transformed by its tenderness, strengthened by the giver's compassion; being met in our emptiness by the fullness of God, being found in our lostness by the Shepherd who cares; being refreshed by his never-failing well-springs, being refilled by his life-giving Spirit; discovering by experience the truth of his promises: 'I will come to you', 'My strength is made perfect in your weakness.'

The more I gave, not only to my husband, my children and my friends but to people in need as well, the more I panted for these times of solitude with God. Catharine de Hueck Doherty's observation seemed particularly relevant:

If we are to witness to Christ in today's market places, where there are constant demands on our whole person, we need silence. If we are to be always available, not only physically, but by empathy, sympathy, friendship, understanding and boundless *caritas*, we need silence. To be able to give joyous, unflagging hospitality, not only of house and food, but of mind, heart, body and soul, we need silence.[13]

In the silence and solitude of my prayer room I would sometimes lie prostrate at the foot of the cross which hung on my wall and admit to God: 'All I have to offer you is my emptiness. Please fill me.' And very often the tenderness of his presence and love would creep over me and the words of this hymn would take on new meaning:

> O the deep, deep love of Jesus!
> vast, unmeasured, boundless, free;
> Rolling as a mighty ocean
> In its fullness over me.
> Underneath me, all around me,
> Is the current of Thy love;
> Leading onward, leading homeward,
> To Thy glorious rest above.
>
> (Samuel Trevor Francis 1834–1925)

Praying for a heart that listens

Just as listening to people is not so much a technique as an attitude, so listening to God is an attitude of heart every would-be people helper needs to cultivate. Solomon summed the situation up right at the beginning of his reign when he prayed: 'Give me, O Lord, a heart that listens.'

That is an amazing prayer in the light of the invitation God had given him: to ask for whatever he wanted. This verse (1 Kgs. 3:9) has been variously translated: an attentive heart, an intelligent heart, a heart full of judgement, a heart full of understanding, a wise heart, a discerning heart. The prayer seems to include all these shades of meaning and many more besides for Solomon was not simply asking for the gift of wisdom which would have boosted his own ego and therefore been a personal enrichment and gain. What he did was to ask for 'that openness of heart which is a preparation for the reception of wisdom'; a soul which listened out for every appeal and whisper from God, which was constantly on the watch for every breath of the Spirit and which so opened itself to people that it offered them 'an interior welcome at a deep level' and a silence so impregnated with love that it tuned in accurately to the groans of sufferers.[14]

That was the kind of prayer that was being born in my own heart. It is the prayer that everyone who would be effective in helping hurting people needs to pray. And we can take courage from the fact that God so obviously delighted in this prayer when it fell from Solomon's lips. But even as I have recalled these early lessons in learning for the sake of writing this chapter and the last, I recognise that it is much easier to know that the heart that listens can be of greater value to the poor and the sick than food or comfort and it is much easier to write about the theory of good listening than to translate that theory into practice. I still break the most basic rules. And so I take comfort from Roger Hurding's observation:

> The Spirit-filled, fruit-bearing Christian is likely to be endowed with a genuineness that arises from goodness and faithfulness, a non-possessive warmth that is fostered by kindness, gentleness and self-control, and an accurate empathy sustained by patience, all undergirded by peace and joy, and motivated by love.[15]

I take heart too from the awareness that God uses as an instrument of healing even our imperfect listening. I was reminded of this fact while I was writing this book.

A girl broke down and wept after a church service where I had been speaking. Another woman and I listened to her story and I was somewhat appalled and critical to hear and see my companion break most of the ground rules of good listening before launching into a long emotional prayer for the person in pain. But at the end of the prayer the girl beamed with joy: 'God has really touched me,' she testified and as she left us her face was wreathed in smiles.

This divine overruling does not excuse us from paying careful attention to the discipline and art form of good listening. Nor must we assume naively that, since God is the one at work, what we do matters little. If we are truly concerned about people and truly concerned to be channels through whom he can work, we will do all in our power to go on and on improving our listening skills so that God's work may be perfected in us.

That this may become more and more true in me, I continue to pray, with Mother Teresa of Calcutta:

Dear Jesus, help me to spread your fragrance everywhere I go. Flood my soul with your spirit and life. Penetrate and possess my whole being so utterly that my life may only be a radiance of yours. Shine through me, and so be in me, that every soul I come in contact with may feel your presence. Let them look up and see no longer me but only Jesus. Stay with me, and then I shall begin to shine as you shine; so to shine as to be a light to others; the light O Jesus, will be all from you, none of it will be mine; it will be you shining on others through me. Let me praise you in the way you love best by shining on those around me. Let me preach you, not by words only, but by the catching force of example, the evident fullness of the love my heart bears to you.[16]

Chapter 7

Listening to the Bereaved

Listening to others is much harder than it sounds. That was the conclusion I reached soon after I began the counselling course at St John's College. That conviction has grown with the years. Indeed listening to others is so complex that I sometimes think we need four ears, not just two – one to listen to the words a person speaks, another to pick up that person's feelings, a third to tune in to God and a fourth inner ear to hear what is going on inside ourselves.

To listen to ourselves. At first it came as a surprise to me to realise that if we are to listen to others accurately we must know how to listen to ourselves.

Myra Chave-Jones[1] explains one reason why this is so important. 'If we're not in touch with ourselves, we shan't be in touch with the people out there.' In underlining that listening is like receiving a gift from someone she challenges would-be listeners to examine the way in which they receive the delicate offerings of a person's innermost thoughts and feelings:

Are you really eager to receive them? Do you handle them with care as you would a valuable present? Or are you just waiting for a pause in the conversation so that you can say something? What kind of people do you find it most difficult to identify with? Why? What makes it hard for you to receive their gift? Do you have any particular fears or phobias: of death, for example, or of cancer? Or are there any bees in your bonnet which might affect the way you listen: 'I must press everyone I meet to make a decision for Jesus.' Or are there things you find it hard to hear from others? Such self-knowledge is vital if we are to be effective in our helping of others.

I discovered the truth of this claim when I made my earliest adventures into self-awareness. I discovered, for example, that I am a warm person who needs to give love and to receive it. This is both a strength and a weakness. The strength is obvious because this love includes the compassion I mentioned at the beginning of this book which is the prerequisite of good people-helping. But the weakness is more subtle. Warm loving people can smother others or cling to them or be possessive and jealous. And warm people are inclined to hug or put an arm around others when what the other person needs is space. This is something I have to be careful of so that I do not invade another person's privacy nor offer protective love when the person would grow faster if I stood back and allowed them time to grow without my support.

I also discovered that, because of the mistakes I made personally when learning to listen to God, I had developed an ingrained suspicion of anyone who claims 'The Lord has told me to do this'. If a young person came to me and said, 'The Lord has told me to marry so and so,' I would feel my tummy muscles tighten, my eyes harden and words of caution rushing to my lips. Often I would catch myself being far more anxious to warn such people against the dangers of self-deceit than to listen to their joy or their pain. I realised too that I had an intolerance of garrulous people who talk at me rather than to me. When such people started telling me their story I would switch off, hear the seemingly-endless stream of words, but fail to tune in to the insecurities which the multiplicity of words were camouflaging. It surprised me to discover that with such people I would feel not compassion, but impatience.

My own impatience would then hurtle me on to a guilt trip. John Powell shows how such 'hidden agendas' block the path to good listening:

> Pain has a way of magnetizing our attention to ourselves . . . Almost continually we experience some feelings of inadequacy, inferiority, anxiety, and guilt. If we let these feelings attract all our attention, we will have little presence to offer others. We will have a neon sign on our foreheads, flashing: 'Not Available'.[2]

Another reason why self-awareness is important is that, when a person is being helped through a crisis, it is easy for them to imagine that their helpers might be critical of them or even despairing of them. 'You must be tired of hearing all my troubles,' one might say. 'You must think I'm terribly boring,' another might suggest. 'I must be a terrible disappointment to you – I mean, your prayers haven't been answered, have they?' a third person might whisper, projecting their own worries on to the person seeking to help.

It is safer to face such fears than to conceal them. But if we are to encourage others to be as honest, open and vulnerable as this, we must be prepared to be equally open about our own feelings so that our response is genuine: 'Well, actually, it may surprise you to hear that I don't find you or your problems boring. Do you?' Or 'I want you to know that *you* are not a disappointment to me. I'm disappointed for you. But *you* certainly haven't disappointed me. Are you disappointed with yourself?'

When it came to responding to situations like this, I encountered a problem – a gross lack of self-awareness. Often I was not sufficiently in touch with my thoughts and feelings to be able to respond with the genuineness, spontaneity and sensitivity which is required. So I had to learn.

Much of that learning was painful. Among other things it involved confronting some soul-searching questions. Why did I want to listen to people? Was it because I enjoyed

having people confide their troubles in me? If so, why?
Was it because this boosted my morale; made me feel
important? Was it because I was curious about the troubles
others face? Was it because I needed to be needed? Or
was I, perhaps, feeding on these people emotionally –
using people in need as a substitute for the mutuality of
friendship?

I also worked hard to understand myself better and, in
order to do this, would liken the various parts of myself to
the segments of an orange. 'When you cut the orange in
half, what do you find?' I would say to myself as I tramped
the hills of Derbyshire, spent a quiet day at the convent or
beavered away at my desk.

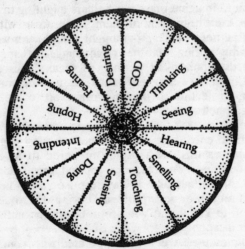

The segments of my orange

What is going on in your mind? What are you thinking
    about?
What is going on in your emotions? What are you
    feeling?
What is going on in your senses? What can you see?
    What can you hear? What can you smell? What

can you feel? What kind of vibes are you picking up?

What is going on in your body? What are you doing with it?

What are your intentions?

What are your hopes?

What are your fears?

What are your desires?

Where are you in your relationship to God?

Listening to pain

Learning to listen to myself in this way became an adventure alongside the other adventures of listening to God and to people. But there were times when listening to myself became almost more painful than I could cope with.

I first became aware of this when the subject we were studying at St John's was bereavement.

Right at the beginning of the seminar we were invited to break up into little groups of three and to talk to the others in our group about a bereavement we had experienced. The word bereavement was used in its widest sense to mean loss through death; or the loss some people feel when they move from a familiar area to a new one; or the losses incurred by redundancy or when a close friend has married and the relationship with them has had to change gear; or a broken engagement. Even as we shuffled our chairs around the lecture room I detected a nervous fluttering in my stomach – as though a thousand butterflies had been let loose inside me. I noticed too a tightening in my throat. Panic gave rise to fear and I was conscious that tears were already pricking my eyes. When my turn came to speak, I described the events leading up to my mother's death.

Mother's death

As so often happens, even though my mother had been ill for so many years the end came suddenly. There had been several 'false alarms' when one of my relatives had phoned our Parkstone home to warn me that my mother might not live much longer. But she had always rallied and resumed her semi-invalid life once more.

So one Sunday night when my sister-in-law telephoned to say that my mother was in hospital again, I saw no need to drop everything and drive to Exeter immediately. I would come in the morning, I promised.

On Monday I drove to Exeter as fast as I could and arrived at the hospital to find my mother already in a coma. I sat by her bed and held her hand, talked to her and prayed with her. But she did not stir. I felt helpless.

The hospital staff warned me that she could linger in this state for days so I drove to Roberts Road to be with my father. We spent most of that day and evening at my mother's bedside, leaving her only to go to my brother's home to eat and to return home to sleep. Early on Tuesday morning we returned. Having been at the bedside for several hours, my father and I decided to return to Roberts Road for an hour or so and to return to the hospital ward that evening. My father kissed my mother tenderly and spoke to her as naturally as though she were fully conscious. 'Cheerio Win! I'll come and see you again later.'

I too kissed her, but though I had been told that a person in a coma can hear the things that are said to them, I now found it impossible to speak. Suddenly I was tongue-tied, not knowing what to say to a mother who was visibly slipping away from us. But I admired my father's lack of inhibition and hoped my mother could hear and feel the warmth and the genuineness of this man who had loved her for so many years and at such great cost to himself.

We had scarcely unlocked the bottle-green door when there was a knock on it. It was Mr Cartwright, the new neighbour in number 38 who was a great friend of my father. Since there was no phone in my parents' home my father had left this man's number at the hospital. Now the request had come. Would my father please telephone.

My father rushed into number 28. A few minutes later he returned looking shocked. All colour had drained from his cheeks and, turning a ghostly white, he simply said:

'She's gone. The Sister said she died about a quarter of an hour after we left.'

I was speechless. While my father slumped into 'his' chair – the one by the wireless where he prayed in the evenings – and put his head in his hands and sobbed, I went into the front room. Dazed.

There on the floor lay a rolled-up carpet which my parents had chosen together a few days before my mother had been admitted to hospital. She would never enjoy it now. I gazed out of the window at the scarlet telephone box across the road. Soon I would need to spend a long time in that box informing relatives and friends. 'Mum died this afternoon.' I wanted them all to know but I did not want to be the one to tell them. It sounded so final. And I was not sure that I believed it. Truths like that are hard to drink in. Yet deep down I knew it was true and in the privacy of that room, where for so many years I had slaved away at my homework, I now gave vent to my feelings in the only way I knew how – with a few stifled sobs.

Grief work

It seemed as though I had only just begun to tell the students this story when Anne called us back so that she could begin her lecture on bereavement.

In telling my story I had not cried. But the exercise had served its purpose. It had brought to the surface the emotions I had felt at the time of my mother's death and now I listened, fascinated, while Anne explained to us what usually happens to a person when a loved one dies or when they are bereaved for some other reason.

There is a recognisable pattern of grief, she explained – stages the bereaved person goes through while they struggle to come to terms with what has happened. The first reaction is shock.

I could identify with that. The feeling of disbelief stayed with me for days after my mother's death. In fact I walked around like someone suffering from concussion. My brain seemed to be paralysed. It refused to function. I felt like a zombie.

This was embarrassing because it meant that I found it almost impossible to make decisions. The day after my mother died I drove my father to the hospital to collect her few belongings. These were neatly piled up on a table. We simply had to check them, then sign for them.

'Do you want to keep her wedding ring?' they asked my father. 'Or shall we leave it on her finger?'

My father looked startled. 'What do you think?' he asked, turning to me. A wave of disgust swept over me preventing me from finding an answer. What did it matter about a ring? It wasn't a ring which either of us wanted at that moment. We wanted the owner of the ring to rise from the dead – at least to say goodbye to us. My father made his own decision. He asked for the ring.

On the way home it was my father who broke the silence. 'I suppose we ought to go shopping. There's nothing for dinner.'

I parked the car. Together we wandered around a supermarket. But it was as though we were in a dream – or perhaps living a nightmare.

'What would you like for your dinner?' I asked. My father replied that he had lost his appetite. I understood. I did not feel like eating anything either. Neither did I feel that I could summon the energy to decide which foodstuffs to buy from the bewildering selection facing me in the supermarket. That indecisiveness worried me. I was not normally like this. What was happening to me? Was I going mad?

After wandering round the maze of shelves for nearly half an hour we decided to buy a packet of sliced ham. 'There's some pickle in the cupboard,' my father recalled. That lunch-time we ate mechanically and because we knew it was the sensible thing to do. But the meal might have been plastic. The ham, pickle and mashed potatoes were tasteless. Bland.

Yes. Anne was correct when she said that the bereaved

person may experience numbness, disorganisation, bewilderment, deep sighing and restlessness. That had certainly been my experience and my father's. It was as though we were viewing life from the double-glazed window of a high tower office block watching the world go by yet not feeling a part of that world – not even wanting to be a part of it.

Emptiness, pining and regrets

The second stage of grief is marked by a persistent longing for the lost one, psychologists warn. There is a feeling of emptiness. The bereaved person may pine for the loved one; they may well weep or attempt to search for the one they have lost.

When I read claims like these I would have more flashbacks to the days following my mother's death. On the evening of her death, my father and I reached for the St Bruno tobacco tin which still sat in the sideboard and still contained the old photographs I had so enjoyed scrutinising as a child. Now my father sorted them out, selecting the ones in which my mother featured. There was a picture of her before she had married my father. There was a picture of them on their wedding day. There was a picture of her with Ray wearing his navy uniform.

More recent photographs were then found in the sideboard drawer. A picture of my mother with Ray's baby daughter, her first grandchild. A picture of her with John, my other brother. Some lovely shots of her with my father on that memorable holiday near Southampton at the time of my graduation. And one of her outside Salisbury Cathedral with my husband on his Ordination day. She looked so petite against my six-foot-tall, well-built husband.

We spent hours too trying to decide what to write as an obituary for the *Express and Echo*, Exeter's evening newspaper. While we toyed with various phrases, she still seemed to be a part of us. And that was what we wanted.

The books on bereavement which I read as part of my training emphasised that the bereaved person will often cherish mementoes of the loved one in an attempt to keep their memory alive. It is a natural, normal reaction. And so is the idealisation of the loved one. I smiled as I recalled the phrases my father insisted on using for my mother's obituary. 'Beloved wife'; 'loving mother of all her children'; 'forty-three years of happily married life'. Of course all of these things were true. But there was another side. We had sometimes felt irritated and frustrated by my mother's refusal to give in. But all memory of that was banished with her death.

During this phase of grieving my father also wanted to see her lying in her coffin. My heart stood still with fear when he announced this was what he wanted and asked whether I wanted to go too.

If I had been brutally honest I would have said no, that was not what I wanted. But by this time Ray had emigrated to Australia. John was suffering from kidney failure, too ill to help, so that left me to accompany him.

'Isn't she lovely!' my father exclaimed when he saw her body. But after that we said nothing. Instead we just gazed, trying to drink in the mystery and, in the silence, said the goodbyes of the heart which we had not been able to say in the hospital. In seeing her lying there in the coffin, it was as though we had found her and that was what we both wanted and needed at that moment.

All the books explained that bereaved people are often oppressed by guilt and feelings of self-reproach. This also rang true in my own experience. In the hours following my mother's death, on the rare occasions when my mind would engage, I would chastise myself: 'If only you'd left Parkstone earlier, you might have arrived at the hospital before she went into a coma.' 'If only you hadn't left the hospital that afternoon you would have been with her at the moment when she went into the presence of Jesus.'

'If only . . .' 'if only . . .' This was a phrase my father used frequently too. 'If only they'd told us that she was about to die we needn't have come home.' It is a phrase which comes quickly to the lips of the grief-stricken person. It expresses one of the phases of grief.

Practical, emotional and spiritual help

At the beginning of the session on bereavement Anne had invited us to recall those who had helped us at a time when we were bereaved. Now she invited us to share our findings.

The exercise made me profoundly grateful to those who had not abandoned my father and me to the desolation of bereavement but who had come to give us practical, emotional and spiritual support.

My sister-in-law was one. While my mother was in hospital and on those traumatic days after her death, Anne cooked a meal for my father and me every evening. That saved us the effort of shopping and cooking and clearing up. I was grateful for that. Both my father and I seemed to be dogged with tiredness. Preparing meals when neither of us had an appetite would have been one burden too many. There were so many things to remember as it was: collecting the death certificate and finding the place to collect it from, visiting the undertaker, selecting hymns for the funeral, choosing a coffin, writing to friends and relatives, ordering wreaths. Yes. That practical help carried us through those days when we seemed to be working on automatic.

The Roberts Road community played their part too. Once the news had sunk in, 'Win is dead,' my father went into the front room and drew the curtains. Then he went to his bedroom and did the same before opening a drawer and taking out a black tie and a black arm band which he proceeded to wear whenever he went out of the house.

These were his ways of announcing to the neighbours that my mother had died. There was no need to say anything. That would have been too painful for everyone. Those who saw the signs interpreted the code. The bush telegraph did the rest.

From the time the curtains were drawn until several days after the funeral, the customary hush enshrouded Roberts Road. People whispered when they passed our house. If neighbours saw me on my own they would ask how my father had taken it. But if they saw him with me they would simply say, 'Hello, Mr Duguid' or 'Hello, Sid', with a tenderness that communicated. They understood. They cared. But they did not want to intrude.

This solidarity with our pain helped. Other people, like the ones shopping in the supermarket we had visited, carried on with the rush and tumble of their normal everyday life. But not our neighbours. They stopped as best they could and identified with our grief by sharing it. This helped to silence within me the protest I had wanted to make on that shopping expedition: 'My mother has just died. How *can* you carry on living as though nothing had happened?'

We were grateful to the Roberts Road community. We were grateful too that some people plucked up the courage to visit us.

Aunt Rene came with her husband and listened while my father related the events of the final hours of my mother's life. Aunt Sally and Aunt Lize, two of my favourite great aunts, came and listened while we went over the story again. Mr Bolt the butcher called even though he had sold his business and now lived fifteen miles away and had to travel in by bus. And Mr Cartwright came from number 28 and just sat with my father and never seemed to mind if he wept.

These listeners comforted us more than they knew. My father and I, like most bereaved people, just longed to talk about my mother. When we were on our own we talked about her most of the time. When compassionate people came to our home and allowed us to talk about our loss, allowing us to cry if the tears flowed, they were God's instruments of healing to us, though they probably never realised it.

Simon Stephens has put the situation well:

To be a compassionate listener, then, is the role of relatives and friends in this particular crisis situation. They must forget self and encourage the bereaved to talk at length and in detail about their loss. There will be tears and long silences. They will hear the life history of the deceased person and the intimate details of his or her death bed over and over again. The compassionate listener need say very little, for his interested presence at the side of the mourner is far more important than anything that he can say. Just to be there and listening to what the mourner has to say is a major contribution to that person's social rehabilitation. It is no easy task! Sometimes it is very painful and distressing.[3]

Others who paid us shorter visits were appreciated quite as much as those who stayed longer. Mr Kettlewell, who used to be headmaster of the School for the Deaf but was now retired, came to offer his sincere sympathy. Our family doctor came. And the vicar came and helped us to plan the funeral.

The funeral! I sometimes wondered how we would get through that service. It all felt so public. But again people ministered God's healing to our heartbreak, not by anything they said but simply by their presence.

When my father and I were disgorged from the funeral car at the top of the stony church drive, we were ushered to our place behind the waiting coffin. The sight of that elm box with its brass handles was like a slap in the face. The last time we had stood together on that spot was on my wedding day when my father was so proud to have me on his arm; dressed in all my wedding finery. Now we were dressed sombrely and together we were giving my mother away. We could no longer deny the harsh reality. Mum was dead. For a few agonising minutes the anaesthetic of grief wore off. Our wounds were exposed. And we stumbled, weeping, behind that flower-studded box into the church. But once we reached the church porch everything changed. 'Look at all those people,' my father whispered. I looked – and gasped. The church was packed. The presence of those people who had taken the trouble to take time off work to come to say goodbye to my mother strengthened us more than anything else could have done in that moment.

I saw my godfather who had given me the Raleigh bicycle when I won my scholarship to grammar school.

I noticed Mrs Furseman who had been a waitress with my mother at Tinlay's Cafe. And I spotted several neighbours: Mr and Mrs Tolman, Mr and Mrs Bolt, and Fred Vosper who lived at 32 Roberts Road, to mention a few.

The strength that flowed into me as I stared at them, emptily but gratefully, took me by surprise. I did not know in those days what I now know; that the word comfort means to strengthen. What I did know was that these people who were not saying or doing anything except by being there were giving me untold comfort.

And so were the words of scripture. As we processed up the aisle, those words of Jesus which the vicar was reading aloud tumbled round my bruised heart and soothed the pain: 'Jesus said: "I am the resurrection and the life. He who believes in me will live, even though he dies; and whoever lives and believes in me will never die"' (John 11:25–26).

'It's not your mother in that box,' these words seemed to say. 'That's only her earthly remains. She lives on.'

I knew that to be true and again I was strengthened – so much so that I could sing the hymns with conviction and confidence. God's presence and love seemed very real. And had not my father and I read together on the night my mother died those wonderful promises penned by the Psalmist:

He who dwells in the shelter of the Most High
    will rest in the shadow of the Almighty . . .
He will cover you with his feathers,
    and under his wings you will find refuge.

(Ps. 91:1,4)

Even so I was grateful for others who incarnated God's love for my father and me.

My eighty-year-old Uncle Bob did this in the funeral car as we travelled to the crematorium. He spent the entire journey quizzing me about my relationship with God.

'I was watching you during the service,' he said. 'You

seemed to believe everything you were hearing and seeing. I wish I could find such assurance of God's love.

'It's strange,' he went on. 'I've been playing the double bass in Handel's *Messiah* every year for as long as I care to remember. I've listened to all those wonderful words. But I still lack the trust in God which seems to be your mainstay.'

In reply I was able to testify to the fact that I was experiencing the divine overshadowing the Psalmist describes and that it was under the wings of God that I found my security in times of testing and trauma. He listened. And giving voice to God's faithfulness increased that sense in me of the peace of God which defies understanding and circumstances and pervades even in the middle of the storm.

Letters and ongoing love

Uncle Bob and the other relatives crowded into number 24 after the funeral. Though I had dreaded this part of the post-funeral proceedings, I found that this too helped. There was only one topic of conversation – my mother. And that continued to be healing.

We all read and re-read the letters which had come trickling in when news of my mother's death had percolated round the city. The appreciation of my mother's pluck, my father's faithfulness, the assurance of people's prayers and their support of us as a family, humbled and helped us. My father had already read these countless times. He was to drink in the consolation they brought very often.

We all admired the bouquet of flowers which someone had delivered for my father and me on the morning of the funeral. 'These are not for the cemetery,' they had said as they thrust them into my arms, 'they are for the ones who are left behind.'

And we all looked at the photographs which my father had stuck in the red leather-bound album he had bought with some money Aunt Sally had given him 'to buy something for yourself to remind you of Win'.

That gathering was rather like a party. A farewell party, it is true. But a most satisfactory and satisfying one none the less.

Then came the slump.

Uncle Bob and his wife left, promising to write to me. Aunt Rene and her husband left, promising to come to see my father soon. David went to fetch our two children who had been looked after for the afternoon by the curate's wife. And my father and I were left with a haze of memories and impressions and a long lonely evening with only the coal fire for comfort.

I shall never forget the relief I felt when Mr Cartwright called that evening. We needed to talk to someone about the wonderful day we had just had. And he came and listened. He would have known nothing of the principles of good listening Anne was teaching us in the St John's course. It did not matter. It was enough that he cared enough to come, to stay, to listen until it was obvious that those pangs of loneliness had been alleviated, at least for that evening. But of course they were to return – especially for my father.

I stayed with him for several days, but David and our two children had returned to Dorset and we all knew that the day would have to come when I would leave my father to work through the remainder of his grieving alone. That day arrived. As I stepped over the brass doorstep to walk to my Dormobile, the pain of the impending separation seemed almost too much to bear.

'Thanks for all you've done, Joycie!' my father managed to mutter through his tears.

'I'll write,' I blurted out, brushing my own tears from my cheeks and kissing him goodbye before climbing into the driver's seat, starting the engine and driving down Roberts Road, past the butcher's, the grocer's, the dairy, the post office and the stationers and turning right into Holloway Street.

'For me, life will rush on as usual,' I mused. 'I have a home to run, a husband and two children to look after, a young wives' group to lead, and a youth group to care for. But dad! He has no one. Nothing. Time will drag.'

Time did drag. During this period my father kept a diary which shows how the few things he did were closely intertwined with the memory of my mother. These entries are typical of many others:

Tuesday	Stayed in.
Wednesday	A fairly quiet morning.
Thursday	Went to see old Mrs Arcott (a lady he and my mother had known forty years earlier).
Friday	Stayed in.
Saturday	Stayed in.
Sunday	Church service.

From time to time he would emerge from this lethargy and enjoy spurts of hyper-activity:

Monday	New carpet laid. Grocery cupboard cleared out.
Tuesday	Shopping and visiting.
Wednesday	Helped Mr Cartwright this evening. Paid funeral expenses.
Thursday	Went for long walk today. Did some shopping in Tinlay's (the cafe where my mother had been a waitress).
Friday	Cleaned right through the house. Did some shopping.
Saturday	Spending the weekend with Reg Bolt at Topsham.

But this outgoing phase would quickly pass to give way to another period of apathy when he would experience that down-drag of bereavement when the loss feels so all-embracing that it seems impossible to get going again in any meaningful way.

A whole variety of people continued to help. The vicar called regularly and encouraged my father to join the Monday meeting for men. My sister-in-law and the

Cart-wrights continued to invite him for meals regularly. People brought him home-made cakes. And all of this eased this pain for which there are no pain killers – the pain of bereavement.

Colin Murray Parkes underlines the value of such practical care:

> The funeral often precedes the peak of the pangs of grief, which tends to be reached during the second week of bereavement. The 'bold face' put on for the funeral can then no longer be maintained and there is a need for some close relative or friend to take over many of the accustomed roles and responsibilities of the bereaved person, thereby setting him or her free to grieve. The person who is most valued at this time is not the one who expresses the most sympathy but the person who 'sticks around', quietly gets on with day-to-day household tasks and makes few demands upon the bereaved.[4]

Meanwhile, for me, life *did* go on much as usual. At times I could even forget that my mother had died so recently and I would imagine that I was recovering from my bereavement quickly, until something happened to jolt me into the painful realisation that the pangs of grief are not easily silenced.

My mother died in January. That March, as Mother's day approached, I went as usual to buy her a card. I had the carefully chosen card in my hand and was about to pay for it when I realised what I was doing.

I put the card back in the rack, and sobbed all the way home. 'I haven't got a mother.' The realisation still stung.

A similar thing happened at Christmas. I went into a shoe shop to buy my mother some slippers for a present, when again the realisation dawned that she would not be needing slippers this year.

But this time I did not sob. I smiled. It was a sign to me that, after eleven months of grieving, I really was recovering. The final phase of grieving, I was to learn at St John's, comes when we are ready to re-negotiate life on a new set of terms. It was not that I loved my mother any less. It simply meant that I was ready to say the necessary goodbye and to live life without her.

My father too seemed to be gaining a new identity. The tone of his letters was changing. He had become verger of the Baptist Church where he worshipped each week and obviously took a pride in polishing the pews and bringing a shine to the silver. He no longer seemed preoccupied with memories of my mother nor did he idealise her any longer. Instead he began to express concern about my brother's failing health. And shortly after the anniversary of my mother's death, he wrote to say he would like to see me because he had something to discuss with me.

When I arrived at number 24, he broke the news that he had met a wonderful widow at church. How would I feel if he married again? They were both lonely and each found in the other the companion they so much needed.

Later that year David preached at my father's wedding at South Street Baptist Church. We rejoiced with him in this new start in life. Since my father was to move to his wife's home, David and I offered to clear number 24 of its furniture. As we loaded into the van the wardrobe and chest of drawers that I had tried so hard to polish when I was still a child, the sideboard which had housed the photographs that had given me so much pleasure, and the carpet my father had laid after my mother died, I realised that this was the end of a chapter. But as we closed the front door of number 24 for the last time and I took a last look at the street which had been home for so many years, it did not occur to me that this painful year had marked a turning point in my life for another reason; that because of it I was to become one of God's wounded healers.

But as I listened to the teaching on bereavement Anne was giving the students at St John's, I knew that, just as others had reached out to me when I was in need, so I wanted to reach out to those who were struggling to find their way through the maze of feelings which confuse most people when they suffer the loss of someone or something they love. Even so, I was aware, as I listened to Anne, that though healing had come to touch and soothe the wounds inflicted by the loss of my mother; and although the reactions my father and I had experienced in the aftermath of her death were perfectly natural and normal, deep inside me there lurked pangs of bereavement that had never been touched. It was when Anne began to describe what can happen to a person who does not grieve when a loved one dies that those butterflies started fluttering in my stomach again and I began to panic.

Chapter 8

Listening to Past Pain

Psychiatrists warn us that one of the most severe strains we ever have to face is the loss of a loved one through death. Even when that person's death is to be expected, because, like my mother, they have been ill for many years, those who are left behind often suffer an acute sense of shock when the news reaches them that their loved one has died. But when one we love dies suddenly so that we have had no time to prepare for it, the shock is greater, the grief may last longer, more long-term damage may be done, and an anxiety state may be precipitated.

And my brother John died suddenly.

Soon after my father remarried, my husband and I moved to Cambridge where David was to serve his second curacy. We had been there just over a year when, one Monday evening, my sister-in-law Anne telephoned with the news: 'John died this afternoon.'

The sense of shock was so great that words seemed to freeze in my throat. 'Oh! No!' was all I could manage by way of reaction at first. After Anne had assured me that she and the children were being well supported by neighbours, I put the phone down. I was in David's study at the time but before I could go to share the news with him I had to cling to his grey, steel desk. Dazed, devastated as I was, everything in the room seemed to be swimming round me as I tried to drink in the news.

John dead? How could he be? He was only thirty-four

years old. He had two young children – just a few years older than my own son and daughter. He had so much to live for: a good job, a comfortable home, the youth group at church. And when they had come to stay a few weeks earlier he had looked so fit – better than he had looked for a year or more. Oh yes. There was that kidney trouble that had been troubling him. But the kidney machine had been dealing with that. The doctor had told him that the prognosis was good – very good. He cannot have died. There must be some mistake.

But there was no mistake. John had died. And a few days later David and I drove to Exeter for his funeral.

Even when I entered John's home I refused to believe he was gone. I looked for him. And as we sat in his lounge waiting for the car to fetch family and friends for the funeral, I felt irritated. What were we all doing there? Why were all these people talking about my brother as though he had ceased to exist?

And everything hurt. John failed to appear. That hurt. Anne seemed to be well in control. That hurt. She read several letters she had received that morning, including one from the Grandmaster of the lodge where my brother had been a freemason. That sent a sharp pain right through me.

The funeral car arrived. I was relieved. I needed to escape from the claustrophobia of that house. The driver was an old friend of John's. They had played the bugles together in the Roberts Road Boys' Brigade. He and I talked about old times all the way to the church. Our reminiscing seemed to make John real again. I needed that. He simply could not be dead.

In contrast to my mother's funeral, going through the motions at John's was like living a nightmare. The church was strange. I recognised few people. David, my husband, walked with Anne. My father was with his new wife. I was alone. Desolate. Even those words of scripture which had seemed so comforting at my mother's funeral: 'I am the resurrection and the life . . .' brought no peace. They seemed to bounce off the cold stone walls of the unfamiliar church, echo round the barn-like building and mock. And a terrible and turbulent darkness seemed to whirl round me with hurricane force and ferocity. Even when the funeral was over the storm refused to subside, and though we drove to John's home I could not face going back into that house where every room and piece of furniture, every picture and cushion reminded me of my tall handsome, fair-haired, impeccably-dressed brother, who would normally be there teasing me and calling me by my pet name 'Joycie', but who had departed this life suddenly and unexpectedly without giving anyone an opportunity to say goodbye. Sobbing on my father's shoulder I begged him to give my apologies to my relatives. And David and I drove home.

The darkness continued to engulf me for the entire journey. David and I scarcely said a word. I could not bring myself to share this inner emptiness even with my husband. Instead I pushed the horrible heaviness of John's tragic death deep inside me and, locking the cellar door, I behaved as though death had not revisited our family. I filled the days that followed with frenetic activity.

A series of losses

At first this proved difficult because, in Cambridge, the expectation of me, the curate's wife, was quite different from the expectations which had been placed upon me in the Parkstone parish. In our first curacy I was expected to be the proverbial 'unpaid curate'. And I loved it. But not so in Cambridge. The vicar we worked with was a bachelor who had had a string of bachelor curates. The parish was not used to a clergy wife and instead of depending on one, several members of the church performed more than adequately the tasks traditionally assigned to the wife of the vicar or his assistant.

In the absence of fixed roles within the fellowship, I looked outside for an outlet for my gifts and found myself a part-time job teaching speech to two pre-school deaf children. I loved these little girls and had great fun helping them to voice their very first words. But within the church I found no immediate natural niche. Perhaps this was one reason why I refused to confront my grief. I do not know. What I do know is that if I had understood then that bereavement means loss – any kind of loss – I hope I would have reacted differently. I now realise that people grieve, not only because a love tie has been severed through death, but they may well grieve in the wake of any other loss: the loss of a limb through surgery or accident, the loss of a job through redundancy or retirement, the loss of treasured possessions, freedom, status or home, the loss of a loved one through a broken engagement or divorce or a move. And the loss of 'what might have been' is a form of bereavement that childless couples recovering from a miscarriage, and some single people who would love to marry, suffer continually.

Gary Collins puts this powerfully:

> Grief is an important, normal response to the loss of any significant object or person. It is an experience of deprivation and anxiety which can show itself physically, emotionally, cognitively, socially and spiritually. Any loss can bring about grief: divorce, retirement from one's job, amputations, death of a pet or plant, departure of a child to college or of a pastor to some other church, moving from a friendly neighbourhood, selling one's car, losing a home or valued object, loss of a contest or athletic game, health failures, and even the loss of confidence or enthusiasm. Doubts, the loss of one's faith, the waning of one's spiritual vitality, or the inability to find meaning in life can all produce a sadness and emptiness which indicate grief. Indeed, whenever a part of life is removed there is grief.[1]

If I had known that, I would have recognised that I had already suffered a whole series of losses. I had lost my mother through death, my cosy Parkstone home and supportive, sensitive friends through the move, my status as the 'unpaid curate', my partnership in the ministry to which David and I believed ourselves to be called jointly, and now my brother. What is more I had exchanged my beloved Purbeck hills for the flatness of Cambridge (a small loss compared with the others but real none the less) and I had slipped a disc playing badminton, so had lost the therapy of releasing tension through energetic competitive sport.

But I could cook. So I baked cakes for the weekly student teas in the vicarage, entertained people for lunch several times a week and served coffee to countless students and young professionals when they shoehorned themselves into our lounge after church on Sunday evenings.

These young adults were members of the church's twenties group. We called it Focus.

During the summer months in Cambridge, students from overseas throng the streets, and that summer, together with members of Focus, I organised a friendship campaign for these students. In this way my relationships with members of Focus deepened. I also started a Bible study in our home for young wives, and preparing for and leading this consumed several hours a week.

I neither grieved for John nor thought about him. And the only way I could cope with the loss of all I held dear in Parkstone was to distance the precious people and places from my mind. For me, the three years there had been such happy ones that I could no longer bear to recall them. The contrast between the past and the present was too painful.

I did not realise at the time that I was on an emotional collision course. Neither did I realise that to bury the memory of loved ones in this way consumes a great deal of energy and is psychologically harmful; that when we lose someone we love we need to give expression to that love; that one way to do this is to weep or mourn; and that to deny ourselves this therapy is to increase the sense of stress.

This busying of myself, this keeping all signs of sadness safely under lock and key, were not deliberate attempts to avoid the painful process of grieving. It was just the way it happened. I knew no other method of coping. People in the church also misinterpreted the signals and read, not signs of sickness, but rather evidence of Christian courage. They applauded this hyper-activity, not recognising that it camouflaged a dangerous vacuum of emotions.

Grief going wrong

Perhaps it is not surprising that, nine months after John's death, I caught flu. This was followed by a severe attack of post-viral depression. David was alarmed and decided that we needed a good holiday. With his customary verve and flair he planned the holiday of a lifetime: a trip to Greece which would include a week in the lovely village of Lindos on the island of Rhodes.

The sun and the sea, time to be quiet with God and together as a family all contributed to the healing process. I regained strength quickly. Even my back improved. As I raced my son along the beach on our last day in Greece, I called out to my husband, 'My back really is better.'

A few hours later I was lying on a trestle table in a crude 'operating theatre' in a primitive hospital in the south of Yugoslavia. While we were driving from Skopje to the Yugoslav-Austrian border, our Dormobile was forced off the road. As it overturned it bounced down a fourteen foot embankment, and my spine was damaged, I sustained head injuries, and we lost most of our possessions.

Instead of spending Easter in Cambridge, as planned, I spent it crowned with bandages in this hospital in the south of Yugoslavia.

'Dear friends, do not be surprised at the painful trial you are suffering, as though something strange were happening to you. But rejoice that you participate in the sufferings of Christ' (1 Pet. 4:12–13). Those were the words on which I had been meditating in Lindos. I had commented on them in a letter to a friend.

David had rescued my Bible from the car, so, propped up in the iron hospital bed, I read these verses from 1 Peter again. I noticed that in the margin near chapter 4 verse 12 I had scribbled: 'these trials will make you partners with Christ in His suffering and afterwards you will have the wonderful joy of sharing his glory'. And against chapter 5 verse 10 I had written this paraphrase: 'After you have suffered a little while, our God, who is full of kindness through Christ, will give you his eternal glory. He personally will come and pick you up and set you firmly in place and make you stronger than ever.'

I marvelled at the way God had seemingly prepared me for yet more losses, but when I returned home it was a different story.

The last straw

Our car was a total wreck – written off. Our cases were ruined. So David packed as many of our belongings as he could salvage into cardboard boxes and, as bedraggled as a refugee family, we travelled across Europe by train. The pain in my back frightened me and I lay on the seat of the train and the ferry for as much of the forty-eight hour journey as I possibly could, hoping I was not causing irreparable damage to my spine.

A friend from church met us in London and drove us to Cambridge. By the time I reached my bedroom I was trembling with shock and fatigue. This friend and David undressed me, put me to bed, made me a drink, and somewhat revived I started to read the letters which had piled up in our absence.

One was post-marked Nottingham. I knew no one in Nottingham in those days and had never visited the city. I was puzzled. But I smiled when I discovered that a girl who had been going out with a member of the Focus group had written to tell me they had decided to get engaged. She ended her letter with a sympathetic sentence which perplexed me: 'I was so very sorry, Joyce, to hear about your father. On top of everything else that must seem like the last straw.'

'Whatever does she mean?' I asked David when he came into the room. He blanched, his jaw dropped open, and clearly he did not know what to say.

'I wasn't going to tell you yet,' he admitted. 'But now I suppose you'll have to know. While you were in hospital your father collapsed at the wheel of his car and died. There was no way anyone here could contact us. But we've missed the funeral, I'm afraid. It was last week. I hid all the letters post-marked Exeter but it didn't occur to me that anyone in Nottingham would know about it. Would you like to see the other letters?'

While David fetched the letters from my family, a few tears found their way to the corner of my eyes. Not many. This sudden severance from my father felt like an amputation performed without anaesthetic. It left me so shocked that after the initial slice of the knife I could feel nothing. This trial seemed too big for me to bear. With a heave I pushed it into the cellar where my unresolved grief for my brother still lay. Stunned, I shared with no one the pain that had pierced my heart when David broke the news. Instead I forced my mind to concentrate on the many signs of God's faithfulness.

That was easy. People at church were wonderful. A student lent us her car for an indefinite period. A businessman gave us an interest-free loan. The women from the Bible study group visited me regularly. My Christian friends commended me for my 'bravery'; 'She's wonderful,' they used to say. 'After all she's been through, she's still smiling.' They were right. I was still smiling. But they could not be expected to know that the smile camouflaged the classic signs of grief going wrong.

In touch with grief

None of us knew that to deny the reality of the death of a loved one, as I was doing, is not bravery but one sign of an abnormal grief reaction. None of us knew that when a person lives in the kind of daze I was in or acts in the kind of wooden, mechanical way I was doing, that these are further signs that things are going drastically wrong. None of us realised that when there is no body to see or bury, the bereaved person can suffer a pathological instead of a normal grief reaction. And none of us was aware that if the grief work we observed in Chapter 7 is postponed or delayed at the time when the loss occurred, then the bereaved person may find that, months or even years later, they will be forced to work through an exaggerated form of the various stages of grief; that until this happens they will not be able to make the necessary adjustments to life without the loved person or thing.

Healing past pain

Four years passed before I learned these facts. It was then that I was introduced to the careful studies of grief reactions made by the Harvard professor, Erich Lindemann. He classified abnormal grief reactions in the following way:

1. A person might be over-active, show no sign of loss and even deny in their subconscious that the loss has occurred.
2. He might acquire symptoms similar to those of the last illness of the deceased. These might be prolonged resulting in the sufferer being labelled an hysteric or a hypochondriac.
3. He might develop a recognised psychosomatic condition: ulcerative colitis, rheumatoid arthritis or asthma.
4. His relationship with his friends and relatives might alter. Sometimes the bereaved person gives up all social contact and lives the life of a recluse.
5. He might go about in a continuous daze, behaving in a formal or mechanical way and avoiding all emotional expression.
6. Anger against specific persons might be spewed out time and time again – the doctor who is accused of neglect, the social worker against whom he threatens to take action.
7. He might lack initiative or drive. The bereaved finds it extremely difficult to make decisions or to complete any course of action without the help of relatives or friends.
8. He might nose-dive into severe depression with insomnia, feelings of unworthiness, great tension, bitter self-reproach and a need for punishment.

With the wisdom of hindsight, I now see that I was manifesting many of these signs of a-typical grief. Though I was physically frail for months, my mind became as hyperactive as ever. Within weeks of the accident David was offered a living in Nottingham. We accepted. The rectory we were to move into had been empty for several months. Every room needed redecorating. I sat in the garden that summer planning colour-schemes, where various pieces of furniture would go in the new home and preparing generally for the move. It never occurred to me that I was about to face yet another mini-bereavement as I left in Cambridge people who had become very special. Neither did I face up to the loss of my father to whom I had drawn so close when my mother died. In fact thoughts of my father were banished from my mind until four years later when Anne asked us to talk about bereavement. Then I panicked.

Inner healing

The reason for the panic became clear when Anne Long turned our thoughts to the subject of healing. Drawing on the teaching of Francis MacNutt, whose ministry was attracting the interest of many Christians at that time, she explained that there are three basic kinds of sickness, each requiring a different kind of touch in prayer:

1. The sickness of our spirit which we have brought upon ourselves because of our personal sin.
2. The emotional sickness and problems which have arisen through no fault of our own but which have been inflicted on us by circumstances or other people.
3. The physical sickness in our body caused by disease, accident or heredity.

She homed in on the second category and helped us to see that the roots of the emotional problems troubling some people are long; that they originate, not from anything the person did, but from things which have happened to them. Such people, she suggested, may benefit from the ministry of inner healing, and she quoted Francis MacNutt to substantiate this claim:

The basic idea of inner healing is simply this: that Jesus, who is the same yesterday, today, and forever, can take the memories of our past and:

1. Heal them from the wounds that still remain and affect our present life.
2. Fill with his love all these places in us that have been empty for so long.[2]

Likening our lives to a house, Anne explained how inner healing works. She gave each of us a picture of a house whose walls were caving in and looking precarious and whose floor area was severely limited because dry rot had left gaping holes through which the occupier might fall headlong at any moment. Under the living room lay a cellar which was not empty but which hid certain stowaways. These stowaways were rather like forceful little people or rebellious children who, though they had been imprisoned, could make their presence felt at the most inappropriate times and in the most inappropriate places. She went on to explain how they had come to live in the cellar area in the first place.

When a child's basic needs are not met, he is filled with fear. The pain is so severe that, in order to survive emotionally, he splits himself from his innermost feelings. Because children are resilient he continues to live and even appears to have forgotten what has happened. But a fundamental part of himself has in fact been pushed away – down into the cellar. The subsequent hurts he experiences as a child, a teenager or an adult force him to fall through the holes in the living room floor and down into the cellar where he is besieged again by all those troubled 'children'. When the storm is over, he pulls himself up to the living room area again and continues to live as though the cellar did not exist. But because of the gaps in the floorboards, the living area is severely restricted.

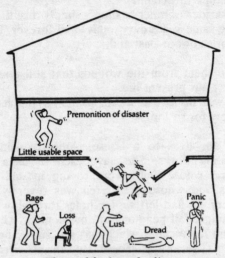

The need for inner healing

The good news which Francis MacNutt, Agnes Sanford, Frank Lake and others were discovering is that these little people need not remain hidden, hurting or needing to hi-jack their owners. On the contrary, they can be brought under the healing and controlling power of Christ. Where this was happening in people's lives, the owner of the house, the troubled person, was unlocking the cellar door, deliberately descending the cellar stairs in the company of Christ, meeting these rioting prisoners, and reliving with them the time and the place when the split had been made. The result was that, for many of these people, the pain disappeared, the person's past and present were so integrated that the cellar area became a peaceful rather than a tempestuous place, the psychological floorboards were mended and consequently the adult could enjoy the spaciousness of the entire living room – or, to translate that into theological language, the spaciousness of salvation, which really means wholeness.

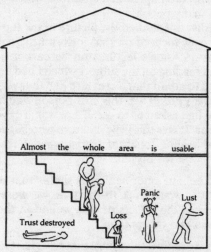

Almost the whole area is usable

Panic

Lust

Loss

Trust destroyed

Going into the cellar with Jesus

These simple pictures[3] made a powerful impact on me for three reasons. First, because at this time I was living in a rectory with a huge cellar area under the lounge. This was approached by a substantial staircase. Part of it was used as storage space and part of it for church meetings. When we arrived, David saw its potential. We carpeted and furnished the biggest room, transforming it from a cold and clinical hall into a church lounge; the other room was converted eventually into an airy office. I could see that something similar could happen in people's lives if emotional cellars were worked over by God.

Secondly, while the counselling course was still going on, a friend invited David and me to see a play about the life of John Wesley. In this play the great Methodist preacher visited a notorious prison. While he was there even the vilest criminals, the murderers, prostitutes and hardened thieves, responded to the love of Christ. Again

I could see that if revival could break out in an English prison in the nineteenth century, God could similarly touch and transform the imprisoned emotions which disturb the stability of many people.

And thirdly, as I studied the picture of the tumble-down house, my eyes focused on that forlorn little figure 'loss'. In the light of Anne's lectures on bereavement and the background reading on the subject which I had been doing, I was forced to admit that a creature like that was crying in the cellar of my life. It was this little person who had stirred when Anne first asked us to recall a personal experience of bereavement. It was this little creature who began to reach out for the healing touch of Christ when I read Francis MacNutt's book for myself:

The idea behind inner healing is simply that we can ask Jesus Christ to walk back to the time we were hurt and to free us from the effects of that wound in the present. This involves two things then:

1. *Bringing to light* the things that have hurt us. Usually this is best done with another person; even the talking out of the problem is in itself a healing process.
2. *Praying the Lord to heal the binding effects of the hurtful incidents of the past.*
   Some of these hurts go way back into the past; others are quite recent.[4]

Asking for help
'Bringing to light the things that have hurt us.' 'With another person.' These were the two points which registered in my mind. Even so I am not sure that I would have acted on them unless God had given me a definite nudge.

C. S. Lewis calls pain God's megaphone through which he speaks to a hard of hearing world. That April, while I was in bed recovering from flu, I realised that I was not only physically weak from the virus, I was also emotionally bruised; that inside the cellar of *my* life lay a part of my personality which had never recovered from the shock and searing pain caused by the series of losses of people and places and prestige I had loved. I was a mere novice in the school of listening to God at the time. Even so, now that I was faced with the reality of my situation, I asked God to show me what to do.

As though in response to that prayer, the story of the Good Samaritan came vividly alive for me. As I lay in bed I tried to imagine what it must have been like to be the man travelling from Jerusalem to Jericho and to be mugged and left lying on the road. I even imagined that *I* was that man; that I had been left bruised, bleeding, abandoned. I watched while two potential helpers hurried by and realised how often I had rushed off to church meetings or Christian Union events rather than stopping to help such a battered person. I became weary and despondent, as this victim of violence in Jesus' story must surely have become. When I heard the sound of the donkey's hoofs I scarcely dared hope that this traveller would stop so much as to look at my wounds. But he did. The sound of his voice was gentle and kind. The feel of his hands on my wounds was sensitive and healing. The taste of his refreshment revived my drooping spirits and the support of his arms restored my dwindling hope.

'I'm sending a Good Samaritan to you,' God seemed to whisper.

The Good Samaritan came in the form of Anne Long. On one of the occasions when she was having lunch with David and me, the conversation revolved around the story of our car crash in Yugoslavia and the sad saga of my father's death. 'How long did it take you to recover from that lot, Joyce?' Anne asked. My reply was spontaneous but took me by surprise: 'I don't think I ever have.'

The subject was not pursued over the meal. It would not have been the right occasion. But it was an important first step for me. I was not the sort of person who found it easy to talk about myself in those days. I had never revealed to anyone, not even myself, just how much I had been affected by the deaths and mini-deaths I had encountered.

But now I had made a beginning. It was only one sentence, it is true. But it was a start. And I had noticed Anne's reaction. She had not registered alarm or disapproval. On the contrary, her accepting, warm response, 'I'm not surprised,' gave me the confidence to phone her at a later date; to ask whether she would be God's Good Samaritan and attend my festering emotional wounds. And she agreed.

Going with Jesus into the cellar

As I drove to Anne's flat I wondered just how I would begin to explain what was troubling me. But I need not have worried. With the skill of someone experienced in listening to God and listening to others, Anne took the initiative. We both love nature. While we drank the coffee she had made we admired the view from her flat: the restful green of the fields surrounding St John's College, the huge oak tree that seemed to exude strength, the flower beds outside her window which were ablaze with colour.

Then, gently, Anne suggested that we offer our time together to God. I was grateful for this prayerful beginning because I knew that, skilful and experienced though Anne was, healing would come, not from her but from the Wonderful Counsellor, Jesus; that if I was to unlock the cellar door with Anne, I would need God's help.

As Anne prayed, the room seemed to be filled with a sense of the presence of God. This gave me the courage to respond to her invitation to take my time to tell her what had prompted me to make the request for help.

At first I struggled to find words to tell her about the anger and panic I had experienced during her first seminar on bereavement. In return, she invited me to tell her more of the story David and I had précised when she came for lunch.

She seemed really interested. And she seemed to care. After the story had tumbled out, Anne asked me a simple but profound question:

'Joyce, have you ever been able to say goodbye to your father?'

The question terrified me. 'Said goodbye? But surely, that means admitting that he's dead,' I thought to myself. 'Well, no. I don't suppose I have,' I admitted.

Anne then explained that it seemed that I had not begun the work of grieving for my father; that the needle of my life was stuck in the groove of denying that he had died. This was not an accusation – just an observation. She went on to explain that in such situations it is important that the work of re-grieving should be done; that a person must admit their loss, face up to its implications and work towards the time when they can wave goodbye to the thing or the person they have been forced to relinquish. The Christian does not have to do this alone. In fact this is where the ministry of inner healing fits in. We can unlock the cellar door, go with Jesus down the staircase and ask him to touch and talk to the bereft and grief-stricken person. Would I like her to be with me while this happened? I wanted to think through the implications of this carefully so we agreed to place a piece of prayer sticking-plaster over the wounds which I had opened up and to meet again when I was ready.

As I drove home that lunch-time it was as though a huge and heavy burden had been lifted from me. In one sense nothing had changed. In another sense everything had changed. Anne had heard my anguish and accepted it as a part of me. She had seen that my capable, coping mask camouflaged a mass of unresolved pain. But she had not rejected me. On the contrary, she had taken my story and me seriously and already the cellar area of my life seemed less formidable.

The Holy Spirit

I have described in *Listening to God* how, shortly after our arrival in Nottingham, the God of surprises took me by surprise by giving me an encounter with himself which transformed my prayer life. This encounter pushed me into making a study of the person and work of the Holy Spirit. The very first reference to him captured my imagination. Before the foundation of the world, we see him brooding over chaos and bringing beauty from it; hovering over emptiness and darkness and creating that many-splendoured thing we call light. His work, it seems, is to replace cacophony with harmony, to bring about integration where there has been fragmentation, and in the words of Isaiah, to give gladness in exchange for mourning.

Somehow I knew that he could do that for me. And I wanted it. So I told Anne that I felt ready to talk again.

Anne suggested that when we next met, she should have another person with her. Two people would be more able than one to discern what was going on in the cellar of my life. Two people would be more effective than one in bringing God's healing to me.

I recognised the value of this suggestion at the time and still do. When someone is being helped in the way Anne was helping me, it is easy to become over-dependent on that person. If the person is also a friend, as Anne was, there is the double danger that the relationship might become over-intense. But an unhealthy dependency and intensity are less likely to become problems when two people are involved in the helping process.

Another reason why two people or even a team of three might be brought in to listen to a person in pain is that to identify with troubled people can be very draining. When more than one helper is involved, while one may take the initiative in the listening and responding and praying process, the others can be tuning in to the person's need and to the still, small voice of God whose wisdom, discernment and knowledge is needed in such circumstances.

The three of us met. There was no need to tell the story all over again. That had been done. Our task this time was to push open the cellar door and go with Jesus to meet the little lost person who lived in the dungeon.

Anne prayed that this would happen and asked that the Holy Spirit would baptise my imagination and bring me in touch with my true feelings. The sense of anticipation in me was high as I imagined myself unlocking the cellar door and walking down that staircase with Jesus. But when we encountered the bereaved person in the cellar, even though Jesus was there, I felt paralysed with pain.

I relived that nightmarish evening when I first learned that my father had died. I felt again that pain which, like a knuckle-duster wound, had left me reeling and stinging all over. Once again, I wanted to escape. But Anne gently and sensitively encouraged me to face it.

I did. I took on board the fact that the father who had rung me the night before I had left for Greece, who had just installed his first-ever telephone so that he and I could more easily keep in touch, had suffered a massive heart attack and had gone without being able to say goodbye. He was dead.

Dead. That word lay on my heart like a lump of lead. It was crushing me, pinning me down.

'Joyce. Is there anything you would like to say to your father or to God?' Anne invited after we had been silent for a while. Suddenly I became conscious of energy filling my body. There was nothing I wanted to say to my father. There was something I wanted to cry out to God. I was angry with him. 'Why did you let him die while I was away? Why couldn't I see him just once more? Why didn't you let me say goodbye?'

The energy generated by that anger seemed to shift the heavy boulder. The anger turned to anguish. I had not thought about my father for four years yet I loved him. That love came surging back.

'Is there anything you want to say to him now?' Anne asked quietly. At last the tears of years came. I don't know how long I wept. What I do know is that I hid my face and sobbed and it was such a relief to cry in that way.

When, eventually, I looked up, Anne was still there, kneeling beside me, watching, caring. Her helper was praying.

Anne smiled – just a sensitive, loving smile. 'Those tears were long overdue,' she said.

I closed my eyes, glad to rest. A few minutes later

Anne's voice broke in on the stillness. 'Joyce. I'm wondering whether you're ready now to say goodbye to your father.'

'Goodbye?' It sounded so final. Yet, when I faced the question I realised that I *was* ready. 'How do I do it?' I asked.

'Do it in whatever way seems right to you,' Anne whispered.

I closed my eyes again. This time I pictured my father as I had last seen him at John's funeral: ruddy with health, full of understanding, supportive, protective love, fulfilled in his role as verger of his beloved Baptist Church, anchored in God and closer to me than he had ever been now that we were weathering this second loss together. I imagined myself driving away from him, leaning out of the window and waving goodbye.

Goodbye to the father who had taught me to pray, to the father who had made endless sacrifices so that I could go to university, to the father who had loved my mother right through to her bitter end and who was now reunited with her in heaven.

The heaviness lifted. Peace flowed into me. I felt whole.

That weekend I walked on my own in the hills of Derbyshire. It was spring. A thrush was sitting on the branch of a tree in the fields where I love to wander. It was singing full throttle, enjoying the sunshine quite as much as I was. The sound of this song arrested my footsteps. I had not been conscious of hearing a bird sing like that since my father died. 'Dad would love to hear you,' I called out to the speckle-breasted fellow. 'He loved songs like that.'

And with that reminder joy and energy, peace and renewed love for my father seemed to flow into me. Suddenly the world seemed so beautiful again that I wanted to embrace it. As I skipped through the fields and over the stile that leads to my home, my heart was light. Suddenly I was happy.

A few days later I was shopping in the fish market in Nottingham. I was about to pay for the prawns I had purchased when I looked up and, for a split second, thought it was my father who was serving me. The ruddy complexion, bright brown eyes and wavy auburn hair of the man behind the counter were so like him.

I paid for the prawns, put them in my basket and smiled. It was a sign to me that real and effective healing had taken place. The heaviness of a-typical grief had been replaced with the searching and finding which are part and parcel of normal grief work. In admitting that my father had died, I had re-found my love for him. This was uniting us now and giving me the courage to renegotiate my life on a new set of terms – without my father's earthly presence but suddenly acutely aware of the many happy hours we had spent together. Gradually I was discovering that saying goodbye to a loved one who has died is not the same as forgetting them or ceasing to think of them. It is simply the way of owning the loss, integrating it, accepting its restrictions and limitations and saying 'yes' to life without the one who has died. This process is painful – but possible.

Helping others
I have no idea why God allowed me to suffer one loss after another in the way I have described. What I do know is that through the help which I received from him and from others, I became one of God's wounded healers.

Shortly after I had said my goodbyes to my father, a member of our own congregation was bereaved. Aware now of the grieving process, I found it a privilege to stay alongside her, to hear her pain, to receive her anger, to assure her that she was not going mad, but that the tangle of emotions which threatened to strangle her were perfectly normal.

At the same time the husband of another friend lay in bed dying of cancer. When I went to visit her one day, I found her hanging her washing on the line. We had not met for some years but she ran into my arms, hid her face and sobbed. I understood. Neither of us spoke. There were no words. It was enough just to be, to let her cry, and to cry with her.

'To cry with her.' A few weeks earlier, while I was still denying the reality of my father's death, I would not have been able to do that. My own hidden grief would have absorbed me. The neon light of non-availability would have flashed from my forehead. But now I counted it a privilege to stay alongside her, comforting her in the same sort of way that I myself had been comforted.

As I learned to stay alongside the bereaved in this way, I discovered that there were certain ways which always seemed to help and certain things which always seemed to hurt.

Listening always helps. As one friend of mine has put it: 'Listening and not trying to judge or pray.' Or if we are not near enough to visit, letters can bring comfort. Because anniversaries – birthdays, Christmas, the anniversary of the death, wedding anniversaries, and so on – can resurrect the sting of bereavement, it helps if we give extra support at such times. Bereavement can last for months, even years, and the person needs to be supported all the way through until they are ready to wave the final farewell.

It is therefore unhelpful to say 'Pull yourself together' or to offer platitudes like 'It'll all work out' or 'Time will heal'. And the inability to listen to the tears and the fears will be as cruel as turning a knife in a gaping wound.

The bereaved person needs to be cherished, they may need company at night for a while, they will appreciate being invited to social functions as long as it is understood that, at the last minute, they might not be able to cope after all.

And although such caring is costly, it brings its own rewards. When the bereaved person does eventually start to re-negotiate life on a new set of terms, we can be assured that the time spent with them has been time well spent. I was glad of the opportunity to give to others what I had received for myself. But what I failed to recognise at the time was the fact that I was still more wounded than whole; that if my heart's desire was truly to draw alongside those entrusted with suffering I would need to open myself further to the healing touch of Christ, because certain emotional hurts, like rebellious children, were still stirring up trouble deep down in the cellar of my life.

Chapter 9

Making Peace with the Past

Several things pin-pointed the fact that there was a pressing need for me to pay further attention to the little people in the cellar of my life. The first was my relationship with David's secretary. But as I traced the manner in which she had been appointed the curious twist in this relationship baffled me.

Because the work in the church was growing, David and I agreed that his need for secretarial help was urgent. We prayed that God would bring across our path someone with secretarial skills who could relieve him of some of the administrative pressures. Within weeks a young vivacious American girl joined the church. While I was talking to her at a fellowship meeting one Monday evening I discovered that she was a qualified secretary and that she was job-hunting. I liked her. When I went home I told David about her. She and her husband came for dinner and we discussed the possibility of her working alongside David in the parish. A few weeks later she took on the thankless task of setting up the church office.

Church office? We had no premises for such an office and so I suggested that our dining room should be used by the secretary during the day and by our family in the evening. This room was conveniently situated near David's study and it seemed an ideal arrangement – until the secretary started work.

She had been working with us for only a few weeks when

I began to behave in an irrational and unreasonable way. Instead of viewing her presence as an answer to prayer, I resented it. Instead of liking her and welcoming the help she gave in answering the telephone and the doorbell, I felt irritated by her presence, which now seemed more an intrusion than a help. And worse, when she and David worked together in his study I found myself hurting inside in rather the same way as I imagine a person who has been stabbed in the chest must feel.

At first I assumed this was the jealousy any wife might feel if her husband is working closely alongside an attractive impressionable young woman. So I gave myself a firm ticking off, confessed my 'sin' to God and expected the situation to change. It did change. It grew worse. And worse. And worse.

It was not that I did not trust David's moral integrity. I did. I knew he was trustworthy. But that belief did nothing to temper the irrationality of the panic which seemed to sweep over me whenever he and the secretary were alone together.

I could not understand myself. I had never felt this way before. It was as though I was consumed by emotions too powerful for me to control. I confessed them, tried to repent of them, asked God to cleanse me of them, but still they refused to budge. Outwardly I was projecting the capable, coping image most clergy wives manage most of the time. Inwardly I was despising myself because the situation seemed so hypocritical and because this conflict was threatening the health and happiness of our home.

This went on for months before my study of the ministry of inner healing, or the healing of the memories as it is sometimes called, brought me hope and also persuaded me to take action.

Several books dealing with the subject of healing past hurts were finding their way from America on to the shelves of Christian bookshops in England at this time. I read them all.

These books reminded me of four facts. First, that time does not necessarily heal memories of past incidents which have been so painful that an individual has had to repress rather than tolerate them. Second, that these memories, though buried deep within the human psyche, can sting quite as effectively twenty or more years after the initial event as they did when they were pushed down into the subconscious. Third, that these memories, though seemingly dormant, possess the power to affect our concepts, our emotions, our behaviour, our view of God, our view of ourselves and our relationships. And fourth, that the ministry of inner healing might benefit those who, though they have confessed and repented, find themselves incapable of making amendments to their behaviour; that there are others who might well be helped through this prayer ministry: those who have become aware that they are held down in any way by ancient hurts from the past or the memory of them; those so held in the grip of unreasonable or irrational fears, anxieties or beliefs that they seem handicapped; incapable of behaving in a normal, loving, Christ-like way. And those who were once excited by the concept of the freedom they could enjoy in Christ but for whom this promise now seemed nothing more than a mirage.

The book which influenced me most was that of the Jesuit Francis MacNutt. His claims made a deep impression on me – in particular the suggestion that the kind of irrational behaviour which I was displaying might spring, not primarily from a person's innate sinfulness but rather from the vulnerability which arises from a hurt inflicted on the person in the dim and distant past:

> Somewhere between our sins and our physical ailments lies that part of our lives where we find many of our real failings as human beings – our emotional weaknesses and problems . . .[1]
> Some of these hurts go way back into the past; others are quite recent. Our experience coincides with the findings of psychologists: that many of the deepest hurts go way back to the time when we were most vulnerable and least able to defend ourselves. There

is a good deal of evidence that some hurts go back
even before birth while the child was still being carried
in the mother's womb. Just as John the Baptist leapt
in Elizabeth's womb when she heard Mary's greeting,
so every child seems sensitive to its mother's moods. If
the mother does not really want the child or is suffering
from anxiety or fear, the infant seems somehow to pick
up the feelings of the mother and to respond to them
. . . These earliest memories up to the time we are two
or three years old seem to be the most important in
setting the patterns of our future behavior – long before
we are free to make our own personal decisions.

If a person has always felt unlovable or has always
been restless or fearful, the need for inner healing
probably goes all the way back to the very earliest
years of life.[2]

The hope in me gave rise to a prayer that Jesus, the
Wonderful Counsellor, would shine his searchlight into
the cellar of my life and expose anything there which was
stunting my growth. 'Lord, if there is anything from my
past which is invading the present and spoiling my walk
with you and my relationship with David, please show
me,' I whispered one night as I went to bed. As though
in answer to that prayer, I woke up next morning with
three distinct childhood memories playing on the video
of my mind.

Childhood hurts

The three childhood memories seemed to be a variation
on one theme. Rejection. Or more accurately, perceived
rejection. The most painful one was of myself lying in
my child-size bed in the corner of my parents' bedroom
in Roberts Road. I was burying my head under the
blankets while they made love, tears were stinging my
eyes but I was fighting them lest I should let out the
sobs of loneliness I wanted to cry. I scarcely dared
breathe because my mind was telling me that I should
not be there. I was intruding. So I lay like a whimpering

puppy, too frightened to let out its yelp. And I felt desolate.

With this picture came the reminder that, when I was little, my father had worked in the bakery at nights and had slept during the day. This meant that at night time there was a spare place in the double bed beside my mother and that is where I slept. But the day came when, for health reasons, my father had to give up his job as a master-baker and then there was a crisis. Where was I to sleep? A child-size bed was bought for me and at first I enjoyed having my own corner of the room. But gradually I missed the warmth and comfort of my mother's presence in bed and wanted to go back to the old arrangement. This of course was neither possible nor appropriate. But I felt isolated in my small dark, make-shift corner.

These feelings of isolation intensified if I was still awake when my parents came to bed. On such occasions my mother would talk to me until I was drowsy and drifting off to sleep. Except when she and my father planned to make love. Then she would pretend to have a headache, tell me she could not talk tonight, that she was rolling over to go to sleep. A few minutes later I would hear them whispering and kissing and fondling one another and I would feel confused, unwanted, unhappy, abandoned. Pushed out.

Each of the books I had read suggested that when painful memories like this were brought to the light of consciousness, the event should be recalled as vividly as possible and relived. The person reconnected with that pain should then seek to discern what Jesus had been wanting to do or to say to them when the original event was taking place. As his presence was revealed, healing would come to the hurt, love would be poured into the loveless places, the effects of the hurtful past could be so bound that its stranglehold would be broken and the sting would be removed. Consequently the past would lose its ability to affect the behaviour of the adult adversely in the present.

I wanted this freedom but did not want to betray or

appear to be blaming my parents. So instead of seeking the help of someone skilled to counsel, I used my own prayer time to ask God to touch this painful memory and so to heal it that my behaviour might be transformed.

In my imagination I returned to the bedroom in Roberts Road and as I lay in the bed in my corner, I could feel the blankets and hear the muffled sounds coming from my parents' bed. I was hurting now just as I had hurt as I lay in that room listening to sounds I should have been protected from. And I cried to God to reach down and rescue me. As I prayed in this way, I plucked up courage to peep out of the blankets and I saw that a screen was now dividing my bed from my parents'. The screen, I noticed, was decorated with angels whose wings stretched almost to the ceiling and touched, giving me the privacy I needed. As I examined the screen those angels seemed to come alive, forming a partition which separated my corner from the rest of the room. And with their presence came the reassuring promise: 'He shall give his angels charge over you to protect you in all your ways.'

I gazed in wonder at the screen. It was enchanting. And as I gazed, that corner of the bedroom lost its terror. It was as though the sting had indeed been removed from this particular memory. I was at peace.

In one sense nothing had changed. The fact remained that I had had to share a bedroom with my parents. The fact remained that I had not been able to cope with feeling on the fringe of their relationship when they were expressing their love for one another. The fact remained that I had interpreted this as rejection of me. Nothing can change those facts. They happened. Yet in another sense everything had changed because the aura that surrounded the memory had changed. Instead of feeling isolated, too frightened even to whimper, I felt bathed in the warmth and light of the love of God communicated to me through these messengers of his – the angels.

I was so convinced that this lay at the root of my irrational behaviour that I expected that once this memory had been touched by God I would change overnight and become warm and outgoing and loving to David's secretary. But, alas, I was to discover that the healing of the memories is not a short cut to maturity or a formula for finding instant freedom. No. It can be a vital and significant start. But it is only a start to a process which may take months or even years to complete. God, after all, is not in a hurry. He is looking for perfection, not quick results.

I did not realise this at the time and since I was unwise enough to seek God's healing touch on my own, no one was there to explain to me that what had happened was that I now understood why my behaviour was so bizarre. I also understood why my jealousy was accompanied by such panic and I felt better inside when I thought about my childhood, but before my behaviour was likely to change there was more work to be done.

Distressed, I went back to God and asked him to touch me again, to set me free from this terrible handicap. As though in answer to this prayer, I participated in a meditation with some students on the counselling course at St John's College.

'I'd like you to imagine that you're lying in bed,' Anne Long invited one afternoon, 'and you are holding a mirror over your head. Look into it and see what you can see.'

At this stage of the meditation I saw myself, not as an adult lying in the bed at the rectory, but as a child lying in the bed in Roberts Road, hedged in by my angels. I could see the mirror over my head but as I looked into it, it became the face of God and I seemed to hear him say over and over again: 'I love you.'

This place which had once been filled with terror had become a place where I was cocooned in love. God's love. And again I sensed that healing was taking place, in the sense – to borrow a phrase from St John of the Cross – that God was pouring love in where love was not.

My love for God deepened as my heart overflowed with gratitude. But still my behaviour did not change. It was as though I was fixed now in a pattern of behaviour which was childish in the sense that I was reacting to the situation in the rectory as though I were a petulant, hurting child and though I could make the connection with past pain and though I had seen God in it all, I could not relate this first phase of inner healing to the irrationality of my thinking and my behaving.

But God, as always, was wonderfully patient. When, on another occasion, I asked him to shed light on the situation, he pieced another part of the jigsaw into place. This time, as I lay in the bed surrounded by my now-familiar angelic companions and still cocooned in the felt love of God, Jesus himself seemed to come to me. He knelt by my bed, held my hand and explained to me that what was happening on the other side of the partition – my parents' love-making – was natural and healthy; that they were not rejecting me but rather expressing love to one another in a rightful God-ordained way. Because he was so tender and sensitive in his explanation of these truths, I could both understand and accept what he was saying. And my mind was renewed.

This time my behaviour did change. But in a way I had not expected.

Until this time, I would squirm if a courting couple came to settle themselves on the benches I could see from the kitchen window of the rectory or if a couple started to make love in a film or play I was watching. One sunny summer lunch-time, however, while I was washing up and a couple were kissing and cuddling on the bench by the rose bushes in the pedestrian precinct below my home, I registered a complete absence of the normal pain and discomfort. 'God *has* been at work,' I marvelled. 'I've never been able to do that before.'

But my gratitude was laced with disappointment. The jealousy problem continued to plague me. And I felt cheated. I had done everything the books described. I had asked the Holy Spirit to show me where the trouble stemmed from. I had invited Jesus to heal the hurts of the past and set me free from their crippling effects. I had experienced his presence in the place of childhood pain, but still I was locked into immature ways of behaving and this was still spoiling my relationship with David, his secretary and God.

A year passed. The secretary left. I knew that I had hurt her. And my emotions were mixed. There was relief that, at last, home could once more be home. But I was riddled with guilt too. And of course the problem did not go away. Other colleagues came to support David in the work and I discovered that the panic of feeling pushed out and rejected flared up, not only when David was working with women, it reared its ugly head when he worked closely with men also because the chief problem was the fear that I was being squeezed out of his life and his love.

The tap root

I was unaware when I embarked on this quest for wholeness that God delights to hand us one piece of the jigsaw at a time. When that one is in place, he provides the next. Another missing piece was to come in the course of the lectures on counselling which I was still enjoying at St John's.

The second term was designed to help us to understand the complex and fascinating ways in which the personality develops. To illustrate one of her lectures on child development, Anne Long used a model created by Christian psychiatrist Frank Lake, which illustrates the importance to the baby of the mother-child relationship particularly during the first nine months of life.[3]

The diagram shows that, just as in the womb the baby is dependent on its mother for physical and emotional sustenance, so after it has been born, the child is helplessly dependent on its mother for the sense of well-being which comes first through unconditional acceptance and second through various kinds of sustenance. Acceptance, according to Frank Lake, is transmitted most effectively through 'the umbilical cord of sight'. He claims that access to the sight of mother is access to life, to knowledge of who I am; to belonging. 'The Infant's Being lives in the light of her countenance. To be shut out is slow death. The way in . . . is opened up by Mother's return; the look in her eyes and the sound of her voice.' Other psychiatrists claim that this acceptance comes through physical contact – particularly when the child is under stress or is confused: 'Holding protects.'

Sustenance, on the other hand, is fed physically through the inflow of milk when the child is at the breast, but equally emotional sustenance flows from the mother to the infant 'on every level of personality'. The child's emptiness is met by mother's fullness, satisfaction and joy. Through relating to her, the child discovers its worth, meaning and sense of well-being as the abundance of her life and love, graciousness and generosity overflows to the baby.

This kind of accepting, sustaining love not only gives birth to trust – the ability to open oneself to warmth and love – it gives rise to the ability to respond to love and it fills the child with the creative energy which enables it to feel, though not necessarily to voice, that joyful confidence: 'I am me. And it's good to be me.'

When such rightful self-confidence surges through a child, that child is strongly motivated to take the initiative in learning the skills which are part of the adventure of life and also to open its arms and heart to others: father, grandparents, aunts, uncles, playmates. It is as though the child has travelled through a tunnel of love. Fed and stimulated by the mother's accepting, sustaining love, the child has discovered the delights of being a person in its own right. It therefore emerges from the tunnel bursting with vitality and spontaneity; filled with a sense of personal well-being, quite capable of taking the initiative.

But where this unconditional love has been withheld for some reason, the trust patterns which have been established in the womb are broken, hope dies, a feeling of worthlessness steals over the infant and he lacks that *joie de vivre* which characterises his more fortunate peers. Such infants will not necessarily grow up lacking in initiative. What they might do as adults is to move round the cycle in the wrong direction – trying to gain acceptance and status through the things that

As the mother gives the baby sustenance on every level, physical and emotional, the child's sense of well-being expands

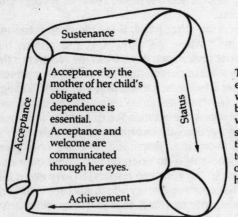

Sustenance

Acceptance by the mother of her child's obligated dependence is essential. Acceptance and welcome are communicated through her eyes.

Acceptance

Status

Achievement

The child now enjoys a sense of warmth and belongingness. Life with mother feels so spacious, yet secure, that the child wants to learn how to love others in the way it has been loved.

The child is now ready for the demands of learning: identification with hurt creatures, patience with other children, gentleness in actions.

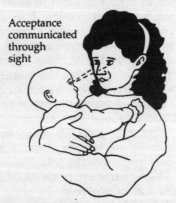

Acceptance
communicated
through
sight

The importance to the child of loving looks

they achieve rather than because of the people they have become.

As I drank in the implications of this particular model, I felt raw inside. It was as though someone had torn the skin from my flesh and left parts of me grazed, exposed and stinging. This pain refused to be pushed below the surface again. But conscious that praying about past pain on my own had not produced the desired fruit on the earlier occasion, I plucked up the courage this time to ask Anne Long to pray over these grazed feelings with me.

Combining good listening with prayer

Again, as I drove to Anne's flat, I wondered how I would begin. But I need not have worried. Anne was an experienced and gifted listener who was well practised in the twin arts of listening to God and listening to others. When I arrived I tuned in to the prayerfulness which pervaded her flat and knew that she would already have committed this session with me to God. I also knew Anne well enough to know that she would offer me her full concentration, try to understand why I was feeling sore, and, as best she could, be the bridge on which God and I could meet. I knew too that she would not hurry me. She had set aside a chunk of her morning to minister to me.

I did my best to describe the inner turmoil that was tormenting me; the fear that my parents loved me, not for who I was but for what I could do. I told her, too, that when she had used that little phrase 'broken trust patterns' to describe what happens when a baby is deprived of the mother-love it craves, it was as though someone had pierced my heart with a dagger. When I tried to translate the pain into words it sounded pathetic and childish but I could tell that Anne understood – that she was not condemning me for being stupid or melodramatic – so I went on to try to explore with her why I was reacting in this way to the diagram she had used.

'I feel uncomfortable talking like this,' I confessed. 'It sounds as though I am criticising my parents and I don't want to do that because I know that they loved me. It's just that, at times, I didn't *feel* loved.'

Anne assured me that she could listen to the details of my story without pointing the finger at my parents. She also pointed out that although children are very quick to pick up messages, they are not so good at interpreting them accurately. Sometimes, therefore, they perceive a hurt like rejection even though the people caring for them had no intention of turning their back on them. Reassured, I told her what was troubling me.

At the beginning of our time together we had asked God to give us wisdom and knowledge and the necessary discernment to make this a healing time. And as we talked, two things my mother had told me more than once as she reminisced about my birth flashed into my mind. They seemed irrelevant, but I voiced them none the less. The first was that I had arrived earlier than expected – so early that she had not even bought a pram for me and had had to borrow one from Mrs Bennett, who lived at the top of Roberts Road and whose son Laurence was born several weeks after me. The second was that it had been a difficult labour and for five days after my birth she had gone blind.

Blind! That word hurt. I thought again of that picture of the mother and the baby enjoying eye contact. No wonder a stab of pain had gone right through me when I saw that. This life-giving look from my mother was a necessity which had been denied me in those earliest hours and days of my life. That pain had been buried all these years but now, like an inflatable ball in water, it refused to be held down any longer; instead, it insisted on bobbing around on the surface of my life so that it could be dealt with.

Anne's acceptance of me and her ability to tune in to the desolation I was experiencing made it safe to share. Indeed it was a relief just to ventilate these feelings. But both Anne and I were aware that, in a situation like this, 'just listening' is not enough. That would simply bring to the foreground of my consciousness and in sharp focus the pain of the past but do nothing to help me to cope with the reality of its crippling presence. This was an occasion when listening paved the way for a more direct touch from God. And so Anne suggested that we should pray.

Prayer for inner healing

As far as I remember, Anne simply prayed that God, who is the Lord of the past as well as the present, would reach back in time to touch and to heal these wounds which had been inflicted on me. Then we waited to see what God would do.

While we were waiting, silently, it was as though I 'became' a baby again. What I mean by this is that I was imagining myself lying all alone in a field on the edge of a wood. I neither struggled nor cried. I just lay there – utterly helpless. But as I lay there alone, empty, helpless, vulnerable, I detected footsteps and later became aware of a presence. It was Jesus. He was emerging from the wood and coming to the field where I lay. When he arrived he bent over me lovingly. With one strong but tender finger I felt him stroke the downy hair on my head. That touch was comforting. He placed his finger in my tiny fist and I clutched it in the way babies delight to do. I liked that. Then my eyes focused on his face. I saw the smile which lighted it as he gazed at me. 'Gazed at me!' Yes. Through his eyes he was loving me in a way in which my mother had been unable to do for no fault of her own. He was bringing me into a new dimension of life.

Warmth, strength, hope, even joy flooded into me as Jesus poured his fullness into my emptiness, as he met my helplessness with his sensitive strength and as he exchanged my desolation for the consolation of his felt presence.

The scene changed. The wood was replaced by a brightly lit room. I was still lying down, a helpless, vulnerable baby. But this time I was surrounded by noise, hyper-activity and panic. None of the attention was centred on me. On the contrary, it was as though I had been abandoned. I was all alone. Frightened. But passive. Alone? No. Here again I sensed that loving, healing presence. Jesus.

I was able to describe little of this to Anne. All I could say by way of explanation was that, whereas I had arrived at her flat hurting all over as though I had been rolled in a bed of stinging nettles, now I seemed to be bathed in peace. Anne was sensitive to the wordlessness of what was happening to me. When she saw that God had answered our prayer and touched me she slipped away, leaving me to luxuriate in his presence.

I do not remember how long I stayed in Anne's flat just drinking in God's love. What I do remember is that a few days later I stumbled on a passage of scripture which I had never consciously encountered before but which seemed to describe graphically the miracle that had happened to me. It was embedded in Ezekiel:

> On the day you were born your cord was not cut, nor were you washed with water to make you clean, nor were you . . . wrapped in cloths. No-one looked on you with pity or had compassion enough to do any of these things for you. Rather, you were thrown out into the open field, for on the day you were born you were despised. Then I passed by and saw you kicking about in your blood, and as you lay there in your blood I said to you, 'Live!' I made you grow like a plant of the field. You grew up and developed and became the most beautiful of jewels. Your breasts were formed and your hair grew, you who were naked and bare. Later I passed by, and when I looked at you and saw that you were old enough for love, I spread the corner of my garment over you and covered your nakedness. I gave you my solemn oath and entered into a covenant with you, declares the Sovereign Lord, and you became mine.
>
> (Ezek. 16:4–8)

Although this passage was originally intended to paint a thumb-nail picture of God's faithfulness to Israel, I could see that, in so many ways, it described his unfailing love to me also. It seemed as though he was telling me that, because my mother went blind at my birth, all the attention had been centred on her and not me; that I had been denied the holding and the cherishing a newborn infant needs. But he, God, had not abandoned me. On the contrary, he had come to me then just as he had come to me when, as a teenager, I had surrendered myself to him.

This moved me very deeply. In speaking to me of the love of God it touched the pain of rejection right at its root.

The next stage

Anne and I met on a subsequent occasion to seek to learn from what I had experienced. It was then that I described to her the pain I had relived in my parents' bedroom. And together we drew the parallels from these two memories. On both occasions I had *felt* frightened, abandoned and pushed out of my rightful place. No one had actually elbowed me out but it felt to me as though they had. On both occasions I had not protested but, on the contrary, had remained quiet and still. On both occasions I had felt unloved. Neglected. And the message which I had absorbed was: 'I'm an intruder. I must keep out of the way or lie very quiet and still. I must not be a nuisance.'

Psychiatrists have a term for the passive kind of reaction I relived. Defensive detachment. Dr Bowlby, in his study of child development, explains that in such situations there is a recognisable pattern of behaviour. A distressed infant will protest in some way – maybe with frantic crying. If the mother or some other significant figure fails to appear, the crying will subside as the child becomes passive and withdrawn. Those caring for him believe that he has calmed down; that he no longer needs attention. But the reverse is true. By this time the child has crossed the threshold of his own tolerance to pain and, in an attempt to survive, he detaches himself from the situation and the people. His silence is not peaceful. It is pregnant with stress and heavy with loss.

Something of this stress reaction contributed, I believe, to the irrational but seemingly real equations I formulated at an early age. And because I believed them I learned to live within their restrictive framework. Even though I was supposed to be an adult, whenever a new member of staff joined our team I would enquire anxiously whether they could cope with a husband-wife partnership 'at the top'. If I sensed that they were finding this difficult, I would panic, withdraw and seek escape rather than run the risk of being proved to be a hindrance to David and his work; rather than run the risk of being pushed out yet again. But whereas, as a child, I would lie passive and refuse to make any response, now that I was an adult I was responding to this new situation with anger. It was this smouldering anger which confused David because I would accuse him of not wanting me beside him in the work and he would look bewildered. He believed, as I do, that we were called by God to minister together. He wanted me alongside him. The last thing he wanted was to exclude me. But when he tried to reassure me of that fact, even after God had touched the memories and restored a vestige of peace, I dared not believe him.

My immature behaviour hurt many of our colleagues. And it distressed me. But through it I discovered what the books at that time had not highlighted: that to seek a touch from God for the emotions can simply be self-indulgent unless we are prepared to follow this up with four more steps. These do not necessarily come in any strict sequence but they are all vital.

One is to forgive. When a person discovers that life has dealt them with a seemingly incomplete pack of cards and that consequently they seem to have been conditioned to play a very inadequate game, they can become consumed with bitterness and resentment.

The resentment against my parents, which I identified as I relived the scene in their bedroom, took me by surprise. 'Why couldn't they have moved?' I complained to God. 'Yes. I know they were poor; that they couldn't afford to buy a house but my godfather who owned 24 Roberts Road had offered them two other bigger properties. We even went to see them and I'd been so excited at the thought of having a room of my own.' As I made this complaint I recalled how my godfather had taken us personally to both of these houses; how he had tried to persuade my parents to move, saying, with a knowing look in his eye: 'It's not good for you to have Joyce in your room any more.' No wonder I felt a nuisance, an intruder. 'Lord, it was so humiliating to have to be there,' I said with some self-pity.

But they had chosen not to move. And the day came when I had to let go of my anger and bitterness and resentment. To forgive. When I did this, feelings of sorrow that they had not been able to see the situation from my perspective persisted but at the same time I realised that they had never intended to scar me in the way they had done. They loved me. 'Father, forgive them. They didn't know what they were doing,' I prayed.

Some hard work

But even this was not enough. I had hurt people with my childish behaviour. Now the time had come to repent. To repent does not simply mean to feel remorse or even sorrow. It does not even mean righting the wrongs of the past. Indeed some wrongs can never be put right. Repentance remains bare and barren until it has effected a change in our behaviour. God had touched my emotions so that I could recall these past hurts without pain. He had also touched my perception so that I saw clearly where I had drawn an inaccurate conclusion from events which had caused me pain. Now I was faced with the task of changing my beliefs and changing my behaviour. This would mean re-learning how to relate to people. It would involve me in taking risks. It would entail a whole new way of thinking about myself and situations. And it demanded that I forsake childish things, to use the language of St Paul; that I learn to live as an adult.

This was easier said than done. The way it eventually became possible for me to achieve my goal was to confront my thoughts and beliefs. To return to the picture of the house, this time I visited not the cellar, where rebellious emotions had lain hidden for so long, but the loft where irrational thoughts and erroneous beliefs ruled the roost: the belief, for example, that I would never change; that the situation was hopeless.

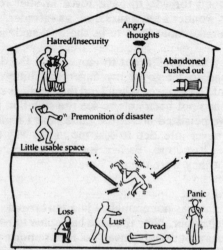

Hatred/Insecurity

Angry thoughts

Abandoned Pushed out

Premonition of disaster

Little usable space

Panic

Loss

Lust

Dread

The need for the second stage of inner healing

I was to discover that just as there is a staircase down into the cellar making that area of one's life controllable, so by the grace of God there is a ladder leading to the loft of our lives. Over a period I learned to climb into that loft, and to put to the little people living there some pertinent questions:

Do you want to change?

How do you feel about the way you are behaving?

How would you advise someone else to behave in the kind of situations which cause you to panic?

Are you prepared to co-operate with God in taking full responsibility for bringing about the necessary changes?

I was able to say a resounding yes to the first question. I did want to change. And my response to the second was equally firm and honest. I admitted that I felt ashamed of the childishness which had dogged me for too long.

The third question brought some much-needed objectivity into the situation because I was highly-motivated to change by this time and to such a person I knew that I would put questions like this:

Is there any evidence to support your fears or are they manifestations of the old irrationality creeping back?

What is the rationale for the way your mind is working?

Are you mistaking feelings and perception for hard facts?

Could there be another way of viewing the situation?

If you're not sure whether your interpretation is accurate, could you ask a trusted friend how they view the situation and learn to take them at their word?

Are you thinking biblically?

Little by little, I learned to apply questions like these to myself. They helped. Most often, when I was tempted to react in the old childish way, it was because I was reacting immaturely rather than responsibly. And I found that by applying my mind to what I was doing, now that the hurts of the past had been touched by God, I could learn to live differently. But it took time and I needed a great deal of support from my husband to help me make the necessary changes in thinking and behaving. The most liberating moment of this whole healing process came when I said my 'I will' to God in response to the question: Are you prepared to co-operate with God in bringing about the necessary changes? After that it was with a sense of excitement that I set myself realistic short-term goals and learned to take the risks involved in reaching them.

These steps towards wholeness were far from pain-free. I soon discovered that, just as my old back injury, although healed to all intents and purposes, can still cause trouble if I ask too much of it or if I am overtired, so these memories which have been touched in the way I have described, are an Achilles' heel in the sense that I am still capable of misinterpreting situations where I feel pushed out. But God's work of transformation continues. I am still changing. Still growing up. And I am so enjoying the experience that I am glad I mounted the ladder that leads to the loft.

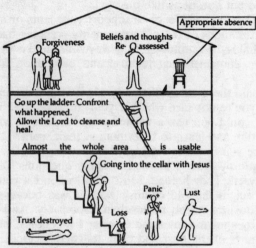

Inner healing after the second stage

Ministering to others

John and Paula Sandford, in their book *The Transformation of the Inner Man*, make this memorable claim: 'Out of the ashes of what we have been and have done has grown the ministry we are . . . Transformation celebrates that the lizard which rode our back is the very thing which will become the noble steed to carry us to victory in the battle for others.'[4]

This has been true to my experience.

Just as God touched and transformed my perception and my behaviour and gave me a taste of that greater wholeness which he always intended his creatures to enjoy, so I have had the privilege of staying alongside others who have been struggling to be set free from the hurts of the past. I have watched some of them enter into the freedom and the abundance of life that there is in Christ. Some seem to have been released from the crippling bondage to past hurts in a remarkable way. Others have relaxed as God has removed the sting from painful memories of the past. And I have wept and laughed with those who have taken courage in both hands and forgiven the people who inflicted such heinous wounds on them when they were weak and vulnerable. Indeed to take the power and love of the crucified, risen, ascended, returning Lord Jesus to a person's pain and watch while he handles it is one of the greatest joys of my counselling ministry. But over the years, alongside this joy has grown an increasing concern about its misuse. Some have seen inner healing as a panacea for all woes. It is not. Some believe that everyone should undergo such spiritual surgery. This is far from the truth. Some believe that inner healing only involves reconnecting the person with the painful past and enabling them to feel the healing touch of Jesus. It does not. Others go on and on peeling off the layers of the onion in 'bless me' sessions while they make no attempt to grow in maturity. And this is a mere caricature of a form of listening to God and to others which can produce prolific growth in personality.

But, as David Watson used to remind us, the antidote to misuse and abuse is not no use but right use. And in a day and age when the ministry of inner healing is being brought into disrepute there is an urgent need to pay attention to its right use and to be aware of the dangers so that we can avoid them.

I was turning these things over in my mind when I travelled from Dover to Calais recently. My husband and I had driven through thick fog to reach the ferry terminal but as we stood on the deck waiting to depart, the sun shone on the white cliffs of Dover even though the rest of the country was still enshrouded in milky-white mist.

As I drank in the crisp autumn air, I watched while the ferry was cast off. It was no longer tied to the harbour. On the contrary, it was free to venture across the English

Channel. But it would not have moved unless someone had started the engine and determined to set sail. 'But even when the ferry docks at Calais, that is not the end of the voyage,' I thought to myself. 'When we arrive in France, a whole new part of the adventure begins. There we have to learn how to drive on the "wrong" side of the road and remember to speak a different language. And that's rather like the ministry of inner healing. When Jesus comes to a person in emotional pain and touches, soothes and heals their innermost sores, it is as though the ferry of their life is cast off. They need remain in bondage to the past no longer. But that person still has to pluck up courage to start the engine of their life and set sail for what might seem like an uncharted sea. They will even have to learn the faith language of radar. And when they seem to have reached their destination, there will be more challenges. The work of growing up never stops this side of eternity.'

The *Pride of Dover* pulled out of the harbour and David and I remained on deck until the famous white cliffs became a white speck on the horizon. And I compared our drive through the fog and this calm crossing to the testimony I have disclosed in this chapter. While I was coming to terms with those patterns of behaviour in me which needed to change, it sometimes felt like driving through fog. But that made the new-found freedom, when it happened, all the more liberating. And it saddened me that a ministry which is so full of potential for people's growth and God's glory should have been brought into disrepute because practitioners had remained unaware of the dangers.

The dangers
Now that many of these dangers have been pin-pointed, however, it is my longing that this method of listening and healing may be exercised with more caution and be restored to its rightful place alongside the healing art of listening, whether the compassionate listening of the caring companion or the more structured expertise of

the professional – the psychiatrist, the psychologist, the psychoanalyst, or the psychotherapist.

But if this is to happen we must beware of *persuading* people to open themselves to this kind of ministry. When the time is ripe and if it seems to be the appropriate way forward for them, they will know. And they are more likely to take responsibility for their actions if they have reached this conclusion for themselves.

If they do conclude that this may be one way in which they can take a step forward into maturity we need to be aware that it is all too easy for us to get out of our depth in such a ministry. It is important therefore, wherever possible, to work alongside someone competent to counsel and not try to go it alone. We are dealing, after all, not with a machine which is easily replaceable but with the complexities of people who are precious to God. We must not run the risk of causing further damage. And if we do find ourselves wading out of our depth, we must be honest enough to say so and call in someone more skilled than ourselves. This is not an admission of defeat. It is wise, loving and responsible.

We must also beware of encouraging certain personality types to explore this avenue of healing. As David Seamands rightly points out in *Healing of Memories*,[5] inner healing is most effective with people who appear to be out of touch with their emotions; those who have repressed the memories of the past and need help in discovering why their path to emotional and spiritual maturity is blocked. When God touches the imagination of these people, they can be helped to take significant steps forward.

But the highly emotional, hysterical kind of person who escapes frequently into the world of fantasy and make-believe will not be helped by this ministry. They will enjoy it. But the exercise could degenerate into an act of self-indulgence. This ego trip for them will prove time-wasting for the listener and could drain him of his last drop of energy. No. This kind of person needs the objectivity of skilled professional counselling and they should be referred whenever possible. That is not to say that their friends will cease to listen. It is to say that friends will help them to see that God is a great God. He has many ways of helping people. Sometimes he uses highly qualified professional people, sometimes he uses the amateur listener, and our role is to make ourselves available, to help as we can and to allow him to be God. After all, as C. S. Lewis has reminded us, Aslan is not a tame lion.

And, unlike us, God is never in a hurry. And so we must let go of our neurotic search for quick cures for personality defects and the quest for instant wholeness. God is changing us from glory into glory, it is true. But the change is almost always slow and gradual with the occasional spurt for our encouragement. Those to whom we are ministering the love of Christ through inner healing, therefore, may need us to stay alongside them for many months until they have discovered how they need to change and how to go about making the necessary changes.

When they have found this key and the inner resources to move forward, they will look back with great gratitude that we stayed alongside them for as long as was necessary and they will marvel at the greatness of God who saw them in their brokenness and loved them enough to rescue and restore them.

At least, those were the emotions that welled up in me as I watched the fog-bound form of England recede into the background and set my face towards France. But that fog reminded me too that God does not always come to the rescue in the way we would like. Sometimes he entrusts us with pain. Even the bewildering pain of depression.

Chapter 10

Listening to the Depressed

My doctor in Cambridge warned me to watch out for signs of depression. 'If someone had been scheming to give you a nervous breakdown, they couldn't have done a better job,' he observed when he examined my back and head injuries on my return to England and when I had told him about my father's death. 'Any one of the traumas you've suffered in the past five years could have triggered off a depressive illness. Now this,' he warned again when he came to see David and myself on a subsequent occasion.

This doctor was a caring Christian whom I admired. I knew he was not gunning for God with these comments. Even so there seemed no need to take his words seriously. I was a committed Christian, after all. In those days I imagined that people who were strong in the faith could not suffer from an emotional disorder, so although I heeded his advice to be careful I failed to spot the tell-tale signs of the predicted illness when they began to flash their amber light.

Even with the wisdom of hindsight I cannot discern how or when the depression started. What I do remember is that, whereas in the first year in Nottingham I threw myself into all the church activities with zest, during the second year I began to withdraw. I recall weeping with exhaustion one Sunday lunch-time just before a church picnic. Sensing that I was particularly fragile that day, a concerned friend encouraged me to stay at home instead of picnicking and even stayed with me, denying herself the pleasure of an afternoon out in the sun. And I recall collapsing in an exhausted heap after catering for a luncheon party in the church hall on another occasion and feeling very angry and sorry for myself, especially since it was Friday – our day off.

But as far as I remember, both times I pulled myself together and busied myself in the home and parish once more. It was some months later that I burst into tears in the middle of the parish prayer meeting and took myself and everyone else completely by surprise.

David had been telling everyone our 'joke' about the plague of mice which had taken up residence in the loft of the rectory while we were on holiday. We had summoned the rodent operative but he had been pessimistic. He doubted whether the mice in the house or the rats in the garden could be controlled. 'They build up an immunity to poison,' he said philosophically. 'You have to learn to live with them in a city centre like this.'

We did. And one morning, we found a mouse dead in our bed. I thought I had felt it wriggling between the sheets during the night but David had told me not to be silly. It was all in my mind, he said. During the night however he had rolled over on to the poor little creature and killed it with the weight of his body. We had laughed at the time. But now, as he was sharing this with everyone and they were laughing, I began to tremble as the tears refused every attempt I made to control them. I had only experienced this kind of physical sign of stress once in my life before – the night I arrived home from Yugoslavia still suffering from the shock of the car crash.

Scratchings and scrabblings at night and clearing up mouse droppings during the day became a way of life. At the same time, as explained in Chapter 9, I was seething with resentment that the privacy of my home was constantly being invaded by a secretary who seemed to have taken over the place I felt was mine – alongside my husband. And though I managed to hide much of my negativity from others, and though the depression was still largely masked from myself, my condition was growing worse. The mice on top of everything else were proving too much.

A bad bout of flu caused me to cave in completely. It dragged on and on and resulted in post-viral depression from which I seemed unable to recover. Eventually it drove me to my doctor. I hated the stigma of that word 'depression' when my doctor used it. Even more I hated the thought of taking the anti-depressants he prescribed. 'Just a crutch', he assured me, 'to help you over the hump.'

Anti-depressants! I dared not admit to anyone that I had a bottle by my bedside. I felt so guilty. And a complete failure – as a clergy wife, a mother and a Christian. And I felt angry with myself for being feeble enough to be incapable of coping.

At the bottom of the pit

I took the anti-depressants for a few days. But they made me feel zombie-like all day. Life was bad enough without feeling 'woozy' from one pill to the next so I determined to stop taking them. I decided that I would work through this crisis without medication. These were early days. My faith had not yet grown dim. I believed firmly in Betsy ten Boom's triumphant testimony: 'There is no pit so deep but God is deeper still.' If necessary I would prove this for myself and I did not need doctor's pills to help me do it.

By refusing to take the anti-depressants I was taking a calculated risk. I could have cracked completely. But, as Jack Dominian, Director of the Marital Research Centre at the Central Middlesex Hospital and Head of the Department of Psychological Medicine there, reminds us so helpfully, this is a choice which the depressed person must be allowed to make for himself. Depression, he claims, is a normal, necessary experience. By 'a necessary experience' he means that some depressions seem simply to be 'a kind of human radar which scans the reality of life and gives our appropriate response'.[1] He goes on to explain that the frozenness of depression may be the only way a given personality can negotiate the changes which are taking place, adapt to them and learn how to cope effectively with them.

Looking back, it would seem that this was what was happening to me. And I was not depressed for twenty-four hours a day and seven days a week, month in, month out as some people are. Mine was what some psychiatrists call a recurrent depression. I would experience episodes of deep darkness bordering on despair which would last for weeks but these would be punctuated by remissions, comparatively normal periods when I could be beguiled into believing that the crisis had passed.

Whenever I was enjoying a respite, I would look up the notes I made at St John's about depression and read the books recommended during this counselling course. The subject of depression now held a fascination for me. There were so many questions in my mind which clamoured for an answer. What *is* depression? What causes it? What is the purpose of it? Can you be totally committed to Christ and suffer from depression?

What depression is
No book offered a succinct definition of the illness we call depression. They all claimed that depression means different things to different people.

Some people, for example, complain of feeling depressed when they are down in the dumps or low in spirits or suffering from an attack of the Monday morning blues. Others claim they suffer from depression for a few days each month. They are using the word depression and premenstrual tension synonymously. Yet others use the same word to describe the disappointment they feel because the purchase of a house has fallen through or the sadness which seeps into them when their budgerigar dies.

This is depression in its mildest form. Uncomfortable but not a serious sickness. This kind of depression is a temporary, passing mood.

Some people however suffer from chronic depression. This may develop only slowly but linger on for two years or more with no remission. For such people everything is literally de-pressed – flattened: their emotions, their ability to appreciate beauty in any form, their capacity to tune in to the still, small voice of God, their ability to give love and receive it. Everything is numb. Grey. They feel lonely, fragile, frightened. As Harry Williams describes it, they feel boringly, saddeningly and terrifyingly alone. Eventually the black cloud does lift but while it hangs over them it feels as though they are condemned to this listless, lifeless existence for ever, and, for some, life no longer seems worth the struggle and they become suicidal or at least live with a persistent death wish.

Another kind of depression is known as psychotic depression. In psychotic depression, the patient's reaction to a severely disturbing set of circumstances impairs his ability to test reality or to function normally. Psychotic depression can last for a very long time and is particularly frightening because it can bring about a complete change of character in the sufferer. Someone who normally copes well with many demands and who enjoys being stretched may, over a period of several weeks, become increasingly irritable and tired, pessimistic and agitated, anxious and irrational. Their outlook on life becomes consistently gloomy and as the gloom thickens their behaviour may become bizarre causing distress to their relatives and friends.

Some people describe depression in rather more spiritual terms. They use words like 'wilderness experience', 'stripping', 'refining', 'pruning' to sum up what they mean by this melancholia. This experience is so much like the dark night of the soul with which the mystics were familiar that it is almost impossible to distinguish between the two.

Then there is that general feeling of discontent which permeates some middle-aged people and which we now call 'the mid-life crisis'. This too can be a form of depression.

Not all psychiatrists view depression with alarm. It is simply a scream of the psyche, some claim, an indication that an area of life is being neglected and needs urgent attention. It is a message the person in pain seems to be reluctant to hear. It is work to be done, lessons to be learnt, the pathway to growth.

In other words depression has many faces, it afflicts the young and the old, the rich and the poor, the successful executive and the unemployed, the Christian and the pagan. It is no respecter of persons. And it can be viewed with dismay or with courage; from man's perspective or from God's.

Causes of depression

But what causes it? The textbooks suggest that the causes are as varied and complex and nebulous as the definitions.

Psychiatrists, I discovered, speak of two kinds of depression. Reactive depression and endogenous depression. Reactive depression, as the label suggests, occurs when a person is coming to terms with a significant loss which is perceived as unpleasant, harmful or devastating: the loss of a spouse through death, separation or divorce, the loss of a job through retirement or redundancy, the loss of reputation through scandal, gossip or immorality, the loss of 'what might have been' through discovering that one is infertile or that a much loved friend or colleague or pastor is moving from the area.

Endogenous depression, on the other hand, comes from within. Its cause cannot easily be traced. The root may never be revealed and the depressed feelings may linger, like a dark shadow, year in and year out.

I recognised that, when the cloud of depression descended on me, it was reactive depression that I was suffering from and so I probed more deeply into some of the possible contributing factors. I discovered that psychiatrists have claimed that depressed feelings often follow some of life's crises like a car crash – particularly if injuries are sustained and more especially if particular parts of the body have been affected: the head, back, eyes, hands, ears, to mention a few.

That made me a front runner for depression, I realised, and in a macabre sort of way it helped to know that there was some concrete, acceptable predisposing factor contributing to my inability to control the gloom which frequently crept into the crevices of my psyche. I took courage from Jack Dominian's claim that in such instances 'sadness is a proper and inevitable reaction which acts as a stimulus to make up for the loss'.[2] It interested me that in developing this theme he suggested that it was depression that often stimulated the healing of the wound and that, until the necessary healing and adjustment had taken place, depression was like a much needed protective layer.

People who had suffered the trauma of an early loss in infancy and who have not had their needs met at this most formative stage of their life were likely to clothe themselves with this protective layer of depression later in life. That was the conclusion some experts had reached after careful research into patterns of behaviour among depressed people. When such people were exposed to stress, it was suggested, they were likely to be prone to depressed feelings because every new stressful situation would seem like a recapitulation of that earlier experience when a psychic wound was inflicted before the personality had developed the resources to combat such an assault.

Some professionals went so far as to claim that the early loss of a loved object – particularly the mother – was the basis of all subsequent depression. This need not be the permanent loss through death. It can be the temporary loss of a prolonged separation through, for example, enforced hospitalisation.

Adults who have been subjected to this degree of pain in infancy, and particularly in the first six months of life, may well re-experience and re-enact this early dread and loss when they nose-dive into depression in later life.

I found these theories particularly intriguing in the light of the childhood memories which had surfaced for me and which are described in Chapter 9. I noted with interest too that many believe that changes in status and environment are thought to contribute to depression in some people. Again, I mused, I was well qualified to fall foul of this melancholia. David and I had had seven homes in ten years. With each move came the challenge of new responsibilities and the loss of familiar surroundings and firm friends. Perhaps it was little wonder that the load-bearing beams of my life were groaning a little.

Furthermore, as Myra Chave-Jones reminds us so helpfully: 'We are inevitably influenced by our surroundings . . . If we live in an emotionally cold environment where we do not seem to be cared for and supported, it is very easy for us to begin to feel undervalued and useless – a quick road to depression.'[3] I thought rather ruefully of the rectory where we lived. Although we had loved it in the early days, the strain of living there was now considerable. It was completely isolated, set as it was in a concrete jungle on Nottingham's inner by-pass. Tramps and drunks called frequently, either to beg for food or money or simply to hurl abuse, and often I would be in the house alone with the children when this happened. Every bus route in the city passed our front door so noise and dirt were a constant problem. And the house had been built over the church hall so whether we were attending a church function or not, the sound of hymn singing would percolate up through our floorboards giving us no rest from parish functions. All of this was imposing its own strain before the problem with the vermin and the saga of the secretary added to the pressure.

And there were the 'vibes'. The house was built over a cemetery and opposite a college where there is the usual occult activity among the students. A few yards up the road there was a meeting hall of the theosophical society. We seemed to be surrounded by evil. Even now, when I go to the church hall I still tune in to that darkness and can be overwhelmed by it. It persuades me to believe that some depression is caused by the principalities and powers of darkness which Paul reminds us of in Ephesians 6:12.

In addition to all this Myra Chave-Jones suggests that, in some people, a hereditary factor might make them susceptible to depression. Such people, she claims, inherit certain genes that predispose them to the illness. My mother, I remember, suffered from depression after Ray enlisted for National Service and again when she became a semi-invalid. My grandmother too suffered several nervous breakdowns and had to be hospitalised. I wondered whether I had inherited a susceptibility to depression from either of them but since there was no way of being certain there seemed little point in dwelling on this factor though I valued the insight.

I also appreciated Myra's reminder that chemical imbalance clearly causes depression in some. This is what triggers off post-natal depression, menopausal depression and, to a lesser extent, pre-menstrual tension. Stress and strain also puts a person under the kind of pressure which might cause them to collapse like a hot air balloon which has run out of fuel. I noted how such physical exertion resulted in Elijah's exhaustion and subsequent depression. And I loved the way God listened, cared for and restored his suffering servant.

But I was especially interested to read that the oldest and most widely accepted explanation of depression seems to be that it almost always involves inverted anger, that is, anger turned in against oneself. A person may seem very sweet and placid on the surface, but underneath their emotions resemble a seething volcano of unexpressed, unacknowledged rage. This frozen rage is thought to be one of the most common causes of depressed feelings. Someone may have been hurt in the past by a teacher or a parent or a relative or they are being hurt or humiliated in the present by an authority figure or peer or colleague who has upset them in some way. Rather than admitting the anger and ventilating it in a healthy way and safe place, they turn it against themselves, blaming themselves for being feeble, a failure or pathetic, and adding insult to injury by piling guilt on top of anguish.

I suspected that frozen rage might lie at the root of my depression. David would sometimes express his hurt and bewilderment that he seemed to have lost the sweet wife he married and exchanged her for a volcano which was liable to erupt at any moment – especially when he and I were alone together.

Christian *and* depressed?

Making a study of the subject in the way I was attempting to do helped me to understand the dynamics of depression and therefore helped me to understand myself. The realisation also crept up on me that it is perfectly possible to be a committed Christian *and* to suffer from depression; that having a firm faith in God is no insurance policy against this dis-ease of the emotions nor even an inoculation against it. I began to see, too, that though I was coping without medication this refusal to resort to anti-depressants would not be appropriate for everyone. Some people need a crutch to help them limp through this wilderness. Just as aspirins cure headaches and antibiotics combat infection, so drugs are sometimes used by God to bring about the cure of a depressive illness caused by chemical imbalance.

I learned too that many great men of God had been entrusted with this mysterious sickness of the soul. In addition to Elijah whom I have already mentioned in this chapter, there was the Psalmist. He summed up my feelings and experiences so succinctly that whenever I felt really low it was to the Psalms that I would turn. These were some of the verses I underlined at the time because they brought me a sorrowful sort of comfort:

Be merciful to me, O Lord, for I am in distress;
   my eyes grow weak with sorrow,
   my soul and my body with grief.
My life is consumed by anguish
   and my years by groaning;
my strength fails because of my affliction,
   and my bones grow weak.

                             (Ps. 31:9, 10)

My tears have been my food
   day and night . . .

all your waves and breakers
   have swept over me.

(Ps. 42:3, 7)

Job too seems well acquainted with the darkness which
was pervading my entire being:

For sighing comes to me instead of food;
   my groans pour out like water . . .
I have no peace, no quietness;
   I have no rest, but only turmoil.

(Job 3:24, 26)

When I lie down I think, 'How long before I get up?'
   The night drags on, and I toss till dawn . . .
so that I prefer strangling and death,
   rather than this body of mine . . .
If I have sinned, what have I done to you,
   O watcher of men?

(Job 7:4, 15, 20)

Then there was J. B. Phillips. Unable to shake off the
symptoms of depression, he had been forced to resign
from his first living and go into hiding in Swanage where he
corresponded with other depressives: Leslie Weatherhead
was one. In a letter to Jack Phillips, this great preacher
who used to thrill huge congregations each Sunday with
his preaching confesses: 'I feel concerned about what you
describe as depression because I went through hell thirty
years ago. I had over two hundred hours of "analysis"
and finally emerged, but it took years . . .' He goes on to
confess that he found a certain drug 'an enormous help'.
'I still take one before a Sunday at the City Temple; a
challenge which still makes me "anxious".'[4] And there
was William Cowper, so becalmed by depression that
when offered a responsible post in the House of Lords
he succumbed to an anxiety state and was so agitated
that he tried several times to kill himself. This was the
description he wrote of himself: 'I am like a slug or snail
that has fallen into a deep well.'

I learned that many of the world's geniuses had suffered similarly: Isaac Newton, Beethoven, Darwin, Van Gogh, Tolstoy, Spurgeon and Martin Luther. Their inner turmoil did not block their creativity. On the contrary, their suffering seemed to contribute to their greatness. While J. B. Phillips was depressed he translated the whole of the New Testament into a powerful paraphrase. While William Cowper was depressed he wrote some of his best hymns and poems. And while C. H. Spurgeon was depressed he preached some of his finest sermons.

How the depressed person feels

This taught me that I must not waste suffering. Instead I must learn to use it. Even so this did nothing to alleviate the pain when I nose-dived into the tunnel once more. The feelings were always the same – or at least a variation on a miserable theme.

One of the most frightening things was the tightness around my head. It was as though someone had clamped an iron frame round my skull. This would bite into my flesh first and then into my brain. It seemed to be obstructing my ability to think clearly. My mind was befogged. Confused. To think became too much of an effort.

To make matters worse, my energy level seemed to have ebbed away. In its place a debilitating lethargy would sweep over the shore of my life and refuse to go away. Because my mind seemed so sluggish, the quick actions and reactions of others felt like a slap in the face. Cruel. Insensitive. Unloving.

Laughter jarred. Singing grated on the exhausted nerves. And because life seemed such an effort and so unlivable, the tiniest mistake anyone made, like allowing the soup to boil over or leaving the door open on a cold day, triggered off an angry reaction from me which filled me with self-loathing and caused the offender to retreat in self-preservation.

Even ordinary household chores seemed to take too much effort: 'I go into the kitchen. The dishes are all there, piled up, dirty, I haven't the energy or inclination to wash them or tidy the house . . . I can't bear to see people laugh or even see them looking well. I feel so jaded in comparison. Lord, I'm feeling dreadful. When will all this end?' That is what I wrote in my prayer journal.

And because everything seemed so grim, the slightest disappointment seemed capable of knocking me off balance and plunging me into a deeper experience of despair.

Even the sun failed to cheer me. 'The sun is shining but everything is dark – very dark. Help me, Lord, please.' In fact when the sun shone I felt worse. Its shafts came as a sharp reminder that normally I respond to them with gratitude and enjoyment. But now, all enjoyment seemed to have evaporated – even from the pleasures of reading, listening to music and walking in Derbyshire. 'I can't concentrate on anything for long; can't enjoy a book. I'm not interested in television, can't feel you [God] there.' Life seemed an ever-darkening shade of grey: joyless, hopeless, dreary.

'Everything hurts' is a phrase that punctuates my prayer journal at this time as I expressed to God the loneliness that was pervading my spirit. 'Will I ever feel energetic again? I'm so lonely, Lord. Desperately lonely. If only there was someone who would come and sit with me, watch me cry, hear my efforts to communicate and tell me that I'm not going mad. I feel as though I'm going mad, Lord. Is there anyone you could send?'

There were people around, of course. But since I hid much of this pain behind my usual smiling countenance they could not be expected to detect that I was wandering around in an inner wilderness. And as I admitted to myself in my prayer journal on one occasion: 'I have wrapped myself round in barbed wire and I sit in its terrifying tangle.' No one could reach me. But if they had been watching they would have seen that church services brought so much pain to the surface that I could scarcely cope. While the music group sang quietly and sensitively during the services of Holy Communion, I would kneel in my pew and weep silently: tears that seemed to flow from some deeply hidden part of myself; tears which were, I knew, a language but a language I had not yet learned to interpret.

These tears seemed such a nuisance. An embarrassment. I would be sitting in the hairdresser's using up all my energy in the attempt to project my normal coping image when suddenly my eyes would fill with tears that looked like pools which threatened to overflow down my unusually pale cheeks. 'If only I could stop crying' was a wish I made frequently.

Insomnia also set in. I would go to bed and toss and turn and turn and toss until two or three o'clock in the morning – even before that night when the mouse met his death in our bed.

But perhaps the worst thing was the guilt and self-loathing. Here was I, a graduate, called by God to serve him alongside my husband in the full-time ministry, a committed Christian, falling apart at the seams. Surely I should be able to pull myself together? Surely I should not feel like this? Whatever must God be thinking about me? Deep down, that is how I reasoned with myself.

Richard Winter, in *The Roots of Sorrow*, claims that when a person is suffering from depression it almost always happens that he is suffering from four or more of the following nine symptoms:

loss of appetite or weight loss
sleep difficulties
fatigue
agitation
retardation (being slowed up)
loss of interest
difficulty in concentration
feelings of guilt
a death wish or thoughts of suicide.[5]

The most alarming moment came for me when I had been staying on my own in Derbyshire one weekend. I missed my bus home by seconds and the frustration spilled over into anger. While I waited impatiently for the next bus to come, I sat in the sun on the banks of the river Derwent and longed for the courage to throw myself into its swollen waters which were heaving their way downstream. After that, the death wish was a recurring one which filled me with terror on the one hand but gave me an escape route, at least in my fantasies, on the other.

Work to be done

I was one of the fortunate ones. As I have explained, mine was a recurrent depression, not a psychotic one. During the short intermissions I could think rationally, read, pray and sense the presence of God. And I was fortunate enough to see a purpose in what was happening to me, at least some of the time. In one of the early remissions, I remember reeling from the shock of what I was going through and talking to God about it. Two passages of scripture and a particular prophecy reassured and strengthened me at this time. First God seemed to remind me that soon after his anointing by the Spirit at his baptism, Jesus was driven into the wilderness where he was tested. This testing, I discovered, was not designed to break the Son of God but rather to strengthen him for the ministry that lay ahead, in the same way as metal must be tested before it is usable. In my strongest moments, even when I was crawling through the endlessly long and dark tunnel of depression, I remembered this and clung on to the hope that maybe this was what was happening to me.

The second scripture came in the form of a promise from Jesus, which again I clung to when the going was tough. 'Simon, Simon,' Jesus had said to his beloved disciple, 'Satan has asked to sift you as wheat. But I have prayed for you' (Luke 22:31–32). Those words 'I have prayed for you' brought such comfort. So much so that I wrote on a piece of paper, JESUS IS PRAYING FOR ME NOW, and stuck it on the wall of my prayer room so that I would be reminded of God's holding hand even when I could no longer feel or experience it.

And the prophecy which I sensed God had given me

takes my breath away even now as I unearth it from my prayer journal:

> Just as nature is about to be stripped bare, the petals will fall from the roses, the leaves will flutter from the trees and the earth will lie hard and bare, so I will strip you. You will lie exposed, naked, in all your vulnerability.
>
> But you must not mistake this stripping for wrathful activity. This is not the stripping of vindictiveness or revenge; it is the stripping of great love. With the nakedness of your winter comes my promise that just as the Spring-time will bring the re-clothing of nature in all its freshness, newness and vitality, so your clothing will be accomplished by me. Your new garments will exceed, in beauty and in usefulness, anything you have previously experienced.
>
> Do not be afraid, neither be dismayed for I am the Lord, your God, and I am covenanting my presence to accompany you wherever you go. Go, therefore, in peace, for I am with you.

Unfortunately there were times when I was afraid. Terrified. There were times when I forgot these precious promises. Times when all hope of recovery disappeared. As I have admitted, there were times when I felt I must be on the verge of madness.

Helping the depressed person

It was then that I discovered that 'just listening' really is a ministry of healing. I recall one Sunday morning when I was in too much inner turmoil to risk darkening the doors of a church. But being alone in the house gave me more time to think than was helpful. The darkness overwhelmed me, the tears flowed and despair held me in such a vice-like grip that I scarcely knew how to live with the emotional pain. The helplessness prompted me to pick up the telephone and dial the number of a friend who happened to be a clergyman. To my astonishment, he was not at church. I was so relieved to hear the sound of a human voice that for several minutes I just sobbed. I do not remember what I blurted down the phone. What I do remember is that it was incoherent. Even so, this perceptive, caring friend responded: 'It sounds as though you're in great darkness. Would it help to come round and talk about it?'

This friend lived out of town so it was not possible to meet that morning. We arranged, instead, that I would go the following day.

When I put the phone down, nothing had changed in one sense. I was still faced with the challenge of driving through the darkness of an emotional pea-soup fog in which I had lost my bearings and in which I had lost my nerve, and yet in another sense everything had changed. Someone had registered my pain, heard it, assured me, through this offer of his time, that I still mattered.

I have sometimes watched a person suffer an asthma attack and gain almost instant relief from the atomiser they draw from their pocket and spray into their mouth. This selfless offer had a similar effect on my emotions. I pulled myself together, dried my eyes, washed my tear-swollen face and cooked lunch for the family.

I am not saying that my husband neither listened nor cared. He did. But it often happens that the people the depressed person loves most become trapped in the irrationality of the threads which weave themselves like a web around the depressed person. There are several reasons for this. One is that because the only thing the depressed person wants is that a miracle cure should be found which will free him from this tangle, if the loved one cannot wave the magic wand or say the perfect prayer which will produce this miracle, the depressed person feels let down and angry and might even lash out in verbal violence. Another is that the relative or close friend who is on the receiving end of this verbal abuse may begin to assume responsibility for the depression and believe 'It's all my fault'. Two people then spiral downwards, hook each other's pain and become incapable of helping one another.

This is what happened to us. Even though David

absorbed much of my anger at great cost to himself and even though, particularly when he knew the death wish was tormenting me, he attempted to prove to me how much he loves and values me, his overtures of loving care, filtered as they were through my negativity and pain, had a hollow ring about them. I seemed incapable of making an appropriate response.

So once again Anne Long came to the rescue. Once again she listened – and listened – and listened. Even when the record seemed stuck in a groove and played the same tale of woe over and over again Anne listened. Every depressed person needs someone like that; someone who will not tire of listening to their main topic of conversation: themselves. Someone who will assure them that, even though they, the listener, may have nothing useful to say, they are prepared to stay in the darkness with the person suffering from depression until they emerge eventually from the tunnel's end. David Augsburger describes this patient listening well:

> When hearing is done as an act of caring, it is a healing process. The exact nature of this process will remain forever a mystery, a gift of grace for which we become profoundly grateful as we see it occurring, before which we are rightfully humble as we know we have, in small measure, participated in it . . .
>
> In caring-hearing, the hurt is opened, the festering bitterness of resentful illusions, the burning of angry demands, the numb frozenness of grief, the staleness of depression are allowed to drain. The light is allowed to pour in, sterilizing the infections and stimulating cells of hope and trust to begin new growth.[6]

New growth
'To begin new growth.' While the hoar frost of depression coated my body, mind and spirit, I was conscious only of the frozenness of this emotional winter time. And yet, as in winter we can stand staring in amazement at an ice-caked landscape and become aware that the hush

conceals the silent sounds of hidden internal growth, that the naked trees and fallow fields are not being killed but being renewed; so during the long winter months of my depression I too was being renewed.

Renewed? No. More accurately, I believe I was experiencing a kind of new birth.

Carlo Carretto's insights, which I had read while I was depressed and recorded in my prayer journal, have helped me to catch a glimpse of what was happening during this time of constriction and darkness.

God is making me his child, claims Carlo Carretto. He uses 'the cosmos and history to make a divine environment for my birth':

> Now I am like an immature foetus, midway between my past and future, between the things I know and those I do not know.
>
> It isn't a comfortable situation.
>
> In fact it hurts.
>
> I suffer from incompleteness, from blindness, from yearning . . .
>
> And it is dark because it is the womb, and it is painful because it is gestation, immaturity.
>
> This is the way God makes us, forming us by matter, making us by events, moulding us by history, as a mother builds a child with her milk and warms it with her love . . .
>
> The gestation of a child lasts for nine months. Our gestation as sons of God, a whole lifetime . . .
>
> [But] God is my father and looks after me. God is my father and loves me.
>
> God is my father and wants me to be with him forever.
>
> If God is my father, I no longer fear the darkness, since he is living in the darkness too and at the appropriate time will turn the darkness into life.[7]

'I suffer from incompleteness, from blindness, from yearning . . .' 'I am like an immature foetus.' Those phrases sum up precisely how I felt as I travelled through that relentless tunnel of depression.

Tunnel of depression? Perhaps Carlo Carretto is right? Perhaps that tunnel which seemed so dark and unwelcoming for much of the time was, after all, none other than the womb of God in which he was re-creating me? Perhaps it may be likened to Frank Lake's dynamic cycle (page 181).

As I think back now to those years of mental and emotional suffering, I see that there are certain parallels to the experience of human birth. But whereas in my infancy, because of my mother's blindness, as explained in chapter 9, I had been denied the evidence of my mother's unconditional love, now as I travelled round the dynamic cycle for a second time – as an adult – God had poured his love into those yawning gaps compensating the love I had lacked the first time round. Contemplative prayer, the prayer of listening to God had played a major part in this profoundly healing experience.

As I had relaxed in his presence, he had come to me. As I had opened myself to an inflow of his grace, he had impregnated me with the gift of his healing Spirit. Even when I had been unable to feel his presence, he had been there, in the tunnel with me, dwelling at the core of my being. As I abandoned myself to him, even when I had been unable to feel his presence, or perhaps more accurately, particularly when I could not feel his presence, he had come to me with the outstretched arms of accepting, unconditional love. And as I had attempted to dwell in him, he had sustained and nourished me: through his word, through stillness, through meditation. When all was dark I could no longer feel him near, but when the depression lifted and the senses sparked to life again, I would become aware that he had been in the tunnel all the time; that he indwelt the very core of my being.

What amazed me most was that he bore the full brunt of my anger. I filled pages of my prayer journal with letters to God which expressed the pain and the anger, the frustration and fear that dogged me. Those tirades are punctuated by messages of love. For even when my feelings were numbed as with frost-bite, God continued to communicate to me that he loved me *with* the depressed feelings. I cannot record that I always believed what I heard at the time. But what I can say is that God was so acting on the raw material of my life that, slowly and gradually, I was discovering that in him I have both worth and status. And when he saw that the time was ripe because I was ready, he brought me to the mouth of the tunnel from which I emerged re-created. Made new. Renewed. Re-energised. Ready to achieve for him, not out of compulsion or neurosis but out of a joyful sense of well-being and with a new understanding of what Jesus might have meant when he said to Nicodemus: 'You must be born again.'

I had no idea when I set out to search for wholeness that the route would lead through this tortuous tunnel of depression, but looking back I believe that every step of that journey was worthwhile. That is not to say that God has now finished with me; that I have reached that much desired state: wholeness. Maturity. No. The learning continues, albeit a little less painfully most of the time. Meanwhile I am left holding the treasures which came from that particular path of personal darkness – not least the richness of the lessons that I learned.

Chapter 11

One Spoke of the Wheel

One of the lessons I learned through my own limited experience of depression was the ability and desire to stay alongside others who suffer the seeming indignity of the temporary change of character, loss of control and absence of the felt presence of God which depression brings in its wake. People who have never groped their way through this particular fiery furnace seem to find it difficult to understand the anguish sufficiently to sit, month after month, with a depressed person. Only those who have been through a similar crisis appear to find deep within themselves the resilience and the resources both to understand and demonstrate their ongoing care. Mary Craig puts the situation well:

> Is it really paradoxical that when we are distressed we turn to the friend who knows what distress can be like? We don't quite know why, but there doesn't seem much point in going for sympathy, the deep-down, understanding kind, to those other friends whose paths have always been smooth. It is as though human beings lack a whole dimension and cannot come to maturity until they have faced sorrow.[1]

Because God entrusted me with this prolonged darkness, met me in it and gave me the resources to work through it, and because I emerged to enjoy a greater degree of wholeness than I ever thought possible, I now count it a privilege, when God asks it of me, to sit alongside others who are being bruised and buffeted in ways which I understand all too well. This patch of personal darkness, I see in retrospect, furthered my growth in that much needed fruit of the Spirit, compassion.

Almost as soon as I emerged from my own dark tunnel I seemed to be drawn to others who were squealing with the pain depression inflicts. And in attempting to help them I learned that, just as there are do's and don'ts which need to be applied to helping the bereaved, so there are do's and don'ts when it is a depressed person who presents himself to us.

Some do's

I discovered, for example, that when a person starts to send out distress signals – they are unusually listless, unkempt, untidy, lacking in energy, irritable, anxious or weepy, or complain of being 'down in the dumps' more than usual – it is wise to take prompt action. And I try to take as my model the way God coped with Elijah when he collapsed in the desert exhausted and depressed (1 Kgs 19).

So the first thing I do is to listen: sensitively and attentively. And just as God gave Elijah the complete freedom to pour out the full gamut of his feelings, so I try to receive the gift of the person's anguish and anger, his tears and his turmoil or the frozenness which prevents him from feeling or expressing even a fraction of his inner emotional pain. I remember so well the gratitude and relief that came to me through those who sacrificed time in this selfless way.

And I take another cue from God. Just as he demonstrated his love and acceptance in practical ways, so I try to put myself in the skin of the depressed person and provide appropriate practical help. A mother with a home to run, small children to look after and the family to feed, for example, will almost certainly feel overwhelmed by the volume of practical tasks to be done. I have learned not

Listening to Others

to ask 'Is there anything I can do?' nor to offer empty promises like 'Ring me if you think of any way I can help.' Instead I prefer to visit the home and, while chatting to this friend or neighbour, sum up the situation for myself. If the sink is full of dirty dishes I wash them without making a fuss about it. If the children are fractious I might suggest that we all go for a walk together or that, while mother has a rest, I take the children to the park. Or if she is struggling with the shopping or the cooking I might help her make a shopping list or suggest that we go to the supermarket together. Or I might bring some ready-cooked casseroles which can be stored in the freezer and heated through when most needed. Although my own experience of depression now lies in the dim and distant past, I have not forgotten the relief I felt when, on numerous occasions, members of our congregation arrived on my doorstep with a ready-made meat pie or chocolate souffle or batch of mince pies which were just what was needed to save me doing what I seemed to have no energy to do: cook for the family.

But I have to remind myself that, though I take God's accepting, practical love as my model, I am not God and there are limits to the amount of help I can give. For one thing, I am aware that depression is infectious. What I mean is that, for me at least, if I sit hour after hour with someone who has nose-dived into depression, some of their darkness seeps into me. I know therefore that common sense demands that I assess just how much time it is wise to spend in pouring love into the bottomless pit of this person's life. And if the situation threatens to be a long-term task, I recognise that the need for other helpers is clear and urgent.

As I listen and give practical help therefore I try to discern whether medical help may be required. If the depressed feelings seem to be dragging on it is always wise to encourage the sufferer to see a doctor. If necessary I go with them to the surgery. The doctor's practised eye may discern that drug therapy would help. Except in situations where the cause of the depression is chemical imbalance, drugs will not cure the depression, but for many people, including Christians, they stabilise the emotions, giving the sufferer the resources to learn the lessons this bout of depression is trying to teach. If the doctor and the depressed person both believe this crutch to be the correct one, I would not advise the patient to refuse medication. Neither would I dissuade them from seeking help from one of the so-called 'talking therapies' – psychotherapy or psychoanalysis – if their doctor prescribed such a course of action. It often happens that such professional people, skilled and trained as they are in understanding the human psyche, can help the depressed person to discover just what it is that they are needing to learn and how best to translate theory into practice.

At the same time I would be listening to God to try to discern what further part he is asking me to play in this person's life. If the symptoms are the forerunners of chronic or psychotic depression, I know that this could last a very long time. There have been occasions when I have sensed that God has asked me to make a colossal commitment to a depressed person. On such rare occasions I have found that I have been given almost supernatural strength to cope. But normally I am aware that I am just one of many helpers; that I can be of most use when I discover what my part is and how it dovetails with the contributions of others. I try to be ruthless with myself; to ask some pertinent questions: 'What can I offer realistically in terms of time and care and love?' Then I offer that and no more, aware that if I offer more I might go under myself and end up helping no one – least of all my own family.

When it becomes clear to me that I am to play a major role in this person's life, like offering counselling or prayer ministry over a period of time, or when I sense that I am being asked to listen to the person's pain week in, week out, I try to ensure that I am supported in four ways: by a group of people who are holding on to me and the entire situation in prayer, by supervision from someone more skilled in understanding the dynamics of depression than I am, by the assent and love of my husband, and by ensuring that I take sufficient time for rest and relaxation and personal prayer so that my own resources will not dwindle to the size of a puddle but can be replenished constantly and be the reservoir God intends them to be. The people who pray for me have no need to know the name of the person I am seeking to help, so confidentiality is not breached in seeking their support. And of course to further ensure that confidentiality is maintained, I ask the depressed person's permission to seek guidance from another counsellor as seems appropriate.

Availability

When I have summed up the situation and decided how involved God is calling me to be, I know that the hard slog is just beginning because I am still near enough to my own years of suffering to recall my greatest longing: 'If only there was someone who would sit with me in the pain – not necessarily to say anything but just to hold my hand and receive my jumbled thoughts and feelings.' By far the best way we can help a person suffering from depression is simply to make ourselves available to stay alongside him in his darkness, prove our love by our faithfulness even when this self-sacrifice is thrown back in our face, spurned or doubted, and by listening over and over again to the same sad tale of woe, the same angry outbursts, the same lack of confidence, the same dreary outlook on life and the same lack of self worth.

This requires patience, stamina, the ability to interpret for the depressed person the sights and sounds of this foreign land through which he finds himself stumbling and the willingness to sit with him in this darkness until the end of the tunnel is reached, remembering that this could take a very long time.

'The ability to interpret the sights and sounds of this foreign land.' One of the sounds will almost certainly be anger because, as we observed in Chapter 10, frozen rage lies at the root of much depression. I have been trying to learn, therefore, to receive a person's anger as a gift and to handle it with care. Anger itself is not a sin. If it were, St Paul would not have written, 'Be angry and sin not.' No. Anger is a natural, neutral response to certain adverse circumstances. It is usually a reaction to fear or frustration. Unless it is defused skilfully it can be used to crush, accuse and blame people and thus be used sinfully. But equally it can be converted into a useful tool. It can point the person to the source of the fear or frustration so that they see clearly where changes must be made.

In receiving the gift of a person's anger therefore, I am listening not only to the angry gestures and the venomous words, but to the base line of the encounter, trying to discern precisely what it is that has triggered off this volcanic eruption. It often happens that the molten lava has to be poured out before these fears and frustrations are discerned. But when these too have been voiced, it is sometimes possible to take prompt and practical action and relieve some of the suffering.

Many of my own fears and frustrations, for example, centred on the rectory, which has since been condemned as 'uninhabitable' by the Church Commissioners. Almost as soon as we moved from that house the depression lifted, at least for a while. I have seen a similar dramatic change take place in others suffering from stress. When the crushing circumstances have been removed, they appear to make a miraculous recovery.

But I try to bear in mind too that an angry person often distorts the truth even though they remain firmly fixed in the opinion that their perception is accurate. My husband reminds me that when I was depressed, if I felt displaced for some reason nothing would dissuade me from the view that he had been guilty of neglecting me or had been particularly insensitive. I needed someone else to confront me, albeit gently, and to help me to see these false beliefs for what they were. Errors of judgement. And I needed someone else's help to discover how to replace falsehood with truth. So in listening to a person's wrath, I try to hear the underlay of terror, to receive the trapped feelings, to accept the person with their rage, to focus more on the hurt than the wrath but, when the time is ripe, to help them to explore whether there are other ways of viewing the situation and other ways of dealing with it. In other words I try to help them to use their anger constructively and not destructively.

Suicide

I also listen for signs which reveal that the depressed person might be feeling suicidal or that they are plagued by the presence of a persistent or recurring death wish: that feeling Elijah expressed so well when he confessed to God: 'I have had enough, Lord . . . Take my life.'

It helped me to be able to confide such feelings in two trusted friends and their healing response stays with me still. One, a clergyman to whom I confessed that, like Elijah, all I wanted to do was to curl up and die, startled me by saying: 'Promise me that if you ever feel like taking your life you will phone me first.' The other, a close friend, simply empathised: 'I didn't know you lived with a death wish too,' she whispered with tears of compassion in her eyes. And she gave me a long, lingering, gentle embrace, wept with me and made a similar request: 'If you should ever contemplate trying to take your life, please phone me first.'

On both occasions the care and concern expressed by these friends penetrated my gloom and I felt cherished.

Jack Dominian helps us to understand that it is almost to be expected that a depressed person will, from time to time, long for an escape route, which may mean that his mind turns in the direction of death:

> The thought that life is too dreadful to go on living crosses the minds of both those who are miserable due to their life situation and of those who have crossed over to the state of depressive illness. In the midst of the various causes of acute unhappiness the desire for relief by ceasing to be is not by itself an unreasonable or surprising reaction.[2]

He goes on to explain that many people live, from time to time, with this kind of death wish but few of them go so far as to contemplate suicide:

> At some moment, however, the real possibility of the removal of oneself occurs to one. From the moment that the act of self-destruction is seriously contemplated as a way out of the predicament . . . such a person, or those to whom the information has been communicated, should ensure that help is sought without further delay.[3]

These words of warning are important, I find. We must always take suicide threats seriously and do all in our power to protect the person from harming himself.

Some don'ts

Just as there are ways of supporting the depressed person, so there are ways which are guaranteed to injure him deeply. One is to tell him, if he admits to suicidal feelings, 'You ought to be ashamed of yourself.' He probably is. And his admission is a cry for help which needs to be met with love and tenderness, not condemnation.

It is equally damaging to say to someone who has plucked up the courage to admit to feeling depressed: 'You shouldn't feel like this' or 'You've been overdoing it, that's what's wrong with you' or 'Pull yourself together'. No one asks to fall prey to the sabotage of depression. When they do they need, not condemnation but listening love. Tenderness.

And sticking-plaster prayers may prove equally painful. By this I mean the kind of prayer prayed by a Christian who understands little of the dynamics of depression, who when faced with a tearful or despondent person believes that the whole complex problem can be unravelled through one prayer or the laying-on of hands, and instead of staying alongside the hurting person expects them to be 'zapped' into wholeness. Such so-called prayer ministry can leave the person deeply distressed, even believing, if no relief comes from it, that they must be beyond help since even prayer fails to pierce their gloom.

No one tried to exorcise me when I was depressed but friends of mine who have suffered from depressive illnesses have been subjected to hours of inappropriate so-called deliverance ministry which has done more harm than good and brought God's ministry of healing into disrepute. There may be occasions when the deliverance ministry will play its part in releasing the depressed person from his tangled emotions. But we must beware of seeing demons under every bed and take advice before jumping to the ready conclusion that the depression is demonic in origin. As people helpers we need to hold two things in tension: the awareness that sometimes there is a Satanic strand contributing to depression, and the realisation that to over-emphasise or exaggerate this possibility is to give Satan more prominence than is appropriate or accurate. Depression needs skilled and sensitive handling if the person is to emerge from the tunnel to enjoy the wholeness which is his, by right, in Christ. And though, from the desperation of their need and the longing for someone to find a quick solution to their pain, they may scream for any kind of prayer or counsel on offer, the wise helper will discern when to pray and when simply to listen, to love and give practical support. The wise helper knows that God, in his infinite wisdom and love, does not always remove our pain instantly. Sometimes he gives us the resources to grow through it, learn from it and thereby enjoy his gift of maturity.

While he is still stumbling along the road that leads to this much desired state – maturity – the depressed person's view of himself will almost certainly reach a low ebb. The temptation then is to try to jolly him along, to try to prove that his perception is clouded, to try to boost his morale by praising and complimenting him. And very often such encouragement will fall flat on its face because our friend will be unable to drink in the implications of what is being said. The helper may then be deflated.

There is a way of giving praise and encouragement which the depressed person might be able to receive. It is to give it in the form of a question: 'Can you see that you did that well?' or 'Does it make sense that you handled that relationship with confidence?' They will turn the memory over in their mind slowly and might even respond: 'Well, yes. I can see that. Yes. That is encouraging.' The encouragement may not last long but it will have brought a glimmer of hope. Whereas if a well-meaning person were to attempt to give gushing praise and applause, it would almost certainly be met with disdain and the response: 'They're trying to convince themselves that I'm better than I am.'

The need for a team
There are no quick cures for depression. And maybe we should not even seek for one because if the lessons are learned thoroughly, depression could be the best thing that ever happened to this person. C. S. Lewis puts the position superbly:

> Imagine yourself as a living house. God comes in to rebuild that house. At first, perhaps, you can understand what He is doing. He is getting the drains right and stopping the leaks in the roof and so on. You knew that those jobs needed doing and so you are not surprised. But presently He starts knocking the house about in a way that hurts abominably and does not seem to make sense. What on earth is He up to? The explanation is that He is building quite a different house from the one you thought of – throwing out a new wing here, putting an extra floor there, running up towers, making courtyards. You thought you were going to be made into a decent little cottage: but He is building a palace.[4]

But while the rebuilding is in progress, the living stones of the depressed person's life need scaffolding to keep them from disintegrating. And no one person can hope to form a structure secure enough to bear this heavy burden on their own. Others must be involved. To admit this is not a sign of weakness or failure on our part but common sense. Gaius Davies, a consultant psychiatrist in London, put the situation well when he made the claim that what is needed to support, not just the depressed, but other people in pain also, is a team of people, each contributing their own unique expertise, each co-operating with the others, each intent on supporting the person until *God's* refurbishment has been completed.

Roger Hurding, another Christian psychiatrist, explains why this cluster of helpers plays such an important part in the life of broken people and he helps to put their problems in perspective.

Man made in the image of God, he claims, was created an essential unity of mind, body and spirit. He was a fully integrated person: his thinking, feeling, creating, intuitive, doing, worshipping, relating and 'simply being' faculties in perfect working order and each in harmony with the rest.

Diagrammatically, man before the Fall looked like this:

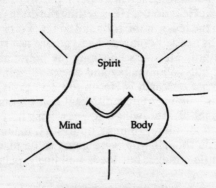

In God's image: WHOLE

But with the Fall came catastrophe. This image was shattered. Man now looked more like this:

Image broken: EVERYMAN

Left to himself he would stay in this state of fallenness and suffer the pain inflicted by imbalance, immaturity and a poor sense of identity for the rest of his life. But if he is exposed to God's love expressed through Christ, his Word, his Spirit and his love incarnated through human carers and counsellors, he will be so transformed that he will be able to enjoy a renewed sense of well-being: balance, maturity, an increased sense of identity and self-worth. He will then look like this:

Balance, Maturity. Sense of Identity

Not perfect. Not fully mature. That happy state will be enjoyed only on the other side of eternity. But enjoying an increased sense of wholeness.

These diagrams have captured my imagination and caused me to dream a dream for the church where I worship and for other Christian communities who are seeking to touch the sores of people who move within their orbit. I have replaced C. S. Lewis's picture of the house with another image: the wheel of a bicycle. Diagrammatically, it will look like this:

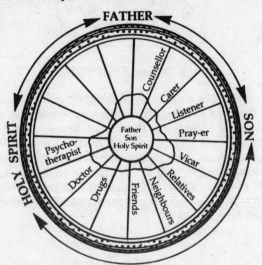

The spokes of the wheel

The mystery is that, within each broken Christian, God the Father, God the Son and God the Holy Spirit have taken up residence. To use the language of St Paul the mystery, the hope of glory, is that Christ is in *us*. Or to quote the language of Jesus, we are indwelt by the three members of the Trinity. But we are also assured that we are *in* Christ. In God. So every damaged personality (and that is each of us) is enfolded in the Trinity and indwelt by the Trinity. But every Christian is also a part of a whole bevy of fellow believers: the body of Christ. My dream is that each member of the body of Christ should discover their gift and use it to the full. When this happens, even though the damage may be severe, the wheel of a person's life may wobble precariously but it will still turn. In this diagram the wheel is supported by a web of spokes who are the burden bearers – the kind of community modelled to me by the residents of Roberts Road which I described at the beginning of this book. In any truly caring community, there will be a similar complex web of spokes. In our own church, even though its geographical setting means that members of the congregation live at a considerable distance from one another, we are setting ourselves the task of creating community. As I write, we are seeking to discern who the 'love therapists' are. By 'love therapists' I mean people who care enough for others to offer practical help when needed: Hoovering, cooking, gardening – those prepared to love with their sleeves rolled up. It has been a sadness to me to discover that fewer people volunteer for this hidden ministry of caring than for the more 'glamorous', up-front tasks of counselling and prayer ministry. Love-in-action, it seems, is the cinderella of today's ministries.

We are also seeking to discover those in whom God has invested a special ability to listen. We are conscious that each of us needs to go on and on learning the art-form of listening but we also recognise that some people have a flair for this particular ministry.

From a large group of listeners, some counsellors are emerging. Some of these have already received counselling training through their secular profession: social workers, probation officers, and Marriage Guidance Counsellors. If no such training has been received we offer basic guidelines to those who appear to be competent to counsel.

But we are aware that it is possible for any counsellor to wade out of their depth and so we have the ear of qualified psychologists, psychiatrists, psychotherapists and psychoanalysts who will advise and supervise when the occasion demands. Similarly other therapists give their support when it is needed: doctors, physiotherapists, occupational therapists and solicitors, to mention a few.

Alongside these other spokes of the wheel, we place the 'prayer therapists'. These are people who will make themselves available to intercede with or for the person in pain. Some of these therapists will have had experience in the ministry of inner healing which I have described in Chapters 8 and 9. Some of them have little experience in listening to people's problems and no experience in counselling. What they bring to people in pain is the gift of faith that God will intervene in some way. When they pray with a person presenting a particular need, they will listen to the description of the problem with one ear and attempt to listen to God with the other ear. They will bear in mind the picture of the person redeemed by Christ but not yet whole (see diagram 3) and they will be leaning heavily on God, relying on him to show them through a word of wisdom or discernment just how he wants to minister to the dents in that person's personality or body or spirit which is causing trouble at the moment.

If the person asking for help is clearly clinically depressed or bereaved, they will pray 'a holding prayer' and refer them to someone more experienced than themselves who can offer appropriate counselling. In some instances, when this seems to be the correct procedure, they might simply pray for the person and the professionals who are attempting to give more long-term help. On other occasions, when the problem is less complex, they might ask God by his Spirit to work in this person's life in any way he chooses. On such occasions, they might look for signs that God's Spirit is at work in the person's life. Because the Holy Spirit is sometimes described as wind, if the person's eyelashes flutter as though they were being blown by the wind while they are being prayed for, the prayer therapists take this as a sign that the perplexed or hurting person is being touched by God in some way. Or, because the Holy Spirit is described as fire, they are not surprised when the person they pray for glows with heat or if their own hands start to burn as they lay them, prayerfully, on the person's head or on injured parts of his body.

And we have seen God work miracles through these untrained people-helpers. By a miracle, I mean a work of healing which cannot be explained in human terms. But, equally, like many others, I have had the distressing task of attempting to piece together the parts of people who have received inappropriate ministry from well-meaning prayer therapists who have made a wrong diagnosis: mistaking, for example, a panic attack for demonisation.

At the same time, I have stayed alongside emotionally immature and hurting individuals who have been brought into wholeness through the talking therapies and drug therapy. But, equally, I have known of some who have remained untouched by psychiatry but who have been wonderfully helped by inner healing or prayer ministry.

For these reasons, the more involved I become in the task of reaching out to hurting people, the more I echo the words of the hymn writer when he wrote: 'God moves in a mysterious way his wonders to perform.' God is mystery. The ministry of healing is a mystery. A mystery is something too complex for the human mind to fathom.

Even so, if we are to be responsible to our calling to be compassionate as our Father is compassionate, we have to try to understand and I, for one, am grateful that, over the years, I have had the privilege of working alongside several professionals who have spent years acquiring learned people-helping skills. But I am grateful, too, that I have also worked with several 'novices' who bring nothing to an encounter with a troubled person other than an awareness that God wants to touch this person's life in some way. Both have challenged me. The professionals challenge me to go on and on learning all that is to be learned about the complexity of the human personality. The novices challenge me to open myself more fully simply to be used by God as and when and how he chooses. Meanwhile God seems to be challenging me to place my dependence in him but to go on with the learning.

And this dresses me down to size. Humbles me. And it has brought me into the realisation that because God is using a whole variety of people in a whole variety of ways to bring wholeness to an individual, I can be content to be just one spoke in the wheel of a person's life. I need never masquerade as the Messiah. Omnicompetent. I need not even make apology for my limitations. On the contrary, I can feel comfortable working within them; content to leave other parts of the burden bearing to those with different expertise.

That is not to say that we can be cavalier or irresponsible in the way we help others. Of course not. We need to learn the discipline of accountability to each other. Loose spokes are dangerous. They cause punctures and even accidents. Christians can cause similar casualties if they insist on operating in isolation. Whether we are listening or counselling, praying for people or offering practical help, we need therefore to keep in touch with the others and with the indwelling Christ so that our goal is achieved – the wheel of the person's life functions freely once more.

Qualifications of a 'spoke in the wheel'

'What kind of qualities are you looking for in people who offer to be spokes in your wheel of caring?' That is a question I am asked frequently. All kinds of characteristics have crowded into my mind in an attempt to answer it.

First and foremost, I look for people who will incarnate the love of Christ. Most of us, from time to time, find that we are rather like the small boy who, for a special treat, went on holiday with his father. Lying in the dark and in that strange bed, he felt alone and frightened. His father, sensing the fear, attempted to reassure him with the comforting thought that there was no need to be afraid because he was not by himself. God was with him. 'Yes,' replied the boy. 'But just for tonight I would like to have a God with skin on.'

And people who incarnate the love of Christ become those much needed 'Gods with skin on' which provide us with the props that are essential to our well-being when we are heavy hearted. The kind of people I have in mind are those who so respect the bruised and bleeding of this world that even in the midst of their pain they offer them warmth, sensitivity, understanding, concern, unconditional love and the Christ-like compassion we focused on in the first chapter of this book. These are the kind of people of whom it is often said as it was of the scientist and priest Teilhard de Chardin, 'Just to speak to him made you feel better; you knew that he was listening to you and that he understood you.' These are the people who bestow, even on the broken-hearted, a sense of their full worth as children of God.

Secondly, I look for people who will learn to listen to God as well as to other people. This ability to tune into the Father heart of God is essential for several reasons. First, as Francis MacNutt reminds us, the creature is dependent on the Creator for the wisdom to know how best to fulfil his role of 'God with skin on'. For, 'just as a doctor looks for the right diagnosis, the Christian helper is seeking discernment – which is the right diagnosis in the realm of prayer.'[8] This discernment comes in a variety of ways, as explained in *Listening to God*. Sometimes it comes in the form of a picture, sometimes through one word which may seem meaningless to the helper but which will cut ice with the person in pain, if, indeed, it has come from God. Or it might come quite naturally in the form of the wisdom to know which questions to ask and which to withhold, when to speak and when to keep silent and in what way one should pray. Unless we listen to God, we shall never graduate from anything higher than our own assessment of a person's pain. But what is really needed is God's perspective. When we have this, we can determine whether the dark valley the person seems to be travelling through has been caused by sin which needs to be confessed and cleansed or whether it is a sickness which needs a healing touch from God or whether it is a mysterious treasure to be seen as a trust from God; the kind of darkness encapsulated in the immortal words of Francis Thompson:

> Is my gloom after all
> Shade of his hand?
>
> (The Hound of Heaven)

Such in-tuneness with God comes most easily to those who have learned to keep silence. And this silent attentiveness before God is important for another reason. Rathbone Oliver, a psychiatrist as well as a priest, puts the situation well:

> The extent of your power to help will depend not on your knowledge of psychiatry, or even on your knowledge of dogmatic or moral theology but on the assurance you bring to human souls that you yourself have been with Jesus . . . People, unhappy, anxious, self-tormented people, are drawn toward real holiness as moths are drawn to a candle.[6]

In other words, what hurting people crave is not the paucity of human help but rather a touch of the divine love, wisdom or healing through God's human agents: his people helpers.

Would-be people helpers need to learn the art of listening to God because none of us has within ourselves the divine love which penetrates and communicates, which heals and consoles or challenges and confronts. But God will add these resources to us. And he will do it while we creep into him ourselves, make a deliberate attempt to lay on one side our preoccupation with our own needs and insecurities, fears and unresolved tensions and add to us sufficient resources to stay alongside broken people. Without this love much of the time we spend with hurting people may well be wasted.

And there is a fourth reason for learning to listen to God. It is here too that we receive forgiveness and cleansing for the sin which would block us from being effective channels of God's power and holding, healing love.

Allow God to be God

People who are aware of the need to depend on God for discernment and resources are those who are most likely to allow God to be God. This, too, I believe to be a quality which should be sought by anyone attempting to help others in the name of Christ. I say this because of the tragic polarisation I detect in certain circles. What I see happening is this. Some skilled psychiatrists, psychoanalysts and other professionals who have spent hours studying the complexities of the human psyche are falling into the trap of assuming that they hold the monopoly when the task in hand is that of straightening bent minds or healing hurt emotions. Very often, of course, God does use them as his chief instrument of healing to hurting people. On the other hand, as Gerard Hughes reminds us, God is a God of surprises. And sometimes he chooses to by-pass the insights of the well-qualified professional and chooses instead to bring peace to one of his heart-broken children through the prayer of faith offered by an amateur who has never even trained in counselling. But such professionals are not the only ones who wear the blinkers. Many prayer therapists, I find, are equally short-sighted and have been heard to claim that unless a person has clearly been touched by God's spirit, the help given to the hurting person has been invalid and ineffective. This claim is naive, inaccurate and arrogant. It results in the failure to discern that sometimes our prayers do not produce the crop of instant cures we anticipate, because on many occasions, God chooses to touch individuals in need through the slow, gradual growth which is effected through psychiatry, drug therapy or counselling. The mystery of God is that he flatly refuses to be tied down by our methodologies. He is a God of variety.

Effective helpers will be those who not only rejoice in whatever method God chooses to bring wholeness to his hurting child, they will be those who have a theology of pain, suffering and death as well as a theology of healing. By this I mean that they will not fall into the trap of demanding that the person being helped should receive instant healing but rather will discipline the clamouring voices inside themselves that demand a miracle every time and learn instead that in the economy of God, pain sometimes has a purpose and that the ultimate healing is, in fact, death itself. One reason I look for people who will allow God to be God is that such people have discovered the unique contribution which other people can make and, instead of feeling threatened by the presence of others, co-operate with them humbly and gratefully in the way I have already outlined in this chapter. So the psychiatrist will support and maybe even supervise someone whose main contribution will be prayer ministry, maybe through the prayer for inner healing; or the counsellor will work alongside the general practitioner, the physiotherapist and the psychologist who are also seeking to bring a certain person into wholeness. Each will make their unique contribution to the person being helped. And in doing so each will learn from the other.

Proficiency, accountability and personal growth

And I look for three more qualities in people who volunteer to be spokes in the wheel of caring. One is proficiency. To become a really effective helper of others demands hard work and a lifetime of learning. While the learning continues, there is a need for each helper to be accountable to others for the way they handle another's hurts. This means that, just as a gifted conductor will draw out the best from a choir or an orchestra, so a gifted, dedicated director of pastoral care will be needed to draw out the full potential of those whom God calls to care in the way I have described. And if this potential is to be realised, each helper will catch a glimpse of the need, not only to be proficient and efficient, but they will make it their quest to grow in personal maturity. This will usually mean that there will need to be someone who will help them to continue to grow in self-awareness, someone before whom they can spread their work load and who will comment on it, someone who will help them to discover how and where their own resources are to be replenished so that they live balanced, healthy lives and avoid burnout.

Who is equal to this task, some readers might ask. And the answer is no one. At least, not in their own strength. But then, we are not asked to serve God in the energy of the flesh but rather we enjoy the privilege of being empowered and energised by his life-giving Spirit. And it is as the indwelling Spirit courses his life through our veins that spiritual fruit matures: love which according to one Harvard professor, is 'incomparably the greatest psychotherapeutic agent . . . something that professional psychiatry cannot by itself create, focus or release',[10] joy, peace, patience, goodness, gentleness, kindness, self-control (Gal. 5:22). The very qualities I have been underlining.

Being one spoke in the wheel of the life of a person in pain, far from being the glamorous ministry people often mistake it to be, is tiring and draining. As Anne Long used to remind her students, it costs 'not less than everything' of the people helping. Human spokes therefore need plenty of patience and plenty of stamina.

But there are rewards. One will be ours to enjoy when the Lord returns. Matthew describes it powerfully:

When the Son of Man comes in his glory, and all the angels with him, he will sit on the throne in heavenly glory. All the nations will be gathered before him, and he will separate the people one from another as a shepherd separates the sheep from the goats. He will put the sheep on his right and the goats on his left. Then the King will say to those on his right, 'Come, you who are blessed by my Father; take your inheritance, the kingdom prepared for you since the creation of the world. For I was hungry and you gave me something to eat, I was thirsty and you gave me something to drink, I was a stranger and you invited me in, I needed clothes and you clothed me, I was sick and you looked after me, I was in prison and you came to visit me.' Then the righteous will answer him, 'Lord, when did we see you hungry and feed you, or thirsty and give you something to drink? When did we see you a stranger and invite you in, or needing clothes and clothe you? When did we see you sick or in prison and go to visit you?' The King will reply, 'I tell you the truth, whatever you did for one of the least of these brothers of mine, you did for me.' (Matt. 25:31–40)

Anything? Hoovering, cooking casseroles, 'just listening', counselling? Yes. Anything. And, if my testimony is an accurate gauge, there is another, more immediate reward. It is the pure joy of watching someone you have been helping crawl out of their joyless chrysalis, not as the caterpillar they once were, but the beautiful butterfly God always intended they should be. Free.

Chapter 12

Listening to Joy

For as long as I remember I have been able to weep with those who weep. Life in Roberts Road seemed to equip me for that. But the realisation dawned on me as the counselling course at St John's drew to a close that I seemed ill equipped to rejoice with those who rejoice. When people were in pain, I slipped very easily into the role of helper. But when it was joy they were wanting to share with me, I felt ill at ease, on the fringe, uncertain of what was expected of me.

This bothered me. So in the third term at St John's I shared my concern with the small group of ordinands and their wives who were part of the same 'growth group' as me. 'This is the area in which I'd most like to mature,' I confided.

I had expected these young people to look shocked when I made this confession. I imagined that the problem was peculiar to me. Instead their eyes expressed empathy and understanding and several heads were nodding as I said my piece.

That term I set myself the task of trying to discover the reason why I was so ambivalent about listening to joy. How *did* one rejoice with those who rejoiced with as much care as one wept with those who weep? What was the secret? While searching for answers to such questions, I asked God to do a further piece of transforming work in me; to set me free to listen to joy with genuineness.

Louis Evely's books, *Joy* and *Suffering*,[1] put the problem into perspective for me and helped me to discover one reason why some people receive sorrow more easily than joy.

This Jesuit priest claims that the inability to receive joy is a universal problem; that though Jesus made us depositaries of his joy and though Christianity is a religion of joy and though God has filled his world with joy, Christian people have not yet learned to cherish this priceless gift. Man has missed his entry into joy, he claims. We are much more inclined to mourn with Christ than to rejoice with him. We are better disposed to be sorrowful with Christ and to share his sufferings than his joy.

At first these claims astonished me. We at St John's, it seemed, were not alone in our problem. I read on.

After the crucifixion, Louis Evely reminds us, a few faithful friends lingered at the foot of Christ's cross. But on the morning of the resurrection, no one was present to witness him bursting the bonds of death or to watch while the angels rolled the stone away. Consequently part of Jesus' post-resurrection task was to convert each of his friends so that they could receive the reality of his joy. But he had to take them by the hand, one by one, and teach them how to receive this joy.

How to receive joy

While I continued to pray that God would convert me in this way, I thought carefully about some further observations of this Jesuit author.

Jesus had already taught his disciples one part of the secret of receiving joy, he explains. It starts with prayer. In the words of Jesus: 'Ask and you will receive, and your joy will be complete' (John 16:24). Now Jesus goes on to show that there is a flip side to this coin. If they are to find themselves in harmony with joy, they must learn to lay aside their preoccupation with themselves.

This is one of the lessons the risen Christ seems to be trying to drum into the minds of the disciples on the road to Emmaus. In his encounter with them, Jesus' first task was to strip them of the prejudices and presuppositions which clouded their perception so that, eventually, their hearts were ready to receive Christ with joy. He deals similarly with Thomas's doubts. When these have been removed the scales fall from his eyes and with joy he cries: 'My Lord and my God.' And, perhaps most movingly of all, we are permitted to eavesdrop as Jesus stands on the shore of the Sea of Galilee and converses with the great deserter, Peter; the one who, that very morning, had resolved to return to his former lifestyle: fishing in the Sea of Galilee. And Jesus takes from his mind the sting of the memory of that night in Caiaphas' palace when Peter denied all acquaintance with Jesus and, in its place, he puts joy: the joy of the awareness that he is still loved and capable of loving; that he is not only usable but recommissioned.

'Yes. Louis Evely is right,' I said to myself. 'Before I can hope to receive joy from another, I must be stripped of my preoccupation with self, be prepared to let go of those things on which my security seems to depend and abandon myself afresh to God. I'll never be able to receive joy with genuineness while another's good news seems to threaten my security.'

I was beginning to see that the block was selfishness on my part. I thought of the occasion when a close friend of mine announced her engagement. She had talked to me at length about her relationship with the young man she was in love with. And through these conversations our closeness with each other had deepened. But when, eventually, she made her commitment to her husband-to-be, I realised that the dynamics of our relationship would need to change. I would have to step back. In time, after she married, I would lose her because she would move away from our area. And because her joy threatened my security, though I made all the right happy noises about being glad for her and though I congratulated him, I had not received their joy with the care I would have received their pain if they had announced that they were separating.

I reflected that I sometimes showed a similar ambivalence when a counselling relationship came to its natural conclusion. I thought of one such relationship in particular. A certain closeness had developed between myself and the girl I had been helping. Over the months, as we worked together, God touched her life in remarkable ways which thrilled and encouraged us both. But this meant, of course, that the time came when there was no more need for counselling sessions and since we are both busy people, our paths no longer crossed. She would write to me from time to time to tell me how God was continuing to touch her with his healing hand. And though I was happy for her, and though I wrote to express my joy, I was aware that there was a hollowness about this so-called joy. It was not a deep emotion. Only superficial. And, again, the problem was self-centredness. I could not really rejoice with her until I had relinquished the selfishness which would have liked to cling to her friendship.

'Detachment! That's the secret!' I recorded in my prayer journal. 'If I am serious about learning to listen to joy, I have to learn the discipline and art form of detachment: detachment from self and detachment from the earth-boundness which still persuades me that my security finds its source in people and possessions rather than in the God who smiles on me constantly with affection and who has sealed his loving promise: "I will never leave you or forsake you."'

I took comfort from Louis Evely's claims: 'Joy is slow to stir in us',[1] 'true joy is attained only gradually – by degrees.' And, I was later to discover, it does come. It came for me as I learned to listen to joy in much the same way as I listen to pain: attentively and with the attitude of mind which determines: 'I'm going to receive this person's gift and handle it with care.'

After I had made this resolve, I learned to read the language of the eyes of the joyful person – to watch them sparkle. Similarly I learned to listen to the tone of the voice as it struggled to contain its excitement. I learned to watch, too, the radiance of the face, to drink its joy and to take this joy deep down into my spirit and sip its nectar. And God gave me so many opportunities to practise these new skills. He continues to give me the privilege of listening to joy.

I am particularly aware of this as I write this chapter. It is December – the time when I write the annual news-letter for our friends. And as I look back over the year and try to decide what to write, I am aware that these last twelve months have been crammed with special joy, not because there has been an absence of pain but because true joy – the kind which comes from sorrows overcome – has dotted my path in the same way as shy primroses dot the hedgerows in spring.

I think, for example, of the occasion when my husband and I were enjoying Cantonese cooking in a Chinese restaurant in China Town in Brisbane, Australia. 'This makes me homesick for Singapore,' I admitted as we ate. Almost before the words had left my lips, I noticed a man smiling at me through the restaurant window. I could scarcely believe my eyes. He was a Singaporean; a friend who, on one of my visits to his country, had begged me to pray for him because he and his wife had been told they were infertile and they both longed for a child.

I did pray. A few months later his wife had written to share their good news. She was pregnant. When the baby was born they sent me a photograph of her which still smiles at me from my kitchen wall.

And now, here they were, grinning from ear to ear and walking through the restaurant door to greet us. As they placed their miracle baby into my arms, it was as though I was handling joy in a physical form. It was a moment of intense and pure joy.

Later that evening, as we talked to these friends in our hotel room, this joy spilled over into heartfelt thanksgiving to God that he had allowed our paths to cross so mysteriously; that we had all 'happened' to be in the same restaurant in the same town at the same time. I gave thanks too, for the fulfilment of Jesus' promise: 'My joy shall be in you and your joy shall be full.'

But joy has also come in less tangible forms. It came in Malaysia one summer when my husband and I enjoyed a reunion with ex-members of our congregation who have now returned to their native land. One of the first people to greet me was a girl I had tried to help when she was a student in Nottingham. She reminded me of the dark days of depression she encountered and of the talks we used to have. And I read the gratitude in her eyes and saw the smile of thanks on her lips and felt the warmth of her embrace, and I found myself receiving and internalising, not only her love and gratitude, but also the joy which seemed to bubble from her. It was another wonderfully joyful moment.

But perhaps the most moving of them all came in the context of a Communion service in a sleepy village in my homeland: England. The service was being conducted by a pastor who, when he had nose-dived into the dark tunnel of depression, had given my husband and me the privilege of staying alongside him in the seemingly-interminable darkness. But just as J. B. Phillips had translated the entire New Testament when he was depressed, and as William Cowper had written some of his most profound poetry and hymns from the dark pit of depression, and as Leslie Weatherhead was capable of enthralling thousands by his preaching even while he was gripped by depression, so this pastor's effectiveness for Christ had not been blunted by the darkness but rather this desert had produced abundant growth.

And as I watched him press his thumbs into the brown loaf which was to become for us the bread of heaven, into my mind flooded memories of the countless times I have watched those thumbs being twiddled aimlessly, listlessly and boringly as they expressed the lifelessness which dogged him. And as I watched in wonder as worship lighted up his face, I recalled the many occasions when that face had been overshadowed by loneliness and anguish. As I listened to the quiver of excitement in his voice as he confessed: 'I'm so excited by God's Word,' I thought of the hours I had heard that voice bemoan the seeming absence of God and the inability to concentrate on his revealed

Word. And I realised that a miracle was unfolding before my eyes.

The miracle was not that this man had experienced a dramatic healing in the sense that one day he was suffering from depression and the next he was enjoying freedom from darkness. His had been a gradual change. God had used drug therapy, the talking therapies, prayer therapy and love therapy to bring him through the dark valley and into this oasis. But just as I had been given the privilege of staying alongside him in the shadowlands, so now I was being given the even greater privilege and joy of being on the receiving end of his ministry.

'The greater privilege and *joy*.' Yes. It was a moment pregnant with profound joy. Not the shallow, transitory, effervescent kind which, like a will o' the wisp, is here one second and disappears the next but the deep down, lasting kind which you savour and ponder and which prompts you to fall on your face at the foot of Christ's cross in wonder, love, adoration and praise; the kind which brings tears to your eyes – tears of JOY.

That day the God of surprises surprised me by joy. Through the transparency of this humble pastor's ministry, he had shown me what he has been creating in the inner recesses of my being: a deep vein of joy. 'My gift to you through others,' he seemed to whisper. 'As you've struggled to absorb their pain so now be enriched by their joy also.'

Some repercussions

And I have been enriched by joy. As I look back in an attempt to trace some of the ways in which God answered that prayer I made in the growth group at St John's, I am aware that, just as Jesus changed the direction of Peter's life when he taught him to receive the joy of the resurrection, so I received a recommissioning from God as I learned to tune in to joy. It was while I listened to the joy the engaged couples in our church were expressing that the idea of organising seminars for engaged couples was conceived. And it was while one particular couple shared their secret joy with me – that they were expecting their first baby – that a seed thought was sown which led to my piloting our first Pregnant Parents' Group in the church. Similarly, it was when married couples invited us to rejoice with them that the marriage seminars which had been held in our home had revolutionised their lives that the urge to set up retreats for married couples pushed me into action.

Engaged Couples' Weekends, Marriage Fulfilment Weekends, Marriage Refreshment Retreats for Christians in Leadership, Pregnant Parents' Group; all have one aim: to focus on the joy which God intended us to give and receive in our relationships in the home and to discover how best to enter into this joy.

These weekends and mid-week retreats are fun as well as hard work. They have opened up for me a whole new dimension of listening to others and encouraged me to dream an even bigger dream for our church. Living as we do, in a troubled, sin-stricken world, there will always be a need for the kind of crisis counselling I have described in this book. But prevention is better than cure. And so my longing for my own church and for the church at large is that, instead of pouring all our resources into gluing together the shattered remains of the broken people who come across our paths and perpetuating the myth that the church is a hospital where sick people come to be cured, we tune in, as well, to the joy and resilience of those who are catching glimpses of the abundant life Christ promised. And we speak to this joyful resilience. We teach those who are coping how to enter more deeply into the joy of their Lord, how to develop good nurturing relationships both in the family and beyond, how to anticipate problems and how to handle them when they arise.

We will teach our parents how to find joy in their children and how to cherish them so that they grow up relishing their uniqueness. Equally we will teach our children how to understand and find joy in their parents; how to show them that they are valued.

We will listen to the joy of teenagers in love and teach

them how to handle the bitter-sweet emotions that come as part of the package of puppy love. We will help our engaged couples to prepare for the joy of marriage, teach our married people how to find more joy in one another as the years fly by and show our single people the special joys of singlehood. And we will not stop there. We will recognise that there are peculiar joys which are denied the young but which make themselves available to the middle-aged and the elderly. So we will whet people's appetites through books and videos, seminars and sermons and show them how to savour the joys of middle age, retirement and even old age.

Best of all, we will point them to the source of all joy, Jesus himself, and to that inexpressible joy which will one day be ours when he returns; that day when the sorrows and sadnesses of this life will be replaced with the ecstasy that will be ours when we see him face to face and exchange our earthly ministry for the heavenly one of serving him tirelessly day and night for ever.

On that great day we shall understand more fully the mysteries of our faith, including the mystery which stares me in the face every time I go to my prayer room. There hangs a banner which was made for me by a nun. Against a blue background which symbolises the vastness of the cosmos, she has placed, in white felt, a representation of the glorified Christ. His arms are outstretched in welcome, reminding me that the glorified Christ is also the welcoming Christ. But as I gaze at his hands and his feet, I see the marks of the nails which she has stitched to remind me that though he is glorified, still he is scarred. And on to the felt she has sewn the figure of the crucified Christ – the one who took upon himself our pain and our shame so that we could take upon ourselves his glory; the one who refused to by-pass Calvary but rather chose to go through the agony of Gethsemane and Good Friday to reach the ultimate joy: Easter day.

Sometimes I feel drawn to this figure because of his aliveness and splendour. At other times it is his vulnerability which compels me. And therein lies the mystery. Joy and pain intertwine. This side of eternity they are bedfellows. Both are essential parts of our humanity.

As I come to the final paragraph of this book, I hear a carol coming from the radio. It is one I learned when I was a child in the Sunday School in Roberts Road – before Barry Hart died:

> What can I give him, poor as I am
> If I were a shepherd, I would bring a lamb
> If I were a wise man, I would do my part
> Yet what I can I give him, give my heart.
>
> (C. Rosetti)

'Give my heart.' Even when I sang that as a child, my heart would be strangely warmed. For years I used to think that that warmth was all that was needed because I was simply required to give my love, my adoration, my worship and my praise. But now I see that it means all of that and much more. For Christ calls us to give to him the compassionate heart that prompts us to serve him in others. He calls us, too, to give him our listening heart – the heart that listens to God and to others; that is sensitive to sorrow but is equally quick to tune into joy.

Postscript

Listening With Love

When I used to lead seminars on listening, I used to summarise my material and project it on to an overhead projector slide:

Listening is a surprisingly difficult discipline to learn. There are certain basic attitudes to be acquired:

1. *Availability:* Giving a person –
   - time
   - concentrated attention
   - your whole person
2. *Listening with your eyes to:*
   - body language
   - eyes
   - hands
   - tears
   - facial expression
   - non-verbal clues that help you to identify painful feelings – like untidiness or the way the person dresses
3. *Listening with your ears* by observing certain do's and don'ts
   - don't interrupt
   - don't put words into a person's mouth
   - don't explain or interpret
   - don't jump to conclusions

- don't give advice
- don't give slick Bible quotations which may make you feel better but do nothing for the person you're listening to

But do:

- listen to the speed and tone of voice
- listen to the language of silences, tears, sighs and pauses
- focus fully on the person as well as being aware of your own reactions
- try to grasp accurately the shades of feeling being expressed
- stay with those feelings and help the person explore them
- use the information you have

4. *Listen with your 'third ear'* (that is, with your intuition and sensitivity),
   - to the vibes
   - to the feelings that may not be named but with which the story may be laced –
     anger
     fear
     resentment
     excitement
   - supremely, listen to God

5. *Listen to Yourself* by asking yourself:
   - How might I feel if I were in this person's shoes?
   - How do I sense this person is feeling?
   - Being aware of what is going on between the person and yourself –
     how they are feeling about you
     how you are feeling about them
   - being aware of your need for God's grace
   - being aware that, just as this person is being confronted with the challenge to grow, so you live on a constant growth curve.

When we listen to a person in this way, as I have shown in Chapters 5 and 6, we flesh out the truth that has been encapsulated so beautifully in a certain worship chorus:

> Each child is special
> Accepted and loved
> A love-gift from Jesus
> To his Father above.

One problem I have faced since my circumstances changed in the way I have outlined in the Preface is that, now that I live and work overseas, I have been stripped of all the props I took for granted when I lived in the West. One of the things I miss most is the proximity and availability of people equipped to listen in depth to my experiences, my joys, my frustrations, my pain, my questions and my prayer journey. I am not alone in experiencing this lack. Most of us who work overseas lament that particular loss. It means that we depend heavily on letters: whether written or spoken on cassette. We rely, too, on the telephone if we are fortunate enough to live in a country where we can be connected to a telephone system.

Since leaving England, therefore, I have given careful thought to the value of letters, cards and telephone calls where, of course, the body language cannot be read, nor, in the case of letters, can the speed or tone of voice be heeded. Yet, for those of us who are aliens in the country of our adoption, as, indeed, for shut-ins, such methods of communication can be life-savers for several reasons. Through them, we can pour out our impressions and our feelings. Through them we can encounter God, feast on his love penned through the words of friends, supporters and relatives. Through them, we can be challenged by God through the confrontation of someone who is faithful enough to draw our attention to inconsistencies in our lives. Through them we can be challenged by God as a faithful listener confronts us about inconsistencies in our lives. In addition, by listening with love to the letters of others, we can offer support and strength. In this way, we keep the wheels of mutuality well oiled. That is why, in this Postscript, we concentrate on three further forms of listening not previously examined in this book:

- listening to letters
- listening to cassettes
- listening to telephone calls

Listening to Letters

Now that my husband and I live in a country where letters are not delivered to our door, part of our own ritual is to make a daily pilgrimage to the post-office box in the small town where we live – just in case there should be a letter or a card from a loved one, a prayer supporter or a well-wisher. And when the fax rings, we jump. It just might be a friendly note rather than a business message.

When letters do come, I remind myself of Macrina Wiederkehr's claim: 'God can be found in the mailbox'.[1] So I look for him and am sometimes surprised by joy when he comes striding across the pages into my heart or my awareness.

I think, for example, of a letter I received just before writing this chapter. It was from someone I have never met but, as I read the four, closely-typed A4 pages, God thrilled me with the reminder of who he is: the Faithful One, the Tender One, the Healer.

My unknown friend begins her letter by describing her first experience of making a retreat. As I read her reminiscences slowly and reflectively and, as I savoured her phrase, 'this gentle and lovely time', I marvelled that God can achieve so much in such a short space of time when people carve out quality time for him. As I read of the emotional battering she had received subsequent to the retreat and of the way God had used a leaf bud to meet her in the hurt, my heart was moved by the mercy of the God who could assure this child of his that, just as a soft, hairy covering protected the leaf bud, so he was protecting her. Just as she detected signs of new life in the garden, so he was detecting new life in her. I was further touched when I read and reread the final paragraph in which she explains the reason why she had shared so much of herself with me: 'I feel that through your writings you have walked with me through the past months and that has caused me to want to write . . .' I felt humbled by those words. At the same time I felt affirmed by God as I read them. And I was grateful because the letter arrived at a time when I was recovering from a long, tiring teaching trip. I needed encouragement. That day God certainly met me through the mail box.

If we are to meet God in the letters we receive, we must do more than skim-read them. Having read a letter right through, we need to return to it, read it as slowly as possible, receive the messages that are being conveyed, not just through the words that have been selected but by reading between the lines also. Some people find it helpful to pause to ask God to enable them to reverence what was written. Some also pray while reading, exposing their reactions to God. Having finished the letter, they lift the author to the God who cares. After reading the letter, it can be helpful to ask ourselves certain questions:

- Why did this person write at this particular moment in time?
- Do certain key phrases, sentences or pen pictures attract me to themselves?
- How was this person feeling when they wrote?
- How has the letter left me feeling?
- How do I want to respond?

When searching for answers to these questions, I often recognise how God comforts and loves us through the affection expressed in the letters of friends. I think, for example, of another letter I received shortly before writing this chapter. It was from a woman in her eighties who loves me like her own daughter. When I asked myself why she had chosen this particular moment to write, the answer left me feeling cherished and loved. She had written because she knew that I had just returned from a demanding five-week trip to India, Pakistan and Nepal. The fact that her letter arrived when it did, during my scheduled

'recovery time', of itself communicated a message: 'I care
about you so much that I want to assure you that I not only
journeyed in prayer with you as I followed your itinerary
but I am with you still.'

The letter exudes such love for me and my family, such
trust in the goodness of God, such gratitude to God for
his faithfulness that I feel warmed, moved, strengthened
and inspired by it. So I have fed from it many times.
This is the value of a letter. As Macrina Wiederkehr
puts it:

> Unlike a telephone call, a letter can be picked up again
> and again. It can be deeply pondered. It can be eaten.
> Always serve letters with a cup of tea and a footstool.
> Celebrate 'the reading' slowly. It is irreverent to read
> a letter fast . . .
> I treasure my letters like early morning sunrises. I
> see the rays between the lines . . . Standing before my
> mailbox holding an original very limited edition in my
> hands is like standing before a feast.[2]

This applies, in particular, to Christmas and birthday
cards, I find. Because at Christmas time an avalanche of
cards and letters descends on our home, we have adopted
a custom we first encountered in a friend's newsletter. In
this letter, she mentioned her practice of putting in a shoe
box early in the new year, all the Christmas cards she
and her husband had received. As the year unfolds, they
remove from the box one card each day, read and relish the
greeting and pray for the sender. My husband and I now
do this at the beginning of our daily Communion Service
so that we lift the sender(s) into God's love in the context
of this love feast. On the day on which I am completing
this chapter, our chosen card comes from a much-loved
relative of mine who writes: 'Hope you are both keeping
well and enjoying your new calling. We follow your lives
with much interest.' Today, there is time to do what we
were unable to do at Christmas – pause to digest and
savour that humbling, loving sentence: 'We follow your

lives with great interest.' Today, there is also time to do what there was no time to do at Christmas – enjoy the picture on the card my cousin sent.

Another letter reached me soon after my return from the trip to Asia I have already mentioned. This one was as loving as the Christmas card and the other letters I have referred to though it was totally different in nature and tone. This one was from a friend to whom I had posted chunks of the journal I had kept while I was travelling. Recognising that I needed to process what had been happening to me and in me on that trip, I had asked her to send me some questions to help me do this faithfully. She did.

I was moved by the method she used. She had spent hours of her precious time reading and rereading what I had written. Subsequently, she selected certain statements I had made, quoted them verbatim and gently and lovingly probed and challenged me.

She writes, for example, 'In Delhi, half-way through the first retreat you led, you wrote, "I am really happy . . . The Mission Partners are spiritually so alive and wide open to receive anything . . . It's like giving water to the parched and thirsty."' She follows this quotation with some suggestions – that I ask myself whether I am in touch with the root of that happiness, for example: 'Did your happiness spring from the Partners' response to what you were offering? And/or the satisfaction of being used by God to quench their thirst for him?'

As I responded to those questions in my prayer journal, I discovered some of the reasons for my contentment. It taught me a great deal about myself, where I am in my relationship with God and what I feel I need to be effective in his service.

On a cassette which she sent me a few days later, this same friend confronted me about feelings of rejection which I had spread before her and before God. This tape demonstrated to me that confrontation need not be aggressive or cause a person to recoil hurt or offended. It can be gentle, loving, wise and growth-inducing. This confrontation was like that. There was no rebuke, no ticking-off – only a string of observations and open-ended questions which set me on the pathway to growth and change:

- I felt for you so deeply because I entered into your pain. You really were feeling the sting of rejection and I empathised with you.
- You know that, if I had been with you I would have read the other person's actions differently. Can you ask yourself where the strength of your emotional reaction is coming from? Does it spring from what the other person did or does the root lie in your own perception which, as you know, is blurred because of wounds from the past?
- Can you talk this through with the person concerned?
- Can you recognise that that person loves you so much that they would not deliberately reject you? Can you help that person to recognise how their behaviour affects you?

Because I could hear from the phraseology she used and from the tone of her voice on the cassette that these questions were asked out of love and with the desire that I might experience God's healing touch, I was able to work through them asking God to show me, not how he wanted the other person to change, but how he wanted me to change.

Listening to Cassettes
The value of letters for the reader, as we have seen, is that they can be read over and over again. We can feast on them. We can be available to the author at a time that is convenient to us and in a place which is conducive to contemplative reading. The value of letters for the sender is that they can choose their words carefully and in their own time knowing that their message will be reverenced by the reader. The *disadvantage* of letters

for the listener, of course, is that we can neither listen with our eyes or our ears so we may well miss the main message the sender intended to communicate. Or worse, we may misunderstand completely what they are trying to say. Similarly, there are advantages and disadvantages in communicating by cassette. One advantage is that, when a message is communicated orally on cassettes, we can listen to the tone and speed of the voice and this undoubtedly helps to reinforce what the sender intended to say. Just before writing this chapter, for example, I listened to a cassette sent to me by a friend. She was chuckling as she recalled some of the things we had done together on holiday. Her chuckle was infectious. I chuckled too. It was a beautiful shared moment even though we are now separated by continents.

Later, the tone of her voice changed dramatically as she shared some of the difficulties she was negotiating at that time. This reminded me of some startling statistics that have been published by communication experts. They claim that, when we communicate, 7 per cent of the message is transmitted through the words we select, 38 per cent through the voice – the tone, speed and pitch together with the pauses and silences – while the other 55 per cent is conveyed non-verbally, through body language. Clearly, then, the main disadvantage of communicating by either letter or cassette is that we are unable to read the body language of the person we are listening to. This underlines the disadvantages as a means of effective communication of both letters and cassettes. There is nothing quite like the personal presence of the person with whom we are communicating. But when that presence is not possible, as well as creating around ourselves a space where we can listen at leisure to the letter or the cassette, giving the person our dedicated time, our concentrated attention, our whole person and as well as listening to the shades of feeling they express, it can be helpful to picture them. What might their body language be like as they write or as they speak? If we could see their eyes as they are communicating with us, what might those mirrors of the soul be saying? And if we could see their facial expressions, what might we read there: a smile of love, maybe, or a look of compassion or . . .?

Another disadvantage of listening to letters or cassettes is that it is impossible to clarify in the way we might do if the person were speaking to us face to face.[3] It is also impossible to check whether the message we have heard and registered is the one the person intended to convey.

Yet there are so many aspects of good listening that can be applied that communicating by cassette is extremely valuable. Like reading letters, we can make ourselves available to the person concerned at a time that is convenient to us and in a place where we can give them our concentrated attention. We cannot interrupt them, put words in their mouths, explain, give advice or interpret what they are saying – at least not to them personally – while we listen. And if we listen carefully to the phraseology, the voice, the pauses, the tears (if there are any), the emotions, we may be able to picture the person – to imagine the look in their eyes, their facial expression, some of the body language we cannot actually see. We can also still pick up the vibes, discern the feelings and listen to God as we listen to the person. In other words, it *is* possible to tune in accurately to the message which is being conveyed.

When we reply, we can also give the person the gift of our respect. We can show them that we empathise with them, that is we feel with them. And we can take up some of the matters they raise, perhaps by asking the kind of question we would ask if they were actually with us, such as, 'Would it help to tell me more about . . .'? And, just as my friend loved me enough to confront me, so we can give the one communicating the gift, if it is needed, of our gentle confrontation as we highlight any inconsistencies they might have divulged. If we are to do this, however, we need to heed the warning Anne Long gives in *Listening*: The gift of confrontation should only be offered if there is good rapport with the other person, if the relationship with them is safe and if our underlying motive is the kind of care that wants the very best for that person. It should not be used if we feel angry with them or irritated by them.[4]

When we are the ones communicating by cassette, there are certain things we can do to ensure that the one with whom we are communicating tunes in accurately to what it is we are trying to tell them.

- When recording a message on cassette, it might help the listener if we start by describing where we are sitting or standing or walking. It might also help them to picture us if we tell them what we are wearing.
- It will be important to avoid confusing the listener by ensuring, as much as possible, that the tone of our voice matches the words we say. If someone says, for example, 'I don't want you to worry about me, I'm all right' in a flat, dull, monotonous voice, the message becomes blurred. Does the listener tune into the optimism of the words or the tone of voice?
- It might help from time to time, to describe our body language: 'The tears are streaming down my face at the moment', 'I'm about to cry', 'I've put on a lot of weight recently and that leaves me feeling down and depressed.'
- It will certainly help the listener if we can give our emotions a name: grief, contentment, happiness, excitement, anger, fear . . .

Listening on the Telephone

One of the disadvantages of communicating by cassette, particularly for those of us who live overseas, is the length of time it takes for a cassette to arrive and for a response to be received. I think, for example, of one friend with whom I correspond in this way. Because of the distance that separates us, it takes at least seven weeks before the one who sends a cassette receives a recorded response. Despite this serious snag, we feel that the warmth and genuineness of the spoken voice as opposed to the written word is well worth waiting for. The lack of immediacy of this kind of communication prompts some people to resort to using the telephone. The advantages are obvious.

There is immediacy in this sort of contact. Warmth can be readily communicated and felt. We can give each other encouragement, support, advice, guidance, love – and the gentle confrontation I mentioned earlier.

That is not to say that communicating by telephone is problem-free, however. Listening to telephone calls demands certain skills which few people learn. This is a great pity because phone calls can be fraught with problems.

With every other kind of listening: listening to a person who has arranged to see us, listening to letters and listening to cassettes, we choose the time when we can be as available to them as possible. A phone call, on the other hand, often comes unexpectedly. For those of us who live overseas, it can come very late at night or even in the middle of the night if the caller has not remembered that they will be crossing time zones with their call! Even if the call comes at a sociable time, it can cut right across what we were doing: having a meal, maybe, breaking into a train of thought or involvement in another project. This means that, often, even when the caller has begun to share their news, the listener is struggling to make themselves available to the unfolding story. They have not had time to lay aside their own agenda or to prepare themselves to listen attentively to the caller. Add to that concern about the cost (something we are always conscious of when making international calls), even the most sensitive, skilful listener can be tempted to cut corners by failing to clarify, by finding easy, take-away answers, by succumbing to those 'don'ts' I mentioned earlier:

- don't explain
- don't interpret
- don't give slick Bible verses
- don't use cliches like: '*Don't worry, everything will be OK*' . . .

Or the temptation might be to believe that we must find a quick solution to the problem being expressed or that we must be inspired with words of wisdom so that the caller feels better before they put the phone down. We might also find ourselves hooked by the seeming helplessness of the one who made the call. Or we might become intimidated by the enormity of the problem they outline.

If telephone conversations are to become healing rather than hurting, we need to recognise the peculiar stress factor of phone calls and to compensate for them. If we want to make regular phone contact with a particular person, for example, it might help to make a 'telephone date' with that person. Since we have lived overseas, we have done that with our son. When he was curate of a parish, we knew it would be difficult to track him down and our movements were equally unpredictable, so we made a 'date' to telephone him at 9.0am (his time) on Sunday mornings. This proved a very effective way of keeping in touch.

There are other things we can do. If we are making the call and, particularly if we want to talk in depth with the listener, it is worth asking them the simple question: 'Are you busy at the moment or may I talk over a few things with you?' If we are the one receiving the call and the call comes at a time when we know we cannot give the person our undivided attention, rather than listening with only half an ear, it may be kinder to be honest and to say: 'I'd love to be able to talk now but it's not really possible. Would you mind if I ring you back?' Most people would understand this question, be grateful for our honesty and happy to fix a time which was mutually agreeable.

Because it is so easy for telephone calls to be misunderstood, when we are listening, we need to listen as carefully to ourselves as to the caller. We can do this by registering our own reactions from time to time or by asking ourselves certain questions:

- How am I feeling about this particular call and the caller?

- What is happening between us?
- Am I hearing what the caller is saying? Are they hearing what I am saying?
- Why did this person call at this particular moment in their life?
- How do I sense they might be feeling about this conversation?
- If my assessment of how they might be feeling is accurate, how appropriate are those feelings?
- Am I communicating warmth and kindness with my tone of voice as well as with my words? Am I affirming the uniqueness of the caller, underlining the fact that he or she is special or am I, perhaps, giving the impression that he or she is a nuisance?
- Does this phone call need to be followed up in any way?

The Deaf and the Blind
Before leaving the subject of listening, I felt urged to mention the special needs of the blind and the deaf. Three things prompt me to do this. One is a letter in the church press which I read a few weeks before writing this chapter. In it the claim is made, in my view correctly, that many Christians avoid conversing with blind people because they are unsure how to establish any kind of rapport. Or worse, they treat blind people as though they were mentally defective. Another is a comment made to me on more than one occasion by the sister of a deaf person: 'People don't even try to talk to her. They ignore her. They think she's not only deaf but dumb and stupid as well. Yet she can speak eloquently and she is, in fact, a very intelligent and interesting woman.' The third is the memories I have of the privilege I was once given of leading a retreat for someone who is blind and her close friend who is partially sighted and partially deaf. The one with the hearing loss expressed in a poem the loneliness that sometimes envelops her and fellow sufferers when hearing people refuse to attempt to speak or to listen to those with impaired hearing:

Noise jangling, a muddle of sound
Voices passing to and fro.
I smile, trying to look as if I know
What is going on.
A joke, shrill laughter,
helpless hilarity.
I laugh, trying to prove to myself
that I belong.
Why do I try?
Why can I never express the cry
that echoes in my heart.
As, in the laughing, talking group,
I sit, cut off,
A person apart.[5]

'A person apart.' That is how the deaf person so often feels. As I have explained in this book, I was trained to teach deaf children. I have also done a certain amount of work with deaf adults and I have been enriched by listening to the faith journey of many fine Christian deaf people. If we are to listen with the heart to such people, we need to apply the same listening skills I have spelled out in this chapter and earlier chapters. We must give them time, attention, respect. We must listen carefully to their eyes, their body language, their tears. We must pay attention to their intonation, the strength of their emotions and how they are coping with the constant challenges life presents them with. We must also be creative as we decide where and how we will listen to them. If the person has a certain amount of residual hearing in one ear but not in the other, it will be most helpful to them if we sit where they can best hear with the good ear. The person concerned will be the best one to advise us about this. If they are to be able to lip-read us, it is essential that the light falls on our face so that they can see our lips clearly. It is equally important that we speak normally and do not try so hard to help them to lip-read that our face becomes contorted making lip-reading impossible. And we must speak slowly. We must be sensitive to the fact that lip-reading is tiring;

sensitive, too, to the realisation that the deaf person
will be reading the language of our facial expression to
see whether they 'hear' the language of acceptance or
rejection. Affirmation may be communicated to them
most powerfully through the love that shines through our
eyes, the smile that lights up our face or the warmth of our
embrace, the touch of a hand. Similarly, listening to the
blind requires the same skills – and more. My experience
of listening to blind people is very limited but I want to end
the book on this note because, even as I am writing this
Postscript, this book is being transcribed into braille by a
blind friend of mine and I am excited to think of sighted
people listening to blind friends and acquaintances and
blind people listening to one another.

Whenever I am listening to anyone, but particularly
when I am listening to blind people, I like to think of
myself as a midwife helping someone else to give birth
to the precious life that has been growing inside them –
maybe for months, maybe for years.

When I think of the word 'midwife', my mind goes to
the woman who helped me to give birth to my first
child. In those days, at least in the area where I lived, there
were no pre-natal classes so, when I went into labour, I felt
a mixture of excitement and the apprehension of naïveté.
I was therefore deeply grateful that this midwife who was
to share with me such a deep and intimate experience as
the birth of my first baby, took the trouble to establish a
rapport which rapidly became a friendship. This generated
trust so that as I went into labour, when she encouraged
me to 'push', I pushed. When she suggested that I should
rest, I lay back on the pillows and rested. Her frequently
repeated affirmation: 'Good girl . . .' assured me that she
could see what I could not see. And I appreciated so much
the sensitive way she used her hands – to stroke mine when
I needed reassurance, to hold mine when I felt fragile and
to guide my son into the world. When, eventually, she
handed to me the bundle which was my baby, she gazed
at him in wonder, marvelling at the perfection of his fingers
and his toes as though she had never seen a newborn baby

before. Her presence felt to me like a gift of God at that important moment in my life.[6]

Just as my midwife took the trouble to forge a relationship with me, so it is vital, if a blind person is to trust us, that we earn their respect and confidence by establishing a good rapport with them. Just as my midwife poured strength into me with her affirming, 'Good girl . . .', so we will need to affirm the blind person who is giving birth to the story of their joy or their pain – that story that needs to come out. And just as the midwife used her hands to comfort me during long, long periods of waiting, we may need to rediscover the value of touch as we listen to a blind person.

Because the blind person will not be able to see us, a gentle hug (where this is appropriate) might help them to sense how we are feeling about them as well as helping them to detect precisely where we are. And, because they cannot see the love and admiration in our eyes, stroking or holding their hand from time to time can convey the warmth, affection and kindness we long to give them. It might also help if the listener describes, from time to time, how they are reacting to the unfolding story.

Since the blind person is unable to read the listener's body language, they may not be able to detect whether that person is feeling full of compassion or even tearful about some of the things they are sharing. So it might help them if the listener explains how they do feel: 'I felt quite tearful when you shared that . . .' 'That made me smile . . .' 'I really felt for you as you told me about . . .' Often, it seems to me, the blind person's ability to see with their inner eyes, their intuition, has been sharpened to compensate for the inability to see with their physical eyes. It will therefore be vital that we give them the gift of genuineness – not saying words which we do not really mean.

Just as a blind person cannot read the language of a sighted person's eyes, neither can a sighted person read the look in the blind person's eyes so they are denied access to this mirror of the soul. That is not to say, however, that listening to a blind person is difficult. Instead of reading the eyes, we can be aware of give-away facial expressions: frowns and smiles, puzzled looks and tears. We can also tune into the body language which communicates so much.

It is particularly important that we clarify that we have understood what the blind person is sharing and that they have understood our response – particularly if we are sighted. The sighted person uses phraseology which is full of images which assume that the other person can see. When talking to a blind person, we may become acutely aware of this and recognise that the words we use may not communicate anything to the one we are with. We need to be sensitive to this and alter our language accordingly – using words which appeal to the other senses: sounds and smells, touch and movement. This is challenging and demanding but abundantly worth while when we bear in mind that our role is to help the person give birth to the joy or the pain which has been growing inside them.

Listening to anyone is so worth while that readers of this book might like to join me in praying this prayer from time to time – particularly when they are given the privilege of becoming someone's spiritual or emotional midwife:

Teach me to listen, Lord,
to those nearest me,
my family, my friends, my co-workers.
Help me to be aware that
no matter what words I hear,
the message is,
'Accept the person I am. Listen to me.'

Teach me to listen, Lord,
to those far from me –
the whisper of the hopeless,
the plea of the forgotten,
the cry of the anguished.

Teach me to listen, Lord,
to myself.

Help me to be less afraid,
to trust the voice inside –
in the deepest part of me.

Teach me to listen, Lord,
for Your voice –
in busyness and in boredom,
in certainty and in doubt,
in noise and in silence.

Teach me to listen, Lord.[7]

Notes

Preface
1. Peter Dodson, *Contemplating the Word* (SPCK, 1987), p. 1.
2. Matthew 25:31, 31, Eugene Peterson's paraphrase, *The Message*, p. 63.
3. Matt. 25:35, 36, ibid., p. 63.
4. Matt. 25:40, ibid., p. 63.

Chapter 1
1. Henri Nouwen, Donald P. McNeill, Douglas A. Morrison, *Compassion* (Darton, Longman and Todd, 1982), p. 4.
2. ibid. p. 27.
3. ibid. p. 16.
4. ibid. p. 18.

Chapter 2
1. Gary Collins's phrase.
2. See Gary R. Collins, *How to be a People Helper* (Regal Books, 1976), pp. 33–4; id., *Christian Counselling* (Word Books, 1980), pp. 24–5.
3. Henri Nouwen, Donald P. McNeill, Douglas A. Morrison, op. cit. p. 32.
4. ibid. p. 24.
5. John A. Sanford, *Ministry Burnout* (Arthur James, 1982), Introduction.

6. F. B. Meyer, *The Shepherd Psalm* (Marshall, Morgan and Scott, 1953), pp. 28, 30.

Chapter 3
1. in Henri Nouwen, *Reaching Out* (Fount, 1975), p. 60.
2. ibid.
3. Katharine Makower, *Follow My Leader* (Kingsway, 1986), p. 116.
4. H. R. Niebuhr, source unknown.

Chapter 4
1. For a fuller discussion, read John Stott, *Issues Facing Christians Today* (Marshalls, 1984), ch. 1.
2. ibid. p. 9.
3. Alan Burgess, *The Small Woman* (Pan, ch. 1. 1957), p. 111.
4. ibid. pp. 143–44.
5. John Stott in *Alive to God Notes*, SU (October/ December 1987).
6. id., *Issues Facing Christians Today*, op. cit. p. 14.
7. ibid. pp. 21–22.
8. See ibid. p. 9.

Chapter 5
1. Henri Nouwen, *Compassion*, op. cit. p. 13.
2. As explained in Joyce Huggett, *Two Into One* (IVP, 1981), Preface.
3. Myra Chave-Jones in a talk given at St Nicholas's Church, Nottingham, September 1986.
4. Anne Long in a handout given to the students at St John's College.
5. Norman Wakefield, 'Learn to be a listener!' *Counsellor's Journal*, CWR, vol. 4, No. (1981), p. 10.
6. Michael Jacobs, *Swift to Hear* (SPCK, 1985), p. 124, 125.
7. John Stott, in Myra Chave-Jones, *The Gift of Helping* (IVP, 1982), Foreword, p. 8.

8. Gary Collins, *How to be a People Helper* (Regal Books, 1976), p. 58.
9. Roger Hurding, *Restoring the Image* (Paternoster Press, 1980), p. 17.
10. Michael Jacobs, *Swift to Hear*, op. cit. p. 28.
11. David Augsburger, *Caring Enough to Hear and Be Heard* (Herald Press, 1982), p. 25.
12. ibid. p. 29.

Chapter 6
1. John Powell, *Will the Real Me Please Stand Up?* (Argus, 1985), p. 113.
2. Myra Chave-Jones, *The Gift of Helping* op. cit. p. 39.
3. John Powell, op. cit. p. 147.
4. ibid. p. 142.
5. ibid. p. 145.
6. Gary Collins, *How to be a People Helper*, op. cit. 1985 ch. 3.
7. Abraham Schmitt, *The Art of Listening With Love* (Abingdon Press, 1977), p. 169.
8. Myra Chave-Jones in a talk given at St Nicholas's, Nottingham.
9. John Powell, op. cit. p. 162.
10. Agnes Sanford, *Sealed Orders* (Logos, 1972), pp. 112, 114.
11. Joyce Huggett, *Listening to God* (Hodder and Stoughton, 1986).
12. Michel Quoist, *Prayers of Life* (Sheed and Ward, 1963), pp. 91, 92.
13. Catharine de Hueck Doherty, *Poustinia* (Fount, 1975), p. 20.
14. Abraham Schmitt, *Listening with Love* (Abingdon Press, 1977), p. 9.
15. Roger Hurding, *Roots and Shoots* (Hodder and Stoughton, 1985), p. 35.
16. Mother Teresa, an adaptation of a prayer by Cardinal Newman quoted in Daphne Rae, *Love Until It Hurts* (Hodder and Stoughton, 1981).

Chapter 7
1. Myra Chave-Jones in a talk given at St Nicholas's, Nottingham.
2. John Powell, op. cit. p. 97.
3. Simon Stephens, *Death Comes Home* (Mowbrays, 1972), p. 66.
4. Colin Murray Parkes, *Bereavement: Studies of Grief in Adult Life* (Pelican, 1972), p. 189.

Chapter 8
1. Gary R. Collins, *Christian Counselling* (Word Publications, 1980), p. 411.
2. Francis MacNutt, *Healing* (Ave Maria Press, 1974), p. 181.
3. Derived from a model created by Frank Lake.
4. Francis MacNutt, op. cit. p. 183.

Chapter 9
1. Francis MacNutt, op. cit. p. 170.
2. ibid. pp. 183–4.
3. Frank Lake, *Clinical Theology* (Darton, Longman and Todd, 1966), p. 140.
4. John and Paula Sandford, *The Transformation of the Inner Man* (Logos, 1982), p. 19.
5. David Seamands, *Healing of Memories* (Victor Books).

Chapter 10
1. Jack Dominian, *Depression* (Fontana, 1976), p. 149.
2. ibid. p. 150.
3. Myra Chave-Jones, *Coping With Depression* (Lion, 1981), p. 16.
4. Vera Phillips and Edwin Robertson, *The Wounded Healer* (Triangle, 1984), p. 103.
5. Richard Winter, *The Roots of Sorrow* (Marshalls, 1985), p. 25.
6. David Augsburger, *Caring Enough to Hear and be Heard* (Herald Press, 1982), p. 152.
7. Carlo Carretto, *Summoned by Love* (Darton, Longman and Todd, 1977), pp. 23, 24, 55, 56.

Chapter 11
1. Mary Craig, *Blessings* (Hodder and Stoughton, 1979), p. 134.
2. Quoted in ibid.
3. ibid. p. 142.
4. Quoted in Mark Gibbard, *Dynamic of Love* (Mowbrays, 1974), p. 1.
5,6,7: Roger Hurding, *Restoring The Image* (Paternoster Press, 1980), pp. 8–11.
8. Francis MacNutt, op.cit. pp. 195–6.
9. Rathbone Oliver, source unknown.
10. Gordon Allport, quoted in Gary Collins, op.cit. p. 25.

Chapter 12
1. Louis Evely, *Joy* (Burns and Oates 1968), p. 39.

Postscript
1. Macrina Wiederkehr, *A Tree Full of Angels* (Harper and Row, 1988), p. 107.
2. Ibid., p. 105.
3. See p. 86.
4. See Anne Long, *Listening*, p. 42. The whole of this chapter (2) of the book contains invaluable insights for the would-be listener.
5. Tracey Williamson.
6. Although I have been using the word 'midwife' to describe the listener for many years, Margaret Guenther's use of this same simile in *Holy Listening* (DLT) has helped me to develop further this imagery.
7. John A. Veltri SJ, *Orientations: A Collection of Helps for Prayer* (Loyola House, Guelph, 1979), p. 46.

Recommended Resources

The Acorn Christian Healing Trust was founded in 1983 by Bishop Morris and Anne Maddocks. Christian Listeners, led by the Rev. Anne Long, is one of several projects organised by this Trust. It comprises a twelve-session training course – normally church-based. Christian listeners become available to doctors, social workers and other health-care professionals for a ministry of listening in the locality of their church.

Christian Caring was established in 1985 on the initiative of a group of evangelical clergy in Cambridge. It has three main aims: to encourage the establishment of pastoral care support groups in the local churches, to train their members and to provide a professional therapy service for Christians in the locality who are in complex emotional need. Further details may be obtained from The Administrator, Christian Caring, Old School, 61, St Barnabas' Road, Cambridge CB1 2BX.

The Post Green Pastoral Centre is one of the many ministries of the Post Green Community which was established in 1974. It organises conferences and camps, offers retreats, counselling and Spiritual Direction and receives individual guests. Its concern is to provide a caring, loving environment where the needs of the whole person can be heard and met. For further details write to: Post Green

Pastoral Centre, 56, Dorchester Road, Lytchett Minster, Poole, Dorset BH16 6JE.

The Clinical Theology Association was formed in 1962 by Frank Lake and is now directed by Peter van de Kasteele. The Association exists to train people in Christian pastoral care and counselling and authorised tutors are currently available in most parts of the UK. Further details are obtainable from The Clinical Theology Association, St Mary's House, Church Westcote, Oxford OX7 6SF.

The Centre for Pastoral Care and Counselling is directed by the Rev. Michael Jacobs. Among other things, the centre provides training for clergy and lay leaders in the dioceses of Derby, Lincoln and Southwell. Short courses and day workshops are arranged which aim to help those involved in listening to brush up and improve their skills. Two audiotapes are available which are best used in conjunction with the book *Swift to Hear*. Further details are available from: The Centre for Pastoral Care and Counselling, Vaughan College, St Nicholas Circle, Leicester LE1 4LB.

Wholeness Through Christ counselling is a form of prayer ministry offered by Christians who have been trained in the Schools of Prayer which The Wholeness Through Christ Trust arranges. A network of these counsellors exists. They offer ministry in their own locality to Christians seeking to be released from bondages and healed from the fears and inner wounds which hinder their spiritual growth and development. Those seeking training must be referred by their pastor, minister or vicar.

The Oxford Christian Institute for Counselling was established in 1985 and has three main aims: to provide a counselling service in a Christian context for people in appropriate need in Oxford and the surrounding districts; to provide support and supervision for those involved in counselling on behalf of the Institute and to provide educational training and study for Christians involved in counselling. Seminars, talks and learning experiences are arranged for counsellors and those wanting to become more effective carers and listeners. Course members must be supported by their local church and are selected by interview.

St John's College Extension Studies Pastoral Counselling Course exists to provide lay people and clergy with an understanding of the way people tick and some skills with which to minister to them. Teaching includes a biblical understanding of man, counselling skills and pastoral care of the depressed and the bereaved. Students are expected to attend two residential weekends at St John's College and to commit themselves to a four-to-six month period of home study. The college also runs an advanced course called Journey Through Life which is run on similar lines and is for those who have some grounding in counselling. Further details may be obtained from St John's Extension Studies, St John's College, Bramcote, Nottingham NG9 3DS.

Caring Seminars is the umbrella title for the Regional Counsellor Training Scheme launched by the Crusade for World Revival (CWR) in 1985 and conducted by Selwyn Hughes and team. These seminars are held on Saturdays and aim to equip Christians to help others with the more simple problems which frequently crop up in the life of the local church. In addition, CWR organise a variety of courses in in-depth counselling at its residential training centre. Further details may be obtained from the centre: Waverley Abbey House, Waverley Lane, Farnham, Surrey GU9 8EP.

Network is a Bible-based, Christian organisation, commissioned in 1986, which seeks to serve the church and the community in three areas: *counselling* of people in need, *training* its own counsellors and others through a programme pioneered by Dr Roger Hurding and general *resources* of library, tapes, local information and short courses for Christians in the Bristol area. Further details may be obtained from Network Christian Counselling, 10 Cotham Park, Cotham, Bristol BS6 6BU.

Recommended Reading

On Listening

Michael Jacobs	*Swift to Hear* (SPCK)
Anne Long	*Listening* (DLT) (Argus Communications)
Abraham Schmitt	*The Art of Listening With Love* (Festival Books)
David Augsburger	*Caring Enough to Hear and be Heard* (Herald Press)

Each of the above books contains valuable insights which show the reader how to listen to others more effectively.

On Counselling

Alistair Campbell	*Rediscovering Pastoral Care* (Darton, Longman and Todd)
Roger Hurding	*Roots and Shoots* (Hodder and Stoughton)
E. Kennedy	*On Becoming a Counsellor* (Gill and Macmillan)
Michael Jacobs	*Still Small Voice* (SPCK)
Myra Chave-Jones	*The Gift of Helping* (Inter-Varsity Press)
Gary Collins	*Christian Counselling* (Word Books)

Roger Hurding	*Restoring the Image* (Paternoster Press)
M. Scott Peck	*The Road Less Travelled* (Rider)
Gary Collins	*Innovative Approaches to Counselling* Vol. 1 (Word)
H. Norman Wright	*Self Talk, Imagery and Prayer Counselling* Vol. 2 (Word)
Frank Lake	*Tight Corners in Pastoral Care* (Darton, Longman and Todd)
Frank Lake	*The Dynamic Cycle* (CTA)

On People Helping

Henri Nouwen	*Compassion* (Darton, Longman and Todd)
Gary Collins	*How To Be a People Helper* (Regal Books)
Jennifer Rees-Larcombe	*God's Gloves* (Marshall Pickering)
Henri Nouwen	*The Wounded Healer* (Fount)
Henri Nouwen	*Reaching Out* (Fount)

Inner Healing

John and Paula Sandford	*The Transformation of the Inner Man* (Logos)
Barbara Leahy Shleman	*Healing the Hidden Self* (Ave Marie Press)
Agnes Sanford	*Sealed Orders* (Logos)
Ruth Carter Stapleton	*The Experience of Inner Healing* (Ecclesia Books)
Francis MacNutt	*Healing* (Ave Maria Press)
Francis MacNutt	*The Power to Heal* (Ave Maria Press)
Barry Kissell	*Walking on Water* (Hodder and Stoughton)

Mary Pytches	*Set My People Free* (Hodder and Stoughton)
David Seamands	*Healing for Damaged Emotions* (Victor Books)
David Seamands	*Healing of Memories* (Victor Books)
Agnes Sanford	*The Healing Light* (Arthur James)
Agnes Sanford	*Healing Gifts of the Spirit* (Arthur James)
Anne White	*Healing Adventure* (Arthur James)
John Wimber	*Power Healing* (Hodder and Stoughton)

I would not endorse all the teaching of each of these writers but the books I mention all contain useful insights into the ministry of inner healing.

Bereavement
How to care for the dying and bereaved:

Ian Ainsworth-Smith	*Letting Go* (SPCK)
Colin Murray Parkes	*Bereavement* (Pelican)
John Hinton	*Dying* (Pelican)
Kathleen Smith	*Help for the Bereaved* (Duckworth)
Elizabeth Collick	*Through Grief: The Bereavement Journey* (Darton, Longman and Todd/Cruse)
Edgar Jackson	*The Many Faces of Grief* (SCM Press)
Jean Grigor	*Loss: An Invitation To Grow* (Arthur James)

Not all the above books are written from a Christian point of view but each of them contains invaluable insights into how best to help the grief-stricken person. The last two are designed to be used by groups of people working through their grief together.

Helpful books to give to the bereaved at the appropriate time

C. S. Lewis   *A Grief Observed* (Faber)

C. S. Lewis' moving and powerful account of his own feelings as he came to terms with the death of his wife.

Wendy Green   *The Long Road Home* (Lion)

Ingrid Trobisch   *Learning to Walk Alone* (Inter-Varsity Press)

Two bitter-sweet books which describe how the authors are coming to terms with widowhood.

Simon Stephens   *Death Comes Home* (Mowbray)

Mary Craig   *Blessings* (Hodder and Stoughton)

Two powerful books which help readers to put themselves in the shoes of parents who suffer the trauma of the death of a child.

Elizabeth Heike   *A Question of Grief* (Hodder and Stoughton)

A sensitive, wise and challenging contribution which will be of help particularly to those who lose a friend through death.

Joyce Huggett   *Facing Death Together* (Creative Publishing)

Joyce Huggett has also produced a tape called *Walking With Jesus Sometimes Hurts* (SU).

**Anthologies which might bring comfort to those
who mourn**

Agnes Whittaker · · · · · · · · *All in the End is Harvest*
· (Darton, Longman and
· Todd/Cruse)

(A beautiful collection of prose and poems, prayers and
reflections which could be given to a Christian or an
unbeliever at any stage of grief.)

Cicely Saunders · · · · · · · · *Beyond All Pain* (SPCK)

(Dame Cicely Saunders' own collection of poems and
prayers written mainly by terminally sick patients in the
St Christopher's Hospice where she is Medical Director.
Could be given to believers and unbelievers.)

Jolanda Miller · · · · · · · · · *Facing Life Again* (Inter-
· Varsity Press)

(Might help some Christians in the later stages of grief.
Read it first to make sure that you feel it is suitable for
the person you have in mind.)

Depression
For befrienders and counsellors:

Myra Chave-Jones · · · · · · *Coping With Depression*
· (Lion)
Jack Dominian · · · · · · · · · *Depression* (Fontana)
Richard Winter · · · · · · · · · *The Roots of Sorrow*
· (Marshalls)
Dorothy Rowe · · · · · · · · · *Depression* (Routledge and
· Kegan Paul)
John White · · · · · · · · · · · · *The Masks of Melancholy*
· (Inter-Varsity Press)
Ross Mitchell · · · · · · · · · · *Depression* (Pelican)

Each of the above make their own important contribution to the understanding of depression.

Biographies which might help a person suffering from depression

Vera Phillips and Edwin Robertson	*The Wounded Healer – J. B. Phillips* (Triangle)
Stanley Baldwin	*Bruised But Not Broken* (Kingsway)
Nancy Anne Smith	*Winter Past* (Inter-Varsity Press)
Alexander Davidson	*Through a Foreign Land* (Lutheran Publishing House)
Don Baker Emery Nestor	*Depression* (Marshalls)

Finding Freedom

Becoming the Person
God Made Me to Be

For Pauline
with love and thanks

CONTENTS

ACKNOWLEDGMENTS

Whenever I finish a book, I find myself overwhelmed by the number of people who partner me in the writing. This book has been no exception but, as always, there is room here to mention only a few.

First, I would like to thank Carolyn Armitage, Editorial Director at Hodder and Stoughton for suggesting that *Living Free* was worth revising. But for her encouragement, I would not have embarked on this project.

Next, I am indebted to my friend and editor James Catford for all the affirmation he has given me both in the past when we have worked together on other books and, in particular, for the way he has believed in the contents of *Living Free* and this revision of that book. Having the opportunity to be back in touch with him and (through him) his wife Clare has been a very great joy.

Then, as always, I want to thank my husband who has given me even more support than usual while I have been giving birth to this 'baby'. He has read each chapter, given me shrewd and thought-provoking critiques and done much of the cooking to release me to write. For these gifts, I am humbled and grateful.

My computer 'died' while I was writing Chapter Ten. So many people rallied round me during the crisis that I felt very cared for. In particular, I would like to thank Derek Knell and Andy Russell of FEBA Radio, David and Margaret Judson of MECO and Carl Armerding at Schloss Mittersill for their help and concern.

Finally, I owe a debt of gratitude to two other groups of people: those who have given me permission to tell their stories to illustrate this book and those who have prayed for the book's conception. Where I have drawn on the experience and testimonies of friends and acquaintances, I have changed their names to protect their privacy but I want the people behind the pseudonyms to know that I am grateful to them for allowing their stories to be used to help others. I am awed, too, that so many of our prayer supporters committed themselves to pray for the book's gestation and growth and for me as I gave birth to it. Their ministry means more to me than I can say. To them and the many readers who have spurred me on by writing to ask when the book is to be published, I also express my appreciation in that simple but profound word, THANKYOU.

My appreciation for permission to quote extracts from various books are due to the following publishers:

Ave Maria Press, Inc., Notre Dame, IN 46556, for: *With Open Hands* by Henri Nouwen (© 1972) pp. 24–5; *Healing* by Francis MacNutt (© 1974) pp 100–1, 116–17; *Heal My Heart, O Lord* by Joan Hutson (© 1976) pp. 104–5; *Praying Our Goodbyes* by Joyce Rupp OSM (© 1988) p. 128. All rights reserved.
Paulist Press for *Hope for the Flowers* by Torina Paulus (© 1972) pp. 21–3; *The Way of Tenderness* by Kevin O Shea CSSR (© 1978 by The Missionary Society of St Paul the Apostle in the State of New York) pp. 111–13, 118.

AUTHOR'S PREFACE

An author's burden frequently gives birth to a book. That, at least, has been my experience. I have carried the burden from which this book emerged for the past twelve years or so, though, during that time, the nature of the burden has gradually changed and evolved.

Let me explain. Twelve years ago, my husband and I were frequently invited to speak at conferences for Christian students. At this time, we were often deeply moved by the zeal, the dedication and the commitment to Christ which was being expressed by some of the fine young people we met. But one thing concerned us. Whereas each student was clearly full of personal, God-given potential, many of them seemed afraid of giving expression to the person God had created them to be and seemed, instead, to be struggling to model themselves on some of the Christian heroes of the day – like John Stott, for example. 'They even try to speak like him,' I observed to my husband on one occasion after I had heard a student attempt to give a scholarly book review.

'Why don't you write a book to help such people?' my then editor invited. I did. As I wrote it, I toyed with the idea of calling it *No Cardboard Cut-outs* because one of my aims was to show that God did not create us to become a replica of anyone else. As someone has expressed it, 'When God made you, he broke the mould.' Since that title sounded rather negative, I chose, instead, to call the book *Growing Into Freedom*, a title which later became *Living Free* and now *Finding Freedom*.

This year sees the tenth anniversary of the publication of the original book.

FINDING FREEDOM

I now no longer move in student circles, live in Cyprus and work for the church overseas. This work takes me to some fascinating parts of the world and I have found that, on my travels, that old burden keeps bothering me. Now, it is not students that concern me but older, often more experienced Christians. They concern me because, although they may be older in years and older in the faith in many cases, the trend seems to le the same. Many of them still strive to become like their heroes in the faith – like Graham Kendrick or John Wimber. And the 'dis-ease' has spread so that it is no longer only individuals who are caught in this trap. Whole fellowships seem collectively to have been ensnared so that while individual Christians are striving to become miniature versions of the platform speakers they most admire, church fellowships try to ape the latest John Wimber meeting or the most recent round of Spring Harvest gatherings.

I am not knocking John Wimber, Graham Kendrick or Spring Harvest. All of these have produced much fruit for the Kingdom and in this I rejoice. What concerns me still is that many Christians have not discerned that God only made one John Wimber and one Graham Kendrick; that this same God created each of us to play faithfully our note without which the great symphony of life will be incomplete.

It seemed important, therefore, to celebrate the tenth year of this book's life by up-dating it, expanding it and publishing this completely revised new edition under a different title and with a different dust jacket. The kernel of the book is the same. And the burden is the same. I long that every Christian person should enter into the freedom which is our heritage as people who are children of God. But, inevitably, over the past years, my perception has changed as I have changed to become, I trust, far more like the person God always created me to be. The thrust of the book is therefore somewhat different. I trust that the original kernel and the new material in which this is now embedded will encourage today's Christian people to find answers to that question which nags at many of us from time to time: 'How can I become the person God always created me to be?' If the revised version of *Living Free* achieves that aim, it will be an anniversary worth celebrating.

1

INSTANT FREEDOM

Someone called Sue once gave me a banner she had made. On a background of blue felt, she had stitched a large, black cross at the foot of which stood two figures. Their backs were turned on a pile of broken chains, their faces were tilted as they contemplated the cross and their arms were raised in ecstasy. Two yellow words soared over the jubilant scene: 'Free indeed'.

I hung the banner in the place where I used to retreat to pray. Sometimes, as I gazed at it, my mind would wander to Ron, a member of the church where I worshipped. A few weeks earlier, Ron's eyes had met mine in the middle of a sermon. The preacher was making some startling claims:

'Jesus heals broken bodies and brings people out of darkness into light. It is possible to rub shoulders with Jesus and yet remain the same person. It is also possible to touch Jesus and be radically changed. We read of the woman with a haemorrhage in Luke 8. She reached out and touched him and "immediately her bleeding stopped". The power of Jesus flowed into her life and she was made whole – completely new. Free.'

A few weeks earlier, Ron had confided in me that he waged a constant war against the lust and sexual fantasies which seemed to hold him in a vice-like grip. He had confessed that this battle left him weary and defeated. Although he frequently stretched out his hand, as it were, and touched the hem of Jesus's garment, no release had come. He had prayed and prayed to be radically changed to become the person God created him to be, but nothing seemed to alter. In the middle of the sermon, his eyes asked a question: 'If Jesus could change that woman instantly, why hasn't he done the same for me? What's wrong with me? Why was hers such a big success story while mine has "failure" written across it?'

When I gazed at the banner hanging there in my prayer room, my heart would go out to Ron and I would ask myself a question: 'Why were the two yellow felt figures so jubilant while Ron remains so defeated?' Then I would think of my own spiritual pilgrimage and of the Christians I meet in the course of my travels and I would ask: 'Why do we Christians so frequently fail in our struggle to become the people our Creator made us to be, and why do we feel frustrated when God loves us so much that, in Christ, he died to secure our freedom?'

Over a period of time, as I prayed the question, an answer evolved. There is a sense in which sermons like the one I have quoted raise false expectations in people like Ron. The Bible nowhere suggests that total, immediate freedom and Christian maturity are experiences enjoyed in all their fullness this side of eternity. The Bible writers envisage Christians enjoying a freedom which comes in instalments and a maturity which develops only gradually and a total transformation which only reaches completion the other side of eternity.

There is another sense, on the other hand, in which the preacher was quite correct to suggest that, when we hand over the reins of our lives to Christ, we can be radically changed because freedom's first instalment comes in the form of salvation. By salvation I mean deliverance from guilt and from the past, deliverance from sin's penalty and from its enslavement, freedom to call God 'Father' and to enjoy intimacy with him, to name but a few of the faces of this multi-faceted gift. As Paul puts it, in Jesus 'we gain our freedom, the forgiveness of our sins' (Colossians 1:13, JB).

The cost of freedom

Christians who can pin-point a time and place in their life when, by faith, they surrendered to the love of God often seem intoxicated by joy for a while. Like the figures in my banner, they feel gloriously different, exhilaratingly free and seem quite uninhibited in giving expression to their joy.

A friend of mine has recently taken the first few intoxicating sips of this joy. She is a tonic to be with. Her eyes sparkle. Her face shines. She is the same as she always was, yet strangely different. Her attitudes are more Christ-like than they used to be. She seems unable to stop marvelling at God's gift of salvation. She is gloriously free. A new creation in very many ways – much more like the person I imagine God created her to be. But she would be the first to admit that she is not yet mature in Christ. Far from it. Whole layers of her personality have yet to be enlightened so that they respond to God.

Christians who have never been encountered by God with a dramatic, Damascus-road-type conversion, on the other hand, are often painfully aware that maturing in Christ takes a life-time. They know, deep down in their innermost beings, that God has set them free but this assurance does not necessarily excite them. Some take their freedom for granted. Others have lost sight of it. For many it has become a mundane part of life like cleaning their teeth or catching the commuter train. God's good news can leave them cold and unmoved, either because it has lodged in their heads and never trickled into their hearts or because they have become so over-familiar with the implications of it that they have lost the ability to marvel at the mystery of it all.

Often, when I detect this kind of indifference lurking in the crevices of my own heart, I reflect on a story Archbishop Anthony Bloom tells. The story is of Natalie, a Russian woman of whom little is known except her name and the fact that she lived in Russia at the turn of the century, when civil war ravaged her country.

As war swept through that land, city after city fell prey to one army after another. In a town which had fallen into the hands of the Red Army, the wife of an officer in the White Army seemed to be caught in a human web. If enemy soldiers discovered her, she and her two children would be killed instantly. What could she do to preserve their lives?

On the outskirts of the city, she discovered a small, wooden cabin. She could hide there until the first surges of conflict were over. Then she would escape.

Towards evening on her second day in hiding, she heard someone knocking on the cabin door. Full of fear, she opened it to discover a young woman of her own age. It was Natalie. She spoke in urgent whispers. 'You must flee at once. You've been discovered. Tonight the soldiers will come. You are to be shot.'

The mother looked down at her two small children. Escape? How could she escape? Her children were too young to walk far. They would be recognised at once. The plan was unthinkable. She must prepare to die.

But Natalie persisted.

'Don't worry about the children. I'll stay here. They won't even look for you.'

'You stay here? But they'll kill you.'

'Yes. But I have no children.'

That night Natalie returned. The mother and her two small boys escaped into the woods. Natalie faced the soldiers alone. Natalie faced death – another woman's death – alone. At any moment, she could have stepped out of the wooden cabin. At any moment she could have become Natalie again. At any moment she could have stepped into freedom. She chose not to. She chose, instead, to stay inside the cabin.

Hours passed. With the cold of morning they came. Members of the Red Army battered down the door and, without bothering to drag her outside, shot her where she was – in bed. That is where friends found her later that day. Dead.

The reason why I like to meditate on that example of self-sacrifice is that it reminds me that two thousand years earlier, a young man of Natalie's age awaited his own death. He was the God-man, Jesus. Just as Natalie died in place of the young mother, so Jesus died in my place. Just as the price Natalie paid was her life-blood, so the price Jesus paid to secure my freedom was his shed blood. I find this awesome and humbling. And I find it even more awesome that God was in Christ giving us a fresh start by forgiving our sins (2 Corinthians 5:19).

This surely must mean that, when the Son suffered the agony

of the Crucifixion, the Father suffered with him. I sometimes seem to see, with the eyes of my imagination, the Father, like a giant shadow, standing behind his Son as he hangs on the Cross. As the nails are hammered into the hands of Jesus, they penetrate the Father's hands also. As the spear pierces Jesus's side, it pierces the Father's also.[1] And I reflect that the Father and the Son suffered, among other things, that I might be set free to become the person God created me to be.

Freedom from guilt

This is deep mystery. Trying to translate a mystery into words is rather like trying to describe a sunset to a person born blind or an oratorio to a person born deaf. It cannot be adequately done. A mystery yields its secrets gradually and slowly to those who pause to ponder, to meditate and to reflect.

I was reminded of this while I was leading a retreat on one occasion. One of the retreatants confessed to feeling a certain distance separating her from God. The reason, she knew, was not that she had committed any spectacular sin which might hit the headlines of the Christian press, yet she discerned a sense of unworthiness as she attempted to spend quality time with God. This seemed to be hindering her spiritual and emotional growth. So I suggested to her that she might spend some time meditating, that is, chewing over and responding to, the meaning of Christ's death. She did. Next day, a hush seemed to descend on the woodland glade where we sat as, with awe and wonder, I examined the pictures she had drawn as a result of her meditation.

The sketch depicted herself with Jesus. From her flowed a polluted stream which flowed into the Saviour. From him flowed a red river of forgiving love which flowed into her and circulated all around her body injecting her with new life. 'It's like a blood transfusion,' she said with a smile. 'All the anti-bodies which were eating me up have gone. They've been replaced by life-giving blood.'

As I studied the pictures and listened to her story, my own love for God was rekindled as I recalled afresh that he loves us so much that, when we come to him, he flushes from us the sin and guilt which soil our lives and renews us with his own life – even when we *have* committed crimes for which we would now condemn ourselves. Like the elderly woman who once told me her story:

> I've lived a terrible life. At times I've been quite evil and done really terrible things. Now I'm growing old, I thought to myself: 'I'd love to go and live near my two beautiful grandchildren.' But my daughter knows the kind of life I've led. Maybe she wouldn't want her mother so near? After all, I could influence her children, couldn't I?
>
> One day I told my daughter what was going on in my mind. She's a Christian and do you know what she said? 'Why don't you put your trust in Jesus, Mummy? He can wipe out the past, set you free from it, give you a completely new start.' At first, I hardly dared to believe what she told me. But I thought it was worth a try. So I told God I was sorry for the past. I asked him to forgive me. And d'you know what happened? He forgave me. He washed me clean. He set me free from all that filth and evil. Even the guilt has gone. I didn't realise it was possible to be so happy. He's given me so much joy and I don't deserve it after what I've done.

That phrase, 'even the guilt has gone', never ceases to move me. Guilts are, among other things, the skeletons we stuff in the cupboard of our memory reminding us of failure and filling us with fear that, one day, the cupboard door could swing open and the skeletons fall in a heap at our feet. Guilt therefore produces an inner restlessness, a lingering dread that the past may yet catch up with us. The guilty person is at enmity with himself, with others and with God. Like Adam whose disobedience prompted him to hide from his wife by covering his nakedness with fig leaves as well as from the God who loved him (Genesis 3:6–10), guilt prevents us from celebrating our creativity and causes us, instead, to hide from ourselves, our nearest and dearest and from God.

The person who places their trust in God's loving plan of salvation, however, no longer needs to hide from their Creator or from others. Although our guilt and self-centredness once held us captive, God in Jesus paid the ransom which set us free from the legacy of the past. As Paul expressed the miracle to Titus: 'Our great God and Saviour, Jesus Christ . . . gave himself for us to redeem us from all wickedness' (Titus 2:13b,14a).

'To redeem' means to buy back or to buy. That is why, in the Book of Revelation, the redeemed celebrate the victory of the Lamb:

'You are worthy to take the scroll and to break its seals and open it: for you were slain, and your blood has bought people from every nation as gifts for God. (Revelation 5:9,LB).

In other words, God sees the skeletons in the cupboard, assures us that he loves us anyway and sets us free from their subtle control over our lives. He guarantees that the past has been dealt with and forgiven and he enables us to enter into the fullness of the abundant life he always intended us to enjoy.

Freedom from the sin-stained past

'Can this really be true? Can I really be forgiven?'

The speaker was a student friend of mine who needed to share the burden of the past with someone. He told me his story. When he was in the sixth form at school, like many young people today, he lived for number one, self. When he fell in love, he seduced his girl-friends on several occasions. Against all the odds, or so it seemed, one of them became pregnant. The child was adopted immediately after its birth. But Paul continued to shoulder the weight of the seriousness of this manifestation of self-centredness: the emotional scars he had inflicted on the girl and the responsibility of bringing an unwanted child into the world. Although it was past history he was describing and he had since responded to the love of God so that, in many ways he knew he was a new person, he continued to ask whether he could ever be sure of being free from *this*?

God has his own unique way of convincing people of the nature of his love and the answer to such questions, so we prayed together, asking him to give us a glimpse of what was in his Father-heart. God seemed to show Paul that the responsibility for the baby was now his and not Paul's. He also seemed to be promising to protect the baby's mother. As for Paul himself, the message of forgiveness which throbs through Luke 15 seemed to be applied specifically to him. In his imagination, he saw the heavenly Father running towards him, the prodigal determined to come home at last. And he felt the enfolding love of the God who embraced him. He wept. As tears of repentance and relief flowed, Paul sensed the mixture of emotions which welled up in God's heart: sorrow, unending love, tender forgiveness, to mention a few. And he knew that the past was forgiven. He could now entrust his son, his girl-friend and himself into God's unfailing love, walk resolutely away from the past and go free.

Undeserved? Yes. But that is what the grace of God is: undeserved love. Pure gift. Our former selves, our unregenerate life-style, our sinful past, our guilt: these were all pinned to the Cross of Christ crucified. They have no more hold over us. The failure which once made us blush, the back-log of guilt which once weighed us down, the sin which engulfed us like the tentacles of an octopus threatening to stifle our personality, have no more hold over us. Their power was destroyed the moment we trusted in Jesus's saving death.

Freedom from the penalty of sin

This is awesome. It is mystery. But equally awesome and mysterious are those words Jesus uttered from the Cross: 'It is finished.'

These words made a powerful impact on me while I was in the middle of writing this chapter. I was gazing at a crude wooden cross which someone had erected in the mountains where I was leading a retreat. As I gazed at the two pieces of wood which had been lashed together by a piece of rope and mounted on a pile of rocks, I spread before God a particular failure I wanted to leave with him. As I expressed my longing to be set free a triumphant roar seemed to come from the cross and echo round the mountain range: 'It is finished!' I was startled by the uncanny power with which those words seemed laced.

'What are you trying to say to me, Lord?' I asked.

The same words reached me with even greater force: 'It is finished.' And I wanted to weep because, suddenly, I knew what those words meant. My failure and I no longer belonged to one another. Jesus, by dying on a crude cross, had separated us. A severance had taken place, setting me free to be me once more. There would be no need to mention this failure to God again. Love for Jesus welled up in my heart reminding me of his claim that those who have been forgiven much, love much.

Because the love within me was so strong, I asked the Beloved to show me how he had felt as he hung nailed to the Cross and I tried, as it were, to step into his skin as he hung there. Whereupon a surge of joy filled me. I felt I understood why the prayer of the penitent thief, 'Jesus, remember me when you come into your Kingdom,' had elicited from Jesus a response of joy, strength and relief: 'Today you will be with me in Paradise.' Even though his body was being tortured, it gave Jesus joy to see that his agony was not in vain. One man, at least, was availing himself of the freedom for which he was paying such a phenomenal price.

Jesus could reassure the penitent because the word 'finished' is a legal word meaning 'accomplished'. It was often scrawled across bills in New Testament times. It means 'Paid!', 'Transaction completed!', 'Score settled!'

Like the thieves hanging either side of the Saviour, we have all offended our holy God in a whole variety of ways – not least by spurning his overtures of love and by refusing to allow God to be God. This is the essence of sin and, as Paul reminds us, 'the wages of sin is death' (Romans 6:23). But just as Jesus rescued the penitent, so he continues to rescue those who repent. Isaiah expresses the inexpressible:

We thought his troubles were a punishment from God, for his *own* sins! But he was wounded and bruised for *our* sins. He was chastised that we might have peace; He was lashed – and we were healed! *We* are the ones who strayed away

like sheep. *We*, who left God's paths to follow our own. Yet
God laid on *him* the guilt and sins of every one of us!

(Isaiah 53:4–6, LB).

In other words, because Jesus died on the Cross and rose again,
we have been set free from the punishment which should have
been ours. The judgment which should have been heaped on us,
fell on him. In God's sight, it is as though, when Jesus died, we
died with him so that God now looks on us as though we had
never ever sinned. Our debt has been cancelled. Paid. We are
free from sin's penalty. God has forgiven us.

When God forgives, he does not play a game of 'Let's
pretend': 'Let's pretend they never sinned'. No. He sees us
as we are: soiled, helpless, innately sinful. He knows what he
is taking on when he promises to love us. Even so, he applies
the righteousness of Jesus to us. When he looks on us, he sees,
not the stain of the sin which has penetrated every particle of
our being, but his pure and holy Son. It is as though we have
been clothed in Jesus's own spotless, unsoiled garment. This is
deep mystery. It can never be fully understood or fully explained
– only contemplated with hearts bowed in adoration, love and
praise as we recall that the freedom it bestows is instant.
Irreversible. Complete. The penalty has been paid. God will
not go back on this act. The deed is done.

Freedom from bondage

In order to appreciate the full extent of this amazing gift of
grace, we need to place our personal short-comings in context
and to recognise that, when the Bible uses the word 'sin,'
it is not referring to acts of disobedience but rather to the
world's orientation against God and towards self-centredness.
This orientation governed Adam and Eve's life. Consequently,
ever since the Fall, men and women have been in bondage to it.
Body, mind and emotions have been snatched from their rightful
owner, God, and enslaved by two terrorists: Satan and self.

A slave is a person who is owned by another; someone
without rights who can be used, abused and disposed of in

any way the owner chooses. A slave is compelled to obey his master. He has no right or power to say 'No' and no opportunity to express his God-given personality in the way it cries out to be expressed. But a slave's former owner has no more authority over him if he becomes someone else's property. He can no longer choke the former slave's potential.

The good news is that when we surrender to Christ, we are rescued from Satan and restored to our rightful owner: God. We are no longer forced to obey the dictates of the Prince of this world, the Evil One. Instead, we are set free to serve the One for whom we were made and to whom our hearts yearn to give glory: Christ our King. We are free to turn our backs on the temptation which peeps through the window of our life and beckons us. We are free to resist what Paul calls 'the ruling spirits of the universe . . . beings who are not gods' (Galatians 4:3, 8, GNB. We are free to bring glory to our Creator by discovering who it is he created us to be.

The chains which held us captive, the powers which once pushed us into self-centred practices, have no more hold over us. God in Christ has destroyed their stranglehold. The door to intimacy with God stands wide open. We are invited to call him Father, to approach him at any time and to enjoy to the full his peace. We are at one with him through the grace of atonement (at-one-ment). We are free indeed.

But, like Ron, with whom I began this chapter, we soon discover that that is not the whole story. Self still beckons. Sin still attracts. Satan still prowls seeking someone to devour. We are only partially free. As John Stott emphasises:

There is more to come . . . Christ 'gave himself to redeem us from all wickedness' (Titus 2:14), to liberate us from *all* the ravages of the Fall. This we have not yet experienced. Just as the Old Testament people of God, though already redeemed from their Egyptian and Babylonian exiles, were yet waiting for the promise of a fuller redemption, 'looking forward to the redemption of Jerusalem', so the New Testament people of God, though already redeemed from guilt and judgment, are yet waiting for the 'day of redemption' when we shall be made perfect.[2]

Ron had not yet appreciated this. By faith and theoretically, he knew that, when he accepted Jesus as Lord and Saviour, he had been set free to become the person God created him to be. He did not know that when we commit ourselves to Christ, we can commit to him only those parts of ourselves with which we are consciously in touch. He had done that but remained oblivious to the fact that these parts are only the tip of the proverbial ice-berg. Deep within our subconscious lie layer after layer of the hidden parts of ourselves. These layers also need to be brought under the Lordship of Christ because, though they lie dormant, their influence over us for good or evil is immense. When Ron's eyes asked me the question, 'Why am I not experiencing the freedom the evangelist promises?' the question was rising, I suspect, from one of these layers which, at that stage of his life, Ron did not even know existed.

But since that Sunday twelve years ago, Ron has discovered that entering into freedom in all its fullness, and watching our true self emerge from its slavery to sin and self is a long-term, life-long project. I sometimes liken it to the life-cycle of an acorn. When an acorn is planted, its full potential is set free. But the release is gradual: first one tiny, tentative root pokes its nose out of the disintegrating shell into the dark earth. Then another and another. Later, the first shoot pushes its head through the soil into the light. All this growth is hidden and even though it is steady and persistent, many years will elapse before a fully mature, fruit-bearing oak tree will have established itself.

In the chapters that follow, we examine ways of ensuring that a similar miracle of growth takes place within each of us so that our full, unique, God-implanted potential is gradually released and we give glory to God by developing into the mature person he created us to be.

For personal reflection

Read the following invitation from God:

> My child, let it be your privilege, each day, to dwell upon
> My sacrifice – made for the whole world.
>   In My suffering love upon the Cross you see a *continuing
> process* . . . the unrequited love which pursues My children
> – yearning for the slightest response, and profoundly
> grateful when one of those children surrenders his or her
> life to Me.
>   On the Cross, you see My heart of love crushed, for the
> moment, by the force of evil which darkens this universe.
> Then you see the bursting forth again of love's *power* . . .
> My Father's victory . . .
>   Here, at the Cross, give Me your heart, anew, every
> day.[3]

Now, gaze at a cross or a picture of one. Ask yourself the
following four questions:

1. What is God saying through this Cross?
2. What is God saying *to me* through this Cross?
3. If I could step into the skin of the Saviour who died on that
   Cross, how might I feel about the world, the penitent thief,
   the by-standers and myself?
4. Write or say a prayer which sums up your response – or
   respond by drawing a picture or by writing a poem.

Notes for Chapter One

1. Here I am drawing on an insight quoted by John Stott in *The Cross
   of Christ* (Inter-Varsity Press, 1986). On p. 158 he describes a
   picture of the Crucifixion which hangs in an Italian church. In this
   picture a vast and shadowy Figure stands behind the figure of
   Jesus. The nail that pierces the hand of Jesus goes through to
   the hand of God. The spear thrust into the side of Jesus goes
   through into God's.

2. John Stott, *The Cross of Christ*, p. 178.
   I would recommend that any reader seeking a deeper understanding of the meaning of Christ's death should read and meditate on the contents of John Stott's book.
3. John Woolley, *I Am With You* (Crown, 1991) p. 3.

2

GRADUAL FREEDOM

Until we come to terms with the fact that God's gift of freedom comes as slowly and gradually as an acorn grows into an oak tree, we are in grave danger of growing disillusioned, we might even tie ourselves in knots of self-condemnation. Like Louise, a girl who once told me her story.

Louise is one of those effervescent Christians I described in the last chapter. She can vividly recall the time when she turned to Christ. She can even describe the exact place where she first sipped the nectar of instant freedom: 'It was a fantastic experience. I knew I was forgiven. I knew God had given me his Spirit. I felt a new and different person.'

Unfortunately, no one helped Louise to understand what freedom in Christ is and what it is not. When she came to see me three years after this dramatic spiritual experience, she confessed to feeling an abysmal failure: 'I really thought that Jesus had given me a completely new life – his life; that I wouldn't be tempted any more, that I was dead to sin, that I couldn't sin again. Then I met Steve. I fell in love with him. He wanted us to sleep together, so we did. I enjoyed it. It never occurred to me that there was anything wrong with it. But then a friend showed me Paul's teaching about sexual immorality[1] and now I've come to see that I'm a hopeless failure. Can God ever forgive me and set me free again?'

My heart went out to Louise. Why hadn't anyone taught her that although Jesus had set her free from her self-centred past, she was not hermetically sealed against sin forever? She was not free from the subtle wiles of Satan.[2] She was not free from temptation's apparent attractions.[3] She was not free from the desires of the flesh or of her old nature. Neither was she free from pain, struggle and the responsibility to make careful choices.

Christians who grow gradually into an awareness of the depth and height and length and breadth of God's love and who respond to that love over a period of time can also become as muddled as Louise. They can also be beguiled into believing that with God as their companion, they have been set completely free from all obstacles hindering their freedom.

Whether we respond to God's invitation to come to him through Jesus suddenly and spontaneously or slowly and after careful thought matters little. What does matter is that we understand what does and does not happen to us at this stage of our pilgrimage.

When we put our faith in Christ, it is true to say that we are translated from the kingdom of darkness into the kingdom of light. Peter assures us of this:

'God called you out of the darkness into his wonderful light' (1 Peter 2:9, LB).

It is also true to say that, though we were once God's enemies, now we are his friends. Paul says just that:

'We were God's enemies but he made us his friends through the death of his Son' (Romans 5:10, GNB).

And it is true that we have moved from death to life. These are unassailable Biblical truths.

But when we placed our trust in God's way of salvation, we did not leap-frog from an egocentric existence straight over the Cross and into God's glorious presence where sin ceases to exist and where suddenly we enjoy full maturity. Neither were we ejected from the kingdom of darkness straight into the new Jerusalem, the world which revolves around God alone.

No. The Cross of Christ penetrated the prison walls which held us captive in the kingdom of darkness. The Cross of Christ also gave us access to God's Kingdom of light. But faith in Christ marks the beginning of the journey, not journey's end. The challenge which now faces us is to travel towards our goal, with Christ. He will accompany us along the path which leads to his Father and the new heaven and the new earth: the new

Jerusalem. Meanwhile there is a great deal of learning to do. We live life in the now, in 'the overlap',[4] the place where the old is restored, renewed and transformed, the place where we are being prepared to receive the new.

We have turned our back on the old life and walked away from it. We have walked, by way of Christ's Cross, towards that stage of the journey where all things will be, not only new, but perfect. But we have not yet reached our destination. We are pilgrims – travelling. We are pupils learning. We are children of the world, being changed so that we can take our place in the Kingdom of God – that Kingdom which, according to Jesus, is both a here and now reality: 'The kingdom of God is within you' (Luke 17:21), and a place we shall enjoy to the full in the future: 'I will not drink again of the fruit of the vine until the kingdom of God comes' (Luke 22:18).

Jesus nowhere uses the term 'the overlap' to describe the present. He does, however, tell parable after parable to help us to understand the nature and purpose of this in-between existence. These parables or metaphors appeal as much, if not more, to our imagination and emotions as to our intellects. They inform us on an intellectual level *and* on a deeper, emotional level also. This was deliberate on Jesus's part. Unlike twentieth-century Western scholars, Jesus did not teach through carefully crafted three-point sermons, through skilfully scripted papers which he proceeded to read to his audiences or even through careful exegesis of the Old Testament. On the contrary, he used stories, picture language, both to inform and *engage* his listeners. This way, he aimed to make an impact on every part of their personality: their minds and emotions, their imaginations and their wills.

The overlap: a place of gradual growth

Take the story of the sower, for example, a parable I frequently picture while I am on a particular prayer walk near my home in Cyprus. As I write, this walk takes me along paths which run beside newly ploughed fields – the kind of fields I imagine Jesus was surveying when he told the story of the 'farmer [who] went out to sow his seed' (Matthew 13:3). These fields are framed by sturdy thistles which wave in the wind, scattering their seeds far and near, reminding me of the picture Jesus paints of the seed that fell among thorns. The fields seem to be studded with impenetrable, sun-baked stones that would take months to remove, reminding me of the seed in Jesus's story which fell on stony ground. My attention is often attracted by the chattering and squawking of the birds that hop from furrow to furrow in the hope of finding tasty morsels. They remind me of the seed which was gobbled up before it could take root. Yet crops grow in these fields just as they did in Jesus's parable – not overnight, but slowly, gradually, persistently. The first sign of growth appears in the form of a green haze which seems to hover over the rich, red earth. Then sturdy little plants appear and, as these are kissed by the sun and watered by the irrigation system, they grow. Little by little, I have the thrill of witnessing a field full of crops and the joy and satisfaction which bring a proud smile to the face of the farmer.

As I walk and reflect, I sometimes try to imagine how Jesus's listeners would have reacted to this story and I am grateful to my friend and mentor Professor Kenneth Bailey for this insight:

> 'The Jews of the first century thought the Kingdom would come with a great apocalyptic revolution. The sun was going to be darkened, the land was going to give up its dead and there would be stars falling from the sky. In the middle of all this would come the Kingdom of God. But Jesus says no. The Kingdom of God comes like a seed quietly planted in the soil . . . There is no such thing as instant discipleship.[5]

And there is no such thing as instant maturity.

Louise, with whom I began this chapter, needed to have this message etched on her heart. Like many other young and not-so-young Christians today, she needed someone gently and patiently to explain to her that there is still no apocalyptic revolution which will result in her becoming a super-spiritual

Christian overnight. In God's economy and in God's Kingdom, we grow only gradually, just as we discover the nature of the person God created us to be only gradually.

The overlap: the place where we are transformed

Jesus painted another powerful pen-picture to underline this fact:

'The kingdom of heaven is like yeast that a woman took and mixed into a large amount of flour until it worked through the dough' (Matthew 13:33).

The implications of this parable were brought home to me in one of those powerful moments when God speaks through the marvels of his created world. I was in New Zealand at the time. My husband and I were visiting one of the wonders of the world: Milford Sound in Fiordland on the South Island. While my husband was buying tickets for the boat which was to take us out to the Tasman Sea via one of the fiords, I stood reading a plaque which described the nature of the water through which we would travel. The plaque informed me that there were two distinct layers of water: the top forty metres consisting of melted snow and providing a home for creatures who thrive in fresh water; and a hidden mass of salt water which never sees the sunshine but which provides a home for certain unique sea creatures.

'The fiord is rather like your life,' a still, small voice whispered. 'You also have an upper layer where you know God's Spirit is at work. You're naming and befriending the creatures which live in that layer. But there is another deep, hidden, mysterious layer which also needs to be owned and explored. Here live parts of your personality which you dismiss because they masquerade as monsters and appear to you grotesque yet these are also parts of your God-given personality which must be both named and befriended.'

The challenge travelled with me as I sat on the boat marvelling at the stunning beauty of the fiord and the mountains, the waterfalls and the water-life. It remains with me still and gives rise to a prayer that the Holy Spirit would, indeed, penetrate every part of my being, transforming me into the likeness of Christ and giving me the joy of ever-increasing maturity.

The overlap: a place of difficulty, tension and struggle

This transformation can only be slow and gradual, for, as Jesus's parable of the sower clearly shows, there are many obstacles to overcome. Although the heavenly sower has sown only good seed into our lives, like a hungry, beady-eyed raven, Satan watches where the seed falls and he is always ready to pounce and snatch it away before it has time to take root. Equally, times of testing and turbulence threaten to choke the seed in the same way as thistles endanger the growth process. Times of triumph and success may also stifle the embryonic life of the plant. Despite these difficulties, the seed and the soil do fuse and the result is lasting fruit. Jesus is at pains to assure us that God does not give up on us. He uses the tempestuous and joyful times to transform us into his likeness so that we are ready to be presented mature in him when Jesus returns.

Paul also assures us that our eventual glorification is guaranteed. In his letter to the Romans he writes:

> God has shown us how much he loves us – it was while we were still sinners that Christ died for us! By his sacrificial death we are now put right with God . . . We were God's enemies, but he made us his friends through the death of his Son. Now that we are God's friends, how much more will we be saved by Christ's life!
>
> (Romans 5:8–10)

Commenting on this passage, John Stott observes:

> What the apostle means is surely this, that our developing, ripening Christian character is evidence that God is at work upon us and within us. The fact that God is thus at work

in our lives gives us confidence that He is not going to give up the job uncompleted. If He is working in us now to transform our character, He is surely going to bring us safely to glory in the end . . .

There is a strong presumption that we shall never be allowed to fall by the way, but shall be preserved to the end and glorified. This is not just sentimental optimism; it is grounded upon irresistible logic. The logic of it is this, that if, when we were enemies, God reconciled us through giving His Son to die for us, how much more, now we are God's friends, will He finally save us from His wrath by His Son's life? If God performed the more costly service (involving His Son's death) for His enemies, He will surely perform the less costly service now that His erstwhile enemies are His friends. Meditate on this until you see the irrefutable logic of Paul's argument.[6]

I once read a charming children's story which engraved these truths on my heart.

The heroine of the story is Yellow, a caterpillar who often dreamed of freedom but whose concept of the world of butterflies and flight was blurred and confused.

One day, when, as usual, thoughts of butterflies were occupying her caterpillar-brain, she came across a curious sight: a grey-haired caterpillar hanging upside-down on a branch. Seeing that he was caught in some kind of hairy stuff, Yellow offered her assistance.

'You seem in trouble . . . can I help?'

'No, my dear, I have to do this to become a butterfly.'

A butterfly! Yellow's caterpillar-heart leapt. Could this be her great opportunity?

'Tell me, sir, what is a butterfly?'

'It's what you are meant to become. It flies with beautiful wings and joins the earth to heaven . . .'

Yellow's heart somersaulted in hope. 'Me! A butterfly? It can't be true! . . . How can I believe there's a butterfly inside you and me, when all I see is a fuzzy worm?'

'How does one become a butterfly?' she added, pensively.

'You must want to fly so much that you are willing to give up being a caterpillar.'

'You mean to die?' asked Yellow.

'Yes and no,' he answered. 'What *looks* like you will die but what's *really* you will still live. Life is changed, not taken away. Isn't that different from those who die without ever becoming butterflies?'

'And if I decide to become a butterfly,' said Yellow hesitantly, 'what do I do?'

'Watch me. I'm making a cocoon. It looks like I'm hiding, I know, but a cocoon is no escape. It's an in-between house where the change takes place. It's a big step, since you can never return to caterpillar life. During the change, it will seem to you or anyone who might peep that nothing is happening – but the butterfly is already becoming. It just takes time!'

Yellow was torn with anguish. What if she became this thing called butterfly and her friends failed to recognize this new self? At least she knew that caterpillars can crawl and eat and love in a limited way. What happens if a caterpillar gets stuck in a cocoon? Could she risk losing the only life she had known when it seemed so unlikely she could ever become a glorious winged creature? All she had to go on was a caterpillar who believed sufficiently to take the leap of faith. And hope.

The grey-haired caterpillar continued to cover himself with silky threads. As he wove the last bit around his head he called:

'You'll be a beautiful butterfly – we're all waiting for you!' And Yellow decided to take the risk.

For courage she hung right beside the cocoon and began to spin her own.

'Imagine, I didn't even know I could do this. That's some encouragement that I'm on the right track. If I have inside me the stuff to make cocoons – maybe the stuff of butterflies is there too.'[7]

And, of course the stuff of butterflies *was* there. Yellow eventually emerged a brilliant, yellow, winged creature – a wonderful sight!

The overlap: a place of hope

There will be times in the overlap when, like Yellow, we are assailed with doubts; when we ask: 'How can I believe there's a butterfly inside me when all I see is a fuzzy worm?' Or, to put it another way: 'How can I believe God's Spirit is at work within me when all I see is a series of constant failures?'

There will be times when life in the overlap will seem as dull and drab and restricted as life in a cocoon; when we seem to be stripped of freedom rather than set free to enjoy life in all its fullness.

And there will be times when we seriously question whether the risk was worth taking; whether we have taken the first gigantic step along the pathway to God for no purpose; whether it would have been better to have remained in the kingdom of darkness than to respond to the finger which beckoned us to cross over into the Kingdom of Light.

But God is the Lord of the overlap. Even when our life seems of little value, even when we detect no spiritual movement, changes *are* taking place; the kind of changes which split open cocoons and produce butterflies. God is changing us. He has guaranteed to make us perfect in the end. He has guaranteed to set us free.

This makes our middle-world existence a place of hope. Hope in the Christian sense does not mean a vain longing. It means certainty. We do not hope for something we already possess. We anticipate it with eagerness, longing and gratitude. This hope motivates and energises us when the waiting seems endless, even futile.

Take the farmer in Jesus's parable, for example. As he scattered his seed, his heart was full of hope. In his imagination, almost certainly, he already saw a field full of wheat.

And what of the seeds he scattered? I was once given a

handful of mustard seeds – some of the smallest seeds in the world. As I held these tiny, black specks on the palm of my hand, I realised that I was holding a handful of hope, for surely, if seeds were sentient, and, like toys in the nursery in children's stories, could talk, they would be whispering to each other: 'I feel full of potential. I hope I'm sown in the kind of earth where a surge of life can flow through me, giving me the strength to push down long, white roots and to push up green shoots. I hope I become the tree I was intended to be.'

In a similar way, hope transforms us. As Henri Nouwen explains, hope influences the way we relate to God, the way we pray and the way we live. He contrasts the prayer of hope with 'the prayer of little faith', claiming that the person of little faith prays like a child who has asked Santa Claus for a present but who runs away frightened as soon as the present is placed into his hands: 'He would rather have nothing more to do with the old bearded gentleman. All the attention is on the gift and none on the one who gives it.'[8]

A person who hopes, on the other hand, prays differently. Their focus is not on the gift, but on the Giver. Their list of requests might be just as long as the list of the person of little faith, but ultimately their desire is not to receive answers to prayer but to affirm unlimited trust in the Giver of all good things.

In other words, hope is based on the belief that God gives only what is good.

Hope inspires an openness to God and his promises even though the way in which these promises will be fulfilled remains a mystery.

Hope sets us free to look at life through a new pair of spectacles.

As Henri Nouwen quoted:

Hope means to keep living
amid desperation
and to keep humming
in the darkness.
Hoping is knowing that there is love, . . .

In the midst of a gale at sea,
it is to discover land.
In the eyes of another·
It is to see that he understands you.
Hope strengthens the awareness that everything we are
given and everything we are deprived of is nothing but a
finger pointing out the direction of God's hidden promise
which we shall taste in full.[9]

The overlap: the place where we deepen our relationship with God

Hope means to nurture a deep-down belief that God understands.

At the beginning of this chapter, I recalled the crisis of faith
which troubled Louise, the young Christian for whom hope had
almost died. Mine was the privilege of staying alongside her
until the embers of hope had been fanned into a flame. Mine
was the privilege of accompanying her a little further along the
pathway of faith. Mine was the joy of watching her discover for
herself that the overlap is not a place of sinless perfection but it
is a place where we may enjoy an ever-deepening relationship
with God.

She discovered this through meditating on Jesus's compelling
story of the son who squandered the inheritance entrusted to
him by his father. She could identify with this youth because,
like him, it was as a member of the family that she had failed.
Like him, she discovered that she had only to take one step
towards the heavenly Father to see that his arms were opened
to her in warmth and welcome and forgiveness. With relief
she ran into those arms and nestled there, rejoicing in God's
reconciling love. It was a humbling and tearful moment rather
than an ecstatic one. But it was life-changing to discover that,
even though she remains flawed, she is deeply loved.

That was twelve years ago. Since then she has experienced
the inevitable intertwining of joy and pain which life in the overlap
affords. She has also found out that the intimacy with God can

be an ongoing and ever-deepening experience. God loves us so much that he meets us where we are rather than demanding that we should be somewhere else. She knows now that, this side of eternity, she will always be vulnerable in the teeth of temptation. She also knows that prayer is a love relationship with God. God is not just her heavenly Father. He is her Friend and her Lover. And I have had the joy of watching her become ever more radiant as she absorbs this divine love. I have had the privilege of watching her become the loving, gifted, creative, compassionate person God created her to be.

For personal reflection

1. Imagine that you have been invited by a publisher to write your autobiography. Look back over your life and recall some of the major milestones – particularly in your journey with God. Write these down as though they were to form the chapter headings of your book. Then decide which incidents you would want to include under each heading. Notice as you do this exercise where your ability to be the person you were created to be has grown in leaps and bounds. Notice, too, where such growth has been slow and hidden.
2. Look back over the past twenty-four hours. Try to detect where God has been active in your life – in the good things and in the difficult circumstances. What do you sense God was attempting to say to you or show you about yourself, about God and about life?
3. Keep a journal, at least while you are reading this book. Write a letter to God in it in which you reflect on your journey through life so far. Write it from the heart.

Notes for Chapter Two

1. See, for example, 1 Corinthians 6:13; 1 Corinthians 6:18; 1 Corinthians 10:8; Ephesians 5:3; 1 Thessalonians 4:3, and my discussion of these verses in *Just Good Friends* (1985) and *Life in a Sex-Mad Society,* (1988) both published by Inter-Varsity Press.
2. See, for example, 1 Peter 5:8.

3. See, for example, Matthew 26:41; 1 Corinthians 10:13; 1 Timothy 6:9.
4. The 'overlap' is a term I first met in Jean Darnall's *Life in the Overlap* (Lakeland, 1977).
5. Here I am quoting from one of Professor Kenneth Bailey's videos: *Jesus, The Theologian: His Parables*. These are available from the Middle East Christian Organisation (MECO) and I would recommend them to anyone seeking a deeper understanding of the parables of Jesus.
6. John Stott, *Men Made New* (Inter-Varsity Press, 1966) pp. 15, 20.
7. Trina Paulus, *Hope for the Flowers* (Paulist Press, 1972).
8. Henri Nouwen, *With Open Hands* (Ave Maria Press, 1976) p. 80.
9. Henri Nouwen, *With Open Hands*, pp. 85, 86.

3

THE HOLY SPIRIT'S ROLE

The transformation of a person like Louise, whom I mentioned in the last chapter, bears the hallmarks of the ministry of the Holy Spirit. As Paul puts it, 'where the Spirit of the Lord is, there is freedom' (2 Corinthians 3:17). Or as Jesus expresses it, the Holy Spirit, the agent of truth, is the One who will lead us into the truth which will set us free (John 14:17 and 16:13). To proceed further in our exploration of how we become the people God always intended us to be without further reference to the Holy Spirit would therefore be as foolish and irresponsible as the way the harvesters looked in a mental picture which God seemed to give to a certain pastor on one occasion.

While the pastor was praying, he saw a mental video which seemed to carry with it the kind of revelatory message which characterised the vision Peter saw while he was praying on the rooftop in Acts 10:9. The pastor saw, not a sheet being let down to earth by its four corners, but a group of harvesters gathering golden grain from a farmer's field. But as the pastor looked at the sequence of pictures closely and carefully, he observed that the workers were using not farming implements but spoons. As the short film continued to play on the screen of his mind, it became apparent that there was no need for their progress to be hampered in this way because parked on a road adjacent to the field stood a farm wagon which was loaded with harvesting tools: sickles, rakes and pitch-forks.

Just as Peter's vision was used by the Holy Spirit to change his perception of Gentiles, so God used this pastor's picture to persuade him that it is possible to attempt to do God's work with the inadequate tools of our own abilities and insights or it is possible to avail ourselves of the Holy Spirit's gifts: among others, his wisdom and counsel and power.

I heard this pastor describe his 'vision' to a group of Tanzanian clergy, including bishops. Since many of them spoke little or no English, one of the Tanzanian bishops translated the experience into Swahili and I still remember him breaking into peals of laughter as he saw, in his mind's eye, the absurdity of the picture: a group of grown-ups harvesting a whole field with small spoons.

Who the Holy Spirit is

It is equally absurd for us to embark on the life-long journey of becoming the person God created us to be without calling on the assistance of God's Spirit to help us. Jesus did, after all, call him the Helper. Yet many of us shun the Holy Spirit's involvement in the process of self-discovery. There are many reasons for this. One is fear. As someone expressed it to me just before I began to write this chapter: 'I've realised that I'm scared of the Holy Spirit. I don't think of him as a person, I think of him as a thing and I avoid reading the Acts of the Apostles because much of it seems weird.'

I, too, used to fear the Holy Spirit's ministry and consequently erected seemingly impenetrable barriers against his intervention in my life. I, too, used to harbour a secret store of doubts about the desirability of opening my life to the 'Holy Ghost', as the Holy Spirit used to be called in the Book of Common Prayer and the Authorised Version of the Bible on which I was reared as a child, so I sensed I understood some of the reasons why this person trembled when the Holy Spirit was mentioned.

When I investigated my own ambivalence towards the third person of the Holy Trinity, I realised that two main factors contributed to it. One covered the excesses and eccentricities of some of the so-called Spirit-filled Christians known to me at then. The other was some of the teaching on the Holy Spirit and his activity which I had received as a child and as a young adult.

I think, for example, of that terrifying word 'ghost' which seemed designed to drive people from the Holy Spirit rather than encourage them to draw near. Or words like 'wind' and 'fire' which my Sunday School teachers had used to help us to understand the Holy Spirit's activity in our lives. Such words had conjured up in my childish mind the fires caused by enemy shelling during the Second World war; fires which had gutted the magnificent cathedral in our city; and fires which had demolished people's homes and business premises, plunging the young and the elderly alike into inexpressible grief and despair. Having witnessed these catastrophes as a child, I wanted nothing to do with God's fire.

Similarly the word 'wind', which describes the Spirit, came to me laced with negative overtones. It would remind me of a poem I learned in school which contrasted the beauty and warmth of the sun with the mischievous, unpredictable behaviour of the wind. It would remind me, too, of the howling wind which would sometimes bite into me while I walked to school or church. The word caused me to recoil from the wind of God's Spirit. And even as an adult, the term 'the empowering Spirit' sounded warning bells inside me. The phrase reminded me of verses describing seemingly wild, uncontrolled and uncontrollable behaviour:

'The Spirit of the Lord came upon [Samson] in power so that he tore the lion apart with his bare hands as he might have torn a young goat. But he told neither his father nor his mother what he had done' (Judges 14:6).

Such violence and deceit repelled me. Consequently I distanced myself from the Holy Spirit and developed a strong dislike of the word 'power'. This dislike deepened in the early 1960s when many seemingly eccentric Christians claimed to have been endued with power from the Holy Spirit. 'If this is power', I concluded, 'I don't want it.' I turned my back on the Holy Spirit because, in the circles in which I then moved, what passed for power communicated itself to me as little more than brashness and the extremes of extrovert enthusiasm. My ambivalence deepened because those who claimed to be Spirit-filled always dressed in T-shirts bearing the slogan: 'Smile, God loves you' and a transfer of a 'smiley

face'. They called their spiritual effervescence joy and, when
challenged, were quick to claim that their behaviour was Biblical.
They would point to verses like 1 Samuel 10:5–7 where we read
of Saul encountering and being influenced by a procession of
zealous men playing lyres and tambourines, flutes and harps,
and praising God in exuberant fashion. The defendants of this
kind of religious fervour seemed totally unaware that someone
else's religious euphoria could communicate itself to others as
an objectionable lack of balance.

Although I rejected the enthusiasm which masqueraded as
power, I detected within myself a deep-down hunger – even an
envy as, slowly, over a period of some eight years, I discerned
that people whose availability to the Holy Spirit was genuine
seemed somehow to change. The only way I can describe the
subtlety of what I observed was that they became a richer
expression of their former selves.

This set me on a quest. I would probe into questions like:
'Who is this Holy Spirit? What is its ministry?'

The Holy Spirit: a person

The first thing I discovered was that, although the Holy Spirit *is*
frequently referred to as wind, water and fire, the Bible makes
it quite clear that, first and foremost, he is a person. As Jesus
puts it, he is a counsellor, a comforter, and an advocate.[1] He
guides us[2] and speaks to us,[3] convinces and constrains us,[4]
transforms and warns us.[5] He can be grieved[6] and lied against.[7]
Moreover, he is not just any person. He is the third person
of the Holy Trinity who, from all eternity, has emanated from
God the Father and God the Son. As someone has summarised
the situation: 'He is the uncreated, creative power of the holy,
loving God. He is personally present to but transcendently other
than the human spirit.'[8] Paul goes so far as to call him, not only
God's Spirit (2 Corinthians 3:3) but God himself (2 Corinthians
3:17). His presence is made known to us by Jesus who refers
to him as the Father's good gift (Luke 11:13).

'The Father's good gift.' Certainly, the words Jesus chooses
conjured up 'good' pictures. The 'advocate' had special meaning

for me at this time. A few months earlier, my husband and I had been involved in a car crash in what was then Yugoslavia. Because I had sustained back and head injuries I became a patient for a week in a primitive hospital. Meanwhile my husband was left with the arduous task of trying to salvage our belongings from the wrecked car, look after our two young children, sort out our financial affairs and try to deal with the legal wranglings surrounding the crash. He would have been totally unable to cope without the help of the village advocate – a man who befriended us and took a great deal of care and trouble to acquaint himself with our plight but who was also fully conversant with the law of the land; a man who could therefore be the go-between in whom the local legal system and our family met and understood each other.

According to William Kelly, this is precisely what the Holy Spirit does. As our Advocate, he identifies with our interests, undertakes our cause, covenants to see us through all our difficulties and becomes our Representative before God. At the same time he is Jesus's Representative. He makes Jesus present to us and reveals all that Jesus is to us. He secures for us all that the Father has to give. He is the One who brings Jesus to us and us to Jesus.[9]

Even though these insights allayed some of my fears, I was startled by Jesus's claim: 'It is better for you that I go away, because if I do not go, the Helper will not come to you. But if I do go away, then I will send him to you' (John 16:7, GNB).

Like many other Christians, there are so many times in my life when I envy the disciples the privilege that was theirs of encountering Jesus face to face when he walked this earth. I, too, would have dearly loved to have seen and heard him, touched him and been held by him. I, too, would have loved to have watched him at work and listened to him pray. 'But no,' he seems to say. 'It is for your good that you cannot see or hear me in the flesh. It is in your best interests that I go away. It is to your advantage that, instead, I infuse you with my Holy Spirit.'

This caused me to question whether the claim that the Holy Spirit is Jesus's Alter Ego – Jesus's 'other self' – might be correct; that this is the reason why it is better for us that the God-man Jesus returned to his Father so that he could come to us in a different guise. If this was true, I reasoned, and it is also true that the Holy Spirit is the breath, the energy and the personality of Jesus, do I not need to do a U-turn and face him rather than flee from him? If it is true that, when the Spirit in-breathes us, little by little, we become more like Jesus, this is another reason why I should draw closer to him rather than run from him. We are created in the image of God and if the Holy Spirit can help me to become more like Jesus, to have him permeating my life is a necessity not a luxury.

The Holy Spirit: a lovely person

The thought challenged me – especially in the light of Galatians 5:22 where Paul spells out the nature of the fruit the Holy Spirit causes to mature in the believer: love and joy, peace and patience, kindness and goodness, faithfulness, gentleness and self-control.

Joy, I reflected, is the ability to rejoice in spite of irksome circumstances, trying people or persistent pain. Love is the unselfish affection which always seeks to promote the well-being of others attempting to meet their deepest needs and facilitate their growth. Peace is the ability to remain calm, tranquil and serene in every circumstance because we entrust all things to the wisdom, sovereignty and omniscience of God, while a patient person keeps on enduring those things they do not enjoy and also accepts people's weaknesses. Gentleness means the ability to place ourselves in another's shoes and so to identify with their feelings and circumstances that we inflict no needless pain on them. Gentleness increases in us the ability to dispense with rudeness, harshness or abrasiveness. Even when the gentle person needs to be firm, the firmness comes laced with compassion, tenderness and the self-control without which these qualities would be impossible.

I understand goodness to mean the rejection of all that is not of God. It is that quality which allows God to be God in our lives. Faithfulness is the loyalty, reliability, dependability and commitment which never disappoints and never lets another down; the quality which can assure another, 'When I say I'll be your friend, I'll always be your friend.' Self-control is the ability to hear the clamour of one's own rebel emotions and inner needs, coupled with the skill to know which to discipline, as we would control an unruly class of children, and which to meet. Like Jesus, the self-controlled person enjoys the inner harmony which stems from a body, mind and soul in perfect working order. And humility was once described to me as that art whereby, when we know we have done something well, we give the glory to God and keep a little bit of encouragement for ourselves.

I remember reading and being beckoned by Robert Frost's reflection on the One who causes this fruit to mature in us:

'Only a *lovely* person can minister *love* . . . Only a *joyful* person can minister *joy* . . . Only a *peaceful* person can minister *peace* . . . Only a *hopeful* person can minister *hope*.'[10]

As I turned this claim over in my mind, I felt further drawn to the Holy Spirit and his ministry. And when I reflected on the way he brooded like a protective bird over the chaos which gradually became the wonderful world of Genesis 1 and 2, the fear in my heart melted and was replaced by awe. This sense of awe increased when, in Psalm 104, I noticed that it is the Holy Spirit who constantly renews the heavens and the earth, the sea and the rivers, the mountains, the moon and the sun, together with all living creatures: birds, plants, trees and the whole of mankind.

Awe was strengthened when I meditated on the Holy Spirit's role in the conception, birth and public ministry of Jesus. It seemed to me that his role had been, in part, an administrative one and, like any good administrator, he had ensured that everything dovetailed together smoothly so that necessary changes could take place as effectively and painlessly as possible.

And fear was further dispelled when I read Jesus's claim that this transforming, life-giving Spirit who inspired the 'letter from home' which is so precious to me (2 Peter 1:21), always glorifies the Son and promotes his Lordship.[11]

So, since John records that Jesus breathed his Spirit into his disciples, and since Luke recalls how the disciples were overwhelmed by the Spirit on the Day of Pentecost, and since John promised that Jesus would likewise 'baptise', that is, clothe, overshadow or immerse believers with his Spirit, I began to pray, in the words of the chorus:

> Spirit of the Living God,
> Fall afresh on me . . .
> Melt me, mould me, fill me, use me,
> Spirit of the living God fall afresh on me.
>   (My version of a familiar chorus)

That was twenty years ago. With the wisdom of hindsight, I sense I can trace some of the ways in which this lovely, third member of the Holy Trinity has been and still is putting me in touch with the person God always created me to be. I discovered, too, that he is showing me some of the characteristics of true, enfleshed freedom. Like Billy Graham, I have drawn the conclusion that 'I need Jesus Christ for my eternal life, and the Holy Spirit of God for my internal life'.[12]

Filled with the Spirit

Before I could discover experientially the precise nature of the Holy Spirit's ministry, however, my eyes were to be opened to the meaning of Paul's injunction to 'be filled with the Spirit' (Ephesians 5:18).

One of the first clues I found seemed a curious one. To enter into the fullness of the freedom God grants and to become the person he always intended us to be, we must surrender ourselves to him. George Matheson sums up this paradox in the first two lines of his well-loved hymn:

> Make me a captive, Lord,
> And then I shall be free.

The Holy Spirit who has been variously described as the Advocate or the Go-Between God or the best man who introduces the Bridegroom (Christ) to the Bride (his church), facilitates this liberating process. He does it, in the words of Paul, by flooding our hearts with God's love (Romans 5:5, JBP).

Will I ever forget the evening when, in a friend's lounge, God gave me the graced moment where I was able to experience this for myself? The friend in whose home it happened had telephoned me to say that he believed he had been baptised with the Holy Spirit and that he had begun to pray in tongues. Still struggling between a desire to be open to the Spirit of God and a disdain for the eccentricities I have already described, my initial response was: 'Oh dear! Maybe we can talk about it on Monday after the meeting.'

The meeting had finished, everyone else had gone home and my friend had told me his story. The genuineness of his experience touched me and although I had gone to the meeting fully intending to 'sort him out' theologically, I knew that to dispute what he had told me would be an affront to him, a trusted friend, and to God. Instead, I simply reverenced his story.

As we had done so often before, we then prayed together. As we prayed, I became aware of him gently and quietly praying in tongues. I became aware, too, at one stage, that he was laying his hands on my head very gently and asking God to touch me afresh. No rushing wind swept through the room and no tongues of flame hovered over our heads but gradually the lounge became holy ground as the sense of the presence and the love of God overshadowed me. As I reflected on this later, it was as though God was pouring into me liquid love. I could almost feel it being spread through every cell of my brain before it percolated round the inner recesses of my being. The sensation stunned me, silenced me and thrilled me. When I left my friend's home and walked through the dark streets to my own, the love seemed to intensify and as I slipped into bed beside my husband, the love continued to overshadow and to overwhelm me. So far as I am aware, sleep eluded me that night but I was glad of the hushed

darkness to absorb the elixir of love in a way I had never before
envisaged, let alone experienced.

For days, although I carried on with my normal routine, I
seemed strangely detached from it all. It was as though I was
watching the world through double-glazed windows. Outside,
my family and friends were acting normally; inside, I felt as
though as I was moving in a womb of love.

'I suppose this is what people call being "baptised with the
Holy Spirit",' I said to my husband. He understood, though
neither of us appreciated what we now know – that, as Andrew
Murray described it one hundred years ago:

'The Spirit is nothing less than the Divine Love itself come
down to dwell in us . . . The Spirit comes to us freighted with
all the love of God and of Jesus: the Spirit is the Love of God
. . . The outpouring of the Spirit is the inpouring of Love.'[13]

When this love-shedding Spirit not only indwells us but also
immerses us in love, he gives far more than the head-knowledge
that God loves us intimately and uniquely. In Paul's words, he
spreads God's love into the nooks and crannies of our lives until,
in that love, we live and move and have our entire being.

He convicts us of sin

This love with which God loves Jesus, ourselves and all his
children, now possesses our hearts and draws from us a
reciprocal love. At least, that was my experience. Love and
praise welled up inside me as from a well-supplied fountain.
Whether I was praying or washing up, worshipping or fetching
the children from school, the cool, coloured waters sprang
spontaneously from the fountain within, and mingled with the
liquid love of God which continued to flow into me and refresh
me. 'But why did I have to wait so long for this?' I once
asked God.

For a whole year I had prayed from the poverty of my parched
and hungry heart that God would meet me in the spiritual desert
in which I had been wandering. I had anticipated that, in answer
to this prayer, water would flow from the mountain top into the
caked clay of my soul, saturate me, fill me and create within me

an oasis where fresh flowers could blossom, where birds would sing and where butterflies of every colour and hue would dance to the music of the spirit.

Instead, for a whole year, I pleaded: 'Lord, drench me with the water of your Holy Spirit if that's what I need,' but no water came – only increased barrenness and the awareness that the emptiness inside me was growing steadily bigger and more cavernous.

'I was preparing you,' he seemed to whisper. And, at last, I understood.

Throughout this year, a horrifying awareness of my own sinfulness crept over me so that I saw myself as I really was: a sinner, coated with grime. I am not implying that the cause of *all* spiritual dryness is sin. It is not. Often it is a gift from God causing us to cry out for a fresh touch of the Spirit. On this occasion, though, I was brought face to face with my innate sinfulness.

It wasn't that I had committed any of the spectacular sins like adultery or murder or theft. Ordinary, humdrum, grubby little sins had accumulated, encrusting me without my noticing. After all, I had been too busy *serving* God to be over-conscious of sin. But during this year, I saw it and felt cheated. Where was the promised energising that the Holy Spirit was supposed to inject (Acts 1:8)? I remember protesting: 'Lord, I asked you for more of your Spirit's life and power. All you have given me is an awareness of sin; not even anyone else's sin. My own!' Now the truth appeared in rather the same way as the rising sun peeps over the mountain range opposite our home ushering in a new day of hope and promise. God *had* been answering my heart-cry, 'Drench me with your Spirit', but he had answered it in a way I had not anticipated or understood because I had not appreciated Jesus's warning that one of the Holy Spirit's main tasks is to convict the world of sin (John 16:8).

Theologians advise us that the word 'convict' was the word customarily used for the cross-examination of a witness or a man on trial. It always carries with it the concept of a cross-examination *process* in that the trial continues until the person admits his wrong-doing.[14] In other words, when the Holy

Spirit permeates and penetrates our innermost beings, he shines the torch of his truth on the inconsistencies which prevent us from becoming the loving and lovable people God created us to be. His purpose in exposing them is not to condemn or to crush us but rather gently to reveal to us how self mars God's image in us, dishonours him and short-changes our personalities. His further purpose is to bring us to that point where we beg him to continue in us his sanctifying work (2 Thessalonians 2:13). But, as the writer of the Epistle to the Hebrews warns us, to be disciplined in this way always feels disconcerting and humiliating rather than consoling.

The scene which greets me as I gaze out of my study window has become, for me, a parable of this aspect of the Holy Spirit's ministry. The vineyards and orange and lemon groves in the valley below bask in the warm sunshine and stretch out to touch the aquamarine Mediterranean sea. The arms of the pampas grass wave in the wind while a blue haze partly masks the mountains which frame the picture. But today this beauty is somewhat marred by a vast expanse of black, scorched land. Two days ago, these terraces were a blond tangle of tall, dried grasses and shoulder-high, unruly weeds. Then, as is the custom at this time of year, a fire was lighted to purge the area of pests and undergrowth. And although the pocked landscape still looks charred, already I am reaping some of the benefits of this seemingly ruthless and dangerous operation. Displaced birds are perching on the branches of the trees in our garden, regaling us with their song and delighting us with the luxuriance of their brightly coloured wings. The path from our home which had been completely overgrown is now not only visible, but usable. And the field rats which were beginning to venture from the field into our house have been driven away.

This parable of nature reminds me that the Holy Spirit's task of purging us of sin is designed, not to humiliate or to destroy us, but rather to set us free from all that would pollute us and mask the Christ-like qualities God has invested in us. The Holy Spirit's part in this double exposure of our sin and our giftedness is crucial. Since he is the one who equipped us to serve God in the first place, he is the one who is most capable of helping us discover precisely the kind of person he created us to be.

He equips us

This aspect of the Holy Spirit's ministry is highlighted in Exodus 31:3–5 where God says of Bezalel:

'I have filled him with the Spirit of God, with skill, ability and knowledge in all kinds of crafts – to make artistic designs for work in gold, silver and bronze, to cut and set stones, to work in wood, and to engage in all kinds of craftsmanship.'

I sometimes wonder how long it took Bezalel to discover that his seemingly natural talents were, in fact, indications of the kind of person God always intended him to be; whether his exploration into self-awareness was as long and difficult as ours sometimes is. We are not told. What we are told is that we cannot make such discoveries on our own. As William Temple once observed:

It is no good giving me a play like *Hamlet* or *King Lear*, and telling me to write a play like that. Shakespeare could do it: I can't. And it is no good showing me a life like the life of Jesus and telling me to live a life like that. Jesus could do it: I can't. But if the genius of Shakespeare could come and live in me, then I could write plays like that. And if the Spirit of Jesus could come and live in me, I could live a life like that.[15]

If the Spirit of Jesus could come? The good news is that the sanctifying Spirit of Jesus *has* come. He hovers over our chaos and inner darkness and, when we give him the go-ahead, gradually reveals to us and connects us with the person God created us to be.

'When we give him the go-ahead.' The way to give him the go-ahead is to heed Paul's injunction to 'be filled with the Spirit' (Ephesians 5:18). One prerequisite for being filled with the Spirit, as I have already indicated, is to acknowledge our need and inner emptiness. As Andrew Murray shrewdly observes:

'The first condition of all filling is emptiness. What is a reservoir but a great hollow, a great emptiness prepared, waiting, thirsting, crying for the water to come?'[16]

Another prerequisite is spelt out by Jesus when he exhorts us to ask:

> 'Ask and it will be given to you; seek and you will find . . .
> Which of you fathers, if your son asks for a fish, will give
> him a snake instead? Or if he asks for an egg, will give him
> a scorpion? If you then, though you are evil, know how
> to give good gifts to your children, how much more will
> your Father in heaven give the Holy Spirit to those who
> ask him?
>
> (Luke 11:9–13)

A third prerequisite is openness to be filled with God's Spirit in whatever way God chooses to in-breathe us.

Like me, countless Christians have discovered that God impregnated them with his Spirit in great gentleness, while the Holy Spirit has come to others in a far more dramatic way. While recognising the authenticity of both and while allowing God to be God in every situation, giving him the spaciousness to enrich our lives in whatever way he chooses, we need to heed Andrew Murray's warning when he observes that the sudden, mighty manifestations of the Holy Spirit, which result in an over-dependence on the fellowship, sometimes have a tendency towards superficiality. The experience reaches the upper, most accessible parts of our personality but leave the hidden depths of the inner life and the current of our will untouched and unchanged. When this happens, our journey towards maturity and our struggle to discover the person God created us to be suffers a set-back. We therefore need constantly to be aware that what is required is not just a past testimony, whether that testimony bears witness to a sudden or gradual conversion experience or an immersion in God's Spirit. No. What is needed is the regular, daily, hourly, ongoing infilling of the Holy Spirit whose further task it is to enlighten us as we feast on God's Word as well as to teach us to pray – the topics on which we shall focus in the next four chapters.

For personal reflection

1. Take a few minutes to still yourself in the presence of God.
2. Read John 20:19–23. Re-read it until you are really familiar with the details of this account of the first Easter Day.
3. Picture the scene as vividly as you can.
4. Now step into the picture so that you are there with the disciples. Notice who is there, what the atmosphere in the room is like, how you feel about being there and where you place yourself – in the middle of the group, for example, or hiding in a corner.
5. Watch the disciples' reactions as Jesus enters the room despite the locked doors. Let the rest of the story unfold and become involved in it – doing as Jesus suggests: gazing at his hands and his side.
6. Be aware that he is breathing his Spirit into the disciples. And he approaches you. Register how it feels to have him close enough to breathe on you. Register, too, how you feel about him breathing his Spirit into you. Are you resisting? Or receiving?
7. Write him a prayer telling him the thoughts and emotions which are clamouring for attention inside you.

Notes for Chapter Three

1. John 14:16 (where the word 'Counsellor' is variously translated 'Comforter' and 'Advocate').
2. Nehemiah 9:19,20; Luke 4:1
3. 2 Samuel 23:2;2 Peter 1:21
4. Acts 13:4
5. Nehemiah 9:30
6. Isaiah 63:10
7. Acts 5:3.
8. *The New Bible Dictionary* (Inter-Varsity Press, 1980) p. 534.

9. William Kelly, quoted by Andrew Murray in *The Spirit of Christ* (Anson D.F. Randolph and Company, New York, 1888) p. 356.
10. Robert Frost, *Set My Spirit Free* (Logos, 1973) p. 39.
11. John 16:14.
12. Billy Graham, *The Holy Spirit* (Fount, 1978) p. 12.
13. Andrew Murray, *The Spirit of Christ*, p. 283.
14. William Barclay, *John's Gospel: The Daily Study Bible* (Saint Andrew Press, 1955).
15. William Temple, quoted by John Stott in *Basic Christianity* (IVP, 1971) p. 102
16. Andrew Murray, *The Spirit of Christ*, p. 306.

4

THE PLACE OF PRAYER

Superficiality and the quest to discover our true identity in Christ are incompatible. As Christians we are called, not to remain shallow, but rather to respond in the deep places of our personality to the deep love of God. That, at least, is the way I understand the Psalmist's phrase, 'deep calls to deep' (Psalm 42:7).

Often, when I lead prayer retreats and Quiet Days, I find people using this phrase of the Psalmist as a prayer: 'May the hidden depths of my being be touched by the depths of your love, Lord.' That is why the Holy Spirit's involvement in our life is so important. As Paul reminds us, the 'Holy Spirit speaks to us *deep* in our hearts' (Romans 8:16, LB, my emphasis). He not only speaks, he helps. In his role as Counsellor or Comforter, he is fully qualified to draw alongside us whenever we are in any kind of need for help.

Prayer is one of the areas into which he delights to move. This is good news because prayer, of all places, is the forum where we discover who and what God created us to be.

By prayer, in this chapter, I am not referring to petitionary prayer or intercessory prayer, nor to spiritual warfare or the prayer of confession, vital though these and other facets of the jewel of prayer are in the life of the believer. I am thinking solely of that aspect of prayer which is an ever-deepening relationship with God. Richard Foster labels this the prayer of home-coming, the prayer which becomes the place where 'we come home to where we belong'.[1] It is the place where we 'come home to that for which we were created',[2] 'the place of deepest intimacy, where we know and are known to the fullest'.[3] This prayer is 'a love relationship: an enduring, continuing, growing love relationship with the great God of the universe'.[4]

The prayer of Jesus

This is the kind of prayer into which Jesus drew his disciples when he called them to 'Come with me by yourselves to a quiet place and get some rest' (Mark 6:31). It is the kind of prayer into which he woos us today.

The context of the original invitation fascinates me. The disciples had just returned from the mission to the villages on which they had been sent by Jesus. It would appear that it had been fruitful. But such missions are draining, as Jesus well knew from personal experience so, instead of sending them straight back into another campaign, he gave them the opportunity of rest, in a quiet place, with him.

Did the disciples protest that there were so many souls to be saved, so many people needing healing, so many others to be delivered from oppression, that to spend time with the Master would be pure self-indulgence? I doubt it. They were well acquainted with his own rhythm of prayer which included frequent forays into the hills where he could be alone with his Father. They knew that when he returned from such times in the Father's presence, he seemed re-energised, empowered and full of wisdom and purpose as though the Father had given him the next piece of the map to guide him on the next phase of the journey. Surely they would have reasoned that, if prayer in a quiet place could re-charge the Master's batteries, it could re-charge theirs also? Jesus not only retreated frequently to quiet places where his relationship with his Father could be nurtured, he applauded Mary of Bethany for turning her back on the tyranny of the urgent in favour of spending leisurely time at the feet of her Beloved, and he gently rebuked Martha for failing to discern the one thing necessary (Luke 10:42).

The place where we know ourselves loved

Why was it that Jesus removed himself from the thronging crowds to spend quality time with his Father? What drew him from his bed to spend the early hours of the morning on the hushed shores of the sea of Galilee? What prompted him to spend the entire night under the star-studded sky?

Do we not find a clue in Matthew 3:17?

The occasion is Jesus's Baptism. His public ministry has not yet begun. The crowds have not yet recognised him as the miracle worker. The Twelve have not yet been called to live in community with him. Yet, as Jesus rises from the waters of the Jordan to face the people he already loved, his Father's cry from heaven echoed round the Jordan valley: 'This is my Son, whom I love; with him I am well pleased' (Matthew 3:17). In other words, the Father seems to be underlining that his Son was uniquely loved not for anything he had achieved but simply for who he was. When we become aware of such love, it not only motivates us for ministry, it reminds us that we are loved, not for what we do but for who we are. It reminds us, as someone has put it, that we were created to be human *beings* and not human *doings*.

The Father's love so energised Jesus that he wanted his disciples to know themselves loved also. That, surely, is the reason why he invited them to escape from the crowds which clamoured so persistently that Jesus and his friends had no time to eat? That, surely, is the reason why he applauded Mary for her foresight and intuitive knowing that when she sat at his feet she was in the right place? That, surely, is the reason why he still pleads with us: '*You* come aside *with me* and get some rest'?

We need to notice that the invitation is not simply to take a break. No. The invitation is to take a holiday with him. Henri Nouwen explains the reason that this emphasis is so crucial to our quest to discover precisely who it is God created us to be. His thesis is that the words 'You are my Beloved' 'reveal the most intimate truth about all human beings'[5] and that 'being the Beloved expresses the core truth of our existence'.[6] He goes on to ask:

> Aren't you, like me, hoping that some person, thing or event will come along to give you that final feeling of inner well-being you desire? Don't you often hope: 'May this book, idea, course, trip, job, country or relationship fulfill my deepest desire.' But as long as you are waiting for that mysterious moment you will go on running helter-skelter, always anxious and restless, always lustful and angry, never fully satisfied . . .
>
> Well, you and I don't have to kill ourselves. We are the Beloved. We are intimately loved long before our parents, teachers, spouses, children and friends loved or wounded us. That's the truth of our lives. That's the truth I want you to claim for yourself. That's the truth spoken by the voice that says, 'You are my Beloved.'
>
> Listening to that voice with great inner attentiveness, I hear at my center words that say, 'I have called you by name, from the very beginning. You are mine and I am yours. You are my Beloved, on you my favor rests. I have molded you in the depths of the earth and knitted you together in your mother's womb. I have carved you in the palms of my hands and hidden you in the shadow of my embrace. I look at you with infinite tenderness and care for you with a care more intimate than that of a mother for her child. I have counted every hair of your head and guided you at every step. Wherever you go, I go with you, and wherever you rest, I keep watch . . . You belong to me . . . We are one.'
>
> Every time you listen with great attentiveness to the voice that calls you the Beloved, you will discover within yourself a desire to hear that voice longer and more deeply. It is like discovering a well in the desert. Once you have touched wet ground you want to dig deeper.[7]

Prayer is the place where we discover, not simply a well, but an oasis. The prayer which is a relationship with God is the place where we hear God say to *us*, 'You are my Beloved.' And, as Henri Nouwen concludes:

'From the moment we claim the truth of being the Beloved, we are faced with the call to become who we are. Becoming the Beloved is the great spiritual journey we have to make.'[8]

The place where we are re-created

But, in order that we might be set free to 'claim the truth of being the Beloved', we need to be re-created or, in New Testament terms, to be born again. That is not as difficult or nonsensical as it sounded to Nicodemus to whom Jesus first used the term. The prayer which is a developing relationship with God can become the womb where, gradually, God sets us free to become the people he always intended us to be.

This theory became a beautiful reality for me one Good Friday. I was leading a retreat at the time and, while the group were having lunch, I went to look at the simple cross one of the other leaders had created with two branches she had found in the garden. As I gazed at this makeshift cross, at the brown cloth surrounding it and the red candle flickering in front of it, I decided to linger rather than to eat with the others.

The longer I lingered, the more I felt drawn into a deep-down stillness as, in my imagination, I pictured Jesus dangling from that cross. The recollection of his agony drew from me a deep, spontaneous and silent adoration. While I was still gazing, contemplating and adoring him, I seemed to see him turn to me as, on that Good Friday, he had turned to John and Mary. Love was streaming from his face. Love flowed from his hands, his side and his heart. It swirled around me and into me. Then, a root seemed gently to push its way out of the tree and wrap itself around me in a protective way so that I found myself in a hidden, underground womb-like space and, although I remained quite still, I knew that, should I want to move, I would simply be responding to the music of liquid love. I could do nothing but stay there and savour the experience. After lingering for an hour or so, the inflow of love seemed to touch a deep fissure at the

core of my being so that, somehow, I knew I was being set free
to give love in a richer measure than ever before; that I could
now operate from a heart which is more healed than hurting.
This love flowed first to Jesus. As I put it later that day in a
letter to a friend: 'I wanted to embrace the cross – to hold it to
myself until it became a part of me, until it entered me. I adore
that man on the cross who has re-created me.'

Such prayer experiences are life-changing gifts from God,
tailor-made by God for each individual. As life-changing as my
contemplation of the 'bush' fire I mentioned in Chapter Three.
There I described how the vine terraces surrounding our home
still bear the scorch marks of the flames which recently burned
them. What I did not say in that chapter was that this planned,
routine fire became the victim of a sudden change in the direction
of the wind. This wind fanned the small, controlled fire into a
blaze sending flames leaping up terraced slopes and racing along
vineyards until in a matter of minutes, they reached our garden
hedge. They singed the roses before starting to lick the jasmine
which climbs up a wooden pergola. We were away from home
at the time, so only heard about the drama when we returned.
But as I now gaze out on to vast stretches of blackness, I am
constantly reminded that, but for the bravery of our neighbours
– a young mother and an elderly widow who were quick-witted
enough to seize the hose pipes in the garden and keep the blaze
under control until the fire engine arrived, our home might not
be here. I am reminded, too, how my attitude towards these
two women has changed. To say that I am grateful would be
an understatement. I am aware that I am indebted to them for
life and find myself yearning to repay them in some way.

When we ponder prayer experiences like the Good Friday
one I have described, the effect is similar. They draw us
closer to Jesus. His gifts of love humble us and stir up within
us the gratitude which gives birth to a desire to serve and
to give him ourselves. In turn, this increases our attachment to him. And the good news is that the deeper this
attachment becomes, the faster we grow into the people he
always intended we should be. For true freedom has nothing to do with pleasing oneself. Paradoxically, true freedom

means to be dominated by Jesus; to be under the influence
of Love.

The place where we are set free to let go

By comparing and contrasting Eve's part in the Fall (Genesis
3:1–24) with the Temptations of Jesus (Matthew 4:1–11), I will
attempt to illustrate what I mean.

When Satan sidled up first to Eve and subsequently to Jesus,
two questions begged to be answered. The first was: 'Whose
Kingdom are you serving?' The second: 'What is your life
principle?' A life principle is the motto we apply to specific
choices and circumstances.[9] When Satan drew Eve's attention
to the seeming lusciousness of the forbidden fruit, she enacted
the answers to these questions showing that she was serving
the kingdom of self and that her motto was: 'I will have what I
want no matter what it costs.' Jesus, on the other hand, gazed on
the stones which must have looked so much like pitta bread, yet,
despite his hunger, he enacted his answers to these questions.
In effect he proclaimed: 'I will not be governed by the pleasure
principle, I will be governed by the Word of God because I am
here, not to please myself, but rather to usher in the Kingdom
of God.'

Just as Satan tempted both of them through the eye gate, by
drawing their attention to something which attracted them, so
he tempted both of them to pursue power. Again, this is where
the similarity begins and ends. While Eve's yearning to 'be as
God' caused her to capitulate, Jesus's submission to the Father
prompted his refusal to be piqued into proving his divinity.

Finally, Satan played his trump card by enticing both of them
to avoid taking responsibility for their actions. Again, while Eve
showed her true colours by stepping into Satan's snare and by
later attempting to pass the blame for her misdemeanours on
to Adam, Jesus neatly side-stepped the trap with a protest.
In effect, he was saying: 'I will not try God's patience for the
sake of prestige or popularity. I will take full responsibility for
my choices.'

The net result of these confrontations was that while Eve lost the freedom to become the poised, responsible person God had created her to be, Jesus emerged empowered. Free. The man of stature and authority his Father created him to be. His attachment to God was so strong that nothing could drag him away from the Father's plan or expressed will. On this occasion, even though he had not eaten for forty days, he could hold a stone on the palm of his hand, know that he possessed the ability to turn it into pitta bread and choose, instead, to say to the Father: 'I'm hungry. I would like to eat. But I am prepared to continue my fast if this is better for the Kingdom.' Even more startlingly, in Gethsemane, he could confess that he did not want to be crucified but he could hold even his life-blood on an open palm and say to his Father: 'You choose.'

This is freedom. This is the life-style of the man who shows us how to become the person God created us to be.

If we piece together the insights of some psychologists, it becomes apparent that Satan is still tempting us through the eye gate, that is, through the lure of the attraction we see. Sigmund Freud suggested that the libido or pleasure principle lies at the heart of every human problem. Alfred Adler questioned this surmise, offering the counter-suggestion that 'the basic drive in people is for power and accomplishment.'[10] The determinist B.F. Skinner contends, however, that we are conditioned by our past and have no alternative other than to abdicate all responsibility for our lives. Who we are and what we become has been decided for us by our up-bringing.

We need not concern ourselves here with a debate about which of these three men is right and which is wrong. We need, rather, to draw on the collective wisdom of all three to recognise that, deep down, all of us have a pleasure-seeking streak, all of us are power-thirsty and all of us are bent towards pride and self-pleasing. We therefore struggle with any principle encouraging us to ensure that it is always God's Kingdom we promote and not our own. If we would be like Jesus, intimacy with God is therefore a must.

Deepening our relationship with God

All friends discover their own methods of becoming more and more intimate with one another. The same is true of closeness with God. And many books are now available to help us in this quest. The book which I have used almost daily for the past nineteen years is Jim Borst's *Coming to God*.[11] In it, he explains that the prayer of relationship or contemplative prayer, as he calls it, sets us free to become the people God intended us to be:

> In the presence of God, we learn the necessity of being absolutely true to ourselves and absolutely honest with ourselves. We learn to see ourselves as we really are – behind the mask of convention and deception, pose and pretence. We grow into truthfulness and genuineness as we grow out of artificiality and falseness in thought, word and deed. The more we live in the presence of God, the more truly we become ourselves – the people God always intended us to be. And as we become more true to ourselves, we become more true to God.[12]

He goes on to claim, and I agree with him, that contemplative prayer also transforms us:

'True spirituality and true prayer must change us, otherwise they are irrelevant and scandalous. We cannot pray day after day, month after month and remain the same.'[13]

One reason why I have used his book so consistently for so many years is that it is a book to be prayed with, rather than a book to be read. Another is that the author takes us by the hand, as it were, and leads us, step by step, out of the fast lane and into a layby with God. There is not space here to do justice to the twelve stages of prayer he mentions in the book – just enough space to whet the appetites of those who sense that they are being drawn into a deeper relationship with God.

The phase of relaxation

The first step is to remind ourselves of Jesus's invitation to 'come . . . and *rest*'. We therefore pull out of life's fast lane for a while, find a suitable layby, take our foot off the accelerator of our heart and relax. It helps, if at all possible, to find a layby into which we can retreat daily: a spare room in our home, a favourite chair in a quiet room, an empty church, a shed in the garden cleaned out specially for the purpose. When we cross the threshold of this place of prayer, it is rather like entering the home of a friend – the opportunity to change gear and to prepare ourselves to deepen the friendship.

Then, just as we might call out our friend's name as we were opening their door, so it can help as we begin our prayer, simply to whisper the name Jesus or to pray: 'Come Holy Spirit', as though we were inviting our indwelling God to come to meet us. Apart from this, during the first few minutes of the prayer time, we say nothing. Instead, just as we might hug a friend on arrival, savouring the richness of the love of this particular relationship, so we spend several minutes tuning in to the presence and love of the Divine Friend who yearns for this time with us even more than we do.

Two friends meeting in this way might then enjoy sharing their news with each other. In the same way, as we become more still in the presence of the Divine Friend, we become aware of the concerns and joys which are uppermost in our minds, letting them tumble out just as they will: the joys, the plans, the worries, the niggles, the questions. As someone has put it, the only way we can come to God is 'just as we are'. And as another teacher of prayer has described the progression as we approach this type of relationship with God, during this first phase of prayer, we become very conscious that it is 'me and him' in that order.

It is at this stage that our prayer differs from a casual conversation with a human friend. For Jesus desires, not simply to hear about the things which concern us, but to lift the burdens from us, at least temporarily, so that we move into a spacious internal place where we can receive his love afresh. So he invites us to transfer our burdens on to him. I sometimes like to picture Jesus in the room where I am praying. When I sense his out-stretched hands, I enact Peter's advice when he says: 'Let him have all your worries and cares, for he is always thinking about you and watching everything that concerns you' (1 Peter 5:7, LB). In other words, I place into those still-scarred hands everything that would prevent me from drawing close to him and him to me. When I have transferred all the clutter from me to him, I stretch out my empty hands as a sign that the hands of my heart are also up-lifted, empty and open, ready to receive anything and everything he desires to give me.

Occasionally, when the burden in my heart seems too big to hold to him, I sense him come to me, lift it from me himself, show me the huge hole which is left when the burden is removed, and remind me that this inner emptiness is the very place into which he will pour fresh and generous portions of his love.

The responding phase

In other words, the encounter begins as we respond to Jesus's invitation: 'Come with me . . . and rest.'

The encounter continues as a deeper response stirs in our hearts and we find ourselves, not only relaxing in his presence, but surrendering to him afresh. This response is not unlike giving a friend a long, leisurely embrace. Not a bear hug. Not a slap on the back. But the kind of non-erotic embrace where genuine love is expressed as your body touches and yields to your friend's. I find Jim Borst's slow, meditative invitation helps me to yield to God in this way:

Before God's face, aware of his presence,
surrender every aspect of your being
your hands, your wrists, your arms;
your senses and brain;
your feet and legs;
each and every nerve and muscle, blood vessel and organ.
Return yourself to him. Seek to withdraw your possessiveness and beg him to possess you, to live in and through you so that you can say with Paul: 'I no longer live, but Christ lives in me' (Galatians 2:20) . . .
urrender your heart, your feelings, your love . . .

Surrender your whole personality, your feelings and all
that is you . . .[14]

The reflecting phase

Just as, often, when we embrace a friend in this healing way, we
marvel at the depth of their love for us, so we may find ourselves
at this stage of our prayer, marvelling at the immensity of the
love in which we are now enfolded. Jesus, God's only son, is here
present with us, attentive to us. This in itself is truly amazing.
Our name is engraved on the palms of his hands.[15] He loves
us so much that he never takes his eyes off us.[16] He indwells
us and we live in him.[17] His life in us is like sap rising to feed
and renew us. His Spirit prays for us continually. He is praying
for us now.[18] He loves us better than we love ourselves. He
knows us better than we know ourselves. Yet he accepts us
as we are. He is using this prayer to change us. We may not
discern precisely how the transformation process works, but it
is happening in the same way as yeast leavens the lump.

He loves us so much that he took the initiative in instigating
this friendship with us.[19]

We sink deeper and deeper into this awareness, deeper and
deeper into his love, and deeper and deeper into heartfelt
gratitude and praise.

The recollecting phase

Or, as we find ourselves enfolded in divine love, we may find
a wave of unworthiness sweeping over us and crashing in a
foaming froth on the shore of our heart. Perhaps this is to
be expected? It so often happens, I find, that when someone
expresses love for me, because I know myself so well, I
know that there is a sense in which I am unworthy of their
affection.

In our relationship with God, we need to refrain from brushing
these feelings to one side and to examine them instead. They
conceal insights which will help us to discover the kind of person
God intended us to be.

So we beg the Holy Spirit to shine the torch-light of his love into the nooks and crannies of our hearts and to expose anything which lurks there which might hinder our relationship with him or which might prevent us from becoming the person God created us to be.

Again, I find Jim Borst's explanation and instructions helpful:

> Many of our 'natural' reactions are expressions and gestures of non-acceptance, of rebellion, of running away from reality, of suppression. Anger flares up, impatience possesses us like an evil spirit; dislikes and grudges harden our hearts; we resent interference and interruption. Without always realising it, we often refuse to accept people, events, situations, conditions, even ourselves as God wills them for us and as he accepts them for us. This non-acceptance of his will in concrete circumstances is experienced in prayer as a barrier, a road-block on the way to God. It is his will that we accept people, circumstances, events; that we do not try to influence people or events except by the power of love, forgiveness, suffering, acceptance and thanksgiving. In daily life, this means that we seek to avoid being judgemental, argumentative, critical and interfering in matters that do not concern us.
>
> Ask God to make you aware of actual barriers of non-acceptance in your life . . .
> Lay down your will and try to discern God's will . . .
> Forgive from the heart . . .[20]

The repenting phase

By this time, unworthiness may be accompanied by conviction or even guilt. But this is not a time or place to grovel. Rather it is an opportunity to confront reality. We are sinful; soiled in so many ways: in our bodies, minds and spirits. We talk to God about our failures and handicaps, lay our sin at the foot of his Cross and stretch out to him stained hands as we beg for pardon. And we give him the privilege and joy of cleansing and renewing us. We may even ask him to show us precisely what it is that he is doing for us.

I remember doing this while praying with a friend on one occasion. She had been pouring into my lap an account of the way in which she had found herself rebelling against God and consequently wounding his love. She now wanted to come back to him in penitence and faith.

As we prayed together over this failure and asked God to cleanse and renew her, a sequence of pictures played on the screen of my mind, showing me, I sensed, the nature of the miracle God was performing at that moment.

In the first picture, I saw a pair of bronzed hands and felt drawn to the long, sensitive fingers. In the second picture, the hands were holding a white, creased piece of fabric which looked like linen. In the third picture, the fingers were shaking out the creases and exposing a large stain which was spoiling the fabric. I then saw that near the hands stood a trough filled with water. As I continued to watch, the hands plunged the cloth into the water, held it there for several minutes and then pulled it out and held it up. The stain had disappeared and the fabric looked new. When I described the pictures for my friend, she expressed her own interpretation – her awareness that, in his love, God had held her in the cleansing waters of his love, removed the stain and renewed her.

He will do the same for us over and over again. That is why, with confidence, we can abandon sin, guilt and discouragement to his immense, unending love, turn away from it and walk away to enjoy the freedom to be the person he made us to be – free in Christ.

The receiving phase

We started this prayer, as I explained earlier, more conscious of ourselves than of God. As the prayer progresses, the emphasis gradually changes until self slips into the wings and we bring Jesus centre-stage. Now the focus changes again. We continue to give Jesus his rightful centre-stage space, but, once again, we draw near.

We concentrate on him, watch him, gaze at him, listen to him. As someone has expressed the purpose of this phase, we look at

him because we love him, we look in order to have our love for
him rekindled and we look until our love is fed and deepened by
our gaze.

And we watch what happens. God responds. He turns to us.
Speaks to us. Fills us afresh with his Spirit. We receive all that
he offers: joy, guidance, encouragement, peace, insight . . .
We bask in the assurance of his love. We submit all that we
know of ourselves to all that we know of him: the Truth. His
presence provides a new perspective. He, the source of truth,
draws us deeper into the truth – the truth about ourselves, the
truth about himself and the strength to move back into the fast
lane to be more true to both; more capable of giving expression
to our authentic selves.

For personal reflection

1. Ask God to deliver you from the curse of superficiality.
2. Re-read p. 48 from 'Aren't you, like me, hoping that some
   person . . . Once you have touched wet ground you want
   to dig deeper.' Reflect on it. Make your personal response
   to it. Write a prayer which is born out of your reflection.
3. Ask yourself the question: 'Whose Kingdom am I serving
   – the Kingdom of Christ or the kingdom of self?' Then ask
   another: 'What is my life principle or motto?'
4. Pray the phases of prayer, paying particular attention to the
   phases of relaxation and receiving.

Notes for Chapter Four

1. Richard Foster, *Prayer* (Hodder and Stoughton, 1992) p. 1.
2. Richard Foster, *Prayer*, p. 1.
3. Richard Foster, *Prayer*, p. 1.
4. Richard Foster, *Prayer*, p. 2.
5. Henri Nouwen, *Life of the Beloved* (Hodder and Stoughton, 1993) p. 26.
6. Henri Nouwen, *Life of the Beloved*, p. 28
7. Henri Nouwen, *Life of the Beloved*, pp. 30–1
8. Henri Nouwen, *Life of the Beloved*, p. 37

9. Here I am drawing on the insights of John Powell in his book *Unconditional Love* (Argus Communications, 1978) ch. 1.
10. Alfred Adler, quoted by John Powell S.J. in *Unconditional Love*, p. 21.
11. Jim Borst, *Coming to God* (Eagle, 1992).
12. Jim Borst, *Coming to God*, p. 57.
13. Jim Borst, *Coming to God*, p. 54.
14. Jim Borst, *Coming to God*, p. 28.
15. Isaiah 49:16.
16. Psalms 139:3.
17. John 17:2–23.
18. Hebrews 7:25.
19. 1 John 4:19.
20. Jim Borst, *Coming to God*, p. 24.

5

SET FREE BY THE TRUTH

The truth is liberating. If we can find it, we discover the secret for which we are searching: who it is we were created to be. And Jesus reveals where this secret may be found:

'If you make my word your home . . . you will learn the truth and the truth will make you free' (John 8:31–2 JB).

In other words, truth needs to be acquired and grasped and learned.

In Hebrew thought, the truth was that which holds water; that which does not give way or collapse; that which is real, correct, a sound basis for conduct. The Bible speaks of a three-pronged truth: the truth is revelation in the form of a person, Jesus; the truth is revelation in the form of a 'letter from home', the Bible; and the truth is God's Word applied to our individual situation by the enlightnenment of God's agent of truth, his Holy Spirit, so that God's truth becomes enfleshed.

'The word', on the other hand, is used to refer both to the written Word, the Bible and the incarnate Word, Jesus himself. As to the concept of setting up home in the Word, Psalm 119 introduces us to a man who seems to have done just that. Here we find the Psalmist striding purposefully in the Law which he respects with his whole being. He brings his entire concentration to bear on each of the commands of the God for whom his heart longs. He thinks constantly about the Word, storing it in his heart (v. 10), treasuring it (v. 11), reciting it (v. 13), meditating on it (v. 15) and delighting in it. The roots of longing burrow deep into his innermost being as he feasts on God's law (v. 20).

He senses that this active Word possesses the power to change him and this gives birth to a holy impatience: 'Wasting

no time, I hurry to observe your commandments' (v. 60, JB).
It also gives rise to a cry from the heart: 'Lord, don't let me
make a mess of things!' (v. 13, LB). 'I am but a pilgrim here on
earth: how I need a map – and your commands are my chart
and guide' (v. 19, LB).

A growing number of Christians, it seems, are detecting
within themselves an envy of the Psalmist. Like beggars holding
out the bowl of their spiritual poverty, they clamour to be led to
the banquet which they sense has been spread for them in the
pages of the Bible. Tired of existing on crumbs, they hanker for
the meat and wine of the Word. When someone shows them
how, they delight to make their home in God's Word just as the
Psalmist did. They discover, with awe, that the many layers of
their being, body, mind and spirit, can be nourished, informed
and set free by God's liberating Word.

Set free by Bible Study

When we find ourselves among those who are hungry for the
Word of God, we need to remind ourselves that, if the Word
is going to change us as well as challenge and inform us, we
need the anointing of God's Spirit. Andrew Murray put this
persuasively one hundred years ago:

> The Word will not take root in us unless the indwelling Holy
> Spirit quickens us – causing us to accept and appropriate it
> in the inner life. The Word is a seed. In every seed there is
> a fleshy part, in which the life is hidden. One may have the
> most precious and perfect seed in its bodily substance, and
> yet, unless it be exposed in suitable soil to the influence of
> sun and moisture, the life may never grow up. And so we
> may hold the words and the doctrines of Scripture most
> intelligently and earnestly and yet know little of their life
> and power. We need to remind ourselves and the Church
> unceasingly, that the Scriptures which were spoken by
> holy men of old as they were moved by the Holy Spirit,

can only be understood as they are taught by the same Spirit. 'The words I have spoken are Spirit and Life; for the apprehending and partaking of them, the flesh profiteth nothing: it is the Spirit that quickeneth, the Spirit of Life within us' (John 6:63).[1]

He goes on to underline that this is one of the solemn lessons which the history of the Jews in the time of Christ teaches us. They were zealous, as they thought, for God's Word and honour and yet events were to reveal that all their zeal was for their human interpretation of God's Word. So Jesus had to rebuke them: 'You diligently study the Scriptures because you think that by them you possess eternal life. These are the Scriptures that testify about me, yet you refuse to come to me to have life' (John 5:39).

They did indeed believe that the Scriptures would lead them to eternal life, yet they failed to see that Jesus was the fulfilment of the Old Testament prophecies and so they refused to come to their Messiah. They studied and accepted Scripture in the light and pride of their human understanding rather than in the light and power of God's illuminating Spirit.

Tragically, the same thing can and does happen to believers today. They study the Bible. They know chunks of it by heart. But it has not touched their will or their emotions because they have not looked to the life-giving Spirit to enlighten them. Andrew Murray concludes:

What is needed is very simple: the determined refusal to attempt to deal with the written Word without the quickening Spirit. Let us never take Scripture into our hand, or mind, or mouth, without realizing the need and the promise of the Spirit. First, in a quiet act of worship within you; then in a quiet act of faith, yield yourself to the power that dwells in you and wait on Him, that not the mind alone, but the life in you, may be opened to receive the Word.[2]

There is no one way of steeping ourselves in the Bible under the guidance of the Holy Spirit but a whole variety of ways. Different personalities, at different stages of their spiritual growth will find different methods helpful.

One option is Bible Study.

In my early years as a Christian, my mentors insisted that I should study the Bible, so I spent hours poring over Scripture with the aid of a pile of Bible commentaries. I found it fascinating. That is why I read Theology at university and even attempted to learn New Testament Greek to help me in my quest to understand the text before me. My mind was enriched by these spiritual gymnastics. More importantly, I discovered that studying the Scripture gave me a glimpse of the kind of person God had created me to be.

Take the Bible's teaching on the person and work of the Holy Spirit, for example, which I outlined in Chapter Three. As I traced the Bible's teaching on these subjects, my mind and heart became like that fertilised soil Andrew Murray mentions. My heart was being prepared to receive the seed-bearing Spirit in a new way so that I found myself begging for the privilege of giving birth to his fruit.

This discovery enabled me to take a stride forward in identifying the me God made me to be because, as I have explained in Chapter Three, it is the Holy Spirit whose ministry it is to transform us until we do become a new creation – the person we were always created to be.

Finding a suitable method

In addition to taking a particular subject like the person and work of the Holy Spirit, noting and looking up all the references on the subject mentioned in the concordance, there are a number of other methods of Bible Study.

One is to read the Bible straight through from Genesis to Revelation just to gain an over-view, among other things, of the kind of people God created us to be. Another is to read the Bible right through, underlining every command we discover or placing a mark against all the promises with which the pages of the Bible are peppered.

Yet another is to learn to pray the Psalms, taking note of the way the Psalmist expressed the full gamut of human emotions and learning to emulate him.

But that is not all. When studying the parables, for example, a great deal can be gleaned about God's plan for us if we ask ourselves some probing questions:

'What is the culture in which Jesus spoke?'

'Who is Jesus's audience on any given occasion: disciples, Pharisees or the crowd? What are they thinking?'

'Is Jesus defending the Gospel or instructing the faithful?'

'How would the listeners have interpreted the metaphor or story?'

When we respond intelligently and in an informed way to these and allied questions, the punch-line of the story becomes obvious, revealing to us the kind of people God created us to be.

Take Jesus's parable of the funeral, for example. The time of Jesus's Crucifixion was fast approaching and he 'resolutely set out for Jerusalem' (Luke 9:51). As he walked along the road, he said to a particular individual: 'Follow me.'

'But the man replied, "Lord, first let me go and bury my father." Jesus said to him, "Let the dead bury their own dead, but you go and proclaim the Kingdom of God"' (9:59. 60)

As Professor Kenneth Bailey reminds us, Jesus's listeners would have known that in Middle Eastern culture, a son was expected to stay at home and serve his parents until they died. Then he was free to leave. So they would have understood the man's response to mean, in effect: 'Let me go and serve my father while he is alive and after he dies I will bury him and commit my life to you.'[4] In other words, the man was in bondage to his culture and therefore not free to follow Jesus. Whereupon Jesus throws down the gauntlet by making it clear that what he expects of us is that we become believers who are prepared to swim against the cultural tide. This is part of the cost of being a disciple. He goes on to say that the spiritually dead can take care of the traditional responsibilities of the local community.

Through studying a parable like this, we are given a clear idea of ways in which we can deal with our culture. This is important because one of the biggest barriers to becoming the person God created us to be is worldliness. 'The world,' according to Michael Green, 'means society which leaves God out of account.'[5] If we accept this definition, worldliness implies the subtle infiltration into our innermost beings by society's philosophies, values and attitudes. The pull of the peer group or the boardroom, the team or the gang, is very strong. So is the tug of the media. So a research student may find himself using the department's photocopier without recording what he owes: 'Everybody does.' The young professional might arrive late for work or leave early and think nothing of it: 'Everybody does.' A sixth-former might remove stationery from school for personal or Sunday School purposes: 'Everybody does.' Tax-payers might find illegitimate ways of avoiding the tax-man's demands: 'Everybody does.' A church fellowship might infringe the copyright of books or cassettes, videos or compact discs: 'Everybody does.' And we remain blissfully unaware that these practices are blocking our pathway to freedom and preventing us from becoming the person God created us to be.

More subtly and perhaps more seriously, the cultural norm has bewitched us. It persuades us that the secret of our identity is to be found in the size of our pay packet or in the geographical area where we live or in the place where we spend our holidays. So we climb the professional ladder, trampling on others if necessary, in order to reach the top so that we can earn yet more money. Prestige and possessions, popularity and power, become the gods we secretly worship. And we remain blinded to the reality that unless these are held on an open palm, they will strangle our God-given personality, refusing us permission to be the humble, generous, care-free, compassionate people God created us to be.

More methods of Bible Study

Another way in which our Bible Study can aid us in our attempt to discover who we are in Christ and what it is he intends us to be is to work our way through a book of the Bible, asking ourselves another series of questions:

'What does this passage or book really mean?'
'Why did the writer express it in that way?'
'Why did he choose that particular word?'
'What was he intending to convey?'
'What would it have communicated to the original readers?'
'What does it imply for today's Christians?'
'What is God saying to me?'

To enable us to respond accurately to such questions, we shall want, from time to time, to reach for the commentaries, the concordances, the Bible dictionaries and other aids to help us deepen our understanding. This spade work is illuminating. It reveals the meaning of the original Greek or Hebrew words as well as the cultural context: the history and geography of Palestine, the social customs of contemporary and ancient village life, and the teaching style of Middle Eastern theologians.

Yet another way of studying the Scriptures is to attempt to discover what God says about pressing problems or particular pleasures like marriage, sexuality, friendship, giving, service, ambition, handling temptation, euthanasia, suffering, Sunday trading, debt, to mention a few.

I find it helpful, from time to time, to home in on a topic which currently concerns me. I sometimes do this while I am on retreat. I think, for example, of the occasion when my husband and I had gone on retreat, in part, to ask God to shed his light on our future. We had resigned from the leadership of the church we had worked in for nineteen years and had been invited to work for the church overseas. As the retreat wore on, the sense that God was calling us to leave England, at least for a while, became increasingly strong. I longed to be able to say a ready and joyful 'Yes' to the new vocation which was beginning to take shape. Instead, my mind seemed to focus on the sacrifices we would have to make if we responded to this call.

At this time, I found myself using the word 'grace' very frequently while I was writing in my prayer journal so I decided to make a study of this little-understood word. First I looked up all the references to the word in the Old Testament, then I turned to the New. After that, I referred to a Bible dictionary where I was reminded that the word 'grace' means, among other things, the love of God expressed as 'mercy' (used one hundred and forty-nine times in the Old Testament), 'kindness' (used thirty-eight times), loving-kindness (used thirty times), and 'goodness' (used twelve times). It also speaks of faithfulness and undeserved favour.

As the Bible translator Moffatt put it, Christianity 'is a religion of grace . . . no grace, no gospel'. Or, as the dictionary I was reading expressed it: 'every process of the Christian life is due to grace.' We are called by grace (Galatians 1:15); we are justified by grace (Romans 3:24); by the grace of God we are what we are (1 Corinthians 15:10), and by the grace of God we enter into the fullness of salvation (Ephesians 2:8).

As my mind juggled with these and other pieces of the jig-saw, I found a two-word picture taking shape. The words were: 'pure gift'. God's grace is pure gift. Our vocation is a gift, our salvation is a gift, our personality is a gift. I knew that I needed this gift to enable me to say 'Yes' to becoming the person God created me to be. I fell asleep that night begging for the gift. At three in the morning, I woke with that 'Yes' on my lips. It was another of those gloriously liberating moments when I knew that my attachment to Christ had been strengthened and that consequently I had been cut free from the need to cling to all I held dear, free to hold everything on an open palm, free to stretch out open hands knowing that whatever came into those hands next would come to me with the God I love.

The purpose of Bible Study

It is vital that we remember that the one purpose of Bible Study is not to accumulate facts *per se*, helpful to our meditation as these facts are. The purpose of Bible Study is that we may go beyond the written Word to encounter the Living Word, Jesus, to deepen our relationship with him and to be changed into his likeness.

Jesus himself makes this quite clear. Addressing a group of

rabbis and approved teachers of the Law on one occasion, he observed:

'You diligently study the Scriptures because you think that by them you possess eternal life. These are the Scriptures that testify about me, yet you refuse to come to me to have life' (John 5:39).

Those of us who delight in making our home in the Word of God through Bible Study need to heed this observation, just as those who clamour for more teaching in churches need to heed it. As Paul discovered, the study of the text can become a substitute for a living encounter with the Living Word. It can even become a way of avoiding such an encounter. When this happens, our study of the Bible could lead to the kind of living death Paul recalls:

'The letter kills, but the Spirit gives life' (2 Corinthians 3:6).

The letter can kill because it can lead to spiritual pride, what C.S. Lewis called 'priggery'. The spiritual prig pleads, 'Give us more teaching.' But the abundance of Bible knowledge inflates him with the puffed-up pride Jesus so loathed in the Pharisees. The spiritual prig boasts about the number of Bible verses he can recite by rote but pays no attention to Jesus's insistence that we should incarnate the Word – flesh it out in the nitty gritty of our daily lives. The spiritual prig insists that his interpretation of the Biblical text is foolproof, irrefutable, right. The implication is that everyone else is wrong.

The letter can kill because it can convince us that all we need to do to grow in grace is to store more and more information about God in the computer of our brain. But knowledge does not necessarily affect behaviour. I was reminded of this while writing this chapter. Since I was awake in the early hours of the morning, I decided to get up while it was still dark and therefore cool. I sat at my desk, switched on the light and began to write. I know, of course, that, in this part of the world, if you sit in a room with the windows wide open and the lights on, a motley collection of wild-life will join the party. First came the moths – some of them drowning in my cup of coffee. Then came the cicadas leaping from floor to desk and back again. These were followed by translucent green insects whose names I have not yet learned. My head told me to close the windows. Instead, I ignored my head-knowledge and continued to allow nature's menagerie to cramp my style.

It is so easy to do the same with the head-knowledge we acquire through Bible study.

We can live with the truth, but not in the truth, let alone living out the truth. There are even times when, like the student who came to see me on one occasion, we rebel at the clear implications of Scripture.

This student described his emotional entanglement with a fellow student and then proceeded to describe in detail their homosexual experimentations. He was clearly troubled, wanting to live life God's way but not knowing what that way was. I invited him to take a look at the Bible's teaching on such sexual practices and to draw his own conclusions. He did. Next time he came to see me, he seemed consumed with anger:

'It's so unfair. The church has explained away divorce. Some heterosexual Christians even manage to disregard the Bible's teaching on promiscuity. In twenty years' time they will have changed their views on homosexual behaviour. I'm just unlucky. Why should I be stuck with the Bible's rigid teaching on the subject? It makes me really angry with God.'

Those prophetic words were spoken fifteen years ago. And my student friend was amazingly accurate. Many Christians have explained away the Bible's teaching on homosexual activity and a whole range of other topics also: the sanctity of life, the need for a day of rest, Sunday trading, the place of women in marriage, the church and the community, to mention a few.

This approach to God, the pride and rebellion which results in a Christian adjusting his life-style to God's revealed Word, is not new. Adam did just this in Genesis 3. It crops up today with monotonous regularity. When we fall into this trap, we wave goodbye to a God-given opportunity of growing into the person he always intended us to become. And it seems inevitable that, from time to time, we will fall into this trap. But we need never remain ensnared. As we have seen, God has given us his Holy Spirit whose mission is to transform us. He is also the One who persuades us that, to become truly effective, our Bible Study must flow into Bible meditation.

For personal reflection

1. Experiment with some of the methods of Bible Study suggested in this chapter. When you find a method which works for you at the moment, use it regularly for a while before moving on to other methods.
2. Re-read Jesus's conversation with his would-be follower on p. 65. Notice that Luke does not record the outcome of the man's encounter with Jesus. Put yourself in the man's sandals, as it were. Imagine that *you* have had this conversation with Christ. How would you want to complete the conversation? What is is about your culture which might tug you away from following Jesus wholeheartedly?
3. Write a prayer from your heart which springs from this meditation.

Notes for Chapter Five

1. Andrew Murray, *The Spirit of Christ* (Anson D.F. Randolph and Company, New York, 1888) p. 90.
2. Andrew Murray, *The Spirit of Christ*, p. 90.
3. Professor Kenneth Bailey has lived and worked in the Middle East for the past forty years and has written a number of books on the parables as well as committing his teachings to audio and video cassettes. I am indebted to him for helping me to place the parables in their cultural context.
4. Professor Kenneth Bailey's insight.
5. Michael Green, *I Believe in Satan's Downfall* (Hodder and Stoughton, 1981) p. 53.

6

THE VALUE OF BIBLE MEDITATION

Bible meditation is to Bible Study what snorkelling is to swimming: an eye-opener, the stunning discovery of a hidden wonder world, a way of marvelling at mysteries.

This realisation dawned on me as I was preparing to write this chapter. I was in Oman at the time. On my first visit to one of Muscat's beautiful beaches, I simply enjoyed bathing in the silk-warm water. But on my second visit someone lent me their snorkel. It was then that I discovered that I was not swimming alone as I had thought. Rather I was being escorted by all kinds of exotic fish: blue fish, striped fish, transparent fish, angel fish, cuttle fish – even a baby turtle. Swimming will never again be the same for me. I shall always wonder what accompanies me or whether corals of every colour lie concealed on the sea bed.

Just as it is possible to swim all your life and remain totally unaware of the treasures of the sea, so it is possible to study the Bible all your life and remain blissfully unaware that it can flow into the method of musing or reflecting on God's revealed Word which the Psalmist describes when he writes: 'Oh, how I love you law! I meditate on it all day long!' (Psalms 119: 97). When God gives us the grace to meditate, however, we find ourselves enthralled or shocked by liberating truths which had formerly remained hidden – for meditation leads us beyond and beneath the surface of the written Word to encounter the Living Word. And the Divine Lover delights, in turn, to reveal to us not only himself but our own selves, gradually to transform us into his likeness.

In other words, whereas the study of Scripture primarily engages the mind, meditation on Scripture deliberately engages every part of our personality: not only the intellect, but the emotions also; not only the will, but the imagination and the body, the affections and the senses. In Bible meditation, God speaks to the most intimate depths of our hearts and encourages us to internalise and personalise his in-breathed Word. Then, gently and gradually, the Word changes us by promoting our growth and by bringing us to maturity and an ever-increasing measure of internal freedom.

Methods of meditation

Bible meditation has been in vogue for centuries. As we observed in the last chapter, the Psalmist meditated on Scripture. So did the prophets, Jesus's mother and Jesus himself. Bible meditation was also recognised by the early church. Bishops and teachers of the first seven centuries make this quite clear. They not only absorbed God's Word in their own hearts and minds, they encouraged the faithful to do likewise, drilling them in specific methods.

One ancient method, in particular, seems to be gaining in popularity today. It is the slow, reflective reading of Scripture which Peter Toon calls formative reading. The purpose of formative reading is to be 'formed' by the Word:

> that is, to be formed by Jesus Christ through the Holy Spirit, who both inspired and interprets the sacred text . . .
>
> I do not hold the Bible in my hand in order to analyse, dissect or gather information from it. Rather I hold it in order to let my Master penetrate the depths of my being with his Word and thus facilitate inner moral and spiritual transformation. I am there in utter dependence upon our God – who is the Father to whom I pray, the Son through whom I pray, and the Holy Spirit in whom I pray.[1]

So effective Bible meditation begins by coming to God and by pausing until we become aware of his presence. Our body can help or hinder this process. By sitting upright in a straight-backed chair, for example, or by kneeling on a prayer stool and by stretching out our hands in expectancy we can whisper to him and ourselves: 'I'm ready to receive whatever the Holy Spirit wants to give to me or show me today.'

It sometimes happens that, as we pause in this way, the sense of the presence of God fills the room in which we sit. Some people sense this more acutely than others. Whether we feel him or not, we know by faith that he is there loving, listening and speaking because he has promised never to leave us or forsake us.

When we are very tired or have been particularly busy, we may find it difficult to unwind in the way I describe in Chapter Four. At such times, playing quiet music can help us to shed the pressures of the day.[2] One of the quickest ways of shedding these pressures is not to deny them nor to push them on one side but rather to recognise them, name them and then place them, one to one, into the hands of the One of whom Peter wrote: 'Cast your cares on him, knowing that he cares about you' (1 Peter 5:7; my paraphrase).

Reflective reading

Some teachers of prayer liken this period of preparation to laying the table before a meal. When we do it with care, creativity and flair, our attitude to the meal and the people with whom we will share it undergoes a subtle but important change. So it is as we approach the banquet of God's Word.

When we are still and aware of his presence and have reached the stage of receptivity I also highlighted in Chapter Four, we are ready for the feast, so we read the chosen passage of Scripture. When selecting the passage or story for meditation, there is value in choosing one which we have previously studied so that the context and exegesis have been clarified for us. Now, we read it as slowly as possible, refusing ourselves permission to hurry. We read it reflectively, reminding ourselves that, on this occasion, our purpose is not to gather information nor to cover new ground. Rather, we read in order to be nourished, touched, healed and set free by the God who loves us. So as we read, we reverence every word. This means that, just as lovers read one another's letters expectantly and attentively, and just as they discover that a single word or phrase or symbol can speak volumes, so we read expecting our hearts to be touched. We read, not only the words, but between the lines also. We read expecting to be blessed and as one who waits to meet the Living Word who inspired the written Word. We therefore open the hidden parts of ourselves, praying that shafts of God's golden light will penetrate any pockets of darkness lurking inside us. And we become aware that there is a sense in which we are embarking on the same kind of slow, patient, ponderous search archaeologists embark on when they dig. We resolve to continue the search until we find our treasure.

Internalising the Word

This treasure will come to us in the form of a word or a phrase, a verse or a pen-picture which seems, somehow, to peep out from the page. When these words beckon and draw us to themselves, we stop, lay the Bible down and say the word or words over and over to ourselves or we dwell on the pen-picture. We then sink our hearts into the Word, to change the metaphor, in the same way as we sink our teeth into a succulent piece of steak. Gradually we reach the stage of wanting to chew what we have bitten off, in order, first, to extract its full flavour and then to prepare ourselves for the process of swallowing and digesting it.

In other words, this is the stage when we personalise and internalise the Word. There are several ways of doing this. We can ask it questions: 'Is there more to you than meets the eye? What are you saying? What are you saying to me?' We can tell it stories from our recent or past experience. We can receive its blessings, listen to its challenges and pause in case a mental picture rises inside us, allowing us to see or hear or sense the richness of the message.

When we are ready, we receive the Word into our innermost beings, allowing its truth to trickle from our heads into our hearts. We trust that, just as vitamins surreptitiously enrich our bodies when we take them, so the Word is working on us and in us as we assimilate it.

When the words have been sampled and savoured, swallowed and relished, it is time to rest and enjoy the afterglow of the meal. We rest with God, surrendering ourselves to his embrace, luxuriating in the sacredness of the moment

This way, we may find ourselves falling in love with God all over again because, very often, we shall be drinking in the incomprehensible: God is in love with us. As we sense his love flowing into us, we not only trust him, we entrust ourselves to him. We stop searching for him and enjoy the experience of being found by him. We become aware that at the centre of our being lies, not the nothingness or emptiness we feared, but God himself.

Responding and returning

This draws from our heart a response.

Sometimes our response will be laced with awe. Sometimes with gratitude. Sometimes we may find ourselves singing with joy. At other times we may weep the tears of years. Sometimes the Word will leave us protesting or doubting, angry or hurting. Even feeling cheated. At other times it will cause us to gaze at God with deep, heart-felt, passionate, adoring love.

Many people find it helpful to put their hearts on paper by recording their response in a prayer journal. Some write a letter to God expressing their feelings as fully as they can encapsulate them. Others simply jot down key words which would mean nothing to a casual reader but which are pregnant with meaning for themselves and God. Some write poetry. Others make their response pictorially using pastels or paints or felt-tip pens.

Each person will respond in their own way. The method we use is unimportant. What is important is that we allow the Word to make an impact on every layer of our being: our mind and our emotions, our imagination and our will, our attitudes and our relationships, our affections and our desires, our bias to sin and our pain and frustration, our successes and our failures, and the well-spring or core of our entire being. This way we gradually discover how to become the people God intended us to be. This way we will find ourselves tasting the experience James describes when he speaks of look[ing] intently into the perfect law that gives freedom . . . doing it . . . and being blessed in what we do (James 1:25 – see also v. 22).

One of the ways in which this verse is fulfilled in us is that when we have made our response, although we return to our daily routine, we do not stop meditating. The Word which we have digested has become a part of us, so whether we are lying in bed or walking to work, standing in the supermarket queue or caught in nose-to-tail traffic, the Word comes with us. And just as cows chew the cud, so we can regurgitate the Word by bringing it to mind, repeating it and pondering it afresh. This way, new insights may flood into our mind and continue to change our perceptions, attitudes and behaviour in the middle of the muchness and manyness of life. Such is the effectiveness of meditation.

I think, for example, of an occasion when I was extremely tired. I had just arrived home from leading a week-long retreat. Since a relative was in hospital, I had spent two hours with her and then returned home to make a meal for the family. But that evening, as I prepared to meditate on God's Word, I handed to him my tiredness and opened myself afresh to his re-energising Word. Then I read Zephaniah 3:14–20. Verse 17 drew me to itself in rather the same way as a magnet attracts pins: The Lord will renew you by his love (JB).

As I sank my heart[3] into these life-giving words, my mood changed from exhaustion to contentment and as I chewed and digested 'my' verse, I relaxed totally. As I rested with the Word, a mental picture helped me to discern what was happening. I found myself imagining that I was a battery lying in the battery-charger of God's love. There were times when I sensed myself being re-energised by this love so that my mood changed again – from contentment to shalom, that sense of well-being from which flows joy.

In my prayer journal, I recorded the relief I felt that Bible meditation had released me from the down-drag of exhaustion:

Dearest Father,

This prayer time reveals to me afresh how very relevant your Word is to my condition. You know how exhausted I feel today, how my batteries have completely run out of juice. Thank you that . . . you've simply encouraged me to rest and while I've been resting, I know *you've* been re-charging the batteries. Thank you that your arms are the cradle in which I lie and where I can be quietened after a hectic, draining week. Please continue to replenish my resources.

That week seemed full of fresh, daily demands but into each demand I regurgitated my verse: 'The Lord will renew you by his love.' So my attitude changed. Consequently I was set free from frustration, set free to receive the fresh supply of energy which flows from the fingers of God every moment of every day and set free to become the creative person God created me to be.

Other effects of Bible meditation

But it would be dishonest of me to imply that Bible meditation always leaves us feeling nurtured and loved. As I have already hinted, there are times when it appears to leave us desolate. I think, for example, of the first day of one retreat I made when I was meditating in a slightly different way on John 20, verses 19–23 – verses which describe Jesus's appearance to his disciples on the first Easter Sunday evening. While meditating on a Gospel story like this, it can be helpful to picture the scene as vividly as possible and then, rather than simply gazing at the picture as though you are watching a video, to imagine that you are able to step into the picture and interact with the characters concerned.

So, using my imagination, I had stepped into the Upper Room where the disciples had locked themselves into their fear and grief, their shock and bewilderment, and while I was there I had the thrill of encountering the Risen Lord. With the ears of my heart, I had heard his excited greeting: 'Shalom! Peace be with you.' Together with the disciples, I had held my breath as I gazed in adoration at his nail-pierced hands and wounded side. I had sensed the mood change in the disciples as joy percolated through their fear, turning their doubt to trust and faith, and I had taken off the sandals of my heart as Jesus drew near and breathed into me his Holy Spirit. But then, it seemed as though the One who had blessed me so richly and undeservedly suddenly slapped me in the face by saying:

'If you forgive people's sins, they are forgiven; if you do not forgive them, they are not forgiven' (v. 23, GNB).

The love which had welled up in my heart turned to anger and, when I left that Upper Room, I felt cheated and hurt, an emotional wreck.

So I asked myself some pertinent questions. Why did that reference to forgiving others prick the bubble? Could it be that Jesus was putting his finger on something in my life which needed addressing rather urgently? And then the pain of months rushed from the hidden recesses of my heart where I had repressed it.

For months a colleague and I had been locked in conflict. We had worked hard to understand and love one another but all our efforts had failed. It seemed that we had only to be in one another's presence to hurt each other – by a look, a sentence or even a silence. So we had recoiled, stunned and bewildered. Now, it seemed, instead of giving me the reprieve I longed for on this week-long retreat, Jesus was encouraging me to re-open the closed file and do the prayer work without which lasting reconciliation would have been impossible.

That day, my journal recorded not messages of love but rather an out-pouring of pain as I told the Lord how deeply I had felt wounded by this woman. I wrote pages explaining why I felt unable to forgive. In doing this, it was as though an abscess was lanced and the pus of bitterness and hatred burst from me on to the unwitting page of my journal. Even when I had completed this diatribe, I confessed that I still felt unable or unwilling to forgive but I added a tentative request: 'Give me the grace to be willing to be made willing to let go of the hurt and hatred: to forgive.'

Next day, I returned, in my meditation, to the same verse:
'If you forgive people's sins they are forgiven; if you do not
forgive them, they are not forgiven.'

In my imagination, I returned, too, to the Upper Room
where, again, I heard Jesus saying to the disciples and to
me: 'Look at my hands. Look at my side.' This time, I not
only looked, I crept up to Jesus and placed my finger in the
hole in his hand and slipped my hand into the wound in his side.
These wounds reminded me of the brutality of his death – the
price he was prepared to pay so that my many failures might
be forgiven. Slowly, my defences crumbled like chalk. Looking
into my Redeemer's eyes, I was able to pray with integrity the
prayer he taught us to pray: 'Forgive us our sins as we forgive
those who have sinned against us.' I knew that he understood
the full implications of this prayer. I knew, too, that not only had
this Bible meditation set my colleague free from the emotional
corner into which I had pushed her but that I had also been set
free from the poison which had been pulsating around my entire
being, polluting me and many other relationships.

I would have preferred to have begun my retreat on a
much cosier, more comforting note but the purpose of Bible
meditation is not necessarily to bring us comfort, though so
often it does do that. It is to bring us into an encounter with
the God who sometimes deems it necessary to help us clear
away the obstacles which bar us from enjoying the intimacy
he so much wants us to enjoy; who sometimes discerns that
ever-deeper levels of our personality need his healing, liberating
touch so that we can enjoy the wholeness into which he is always
leading us.

Use of the imagination

Some Christians balk at the idea of Bible meditation when
they realise that it involves engaging the imagination. Someone expressed the dilemma in this way when she put the
following in the Question Box during a retreat I was leading:

If I am honest, I do have doubts about the use of the imagination. There are several reasons for this. One is that in Genesis 6:5–6 we read that God was sorry he had made mankind 'for the imagination of his heart was evil continually'. Another is that the tower of Babel surely began in the imagination of man's heart. And in 2 Corinthians 10:5, we read about using spiritual weapons to 'cast down imaginations' (KJV). The imagination, like the rest of us, needs to be redeemed – it *is* being redeemed through the ongoing process of sanctification. But until this work is complete in eternity, do we not need to be cautious with our imagination? Cannot the Evil One who gained access to human imagination in Genesis, all too easily tinker with it today even in the case of a Christian?

If we take comments like these to their logical conclusions, it would appear that we are claiming that whereas at the Fall, Satan gained access to our imaginations, our minds remained gloriously untainted from his malicious meddling. But, of course, that is not true. As a result of the Fall, every part of our personality was affected and can now be used for good or for evil, channelled constructively or destructively. This includes the mind.

As we observed in the last chapter, our mind can convince us of the seeming necessity to live as children of our culture or it can persuade us to challenge our culture by ushering in the counter-culture of God's Kingdom.

Moreover, Paul's reflections on the mind are worthy of note. 'The mind of sinful man is death,' he claims (Romans 8:6). 'The sinful mind is hostile to God. It does not submit to God's law, nor can it do so' (Rom. 8:7). It cannot do so because 'the God of this age has blinded the minds of unbelievers, so that they cannot see the light of the gospel of the glory of Christ, who is the image of God' (2 Corinthians 4:4). Only the mind which is controlled by the Spirit is life and peace (Romans 8:6). We therefore live in constant and urgent need of that ministry Paul calls the renewal of the mind (Romans 12:2).

We also need to note that it is only the Authorised Version

(AV) or King James Version (KJV) which uses the word 'imagination' in the verses from Genesis quoted above. More modern translations seem to recognise that the word 'imagination' in earlier English meant not only the ability to see pictures, but was also shorthand for the thought-patterns of the unregenerate. So, for example, the NIV rendering of Genesis 6:5 reads: 'The Lord saw how great man's wickedness on the earth had become, and that every inclination of the thoughts of his heart was only evil all the time' instead of the older version: 'the imagination of his heart was evil continually'.

But there are other, more positive reasons why we should engage not just our minds but our imaginations also when we meditate on the Bible. The chief reason is that Jesus clearly expected us to do so.

As I underlined in *Open to God*,[4] unlike many of today's scholars and Christian teachers and writers, Jesus was not a Western theologian. He was a Middle Eastern theologian. He did not, therefore, appeal primarily to the intellect. He appealed first and foremost to the imagination, which was why he taught, not through carefully crafted three-point sermons, but through stories which he often left suspended so that his listeners would complete them for themselves. He also appealed to the eye gate, appearing to expect his hearers to visualise what he was describing: the farmer scattering his seed in the way some farmers in the Middle East still sow their crops; the woman sweeping her house with the vigour with which my neighbours here in the Eastern Mediterranean still sweep their homes: the shepherd who, at cost to himself, searched the ditches and dells until he had found and rescued the sheep who was as dear to him as a child. Similarly, Jesus appears to have expected his audience to enter into the parables, using their senses in the way some creatures use their antennae. So he appears to expect us to smell the yeast, to marvel at the effect it has on a lump of lifeless dough, to watch the loaf rising before our eyes.

This causes Richard Foster to conclude, and I agree with him:

We simply must become convinced of the importance of

thinking and experiencing in images. It came so spontaneously to us as children, but for years now we have been
trained to disregard the imagination, even to fear it . . .
The imagination is stronger than conceptual thought and
stronger than the will.[5]

Or, as Gerard Hughes expresses it:

The imagination is a wonderful and much neglected faculty.
It enables us to enter into the scenes of the Gospel with
our senses and our feelings as well as with our minds,
but it also projects into our conscious minds thoughts,
memories and feelings which, although hidden from us in
our subconcious, are, in fact, influencing our perception,
thinking and acting.[6]

Indeed, through using what C.S. Lewis referred to as the
'baptised imagination', our meditation may reveal to us that
our image of God is distorted, that we are riddled with guilt,
paralysed by past pain, crippled by an overwhelming sense of
worthlessness, or full of doubt rather than faith. We therefore
need to discover how to process our meditation so that,
whatever it reveals, we can use it, not to condemn ourselves,
but rather to find a new dimension of freedom.

Processing our meditation

One way of processing our meditation so that it helps us to
discover the kind of people God created us to be is to pause
when we have completed it and ask ourselves some pertinent
questions:
    'What was my predominant mood while I was meditating: joy
or sadness, peace or anxiety, strength or exhaustion, doubt or
hope, fascination or boredom or . . . ?'
    'Or did my moods fluctuate? If so, how? Did I lurch from fear
to faith or . . .'

'Were there times when my mind seemed to go blank or when nothing seemed to be happening? If so, what was happening in the seeming nothingness?'

'Which words or pen-pictures, phrases or experiences seemed particularly helpful?'

'When did negative feelings sweep over me and what name would I give to these feelings?'

'Were there any other obstacles which seemed to block my path to God: guilt, worthlessness, the memory of past hurts, a negative image of God, for example? If so, how have these left me feeling?'

Our response to these questions will determine what happens next. If the meditation left us feeling loved or comforted by God, for example, processing this discovery poses few problems. We can round off our time of prayer by relishing the memories of this fresh encounter with the indwelling Christ, allowing them to re-energise us and equip us for the tasks ahead.

If, on the other hand, our path to God seems blocked for some reason, or if the meditation has left us filled with a feeling of sadness or bogged down with worry, we will need to adopt a different procedure. Take guilt feelings, for example. Guilt can be a healthy reaction to our own wrong-doing. In this event, when guilt surfaces during our meditation, we need only acknowledge our failure and ask for the grace to receive God's free-flowing forgiveness. If we detect an internal struggle, which is not unlike a civil war when one part of our personality longs to repent while the other part remains in a stubborn state of rebellion, it is wise to allow the repentant part of ourselves to pray so that, in time, the other part of us can catch up.

But what about those occasions which happen to most of us from time to time, when guilt overwhelms us with a sense of worthlessness and seems out of all proportion to any misdemeanour we may have committed? What happens when we feel persistently unloved and unlovable? Gerard Hughes speaks helpfully of this not uncommon state of mind when he writes:

Salvador Dali has painted the crucified Christ suspended

above the globe of the earth. Let your imagination work on that image and speak to Christ dying on the cross. He has become the sin of the world and there is no crime, however hideous, which he has not taken on himself and forgiven. Tell Christ that although he has succeeded with the rest of the human race, he has met his match in you, and that not even his death can overcome your guilt. He may find all other human beings to be lovable, but you are God's mistake which he can never put right. If you can persist in this prayer, he will uncover a hidden source of guilt, which is pride, the refusal to let God be God to you, clinging to your guilt as though it were more powerful than his love.[7]

Silence

Gerard Hughes continues:

Another method is to sit in silence with your feelings of guilt and worthlessness, as though they formed a heap of rotting rubbish in front of you, and then pray to Christ to show himself through the mess. This is a useful exercise because in it you are not pretending, not hiding your guilt from yourself; you are acknowledging your own inability to remove it and allowing him to be what we can so easily express with our lips, but not with our inner being – our Saviour.[8]

Our liberator. The One who alone is able to set us free, not only from our guilt and shame but from ourselves also.

And if nothing seems to have happened, we do well to examine the nothingness. Like the man who attended a retreat I was leading on one occasion. I led the group in a meditation on Revelation 3:20 where Jesus says: 'Listen! I stand at the door and knock; if anyone hears my voice and opens the door, I will come into his house and eat with him, and he will eat with me' (GNB).

'Imagine you are in your own home,' I invited the group,

'and you hear a knock at the door. You know it is Jesus, so notice whether you decide to open the door or to pretend there is no one at home. If you open the door, notice whether you do it with a flourish, showing that you are pleased to welcome him or whether you do it reluctantly, aware that the beds are not made or that the washing up has not been done.'

As I continued in this vein, I noticed that this particular man was looking extremely uncomfortable, so during the coffee break which followed, I asked him how he had found the experience.

'It was a complete waste of time,' he retorted angrily.

'Would you like to tell me what happened?' I invited.

'Nothing happened,' he replied curtly. 'I've already told you that it was a complete waste of time.'

'Tell me about the nothing,' I persisted. Whereupon he explained that he lives in a mews flat in London. 'The door of my flat opens outwards,' he went on. 'When you told us Jesus was knocking on the front door, I went to it and opened it with such a flourish that I knocked Jesus over and had to help him to his feet again. That just shows you how stupid the experience was.'

Suddenly his anger evaporated, his jaw dropped and he exclaimed: 'Joyce! That's the story of my life. I've been so busy making money that I've had no time for Jesus recently. It's as though I've been knocking him over whenever he has attempted to come near to me. I see now that it's time to help him to his feet and invite him back into my life again.'

I was touched by the humility of this confession and moved to discover once more that, through Bible meditation, God had begun to put this man back in touch with the person he was created to be.

Such experiences are not rare. Such stories are numerous. The genius of Bible meditation is that it has the capacity to touch the many layers of our personality so that, little by little and bit by bit, more and more parts of our being are set free by God's liberating Spirit.

For personal reflection

1. Re-read the pages on reflective reading and internalising the Word (pp. 75–7). Then turn to Psalm 139 or a passage of Scripture you have been studying recently, and meditate on it in the way I describe. Try too make sure that you leave time to make your response.

2. Read John 20:19–23. Picture the scene as vividly as you can. Ask yourself the questions on pp. 84–5:

   'What was my predominant mood while I was meditating: joy or sadness, peace or anxiety, strength or exhaustion, doubt or hope, fascination or boredom or . . . ?

   'Or did my moods fluctuate? If so, how? Did I lurch from fear to faith or . . . ?

   'Were there times when my mind seemed to go blank or when nothing seemed to be happening? If so, what was happening in the seeming nothingness?'

   'Which words or pen-pictures, phrases or experiences seemed particularly helpful?'

   'Did negative feelings sweep over me at any time? If so, what name would I give to these feelings?'

   'Did anything obstruct my path to God: guilt, worthlessness, the memory of past hurts, a negative image of God, for example? If so, how have these left me feeling?'

   Make your response, bearing in mind p. 85.

3. There are two cassettes which can help people explore the methods of Bible meditation mentioned in this chapter: *Teach Us to Pray* published by Hodder and Stoughton, and *Teach Me to Pray*, published by Eagle. Both include music to bring listeners into stillness and guided meditations.

Notes for Chapter Six

1. Peter Toon, *Meditating as a Christian*, (HarperCollins, 1991) p. 58.
2. Several cassettes have been produced to help people come into this kind of stillness. Among them are: *Open to God* by Joyce Huggett, published by Hodder and Stoughton; *Reaching*

Out, *Impressions* and *In the Beginning* by John Gerightey and Simeon Wood, published by Eagle. And many people find music from the Taizé community, particularly the cassette, *Laudate*, is especially helpful.

3. Here I am drawing on the insights of Macrina Wiederkehr in her book, *A Tree Full of Angels* (Harper and Row, 1988) pp. 49–63.

4. Joyce Huggett, *Open to God* (Hodder and Stoughton, 1989) pp. 53–6.

5. Richard Foster, *Celebration of Discipline* (Hodder and Stoughton, 1980) p. 22.

6. Gerard Hughes SJ, *God of Surprises* (Darton, Longman and Todd, 1986) p. 37.

7. Gerard Hughes SJ, *God of Surprises*, pp. 84–5.

8. Gerard Hughes SJ, *God of Surprises*, p. 85.

HINDERED BY HURTS

Over and over again the Holy Spirit uses the medium of Bible meditation to remind us that we were created for love: both to give love and to receive it. One reason why he does this is to impress on us that we were created in the image of God – that is, in the image of the Holy Trinity: the Father, the Son and the Holy Spirit. This means that we were created to be like this tri-une God. A careful survey of the nature of the love which flows between these three persons who are so mysteriously one, helps to put us in touch with our potential.

Love is mutuality

Take Genesis 1, for example, where we eavesdrop on a conversation taking place within the sacred precincts of the heavenly places. 'God said, "Let *us* make man in our own image, in the likeness of ourselves"' (v. 26, JB, my emphasis). The unmistakable and undeniable use of the plural suggests that, as the Father, the Son and the Holy Spirit discussed the creation of the world, they dreamed another dream – of creating people who, like themselves, would be capable of communicating with each other and co-operating with each other – who could become co-creators with God.

Jesus invites us to take a further peep behind the curtains of the heavenly realms. During the Last Supper, while he prepares his disciples for his imminent departure, he reminisces in prayer: 'And now, Father, glorify me in your presence with the glory I had with you before the world began' (John 17:5). John provides

us with a thumb-nail sketch of that glory when, in the prologue
of his Gospel, he writes:

'Before the world was created, the Word already existed; he
was with God, and he was the same as God . . . Through him
God made all things; not one thing in all creation was made
without him' (John 1:1, 3, GNB).

Many Bible scholars also believe that Proverbs 8:27-31 (JB)
refers to Jesus's relationship with his Father before the Holy
Spirit shone like the sun over the darkness which was to become
the world:

> When he fixed the heavens firm, I was there,
> when he drew a ring on the surface of the deep,
> when he assigned the sea its boundaries . . .
> when he laid down the foundations of the earth,
> I was by his side, a master craftsman,
> delighting him day after day,
> ever at play in his presence,
> at play everywhere in his world.

By putting together these pieces of the jig-saw, it becomes
apparent that, before the beginning of creation, a relationship
existed between three co-equal persons. This relationship
was characterised by co-operation, communication and two-
directional love – giving love and reciprocal love. Since we
were born in the image of this tri-une God, it follows that
we were born capable of and needing relationship. Indeed, the
author of Genesis goes on to underline that even in Paradise
an intolerable loneliness held the first man in its deathly grip
until the opportunity for relationship with a like-minded person
was provided. God's profound statement, 'It is not good for the
man to be alone,' seems to have been etched on our souls ever
since. It is a cry which finds an echo in so many hearts today.
Like Andy – a young man who came to see me while I was in
the middle of writing this chapter.

'Impoverished. That's a good word to sum me up. That's just
how I feel,' he admitted and went on to relate the way in which
this realisation had surfaced for him that very evening.

'I was driving home through the country lanes this evening and the sun was low in the sky, just peering through the trees. It was beautiful. And I thought back to last week when I was on a skiing holiday in the mountains. It was magic, you know. As we reached the top of one mountain, you could look ahead and see mile after mile of virgin snow. Not a single foot-mark marred it. It was wonderful. So much beauty. Such good health. I've got a fulfilling job, too – in fact I have to tear myself away from it, I enjoy it so much. Yet some days I wake up and wonder: is this all life is? And inside me there's an emptiness. I'm hollow, an empty shell. The dull ache gnaws away inside me and I wonder if I can live for another forty years carrying the burden of my aloneness.'

My heart went out to this young man who had grown so keenly aware that a person's deepest need is for relationship because, as we talked, he admitted that he had never learned how to forge close friendships and even now, successful though he was in so many ways, he would not know where to begin.

Difficulties in loving

This problem is not unique to Andy. Many of us would confess to loving with a limp which has handicapped us for years, if not all our lives. We stumble in and out of relationships because we lack self-esteem and, as the contemporary author and psychiatrist Jack Dominian so rightly reminds us: 'To be and feel good in being oneself is the key to self-love and self-love is the key to all personal loving.'[1]

Dr Dominian goes on to put his finger on another reason why many of us become emotional cripples, in his shrewd observation that 'so much hinges on the way our constitutional make-up interacted with the way our parents behaved towards us'.[2] I like this emphasis because the assumption is frequently made that we are who we are because of the things that our parents or other significant people in our lives did or neglected to do. That is not strictly correct. Our parents may have given us what is commonly called today, 'good enough parenting',[3] yet the way we received and perceived their love may have caused us to emerge from childhood into adulthood feeling insecure or of little worth, lacking in self-esteem or self-confidence, unable to receive either affection or affirmation, feeling unloved and unlovable. We may feel so bad about ourselves that, deep-down, we are convinced that who we are and what we have to offer in relationships is worthless.

Childhood vulnerability

Because we come into the world as helpless babies and because the maturing process takes us through the vulnerability of childhood and adolescence, there are endless opportunities for seemingly irrevocable damage to be done.

Take our arrival into the world, for example. For some babies, this is the first joyous adventure into a new environment where clearly they are wanted, loved and cherished: But for others, birth is not an adventure but a trauma. As author and counsellor Edward Moss reminds us:

> there is a good deal of evidence to suggest that if a baby
> is unwanted or resented, or if the mother herself is ill or
> miserable or insecure during the pregnancy or the birth,
> this can make the process more of an exhausting ordeal,
> less of a joyful venture.[4]

He goes on to explain that such birth traumas can cast long shadows over the person's future.

But our vulnerability accompanies us beyond babyhood and into childhood. Since these are the phases of our lives where important foundations are laid, like trust, self-acceptance, pride in achieving and pleasure of self-expression, our propensity for being badly hurt accelerates. Because children are resilient, they find coping mechanisms to over-ride emotional knocks and bruises at the time they occur. But the patterns of behaviour they devise are not necessarily healthy, neither does the memory of them die. It lives on, capable of being activated in adulthood, when a person comes under stress or, like Andy, flounders in the attempt to make close relationships. The consequences can then be dire.

In *Habitation of Dragons*, Keith Miller records the tragic tale of Alice – a woman whose inability to forge close friendships in adulthood was traced to the emotional injuries inflicted on her when she was a child:

> When I was a tiny little girl, I was put in an orphanage. I was not pretty at all, and no-one wanted me. But I can recall longing to be adopted and loved by a family as far back as I can remember. I thought about it day and night. But everything I did seemed to go wrong. I tried too hard to please everybody who came to look me over, and all I did was drive people away. Then one day the head of the orphanage told me a family was going to come and take me home with them. I was so excited, I jumped up and down and cried. The matron reminded me that I was on trial and that it might not be a permanent arrangement. But I just knew it would be. So I went with this family and started school in their town – a very happy little girl. And life began to open up for me, just a little.
>
> But one day, a few months later, I skipped home from school and ran in the front door of the big old house we lived in. No-one was at home, but there in the middle of the front hall was my battered old suitcase with my little coat thrown over it. As I stood there and looked at that suitcase, it slowly dawned on me what it meant . . . they didn't want me. And I hadn't even suspected . . . That happened to me seven times before I was thirteen years old.[5]

Sadly, this is not an isolated incident. Alice's heart-rending testimony could be echoed by far too many people whose ability to trust has been destroyed by repeated rejections. As Jack Dominian explains:

> The absence of a safe physical and emotional attachment primes such a person to regard its surrounding world

with suspicion. Instead of security it acquires the fear of being abandoned, unwanted or rejected. This fear becomes gradually a part of its life so that it expects those close to it to act in a similar manner. Such a person expects to be let down, rejected, hurt, attacked or even destroyed by others. They are particularly vulnerable to suspicion about the intentions of others. Such vulnerable people find it hard to establish relationships of trust and both their freedom and integrity of relating are restricted.[6]

But Simon was not rejected by his parents. They loved him so much that they wanted the very best for him. They even made huge personal sacrifices so that Simon could be sent to boarding school. Unfortunately, it had not occurred to them to explain to their son why they believed that this particular plan lay in his best interests. So Simon, a sensitive, creative child, was devastated at the age of eleven to be presented with a *fait accompli*: he was to become a boarder at the nearby school.

'Why?' was the question which burned inside him as he struggled to adjust to life away from home. 'What have I done wrong? Why don't they want me at home?' He dared not voice these questions lest his parents should accuse him of being insolent and, as he thought, love him even less. So he fought back the tears which frequently threatened to betray the river of sorrow continually flowing inside him.

He tried to come to terms with the hurly-burly of boarding school which so many of his peers seemed to relish. But he was not the sporty type who quickly gathered round himself a group of like-minded, out-going friends. He was a bookworm who sought privacy and peace where he could indulge in the fascinating world of ideas.

Term after term saw no improvement in his ability to adjust to boarding-school life. At the beginning of every holiday, he determined to pluck up courage to ask his parents if he could become a day boy. Each holiday his courage failed. Gradually, as the years wore on, his ability to give and receive love dwindled to a puddle. But the lovelessness hurt. The hurt gave rise to hatred and anger. No one suspected the inner ferment because Simon succeeded in camouflaging the real situation with a plastic smile.

Simon's story, too, will resonate with many readers – not necessarily because they were packed off to a boarding school against their will or better judgment, but because they have been caught up in other transitions for which they were unprepared.

As Edward Moss reminds us, if these transitions are abrupt:

> there may well be a tendency to create a sort of shell round the inner personality. This shell becomes the outward personality of the child, while the inner, more sensitive side finds no expression, is not encouraged or developed, and gradually disappears from consciousness. This can produce in later years an adult who is rigid in conforming to an image, rather than spontaneous in expressing his or her true self, one who finds it hard to be in touch with his or her emotions, one who is afraid of losing control and whose emotional life is in some degree underdeveloped and immature.[7]

Adulthood

Unfortunately, the human psyche remains vulnerable beyond childhood and into adulthood. Human beings are capable of being emotionally wounded to the day they die.

I recall, for example, a conversation I once had with an elderly member of the church I once attended. When she worshipped, this woman's face would glow with wonder, love and praise, and I loved to watch her. But sometimes, when she and I spent quality time together, she would show me the hurting side of herself. Her husband had died, her daughter had committed suicide and, one by one, the friends with whom she had spent so much of her life had 'died off', as she put it. This left, not only the inevitable ache of bereavement, but a reluctance to reach out to others in love. 'It hurts so much when someone you love is taken away,' she explained.

I understood. We do not need to wait until we are in the upper eighties to experience the sense of loss which sweeps over us when a loved one is removed through death, divorce, or some other separation. We do not need to wait until we are old to discover the reluctance we feel in the wake of such separation to reach out to others and to explore new friendships.

Young adults may find their ability to love blocked for different reasons. I think, for example, of a young man I met on one of my trips to the Far East. We will call him Gee Ming.

Gee Ming used to lead the youth group of the church he attended. He loved the young people and they responded positively and warmly to his leadership. But Gee Ming, a new convert, was a young man with heavy financial commitments. Over a period of time, unknown to anyone in the church, he got into serious debt. Shame about his predicament prevented him from discussing the situation with his pastor or with the elders of the church. Instead, he fell back into a way of coping which had been all too familiar to him before he committed his life to Christ: gambling, speculating, embezzlement and even overt theft. He knew that these practices were wrong but a voice inside him would whisper: 'It will only be for short while, then you can live like a Christian again.' This voice sounded so sensible and so wise. But by the time I met him, he had withdrawn from the fellowship, resigned from leadership of the youth group and was actively avoiding any encounter with his former Christian friends.

'It's over now – the church, I mean. They were my family. It's left a big hole in my life and I don't know how to fill it.'

Gee Ming had become a lonely, lost and forlorn man whose life, at that moment, seemed to be devoid of love.

Again, such incidents are not rare in the experience of young adults. They venture into the big, uncharted sea of work with no one to guide them. Having little or no experience to draw on, they rely on the few insights and strengths they have acquired during their teenage years. When they are brought face to face with situations which challenge their youthful idealism, their limited expertise and even their faith – relationship problems, problems with management, work problems, financial problems, the inability to find employment and so on, their ability to give and receive love may well suffer a severe set-back. Even so, what they urgently need at this time is a great deal of understanding and tender loving care.

If someone like Alice so much as sniffs rejection, she may well curl up in a prickly ball like a hedgehog and become uncommunicative. Or, someone like Simon may well appear to be charming – or sweet if they are a woman – but this charm and sweetness may well camouflage a seething volcano. Unexpected change like redundancy, divorce, adultery, betrayal of other kinds, could cause the volcano to erupt.

Some solutions

That is the bad news. It is bad news because it restricts our freedom to become the loving and lovable people God created us to be. The good news is that we need not live for ever out of an 'unhealed centre'. Healing is available. Very occasionally this healing is instant. Almost always it is gradual. It comes in a vast variety of ways. In this chapter, we high-light two of these ways and in the next chapter home in on many more.

One way is through pastoral counselling or even through psychotherapy. I like the way Edward Moss defines this instrument of healing:

'It is the function of counselling or psychotherapy to provide the framework of concerned attention, love and support, within which the individual is enabled to complete this bit of growing up.'[8]

In other words, a counsellor or psychotherapist may help the person being counselled to trace the problem back to its source and will seek to help them to establish new patterns of behaviour so that they can be set free to become the loving, lovable people God created them to be.

While I was in the middle of writing this chapter, the telephone rang. The caller was a friend who has been on the receiving end of professional counselling for the past two years. 'Outwardly nothing has changed,' she confessed. 'But inwardly, a lot is happening. I know that I am being set free. I know that I am becoming more "me". There's a long way to go yet but I'm getting there.'

Many of us who have benefited from the wisdom, insights and love of sensitive, professional counsellors would echo that confident cry. Like Simon, the young man whose ability to love was impaired by his reaction to his parents' decision to send him to boarding school. He received counselling over a period of many months. During the sessions, he was brought face to face with the questions he longed to put to his parents at the age of eleven. He was able, too, to process the anger which had blazed inside him throughout his childhood and early adult years. He was also able to confront the methods he had used to cope with the problems he encountered at boarding school, face the lessons the experience had taught him about himself and discover how he could re-negotiate life on a new set of terms. Slowly, his latent, God-given ability to love re-emerged.

Simon once likened the healing process to the drip-by-drip thaw which happens when snow and icicles begin to respond to the warmth of rising temperatures. At first he found the melting process alarming. But when he realised that the thaw could be slow and steady, persistent and gentle, his plastic smile was replaced with a genuine one. Little by little he found within himself the resources to reach out a rescuing hand to others in need and, eventually, to learn to ask others for help. He was even able to understand why his parents had acted in the way they did and to let go of the resentment he had harboured against them from puberty on.

Inner Healing

There used to be a time when it was believed that professional counselling was the only route towards wholeness that a person could take. But the past twenty years or so have produced enough evidence to show that God is using other ways to set people free to love and be loved.

I think, for example, of the ministry of inner healing.

Francis MacNutt, a man who has been used by God in the

healing ministry for the past thirty years or so, defines inner healing in this way:

> The basic idea of inner healing is simply this: that Jesus, who is the same yesterday, today, and forever, can take the memories of our past and:
> 1. Heal them from the wounds that still remain and affect our present life.
> 2. Fill with his love all these places in us that have been empty for so long.
>
> The idea behind inner healing is simply that we can ask Jesus Christ to walk back to the time we were hurt and to free us from the effects of that wound in the present. This involves two things then:
> 1. *Bringing to light* the things that have hurt us. Usually this is best done with another person; even the talking out of the problem is in itself a healing process.
> 2. *Praying the Lord to heal the binding effects of the hurtful incidents of the past.*
>
> Some of these hurts go way back into the past; others are quite recent.[9]

As I have explained in *Listening to Others*,[10] I have benefited enormously from this gentle, sensitive ministry. So did Gill.

Gill once worshipped in the same church as me. By her own confession, she was an inquisitive little girl. Like many chidren, she frequently tuned in to adult conversations and, like many children, was quick to absorb facts but slow to interpret them accurately. Since she was a sensitive child, snippets of conversations she overheard would tumble round in her mind as clothes tumble round in a washing machine. Some of the things she overheard seriously dented her self-esteem. When she came to see me on one occasion she vividly recalled and described one such incident.

She was six years old at the time and had gone, with her mother, to the family doctor who was also a friend of the family. After the doctor had given her a routine medical examination,

Gill dressed herself behind the curtained screen where she was out of sight but not out of ear-shot. So she heard the doctor say in a casual, jocular kind of way: 'Of course, you realise that Gill will never be a teacher or anything like that? She's not clever enough.'

This observation not only tumbled round her head, it wormed its way into her heart and lodged there – hidden but neither lifeless nor powerless. Although Gill never consciously recalled the incident as she grew up, from that moment she lived within its limitations.

Throughout her late teens, for example, and even into her early twenties, whenever she was invited to accept responsibility at work or in the church, she would giggle nervously and brush such invitations aside with a dismissive comment like, 'Oh! Thank you ever so much for inviting me but I couldn't do anything like that – I'm not good enough.' It was as though her memory played on her perception of herself the kind of tricks a hall of mirrors plays on peoples' bodies. The reflection she saw was grossly misshapen.

This reflection was unexpectedly exposed when I invited her to become a Sunday School teacher. She refused. But some time later she reopened the conversation:

'You know, I don't understand myself. I really love children, as you know. I think they're really lovely. But when you asked me to be a Sunday School teacher recently, I panicked. "I couldn't. Oh! I couldn't," I said to myself. "Think of all the responsibility. I'm not capable of coping with that. Not good enough." But there's another part of me that knows I *could* do it. And that makes me really cross with myself. I really want Jesus to set me free from whatever it is that's holding me back so that I can serve him as I want to.

When we prayed together, asking God to expose the source of her feelings of inferiority, the old memory of the doctor's surgery flooded into Gill's mind.

I invited her to return, in prayerful imagination, to that surgery; to become, as far as she was able, in her imagination, little six-year-old Gill. She did.

'Yes. I'm there. I can see it all clearly. And I can hear the doctor telling my mother that I wouldn't be clever enough to be a teacher.'

We then went on to ask God to reveal to us whatever he wanted to show Gill about herself.

In the silence which followed, some words from Isaiah came into my mind. Although these words were originally a message for the nation of Israel, they convey comfort for every child of God and I sensed that God was wanting to remind Gill of them now:

> Fear not, for I have redeemed you . . .
> you are precious and honoured in my sight
> and . . . I love you.
>
> (Isaiah 43:1, 4)

> You will be like a beautiful crown for the LORD.
> No longer will you be called 'Forsaken,' . . .
> Your new name will be 'God Is Pleased with Her' . . .
> Because the LORD is pleased with you.
>
> (Isaiah 62:3–4, GNB)

As I read these promises aloud, I heard Gill gasp. She told me what had been happening to her in the silence. In her mind's eye she had seen a picture of a huge hand which she took to be the hand of God. On the open palm, held up for all to see, lay a priceless jewel which God seemed to assure her was the way he viewed her. We had asked him to show us what his perception of Gill was and, with awe, we sensed that he had spoken: through the prophet and through a picture.

It was a liberating moment in that it was as though the finger of God had lifted the arm of the record player from the disc which used to pound out the message: 'You're not clever Gill . . .,' then taken the old record and smashed it. Instead, he sang a new song which was to tumble round Gill's head for a very long time:

> You are precious . . .
>   and honoured . . .

I love you
And I'm pleased with you.

Although the past was still the past, although what had happened in that surgery all those years ago could not be reversed, the sting had now been removed from Gill's memory so that, gradually, it lost its power to restrict her freedom.

I would like to emphasise that word 'gradually'. It is rare that a single prayer reverses the message that the unhealed areas of our lives pump into our consciousness. Inner healing is almost always a process. It was for Gill. Over the months, as she assimilated the new song which now carolled through her brain, she gained in self-confidence and blossomed. She did become a Sunday School teacher and loved it so much that she went on to train as a primary school teacher. While she was training, she also became the worship leader of the church she attended. Some two years after our prayer time together, I talked to her after a meeting. She grinned broadly, brought me up to date with her progress and made the telling comment: 'It's as if I've finally grown up. It's great.'

For personal reflection

1. Read, as slowly and reflectively as possible, Psalm 139:1–18. Just as the Psalmist here reviews his life, take time to review yours. One way of doing this is to write down eight to twelve significant events of your life, beginning with your birth and ending with the present moment. As you recall the past, ask yourself the question:

   'How has God revealed his love to me at various stages of my journey through life?' Relish every memory of his love. Write a prayer of praise and thanks.

2. Or echo this prayer:

   Lord God, we your human children are learning from experience that we must have love; without it we go wrong. We see how little ones without the warm love of father and mother, never really recover. Every soul cries out, 'I want to be loved'. Lord, it takes a lot of faith to think that out of the billions of souls you love each one, as if he were an only child. Nothing can kill your love for me . . . nothing I do, whatever happens to me, wherever I go, even in the hells I make for myself. O Father and Mother God.[11]

3. Reflect on Jeremiah 31:3, (GNB):
   'I have always loved you, so I continue to show you my constant love.'
   And this promise from God:

Your days as a small child are too complicated for you to remember. I, your Creator, see the ways circumstances crippled you. I haven't forgotten one joy or one sorrow that you experienced. I know how these joys and sorrows have reached down through all the years of your life, freeing you, or binding you, making your heart sing, or making your heart cry. I know the healing that your life-tossed child soul needs. I can loose the tethers and free you from all that began to bind you from the moment you were conceived . . . for you were conceived from My heart . . . in My heart, and of My heart.

With a father's love let Me dissolve all that binds you . . . let Me set you free! Let Me loosen the grips of crippling experiences.

Notes for Chapter Seven

1. Jack Dominian, *The Capacity to Love* (Darton, Longman and Todd, 1985) p. 13.
2. Jack Dominian, *The Capacity to Love*, p. 13.
3. Winnicott's phrase.
4. Edward Moss, *Growing Into Freedom* (Eagle, 1993) p. 8.
5. Keith Miller, *Habitation of Dragons* (Word Books, 1970) pp. 185–6.
6. Jack Dominian, *The Capacity to Love*, p. 74.
7. Edward Moss, *Growing into Freedom*, pp. 22–3.

8. Edward Moss, *Growing into Freedom*, p.11.
9. Francis MacNutt, *Healing* (Ave Maria Press, 1984) pp. 181–2.
10. Joyce Huggett, *Listening to Others* (Hodder and Stonghton, 1988).
11. George Appleton, *Prayers From a Troubled Heart* (Darton, Longman and Todd, 1983) p. 48.
12. Joan Hutson, *Heal My Heart, O Lord* (Ave Maria Press, 1976) p. 7.

8

BECOMING THE PERSON GOD MADE ME TO BE

Inner healing and counselling need not compete with each other. It is not unusual for a person gripped in the winter of lovelessness to benefit from both. An experienced Christian counsellor might use counselling skills during one session and prayer ministry insights in another. Alternatively, a psychotherapist might call on someone involved in prayer ministry to work in partnership with him, the one working with the client using therapeutic skills, and a pastor or other mature Christian praying with the same client on other occasions. With the client's permission, they will keep in touch with one another until the client takes significant steps towards wholeness.

People like Alice, the little girl I mentioned who was so emotionally battered during her childhood, may well need both systematic counselling and inner healing if they are to be set free to love in the way I described at the beginning of the last chapter. She will neither find it easy to trust enough to receive love again nor to take the risk of giving love. After all, she runs the risk of being rejected all over again, and then what? Nor will she find it easy to learn to communicate her truest feelings or to co-operate with others in the way we see the members of the Holy Trinity relating.

It may be that, with someone like Alice, another of the many methods God uses to bring people into greater wholeness will be the route he takes. For when a person has been so damaged that they dare not lift the lid of Pandora's box for fear that the past will somehow swamp them again, God gently woos them with an undemanding healing touch. I think, for example, of the prayer ministry which John Wimber, David and Mary Pytches, Leanne Payne and others have brought to our notice, as a result of which numerous emotionally crippled Christians have learned to love again.

This form of ministry differs from the method of inner healing I described in the last chapter, though technically this could also be called inner healing since it brings about a greater internal wholeness. It differs in this way. Instead of asking the person to go back, using the vividness of their imagination, to the place and time when they were wounded, and instead of asking the hurting person to picture Jesus in the scene as I did with Gill in chapter seven, we give the person the opportunity to share with us as much or as little of their story as seems appropriate, and then we make it clear that we are going to ask the Holy Spirit to fall upon them to do in them and for them whatever it is that he discerns is right at that moment. We invite the person simply to relax and to open themselves to receive God's Spirit. Then we call on the Holy Spirit to come in whatever way he should choose.

The person may not see anything in the way Gill saw the picture of God's hand holding the jewel. But very often they become aware of an indescribable overwhelming of the Spirit which is perhaps not unlike the way he overshadowed Mary when Jesus was conceived.

Just as that overshadowing produced the miracle of the Son of God's conception within a woman's womb, so the results of this kind of prayer suggest that deep, vital and lasting changes frequently occur.

Francis MacNutt quotes from a letter written to him by a woman he once prayed for in this way:

> As you placed your hands very lightly on my forehead, a feeling of weightlessness came over me . . . There was this feeling of peace. Although I was semi-conscious, it was as if I were in another world which was very peaceful . . . so I just stayed there realizing for the first time in my life that Jesus loved me and forgave me my sins.[1]

Such testimonies are not rare. Such healing takes place frequently. It cannot be analysed or explained but it changes the lives of severely damaged people and brings them closer to discovering the person who lives inside them who has been trapped for decades by the haunting memories of past hurts.

Sometimes, as in the case of the woman Francis MacNutt mentions, when the Holy Spirit falls on a person in this way, the feeling of weightlessness referred to causes them to fall to the ground. As this woman put it in her letter:

'I got this feeling like I was falling and I could feel Father's hands grasping my head . . . Then I just went down like a feather, so softly. I felt weightlessness, but I was always conscious; I just had no control over my body.'[2]

Bible Meditation

When such healing comes, however it comes, it is like putting on a new pair of spectacles or suddenly hearing the first blackbird in Spring. And the years have shown me that, very often, the healing comes softly and gently, not when we are clamouring for it in a counselling session or a healing service, but when we least expect it, when we are on our own praying or meditating on a passage of Scripture or 'just being'.

That, at least, has been my experience.

In *Listening to Others*,[3] I have referred to my own birth trauma – how my mother went blind at my birth and the effect that had on my ability to love and be loved. In that same book, I referred to the healing which has trickled into my life over the years – through counselling and through prayer ministry. But inner healing, as I have said, is a process. It is as though God gives us as much healing as we need to bring us to a plateau from which we can live and relate with increasing freedom and maturity, and then surprises us with the joy of a fresh healing touch.

I have known the theory of this for many years but it had not occurred to me that my own healing process in this area was incomplete until I was meditating on Isaiah 66 on one occasion

some eighteen years after the first counselling session I had
received. This was what I read:

> Oh, that you may suck fully
> of the milk of her comfort,
> That you may nurse with delight
> at her abundant breasts.
> As nurslings, you shall be carried in her arms
> and fondled in her lap;
> As a mother comforts her [child],
> so will I comfort you.
>
>   (Isaiah 66:11,12, JB)[4]

'Picture God as a comforting mother holding your inner child
close to her breasts,' suggested the author of the book I was
using to help me in my meditation. When I read that suggestion,
my first reaction was to recoil. Then I felt my heart freeze.
Something inside me refused to continue meditating. I closed
the book, put it down and, with a mighty heave, pushed away
the ambivalence which had risen unbidden to the surface of my
mind. I was overseas on a teaching tour at the time and faced a
busy day, so I spent the rest of my prayer time preparing myself
for the day ahead and thought no more about this curious act of
avoidance.

Two days later, however, while I was still 'coming to' as it
were after a good night's sleep, it was as though the bedroom
where I was staying was filled with the presence of God. It
almost seemed as though the Beloved had come through the
open window and enfolded me in tenderness. In fact, when I
tried to explain it later to the person in whose home I was
staying, I simply said: 'I had a visit from the Tender One this
morning,' and I remember being relieved when she asked no
questions but seemed to know what I meant.

I did not know that morning what I now know; that God
was preparing to take me on another lap of the journey
into wholeness. That morning, I simply luxuriated in the tender,
gentle, motherly love which enfolded me. Over the next few
days, while I stayed in that home, every morning started in the

same way: with the acute awareness of the enveloping presence of the Tender One. This continued for several days after I had left that place which had become holy ground for me. In the retreat house where I was leading the Easter retreat I referred to in Chapter Four, I was still conscious of the overshadowing of the Tender One. But then everything changed.

For no apparent reason, I found myself re-living, in my dreams and in my prayer times, the trauma of my birth. I was still on the teaching tour, still busy, still coping outwardly, but inwardly, I was in turmoil. At first, I thought the Tender One had deserted me but one warm, sunny day, as I sat on the shore of a lake trying to understand the inner turmoil and trying to spread it before God, the loving presence was there for me again – me the adult and me the baby. As memories of my birth flooded my memory yet again, I felt tender arms receiving me into the world and instinctively I knew that the deep inner wound which had been touched as I knelt at the foot of the Cross on Good Friday had been healed once and for all.

At first I failed to appreciate the connection between the visit of the Tender One and the exposure of this primal pain but during the retreat which sandwiched these two events, I 'happened' to discover a little book on the bookshelves of the retreat house: *The Way of Tenderness* by Kevin O'Shea. In it, he explains that tenderness

is not something efficient, executive, managerial. It does not belong to the domain of getting things done. There is nothing violent in it, nothing strong in it. It is not manipulative, not task-oriented, not a thing of action. It belongs to being, rather than to doing, and to feeling, and to resting, in peace, at depth. It is a quality of being related, it is the limitlessness of being so, without strain or fear. There is something of love in it. It is the relaxedness that comes from knowing by experience that one is thoroughly and totally loved . . . If we could ask ourselves, 'at this very moment, right here, do I honestly believe that God likes me – not loves me, since He has to do that theologically, but likes me?' and if we could say,

'Yes He does,' and mean it, there would be a relaxedness
and a gentleness with us that is close to what we are
calling 'tenderness' . . . We could feel that we could
love our whole life-story, that we are graced, and made
beautiful, by the providence of our own history. That is
what 'tenderness' might mean.[5]

The phrase, 'knowing by experience that one is thoroughly
and totally loved,' and the sentence, 'We could feel that we
could love our whole life-story,' seemed to sum up what I
was experiencing, in greater depth than ever before. After I
had pondered these insights, I read on.

The little booklet helped me to see that when we have experienced true tenderness, we are less afraid to come close to the
pain and hurt which lies embedded in us. Instead of fighting it
or denying it, we discover within us the resources to take 'a
good, soft look at it'.[6] We can be calm about it, linger over it,
not be overwhelmed by it. And we discover that it has lost some
of its terror. Now that we have experienced true tenderness,
the trauma seems, somehow, to be more manageable. There
comes a moment of 'recognition' – a moment which proves to
be constructive, creative, integrative and curiously healing. It
is a quiet moment, a moment of intense and deep experience
and awareness. Although we could not describe it in words,
we are aware that it is having a profound effect on us. It is as
though the safe boundaries we had set in place inside us were
gradually dissolving. Yet we are at peace. Our whole being is
touched, hushed, held.

We can remain at peace because tenderness opens our eyes
to the reality that inner integration does not necessarily lie
ahead of us in the realm of the 'not yet': 'It opens out to
us a unity and an integrity we could never have claimed for
ourselves, or found our path to arrive at it.'[7] But it is for
now. And when our barriers melt inside us, our eyes refuse
to focus fully on ourselves. Instead, we become more fully
involved with the gift and the Giver. Instinctively, we trust
both. They make us not so much vulnerable as transparent,
that is, being consciously and completely open to a Presence

which cannot and will not inflict hurt but which will, instead, touch totally the core of our being. Such is the level of our trust that we open more and more of ourselves to both the Giver and the gift. This is 'frailty smiled at'.[8] As we continue to unfold in the warmth of tenderness, we find ourselves able to befriend the dark depths of ourselves. When we do this, what we find in these hidden depths no longer masquerades as destructive forces but rather reveals themselves for what they are: qualities and events which can be redeemed and recycled.

With the wisdom of hindsight, as I reflect on the sequence of events which brought to me a greater degree of inner wholeness than I had previously encountered, I am once again awed by the depth and mystery of the love of the God whose longing is to set us free to become the people he created us to be.

The living word

In the climate in which we live, when scores of books have been written about counselling, inner healing and prayer ministry, it seems timely to underline that God's healing can and frequently does come in the quiet, undramatic moments when he encircles us with love – as we walk, as we work, as we contemplate the wonders of creation or as we meditate on the Scriptures. It is one of the reasons why, in Chapter Five, I stressed the importance of processing the fruit of our Bible meditation.

It happens not infrequently, for example, that we can be reading a familiar Gospel story or a passage like the one from Isaiah which I was reading that morning in my friend's house, when, if we are tuned in to our innermost self, we will detect an inner reaction or some strong feelings. If we listen to those emotions, moods and responses, they can point us to the need for inner healing. We may, for example, be meditating on the miracle Jesus performed at the Wedding at Cana in Galilee. While others might marvel at the way glimpses of his divinity shone through the young rabbi Jesus, we might detect within ourselves jealousy or anger or ambivalence towards Mary, or we might find ourselves hooked by the manner in which Jesus appears to have rebuked his mother on this occasion.

If we chide ourselves for harbouring unholy thoughts and feelings and, with a mighty effort, force ourselves to rejoice with the host of the wedding, we shall miss a golden opportunity. If, on the other hand, we will listen and talk to our jealousy, our anger or ambivalence, we may find ourselves being touched and healed by the Tender One.

Suppose we feel irritation with Mary who appears, to us, to be interfering. If we acknowledge this to ourselves and become a guest at that wedding, using the gift of the imagination in the way I described in Chapter Five, we may find ourselves talking to Jesus about this ambivalence. Perhaps we will ask him how he felt when his mother seemed to demand a miracle. Or maybe will find ourselves sympathising with him: 'Poor you! I know how that feels. My mother was always interfering too.' Or maybe the strength of our emotions will alarm us and we will find ourselves talking to Jesus about that. It could be that, if we are Protestants, we have been schooled to dismiss the role of Mary and that God will use this meditation to bring more balance into our view of the woman he chose to become the mother of his Son.

No one can predict ahead of time what the outcome of such a meditation might be. But if painful, inhibiting memories are triggered by praying with Scripture, these should not be pushed to one side. They need to be confronted and prayed over until our hearts are healed.

Healing might well come to us if we return more than once to this story of the Wedding at Cana. As we do so, we recall where we left off our conversation with Jesus last time and start our prayer by resuming the conversation at that point, in the same way as we might address a friend. We do this until, intuitively, we know that this passage has shown us all we need to know at this stage of our pilgrimage. Alternatively, or as a follow-up, we turn to John 19: 25–7 and watch and learn from the way Jesus relates to his mother there:

'Standing near the cross were Jesus' mother, Mary, his

aunt, the wife of Cleopas, and Mary Magdalene. When Jesus saw his mother standing there beside me, his close friend, he said to her, "He is your son." And to me he said, "She is your mother!" And from then on I took her into my home' (LB).

As we stand there, still recalling perhaps the conversations we have already had with Jesus about our relationship with our mother, we might allow him to draw from us any bitterness or resentment which we recognise we are still harbouring. Or we might find our hardness towards our own mother melting as we contemplate Jesus's example. Despite his own anguish of body, mind and spirit, he forgets himself and concentrates, instead, on his mother's urgent need of friendship and human love. So he gives her his closest friend as companion, confidante and comforter.

As Gerard Hughes observes in *God of Surprises*, the effect such prayer can have is astonishing, lifting heavy burdens from people's lives, 'bringing back to them a capacity for joy and delight in life which may have been stifled for years and, in some cases, restoring to physical health people who had been suffering for years from illnesses which did not respond to medical treatment.'9

Deliverance

The Holy Spirit sometimes uses this kind of meditation to deliver us from the negativity which would prevent us from becoming the person he created us to be.

Like the young man who once described for me what had happened while he was meditating on the raising of Lazarus. He related how, in his imagination, he had 'become' Lazarus lying in the grave of his felt lovelessness. While lying there, the voice of Jesus pierced the darkness of the grave and of his consciousness: 'Lazarus, come out!' (John 11:43, LB). He obeyed. Still wrapped in his grave clothes, he hobbled to the entrance of the tomb and stood waiting at the foot of the flight of stairs which separated him from Jesus and his sisters: 'But as I came out of the darkness, all kinds of other things rushed out in front of me,' he said, 'like snakes and rats. It was as though I was not only being given a brand new start in life, but at the same time, God was ridding me of all the negativity which had been polluting my life for years: hatred and bitterness, resentment and jealousy.'

He then went on to tell me what had happened when Jesus invited the by-standers to 'Unwrap him and let him go!' (John 11:44, LB). He found himself valuing and responding to the tenderness with which his sisters and friends removed the bandages which still bound him: 'That's symbolic too. I know my negativity has prevented me from reaching out to others in love but this encounter with Christ has given me new hope and the courage to start again.'

I was deeply moved by this testimony for two reasons. One, because I sensed that God had silently and secretly exercised what is sometimes called 'the deliverance ministry'. And two, because of the role played by the sisters and friends in the meditation. We look at these in turn. First, the deliverance ministry.

Deliverance Ministry

Francis MacNutt defines this as 'a process, mainly through prayer, of freeing a person who is *oppressed* by evil spirits'.[10] He draws an important destinction between possession and oppression, making it clear that the deliverance ministry is not the same as exorcism. He admits to trying to avoid any involvement with the ministry of deliverance but found himself a practitioner because, as he puts it in *Healing*: 'there were some people I simply could not help merely by praying for inner healing. Prayer for deliverance sometimes was called for.'[11]

He highlights some of the indications that deliverance ministry may be needed instead of, or as well as, the prayer for inner healing. One is that the prayer for inner healing seems to accomplish nothing. He explains:

I have come to expect that prayer for inner healing will ordinarily have a perceptible effect. If, after prayer, a

person says, 'I still have a feeling of being tied up inside,'
it may indicate a need for further counselling or support
in community, or more prayer for inner healing – or,
possibly, for deliverance.[12]

He highlights, too, the differences between the prayer for
deliverance and the prayer for healing:

> 1. Whereas prayer for healing is addressed to God, a
> prayer of deliverance . . . is directed to the oppressing
> demons.
> 2. Whereas prayer for healing is ordinarily a petition,
> prayer for deliverance is a *command* . . . to the demonic
> forces, ordering them to depart in the name of Jesus
> Christ, as did Paul to the spirit influencing the soothsaying
> girl: 'I order you in the name of Jesus Christ to come out
> of her' (Acts 16:18b).[13]

I have found, when exercising this kind of ministry, that there
is no need to shout or rant or rave. There is a need to be as
firm as we might be with a yapping dog when we round on it
with an authoritative 'Be quiet!' I have also found that, before
embarking on this ministry, we need to beg God for the gift
of discernment lest we minister inappropriately and do more
harm than good.

But, like Francis MacNutt, I have also discovered that
there are people whose need for healing is urgent but who
are incapable of receiving it because they are blocked by
the demonic. Like the girl I once prayed for on one of our
overseas trips. She had been describing for me the hatred and
bitterness with which she seemed consumed and, together,
we had prayed for the healing of her heart. In the middle of
the prayer, it became apparent that, before she could receive
healing, she needed deliverance. I simply commanded, in the
Name of the Lord Jesus Christ, that the bitterness and hatred
should depart. She coughed a choked kind of cough and then
clung to me as she said: 'Something's gone . . . It went over

there,' she added, pointing to a nearby swimming pool. 'I feel suddenly free.' She was free. Free to receive the healing she needed to turn her back on years of compulsive bitterness so that she could learn to love again.

The role of friends

One of the reasons God brings us into healing is so that we may learn to relate to others in the way I described at the beginning of the last chapter: in the way the three members of the Holy Trinity love, co-operate and communicate with each other. Is that why God almost always brings someone else alongside us when he heals our hearts, I wonder?

The fact of the matter is that other people are almost always given the privilege of incarnating for us the healing love which is being applied to our heart's hurts by the Holy Spirit. Sometimes, as we have seen, the person is a highly qualified counsellor or psychotherapist. At other times, it is someone who has been entrusted with the sensitivity and gifts required to pray for inner healing for others. On other occasions it is a skilled spiritual director who is trained and experienced in discerning the movement of God's Spirit in us. And sometimes it is close friends or relatives – those capable of embodying for us the tenderness which flows from the Tender One but which we need to feel in human form.

As Kevin O'Shea explains, the tenderness which gives rise to the re-birth of trust begs to be shared: 'There is no way of keeping reserved or enclosed what is by nature transparent. It is already *an overture to others*. This overture is the beginning of a new kind of trust in others.'[14]

He goes on to explain the importance of this re-orientation. Before the healing touch was felt, we operated from a place of inner hurt behind the defences which we had built to protect ourselves from being injured further. As the defences dissolve, a new 'self' emerges, a 'self' more like the person we were created to be. Consequently, we grow in our awareness of who we are by grace and by the changes which are taking place inside us. Our need for a person or people with whom to share this new 'self' is urgent. It is as we share that we mature and are assured that another can resonate to the same tenderness. It is in the face, the smile, the eyes, the touch, the embrace of another that the fruit of this tenderness matures. It does not mature suddenly or quickly – but slowly and sometimes with a struggle. Like the lemon tree in my garden. In its first season, four years ago, it was the proud bearer of one lemon. Then it appeared to have died. Yet we detected signs of life. The more the tree battled, the more we cared for it – fertilising the soil around it, watering it, talking to it, cherishing it. Now, at last, it is showing promising signs of growth and we have every hope of fruit next year.

God, similarly, watches over our progress and yearns, for our sakes, that we will bear the fruit of the tenderness and healing with which he fertilises and waters our lives. And when the fruit does appear, we shall find within ourselves an ever-increasing capacity to become the loving and lovable people God created us to be.

For personal reflection

1. Read the following poem:

> My friend . . .
> you who are part of me
> please take away the veil
> that covers me – please set me free.
>
> You know that we belong, are deeply one.
> I cannot see you clearly
> there is this veil,
> that covers heart and mind and soul.
>
> Did people put it there
> or did I choose this cover
> To protect, to hide
> my insecurity, my wounded self?

Or is it just the final skin
of my unfinished birth
to personhood, to self
which you possess already?

Please take it off with tender care;
I am so insecure, so easily hurt.
Your love can set me free.
Your trust will melt my veil.

Then we can fully meet
in giving and receiving
in seeing, understanding.
We will be whole and free and one.

In oneness we will look
into the world, towards people, God,
uplifting many veils
and freeing hidden beauty – life.

2. Look back over your life and recall the people who have
   lifted your many veils. Thank God for them. If they are
   still alive, you might like to write to some of them or thank
   them on the telephone.
3. Write a prayer in your journal thanking God for bringing
   these friends and mentors across your path.

Notes for Chapter Eight

1. Francis MacNutt, *Overcome by the Spirit* (Eagle, 1991) p. 37.
2. Francis MacNutt, *Overcome by the Spirit*, p. 37.
3. Joyce Huggett, *Listening to Others* (Hodder and Stoughton, 1988).
4. Quoted Mary Meehan SSC, *Exploring the Feminine Face of God* (Sheed and Ward, 1991) p. 63.
5. Kevin O'Shea CSSR, *The Way of Tenderness* (Paulist Press, 1978) pp. 9–10.
6. Kevin O'Shea CSSR, *The Way of Tenderness*, p. 11.
7. Kevin O'Shea CSSR, *The Way of Tenderness*, p. 14.
8. Kevin O'Shea CSSR, *The Way of Tenderness*, p. 19.

 9. Gerard Hughes SJ, *God of Surprises* (Darton, Longman and Todd, 1986) p. 86.
10. Francis MacNutt, *Healing* (Ave Maria Press, 1984) p. 208.
11. Francis MacNutt, *Healing*, p. 209.
12. Francis MacNutt, *Healing*, p. 217.
13. Francis MacNutt, *Healing*, p. 218.
14. Kevin O'Shea CSSR, *The Way of Tenderness*, p. 19.
15. Henry Rohr, *Set Me Free* (Spectrum Publications, 1972).

9

FREE TO LOVE

Even though we may have been emotionally wounded on
numerous occasions, when we begin to yield to the healing
touch of the Tender One, our view of the world and of ourselves
will begin to change. Among other things, perhaps for the first
time in our lives, we may find ourselves believing that we have
been created in the image of God; that he has adopted us into
his family; that just as every child in a human family is unique,
with its own distinct personality, its own set of fingerprints and
its own way of loving its parents, so, too, we are unique to God
and the world. We shall begin to warm to the description of
ourselves as 'friends of God' (Exodus 33:11; John 15:14) and
recognise that, just as God once said to Moses, 'there is a place
near me where you may stand' (Exodus 33:21), so there is a
special place at his side ear-marked for us.

And some of the Bible's other pen-pictures will take on new
meaning for us. Like Paul's picture of the body of Christ in 1
Corinthians 12:12–31, for example. We shall discern that, through
Paul, God is underlining that, as the song puts it, 'each child is
special, accepted and loved, a love gift from Jesus from his Father
above', and that that 'specialness' includes us. We shall be able to
look in the mirror as well as into the inner recesses of our being
and echo the Psalmist's awed hymn of praise:

You created *my* inmost being;
you knit *me* together in my mother's womb.
I praise you because I am fearfully and wonderfully made;
your works are wonderful

(Psalm 139:13, my emphasis)

We shall even be able to add our personal, authentic, resounding 'Amen' to this prayer:

> Lord my God, when your love spilled over
> into creation
> You thought of me.
> I am
> from love   of love   for love.[1]

And when we are assured that, indeed, we are from love and of love, then an important foundation stone will have been laid in our lives on which we can build for the future. We shall be ready to make the life-long experiential exploration into what it means to have been created 'for love'.

Jesus's love

The true meaning of the word 'love' has not only been devalued over the centuries, it has been almost eroded. That is why, in this chapter, we place the spotlight on Love incarnate, love in human flesh, Jesus himself. He is the only person who has lived on earth who has personified love in all its purity, so he is the only one qualified to show us how to become the loving and lovable people we were created to be.

Love is what God is. So when Jesus lived on earth, love flowed out of him in ever-expanding concentric circles. At the centre of those circles, after he had left his home in Nazareth, we see him relating intimately with one person: John the beloved. From that smallest circle of love spread a bigger one, his relationships with the privileged three: Peter, James and John. But these close relationships were by no means exclusive. From them emerged an even bigger circle which embraced the Twelve, and after that the circles of love seemed limitless, drawing in friends like Lazarus, Martha and Mary, Mary Magdalene, Salome, 'the women from Galilee' who supported Jesus with their presence as well as their presents, beggars, lepers, widows, children . . . The list is endless. In other words, it would appear that, in his earthly ministry, Jesus did not love everyone with the same degree of intensity, even though his love embraced everyone. It would also appear that he chose carefully and prayerfully those with whom he would relate most closely, and that he chose not independence but interdependence as the base from which he would establish his Kingdom. Clearly, just as his Father once pronounced, 'It isn't good for man to be alone' (Genesis 2:18 LB), so Jesus recognised that inter-relatedness and inter-connectedness with others was vital to his wholeness and effectiveness.

Was this the reason why he retreated to the hills for a whole night of prayer prior to selecting the Twelve? We are not told. It would appear, however, that when he returned from that nocturnal retreat, there was no doubt in his mind that there were twelve particular men with whom God wanted him to live in community. We also know that the principle of the concentric circles is an important one for us if we are to become the loving people God created us to be. John Powell paints the picture helpfully and persuasively:

'I cannot enter into a love-relationship with many people. I would be exhausted in the effort. So I must choose . . . Since love can exist on many levels, it is extremely important not to offer a commitment of love which I may not be able to honour.'[2]

We, too, must therefore make choices. Such choices should be made, not in the heat of the moment, but after careful thought and prayer. Certain probing questions sometimes help us in the selection process. The first is a particularly penetrating one:

'Am I squeezing relationships into my spare time or are they the base from which I work?'

There are five more:

1. 'What do I want from this relationship and what can I give to it?'
2. 'Within the apparent givenness of my profession or vocation, if I am realistic, how much time do I have to forge close friendships?'

3. 'To whom do I owe my primary commitment?'
4. 'Whom else do I love and in what way?'
5. 'What are the demands on my time and energy to which I must fully respond in order to become fully myself?'

Although on paper this may look rather cold and clinical, it is important to confront such questions, particularly before embarking on any new close relationship. John Powell outlines the possible consequences of failing to do this:

> Most people lurk behind protective walls . . . 'security operations'. These are designed to protect an already injured ego from further vulnerability. At the call of love, these people come out, perhaps haltingly at first, but they do come out, reassured by the promises of love. If I have made a premature or overstated commitment, I will later have to take back my promises made to such a person. I will have to explain that I really did not mean what I said or that I have changed my mind. I will leave that person standing painfully naked and unprotected. He will . . . go back behind a higher and more impenetrable wall. And, once burned, doubly cautious, it may be a long time before anyone will ever successfully call him out again, if that be possible at all.[3]

A close, committed love

Jesus did not make that cruel mistake. Having made his careful, prayerful choice of friends, he dedicated himself wholeheartedly to making the relationships work. Even though his chosen ones misunderstood him,[4] challenged him,[5] quarrelled with each other,[6] and let him down,[7] he loved them to the end.

He was so committed to them that he made himself available to them. He did this by reading their hearts:

'There was no need for anyone to tell him about them because he himself knew what was in their hearts' (John 2:25 GNB).

He not only read them, he felt for them, and created the warm, accepting climate where they could discover what it meant to be privileged children of the Kingdom.

His concern for and promotion of their growth was typically Middle Eastern. It was expressed through the intimacy of loving looks, affectionate touch and warm words. As a born and bred Westerner, it is good for me to live in the Middle East and encounter local Christians publicly expressing their love for one another. I think, for example, of the retreat my husband and I were leading just before I settled down to write this chapter. Most of the retreatants came from the Middle East. God had drawn us very close to one another during our short time together. So, as the retreat drew to its close, it seemed natural for the men to sit with their arms around each other, enjoying to the full this non-erotic touch. It seemed natural, too, for the women to embrace each other, not with a quick hug, but with long, leisurely, loving embraces.

Jesus is a model for this kind of intimacy. He was unafraid to express affection. John reminds us that, at the Last Supper, he 'was reclining next to him' (John 13:23). When Jesus warned them that one of them would betray him, his distress was clear for all to see.

Simon seems to have motioned John to ask Jesus which of them was to turn traitor, whereupon John leaned back against Jesus (v. 25). Again, here in the Middle East, that would seem neither inappropriate nor unseemly. No one would recoil from such demonstrations of affectionate understanding: rather they would recognise that, with John, Jesus is simply modelling warm, affectionate, non-genital, same-sex loving.

But, contrary to his culture, he expressed, openly and in public, love across the sex divide as well. Luke records how, on one occasion, while Jesus was dining with Simon, the Pharisee, a prostitute approached him with her heart obviously brim-full with love for him. This love overflowed in the form of tears as she knelt at his feet. Her tears washed his feet, so she wiped them, not with a towel but with her long, flowing hair. Then she anointed them with the expensive perfume she had brought as a gift for him (Luke 7:36–8). When Simon poured scorn on the woman's actions, Jesus defended her, highlighting and applauding the genuineness of her love and contrasting it with Simon's seeming hostility and lack of hospitality.

Warm, genuine, tactile, verbal love. This is the pattern of Jesus's love. The Holy Spirit's task is to set us free to love like that.

People in the West, as I have hinted, may find that it takes time for them to learn to feel comfortable with non-erotic touch. But, as Joyce Rupp explains in *Praying Our Goodbyes*:

> Touch fills a person's being with the energy of bonding and love. Without ever saying a word, the message is given: 'I care. I am here for you. Here is some strength of mine to go on; here is some love to energize you when you need it so much.' Touch connects one to another in care, makes contact with heartache . . . warms the cold or exhausted spirit. Touch can penetrate barriers of despair, anguish, hardness or bitterness.[8]

Words and looks

Jesus's love was expressed, not only in touch, but also in looks and words. What did Peter read in the Lord's eyes in the courtyard on that unforgettable Good Friday? The Bible does not tell us, so we can only guess. Could it have been hurt love, the pain a person feels when a dear friend has rejected him? And what did the woman caught in the act of adultery see in Jesus's eyes? Again, the Bible remains silent. Could it have been accepting love? What did Mary and John see in Jesus's blood-shot eyes as he hung from the Cross? Undoubtedly, tender, suffering but generous love.

Though we are left to draw our own conclusions about what people saw shining through Jesus's eyes, the Bible makes it patently clear that Jesus was a man who was unafraid to vocalise the love which he felt for his disciples. Take the conversation he had with them in the Upper Room, for example. Here he repeatedly tells and shows them just how deep and extensive his love for them is:

'As the Father has loved me, so have I loved you' (John 15:9).

Did John remind the disciples of this amazing declaration of love during those agonising hours sandwiched between Christ's Crucifixion and that sensitive Resurrection appearance in that same Upper Room on Resurrection Day? Did they deliberate on the other references he made to his love for them – such as:

'Love one another *as I have loved you*? (John 15:12, my emphasis).

Or did they remind each other that he made comments like this more than once?

'As I have loved you, so you must love one another' (John 13:34).

Again, we are not told. What is clear, however, is that Jesus felt uninhibited about expressing the love he felt for people. We will know that we are becoming the people God created us to be, that is, those formed in the image of his all-loving Son, when we, too, grow in our capacity to give love and to receive it. For some of us, as we have observed in a previous chapter, this may take a long time, so we shall have to exercise patience, contrasting Jesus's example with that of an elderly man I once read about.

This man had a close friend with whom he lived in a Christian community. Over the years they had learned to understand each other, empathise with each other and support each other. When one was sick, the other was there, available to him. Or when one had good news to share, the other was there, entering into his joy. One day, unexpectedly and tragically, one of the men was run over by a car in the road opposite the community's home. He was killed instantly. As soon as his friend heard the news, he rushed into the street, knelt beside his friend's body, wrapped his arms around him and cried: 'Wake up! You can't die yet. I never told you that I loved you.'

Affirmation

Jesus *did* tell his friends how much he loved them. He also demonstrated this love in non-verbal ways. For example, he affirmed them.

Jack Dominian reminds us that 'the word affirmation comes from the Latin "affirmare" and it means to make firm, to give strength to . . . the human personality'.[9] He also explains what

affirmation does, suggesting that it answers two questions
which are pertinent to the subject of this book. The questions are:

'Who am I?'

'What do I mean to myself in relation to myself and others?'

Affirmation helps us to find the solutions to these questions in a variety of ways. When someone reflects back
to us the way they value and appreciate us, they increase
our sense of self-worth and therefore help us to discover
who we really are. And when someone increases our sense
of self-worth, they give us a priceless gift – the awareness that we are full of potential, some clues to help us
identify the specific nature of that potential, and therefore
some hints to help us find an answer to the second question: 'What do I mean to myself in relation to myself and
others?'

Notice the way Jesus did this for Peter. Before Peter had
even started to serve his apprenticeship with Jesus, and while
he was still protesting his unworthiness to keep company with
the Master, he heard these affirming words pouring from the
Lord's lips:

'Don't be afraid [Simon], from now on you will catch men'
(Luke 5:10b). In other words, Simon, you have a unique role
to play in the Kingdom.

Even more astonishingly, many months later, yet more
affirmation came Peter's way as Jesus gave him a new symbolic name:

'You are Peter, and on this rock I will build my church'
(Matthew 16:18).

Up to this point, Peter's track record had not been particularly
impressive and, as time went on, it was to grow steadily
worse. He was the one who acted as the mouth-piece of
those trying to dissuade Jesus from travelling to Jerusalem.
He was the one who, during the Last Supper, refused to
allow Jesus to wash his feet. He was the one who would
deny Jesus three times. But Jesus detected his potential
and carefully and sensitively drew this out. In doing so, in
the language of John Powell, Jesus was underlining Peter's

value as 'an unique, unrepeatable and even sacred mystery of humanity'.[10]

Assumed responsibility for people

One of the reasons why Jesus possessed this great capacity for affirming others was that he loved from a healed rather than from a hurting centre. This, in turn, gave him the inner freedom and space, not only to read people's hearts, but to recognise and meet their needs. To meet the needs of another is 'the fruit of friendship'.[11] It is one of the many faces of love, for love not only gives itself to others, it walks a mile in another's moccasins, to quote the old Indian proverb, and through empathy, discerns their real needs. At the same time, love remains separate from the need in order to make itself available to the needy person without being overwhelmed by them.

Was this the reason why, in Mark 1, for example, when Jesus's disciples sought him out insisting that he should leave that prayer-saturated place to return to the clamouring crowds, Jesus made the astonishing suggestion: 'Let's go somewhere else'?

We cannot know for certain what prompted that decision. We must, however, recognise that, if we are to love effectively, we too must set boundaries and refuse to be in bondage to the person in need. This is what Jesus modelled. In doing so, he gave his friends the greatest gift anyone can give another: 'the gift of belovedness'. I never cease to marvel at the methods Jesus used to give his closest friends this gift.

I think, for example, of those gruelling hours leading to his arrest in the Garden of Gethsemane. Although, during the Last Supper, he must have experienced a great deal of personal anguish, with painstaking care he prepared his disciples for the shock and trauma of their forthcoming bereavement:

'Do not let your hearts be troubled . . . In my Father's house are many rooms; if it were not so, I would have told you. I am going there to prepare a place for you. And if I go and prepare a place for you, I will come back and take you to be with me that you also may be where I am' (John 14:1–3).

This self-giving love which detected and ministered to the inner needs of the loved one was in evidence after the Resurrection also. Think of Mary weeping at the empty tomb. Jesus saw. Jesus cared. Jesus came. With one, economical, power-filled word he consoled her: 'Mary' (John 20:16). Or think of Thomas. Into the empty shell of his doubt, the risen Lord came with the much-needed invitation:

'Put your finger here; see my hands. Reach out your hand and put it into my side. Stop doubting and believe' (John 20:27).

Forgiveness

Even more astonishingly, perhaps, Jesus forgave his failing friends. The Greek word for 'to forgive' is *aphesis*. It is the word Jesus used at the grave of Lazarus. Having called Lazarus from the tomb, he invites the by-standers to *aphesis* – that is, to set him free from the grave-clothes so that he can go. In other words, 'to forgive' actually means 'to let go', 'to drop'.

This is precisely what we see Jesus doing in his relationships with his disciples. They failed him so many times. Although they lived with him and listened to his teaching, they failed to understand the true nature of his mission. Even at the Last Supper, some of them were arguing about which of them would be the greatest in Christ's Kingdom. Worse was to come when, instead of supporting him through the agonising hours of his arrest, trial and crucifixion, they deserted him.

Jesus was human. He must surely have been hurt by their rejection and neglect. Yet, on the first Easter Day, he made it clear that he was clinging to no grudges, no resentment, no hatred. Rather, he was ready to reach out to them in love.

On my desk, as I write, lies a photograph of a statue which stands on a small beach on the shores of the Sea of Galilee – the spot where it is believed Jesus re-commissioned Peter. As I have been gazing at this picture, I have been trying to place myself in Peter's shoes. If the other disciples had failed their Lord, he was the failure *par excellence*. Not only had he deserted Jesus, like all the rest, he had denied that he even knew this man he so fervently loved. Did he have trouble

looking the Resurrected Jesus in the eye, I wonder? Did he
shuffle along the beach shamefacedly? We are not told. But
we know that Jesus did not humiliate him in any way. On the
contrary, he seemed eager to restore this leader designate of
the early church. Just as Peter had denied him three times, now
Jesus gives him three opportunities to declare his love. Then
Jesus commissions him – feed my sheep, feed my lambs.

Peter's posture in this picture before me speaks of unworthiness, helplessness and renewed commitment. He kneels at
Jesus's feet with one hand held out in despair while the other
is receiving the shepherd's crook which Jesus is handing to him.
The figure of Jesus, on the other hand, exudes tenderness, trust
and tranquil strength.[12] Qualities I imagine we shall enjoy as we
become more and more like the warm, affectionate, affirming,
forgiving people he made us to be.

Transparency

But Jesus's loving of his disciples and friends was memorable,
not just because of what he did for them, but also because of who
he was. Most of us, as we have already seen, defend ourselves
with masks. Many of us carry around, as it were, a brief-case
full of them so that we can change them as circumstances
demand.

Jesus, on the other hand, was transparent. He revealed both
personal strengths and personal limitations. There were times,
for example, when his divinity peeped through his humanity – as
when he changed the water into wine at the Wedding at Cana
in Galilee. There were times, too, when his divinity streamed
through – as on the Mount of Transfiguration. But there were
other occasions when he was transparently weak and helpless:
at his birth, for example, or as he stumbled under the weight
of his Cross on the Via Dolorosa.

There were other limitations also. When James and John made
their request for preferential treatment in the Kingdom, Jesus
replied: 'I do not have the right to choose who will sit at my
right and my left. It is God who will give these places to those
for whom he has prepared them' (Mark 10:40, GNB). In other

words, Jesus was a man under authority, a man in submission, a man with set limits and yet one who was gloriously free – the person his Father created him to be.

What was the secret of his transparency? What kind of person is it who detects the strengths in others and affirms them? What kind of person is it who is more concerned for the welfare of the loved one than his own well-being? What kind of person is it who readily forgives? What kind of person is it who has no need to project a psuedo-self; who clearly states what his limitations are? If we can discover the answers to those questions, we may draw a little closer to discovering who it is we are intended to be.

As we study the life-style of Jesus, it becomes clear that the person who loves in this way enjoys a double sense of security. Such people are secure in the love of God and therefore secure in their God-given identity. Jesus seems to have reached this enviable, liberating state by the age of twelve! So, in Luke 2:46–9, we see him in the temple, able to hold his own with the teachers of the Law, a poised, secure, purposeful youth who had already discovered his mission in life. As he expressed it to Mary and Joseph, 'I must be busy with my Father's affairs' (Luke 2:49, JB). He had had a normal, village home life in Nazareth where doubtless he experienced the warmth of human parenting from Mary and Joseph, but now he had reached the stage of maturity where, unashamedly, he could separate himself from them and insist on the appropriateness of establishing himself as his own person in relationship with his heavenly Father and the world at large. He was not rejecting his parents; indeed, he remained 'obedient to them' (Luke 2:51, LB). But he refused to remain in bondage to them.

We will know that we are more like the person God created us to be when we, too, refuse to remain in bondage to anyone: parents, the past, friends, culture. We will also recognise that we are becoming increasingly free when we, too, feel sufficiently secure in God, in ourselves and about ourselves, that we can affirm others and extend to them warm, accepting love.

In Cyprus a phrase which is often used is, 'Slowly, slowly!'

And because we are novices in this art-form of loving, it is a phrase we need to whisper to ourselves while we learn this particular skill. That is why I value Antoine de Saint-Exupéry's charming story, *The Little Prince*.

In this book, a prince from another planet visits planet earth. While on earth, he finds himself gripped by loneliness. Until, one day, he meets a fox:

> 'Come and play with me,' proposed the little prince, 'I am so unhappy.'
>
> 'I cannot play with you,' the fox said, 'I am not tamed.' . . .
>
> 'What does that mean – "tame"?'
>
> 'It is an act too often neglected,' said the fox. 'It means to establish ties.'
>
> '"To establish ties"?'
>
> 'Just that,' said the fox. 'To me, you are still nothing more than a little boy who is just like a hundred thousand other little boys. And I have no need of you. And you, on your part, have no need of me. To you, I am nothing more than a fox like a hundred thousand other foxes. But if you tame me, then we shall need each other. To me, you will be unique in all the world. To you, I shall be unique in all the world . . .'
>
> 'What must I do, to tame you?' asked the little prince.
>
> 'You must be be very patient,' replied the fox. 'First you will sit down at a little distance from me – like that – in the grass. I shall look at you out of the corner of my eye, and you will say nothing . . . But you will sit a little closer to me, every day . . .' The next day the prince came back . . .
>
> So the little prince tamed the fox.[13]

Just as the little prince tamed the fox, so Jesus tamed his disciples. After they had lived with Jesus for three years, the disciples were fast reaching the stage when they could tame each other.

A touching scene in the musical *Godspell* highlighted this.

Many Christians, myself included, were disturbed by the portrayal of the person of Jesus in this musical, but the scene I refer to was a powerful one.

It is the Last Supper. Jesus has washed his disciples' feet. He prepares for the final farewells. He moves around the table, embracing, kissing or playfully ruffling the hair of one disciple after another. Then he does a curious thing. He holds up a mirror in front of each of the disciples in turn. As he does so, the disciple's make-up is removed – not by the disciple himself but by his neighbour.

This was a moment of great significance. To allow someone else to wipe off the make-up which masks our real self requires a great deal of trust. And if we are to become the loving and lovable, maskless people God created us to be, we must be lured out of the false security of life behind the mask and take the risk of allowing others to discover who we really are. This interdependence modelled to us by Jesus transforms us. No one has taught me this more clearly than Chris.

When Chris first came to see me, he was one of the loneliest people I had ever encountered. He was in his late twenties but had only ever experienced even a modicum of closeness with one other person in his entire life. This friend, a flat-mate, had just moved, leaving Chris bereft. The pain of separation seemed unbearable. When he came to see me, he gave voice to his feelings of loss and bereavement. We invited God to come into the lonely void. And we looked at Chris's circle of acquaintants. Where could he, a single, shy introvert, find security, warmth and a place to belong? He doubted whether he could take the risk of reaching out to others again. I happened to know of a church in the town where Chris lived and suggested he tried it. Three months later, he visited me again. I scarcely recognised him. His eyes were shining. He smiled. He was full of news about his fulfilling job and the new church.

'Chris. You're so different. What's happened?'

He laughed. 'It's the house group at that church you suggested I should try. The services on Sunday aren't at all what I'm used to but the house group is great. They were pleased to see me, welcomed me and even looked out for me on Sundays at church. They're so friendly that I feel wanted, accepted and even appreciated. I didn't know it could be like this.

The members of that house group were probably totally unaware that they were taming Chris – becoming instruments of God's healing for him. Yet they conveyed to him the message we all need to hear:

'I am lovable! I don't have to do anything or be anything but myself.'[14]

In this way, they drew him out of his self-protecting fortress and set him free to give and receive love again. When people do this for us so that the 'I am lovable' message is etched on our hearts, then we are free to serve.

For personal reflection

1. Recall the claim that Jesus's ministry flowed from the relationships he established. Compare this with your own philosophy and life-style.
2. Write a prayer out of the experience.
3. Take a fresh look at the six questions on pp. 125–6, and spend time reflecting on them and answering them.
4. What has the experience shown you about yourself? Do you need to make changes in your life-style or relationships? What are you going to do about this?
5. Write a prayer asking the Holy Spirit to continue to transform you into the loving and lovable person God created you to be.

Notes for Chapter Nine

1. Jacqueline Syrup Bergan and S. Marie Schwan, *Love: A Guide for Prayer* (Saint Mary's Press, Minnesota, 1985) p. 11.
2. John Powell, *The Secret of Staying in Love* (Argus Books, 1974) p. 48.
3. John Powell, *The Secret of Staying in Love*, p. 48.
4. Luke 18:34.
5. Luke 8:45.
6. Luke 22:24.
7. Luke 22:46.

8. Joyce Rupp, *Praying Our Goodbyes* (Ave Maria Press, 1991) p. 91.
9. Jack Dominian, *Cycles of Affirmation* (Darton, Longman and Todd, 1977) p. 154.
10. John Powell, *The Secret of Staying in Love*, p. 56.
11. Henri Nouwen's phrase.
12. This photograph has been reproduced in my book, *The Smile of Love* (Hodder and Stoughton, 1990).
13. Antoine de Saint-Exupéry, *The Little Prince* (Piccolo, 1982) pp. 63–6.
14. John Powell, *The Secret of Staying in Love*, p. 19.

10

FREE TO SERVE

Until we know who we are and what our gifts are, we cannot
discover how we might most effectively make an impact for
Christ in our small corner of the universe. We might even
find zealous, well-meaning Christian leaders or peers steering
us towards ministries for which we are ill-equipped. And that
would be a tragedy because, when every part of our being
responds to the orchestration of the Spirit, a surge of energy
seems to flow through us and thrill us in rather the same way
as musicians thrill to the harmony they are helping to create.

One reason for this tremendous surge of energy is that when
we allow God to conduct our lives, we enjoy a foretaste of
heaven and we catch a glimpse of the person he created us
to be. Paul put it this way: we were created 'to praise the
glory of his [God's] grace' (Ephesians 1:6, JB).

The catechism on which Christians used to be reared put it
another way:

'God made me to know him, love him and serve him in this
world and to be happy with him in the world to come.'

The contemporary author, Gerard Hughes, commenting on
the same theme, writes:

'Before the world was made we were chosen to live in love
in God's presence by praising, reverencing and serving him in
and through creation.'[1]

The Book of Common Prayer draws the seemingly paradoxi-
cal conclusion that 'his service is perfect freedom'.

In other words, when we serve God we are truly free because
he created us in such a way that we will only enjoy complete
fulfilment in life when we are reverencing him and everyone

and everything he has made, and when we are serving him and them. This lies at the very heart of who we are.

The big lie

There is a snag, however. As children of our first parents, Adam and Eve, we have become victims of the Fall.

Just as our first parents believed the big lie Satan whispered in their ears – that God is a spoil-sport, out to deprive us of joy rather than to delight us with his love, so we are easily beguiled into believing in this caricature of God. This means that a civil war may frequently rage inside us. While some parts of our personality will struggle to be true to our calling, to serve Christ and the world, to serve Christ in the world, other parts of us will rebel and insist on putting self before our Master. One of the challenges which faces us, therefore, is to discern and to discipline those parts of ourselves which seem intent on ensuring that our world revolves around 'number one', self, rather than God.

Someone has suggested that the way to do this is to become like the woman who owned two dogs: one white and one black. These dogs used to fight frequently and ferociously. But over a period of time, a friend of the woman observed that while one week the white dog would win the fight, the following week the victor would be the black dog. Because the pattern persisted with monotonous regularity, the friend could contain her curiosity no longer so she asked the dog's owner if there was an obvious reason for this pattern. Whereupon her friend explained that the answer was simple: 'One week I feed the white dog and starve the black one, while the following week, I feed the black one and starve the white. The dog which is being fed is the one which wins.' We, similarly, need to ensure that, while the God-pleasing, God-serving part of our personality is fed and nurtured and therefore strengthened, the narcissistic parts of our personality are gradually starved into defeat.

Saying 'Yes' to God

That is not to imply, however, that the main initiative in winning this perennial battle is ours. It is not. God takes the initiative. I discovered this while I was on retreat on one occasion. One of the questions I had taken with me was: 'Lord, do you want me to go to live in Cyprus?' The answer came within the first few days of this five-week-long holiday with God.

But the answer faced me with a bigger, more pressing question. Now that I felt as certain as I could that God was, indeed, calling me to make the island my base, the question was: 'How do I say "Yes" to this request?'

For weeks, I wrote eloquent prayers telling God that I wanted to say 'Yes'. I wrote a poem which brought into sharp focus my fears and longings now that I was confronted with the need to say 'Yes'. I even studied and meditated on the Incarnation of Jesus in the hope that I would gain courage and inspiration from the example of the ready, generous, all-embracing 'Yes' which Mary uttered when the angel invited her to become the mother of the Messiah. Yet, although a burning desire to capitulate consumed me, no 'Yes' so much as squeezed through my lips.

It was on this retreat that I meditated on the word 'grace' which I mentioned in Chapter Five – the grace which is variously translated 'mercy', 'kindness' and 'pure gift'. It was on this retreat that I fell asleep begging for a generous slice of this free gift. It was in the middle of the last night of this retreat, at three in the morning to be precise, that I woke with a joyful, spontaneous 'yes' rising from somewhere deep inside me. It was then that I realised that though we may have earned a degree in theology and have many years of Christian ministry to our credit, left to our own devices, self would still prevent us from saying 'yes' to the freshness and newness of God's unexpected call. Grace is the midwife which gives birth to the desire and the ability to say the 'Yes' which is gestating and growing within us.

Some obstacles to overcome

As I look back on that retreat and as I read the pages of the prayer journal in which I was writing at the time, I notice that a word I used frequently was 'fear'. I was afraid of leaving the English home I loved for a much smaller house in a country where I would always be a foreigner who carried on her person an identity card marked *'ALIEN'*. I was afraid that, at a time when the world seemed gripped by recession, the financial support we would need would not be forthcoming. And I was afraid that, if I were stripped of all the support structures which I had taken for granted for years – the team who worked with me, my spiritual director and others who were there 'for me' whenever I needed them, the quiet places to which I could retreat when I needed a place 'just to be' with God – I would find myself unable to cope.

Others facing the enormity of the 'Yes' which confronts them have spoken to me of similar fears. They are not only natural, they are a gift because they reveal to us that, though we may have been claiming to find our security in God, we have, in fact, been seeking our security in our homes and our salary, our roles and our successes. As Jean Vanier puts it:

We get seduced by riches and power;
     by status and by superficial pleasures.
We begin to doubt
     and thus tend to float along with the current.[2]

Or, as Ronald Rolheiser points out, as human beings who are creatures of our culture, we spontaneously draw support from fame, hedonism, pleasure, power, possessions, sex and so on. When we are faced with counting the cost of the 'Yes' God wants us to whisper, we are brought face to face with our need to draw strength instead from the resources of God, through the 'littleness' of dependence on him and on his people.

This diagram reminds me of an insight of Jean Vanier's which never ceases to challenge me: 'We all have to choose between two ways of being crazy: the foolishness of the Gospel and the nonsense of the values of the world.'[3]

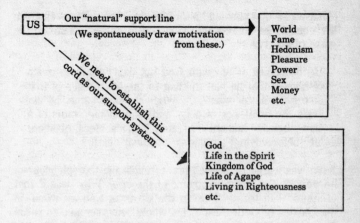

Reproduced from Ronald Rotheiser's *The Restless Heart* (Hodder)

The dynamic of love

Those who most easily choose the foolishness of the Gospel are those who are most aware that God is in love with them, that prayer is a love affair with their Creator. The reason for this is that, when we are overtaken by the awareness that we are loved, we are humbled. In particular, we are humbled when the love of *God* overwhelms us. As the Jesuit, John English, observes: 'The intensity of the experience of love is, of course, a great grace. It cannot be obtained by human effort.'[4]

This gift of grace brings in its wake the realisation that we are utterly dependent on Love for our very existence. This realisation opens our eyes to the amazing truth that we are loved, not for anything we can do, but for who we are. We are therefore beings of love – loved even while we were steeped in our sinfulness. This awareness, in turn, draws from us awe, adoration, freedom and a deep desire to serve.

We see this dynamic of love operating so beautifully in Jesus.

What was it that enabled him, of his own free will, to renounce the equality he shared with God and to assume, instead, the guise of a servant?

> He had equal status with God but didn't think so much of himself that he had to cling to the advantages of that status no matter what . . . When the time came, he set aside the privileges of deity and took on the status of a slave, became human! . . . [and] lived a selfless, obedient life [before dying] a selfless, obedient death.[5]

What was it that persuaded him to exchange the splendour of heaven for the rough exposure of the crib? What was it that prompted him to say 'Yes' to the Cross of Calvary when, in the Garden of Gethsemane, his whole being seemed to recoil from the price he had to pay for our salvation?

It was love. Love for the Father. Love for us. In the vocabulary of Jesus, love and service seem to be synonymous. What the Father asked, he did. He could do it because he was motivated by a deep, sustained and sustaining love. As he summed it up on the night before he died: 'I have obeyed my Father's commands and remain in his love' (John 15:10).

When we, too, immerse ourselves in the felt love of God, we will find ourselves wanting to serve. Compelled to serve, not by a Sergeant Major God who barks his commands until we obey, but compelled by love. For the essence of love is service. Lovers delight to find little ways of serving one another – simply to bring delight to the other. Christian service is like that. It is a grateful abandonment and dedication of all that we know of ourselves to all that we know of God. It is as simple, as profound and as costly as that. It is why Paul could call himself, with obvious pride, 'the servant of Christ' (Romans 1:1; Philippians 1:1). It is why Jesus 'consented to be a slave' (Philippians 2:8, JBP); why he could claim: 'The Son of Man did not come to be served, but to serve' (Mark 10:45).

It is why, paradoxically, when we can take for ourselves a life principle which asserts our servanthood, like the caterpillar

entering the chrysalis, we find ourselves on the verge of
true freedom. Like voluntary slaves who have renounced all
personal rights to ownership of possessions, decision-making
and self-aggrandisement, and like voluntary slaves who have
vowed to spend and be spent in the service of the master they
love, we, too, can be slaves, yet gloriously and wonderfully
free. This is the foolishness of the Gospel.

How to Serve

There are as many ways of serving God as there are people,
and it is vital that we recognise that the first and most important
way is simply to be the person he intended us to be.

As someone has summed up this liberating truth: 'A tree
brings most glory to God simply by being a tree.'

Yet, so often, as human beings, we strive to become what we
are not and consequently grow discouraged and disillusioned in
the attempt. We therefore do well to heed another pithy piece
of advice: 'Bloom where you are planted.'

A medical student called Vicki helped me to see how profound
these simple statements are when I was a patient in the hospital
where she was working. I was facing major surgery for the first
time in my life. When feelings of apprehension surfaced in me
or when fear gripped me, somehow Vicki was always there:
to listen, to pray or simply to hold my hand. When I was
wheeled into the operating theatre, Vicki was there – grinning
broadly with a grin I could interpret as 'I'm praying. I care.'
When I came round from the anaesthetic, Vicki was there –
still wearing her white coat, still smiling, her china-blue eyes
saying: 'I'm glad you survived. I'm still here "for" you.' In the
days that followed, she sacrificed much-needed time off to be
with me. Her presence was a ministry to me and a witness to
the ward. Fellow patients would ask me, 'Who is that young
doctor with the beautiful smile?'

And I would tell them: 'She's a member of our church.'

'Church!'

The mention of that word opened up several opportunities for me to speak of God's love and, in particular, to draw alongside a Roman Catholic patient whose need for support and prayer was urgent – all because Vicki was blooming where she was planted, becoming the good doctor God created her to be.

Or I think of another friend who serves God simply by being the person God created her to be. People who meet her often comment: 'I don't know what it is about you, but it's good to be with you.' I felt this even before she became a close friend because, when she prays, it is as though she is really making contact with God. When people speak, she reverences the things they say; when she responds, she is caring and wise; and she seems to find it so easy to affirm others, helping even strangers to feel at home and at peace. She will never wear a recognisable label like 'doctor' or 'politician', but that matters little. She, too, is blooming where she is planted, becoming the beautiful, praying, caring person God created her to be.

In *Call to Conversion*, Jim Wallis underlines the importance of incarnating the love of Christ in this way:

> When I was a university student, I was unsuccessfully evangelised by almost every Christian group on campus. My basic response to their preaching was, 'How can I believe when I look at the way the church lives?' They answered, 'Don't look at the church – look at Jesus.' I now believe that statement is one of the saddest in the history of the church. It puts Jesus on a pedestal apart from the people who name his name. Belief in him becomes an abstraction removed from any demonstration of its meaning to the world. Such thinking is a denial of what is most basic to the gospel: incarnation. People should be able to look at the way we live and begin to understand what the gospel is about. Our life must tell them who Jesus is and what he cares about.[6]

Serving the poor

The briefest of glances at the Gospels reveals that, when Jesus walked this earth, there was a particular group of people he cared about: the poor. As Jean Vanier, himself a champion of the poor, puts it:

> It is as though he is attracted in a special way,
> almost like a magnet,
> to those who are suffering, or broken or rejected.'[7]

It follows that when we find ourselves being drawn closer and closer to Jesus, we shall also find ourselves becoming more and more concerned for the poor. To be with Jesus is to be in the presence of Love and compassion. This compassion is contagious. It will rub off on us and overflow from us, and we will find ourselves asking: 'Who, for me, are the poor?'

I once asked a friend and mentor that question. His answer surprised and challenged me: 'Don't we discover the answer to that question by asking, "How am I poor?"'

The question intrigued and challenged me and, like many such questions, helped me to move forward. I was standing at one of life's cross-roads at the time, sensing that the finger of God was beckoning me to become involved with the poor in some way. When I asked myself the question: 'How am I poor?' the answer rose from somewhere within me:

'My poverty, so often, is a poverty of spirit. I write about prayer as relationship with God and attempt, on retreats and Quiet Days, to lead others to the Fountain of Life, Jesus, but sometimes I do it from the barrenness which can be born of busyness so I feel as though I am scraping the bottom of an empty barrel.'

It was a humbling moment and an important one. Other Christians in leadership, I know full well, suffer from the same dis-ease – particularly Christians who live and work overseas where the resources that people in the West take for granted are so few and far between. As I faced my own poverty, I also found the answer to my question: 'Who, for me, are the poor?'

I not only found the answer to my question, I discovered the nature of my new vocation. I now work full-time with my 'poor' – those who have given everything they have and are for

the extension of Christ's Kingdom overseas. Together with my
husband, I now have the privilege of leading prayer retreats for
them where we seek to take them by the hand, as it were, and
stay alongside them in love as they feast on food no money can
buy – the banquet of God's love.

While writing this chapter, we have been leading one such
retreat and here I have seen the spiritual principle I am
spelling out – the interplay between closeness with Christ
and compassion for others – transform the perception of a
young man in whom God's Spirit is clearly at work. He is
someone whose desire to spend quality time with God is
deep. While I have been giving him a retreat 'in the stream
of life', he has needed to renew his visa so that he can remain
in the country where he works. So, together with the refugees
who have swarmed into the country where he lives, he joined
the long queue of those seeking permission to stay. This gave
him ample time to gaze into the lined, helpless, hopeless faces
of foreigners far away from home, who, like him, were still
struggling to cope with filling in forms in a foreign language.
His heart went out to these people in love and in prayer and
in the desire to strengthen them in whatever way he could.
But, as often happens in such circumstances, this growing
desire to help the poor brought him face to face with his
own helplessness. As he expressed it to me: 'The task is so
enormous. Where do I begin?'

The service of hiddenness

We begin where Jesus began at his birth – by entering into
the seeming hopelessness of the situation. Until, like him, we
feel to the full the despair and the helplessness, we have not
fully identified with the thousands for whom there is no hope
of anything but poverty. In two thirds of the world, people are
pawns in a political game. They no longer hold the reins of their
own lives. The controls were snatched from them or from their
forebears decades ago and, like little sticks being swept along by
the current of a swollen, fast-flowing river, they simply survive
the best they can. Many face abject poverty, starvation, day-in,

day-out grief as they watch children and loved-ones young and old die in their arms or, worse, helplessly in the streets. Such destitution may draw the worst rather than the best from them. They may resort to theft, violence or greed but they need the help, the support and the prayers of those God sends across their path – in a queue for a visa, through the medium of the television screen, in the streets of the city where they live.

But where do we begin to make an impact on such a sea of need? The key to that question lies in Matthew 25 where Jesus describes what will happen when he returns, not as a tiny baby but 'in glory'. All the nations will be gathered before him and, just as a Middle Eastern shepherd separates his sheep from his sleek goats, Jesus will call his 'sheep' to him. 'Come!' he will say to them, and he will commend and applaud them for championing the stranger and the starving, the sick and the destitute and those in prison. Whereupon the 'sheep' will express their surprise: 'Lord, when did we see you hungry and feed you, or thirsty and give you something to drink?' And Jesus will reply: 'I tell you the truth, whatever you did for one of the the least of these brothers of mine, you did for me' (Matthew 25:37, 40).

We may have the time, the energy and the resources to minister to only one of the world's needy ones. It is enough. It may be all that is required of us. Or it may be that our involvement with a sick and suffering world may be through the ministry of hiddenness – either in our own home country or overseas. In *City of Joy*, Dominique Lapierre highlights the value of hiddenness by showing how some of the world's unsung heroes felt called by God to leave home and go to live in one of the worst of India's slums – not to preach, not to engage in overt evangelism, but simply to be a praying presence which incarnated the love of Christ. It was no easy task but it bore fruit for Christ and his Kingdom. Over the long, testing months and years, one young man, in particular, established his rhythm of prayer and involvement with his neighbours, and inspired the kind of trust from which the mutuality of love is born. The impact he made on this forgotten corner of the world can never be fully assessed.

It has been my privilege to visit many such hidden ones – people who could be climbing the professional ladder in their home country, people who could be lining their pockets with the world's gold, but who have chosen, instead, to live and work quietly in parts of the world where the only thing they can do for Christ is to incarnate his love and to pray.

Intercessory prayer

The only thing they can do? Yes. Sometimes, such people see little apparent fruit for their love and their labour. In the countries where they work, they do not enjoy the kudos of seeing thousands flock to meetings they speak at. Indeed, there are no meetings – just a day-in, day-out rhythm of prayer and overflowing love. Often they feel spiritually drained and dry. Sometimes they wonder how effective they are. Sometimes the only sign that God is working through them is that, when they pray, they weep and they groan as they confront the darkness in which their part of the world is enveloped. Rather, I should say, the Holy Spirit weeps through them in the way Paul describes:

'The Spirit helps us in our weakness. We do not know what we ought to pray for, but the Spirit himself intercedes for us with groans that words cannot express. . . . [and] in accordance with God's will' (Romans 8:26–7).

They groan with the Spirit because the going seems so hard, because people's hearts seem so hard and the sense of oppression hangs over them like a thick and menacing cloud. And yet they stay and they pray and they work and they love just as Jesus before them stayed and prayed and worked and loved. The fruit of their labours may not be reaped for decades. That does not invalidate, rather it authenticates, the power of the praying presence.

History highlights this. I think, for example, of a letter I received recently from a friend who spent many years as a missionary doctor in a little-evangelised country before returning to his home-land. Some fifteen years later, he was invited to return to lead seminars in the country where he had once served. It proved to be a moving experience as he discovered that people who were young in years and young in the faith when he had worked with them, had now assumed leadership of the indigenous church. The little fruit he had seen during his time overseas had multiplied one-hundred-fold.

But, of course, we need only to pack our bags and travel overseas if we hear a clear call from God to do so. It is equally possible to work in this hidden way in our own home country. Those of us who do work overseas often testify to sensing the power of the prayer of our supporters, some of whom intercede for us spasmodically, some regularly – like the friends who have our engagement diary tucked into their Bibles or on their notice-board. When some of them write to tell us of the times and ways in which the Holy Spirit has prayed through them or inspired them to pray, the timeliness and aptness of these letters trigger within me tears of gratitude – to God for his faithfulness in raising up such prayer partners and to them for their openness to the Spirit.

The use of our gifts

'But how do I know where I am meant to be serving and what I am supposed to be doing?'

This is a question I am frequently asked. One way of discovering the answer to it is to try to discern the gifts God has entrusted us with.

I make this claim because, as I explained in an earlier chapter, it is the Holy Spirit who, at our creation, and in our re-creation, pours into us the gifts and the talents which are the tools we need for the task to which he calls us. In that chapter, I referred to the way he had equipped Bezalel for the uniqueness of his ministry:

Then the LORD said to Moses, 'See I have chosen Bezalel . . . and I have filled him with the Spirit of God, with skill, ability, and knowledge in all kinds of crafts – to make

artistic designs for work in gold, silver and bronze, to
cut and set stones, to work in wood, and to engage in
all kinds of craftsmanship.

(Exodus 31: 1–5)

God continues:

I have given skill to all the craftsmen to make everything
I have commanded you: the Tent of Meeting, the ark of
the Testimony with the atonement cover on it, and all the
other furnishings of the tent – the table and its articles,
the pure gold lampstand and all its accessories, the altar
of incense, the altar of burnt offering and all its utensils,
the basin with its stand – and also the woven garments,
both the sacred garments for Aaron the priest and the
garments for his sons when they serve as priests, and the
anointing oil and fragrant incense for the Holy Place.

(Exodus 31: 6–11)

I find myself moved by this hive-of-activity picture of a group
of God-gifted people all donating their talents to the glory of
God. I am moved, too, to recall the way in which men and
women of God down the ages have responded to the call to
donate their giftedness to the glory of God.

The day before I began this chapter, for example, I
visited a friend who was listening to Handel's *Messiah*.
How impoverished millions of people would have been if
Handel had failed to translate into that memorable oratorio
the clear prompting of God's Spirit. I think of the short time
I spent in the prayer-saturated studio of an artist in Auckland
on one occasion. I had never met this artist before, though
God had spoken to me through her art. In *Finding God in
the Fast Lane*,[8] I have related how I felt drawn to one of
her paintings which is reproduced in that book. The impact
of that visit continues to bear fruit in my life, bringing me
seemingly endless insights and healing. But we do not need
to be a musician or an artist, an author or a pastor to be
used by God. Some of us have been entrusted with the gift

of hospitality, others with the gift of listening, yet others with a gift of letter writing which God uses to strengthen and comfort the recipients.

When God uses the gifts which he has entrusted us with and gives us glimpses of the ways in which he is using us, we enter into the joy of partnership with our Creator and we take a few further steps along the road to freedom. But God has not only given us gifts; he has created us in rather the same way as he creates children – full of potential. The challenge comes to us at various stages of our lives therefore, to respond to invitations for which we have no experience and for which we do not feel particularly gifted or qualified. When such challenges come from God, we shall find that, latent within us, though we had never discerned them, lie the talents we need for such tasks.

Many Christians would testify that one of the treasures which have come out of the darkness and grimness of the world-wide recession of the 1990s has been the discovery by skilled, professional people that they have gifts which had previously been overlaid by busyness and seeming success. I think of a former director of a company in England.

This businessman, like countless others, was made redundant by the firm he had served faithfully for many years. As he listened to the medley of emotions which vied for his attention – feelings of anger and humiliation, disappointment and loss, he also began to ask God what he was to do with the rest of his life. There seemed little hope that he would be offered secular employment. But did that matter? The question startled him and jolted him out of despondency and into creative thinking. He examined his real situation and realised that although for years he had enjoyed a handsome salary and the high standard of living which went with it, these were not essentials. They were, in fact, luxuries. If he and his family could lower their standard of living, they would have quite enough money to live on.

His family agreed to make the necessary sacrifices and everything changed. As he held on an open palm his perceived need to find new employment, a whole new area of ministry opened up for him. He now finds that he has the time with

God which formerly eluded him and that, from that still place, God is frequently sending him into Eastern Europe to touch the lives of needy believers who so thirst for the ministry of encouragement which he and his wife bring. If my perception is accurate, this family are poorer financially but richer spiritually than they have ever been. They would also be among those who would testify to enjoying more of this mysterious thing called freedom than ever before, because they are allowing God to draw out their full and fine potential.

For personal reflection

1. Make a list of your gifts and abilities. If you find it difficult to do this on your own, ask someone who knows you well to help you. When you have become aware of the way in which God has endowed you, if you feel you can, surrender afresh to him all that you have and all that you are.
2. If you can, pray this prayer

> Take, Lord,
> and receive all my liberty,
> my memory, my understanding
> and my entire will,
> all that I have and possess.
>
> You have given all to me,
> to you, Lord, I return it.
>
> All is yours:
> do with it what you will.
> Give me only your love
> and your grace,
> that is enough for me.[9]

3. Write down your life's motto.
4. Reflect on the following:
   'To love is not to give of your riches but to reveal to others their riches, their gifts, their value and to trust them and their capacity to grow.'[10]

Notes for Chapter Ten

1. Gerard Hughes SJ, *God of Surprises* (Darton, Longman and Todd, 1986) p. 63.
2. Jean Vanier, *The Broken Body* (Darton, Longman and Todd, 1988) p. 118.
3. Jean Vanier, source not traced.
4. John English SJ, *Spiritual Freedom* (Loyola House, 1987), p. 44
5. Philippians 2:6, Eugene Peterson, *The Message* (NavPress, 1993) p. 11
6. Jim Wallis, *Call to Conversion* (Lion, 1981) p. 108.
7. Jean Vanier, *The Broken Body*, p. 13.
8. Joyce Huggett, *Finding God in the Fast Lane* (Eagle, 1993).
9. *The Spiritual Exercises of St Ignatius of Loyola*.
10. Jean Vanier, *The Broken Body*, p. 80.

11

SET FREE BY DIFFICULTIES

I do not want to imply that those who dedicate their lives to the service of God live happily ever after in this world as well as in the next. That would be a travesty of the truth. There is a price to pay for the freedom we seek.

This was brought home to me a few minutes before starting this chapter when I had lunch with a missionary whose husband had died recently and tragically of a heart attack. In the aftermath of his death, his widow and many of his friends found themselves asking that question which has no answer this side of eternity: 'Why?' 'Why, when his ministry was bearing so much fruit, was he taken? Why now?'

While I write, I find myself pausing frequently to pray for two of our own prayer partners whose lives are in turmoil because of the sudden onslaught of life-threatening illness. Having benefited so much from the ministry of this couple, I, too, was tempted to ask the question: 'Why?' But I know from past experience that that question has no answer. Instead, I asked God how I should pray.

As though in answer to that prayer, in the wakeful hours of one night, I was reminded of a silversmith I once watched while I was on holiday in Greece. I had been browsing in his shop for several minutes, admiring his hand-made filigree work and fingering the goblets, chalices and rose bowls he had made when, out of the corner of my eye, I saw him take a pair of tongs and lift a chalice from the shelf in his work corner. Intrigued, I moved to the nearby furnace and watched as he held the chalice in the flames. One part of me wanted to protest. In my *naïveté*, I thought that the gleaming chalice would be spoiled. But patiently and calmly, he held it in the intensity of the heat. Then, when his experienced eye detected that the chalice had been held in the furnace long enough, he withdrew it. Smiling, he took a soft cloth with which he rubbed his blackened masterpiece and even I could see that the refining had made his creation even more beautiful and even more precious than it had been before its ordeal.

This memory reminded me of a chorus which it is fashionable to sing in certain Christian circles:

Purify my heart, let me be as gold and precious silver,
Purify my heart, let me be as gold, pure gold.
Refiner's fire, my heart's one desire is to be holy,
set apart for You, Lord . . .

Such powerful, profound and far-reaching words! But if we think about them and sing them with integrity, perhaps we should not be surprised when God holds us or those we love and admire in the flames? If we believe those words, we shall know, with a deep-down certainty, that he will hold us there just long enough for the refining to take place but he will never abandon us to the flames. As someone has put it: 'He who is near me is near the fire.' Even so, being purified in this way will inevitably hurt. It is part of the price we pray for our freedom.

The pruning principle

We must remember, too, that when Jesus likened himself to the whole vine and likened us to individual branches, he warned us that his Father is a faithful vine-dresser. Faithful vine-dressers always prune the branches that have borne fruit so that they can bear more fruit. When I watch the vine-dressers near my home lopping off branch after branch from their vines, leaving little more than a leprous stump, I sometimes wonder how the vine might feel if it were sentient. Would it protest: 'Why this cruelty? Why this waste?' Or would it look back on past prunings and recognise that the cutting back is, indeed, an essential part of the fruit-bearing process?

We have no way of telling how a vine might feel. Many of us, however, have felt the pain of loss as the heavenly vine-dresser has lopped off the muchness and manyness of our ministries and brought us to the place where we are prepared to do the one thing he asks and to do it with all the wisdom and energy he gives. We have recognised that this is part of the price we pay for our freedom. We have also discovered the paradox that, when we submit to such drastic pruning, we find ourselves feeling not empty but full, not restricted or deprived but enriched and liberated. We find ourselves free to blossom in the place where he wants us to be. Free to bear fruit in the manner in which he always intended. Free to become the people he always created us to be.

Spiritual warfare

But there is another reason why the price of freedom is high. As Peter warns us, we have an Arch-enemy to contend with. This enemy 'prowls around like a roaring lion looking for someone to devour' (1 Peter 5:8). Although he does not seem to trouble Christians whose lives resemble the Sadducees Jesus once confronted with the condemnation: 'You do not know the Scriptures or the power of God' (Matthew 22:29), he does torment believers who perceive Jesus to be the pearl of great price for whom it is worth sacrificing everything. Such Christians often find themselves paying a very high price for the freedom to become the people God created them to be. They know what Michael Green means when he warns that, when we surrender our lives to Christ, 'we pass from security into the firing line'.[1] They understand, too, John's description of the enemy in the Book of Revelation where he is likened to a blood-thirsty dragon which wages constant war against those who keep God's commandments and bear testimony to Jesus (Revelation 12).

Because the enemy's wiles are so subtle and so potentially

lethal, it can be helpful to highlight them so that when he does his worst, we recognise what is happening and recognise who holds the reins and what is really happening to us.

The accuser

One way of clarifying the mystery is to become conversant with the enemy's many names. These indicate his many activities. One name is Satan and, as Michael Green reminds us in *I Believe in Satan's Downfall*, the word 'Satan' means 'accuser' or 'slanderer'. We may expect, therefore, to suffer the indignity of being accused before God by Satan and others who insist that we are unacceptable. In Zechariah 3:1, we see the high priest Joshua being assailed in this way:

'Then the Angel showed me (in my vision) Joshua the High Priest standing before the Angel of the Lord; and Satan was there too, at the Angel's right hand, accusing Joshua of many things' (LB).

We see Satan playing a similar trick in Job 1:6–14 (LB):

One day as the angels came to present themselves before the Lord, Satan, the Accuser, came with them.

'Where have you come from?' the Lord asked Satan. And Satan replied, 'From patroling the earth.'

Then the Lord asked Satan, 'Have you noticed my servant Job? He is the finest man in all the earth – a good man who fears God and will have nothing to do with evil.'

'Why shouldn't he, when you pay him so well?' Satan scoffed. 'You have always protected him and his home and his property from all harm. You have prospered everything he does – look how rich he is! No wonder he "worships" you! But just take away his wealth, and you'll see him curse you to your face!' . . .

So Satan went away; and sure enough, not long afterwards when Job's sons and daughters were dining at the oldest brother's house, tragedy struck.

And just as we read of Satan entering into Judas during the Last

Supper (Luke 22:3), so Satan seems to have entered into Job's wife and 'Job's comforters' as his so-called friends are often described. Through them, Satan accuses Job before God and the result is that Job is filled with self-loathing, self-condemnation and the desire to die:

'Oh, that God would grant the thing I long for most – to die beneath his hand, and be freed from his painful grip' (Job 6:8–9, LB).

The pattern spelled out so painstakingly in the Book of Job has been repeated countless times down the centuries so that Christian is set against Christian. Where love, compassion and tenderness should abound, hatred, bitterness and a critical spirit reign. Instead of learning to understand each other and rejoicing in the insights which God has entrusted to others, so-called followers of Jesus revile each other, become entrenched in the narrowness of their cherished beliefs, and fight tooth and nail to defend the little portion of the truth which they believe to be the whole truth.

Though most would not stoop to actual murder, they crucify others with hatred in their eyes, and vehemence, cruelty and bigotry in their verbal attacks. And Satan chuckles because, as anyone with a grain of sensitivity knows, the adage, 'sticks and stones may break my bones but words will never hurt me' is far from the truth. Words do hurt. They inflict deep and lasting wounds which may take years to heal.

Worse, Satan rubs his hands with glee because, while Jesus continues to pray 'that they may be one' (John 17:11), the Accuser has kept on the boil the scandal of the disunity, distrust and discord which has riddled the church for centuries, marring the image of Christ it presents to a world which is rightly scandalised by this perennial denial of the power of the Gospel.

The tempter

Satan is also known as the Tempter (Matthew 4:3; 1 Thessalonians 3:5). Just as the Tempter sidled alongside Adam and Eve in Genesis 3 and alongside Jesus in the Wilderness, so he will frequently sidle alongside us, seeking to alienate us from God. For Satan is the Antichrist,

> the embodiment of opposition to our Lord . . . He is set for our downfall, and will come at us either as the king of the jungle, the 'roaring lion seeking whom he may devour' (1 Peter 5:8) or else seductively, as the 'angel of light' (2 Corinthians 11:14) seeking whom he may deceive.[2]

He is not only the tempter *par excellence*, he is a liar. Jesus goes so far as to call him 'the father of lies' (John 8:44). We hear him whispering lies into the ears of Adam and Eve in the Garden of Eden and, similarly, we shall hear him whispering lies into our minds and hearts, causing us to doubt God's love and promises.

Sadly, that is not all. This subtle liar and tempter does not work alone. He is the prince of the power of the air who has hosts of evil spirits on whose help he draws. As Paul describes this network of evil:

> We are not fighting against people made of flesh and blood, but against persons without bodies – the evil rulers of the unseen world, those mighty satanic beings and great evil princes of darkness who rule this world; and against huge numbers of wicked spirits in the spirit world.
>
> (Ephesians 6:12, LB)

The novels of Frank Peretti have opened our eyes and imaginations to the reality of that claim as it might well be fleshed out in our materialistic, Western, secular society, so that it is now easy to see how leaders in all walks of life, including the church, have been influenced by this enemy Jesus calls 'the prince of this world' (John 12:31; 14:30).

As Richard Foster perceives the situation:

> Behind absentee landlords of ghetto flats are the spiritual forces of greed and avarice. Behind unreasoned and excessive resistance to the Gospel message are

demonic forces of disobedience and distraction. Underneath the organized structures of injustice and oppression are principalities of privilege and status. Aiding and abetting the sexual violence and the race hate and the child molestation that are such a part of modern society are diabolical powers of destruction and brutality. Therefore, says Paul, when we face, for instance, people who are deaf to the Gospel or laws that are cruel and unjust or leaders who are oppressive, then we are also dealing with cosmic principalites and powers that are straight from the pit.[3]

Or, as Michael Green sums up the situation:

Satan attacks the minds of men with doubts, fears and propaganda. Satan assails the spirits of men with lust, pride and hatred. Satan assaults the bodies of men with disease, torture and death. Satan assails the institutions of men (which he seeks to impregnate) with structural evil. In the Bible itself we find him manipulating nations (Daniel 10), city councils (1 Thessalonians 2:18), rioting mobs (John 8:44, 59) and the very elements themselves (Mark 4:39). Satan is immensely powerful. It is unwise to underestimate him.[4]

The oppressor

In particular, it is unwise to underestimate his ability to oppress us and, through constant discouragement, over-work, criticism or sickness, to grind us into the ground like powder until we reach the conclusion that only one option faces us – to give up.

Just as we have observed him doing just this to Job, so we watch him achieve the same aim with the prophet Elijah. Having won an immense prayer victory for God on Mount Carmel, the exhausted Elijah falls prey to the twin curses of a distorted perception of his person and ministry, and the discouragement which led to depression and a gnawing, numbing death wish. So we hear this great prayer warrior bleating before God:

'I have had enough, LORD . . . Take my life' (1 Kings 19:4).

The first part of that pain-wracked prayer is being echoed today by countless Christians seeking to become the people God created them to be. I have met them in England – fine, dedicated people, including Christians in leadership, who sacrifice so much for God. In particular, since I have had the privilege of working overseas, I have met such people in countries where the going is tough because the blanket of spiritual darkness never seems to lift; where the signs of the movement of the Spirit in people's lives are so few and far between that they wonder why they are there, question whether they should pack their bags and return home, or ask soul-searching questions like: 'What are we doing wrong?' or 'Why can't we make more impact for God?' And I have encountered such spiritual oppression myself.

Just before writing this chapter, for example, my husband and I were speaking at a conference where the hardness of hearts of some of the so-called believers crushed us so effectively that I felt powerless to speak or to minister in the way I had planned. Like Elijah, I, too, wanted to escape – to run away, to lick my wounds, to give up. I resisted that temptation and faced, instead, the heartbreak of watching Jesus's parable of the sower being enacted before my eyes: God's precious seed falling on calloused hearts; some being swept away in the foaming sea of frivolity and the desire some Christians have to be entertained rather than taught; other seed being choked by cynicism and the pull of the peer group. Although there *was* the joy, too, of watching some seed bear beautiful fruit for the Kingdom, I came away with the overwhelming and growing sense that we had been embroiled in enemy activity and that we and the group with whom we had been working had been ill-equipped to combat God's Arch-enemy.

The seducer

But perhaps we need to remember that Satan comes to us most subtly, not through external circumstances or other people, but through our own attitudes, thought patterns, personality, emotions and imagination. As John English emphasises, Satan's aim is to enslave us, to turn us in on ourselves, to make us self-centred, to make obsessions of our own egotisms: 'No single individual of any state in life is overlooked: Satan wages a war that involves the whole universe. His intention is to reduce [people] to slavery and thus prevent them from reaching their completion and fulfilment.'[5]

He seduces us, too, by attacking our Achilles' heel – particularly in those unguarded moments which creep up on us all when we are exhausted or suffering from any kind of stress.

'Is it worth it?' That is the question some Christians ask when they find themselves, like Job and Elijah, being jolted through month after month of turbulence. The answer to that question, if Jesus is to be believed, is a resounding 'Yes'. In the Book of Revelation, he piles promise after promise upon 'the overcomers'. As John describes the triumphant scene:

> I, John, saw the Holy City, the new Jerusalem, coming down from God out of heaven. It was a glorious sight, beautiful as a bride at her wedding.
>
> I heard a loud shout from the throne saying, 'Look, the home of God is now among men, and he will live with them and they will be his people; yes, God himself will be among them. He will wipe away all tears from their eyes, and there shall be no more death, nor sorrow, nor crying, nor pain. All of that has gone forever.'
>
> And the one sitting on the throne said, 'See, I am making all things new!' . . . Everyone who conquers will inherit all these blessings and I will be his God and he will be my son.'
>
> (Revelation 21:2–5,7, LB)

But the good news is that we do not need to wait until the Lord's return to enter into our inheritance. We can enjoy foretaste after foretaste of the promised freedom now. For just as a woodcarver takes a sleeping piece of wood into his hands and with a skilled stroke here and a deft cut there sets the wood free to be the carved bird or figurine it begs to be, so the eye of God sees our potential and makes of life's problems, and even the murderous wiles of the Evil One, the chisel which transforms us rather than the axe which destroys us.

Co-operating with God

Think again of Job, for example. Bruised, battered and bleeding though he was, God granted him graced moments when, clearly, he was being set free to emerge as the person of faith God created him to be. Even before God had restored his fortunes, he could give that immortal testimony:

'I know that my Redeemer lives, and that he will stand upon the earth at last. And I know that after this body has decayed, this body shall see God! Then he will be on *my* side! Yes, I shall see him, not as a stranger, but as a friend! What a glorious hope!' (Job 19:25–7, LB).

And as he emerged from the crucible, he could make this jubilant faith statement before God:

'I had heard about you before, but now I have seen you' (Job 42:5).

God's longing is that each of us should emerge equally unscathed, humbled, yet triumphant. So he suggests a series of coping mechanisms for those times when the going is tough. Peter highlights one:

Be careful – watch out for attacks from Satan, your great enemy. He prowls around like a hungry, roaring lion, looking for some victim to tear apart. Stand firm when he attacks. Trust the Lord; and remember that other Christians all around the world are going through these sufferings too.

(1 Peter 5:8–9, LB)

Or, as Richard Foster puts it:

Spiritual warfare is not something we talk about; it is something we do. How do we do it? . . . We do it by coming against every 'mountain' that hinders our progress

in God. . . . We stand against evil thoughts and suspicions
and distortions of every sort. . . . We do it by demon
expulsion. Wherever we find evil forces at work, we firmly
demand that they leave. We are in charge, not them. In
the ministry of power we take authority over whatever is
opposed to our life in the kingdom of God.[6]

When we do stand firm and learn to take authority over our
sexual fantasies, worldly attitudes and self-centred thoughts,
instead of caving in to every temptation which comes our way,
eventually we experience a curious sense of exhilaration, joy
and lightness of spirit. Although we may have learned from
the bitterness of experience that Ole Hallesby was correct
when he claimed that 'the secret prayer chamber is a bloody
battle-ground. Here violent and decisive battles are fought out',[7]
we now know from experience that, when those battles are won,
we find ourselves in touch with the person God always intended
us to be. It is a jubilant and triumphant moment.

Striving together

Such moments motivate us to heed other injunctions given by
God – like his exhortation to learn to fight the enemy rather than
each other. Through his mouth-piece, Paul, God encourages us
to arm ourselves for battle, and, like Roman soldiers, to take
up our shields and form a solid phalanx of faith which can resist
all the fiery darts of the enemy (Ephesians 6:13–16). This way
we shall experience that unity of the Spirit with which we can
contend those who oppose us 'as one man', not frightened by
anything (Philippians 1:27). This way, the truth of James 4:7
becomes experiential rather than theoretical: 'Resist the devil
and he will flee from you.'

This resistance includes Satan's activity within the innermost
core of our own being. And, if we are to detect his activity
accurately, like Elijah, we need times of stillness and reflection
so that we can hear God's still small voice:

'Go out and stand before me on the mountain,' the Lord

told [Elijah]. And as Elijah stood there the Lord passed by, and a mighty windstorm hit the mountain; it was such a terrible blast that the rocks were torn loose, but the Lord was not in the wind. After the wind, there was an earthquake, but the Lord was not in the earthquake. And after the earthquake, there was a fire, but the Lord was not in the fire. And after the fire, there was the sound of a gentle whisper. When Elijah heard it, he wrapped his face in his scarf and went out and stood at the entrance of the cave.

And a voice said, 'Why are you here, Elijah?'

(1 Kings 19:11–13, LB)

There is value, I find, in establishing a rhythm of prayer which includes daily times of stillness during which God can gently help us to sense where his Spirit has been at work within us and where the Evil One has been undermining the Holy Spirit's work. This can connect us so powerfully with the person we were created to be that it is well worth the discipline.

One way of embarking on this form of listening to God and one's self is to set aside a few minutes each day when we watch an action replay of the past twenty-four hours. The aim is not to condemn ourselves but simply to be aware of the things we have done and left undone; the things, too, we have thought and the way we have reacted. Often we will see clearly that the Holy Spirit has been very active in our lives, keeping us focused on God and keeping us journeying in a God-ward direction. From time to time, however, as we reflect, we may well become conscious that, though we began the day well, gradually our attitudes and actions became more self-centred than God-centred. On such occasions, we should suspect that the Evil One has been at work and that we have colluded with him. When we detect his devilish dealings there is further value in tracing the thought or attitude or reaction back to its beginning. This way, we shall not only deal a death-blow to this current insurrection, but we shall learn how to detect the deceiver's presence more quickly and, in future, to nip his activities in the bud.

Another way of discerning the intrusion of the Evil One is to listen to the language of our moods. As Ignatius of Loyola pointed out so helpfully, when we are becoming the person God created us to be, entering into the fullness of his freedom, the Holy Spirit's activity in us 'is very delicate, gentle, and often delightful. It may be compared to the way a drop of water penetrates a sponge.'[8] When Satan 'tries to interrupt our progress, the movement is violent, disturbing, and confusing. It may be compared to the way a waterfall hits a stone ledge below.'[9]

Looking to Jesus

When our reflection reveals the presence of the Evil One, there is no need to despair. As we have already seen, God, not Satan, holds the reins because God and not Satan is in ultimate control. And if we listen carefully, we may hear the kind of heavenly music Joshua heard when he was being accused before God by Satan:

'And the Lord said to Satan, "I reject your accusations, Satan; yes, I, the Lord, . . . rebuke you. I have decreed mercy to Joshua and his nation; they are like a burning stick pulled out of the fire."' (Zechariah 3:2 LB).

Or we may hear God rebuke our accusers as Job heard him rebuke his three friends:

'I am angry with you . . . for you have not been right in what you have said about me, as my servant Job was' (Job 42:7, LB).

For, on the Cross, Jesus conquered evil and the Evil One. By his death, Jesus rescued us from the clutches of all dark, Satanic principalities and powers. That is why Luther's hymns and catechisms 'reverberate with joy that God has rescued us from the "monster" or "tyrant" the devil, who previously held us in the captivity of sin, law, curse and death'. That is why we can echo Paul's cry:

I am convinced that nothing can ever separate us from [God's] love. Death can't, and life can't. The angels won't, and all the powers of hell itself cannot keep God's love away. Our fears for today, our worries about tomorrow . . . nothing will ever be able to separate us from the love of God demonstrated by our Lord Jesus Christ when he died for us.

(Romans 8:38–9, LB)

That is why, even when the world and Satan have done their worst, like Jesus returning to Galilee from the Wilderness of Temptation, we shall be able to return to our Galilee 'full of the Holy Spirit's power' (Luke 4:14, LB) – a little more like the person God always intended us to be.

For personal reflection

1. Watch an action replay of the past twenty-four hours. Try not to judge yourself but simply to recall the events and your reactions to them. Ask the Holy Spirit to shed his light on the memories, showing you where you have been responding positively to his promptings and where and how Satan has been active in your life: by accusing you before God, tempting you, oppressing you, seducing you. . . .
2. While these memories are fresh in your mind, if you recall occasions when you have resisted the Evil One, thank God for giving you the grace. If you recall occasions when you failed to resist temptation, refuse to grovel. Instead, remind yourself that we shall regularly fail unless we receive from God the grace we need to resist. Receive his forgiveness and stride on towards freedom.
3. Re-read the story of the silversmith on pp. 157–8. Do you know of anyone who is being 'held in the fire' at the moment? If so, hold them in the love of God.
4. Pray, too, for those whose ministries and lives are being pruned in any way and especially for those who work in countries where the sense of oppression is marked and persistent.

Notes for Chapter Eleven

1. Michael Green, *I Believe in Satan's Downfall* (Hodder and Stoughton, 1984) p. 60.
2. Michael Green, *I Believe in Satan's Downfall*, p. 48.
3. Richard Foster, *Prayer* (Hodder and Stoughton, 1992) pp. 254–5.
4. Michael Green, *I Believe in Satan's Downfall*, p. 50.
5. John J. English SJ, *Spiritual Freedom* (Loyola House, Guelph, 1987) p. 164.
6. Richard Foster, *Prayer*, p. 256.
7. Ole Hallesby, quoted by Richard Foster, in *Prayer*, p. 255.
8. *The Spiritual Exercises of St Ignatius*, trans. David L. Fleming SJ (The Institute of Jesuit Resources, 1985) p. 217.
9. *The Spiritual Exercises of St Ignatius*, trans. David L. Fleming SJ, p. 217.
10. John Stott, *The Cross of Christ* (Inter-Varsity Press, 1986) p. 229.

12

FREE AT LAST

Most days when I am at home, I go on an hour-long prayer walk. It takes me past the vineyards which I have described in an earlier chapter, through the orange and lemon groves, along the beach and back through the vineyards again. I did this walk just before starting to type this chapter and I am glad I did because what I saw seemed to sum up much of the content of this book.

As I wandered along those now-scorched vine terraces, I noticed first that tufts of lush, resilient grass had already begun to push their way through the parched earth and past the layer of ashes. Then, when I stooped down on a certain hillock to examine this seeming miracle more closely, I marvelled. At my feet lay a carpet of tiny, blue flowers – like wild grape-hyacinths. These, too, had survived the flames, broken through the rock-hard earth and blossomed in the way their Creator intended. They seemed to smile in the warm, autumn sunshine. They seemed free indeed.

Their simple but stunning beauty reminded me of the freedom we shall all enjoy one day. John's description of it never ceases to enthrall me:

'Dear friends, now we are children of God, and what we will be has not yet been made known. But we know that when he appears, we shall be like him, for we shall see him as he is' (1 John 3:2).

'When he appears.' When Jesus appears again we shall be free at last: free from every vestige of self-centredness, free from sin, free from temptation, free to be with him, free to become the person he always intended us to be. The world

may scoff and scorn but it cannot steal our joy as we anticipate
that day.

This waiting reminds me of a moving scene in Richard
Attenborough's memorable, award-winning film, *Ghandi*. The
cameras take us to a remote railway station in India. There
we see a platform teeming with waiting Indians. Two British
soldiers survey the scene from their hill-top vantage-point.
Nodding towards the crowd as a steam train approaches, one
asks: 'What are they doing? What are they waiting for?'

His colleague replies: 'I've no idea. All I know is they received
a telegram a few days ago. On it were three words: "He is
coming".'

The train snorted to a halt. A small, middle-aged Indian
dressed in white home-spun cloth alighted. The people surged
forward to greet him. Dark eyes lit up, weary faces creased
with smiles. And the soldiers mocked at the reverence with
which this seemingly insignificant native was being treated. Why
the euphoria? Here was just another Indian, here today, gone
tomorrow. Gone tomorrow? They were not to know that this
charismatic figure, Ghandi, would one day lead his country into
freedom from British rule. The thought had never even crossed
their minds.

Neither can the world concede that our telegram from heaven
has arrived. 'I am coming soon,' Jesus promises (Revelation
3:11). The world cannot detect the joy which wells up within
us like a fountain as we read his further promise, 'I am
making everything new!' (Revelation 21:5). The world does
not understand that when he comes, we shall be transformed
into the people he created us to be. We shall be free at last. Yet
this is the theme which throbs through the Book of Revelation.
Whenever we meditate on the mysteries concealed in the pages
of this book, we stand on the threshold of Paradise found.
Freedom found.

Has anyone captured the atmosphere more accurately than
C.S. Lewis as he concludes his famous Narnia tales? Here
he claims that the things which happened to his characters
after the books ended were so great and beautiful that he
could not write them. Although for us it was the end of

all the stories, for them it was the beginning of the real story.

> All their life in this world and all their adventures in Narnia had only been the cover and the title page: now at last they were beginning Chapter One of the Great Story which no one on earth has read: which goes on for ever: in which every chapter is better than the one before.[1]

In the Book of Revelation, too, every chapter is more thrilling than the one before. Reading the book at one sitting is as tantalising as hearing the sound of running water when climbing in the mountains on a hot summer's day, and as thirst-quenching as drinking long draughts from such crystal-clear streams. Each promise is precious: the promise of 'a new heaven and a new earth', the promise that God will 'wipe away every tear from [our] eyes', the promise that 'death shall be no more, and never again shall there be sorrow or crying or pain' (21:1–4). But the greatest thrill of all will be that we shall see the Beloved face to face. He will make our home with us and we with him. We shall be his people and he will be with us. We shall delight, not in his presents, but in his everlasting presence.

Free to worship

And, for the first time in our lives, we shall be set free truly to worship. Some of us have already received a foretaste of what the worship of heaven might entail – complete self-forgetfulness, utter self-abandonment. As John describes it:

> Day and night they never stop saying:
>
> > 'Holy, holy, holy,
> > is the Lord God Almighty,
> > who was and is, and is to come.' . . .
>
> Then I looked and heard the voice of many angels, numbering thousands upon thousands, and ten thousand times

ten thousand. They encircled the throne and the living creatures and the elders. In a loud voice they sang:

'Worthy is the Lamb, who was slain, to receive power
and wealth and wisdom and strength
and honour and glory and praise!'

Then I heard every creature in heaven and on earth and under the earth and on the sea, and all that is in them, singing:

'To him who sits on the throne and to the Lamb
be praise and honour and glory and power,
for ever and ever!'

The four living creatures said, 'Amen,' and the elders fell down and worshipped.

(Revelation 4:8; 5:11–14)

I am tempted to say, 'Fantastic!' and to leave it at that. But there is more.

Free for Intimacy

Zephaniah puts it beautifully:

'Do not fear . . . do not let your hands hang limp. The LORD your God is with you, he is mighty to save. He will take great delight in you, he will quiet you with his love, he will rejoice over you with singing', (3:16–17).

There is a sense in which that prophecy has already been fulfilled. There is another sense in which we have yet to enter into a full experiential awareness of its meaning. Here in this world, God's felt presence is, at best, fleeting, intermittent, transitory. Not so in heaven. There we shall enjoy a permanent intimacy with God. There, we shall know, not with the eye of faith, but experientially that we belong to God and that he belongs to us. There the words from the Song of Solomon will find their fulfilment:

'I am my Beloved's, and my Beloved is mine' (6:3, JB).

We shall know what it means to be the Bride of Christ. Michael Wilcock's description of the heavenly Bride never ceases to excite me:

We have passed beyond the bounds of space and time into regions of eternal light, unshadowed by the slightest imperfection, not to say evil; where the eyes of every created thing are fixed in adoration upon the Lamb alone. *Yet he is not alone.* For sharing the Scene with him – indeed, taking its very title role – is a radiant stranger whose features, as we consider them, are nonetheless familiar. Can it be . . .?

It is 'the Bride, the wife of the Lamb.' It is the church of Christ. *It is you; it is I.* Whatever other metaphors we may use to describe our relationship with Christ, the last Scene of the Bible shows us ourselves married to him, 'cleansed . . . by the washing of water with the word', presented before him 'in splendour, without spot or wrinkle or any such thing' (Ephesians 5:26–7).

Although there we must leave the portals of heaven, we may continue to feast our minds on these mysteries remembering that, while we live life in the overlap, we are rather like butterflies testing our wings in a vast auditorium. We are no longer caterpillars. We have multi-coloured wings already. And we have learned that flying is fun. But, from time to time, we press against the window-pane sensing that a greater freedom is only a pane of glass away. It is. And Christ is coming soon. When he comes, the glass panels will be removed. We shall be free at last. Free to become the people he always created us to be.

Even so, come Lord Jesus!

Notes for Chapter Twelve

1. C.S. Lewis, *The Last Battle* (Puffin, 1964) p. 165.
2. Michael Wilcock, *I Saw Heaven Opened* (Inter-Varsity Press, 1975) p. 205.